Is

CW00923137

(30 May 2008)

CASTLES, TOWN DEFENCES AND ARTILLERY FORTIFICATIONS IN THE UNITED KINGDOM AND IRELAND

A BIBLIOGRAPHY
1945–2006

Dolbadarn

Frontispiece (overleaf): Dolwyddelan Castle, Caernarvonshire (Cadw, Crown Copyright).

CASTLES, TOWN DEFENCES AND ARTILLERY FORTIFICATIONS

IN THE UNITED KINGDOM AND IRELAND

A BIBLIOGRAPHY 1945–2006

by

JOHN R. KENYON

SHAUN TYAS
DONINGTON
2008

Typeset and designed from the discs of the author by the publisher

Published by

SHAUN TYAS
1 High Street
Donington
Lincolnshire
PE11 4TA

ISBN 1 900289 89X (ten digits)
978-1900289-894 (thirteen digits)

Printed and bound by Biddles Ltd of King's Lynn

I dedicate this volume to the memory
of my great and much missed friend,

RICHARD AVENT,

Chief Inspector of Ancient Monuments
and Historic Buildings, Cadw

CONTENTS

CONTENTS

CONTENTS

ACKNOWLEDGEMENTS

My first debt must be to the Society of Antiquaries of London, as it was in the Society's library, as a member of staff, that I started to compile the original *Bibliography*, and I have used that library ever since in order to consult journals that are not taken in any Cardiff library. My thanks are also due to the Society's Librarians, John Hopkins and his successor Bernard Nurse, for their patience, not forgetting Adrian James. The National Museum of Wales has allowed me to work on this book as part of my duties, and I owe a great debt to David Dykes, the late George Boon and Eurwyn Wiliam.

The British Academy and the Royal Irish Academy funded various periods of study in Dublin, largely at the Royal Irish Academy; without such visits, the Irish section would have been far from complete. I am most grateful to the staff of the RIA's library for their assistance; it has been a great pleasure to study there. The libraries of the Society of Antiquaries of Ireland and Trinity College, Dublin, also gave me access to their Irish journals sections.

The Castle Studies Group and the Fortress Study Group have contributed to the cost of the production of the book, and I am indebted to these organisations for this assistance.

Numerous people have helped me over the years by providing references or sending me copies of their publications, too many to mention here; their assistance has also been invaluable. However, I must mention Derek Renn and Andrew Saunders; they both supported my applications for funding from the British Academy.

I thank most sincerely Shaun Tyas for agreeing to publish this book. He was the first publisher that I approached after the Council for British Archaeology had said 'No', and the alacrity in which he accepted the proposal was a great relief!

A draft of the text was examined a few years ago by Derek Renn (Part 1 and England), the late Richard Avent (Wales), Geoffrey Stell (Scotland) and Conleth Manning (Ireland), to whom I am indebted for their comments. In particular, Geoff pointed out the error of my ways regarding some counties in Scotland, whilst Con added a number of publications that I had not seen. However, I must stress that errors and omissions must be laid firmly at my door!

I have dedicated this book to the memory of a dear friend, Richard Avent, who, with his younger son Rhydian, died tragically in a diving accident off Gozo in the summer of 2006. I will always have great memories of our castle jaunts,

ACKNOWLEDGEMENTS

whether at castle conferences or out in the field. His contribution to the subject was great. He was also a calming influence whenever I ranted about some of the more useless publications that have appeared in the field of castle studies in recent years!

Last, but by no means least, I must record my indebtedness to my family – Chris, Pip and Jo, not forgetting several labradors. Their tolerance of my castle activities over the past thirty years or more has made them saints!

John R. Kenyon
The Epiphany of Our Lord 2007

FORTIFICATIONS BIBLIOGRAPHY

INTRODUCTION

This bibliography covers books and articles on fortifications in the United Kingdom and Ireland from the time of the Norman Conquest of England up to the twentieth century. No bibliographer should ever claim that his or her work is definitive, and all I would say is that I hope that I have over 99 per cent of the *key* material in this field, and possibly at least 95 per cent of material published as a whole.

I am sure that there are a number of guide books to sites not in State care, and in several editions, that I have missed, and several articles in county magazines and similar publications. Of the books and articles listed, I have seen 99.99 per cent! Occasionally I have not been able to follow up a publication, but it has been included if I have been satisfied that it is bona fide. In spite of being able to use various libraries in Dublin, I know that there are a number of Irish local history journals that I have not been able to examine. The following website is well worth exploring for anything that I may not have seen:

http://www.rhs.ac.uk/bibl/ireland.asp

Readers should be aware that the key pre-1945 publications on castles in England and Wales are listed in David Cathcart King's two-volume work *Castellarium Anglicanum* (Kraus, 1983). I started on the *Bibliography* whilst working at the Library of the Society of Antiquaries of London in the early 1970s, and had not thought of publication until this was suggested to me by Derek Renn. After an initial, unsuccessful, approach to the Royal Archaeological Institute, Henry Cleere, then Director of the Council for British Archaeology, suggested that it could form a volume in the CBA's research report series. The CBA in the end published three volumes (1978, 1983 and 1990), and I am indebted to that body for doing so, and was to some extent sorry to see that this final volume, which incorporates the first three with numerous additions, together with post-1990 material, is not a CBA publication.

However, these things often work out for the better, and I am deeply indebted to Shaun Tyas for agreeing to accept my proposal so promptly and seeing the merits of a bibliography in book form, rather than electronic. At a straw poll taken a few years ago at a meeting of the Castle Studies Group, particularly of members who would use the bibliography professionally, the overwhelming response was for a hard copy, so that it was immediately to hand in members' offices. It was considered that an electronic version would be a bonus, but not at the expense of a traditional book.

1

A feature of the three CBA volumes is an overview of the main publications cited in each volume. I have avoided that here, because of the lack of space and time; in fact the history of castle studies would make a book in its own right. The introductions to those three CBA research reports still stand as an overview of the literature. Also, since the formation of the Castle Studies Group in 1987, there has been an annual bibliography of the main publications on medieval fortifications, and in more recent years, particularly since the CSG bibliography became a separate publication from the original newsletter in 1997, there has been a lengthy critique before each listing. The latest issue, number 20, was published in the summer of 2007.

In recent years various people have sent me lists of publications to consider, and whereas some of the material had already been included since 1990, and I had noted others, a certain amount tended to be duplicated typescripts of interim reports and similar items, and I have usually excluded these, especially when the final reports have been published.

Details of any additions and corrections would be most welcome, and they will probably be listed in a separate section of the CSG's annual bibliography, even the post-medieval and modern material, as that publication would seem to be the best outlet for publishing addenda and corrigenda. The information should be sent to me at The Library, Amgueddfa Cymru – National Museum Wales, Cathays Park, Cardiff CF10 3NP, or e-mailed to me at my current (2008) email addresses:

     john.kenyon@museumwales.ac.uk

or   john.r.kenyon@ntlworld.com

The Bibliography

This work, covering Great Britain, Northern Ireland and Ireland, as well as the Channel Islands, the Isle of Man and the Scillies, is in two parts, following the format in the three CBA volumes. Part 1 covers general books and pamphlets, periodical articles and miscellaneous items, mainly articles in books of essays. Part 2 covers publications on specific counties and the individual sites within them, arranged by country, starting with England. The historic counties have been used, and the section on Ireland has the counties of the North and the Republic in one sequence. Although many may be unfamiliar with the historic counties nowadays, the index of places has been compiled to address this potential problem.

Scholarly and popular books and articles have been included, and some of the more important children's books are also listed. Castles which are not medieval in origin, such as Victorian Penrhyn in Caernarvonshire, have been omitted. It has not always proved possible to locate and list every edition of an item, especially guidebooks, for example the numerous editions of the guide to Dunnottar in Kincardineshire. The various area archaeological units have generated a vast amount of grey literature as part of their official duties, and these in-house reports have been omitted, although such work often leads to full academic publication, and hence inclusion.

A number of continental publications have been included, as having a direct bearing on castles in the UK and Ireland, notably books in German on Irish and Scottish castles, together with several French papers on the medieval castle in France and England.

The main entries in the inventories compiled by the Royal Commissions and sister bodies have been extracted, for example the survey of Corfe Castle in one of the Dorset volumes. However, those in the Glamorgan volumes have not been extracted as there are two volumes devoted solely to the castles. Some entries in the *Victoria County History* volumes have also been cited.

Within each county entry, general material is listed first, and then come the sites in alphabetical order. Within an individual site, any monographs and guidebooks are listed first, in alphabetical order by author (with Anon at the beginning), and then come essays in books, again in author sequence, followed by periodical articles, arranged in alphabetical order by the journal title, papers in the same journal coming in order of volume number.

ABBREVIATIONS

anon	anonymous
BAR	British Archaeological Reports
CAA	Cambrian Archaeological Association
CBA	Council for British Archaeology
ch	chapter
CUP	Cambridge University Press
DoE	Department of the Environment
espec	especially
HBMCE	Historic Buildings and Monuments Commission for England
HMSO	Her/His Majesty's Stationery Office
MoLAS	Museum of London Archaeology Service
n d	no date
OPW	Office of Public Works
OUP	Oxford University Press
RAI	Royal Archaeological Institute
RCAHMS/RCAMS	Royal Commission on the Ancient and Historical Monuments of Scotland
RCAHMW	Royal Commission on the Ancient and Historical Monuments of Wales
RCHM/RCHME	Royal Commission on the Historical Monuments of England
S l	Sine locum
S n	Sine nomine
ser	series
TSO	The Stationery Office

* An asterisk at the end of an entry means that the publication is illustrated.

PART 1 – GENERAL

(a) BOOKS AND PAMPHLETS

Anon
Ancient monuments of Northern Ireland. **1**. *In State care*. 5th edition. Belfast: HMSO, 1969*

Ancient monuments of Northern Ireland. **2**. *Not in State care*. 3rd edition. Belfast: HMSO, 1969*

Castles, kings and princes: warriors and fortresses of Wales through the ages. [Gillingham, Suffolk]: Old Orchard Press, [1991]*

English castles almanac. London: English Tourist Board, 1992*

English castles: history & building, map & gazetteer. London: English Heritage, [c 2004] (Z guides)*

Forts and castles. London: Macdonald Educational, 1980*

The national monuments of Ireland. Dublin: Bord Failte Eireann, 1964*

Aalen, F H A (ed), with O'Brien, C
England's landscape [7]: the north east. London: Collins, in association with English Heritage, 2006* [espec ch 4, by R Lomas and R Muir]

Adams, B
Medieval castles. London: Gloucester Press, 1989*

Adkin, M
The Daily Telegraph guide to Britain's military heritage. London: Aurum, 2006*

Ainslie, A D
Historic castles of Scotland. Privately published, [c 1982]*

Aldred, D
Castles and cathedrals: the architecture of power 1066–1550. Cambridge: CUP, 1993*

Alexander, C
Ironside's line: the definitive guide to the General Headquarters' Line planned for Great Britain in response to the threat of German invasion 1940–42. Storrington: Historic Military Press, 1999*

5

Allibone, J
Anthony Salvin: pioneer of Gothic revival architecture. Cambridge: Lutterworth Press, 1988*

Ambrus, V
Drawing on archaeology: bringing history to life. Stroud: Tempus, 2006*

Ambrus, V and Aston, M
Recreating the past. Stroud: Tempus, 2001*

Anderson, W
Castles of Europe from Charlemagne to the Renaissance. London: Elek Books, 1970*

Ardagh, P
Why are castles castle-shaped? 100½ questions about castles answered. London: Faber and Faber, 2002*

Aris, M and Burns, J
The development of the castle in Wales. [S l]: Gwynedd Archives Service/Language Studies Centre, 1993*

Armitage, E S
The early Norman castles of the British Isles. Farnham: Gregg Press, 1971* [reprint of 1912 edition]

Avent, R
Cestyll tywysogion Gwynedd/Castles of the princes of Gwynedd. Cardiff: HMSO, 1983*

Babington, C, Manning, T and Stewart, S
Our painted past: wall paintings of English Heritage. London: English Heritage, 1999*

Barrett, P
The walled towns of Wales and Chester. Cardiff: Wales Tourist Board, 1995*

Barry, T B
The archaeology of medieval Ireland. London: Methuen, 1987*

Bartlett, T and Jeffery, K (eds)
A military history of Ireland. Cambridge: CUP, 1996* [espec chs 3 & 4]

Barton, S
Castles in Britain: an illustrated guide. Worthing: Lyle, 1973*

Baxter, C and Havord, B
Scottish castles. Edinburgh: Lomond Books, 1995*

Beaton, E
Scotland's traditional houses: from cottage to tower-house. Edinburgh: TSO, 1997* (Discovering historic Scotland)

Bebb, W A
Hil a hwyl y castell: llyfr hanes cestyll Cymru i blant Cymru. Aberystwyth: Gwasg Aberystwyth, 1946*

Beffeyte, R
Les machines de guerre au Moyen Age. Rennes: Editions Ouest-France, 2000*

Bimberg, C
Introducing castles. Brighton: Young Library, 1989*

Binding, G
Medieval building techniques. Stroud: Tempus, 2004*

Bottomley, F
The castle explorer's guide. London: Kaye and Ward, 1979*

Brabbs, D
England's heritage. London: Cassell, in association with English Heritage, 2001* [espec ch 3]

Bradbury, J
The medieval siege. Woodbridge: Boydell Press, 1992*

Bradley, J
Walled towns in Ireland. Dublin: Town House and Country House, 1995*

Braun, H
The English castle. 3rd edition, revised. London: Batsford, 1947–8*

Breeze, D J
Historic Scotland: 5000 years of Scotland's heritage. London: Batsford, in association with Historic Scotland, 1998*

A queen's progress: an introduction to the buildings associated with Mary queen of Scots in the care of the Secretary of State for Scotland. Edinburgh: HMSO, 1987*

Brice, M
Forts and fortresses. Oxford: Facts on File, 1990*

Stronghold: a history of military architecture. London: Batsford, 1984*

Brooke, C J
Safe sanctuaries: security and defence in Anglo-Scottish border churches 1290– 1690. Edinburgh: John Donald, 2000*

Brown, R A
Allen Brown's English castles. Introduction by J Coad. Woodbridge: Boydell Press, 2004* [reprint of 1976 edition]

The architecture of castles: a visual guide. London: Batsford, 1984*

Castles. Princes Risborough: Shire Publications, 1985* (Shire archaeology; 36)

Castles, conquest and charters: collected papers. Woodbridge: Boydell Press, 1989*

Castles from the air. Cambridge: CUP: 1989*

English medieval castles. London: Batsford, 1954*; 2nd edition, *English castles*, Batsford, 1962* [paperback only]; 3rd edition, Batsford, 1976*

Brown, R A (ed)
Castles: a history and guide. Poole: Blandford Press, 1980*

Bryant, J
Turner: painting the nation. English Heritage properties as seen by J M W Turner. London: English Heritage, 1996*

Bur, M
Le château. Turnhout: Brepols, 1999* (Typologie des sources du moyen âge occidental; 79)

Burke, J
Life in a castle in medieval England. London: Batsford, 1978*; New York: Dorset Press, 1992*

Burton, N
English Heritage from the air. London: Sidgwick and Jackson, 1989*

Cadw: Welsh Historic Monuments
Castles in Wales: an educational publication. Cardiff: Cadw: Welsh Historic Monuments, 1994*

Exploring and conserving the castles of the Welsh princes/Archwilio a diogelu cestyll tywysogion Cymru. Cardiff: Cadw: Welsh Historic Monuments, [2002]* [leaflet to accompany an exhibition]

Cairns, C
Medieval castles. Cambridge: CUP, 1987*

Caldwell, D H
Scotland's wars and warriors: winning against the odds. Edinburgh: TSO, 1998*

Carpenter, A C
Guns and carriages: the construction of the world's first reproduction Moncrieff depression mounting. Tiverton: Halsgrove, 1999*

Clarke, G S
Fortification: its past achievements, recent development, and future progress. Liphook: Beaufort Publishing, 1989* [reprint of 1907 2nd edition]

Clarke, H
The archaeology of medieval England. London: British Museum Press, 1984*
[espec ch 4]

Cleator, P E
Castles and kings. London: Hale, 1963*

Clements, G
The truth about castles. London: Macmillan Children's Books. 1991*

Clements, W H
Defending the north: the fortifications of Ulster 1796–1956. Newtownards: Colourpoint Books, 2003*

Towers of strength: the story of the Martello towers. Barnsley: Leo Cooper, 1999*

Cocroft, W D and Thomas, R J C
Cold War: building for nuclear confrontation 1946–1989, edited by P S Barnwell. Swindon: English Heritage, 2003*

Cocroft W D [et al]
War art: murals and graffiti – military life, power and subversion. York: CBA, 2006* (Research report; 147)

Colvin, H M (ed)
Building accounts of King Henry III. Oxford: Clarendon Press, 1971*

The history of the king's works. 1–2. The middle ages. 2 volumes and plans. London: HMSO, 1963*

The history of the king's works. 3. 1485–1660 (part I). London: HMSO, 1975*

The history of the king's works. 4. 1485–1660 (part II). London: HMSO, 1982*

Condit, T
Ireland's archaeology from the air. Dublin: Country House, 1997*

Connolly, R E
If walls could talk: great Irish castles tell their stories. Dublin: Mentor Books, 2004*

Cook, D
Castles of Scotland. Edited by V Brett. Norwich: Jarrold, 2002*

Castles of Wales and the Welsh Marches. London: Pitkin Pictorials, 1984*; 2001*

Copeland, T
A teacher's guide to using castles. London: English Heritage, 1994*

Corbishley, M
Aerial photography. London: English Heritage, 2004* (Education on site)

Corfis, I V and Wolfe, M (eds)
The medieval city under siege. Woodbridge: Boydell Press, 1995*

Cormack, P
Castles of Britain. Cleveland, Ohio: Artus, 1982*; new edition, Godalming: Peerage Books, 1989*

Corneweyle, R
The manner of fortification of cities, townes, castelles and other places. Edited with an introduction by M Biddle. [S l]: Gregg International, 1972* [facsimile reprint of 1559 edition]

Cosgrove, A (ed)
A new history of Ireland. 2. Medieval Ireland 1169–1534. Oxford: Clarendon Press, 1987*

Coulson, C
Castles in medieval society: fortresses in England, France, and Ireland in the central Middle Ages. Oxford: OUP, 2003*

Coventry, M
The castles of Scotland: a comprehensive reference and gazetteer to more than 2700 castles and fortified sites. 3rd edition. Musselburgh: Goblinshead, 2001* [previous editions 1995 and 1997]

The castles of Scotland. 4th edition. Edinburgh: Birlinn, 2006*

Craig, M
The architecture of Ireland from the earliest times to 1880. London: Batsford, 1982*

Craig, M and the Knight of Glin
Ireland observed: a guide to the buildings and antiquities of Ireland. Cork: Mercier Press, 1970*

Creighton, O H
Castles and landscapes. London: Continuum, 2002*

Castles and landscapes: power, community and fortification in medieval England. London: Equinox, 2005* [paperback edition of above book, with enhanced photographs]

Creighton O [H] and Higham, R [A]
Medieval castles. Princes Risborough: Shire Publications, 2003* (Shire archaeology; 83)

Medieval town walls: an archaeology and social history of urban defence. Stroud: Tempus, 2005*

Cross, M
Bibliography of monuments in the care of the Secretary of State for Scotland.
Glasgow: The University, Department of Archaeology, 1994

Crossley, D
Post-medieval archaeology in Britain. Leicester: Leicester University Press, 1990*
[espec ch 4]

Crossley, F H
Timber building in England from early times to the end of the seventeenth century. London: Batsford, 1951* [espec ch 9]

Cruden, S
The Scottish castle. Edinburgh: Nelson, 1960*; revised edition, 1963*; 3rd edition, Edinburgh: Spur Books, 1981*

Cruickshank, D
Invasion: defending Britain from attack. London: Boxtree, 2001*

Cunliffe, B (ed)
England's landscape [4]: the west. London: Collins, in association with English Heritage, 2006* [espec ch 5, by J Bond]

Dargie, R
Scottish castles and fortifications. Thatcham: G W Publishing, 2004*

Davies, S
Welsh military institutions, 633–1283. Cardiff: University of Wales Press, 2004 [espec ch 5]

Davis P R
Castles of the Welsh princes. Swansea: Christopher Davies, 1988*

Davison, B K
Explore a castle. London: Hamish Hamilton, 1982*

Looking at a castle. London: Kingfisher, 1987*

The observer's book of castles. London: Warne, 1979*; 2nd edition, *The new observer's book of castles*. Harmondsworth: Warne, 1986*

Picturing the past through the eyes of reconstruction artists. London: English Heritage, 1997* (Gatekeeper series)

Davison, B K and Dennis, P
Exploring a castle. London: Kingfisher Books, 1992* [revised edition of *Looking at a castle*]

De Breffny, B
Castles of Ireland. London: Thames & Hudson, 1977*

De Breffny, B and Ffolliott, R
The houses of Ireland. London: Thames & Hudson, 1975*

DeVries, K
Medieval military technology. Peterborough, Ontario: Broadview Press, 1992*

DoE for Northern Ireland
Historic monuments of Northern Ireland: an introduction and guide. 6th edition. Belfast: HMSO, 1983*

Dobinson, C
AA command: Britain's anti-aircraft defences of World War II. London: Methuen, 2001*

Donnelly, C J
Living places: archaeology, continuity and change at historic monuments in Northern Ireland. Belfast: Institute of Irish Studies, The Queen's University, 1997* [espec chs 8–10]

Donnelly, M P and Diehl, D
Siege: castles at war. Dallas: Taylor Publishing, 1998*

Dorward, L
Castles in Scotland: resource book for teachers, edited by M Fry and C Tabraham. Edinburgh: Historic Scotland, [1999]*

Douet, J.
British barracks 1600–1914: their architecture and role in society. London: TSO for English Heritage, 1998*

Draper, P
The formation of English Gothic: architecture and identity. London: Yale University Press, 2006*

Duffy, C
The fortress in the age of Vauban and Frederick the Great 1660–1789. Siege warfare volume 2. London: Routledge and Kegan Paul, 1985*

Siege warfare: the fortress in the early modern world 1494–1660. London: Routledge and Kegan Paul, 1979*

Dunbar, J G
The historic architecture of Scotland. London: Batsford, 1966*

Scottish royal palaces: the architecture of the late medieval and early Renaissance periods. East Linton: Tuckwell Press, 1999*

Dyer, N
British fortification in the late 19th and early 20th centuries. Fareham: Palmerston Forts Society, 2003*

Dykes, D W
Alan Sorrell: ail-greu'r gorffennol. Cardiff: National Museum of Wales, 1980*

Alan Sorrell: early Wales re-created. Cardiff: National Museum of Wales, 1980*

Emery, A
Greater medieval houses of England and Wales 1300–1500. 1. Northern England. Cambridge: CUP, 1996*

Greater medieval houses of England and Wales 1300–1500. 2. East Anglia, central England, and Wales. Cambridge: CUP, 2000*

Greater medieval houses of England and Wales 1300–1500. 3. Southern England. Cambridge: CUP, 2006*

Endres, G and Hobster, G
Castle ruins of medieval England and Wales. Ramsbury: Airlife Publishing, 2003*

English Heritage
A poster pack for looking at castles. London: English Heritage, [1994]*

Enoch, V J
The martello towers of Ireland. Privately published, [1975]*

Evans, D
Arming the fleet: the development of the Royal Ordnance Yards 1770–1945. Gosport: Explosion! Museum of Naval Firepower, in association with English Heritage, 2006*

Evans, L
The castles of Wales. London: Constable, 1998*

Fawcett, R
Scottish architecture: from the accession of the Stewarts to the Reformation 1371–1560. Edinburgh: Edinburgh University Press, in association with Historic Scotland, 1994*

Fenlon, J
Goods and chattels: a survey of early household inventories in Ireland. Kilkenny: The Heritage Council, 2003*

Fenwick, H
Scotland's castles. London: Hale, 1976*

Fernie, E
The architecture of Norman England. Oxford: OUP, 2000* [espec ch 3]

Fissel, M C
English warfare, 1511–1642. London: Routledge, 2001*

FitzPatrick, E
Royal inauguration in Gaelic Ireland c 1100–1600: a cultural landscape study.
Woodbridge: Boydell Press, 2004*

Foot, W
Beaches, fields, streets, and hills ... The anti-invasion landscapes of England, 1940. York: CBA, 2006* (Research report; 144)

The battlefields that nearly were: defended England 1940. Stroud; Tempus, 2006*

Forde-Johnston, J
Castles and fortifications of Britain and Ireland. London: Dent, 1977*

Great medieval castles of Britain. London: Bodley Head, 1979*

A guide to the castles of England and Wales. London. Constable, 1981*

Foster, J
Guns of the north-east: coastal defences from the Tyne to the Humber. Barnsley: Pen & Sword Military, 2004*

Fraser, S
Castles and cathedrals. London: Hodder & Stoughton, 1992*

Friar, S
The Sutton companion to castles. Stroud: Sutton Publishing, 2003*

Fry, P S
British medieval castles. Newton Abbot: David and Charles, 1974*

Castles of Britain and Ireland. Newton Abbot: David and Charles, 1996*

Castles: England, Scotland, Wales, Ireland. Newton Abbot: David and Charles, 2005* [new edition of the previous title]

The David and Charles book of castles. Newton Abbot: David and Charles, 1980*

Furtado, P [et al] (eds)
The Ordnance Survey guide to castles in Britain. [Southampton]: Ordnance Survey; Country Life Books, 1987*

Gander, T
Military archaeology: a collector's guide to 20th century war relics. Cambridge: Stephens, 1979*

Gascoigne, B and C
Castles of Britain. London: Thames & Hudson, 1975*

Gaunt, P
The Cromwellian gazetteer: an illustrated guide to Britain in the Civil War and Commonwealth. Gloucester: Alan Sutton, 1987*

A nation under siege: the Civil War in Wales 1642–48. London: HMSO for Cadw: Welsh Historic Monuments, 1991*

Gerrard, C
Medieval archaeology: understanding traditions and contemporary approaches. London: Routledge, 2003*

Gianazza, G
Castles from the air. London: Frances Lincoln, 2003*

Châteaux forts: vus du ciel. Paris: Hazan, 2003*

Gies, J and F
Life in a medieval castle. London: Abelard, 1975*; London: Folio Society, 2002*

Glover, R
Britain at bay: defence against Bonaparte, 1803–14. London: Allen and Unwin, 1973*

Goodall, J S
The story of the castle. London: Deutsch, 1986*

Graham, B J
Anglo-Norman settlement in Ireland. [S l]: Group for the Study of Irish Historic Settlement, 1985*

Medieval Irish settlement: a review. [S l]: Historical Geography Research Group, 1980*

Graham, B J and Proudfoot, L J (eds)
An historical geography of Ireland. London: Academic Press, 1993* [espec chs 2 and 3]

Grant, A and C
The castle companion: a guide to historic castles of south Wales. Pontypool: Village Publications, 1991*

Gravett, C
Castle. London: Dorling Kindersley, 1994* (Eyewitness guides; 49)

The history of castles: fortifications round the world. Guilford, Ct: Lyons Press, 2001*

Medieval siege warfare. London: Osprey, 1990* (Elite series; 28)

Norman stone castles (1): the British Isles 1066–1216. Oxford: Osprey, 2003* (Fortress; 13)

Gravett, C and Nicolle, D
The Normans. Oxford: Osprey, 2006* [dust jacket subtitled *Warrior knights and their castles*]

Gregor, H
Castles for young people. London: HMSO, 1977*; 2nd edition, 1982*

Grenville, J
Medieval housing. London: Leicester University Press, 1997*

Griffiths, R A
Boroughs of mediaeval Wales. Cardiff: University of Wales Press, 1978*

Grimble, I
Castles of Scotland. London: BBC Books, 1987*

Grose, D
The antiquities of Ireland: a supplement to Francis Grose, edited by R Stalley. Dublin: Irish Architectural Archive, 1991*

Guinness, D and Ryan, W
Irish castles and houses. London: Thames & Hudson, 1971*

Halpin, A and Newman, C
Ireland: an Oxford archaeological guide to sites from earliest times to AD 1600. Oxford: OUP, 2006*

Hammond, M
Castles of Britain. 1. England. London: Ian Allan, 1963*

Castles of Britain. 2. Scotland. London: Ian Allan, 1964*

Castles of Britain. 3. Wales and Northern Ireland. London: Ian Allan, 1964*

Harbison, P
Beranger's views of Ireland. Dublin: Royal Irish Academy, 1991*

Cooper's Ireland: drawings and notes from an eighteenth-century gentleman. Dublin: O'Brien Press, 2000*

Guide to the national monuments of Ireland. Dublin: Gill and Macmillan, 1975*

'Our treasure of antiquities': Beranger and Bigari's antiquarian sketching tour of Connacht in 1779, based on material in the National Library of Ireland and the Royal Irish Academy. Bray: Wordwell, 2002*

Hardy, C
Francis Frith's English castles. Salisbury: Frith Book Company, 1999*

Francis Frith's Scottish castles. Salisbury: Frith Book Company, 1999*

Francis Frith's Welsh castles. Salisbury: Frith Book Company, 2000*

Harrington, P
Archaeology of the English Civil War. Princes Risborough: Shire, 1992* (Shire archaeology; 68)

English Civil War archaeology. London: Batsford, in association with English Heritage, 2004*

English Civil War fortifications 1642–51. Oxford: Osprey, 2003* (Fortress; 9)

Harris, N
Castles of England, Scotland and Wales: a guide and gazetteer. London: G Philip, 1991*

Harrison, P
Castles of God: fortified religious buildings of the world. Woodbridge: Boydell Press, 2004*

Harvey, J H
English mediaeval architects: a biographical dictionary down to 1550. Gloucester: Alan Sutton, 1984

English mediaeval architects: a biographical dictionary down to 1550. Supplement to the revised edition of 1984. Hulverstone Manor: Pinhorns, 1987

Harvey, P D A
Maps in Tudor England. London: Public Record Office, 1993* [espec ch 2]

Hayes-McCoy, G A (ed)
Ulster and other Irish maps c 1600. Dublin: Stationery Office for the Irish Manuscripts Commission, 1964*

Henry, C
British Napoleonic artillery 1793–1815 (2): siege and coastal artillery. Oxford: Osprey, 2003* (New vanguard; 65)

Higham R (ed)
A guide to the sources of British military history. London: Routledge and Kegan Paul, 1972

Higham, R and Barker, P
Timber castles. London: Batsford, 1992*

Timber castles. Exeter: University of Exeter Press, 2004* [reprint of the Batsford book with new preface]

Hill, D
Turner in the north. London: Yale University Press, 1996*

Hill, O
Scottish castles of the 16th and 17th centuries. London: Country Life, 1953*

Hill, P and Wileman, J
Landscapes of war: the archaeology of aggression and defence. Stroud: Tempus, 2002*

Hilling , J B
The historic architecture of Wales: an introduction. Cardiff: University of Wales Press, 1976*

What style is it? A pocket guide to architecture in Wales. Cardiff: Cadw: Welsh Historic Monuments, 1995*; revised edition, 2005*

Hindle, B P
Medieval town plans. Princes Risborough: Shire, 1990* (Shire archaeology; 62) [espec ch 6]

Hindley, G
Castles of Europe. Feltham: Hamlyn, 1968*

Hinton, D A
Archaeology, economy and society: England from the fifth to the fifteenth century. London: Seaby, 1990*

Hinz, H
Motte und Donjon: zur Frügeschichte der mittelalterlichen Adelsburg. Cologne: Rheinland Verlag, 1981*

Hislop, M
Medieval masons. Princes Risborough: Shire, 2000* (Shire archaeology; 78)

Hogg, G
Castles of England. Newton Abbot: David and Charles, 1970*

Hogg, I V
Coast defences of England and Wales 1856–1956. Newton Abbot: David and Charles, 1974*

Fortress: a history of military defence. London: Macdonald and Jane's, 1975*

The history of fortification. London: Orbis, 1981* [reprinted as *The history of forts & castles*. London: Macdonald, 1988*]

Hooke, D
England's landscape [6]: the west midlands. London: Collins, in association with English Heritage, 2006* [espec ch 4]

Hopkinson, C and Speight, M
The Mortimers, lords of the March. Almeley: Logaston Press, 2002* [espec ch 10]

Horan, M
Scottish castles. Edinburgh: Chambers, 1994*

Howard, D
Scottish architecture: Reformation to Restoration 1560–1660. Edinburgh: Edinburgh University Press, 1995*

Hughes, Q
A chronology of events in fortification from 1800 to 1914, and An illustrated English glossary of terms used in military architecture. Liverpool: Fortress Study Group, 1980*

Military architecture. London: Evelyn, 1974*

Military architecture: the art of defence from earliest times to the Atlantic Wall. 2nd edition. Liphook: Beaufort Publishing, 1991*

Hugill, R
Borderland castles and peles. Newcastle: Frank Graham, 1970*

Hull, L [E]
Britain's medieval castles. Westport, Conn: Praeger, 2006*

The great castles of Britain & Ireland. London: New Holland, 2005*

Humble, R
English castles. London: English Tourist Board; Weidenfeld and Nicolson, 1984*

Humphries, P H
Castles of Edward the First in Wales. [Cardiff]: HMSO, 1983*

Engines of war: replica medieval siege weapons at Caerphilly Castle. Cardiff: Cadw: Welsh Historic Monuments, 1992*; 2nd edition, 1996*

On the trail of Turner in north and south Wales. Cardiff: Cadw: Welsh Historic Monuments, 1995*; revised edition, 2001*

Hutchinson, G
Martello towers: a brief history. [S l]: the author, 1994*

Imrie J and Dunbar, J G (eds)
Accounts of the masters of works for building and repairing royal palaces and castles. 2. 1616–1649. Edinburgh: HMSO, 1982

Ive, P
The practise of fortification. Edited with an introduction by M Biddle. [S l]: Gregg International, 1972* [facsimile reprint of 1589 edition]

James, T and Simpson, D
Ancient west Wales from the air. Carmarthen: Carmarthenshire Antiquarian Society, 1980*

James, T B
The palaces of medieval England c 1050–1550. London: Seaby, 1990*

Johnson, D N
The Irish castle. Dublin: Eason, 1985*

Johnson, M
Behind the castle gate: from medieval to Renaissance. London: Routledge, 2002*

Johnson, P
Castles from the air: an aerial portrait of Britain's finest castles. London: Bloomsbury, 2006*

Castles of England, Scotland and Wales. London: Weidenfeld and Nicolson, 1989* [text is taken from Johnson's 1978 book below, but there are several new illustrations]

The National Trust book of British castles. London: National Trust; Weidenfeld and Nicolson, 1978*

Jones, B M

Raise the drawbridge: stories and legends of Welsh castles. Llandybie: Dinefwr Press, 1999* [first published 1938]

Jones, G R [*et al*]
Herio'r cestyll. Cardiff: University of Wales Press, 1983*

Jones, M
Knights and castles. London: Batsford, 1991*

Kain, R J P (ed)
England's landscape [3]: the south west. London: Collins, in association with English Heritage, 2006* [espec ch 6, by R A Higham]

Kaufmann, J E and Jurga, R M
Fortress Europe: European fortifications of World War II. London: Greenhill Books, 1999*

Keen, M (ed)
Medieval warfare: a history. Oxford: OUP, 1999*

Keevill, G
Medieval palaces: an archaeology. Stroud: Tempus, 2000*

Kemp, A
Castles in colour. Poole: Blandford Press, 1977*

Kent, P
Fortifications of East Anglia. Lavenham: Dalton, 1988*

Kenyon, J R
Castle studies: recent publications – 12. [S l]: Castle Studies Group, 1999 [previous issues listed in Part 1(b)]

Castle studies: recent publications – 13. [S l]: Castle Studies Group, 2000

Castle studies: recent publications – 14. [S l]: Castle Studies Group, 2001

Castle studies: recent publications – 15. [S l]: Castle Studies Group, 2002

Castle studies: recent publications – 16. [S l]: Castle Studies Group, 2003

Castle studies: recent publications – 17. [S l]: Castle Studies Group, 2004

Castle studies: recent publications – 18. [S l]: Castle Studies Group, 2005

Castle studies: recent publications – 19. [S l]: Castle Studies Group, 2006

The Library catalogue. [Liverpool]: Fortress Study group, [1990]

Medieval fortifications. Leicester: Leicester University Press, 1990*; paperback, 1991* [with corrections, and new publications cited in extended preface]

Medieval fortifications. London: Continuum, 2005* [re-issue of 1991 paperback edition]

Kenyon, J R and Avent, R
Castles in Wales and the Marches: essays in honour of D J Cathcart King. Cardiff: University of Wales Press, 1987*

Kerr, N and M
A guide to medieval sites in Britain. London: Grafton, 1988*

A guide to Norman sites in Britain. London: Granada, 1984*

Kerrigan, P
Castles and fortifications in Ireland 1485–1945. Cork: Collins Press, 1995*

Kightly, C
Strongholds of the realm: defences in Britain from prehistory to the twentieth century. London: Thames & Hudson, 1979*

Castles: the north Wales borderlands/Cestyll: gororau gogledd Cymru. Ruthin: Denbighshire County Council, 2002*

Living rooms: interior decoration in Wales 400–1960. Cardiff: Cadw, 2006*

King, D J C
The castle in England and Wales: an interpretative history. London: Croom Helm, 1988*; paperback, Routledge, 1991* [includes final paragraphs of ch 13 omitted in error from the hardback edition]

Castles and abbeys of Wales. London: HMSO, 1975*

Castellarium Anglicanum: an index and bibliography of the castles in England, Wales and the islands. Millwood: Kraus International, 1983, 2 vols*

King, R
Castles in Wales. Shepperton: Dial House, 1996*

Lake, J
Twentieth-century military sites: current approaches to their recording and conservation. Swindon: English Heritage, 2000, republished 2003*

Langley, A
Castle at war: the story of a siege. London: Dorling Kindersley, 1998*

Leask, H G
Irish castles and castellated houses. 2nd edition, revised reprint. Dundalk: Dundalgan Press, 1951*

Lepage, J-D G G
Castles and fortified cities of medieval Europe: an illustrated history. Jefferson: McFarland, 2002*

Lesberg, S
The cottages and castles of Ireland. Leicester: Peebles Press, 1975*

Liddiard, R
Castles in context: power, symbolism and landscape, 1066–1500. Macclesfield: Windgather Press, 2005*

Liddiard, R (ed)
Anglo-Norman castles. Woodbridge: Boydell Press, 2003*

Lindsay, M
The castles of Scotland. London: Constable, 1986*

Lines, C
Exploring castles. Hove: Wayland, 1989*

Linsell, D
Castles 1066–1500 (Collins living history). London: Collins Educational, 1991*

Castles 1066–1500: teacher's notes (Collins living history). London: Collins Educational, 1991*

Little, B
Architecture in Norman Britain. London: Batsford, 1985* [espec chs 2 & 3]

Debrett's the castles of Britain. Camberley: Webb and Bower, 1990*

Loeber, R
A biographical dictionary of architects in Ireland 1600–1720. London: Murray, 1981

Lowerre, A
Placing castles in the Conquest: landscape, lordship and local politics in the south-eastern midlands, 1066–1100. Oxford: J and E Hedges, 2005* (BAR British series; 385)

Lowry, B
British home defences 1940–45. Oxford: Osprey, 2004* (Fortress; 20)

Discovering fortifications from the Tudors to the Cold War. Princes Risborough: Shire Publications, 2006* (Discovering series; 296)

20th century defences in Britain: an introductory guide. York: CBA, 1995* (Practical handbook in archaeology; 12)

Ludlow, J and Jameson, N (eds)
Medieval Ireland: the Barryscourt Lectures I–X. Kinsale: Gandon Editions, 2004*

McAleavy, D
Life in a medieval castle. London: English Heritage, 1998* (Gatekeeper series)

Macaulay, D
Castles. London: Collins, 1977*

McCord, M and Graham, R
Tower houses and ten pound castles. Belfast: Crannog Press, 1970*

McCullogh, N and Mulvin, V
A lost tradition: the nature of architecture in Ireland. Dublin: Gandon Editions, 1987*

Macdonald, F and Bergin, M
A medieval castle. London: Simon and Schuster, 1990*

McEnery, J H
Fortress Ireland: the story of the Irish coastal forts and the river Shannon defence line. Bray: Wordwell, 2006*

MacIvor, I
A fortified frontier: defences of the Anglo-Scottish border. Stroud: Tempus, 2001*

McKean, C
The Scottish château: the country house of renaissance Scotland. Stroud: Sutton Publishing, 2001*

McNeill, P and Nicholson, R (eds)
An historical atlas of Scotland c. 400-c. 1600. St Andrews: Atlas Committee of the Conference of Scottish Medievalists, 1975*

McNeill, T E
Anglo-Norman Ulster: the history and archaeology of an Irish barony, 1177–1400. Edinburgh: John Donald, 1980*

Castles. London: Batsford, in association with English Heritage, 2006*

Castles in Ireland: feudal power in a Gaelic world. London: Routledge, 1997*

English Heritage book of castles. London: Batsford, in association with English Heritage, 1992*

Mallory J P and McNeill, T E
The archaeology of Ulster from colonization to plantation. Belfast: Institute of Irish Studies, The Queen's University, 1991*

Mallory, K and Ottar, A
Architecture of aggression: a history of military architecture in north west Europe 1900–1945. London: Architectural Press, 1973*

Mannion, J
Castles from above. London: Myriad, 2005*

Matarasso, F
The English castle. London: Cassell, 1993*

Matthews, R
Building a castle. Hove: Firefly, 1990*

Castles. Harmondsworth: Puffin, 1990*

Living in a castle. Hove: Firefly, 1990*

Maurice-Jones, K W
The history of coast artillery in the British Army. London: Royal Artillery Institution, 1959*

Mehl, H
Naval guns: 500 years of ship and coastal artillery. London: Chatham Publishing, 2002*

Merlen, R H A
The motte-and-bailey castles of the Welsh border. 2nd edition. Ludlow: Palmers Press, 1987*

Metternich, W
Burgen in Irland: Herrschaftsarchitektur im Hochmittelalter. Darmstadt: Wissenschaftliche Buchgesellschaft, 1999*

Montagu of Beaulieu, *Lord*
English Heritage. Edited by P H Reed. London: Queen Anne Press, 1987*

Moore, D
Arming the forts: the artillery of the Victorian land forts. Fareham: Palmerston Forts Society, 1994*

A handbook of military terms used in connection with fortifications of the Victorian era. Fareham: Palmerston Forts Society, 1991*; 2nd edition, 1993*

The Moncrieff story. Gosport: D Moore for the Palmerston Forts Society, 1992*

[Moore, D]
Yr arlunydd a'r castell/The artist and the castle. Aberystwyth: National Library of Wales, 1984*

Morant, R W
The monastic gatehouse and other types of portal of medieval religious houses. Lewes: Book Guild, 1995*

Morley, B M
Henry VIII and the development of coastal defence. London: HMSO, 1976*

Morris, M
Castle: a history of the buildings that shaped medieval Britain. Basingstoke: Channel Four Books, 2003*

Morris, R
Churches in the landscape. London: Dent. 1989* [espec ch 6]

Morris, W R
Cestyll y Norman. [?Cardiff: Welsh Office]/Y Gyfadran Addysg, Coleg Prifysgol Cymru, 1984* [reference taken from a footnote; the compiler has been unable to trace a copy of this publication, not even in the National Library of Wales]

Mountfield, D
Castles and castle towns of Great Britain. London: Studio editions, 1993*

Muir, R
Castles and strongholds. London: Macmillan, 1990*

The new reading the landscape: fieldwork in landscape history. Exeter: Exeter University Press, 2000* [espec ch 9]

Musson, C
Wales from the air: pattern of past and present. Aberystwyth: RCAHMW, [1994]*

Neaverson, E
Mediaeval castles in north Wales: a study of sites, water supply and building stones. Liverpool: Liverpool University Press; London: Hodder and Stoughton, 1947*

Newman, R
The historical archaeology of Britain c. 1540–1900. Stroud: Sutton, 2001* [espec pp 13–20, 138–41]

Newson, B
Castles of England: book one. Norwich: Jarrold, 1973*

Castles of England: book two. Norwich: Jarrold, 1973*

Nicolle, D
Medieval siege weapons (1): western Europe AD 585–1385. Oxford: Osprey, 2002* (New vanguard; 58)

Noonan, D
Castles & ancient monuments of England. London: Aurum Press, 2000*

Castles & ancient monuments of Ireland. London: Aurum Press, 2001*

Castles & ancient monuments of Scotland. London: Aurum Press, 2000*

Norris, J
Early gunpowder artillery c. 1300–1600. Ramsbury: Crowood Press, 2003*

Welsh castles at war. Stroud: Tempus, 2004*

Nutt, C
The English castle story. London: English Heritage, in association with Thames House Books, 2005*

O'Brien, J and Guinness, D
Great Irish houses and castles. London: Weidenfeld and Nicolson, 1992*

O'Brien, J and Harbison, P
Ancient Ireland from prehistory to the middle ages. London: Weidenfeld and Nicolson, 1996*

O'Conor, K
The archaeology of medieval rural settlement in Ireland. Dublin: Royal Irish Academy, 1998* (Discovery Programme monograph; 3)

O'Keeffe, T
Barryscourt Castle and the Irish tower-house. Carrigtwohill: Barryscourt Trust, 1997* (Barryscourt lecture; 1)
Medieval Ireland: an archaeology. Stroud: Tempus, 2000* [espec chs 1 and 2]

Oman, C W C
Castles. [S l]: Beekman House, 1978* [reprint of 1926 edition]

O'Neil, B H St J
Castles and cannon: a study of early artillery fortifications in England. Oxford: Clarendon Press, 1960*
Castles: an introduction to the castles of England and Wales. 2nd edition. London: HMSO, 1973*

Oram, R and Stell, G (eds)
Lordship and architecture in medieval and renaissance Scotland. Edinburgh: John Donald, 2005*

Osborne, M
Defending Britain: twentieth-century military structures in the landscape. Stroud: Tempus, 2004*
Sieges and fortifications of the Civil Wars in Britain. Leigh-on-Sea: Partizan Press, 2004*

O'Sullivan, A
The archaeology of lake settlement in Ireland. Dublin: Royal Irish Academy, 1998* (Discovery Programme monograph; 4)

Partridge, M S
Military planning for the defense of the United Kingdom, 1814–1870. New York: Greenwood Press, 1989*

Patullo, N
Castles, houses and gardens of Scotland. Edinburgh: Blackwood, 1967*

Peters, E and Morgan, R
Strongholds and sanctuaries: the borderland of England and Wales. Stroud: Alan Sutton, 1993*

Pettifer, A
English castles: a guide by counties. Woodbridge: Boydell Press, 1995*

Welsh castles: a guide by counties. Woodbridge: Boydell Press, 2000*

Phillips, G
Scottish castles. Glasgow: Drew, 1987*

Phillips, G
The Anglo-Scots wars: a military history. Woodbridge: Boydell Press, 1999*

Planel, P
Locks and lavatories: the architecture of privacy. London: English Heritage, 2000* (Gatekeeper series)

A teacher's guide to battlefields, defence, conflict and warfare. London: English Heritage, 1995*

Platt, C
The architecture of medieval Britain: a social history. London: Yale University Press, 1990*

The castle in medieval England and Wales. London: Secker and Warburg, 1982*

Medieval Britain from the air. London: G Philip, 1984*

Medieval England: a social history and archaeology from the Conquest to AD 1600. London: Routledge and Kegan Paul, 1978*

Pluckrose, H
Castles. London: Franklin Watts, 1991*

Let's go to a castle. London: Watts, 1979*

Porter, P
Medieval warfare in manuscripts. London: British Library, 2000*

Porter, S.
Destruction in the English Civil War. Stroud: Alan Sutton, 1994*

Pounds, N J G
The medieval castle in England and Wales: a social and political history. Cambridge: CUP, 1990*

Prior, S
A few well-positioned castles: the Norman art of war. Stroud: Tempus, 2006*

Pritchard, D
Irish castles. Bray: Real Ireland Design, 1988*

Quiney, A
Town houses of medieval Britain. London: Yale University Press, 2003*

Ramm, H G [et al]
Shielings and bastles. London: HMSO, 1970*

Redknap, M
Ail-greu: delweddu ein gorffennol. Cardiff: National Museums & Galleries of Wales; Cadw: Welsh Historic Monuments, 2002*

Re-creations: visualizing our past. Cardiff: National Museums & Galleries of Wales; Cadw: Welsh Historic Monuments, 2002*

Reeves, M
The medieval castle. 2nd edition. Harlow: Longman, 1988*

Reeves-Smyth, T
Irish castles. Belfast: Appletree Press, 1995 (2006)*

Irish gardens and gardening before Cromwell. Carrigtwohill: Barryscourt Trust, 1999* (Barryscourt lecture; 4)

Reid, A
The castles of Wales. London: G Philip, 1973*

The castles of Wales. Ruthin: John Jones Publishing, 1998* [unedited reprint of the above]

Reid, S
Castles and tower houses of the Scottish clans 1450–1650. Oxford: Osprey, 2006* (Fortress; 46)

Renn, D F
Norman castles in Britain. London: John Baker, 1969*; 2nd edition, 1973*

Reyerson, K and Powe, F (eds)
The medieval castle: romance and reality. Dubuque: Kendall/Hunt Publishing, 1984*

Rickard, J
The castle community: the personnel of English and Welsh castles, 1272–1422. Woodbridge: Boydell Press, 2002*

Roberts, G
Welsh castles. Talybont: Y Lolfa, 2001*

Roberts, J A
Real Welsh castles. Caernarfon: Cyhoeddiadau Mei, 1981*

Robinson, D M
Heritage in Wales: a guide to the ancient and historic sites in the care of Cadw: Welsh Historic Monuments. London: Queen Anne Press, 1989*

Robinson, D M and Thomas, R S (eds)
Wales: castles and historic places. Cardiff: Wales Tourist Board; Cadw: Welsh Historic Monuments, 1990*

Robottom, J
Castles and cathedrals 1066–1500. Harlow: Longman, 1991*

Ross, S
The castles of Scotland. London: G Philip, 1973*

Chambers guide to the castles of Scotland. Revised edition. Edinburgh: Chambers, 1987*

Scottish castles. Moffat: Lochar, [c 1990]*

Ross, W G
Military engineering during the Great Civil War 1642–9. London: Ken Trotman, 1984* [first published 1887]

Rowley, T
The landscape of the Welsh Marches. London: Michael Joseph, 1986* [espec ch 6]

The Norman heritage 1055–1200. London: Routledge and Kegan Paul, 1983* [espec ch 3]

Ruddy, A J
British anti-invasion defences 1940–1945: a pocket reference guide. Storrington: Historic Military Press, 2003*

Rutland, J
Knights and castles. London: Kingfisher Books, 1987*

Ryan, M (ed)
The illustrated archaeology of Ireland. Dublin: Country House, 1991*

Salariya, D
A medieval castle. Hemel Hempstead: Simon and Schuster Young Books, 1990*

Salter, M
Castles and stronghouses of Ireland. Malvern: Folly Publications, 1997*

The castles of north Wales. Malvern: Folly Publications, 1997*

The castles of south-west Scotland. Malvern: Folly Publications, 1993*

The castles of the heartland of Scotland. Malvern: Folly Publications, 1994*

Discovering Scottish castles. Princes Risborough: Shire Publications, 1985*

English castle books by Mike Salter: index and amendments. Malvern: Folly Publications, [2002]

Midland castles. Bartley Green: Quercus, 1993*

Salzman, L F
Building in England down to 1540: a documentary history. Oxford: Clarendon Press, 1952* (corrected reprint, 1967*)

Sancha, S
The castle story. London: Kestrel Books, 1979*; Harmondsworth: Penguin Books, 1981*

Saunders, A D
English Heritage book of Channel defences. London: Batsford, in association with English Heritage, 1997*

Fortress Britain: artillery fortification in the British Isles and Ireland. Liphook: Beaufort Publishing, 1989*

Fortress builder: Bernard de Gomme, Charles II's military engineer. Exeter: University of Exeter Press, 2004*

Saunders, A D [*et al*]
Five castle excavations: report on the Institute's research project into the origins of the castle in England. [London]: Royal Archaeological Institute, 1978*

Sauvain, P
What to look for at the castle. Harlow: Longman, 1985*

Schofield, [A] J (ed)
Modern military matters. Studying and managing the twentieth-century defence heritage in Britain: a discussion document. York: CBA, 2004*

Monuments of war: the evolution, recording and management of twentieth-century military sites. London: English Heritage, 1998*

Schofield, J and Palliser, D (eds)
Recent archaeological research in English towns. London: CBA, 1981*

Schofield, J and Vince, A
Medieval towns. London: Leicester University Press, 1994*

Scott, D
Caisleáin Eireannacha. Dublin: An Foras Riaracháin, 1968*

Sellman, R R
Castles and fortresses. 2nd edition. London: Methuen, 1962*

Shelby, L R
John Rogers: Tudor military engineer. Oxford: Clarendon Press, 1967*

Short, B
England's landscape [1]: the south east. London: Collins, in association with English Heritage, 2006* [espec ch 4, although little information on castles compared to the other titles in the series]

Shuter P and Reynoldson, F
Castles and cathedrals. Oxford: Heinemann Educational, 1991* + assessment and resource pack*

Simpson, W D
Castles from the air. London: Country Life, 1949*

Castles in Britain. London: Batsford, 1966*

Castles in England and Wales. London: Batsford, 1969*

Exploring castles. London: Routledge and Kegan Paul, 1957*

Scottish castles: an introduction to the castles of Scotland. Edinburgh: HMSO, 1959*

Smith, J S (ed)
North east castles: castles in the landscape of north east Scotland. Aberdeen: Aberdeen University Press, 1990*

Smith, V T C
Defending London's river. Rochester: North Kent Books, 1985*

Sorrell, A
British castles. London: Batsford, 1973*

Reconstructing the past, edited by M Sorrell. London: Batsford, 1981*

Soulsby, I
The towns of medieval Wales: a study of their history, archaeology and early topography. Chichester: Phillimore, 1983*

Stalley, R A
Architecture and sculpture in Ireland 1150–1350. Dublin: Gill and Macmillan, 1971*

Early medieval architecture. Oxford: OUP, 1999* [espec ch 4]

Stanford, S C
The archaeology of the Welsh Marches. London: Collins, 1980*; 2nd edition, Leinthall Starkes: the author, 1991* [espec ch 9]

Starkey, D (ed).
The inventory of King Henry VIII: Society of Antiquaries Ms 129 and British Library Ms Harley 1419. The transcript. London: Harvey Miller for the Society of Antiquaries, 1998 (Research report; 56)

Steane, J M
The archaeology of medieval England and Wales. London: Croom Helm, 1985* [espec ch 2]

The archaeology of power: England and northern Europe AD 800–1600. Stroud: Tempus, 2001* [espec ch 7]

Steele, P
The best-ever book of castles. London: Kingfisher, 1995*

Stewart, R W
The English Ordnance Office 1585–1625: a case study in bureaucracy. Woodbridge: Boydell Press for the Royal Historical Society, 1996

Stocker, D
England's landscape [5]: the east midlands. London: Collins, in association with English Heritage, 2006* [espec ch 6]

Sutcliffe, S
Martello towers. Newton Abbot: David and Charles, 1972*

Sweetman, D
Irish castles and fortified houses. Dublin: Town House and Country House, 1995*

Medieval castles of Ireland. Cork: Collins Press, 1999*; Woodbridge: Boydell Press, 2000*

The origin and development of the tower-house in Ireland. Carrigtwohill: Barryscourt Trust, 2000* (Barryscourt lecture; 8)

Tabraham, C
Castles of Scotland: a voyage through the centuries. London: Batsford, 2005*

Scotland's castles. London: Batsford, in association with Historic Scotland, 1995*; new edition, 2005*

Scottish castles and fortifications: an introduction to the historic castles, houses and artillery fortifications in the care of the Secretary of State for Scotland. Edinburgh: HMSO, 1986*

Scottish castles and fortifications. Revised edition [of the above]. Edinburgh: Historic Scotland, 2000*

Tabraham, C and Grove, D
Fortress Scotland and the Jacobites. London: Batsford, in association with Historic Scotland, 1995*

Taylor, A J
The king's works in Wales, 1277–1330. London: HMSO, 1974*

Studies in castles and castle-building. London: Hambledon Press, 1985*

The Welsh castles of Edward I. London: Hambledon Press, 1986*

Taylor, C and Muir, R
Visions of the past. London: Dent, 1983* [espec chs 15, 15 & 21]

Telling, R M
English martello towers: a concise guide. Beckenham: CST Books, 1997*

Handbook on martello towers. Beckenham: CST Books, 1998*

Thomas, A
The walled towns of Ireland. Blackrock: Irish Academic Press, 1992, 2 vols*

Thomas, R (ed)
Castles in Wales: history, spectacle, romance. Basingstoke: Automobile Association; Cardiff: Wales Tourist Board, 1982*

Thompson, A H
Military architecture in medieval England. Wakefield: EP Publishing, 1975* [first published in 1912 as *Military architecture in England during the Middle Ages*]

Thompson, M W
The decline of the castle. Cambridge: CUP, 1987*

Medieval bishops' houses in England and Wales. Aldershot: Ashgate, 1998*

The medieval hall: the basis of secular domestic life, 600–1600 AD. Aldershot: Scolar Press, 1995*

The rise of the castle. Cambridge: CUP, 1991*

Ruins reused: changing attitudes to ruins since the late eighteenth century. Great Dunham: Heritage Marketing and Publications, 2006*

Ruins, their preservation and display. London: British Museum, 1981*

Thurlby, M
The Herefordshire school of Romanesque sculpture. Almeley: Logaston Press, 1999*

Romanesque architecture and sculpture in Wales. Almeley: Logaston Press, 2006*

Times Newspapers
Castles of Britain. London: Times Newspapers, 1980* [wallchart]

Tomlinson, H C
Guns and government: the Ordnance Office under the later Stuarts. London: Royal Historical Society, 1979

Toy, S
The castles of Great Britain. London: Heinemann, 1953*; 2nd edition, 1954*; 3rd edition, 1963*; 4th edition, 1966*

A history of fortification from 3000 BC to AD 1700. London: Heinemann, 1955*; Barnsley: Pen & Sword Books, 2006*

Tranter, N

The fortified house in Scotland. 1. South-east Scotland. Edinburgh: Oliver and Boyd, 1963*

The fortified house in Scotland. 2. Central Scotland. Edinburgh: Oliver and Boyd, 1963*

The fortified house in Scotland. 3. South-west Scotland. Edinburgh: Oliver and Boyd, 1965*

The fortified house in Scotland. 4. Aberdeenshire, Angus, and Kincardineshire. Edinburgh: Oliver and Boyd, 1966*

The fortified house in Scotland. 5. North and west Scotland and miscellaneous. Edinburgh: W and R Chambers, 1970*

Tuck, A

Border warfare: a history of conflict on the Anglo-Scottish border. London: HMSO, 1979*

Turner, H L

Town defences in England and Wales: an architectural and documentary study AD 900–1500. London: John Baker, 1970*

Tuulse, A

Castles of the western world. London: Thames and Hudson, 1958; Newton Abbott: David & Charles, 2002*

Unstead, R J

Castles. London: Black, 1970*

Vance, M

Castles: monographs. Monticello: Vance Bibliographies, 1984

Vaughan-Thomas, W

The splendour falls: the story of the castles of Wales. Cardiff: HTV Cymru/Wales, 1973*

Villena, L

Glossaire: fichier multilangue d'architecture militaire médiévale, sous assistance de L Crespi, F Enaud, W Meyer & A Taylor. Frankfurt am Main: Edition Wolfgang Weidlich, 1975*

Vine, P A L

The Royal Military Canal: an historical account of the waterway and military road from Shornecliffe in Kent to Cliff End in Sussex. Newton Abbot: David and Charles, 1972*

Warner, P

A guide to castles in Britain: where to find them and what to look for. London: New English Library, 1976*; revised edition, 1981*

The medieval castle: life in a fortress in peace and war. London: A Barker, 1971*
[+ later impressions, eg Book Club Associates]

Sieges of the Middle Ages. London: Bell, 1968* (reprinted in 2000 in Penguin's 'Classic military history' series)

Watson-Smyth, M (ed)
Deserted bastions: historic naval and military architecture. London: SAVE Britain's Heritage, 1993*

Wheatley, A
The ideas of the castle in medieval England. Woodbridge: York Medieval Press, 2004*

Wickham-Jones, C R
The landscape of Scotland: a hidden history. Stroud: Tempus, 2001*

Wiggins, K
Siege mines and underground warfare. Princes Risborough: Shire Publications, 2003* (Shire archaeology; 84)

Wilcox, R P
Timber and iron reinforcement in early buildings. London: Society of Antiquaries, 1981* (Occasional paper (new series); 2)

Wilkinson, F
The castles of England. London: G Philip, 1973*

Williams, G
Stronghold Britain: four thousand years of British fortifications. Stroud: Sutton Publishing, 1999*

Williams, W
Cymru'r cestyll 1282–1400. [Cardiff: Welsh Office], 1987*

Williamson, T
England's landscape [4]: East Anglia. London: Collins, in association with English Heritage, 2006* [espec ch 6]

Wills, H
Pillboxes: a study of UK defences 1940. London: Leo Cooper, 1985*

Winchester, A J L (ed), with A G Crosby
England's landscape [8]: the north west. London: Collins, in association with English Heritage, 2006* [espec ch 9, by A J L Winchester]

Wise, T
Forts and castles: the story of defence works from ancient times to the present. New Malden: Almark, 1972*

Wood, D A
An illustrated guide to Victorian forts and equipment. Ipswich: the author, 1989*

Wood, M
The English mediaeval house. London: Phoenix House, 1965* [and later reprints, e g Bracken Books, 1983*]

Norman domestic architecture. [Revised edition]. [S l]: RAI, 1974* (first published in *Archaeological Journal* 92 (1935), 167–242)

Thirteenth-century domestic architecture in England. [S l]: RAI, 1950* (supplement to *Archaeological Journal* 105)

[Wood, S]
Understanding people in the past: a teacher's guide to Historic Scotland's properties, edited by M Fry. Edinburgh: Historic Scotland, 1995*

Wood, T
Spotlight on castles. London: Franklin Watts, 1989*

Woolgar, C M
The great household in late medieval England. London: Yale University Press, 1999*

The senses in late medieval England. London: Yale University Press, 2006*

Wright, N
Beautiful castles of Britain. London: Marshall Cavendish, 1978*

Yeoman, P
Medieval Scotland: an archaeological perspective. London: Batsford, in association with English Heritage, 1995* [espec chs 6 & 7]

Yerburgh, D S
An attempt to depict the castles of the Welsh princes: a pictorial journey through Wales to the remains & sites of the castles which were built by the Welsh princes. Salisbury: Revd Canon D S Yerburgh, [2006]*

Yorke, T
English castles explained. Newbury: Countryside Books, 2003*

Young, P
Civil War England. London: Longman, 1981*

Young, P and Emberton, W
Sieges of the Great Civil War 1642–1646. London: Bell and Hyman, 1978*

Zeune, J
The last Scottish castles: investigations with particular reference to domestic architecture from the 15th to the 17th century. Buch am Erlbach: Verlag Marie L Leidorf, 1992*

The long pause: a reconsideration of Scottish castle-building c 1480–1560. Munich: [the author?], 1984*

Der schottische Burgenbau vom 15. bis 17. Jahrhundert. Marksburg: Deutsches Burgeninstitut, 1989*

(b) PERIODICAL ARTICLES

Anon
'North Wales castles from the air', *Popular Archaeology* 5.1 (1983), 9–15*

'Iron traversing platforms – 1', *Ravelin* 23 (1991), 19–20*

Anderton, M and Schofield, J
'Anti-aircraft gunsites: then and now', *Conservation Bulletin* 36 (1999), 11–13*

Ashbee, J
'"The chamber called *Gloriette*": living at leisure in thirteenth- and fourteenth-century castles', *Journal of the British Archaeological Association* 157 (2004), 17–40*

'Cloisters in English palaces in the twelfth and thirteenth centuries', *ibid* 159 (2006), 71–90*

Attar, R and Ho, Sheu
'King's castles', *BBC History Magazine* 7.5 (2006), 82–83* [Edward I's castles in north Wales]

Austin, D
'The castle and the landscape: annual lecture to the Society for Landscape Studies, 1984', *Landscape History* 6 (1984), 69–81*

Avent, R
'Cadw and castle conservation', *Castle Studies Group Newsletter* 13 (1999–2000), 56–59*

'Castles of the Welsh princes', *Château Gaillard* 16 (1994), 11–20*

'Gwlad y cestyll eraill', *Etifeddiaeth y Cymro* 7 (1997), 7–10*

'Cofio Arnold Taylor, 1911–2002', *ibid* 24 (2003), 7–8*

'The land of other castles', *Heritage in Wales* 7 (1997), 7–10*

'Remembering Arnold Taylor', *ibid* 24 (2003), 7–8*

'The castles built by King Edward I in Wales between 1277 and 1300', *IBI Bulletin* 47 (1990–1), 49–58*

Awty, B G

'The Arcana family of Cesena as gunfounders and military engineers', *Transactions of the Newcomen Society* 59 (1987–8), 61–80*

'Parson Levett and English cannon founding', *Sussex Archaeological Collections* 127 (1989), 133–45

B, F S

'Ordnance stores in Ireland, 1769', *Irish Sword* 2 (1954–6), 233–35

Bachrach, D S

'The organisation of military religion in the armies of King Edward I of England (1272–1307)', *Journal of Medieval History* 29 (2003), 265–86

Ball, T

'Castles on paper', *Fortress* 2 (1989), 2–15*

Barker, P A

'Rabies archaeologorum: a reply', *Antiquity* 54 (1980), 19–20

'Rabies archaeologorum: a reply', *Château Gaillard* 9–10 (1982), 22–22

Barrett G F and Graham, B J

'Some considerations concerning the dating and distribution of ring-forts in Ireland', *Ulster Journal of Archaeology* 3 ser 38 (1975), 33–45*

Barry, T B

'Harold Leask's 'single towers': Irish tower houses as part of larger settlement complexes', *Château Gaillard* 22 (2006), 27–33*

'Rural settlement in Ireland in the Middle Ages: an overview', *Ruralia* 1 (1996), 134–41*

Beamish, H

'Defence review: the modern defence heritage and the National Trust', *National Trust Annual Archaeological Review* 7 (1998–9), 11–17*

Beanse, A

'The Twydall profile', *The Redan* 43 (1998), 25–28*

Beanse, A and Gill, R

'The London mobilisation centres', *ibid* 43 (1998), 12–24*

'London mobilisation centres: gazetteer – 1', *ibid* 44 (1998), 22

Beeler, J H

'Castles and strategy in Norman and early Angevin England', *Speculum* 31 (1956), 581–601

Brown, D M

'Dendrochronological dated buildings from Ireland', *Vernacular Architecture* 33 (2002), 71–73*

Brown, G and Field, D
'Principles of defence: military trenches', *Conservation Bulletin* 44 (2003), 26–27*

Brown, R A
'An historian's approach to the origins of the castle in England', *Archaeological Journal* 126 (1969), 131–48

'Castle gates and garden gates', *Architectural History* 27 (1984), 443–45 [this particular issue of the journal is titled *Design and practice in British architecture: studies in architectural history presented to Howard Colvin*]

'Les châteaux féodaux', *Cahiers de Civilisations Médiévale* 29 (1986), 37–39*

'The Norman Conquest and the genesis of English castles', *Château Gaillard* 3 (1969), 1–14

'Royal castle building in England, 1154–1216', *English Historical Review* 70 (1955), 353–98

'A list of castles, 1154–1216', *ibid* 74 (1959), 249–80

Bruce, D and Creighton, O
'Contested identities: the dissonant heritage of European town walls and walled towns', *International Journal of Heritage Studies* 12 (2006), 234–54*

Bryce, I B D and Roberts, A
'Post-Reformation Catholic houses of north-east Scotland', *Proceedings of the Society of Antiquaries of Scotland* 123 (1993), 363–72*

'Post-Reformation Catholic symbolism: further and different examples', *ibid* 126 (1996), 899–909*

Bur, M
'The social influence of the motte-and-bailey castle', *Scientific American* 248.5 (1983), 132–38, 140*

Burke, J
'The New Model Army and the problems of siege warfare, 1648–51', *Irish Historical Studies* 27 (1990), 1–29

Burne, R V H
'The evolution of the English castle with special reference to the castles of north Wales', *Journal of the Chester and North Wales Architectural, Archaeological and Historic Society* 50 (1963), 15–26*

Burridge, D
'The Maunsell forts', *Byegone Kent* 11.2 (1990), 58–65*

'Designing the forts', *The Redan* 21 (1991), 11–12

Bury, J
'Early writing on fortifications and siegecraft: 1502–1554', *Fort* 13 (1985), 5–48*

Butler L

'Dolforwyn Castle and the Welsh castles of north Wales', *Fortress* 9 (1991), 15–24*

'Masons' marks in castles: a key to building practices', *Château Gaillard* 18 (1998), 23–27*

'Castles of the Welsh princes in north Wales', *IBI Bulletin* 47 (1990–1), 41–48*

'Eight Duchy of Lancaster castles', *Castle Studies Group Journal* 19 (2006), 245–46*

Buttimer, J

'The treaty ports', *An Cosantóir* 38 (1978), 195–99*

Caen Colloquy

'Les fortifications de terre en Europe occidentale du Xᵉ au XIIᵉ siècles (Colloque de Caen, 2–5 Octobre 1980)', *Archéologie Médiévale* 11 (1981), 5–123*

Cairns, C

'The Irish tower house – a military view', *Fortress* 11 (1991), 3–13*

Caldwell, D H

'A sixteenth-century group of gun towers in Scotland', *Fort* 12 (1984), 15–24*

Cantwell, A and Moore, D

'The Victorian army and submarine mining', *Fortress* 18 (1993), 32–47*

Carpenter, A C

'Cannon on historic monument sites: a personal recollection', *Journal of the Ordnance Society* 12 (2000), 59–69*

Cherry, J

'Imago castelli: the depiction of castles on medieval seals', *Château Gaillard* 15 (1992), 83–90*

Chrismas, R

'Guthrie's self balanced rolling bridge: some further consideration', *The Redan* 16 (1989), 13–15* [see also D Moore, below]

Clark, N H

'Twentieth century coastal defences of the Firth of Forth', *Fort* 14 (1986), 49–54*

Coad, J G

'New warfare into old castles: a study of the adaptability of some fortifications in south east England, 1740–1940', *Château Gaillard* 14 (1990), 61–76*

'Warfare and defence: what next?', *Post-Medieval Archaeology* 39 (2005), 224–32*

Cobb, P

'The commercial ports defence scheme 1885–70 [*sic*]', *Palmerston Forts Society Newsletter* 14 (1988), 24–28

'The follies of war: the war-time uses of the Royal Commission forts', *The Redan* 18 (1990), 1–5

'Aviation and the forts', *ibid* 34 (1995), 37–47*

Coldstream, N
'Architects, advisers and design at Edward I's castles in Wales', *Architectural History* 46 (2003), 19–36*

Colvin, H M
'Castles and government in Tudor England', *English Historical Review* 83 (1968), 225–34

Conolly, A
'Castles and abbeys in Wales: refugia for 'medieval' medicinal plants', *Botanical Journal for Scotland* 46 (1994), 628–36

Costello, H
'Into the breach', *BBC History Magazine* 3.5 (2002), 38–39* [native Welsh castles]

Coulson, C
'Specimens of freedom to crenellate by licence', *Fortress* 18 (1993), 3–15*

'The state of research: cultural realities and reappraisals in English castle studies', *Journal of Medieval History* 22 (1996), 171–207*

'Structural symbolism in medieval castle architecture', *Journal of the British Archaeological Association* 132 (1979), 73–90

'Hierarchism in conventual crenellation: an essay in the sociology and metaphysics of medieval fortification', *Medieval Archaeology* 26 (1982), 69–100*

'Licences to crenellate', *ibid* 26 (1982), 162

'Freedom to crenellate by licence: an historiographical revision', *Nottingham Medieval Studies* 38 (1994), 86–137

Coulson, I and Culpin, C
'Castles in context: interpreting sites for secondary history', *Heritage Learning* 30 (2004), 3–4*

Counihan, J
'Ella Armitage, castle studies pioneer', *Fortress* 5 (1990), 51–59*

'Mottes, Norman or not!', *ibid* 11 (1991), 53–60*

Cowie, L W
'The Martello towers', *History Today* 29 (1979), 603–9*

Credland, A G
'Crossbow remains', *Journal of the Society of Archer-Antiquaries* 23 (1980), 12–19*

Creighton, O H

'"The rich man in his castle, the poor man at his gate": castle baileys and settlement patterns in Norman England', *Château Gaillard* 21 (2004), 25–35*

'"Castles of communities": medieval town defences in England, Wales and Gascony', *ibid* 22 (2006), 75–86*

'Castles, lordship and settlement in Norman England and Wales', *History Today* 53.4 (2003), 12–19*

'Early castles and rural settlement patterns: insights from Yorkshire and the east midlands', *Medieval Settlement Research Group Annual Report* 14 (1999), 29–33*

Creighton, O H and Higham, R A

'Castle studies and the "landscape" agenda', *Landscape History* 26 (2004), 5–18*

Crick, T

'Fortifications from Vauban to Jervois', *Fort* 24 (1996), 37–41*

Currie, C K and Rushton, N S

'Dartington Hall and the development of the double-courtyard design in English late medieval high-status houses', *Archaeological Journal* 161 (2004), 189–210*

Davies, O

'A summary of the archaeology of Ulster, part II', *Ulster Journal of Archaeology* 3 ser 12 (1949), 43–76* [espec pp 56–64]

Davison, B K

'The origins of the castle in England', *Archaeological Journal* 124 (1967), 202–11*

'Three eleventh-century earthworks in England', *Château Gaillard* 2 (1967), 39–48* (Beihefte der Bonner Jahrbücher; 27)

'Early earthwork castles; a new model', *ibid* 3 (1969), 37–47*

'The origins of the castle', *Current Archaeology* 1 (1967–8), 129–30*

Dawson, J E and Lalor, C

'Coast defence artillery', *An Cosantóir* 33 (1973), 391–96*

de Cardi, B

'The Scottish castle: report of the third Scottish Summer School, Aberdeen, 1954', *Archaeological News Letter* 5 (1954–5), 79–84*

de hOir, S

'Guns in medieval and Tudor Ireland', *Irish Sword* 15 (1982–3), 76–88*

Denison, S

'Tracing the relics of wartime defence', *British Archaeology* 3 (1995), 8–9*

'Fortress Britain', *ibid* 65 (2002), 8–11*

Dix, B and Thomas, E
'Castles and plantation sites [in NW Ulster]', *Archaeological Journal* 159 (2002), 298–311*

Dixon, P
'Shielings and bastles: a reconsideration of some problems', *Archaeologia Aeliana* 4 ser 50 (1972), 249–58

'Towerhouses, pelehouses and border society', *Archaeological Journal* 136 (1979), 240–52*

'Come into my castle, little man', *British Archaeological News* new ser 11 (1994), 4*

'Design in castle-building: the controlling of access to the lord', *Château Gaillard* 18 (1998), 47–57*

Dixon, P and Lott, B
'The courtyard and the tower: contexts and symbols in the development of late medieval great houses', *Journal of the British Archaeological Association* 146 (1993), 93–101*

Dobinson, C S, Lake, J and Schofield, A J
'Monuments of war: defending England's 20th-century defence heritage', *Antiquity* 71 (1997), 288–99*

Dollen, B von der
'Die Entwicklung des Burgenbaus in Irland seit der anglo-normannischen Eroberung: ein Überlick unter Berücksichtigung neuerer Forschungen', *Burgen und Schlössen* 37 (1996), 50–58*

Doninck, K van
'Martello towers', *Mededelingenblad van de Simon Stevinstichting* 1.1 (1986), 14–20*

Donnelly, C J
'Passage or barrier? Communication between bawn and tower house in late medieval Ireland – the evidence from County Limerick', *Château Gaillard* 21 (2004), 57–64*

'John Henry Parker and his contribution to Irish tower house studies', *Group for the Study of Irish Historic Settlement Newsletter* 5 (1995), 5–7

'Frowning ruins: the tower houses of medieval Ireland', *History Ireland* 4.1 (1996), 11–16*

Donnelly, J A
'A study of the coastal forts built by Henry VIII', *Fort* 10 (1982), 105–26*

Dracop, J
'Edward's castles: defence or aggression?', *Archaeology Today* 8.6 (1987), 40–45*

Earle, J

'The peculiar ways of defending Britain', *British Archaeology* 26 (1997), 8–9*

'The outer London defence ring', *Defence Lines* 4 (1996), [11]*

'The Defence of Britain Project: progress to date', *Museum Archaeologist* 23 (1998), 52–54*

'The Defence of Britain Project', *Sanctuary* 25 (1996), 13

Easton, D and Stell, G

'RCAHMS and the Defence of Britain Project', *Monuments on Record: Annual Review 1998–9* (1999), 44–46*

Edwards, J G

'Edward I's castle-building in Wales', *Proceedings of the British Academy* 32 (1946), 15–81

'The Normans and the Welsh March', *ibid* 42 (1956), 155–77*

Ellington, M

'New view on an old vision: tower house restoration in Scotland', *Country Life* 180 (1986), 1332–34*

Etienne, D

'Les châteaux de Guillaume fils Osbern dans le sud des Marches Galloises', *Annales de Normandie* 56 (2006), 29–60*

Evans, D

'A proposed installation of a tide gauge in the Palmerston sea forts', *Fort* 15 (1987), 101–4

Evans, D M

'Et in arcadia? The problems with ruins', *Antiquaries Journal* 84 (2004), 411–22

Everson, P

'Delightfully surrounded with woods and ponds: field evidence for medieval gardens and large-scale designed landscapes', *Garden History Society Newsletter* 49 (1997), 23–25 + illus on page 1*

Faulkner, P A

'Domestic planning from the twelfth to the fourteenth centuries', *Archaeological Journal* 115 (1958), 150–83*

'Castle planning in the fourteenth century', *ibid* 120 (1963), 215–35*

Fawcett, R

'Castle and church in Scotland', *Château Gaillard* 18 (1998), 87–92*

Ferguson, K

'Castles and the Pallas placename: a German insight', *Irish Sword* 22.89 (2001), 241–48*

Finn, C
'Defiant Britain', *Archaeology* 53.3 (2000), 42–49* [WWII defences]

Foot, W
'The lost defensive ditches of wartime', *British Archaeology* 37 (1998), 10–11*

'Landscape of war', *ibid* 54 (2000), 18–23*

'Public archaeology: defended areas of World War II', *Conservation Bulletin* 44 (2003), 8–11*

'The forgotten last ditches', *Defence Lines* 11 (1998), 4–6*

'Pillboxes in the modern landscape', *ibid* 12 (1999), 11–12*

Forman, S G
'Border towers', *Country Life* 101 (1947), 128–30*

Freeman, A Z
'Wall-breakers and river-bridgers: military engineers in the Scottish wars of Edward I', *Journal of British Studies* 10.2 (1971), 1–16

Fry, M F
'Preserving ancient and historic monuments and sites in State care in Northern Ireland, c 1921 to c 1955. Part one: establishing a system of care', *Ulster Journal of Archaeology* 3 ser 62 (2003), 161–75*

Gardiner, M
'Britain's finest hour', *Fortress* 5 (1990), 55–60* [1939–45 defence structures]

Gardner, K S
'The archaeology of the fortifications of the Great Civil War in the south west', *Council for British Archaeology South West* 11 (2003), 8–14*

Gee, E
'Heating in the late Middle Ages', *Transactions of the Ancient Monuments Society* new ser 31 (1987), 88–105*

Gilyard-Beer, R
'Artillery fortifications in Britain', *IBI Bulletin* 29 (1971), 28–31*

Glasscock, R E
'Mottes in Ireland', *Château Gaillard* 7 (1975), 95–110*

Glasscock, R E and McNeill T
'Mottes in Ireland: a draft list', *Bulletin of the Group for the Study of Irish Historic Settlement* 3 (1972), 27–51

Goodall, J
'When an Englishman's castles was his house', *Country Life* 192.15 (1998), 68–71*

Goodwin, J E

'Circular masonry redoubts', *Fort* 2 (1976), 5–6*; pp 19–26* in revised edition of *Fort* vols 1–3

'Naval and military co-operation and control over invasion warnings, 1803', *Fortress* 15 (1992), 31–36*

Gowen, M

'17th century artillery forts in Ulster', *Clogher Record* 10.2 (1980), 239–57*

'A bibliography of contemporary plans of late sixteenth and seventeenth century artillery fortifications in Ireland', *Irish Sword* 14 (1980–1), 230–36

Graham, B

'Twelfth and thirteenth century earthwork castles in Ireland: an assessment', *Fortress* 9 (1991), 24–34*

'Twelfth- and thirteenth-century earthwork fortifications in Ireland', *Irish Sword* 17 (1987–90), 225–43*

'Medieval timber and earthwork fortifications in western Ireland', *Medieval Archaeology* 32 (1988), 110–29*

Gravett, C

'Kitchens and keeps: domestic facilities in Norman castles', *Royal Armouries Yearbook* 3 (1998), 168–75*

'Siege warfare in Orderic Vitalis', *ibid* 5 (2000), 139–47

Gray, M

'Castles and patronage in sixteenth century Wales', *Welsh History Review* 15 (1990–1), 481–93

Green, M

'The last lines of defence', *Living History* 10 (2004), 30–35*

Greeves, I D

'The construction of the GHQ stop-line: Eridge to Newhaven, June–November 1940', *Fortress* 16 (1993), 52–61*

Griffiths, R A

'Prince Henry's war: armies, garrisons and supply during the Glyndŵr rising', *Bulletin of the Board of Celtic Studies* 34 (1987), 165–73

Grigson, G

'Invasion forts of the Normans', *Country Life* 134 (1963), 1616–17*

Gruffydd, K Ll

'Maritime defences and Wales during the later Middle Ages', *Cymru a'r Môr/Maritime Wales* 18 (1996), 10–32*

Guy, N
'The 2003 'Castles at risk' register', *Castle Studies Group Newsletter* 17 (2004), 67–74*

Hamilton-Baillie, J R E
'The fixed fortifications of the sixteenth to nineteenth centuries illustrated by the defences of Chatham', *Royal Engineers Journal* 88.1 (1974), 2–14*

Harbison, P
'Irish castles', *An Cosantóir* 36 (1976), 79–82*

Harfield, C G
'A hand-list of castles recorded in the Domesday Book', *English Historical Review* 106 (1991), 371–92

Harrington, P
'English Civil War fortifications', *Fort* 15 (1987), 39–60*

'Siegefields: an archaeological assessment of 'small' sieges of the British Civil Wars', *Journal of Conflict Archaeology* 1 (2005), 93–113*

Haslam, C
'Landmarks in coastal defence', *Fortress* 4 (1990), 3–12*

Haslam, R
'Princely buildings: architecture and the princes of Wales', *Country Life* 170 (1981), 428–30*

Hawes Richards, D
'The chimney', *Journal of the British Archaeological Association* 3 ser 24 (1961), 67–79*

Hayes-McCoy, G A
'The first guns in Ireland', *An Cosantóir* 34 (1974), 3–7

Héliot, P
'L'évolution du donjon dans le nord-ouest de la France et en Angleterre au XIIᵉ siècle', *Bulletin Archéologique du Comité des Travaux Historiques et Scientifiques* new ser 5 (1969), 141–44*

'La genèse des châteaux de plan quadrangulaire en France et en Angleterre', *Bulletin de la Société des Antiquaires de France* (1965), 238–57*

'Les origines du donjon résidentiel et les donjons-palais romans de France et d'Angleterre', *Cahiers de Civilisation Médiévale* 17 (1974), 217–34*

'Le Château de Saint-Gobain et les châteaux de plan concentrique en Europe occidentale', *Gladius* 12 (1974), 43–58*

Hellis, J
'The Wessex wall: the pillbox defences of the south-west during the 2nd World War', *Ravelin* 23 (1990), 6–11

Higham, R A
'Current debates in British castle studies: a personal note', *Castle Studies Group Newsletter* 12 (1998–9), 47–50

'The study and interpretation of British town walls: medieval urbanism and urban defences in south west England', *Europa Nostra Bulletin* 53 (2000), 43–52*

'Ambienti regionali e castelli in terra, legno, pietra', *ibid* 54 (2001), 113–16

'Archaeology and the study of British castles: the XX century in retrospect', *ibid* 55 (2001), 142–52*

'Timber castles – a reassessment', *Fortress* 1 (1989), 50–60*

Higham, R A and Saunders, A
'Public and private defence in British medieval towns', *IBI Bulletin* 50 (1994–5), 117–28*

Hillaby, J
'Hereford gold: Irish, Welsh and English land: part 2. The clients of the Jewish community at Hereford 1179–1253: four case studies', *Transactions of the Woolhope Naturalist's Field Club* 45.1 (1985), 193–270*

Hislop, M.
'John Lewyn of Durham: a north country master mason of the 14th century', *Journal of the British Archaeological Association* 151 (1998), 170–89*

Hodges, R
'The Danish contribution to the origin of the English castle', *Acta Archaeologica* 59 (1989), 169–72*

Hoey, L R and Thurlby, M
'A survey of Romanesque vaulting in Great Britain and Ireland', *Antiquaries Journal* 84 (2004), 117–84*

Hogg, A H A and King, D J C
'Early castles in Wales and the Marches: a preliminary list', *Archaeologia Cambrensis* 112 (1963), 77–124*

'Masonry castles in Wales and the Marches', *ibid* 116 (1967), 71–132*

'Castles in Wales and the Marches: additions and corrections', *ibid* 119 (1970), 119–24*

Hogg, I V
'Notes on the identification of coast artillery gun emplacements', *Fort* 8 (1980), 61–70*

Honeyman, H L
'The standard axial dimensions of English mound-and-bailey castles', *Proceedings of the Society of Antiquaries of Newcastle upon Tyne* 4 ser 10 (1942–6), 294–98*

Hope-Taylor, B
'New light on mottes', *Country Life* 109 (1951), 1528–30*

Hopkinson, M F
'Living in defended spaces: past structures and present landscapes', *Landscapes* 1.2 (2000), 53–73*

Hornyold-Strickland, H
'Pele towers of the border', *Transactions of the Ancient Monuments Society* new ser 2 (1954), 44–54

Household, H
'Mine and countermine', *Country Life* 155 (1974), 743–44, 747*

Howell-Everson, D
'Victorian fortress strategy in the United Kingdom', *Fort* 15 (1987), 91–100*

Hubberstey, N J
'Exercise Welsh border', *Sanctuary* 26 (1996), 12–13* [fieldwork on WWII defences in the Welsh Marches]

Hughes, Q
'Considerazioni e teorie sulla difesa costiera inglese', *Castellum* 25–6 (1986), 25–44*

'Russian views on the English defences in 1864', *Fort* 7 (1979), 69–79*

'Letters from the Defence Committee in 1861', *ibid* 8 (1980), 71–102*

'The Duke of Wellington's warning of invasion', *ibid* 9 (supplement) (1981), 54–76

'Some thoughts on the rotating gun platform', *ibid* 19 (1991), 59–72*

'Medieval firepower', *Fortress* 8 (1991), 31–43* [Edwardian castles of north Wales]

'The British use of bastion fortifications', *IBI Bulletin* 40 (1982), 51–69*

'The Dutch connection: the impact on British fortifications from the sixteenth to the early nineteenth century', *Jaarboek Stichting Menno van Coehoorn* (1983), 12–19*

Hull, L
'Standing guard', *In Britain* (Oct.Nov 2006), 44–49* [south Wales castles]

Humphries, P H
'Elegance and simplicity: the castle chapel', *Castle Studies Group Newsletter* 10 (1996–7), 49–51 [reprint of below]

'Urddas a symlrwydd: capel y castell', *Etifeddiaeth y Cymro* 4 (1996), 17–18*

'Cestyll – y rhyfel olaf', *Etifeddiaeth y Cymry* 16 (2000), 11–14*

'Elegance and simplicity: the castle chapel', *Heritage in Wales* 4 (1996), 17–18*

'Castles – the last stand', *ibid* 16 (2000), 11–14*

Hunt, J
'Heritage in stone. 5. Castles great and small', *North Munster Antiquarian Journal* 20 (1978), 71–73*

Hunter, R J
'Carew's survey of Ulster, 1611: the "voluntary works"', *Ulster Journal of Archaeology* 3 ser 38 (1975), 81–82

Impey, E
'The seigneurial residence in Normandy, 1125–1225: an Anglo-Norman tradition?', *Medieval Archaeology* 43 (1999), 45–73*

Iorwerth, D
'Codi cestyll paent: gwaith Terry Ball, arlunydd sy'n ail-greu', *Etifeddiaeth y Cymro* 12 (1999), 9–12*

'Ddoe in fyw?', *Etifeddiaeth y Cymry* 22 (2002), 11–14*

'Building paper castles: the work of Terry Ball, reconstruction artist', *Heritage in Wales* 12 (1999), 9–12*

'Back to life?', *ibid* 22 (2002), 11–14*

Jones, P M
'A towering misconception?', *Gwent Local History* 98 (2005), 3–7*

Jones, P N and Renn, D
'The military effectiveness of arrow loops: some experiments at White Castle', *Château Gaillard* 9–10 (1982), 445–56*

Jope, E M
'Scottish influences in the north of Ireland: castles with Scottish features, 1580–1640', *Ulster Journal of Archaeology* 3 ser 14 (1951), 31–47*

'Moyry, Charlemont, Castleraw, and Richhill: fortification to architecture in the north of Ireland', *ibid* 3 ser 23 (1960), 97–123*

Joyner, P
'Some Sandby drawings of Scotland', *National Library of Wales Journal* 23 (1983–4), 1–16*

Keay, A
'The presentation of guardianship sites', *Transactions of the Ancient Monuments Society* 48 (2004), 7–20*

Kendall, C P

'Securing a future for martello towers', *Conservation Bulletin* 31 (1997), 6–7*

Kent, P

'The military trinity: the role of Wellington, Burgoyne and Palmerston in fortification policy, 1830–1860', *Fort* 14 (1986), 39–47

'East Anglian fortifications in the twentieth century', *Fortress* 3 (1989), 43–57*

Kenyon, J R

'Early artillery fortifications in England and Wales: a preliminary survey and reappraisal', *Archaeological Journal* 138 (1981), 205–40*

'Country houses behind castle walls', *British Archaeology* 22 (1997), 8–9*

'Castle-studies: recent publications', *Castle Studies Group Newsletter* 1 (1987), [3–5]

'Castle-studies: recent publications', *ibid* 2 (1988), 7–10

'Castle-studies: recent publications', *ibid* 3 (1989), 15–18

'Castle-studies: recent publications', *ibid* 4 (1990), 13–19

'Castle studies: recent publications', *ibid* 5 (1991), 10–17 [issue dated 1992 in error]

'Castle studies: recent publications', *ibid* 6 (1992–3), 11–17

'Castle studies: recent publications', *ibid* 7 (1993–4), 10–19

'Castle studies: recent publications – 8', *ibid* 8 (1994–5), 19–31

'Castle studies: recent publications – 9', *ibid* 9 (1995–6), 9–25

'Castle studies: recent publications – 10', *ibid* 10 (1996–7), 17–35

'Castle studies: recent publications – 11', *Castle Studies Group Newsletter: Bibliography Supplement* 11 (1997–8), 1–31 [later issues listed in Part 1(a)]

'Fluctuating frontiers: Normanno-Welsh castle warfare *c* 1075 to 1240', *Château Gaillard* 17 (1996), 119–26*

'Early artillery fortification in England and Wales', *Fort* 1 (1976), 22–25*; pp 33–36* in 1993 revised edition of *Fort* vols 1–3

'Early gunports: a gazetteer', *ibid* 4 (1977), 4–6*; pp 75–85* in 1993 revised edition of *Fort* vols 4–5

'James Fergusson: a critic of early Victorian military architecture', *ibid* 8 (1980), 47–54*

'Terminology and early artillery fortification', *ibid* 11 (1983), 31–34

'A hitherto unknown early seventeenth century survey of the coastal forts of southern England: a preliminary outline', *ibid* 11 (1983), 35–56*

'The library catalogue: supplement one', *ibid* 15 (1987), 153–58

'The state of the fortifications in the West Country in 1623', *ibid* 16 (1988), 45–52*

'David Cathcart King and castles in Wales and the Marches', *Fortress* 8 (1991), 44–50*

Kenyon, J R and Thompson, M W

'The origin of the word "keep"', *Medieval Archaeology* 38 (1994), 175–76*

Kerr, A G

'Pillbox defences of S Wales aerodromes', *Ravelin* 39 (1994), 11–12

Kerr, N

'Welsh castles: Cestyll 83, the year of the castle', *Popular Archaeology* 5.1 (1983), 3–8*

Kerrigan, P M

'Defences of Ireland 1793–1815', *An Cosantóir* 34 (1974), 107–9

'The defences of Ireland 1793–1815: 2. The martello towers', *ibid* 34 (1974), 148–49*

'The defences of Ireland 1793–1815: 3. The signal towers', *ibid* 34 (1974), 225–27*

'The defences of Ireland 1793–1815: 4. The Dublin area and Wicklow Mountains', *ibid* 34 (1974), 285–87, 289–90*

'The defences of Ireland 1793–1815: 5. The Shannon estuary', *ibid* 34 (1974), 310–14*

'The defences of Ireland 1793–1815: 6. The Shannon – Portumna to Shannon Harbour', *ibid* 35 (1975), 59–63*

'The defences of Ireland 1793–1815. Part 7: Shannonbridge', *ibid* 35 (1975), 398–403*

'The defences of Ireland 1793–1815. Part 8. Athlone', *ibid* 37 (1977), 150–53*

'The defences of Ireland 1793–1815. Part 9: Waterford and Wexford', *ibid* 37 (1977), 245–47*

'The defences of Ireland 1793–1815. Part 10: Cork Harbour and Kinsale', *ibid* 38 (1978), 145–50*

'The defences of Ireland 1793–1815. Part 11: Bantry Bay', *ibid* 41 (1981), 2–7*

'The defences of Ireland 1793–1815. Part 12: the west coast, Kerry to Sligo', *ibid* 42 (1982), 39–44*

'The defences of Ireland 1793–1815. Part 13 – the north west', *ibid* 42 (1982), 39–44*

'The defences of Ireland 1793–1815. Part 14: the north east', *ibid* 43 (1983), 115–18*

'The defences of Ireland. Part 15: naval and military aspects (1793–1815) and general', *ibid* 43 (1983), 142–49*

'Irish castles and fortifications in the age of the Tudors. Part 1 – 1485–1558', *ibid* 44 (1984), 199–203*

'Irish castles and fortifications in the age of the Tudors. Part 2 – 1558–1603', *ibid* 44 (1984), 275–76, 278–79*

'The defences of the south-eastern coast of Ireland, 1903–14', *Decies* 10 (1979), 29–31

'Fortifications in Tudor Ireland 1547–1603', *Fortress* 7 (1990), 27–39*

'An early proposal for signal towers, 1803', *Irish Sword* 12 (1975–6), 155–56

'A military map of Ireland of the late 1790's', *ibid* 12 (1975–6), 247–51

'Seventeenth century fortifications, forts and garrisons in Ireland: a preliminary list', *ibid* 14 (1980–1), 3–24, 135–56*

'Minorca and Ireland – an architectural connection: the martello towers of Dublin Bay', *ibid* 15 (1982–3), 192–96*

'Coastal signal towers in Ireland, 1814', *ibid* 24.98 (2005), 462–63*

'The defences of Ireland 1793–1815: the Shannon estuary', *Old Limerick Journal* 25 (1989), 100–3* [reprinted from *An Cosantóir* vols 34 and 35]

King, D J C
'The defence of Wales, 1067–1283: the other side of the hill', *Archaeologia Cambrensis* 126 (1977), 1–16*

'The field archaeology of mottes in England and Wales: eine kurze Übersicht', *Château Gaillard* 5 (1972), 101–12*

'The trebuchet and other siege-engines', *ibid* 9–10 (1982), 457–70

'Castles and the administrative divisions of Wales: a study of names', *Welsh History Review* 10 (1980–1), 93–96

King, D J C and Alcock, L
'Ringworks of England and Wales', *Château Gaillard* 3 (1969), 90–127*

King, E
'The parish of Warter and the castle of *Galchlin*', *Yorkshire Archaeological Journal* 52 (1980), 49–58*

Kitchen, F
'Aspects of the defence of the south coast of England: 1756–1805', *Fort* 19 (1991), 11–22*

Knight, J K
'Welsh fortifications of the first millennium AD', *Château Gaillard* 16 (1994), 277–84*

Leask, H G

'The Irish tower-house castle', *Belfast Natural History and Philosophical Society, Proceedings and Reports* 2 ser 3 (1945–50), 28–34*

'Redoubts occupied by the Royal Scots in Ireland in the eighteenth century', *Irish Sword* 1 (1949–53), 188–90

'Castles and their place in Irish history', *ibid* 10 (1971–2), 235–43

Le Clerc, P

'Development of castles and historic houses: 2. Ireland', *IBI Bulletin* 13 (1960), 16–19*

'Protection and repair of castles and historic houses: 2. Ireland', *ibid* 13 (1960), 23–25

Lemman, C H

'The story of the martello tower', *Rye Museum News Letter* 10 (1961), 43–48*

Le Patourel, J

'Fortified and semi-fortified manor houses'. *Château Gaillard* 9–10 (1982), 187–98*

Loeber, R

'Biographical dictionary of engineers in Ireland, 1600–1730', *Irish Sword* 13 (1977–9), 30–44, 106–22, 230–55, 283–314*

Lowry, B C

'The anti-invasion defences of Western Command in 1940', *Fort* 27 (1999), 159–78*

Lynn, C J

'Some 13th-century castle sites in the west of Ireland: note on a preliminary reconnaissance', *Journal of the Galway Archaeological and Historical Society* 40 (1985–6), 90–113*

'The medieval ringfort – an archaeological chimera?', *Irish Archaeological Research Forum* 2.1 (1975), 29–36

'The dating of raths: an orthodox view', *Ulster Journal of Archaeology* 3 ser 38 (1975), 45–47

McAuliffe, M

'The tower house and warfare in Ireland in the 14th and 15th centuries', *Irish Sword* 18 (1990–2), 297–302*

'The use of tower houses and fastness in the Desmond rebellions 1565–1583', *Journal of the Kerry Archaeological and Historical Society* 24 (1991), 105–12

MacCauley, J A

'General Dumouriez and Irish defence', *Irish Sword* 9 (1969–70), 98–108, 165–73

McComish, J A
'The survival of the Irish castle in an age of cannon', *ibid* 9 (1969–70), 16–21*

Macdonnell, E
'Border strongholds', *Country Life* 171 (1982), 486–87*

McKean, C
'Sir James Hamilton of Finnart: a renaissance courtier-architect', *Architectural History* 42 (1999), 140–72*

'A Scottish problem with castles', *Historical Research* 79 (2006), 166–98*

'The Scottish château', *Review of Scottish Culture* 12 (1999–2000), 3–21*

'Galleries, girnals, yards and the woman house: the ancillary structures of the Renaissance country house in Scotland', *ibid* 16 (2003–4), 19–34*

McKenna, M E
'Evidence for the use of timber in mediaeval Irish tower houses: a regional study in Lecale and Tipperary', *Ulster Journal of Archaeology* 3 ser 47 (1984), 171–73 + microfiche*

McKenna, R
'Martello towers and other coastal defenders of the 19th century', *Time & Tide* 3 (2001), 105–12*

McLees, D
'Henry Yevele: disposer of the king's works of masonry', *Journal of the British Archaeological Association* 3 ser 36 (1973), 52–71

McNeill, T E
'The origins of tower houses', *Archaeology Ireland* 6.1 (1992), 13–14*

'Hibernia pacata et castellata', *Château Gaillard* 14 (1990), 262–75*

'Castles of ward and the changing pattern of border conflict in Ireland', *ibid* 17 (1996), 127–33*

'Dunineny Castle and the Gaelic view of castle building', *ibid* 20 (2002), 153–61*

'Medieval raths? An Anglo-Norman comment', *Irish Archaeological Research Forum* 2.1 (1975), 37–39

'Ulster mottes: a checklist', *Ulster Journal of Archaeology* 3 ser 38 (1975), 49–56*

McNeill, T E and Pringle, M
'A map of mottes in the British Isles', *Medieval Archaeology* 41 (1997), 220–23*

Manning, C
'Low-level roofs in Irish great towers', *Château Gaillard* 20 (2002), 137–40*

'Artillery defences and Irish towns in the XVI and XVII centuries', *Europa Nostra Bulletin* 56–7 (2003), 133–38*

'Some unpublished Austin Cooper illustrations', *Journal of Irish Archaeology* 9 (1998), 127–34*

Marshall, P

'The ceremonial function of the donjon in the twelfth century', *Château Gaillard* 20 (2002), 141–51*

Mathieu, J R

'New methods on old castles: generating new ways of seeing', *Medieval Archaeology* 43 (1999), 115–42* [Edwardian castles of north Wales]

Maxwell-Irving, A M T

'Early firearms and their influence on the military and domestic architecture of the borders', *Proceedings of the Society of Antiquaries of Scotland* 103 (1970–1), 192–224*

'Scottish yetts and window-grilles', *ibid* 124 (1994), 433–54*

Mead, H P

'The martello towers of England', *Mariner's Mirror* 34 (1948), 205–17, 294–303*

Meek, M

'Conservation at historic monuments: a selection of works from April 1980 to March 1985', *Ulster Journal of Archaeology* 3 ser 48 (1985), 103–12*

Merlen, R H A

'Castles of mystery on the border', *Country Quest* 30.11 (1990), 26–27* [mottes in the Welsh Marches]

Merriman, M

' "The Epystle to the Queen's Majestie" and its "Platte"', *Architectural History* 27 (1984), 25–32* [this particular issue of the journal is titled *Design and practice in British architecture: studies in architectural history presented to Howard Colvin*]

'Realm and castle: Henry VIII as European builder', *History Today* 41 (June, 1991), 31–37*

Mesqui, J

'La fortification des portes avant la Guerre de Cent Ans: essai de typologie des défenses des ouvrages d'entrée avant 1350', *Archéologie Médiévale* 11 (1981), 203–29*

Miers, M

'To restore or not to restore?', *Country Life* 199.38 (2005), 98–103*

Milliken, M

'Defence of the realm', *English Heritage Magazine* 13 (1991), 14–15*

Moore, D

'Guthrie's self balanced rolling bridge', *Palmerston Forts Society Newsletter* 15 (1989), 14–15*

'The Moncrieff story: part one', *ibid* 12 (1988), 18–23*

'The Moncrieff story: part two', *ibid* 13 (1988), 12–21*

'The Moncrieff story: part three', *ibid* 14 (1988), 17–23*

'The Moncrieff story: part 4', *ibid* 15 (1989), 23–31*

'The Moncrieff story: part 5', *The Redan* 16 (1989), 16–22*

'The Moncrieff story: part 6', *ibid* 17 (1989), 23–33*

'The Moncrieff story: part 7', *ibid* 18 (1990), 27–32

'An index of military terms used in connection with fortifications of the Victorian era', *ibid* 19 (1990), 34–36

'Designing the forts', *ibid* 20 (1990), 26–38*

'Military terms: part 2', *ibid* 20 (1990), 33–37

'Wood traversing platforms', *ibid* 20 (1990), 7–11*

'Military terms: part 3', *ibid* 21 (1991), 32–37

'Wood traversing platforms – part 2', *ibid* 21 (1991), 13–19*

'Firing the guns – 2: Watkin depression finders', *ibid* 34 (1995), 5–16*

'Identifying gun emplacements: an introduction to Victorian gun positions', *ibid* 36 (1996), 9–16*

'Racers for heavy RML guns', *ibid* 36 (1996), 17–18*

'High angle fire batteries', *ibid* 36 (1996), 19–31

'Garrison carriages and slides – 10: the 11 & 12-inch RML of 25–tons', *ibid* 38 (1996), 7–11*

'Laboratories in forts', *ibid* 38 (1996), 19–28*

'Laboratory implements in land forts & batteries', *ibid* 38 (1996), 29–31*

'Garrison carriages and slides – 11: the 12.5 inch RML of 38–tons', *ibid* 39 (1997), 2–14*

'Laboratories in forts: extract from the Department of the Director of Artillery 1884', *ibid* 39 (1997), 15

'Garrison carriages and slides – 12: the 12.5 inch RML of 38 tons small port mountings', *ibid* 40 (1997), 2–12*

'The guns that disappeared. 2. The Moncrieff pattern I carriage', *ibid* 45 (1999), 28–34*

'The guns that disappeared (part 3). The pattern II carriage', *ibid* 46 (1999), 28–35*

'The guns that disappeared (part 4): the 9–inch RML of 12 tons', *ibid* 48 (2000), 9–18*

'The guns that disappeared (part 5): hydropneumatic mountings', *ibid* 49 (2000), 20–29*

'Arming the forts: the 6.6–inch howitzer', *ibid* 52 (2001), 37–44*

'The evolution of the caponière 1', *ibid* 54 (2002), 47–53*

'The evolution of the caponière 2', *ibid* 55 (2002), 17–27*

'Lighting the forts – part 2', *Ravelin* 23 (1991), 2–8*

Morris, M

'Marc Morris on castles', *Living History* 1 (2003), 12–18*

Morton, R G

'Plans for Ulster defence, 1795–97', *Irish Sword* 2 (1954–6), 270–74

Nevin, M

'The defence of the southern part of Ireland by General Vallancey, Chief Engineer', *Journal of the Royal Society of Antiquaries of Ireland* 125 (1995), 5–9

Nicholls, K W

'Anglo-French Ireland and after', *Peritia: Journal of the Medieval Academy of Ireland* 1 (1982), 370–403 [espec pp 389–91]

Nickell, L J

'In the steps of Richard III', *Country Life* 174 (1983), 612–13*

O'Brien, B M

'Martello towers', *An Cosantóir* 25.7 (1965), 329–36*

O'Conor, K

'Motte castles in Ireland: permanent fortresses, residences and manorial centres', *Château Gaillard* 20 (2002), 173–82*

'Irish earthwork castles', *Fortress* 12 (1992), 3–12*

'The later construction and use of motte and bailey castles in Ireland: new evidence from Leinster', *Journal of the Co Kildare Archaeological Society* 17 (1991), 13–29*

'The Discovery Programme's recent research on medieval rural settlement in Ireland', *Medieval Settlement Research Group Annual Report* 12 (1997), 10–16

Ó Danachair, C

'Irish tower houses and their regional distribution', *Béaloideas: the Journal of the Folklore of Ireland Society* 45–7 (1977–9), 158–63*

Ó Drisceoil, C

'Recycled ringforts: the evidence from archaeological excavation for the conversion of pre-existing monuments to motte castles in medieval Ireland', *Journal of the County Louth Archaeological and Historical Society* 25.2 (2002), 189–201*

'The Shannon in military history', *North Munster Antiquarian Journal* 14 (1971), 53–64

O'Farrell, P

'Withdrawal from the harbour defences in 1938', *An Cosantóir* 48.7 (1988), 16–17*

O'Keeffe, T

'The archaeology of Norman castles in Ireland. Part 1: mottes and ringworks', *Archaeology Ireland* 4.3 (1990), 15–17*

'The archaeology of Norman castles in Ireland. Part 2: stone castles', *ibid* 4.4 (1990), 20–22*

'Concept of 'castle' and the construction of identity in medieval and post-medieval Ireland', *Irish Geography* 34 (2001), 69–88*

'The fortifications of western Ireland, AD 1100–1300: another interpretation', *Journal of the Galway Archaeological and Historical Society* 50 (1998), 184–200*

'Were there designed landscapes in medieval Ireland?', *Landscapes* 5.2 (2004), 52–68*

Olsen, O

'Rabies archaeologorum', *Antiquity* 54 (1980), 15–19

'Rabies archaeologorum', *Château Gaillard* 9–10 (1982), 213–19

O'Neil, B H St J

'Stefan von Haschenperg, an engineer to King Henry VIII, and his work', *Archaeologia* 91 (1945), 137–55*

Oram, R D

'Prelatical builders: lordly symbolism in episcopal and monastic residences in Scotland c 1124–c 1500', *Château Gaillard* 20 (2002), 183–93*

'Castles and colonists in twelfth- and thirteenth-century Scotland: the case of Moray', *ibid* 22 (2006), 289–98*

Osborne, M

'The magic mushroom: FC construction pillboxes', *Loopholes* 20 (1997), 7–14*

Oswald, A S

'Castles from the air', *Country Life* 102 (1947), 72–75*

'Castles from the air – II: walls and towers', *ibid* 104 (1948), 572–74*

'Castles from the air – III: the river passage', *ibid* 104 (1948), 1042–44*

'Castles form the air – IV: guardians of the coast', *ibid* 105 (1949), 134–36*

'Castles form the air – V: the moated castle', *ibid* 105 (1949), 542–44*

'Castles from the air – VI: castle into country house', *ibid* 106 (1949), 28–30*

Pegden, B K

'The purchase of bricks for martello towers in the year 1804', *Fort* 8 (1980), 55–60*

'Martello towers & related works, 1778–1873: an introduction to published material and official records', *Ravelin* 42 (1995), 19–22

'Martello towers & related works, 1778–1873', *ibid* 44 (1996), 14–16

'Martello towers & related works, 1778–1873: an introduction to published material and official records', *ibid* 45 (1996), 16–19

'Martello towers & related works, 1778–1873: an introduction to published material and official records', *ibid* 46 (1997), 24–28

'Martello towers & related works, 1778–1873: an introduction to published material and official records', *ibid* 49 (1998), 10–13

Petre, J

'Historians and the role of castles in the Wars of the Roses', *Fort* 12 (1984), 5–9

Petrie, G

'An essay on military architecture in Ireland previous to the English invasion', *Proceedings of the Royal Irish Academy* 72C (1972), 216–69* [originally read on 28 April 1834]

Phillips, B

'Past master', *Heritage Today* 65 (2004), 40–43* [the artist Peter Dunn]

Pinsent, M

'The defences of the Bristol Channel in the last two centuries', *Fort* 11 (1983), 63–76*

Piper, J

'Martello towers', *House of Whitbread Magazine* 18.1 (1958), 12–15*

Porter, S

'Property destruction in the English Civil Wars', *History Today* 36 (August, 1986), 36–41*

Portlock, J E and Nugent C H

'The state of the art of fortification towards the end of the nineteenth century', *Fort* 9 (1981), 43–101*

Pounds, N J G

'The chapel in the castle', *Fortress* 9 (1991), 12–20*

Powter, A

'History, deterioration, and repair of cement and concrete in nineteenth century fortifications constructed by the Royal Engineers', *Bulletin of the Association for Preservation Technology* 10.3 (1978), 59–77*

'Concrete in nineteenth century fortifications constructed by the Royal Engineers', *Fort* 9 (1981), 31–42

Prestwich, M

'English castles in the reign of Edward II', *Journal of Medieval History* 9 (1982), 159–78*

Price, G

'Castle ownership: politics and power in high medieval England', *Medieval Life* 4 (1996), 11–17*

Purcell, S

'Airfield defence, part 2: fieldwork', *Loopholes* 22 (1999), 3–8*

Purton, P

'The myth of the mangonel: torsion artillery in the Middle Ages', *Arms & Armour: Journal of the Royal Armouries* 3 (2006), 79–90*

'Donjons: some heretical thoughts', *Castle Studies Group Newsletter* 16 (2002–3), 86–88*

'Medieval siege artillery and the disappearance of the torsion weapon', *Postern* 14 (2002–3), 8–10

Quiney, A

'Hall or chamber? That is the question. The use of rooms in post-Conquest houses', *Architectural History* 42 (1999), 24–46*

Redfern, N

'Anti-invasion defences of Scotland, Wales and northern England, 1939–45: insights and issues', *Defence Lines* 12 (1999), 6–9*

Remfry, P M

'The dating of medieval military architecture', *Castle Studies Group Newsletter* 15 (2001–2), 86–95*

Renn, D F

'Mottes: a classification', *Antiquity* 33 (1959), 106–12*

'Mottes: a correction', *ibid* 33 (1959), 213

'The round keeps of the Brecon region', *Archaeologia Cambrensis* 110 (1961), 129–43*

'Master Jordan, who made the king's trébuchet', *Arms & Armour: Journal of the Royal Armouries* 1.1 (2004), 25–32*

'The Anglo-Norman keep, 1066–1139', *Journal of the British Archaeological Association* 3 ser 23 (1960), 1–23*

'The first Norman castles in England (1051–1071)', *Château Gaillard* 1 (1964), 125–32*

'English fortification in 1485', *ibid* 13 (1987), 169–74*

'The castle at Goseford', *Surrey Archaeological Society Bulletin* 41 (1968), 3

Rigold, S E

'Timber bridges at English castles and moated sites', *Château Gaillard* 6 (1973), 183–93*

'Structural aspects of medieval timber bridges', *Medieval Archaeology* 19 (1975), 48–91*

'Structural aspects of medieval timber bridges: addenda', *ibid* 20 (1976), 152–53

Roberts, B K
'Moats and mottes', *ibid* 8 (1964), 219–21*

Roche, T W E
'Castle-hunting in the south of England', *Amateur Historian* 4 (1958–60), 62–65, 95–97*

Rogers, A
'Edward I and the castles of north Wales', *History Today* 19 (1969), 445–52*

Rogers, R
'Aspects of the military history of the Anglo-Norman invasion of Ireland 1169–1225', *Irish Sword* 16 (1984–6), 135–44

Rowan, A
'The Irishness of Irish architecture', *Architectural History* 40 (1997), 1–23*

Ruckley, N A
'Water supply of medieval castles in the United Kingdom', *Fortress* 7 (1990), 14–26*

Rudd, A
'The military defences of the north of England 1939–45', *Archaeology North* 9 (1995), 41–42

Ryder, P F
'Do peel towers exist?', *CBA Group 3 Newsbulletin* [3.10] (1988), 18–20

Salter, M
'Summary survey of Irish castles', *Postern* 19 (2006–7), 9–12*

Samson, R
'Knowledge, constraint, and power in inaction: the defenseless medieval wall', *Historical Archaeology* 26.3 (1992), 26–44*

Saunders, A D
'Five castles excavations: reports on the Institute's research project into the origins of the castle in England: introduction', *Archaeological Journal* 134 (1977), 1–10

'The English medieval castle as country house', *IBI Bulletin* 49 (1993), 49–54*

'Attitudes towards defence at English monastic houses and granges', *ibid* 50 (1994–5), 51–54*

'From Kronstadt to Portsmouth', *Europa Nostra Bulletin* 51 (1999), 85–90* [formerly *IBI Bulletin*]

'La *grande torre* – fortezza o palazzo?', *ibid* 54 (2000), 117–24*

'"Palmerston's follies" – a centenary', *Journal of the Royal Artillery* 87 (1960), 138–44

'The coastal defences of the south-east: a reassessment', *Ravelin* 39 (1994), 3–7

'Artillery fortifications in Britain: recent research and conservation', *Teka Komisji Urbanistyke i Architekury* 27 (1995), 231–39*

Schmidtchen, V
'Castles, cannon and casemates', *Fortress* 6 (1990), 3–10*

Schofield, J
'Surveying 20th century fortifications', *Conservation Bulletin* 31 (1997), 13*

'Military archaeology: past practice – future directions', *ibid* 44 (2003), 4–7*

Schofield, J and Lake, J
'Defining our defence heritage', *ibid* 27 (1995), 12–13* [correction to illustration can be found in 28 (1996), 22*]

Shelby, L R
'Guines Castle and the development of English bastioned fortifications', *Château Gaillard* 3 (1969), 139–43*

Simpson, G G
'Claves castri: the role of the gatekeeper in Scottish medieval castles', *ibid* 15 (1992), 319–24*

Simpson, G G and Monro, R W
'A checklist of western seaboard castles on record before 1550', *Notes and Queries of the Society of West Highland and Island Historical Research* 19 (1982), 3–7

Simpson, G G and Webster, B
'Charter evidence and the distribution of mottes in Scotland', *Château Gaillard* 5 (1972), 175–92*

Simpson, W D
'"Bastard feudalism" and the later castles', *Antiquaries Journal* 26 (1946), 145–71*

Sitwell, S
'Plastic baronial: Scottish castles of the 16th and 17th centuries', *Architectural Review* 115 (1954), 297–301*

Skelton, R A
'The military surveyor's contribution British cartography in the 16th century', *Imago Mundi* 24 (1970), 77–93

Skurdenis, J
'The Welsh castles of Edward I', *Archaeology* 40.5 (1987), 74–75, 88*

Smith, T P
'Why did medieval towns have walls?', *Current Archaeology* 8.12 (1985), 376–79*

Smith, V T C
'Defending the Forth: 1880–1910', *Fort* 13 (1985), 99–102*

Sneyd, S
'A castle by any other name', *Postern* 8 (1998), 5–8*

'The search for the green knight's castle', *ibid* 10 (2000), 19–24*

'The search for the green knight's castle: part II', *ibid* 11 (2000), 4–8*

'Who or what lies under the hill?', *ibid* 15 (2003–4), 25–28

Speight, S
'Castle warfare in the *Gesta Stephani*', *Château Gaillard* 19 (2000), 269–74

'Religion in the bailey: charters, chapels and the clergy', *ibid* 21 (2004), 271–80*

'British castle studies in the late 20th and 21st centuries', *History Compass* 2 (2004), 1–30*

Spiteri, S C
'Illustrated glossary of military architecture terms', *Fort* 21 (1993), 105–14*

Stalley, R A
'A twelfth century patron of architecture: a study of the buildings erected by Roger bishop of Salisbury', *Journal of the British Archaeological Association* 3 ser 34 (1971), 52–83*

'William of Prene and the royal works in Ireland', *ibid* 131 (1978), 30–49*

Stanford, C
'On preserving our ruins', *Journal of Architectural Conservation* 6.3 (2000), 28–43*

Stell, G
'Medieval secular architecture' [in west central Scotland], *Archaeological Journal* 143 (1986), 6–7

'War-damaged castles: the evidence from medieval Scotland', *Château Gaillard*

19 (2000), 275–85*

'Unfinished works', *History Scotland* 5.2 (2005), 14–21*

'The Scottish medieval castle: form, function and evolution', *Prospect* 14 (1982), 14–15*

'Destruction, damage and decay: the collapse of Scottish medieval buildings', *Review of Scottish Culture* 2 (1986), 56–69*

Stevenson, I V
'The defences of Cork Harbour in Ireland', *Fort* 27 (1999), 113–42*

'Ireland – two treaty ports and one that never was', *Fortress* 12 (1992), 51–60*

'Ireland – two treaty ports and that that never was', *ibid* 13 (1992), 34–45*

'Two Irish loughs', *The Redan* 35 (1995), 11–28*

'Three Scottish ports', *ibid* 46 (1999), 36–48*

'The defences of the commercial ports of Great Britain: a short survey', *ibid* 65 (2005), 11–20*

Stocker, D
'The shadow of the general's armchair', *Archaeological Journal* 149 (1992), 415–20 [review article]

Stout, G
'Pillboxes on the Boyne (1939–45)', *Journal of the Old Drogheda Society* 12 (2000), 244–55*

Sturdy, D
'Cestyll mewn inc', *Etifeddiaeth y Cymro* 13 (1999), 18–20*

'Castles with a Welsh view', *Heritage in Wales* 13 (1999), 18–20*

Sutcliffe, S
'England's Napoleonic heritage', *Country Life* 146 (1969), 686, 688*

Sweetman, D
'Dating Irish castles', *Archaeology Ireland* 6.4 (1992), 8–9*

'Earthwork castles', *IAPA Newsletter* 22 (1996), 7*

'The hall-house in Ireland', *Irish Archaeology* 12.3 (1998), 13–16*

Tabraham, C J
'The Scottish medieval towerhouse as lordly residence in the light of recent excavation', *Proceedings of the Society of Antiquaries of Scotland* 118 (1988), 267–76*

Tait, A A
'The Protectorate citadels of Scotland', *Architectural History* 9 (1965), 9–24*

Talbot, E J
'Early Scottish castles of earth and timber: recent fieldwork and excavation', *Scottish Archaeological Forum* 6 (1974), 48–57

Tatton-Brown, T
'The use of Quarr stone in London and east Kent', *Medieval Archaeology* 24 (1980), 213–15

Taylor, A J
'The north Wales castles', *Archaeological Newsletter* 3 (1950–1), 161–62

'Castles and castle building in the Middle Ages', *Transactions of the Architectural and Archaeological Society of Durham and Northumberland* new ser 3 (1974), 39–46*

'Castle-building in thirteenth century Wales and Savoy', *Proceedings of the British Academy* 63 (1977), 265–92*

'Master James of St George', *English Historical Review* 65 (1950), 433–57

'Who was "John Pennardd, leader of the men of Gwynedd"?', *ibid* 91 (1976), 79–97

'Some notes on the Savoyards in north Wales, 1277–1300, with special reference to the Savoyard element in the construction of Harlech Castle', *Genava* new ser 11 (1963), 289–315*

'The rehabilitation of castles in the country districts of England', *IBI Bulletin* 22 (1966), 71–74*

'English builders in Scotland during the War of Independence: a record of 1304', *Scottish Historical Review* 34 (1955), 44–46

Taylor, C
'Medieval ornamental landscape', *Landscapes* 1.1 (2000), 38–55*

Thompson, M W
'Associated monasteries and castles in the Middle Ages: a tentative list', *Archaeological Journal* 143 (1986), 305–21

'The military interpretation of castles', *ibid* 151 (1994), 439–45*

'Keep or country house? Thin-walled Norman "proto-keeps"', *Fortress* 12 (1992), 13–22*

'A suggested dual origin for keeps', *ibid* 15 (1992), 3–15*

'Motte substructures', *Medieval Archaeology* 5 (1961), 305–6

Tierney-Jones, A
'Dad's army's secret weapons', *The Field* 300.7180 (2002), 92–94*

Tod, R
'Scottish castles', *Fort* 5 (1978), 3–11*; pp 8–21* in 1995 revised edition of *Fort* vols 4–5

Tomlinson, H [C]
'The Ordnance Office and the king's forts, 1660–1714', *Architectural History* 16 (1973), 5–25*

Turnbull, S
'The passing of the medieval castle', *Medieval History Magazine* 9 (2004), 22–27*

Turner, J L
'Castles by the sea', *Country Life* 116 (1954), 1150–51*

Turvey, R
'The defences of twelfth-century Deheubarth and the castle strategy of the Lord Rhys', *Archaeologia Cambrensis* 144 (1995), 103–32*

Twohig, D C
'Norman ringwork castles', *Bulletin of the Group for the Study of Irish Historic Settlement* 5 (1978), 7–9

Vachell, E T
'The development of castles in England', *Proceedings of the Devon Archaeological Exploration Society* 5 (1953–8), 95–116*

Walker, B
'The use of 'skailie' in medieval and post-medieval Scotland', *Antiquity* 75 (2001), 163–71*

Wallace, C, Lawson, J A and Reed, D
' 'ye toun salbe wallit & stanke it about, with ane substantious wall': mural ideology in 16th century Edinburgh and southern Scotland?', *History Scotland* 4.6 (2004), 35–42*

Walton, C
'The Welsh castles of Edward I – in a weekend', *Medieval History Magazine* 2.5 (2005), 40–45*

Ward, S G P
'Defence works in Britain, 1803–1805', *Journal of the Society for Army Historical Research* 27 (1949), 18–37*

Waterman, D M
'Somersetshire and other foreign building stone in medieval Ireland, c 1175–1400', *Ulster Journal of Archaeology* 3 ser 33 (1970), 63–75*

Whistler, L
'Ordnance Vanbrugh. Military buildings in the Vanbrugh-Hawksmoor manner', *Architectural Review* 112 (1952), 376–83*

White, P
'Castle gateways during the reign of Henry II', *Antiquaries Journal* 76 (1996), 241–47*

White, T B
'Towers of the English and Scottish borders', *IBI Bulletin* 7 (1954), 1–3*

Whitehead, T
'Re-use: strategies for historic buildings', *Sanctuary* 24 (1995), 18–19*

Wiggins, K
'Warfare underground', *British Archaeology* 71 (2003), 8–13*

Wilcox, R [P]
'Timber reinforcement in medieval castles', *Château Gaillard* 5 (1972), 193–202*

Williams, D
'Fortified manor houses', *Transactions of the Leicestershire Archaeological and Historical Society* 50 (1974–5), 1–16

Williams, G
'Henry de Gower (?1278–1347): bishop and builder', *Archaeologia Cambrensis* 130 (1991), 1–18*

Williams, G A
'Welsh raiding in the twelfth-century Shropshire/Cheshire March: the case of Owain Cyfeiliog', *Studia Celtica* 40 (2006), 89–115*

Williams, J G
'The castles of Wales during the Civil War, 1642–47', *ibid* 137 (1988), 1–26*

Wills, H
'Pillboxes: a study of UK defences 1940–41', *Current Archaeology* 6 (1978–80), 304–6*
'The pill-boxes that went to war', *Popular Archaeology* 1.5 (1979), 16–17*

Wood, D
'Mantlets', *The Redan* 57 (2003), 2–7*

Wood, J
'Six northern castles: a review of recent work undertaken by the Lancaster University Archaeological Unit', *Castle Studies Group Newsletter* 6 (1992–3), 18–21

Yeoman, P
'Mottes in northeast Scotland', *Scottish Archaeological Review* 5 (1988), 125–33*

Zadora-Rio, E
'Les essaies de typologie de fortifications de terre médiévales en Europe: bilan et perspectives', *Archéologie Médiévale* 15 (1985), 191–96

Zeune, J
'Die frühen Steinburgen in den westlichen Inseln und Hochlanden Schottlands', *Burgen und Schlosser* 24.1 (1983), 13–26*

'Perfecting the tower house: post-medieval Scottish castellated architecture. Part 1: the L-plan tower house', *Fortress* 10 (1991), 23–30*

'Perfecting the tower house: post-medieval castellated Scottish architecture. Part 2: the Z-plan house', *ibid* 11 (1991), 14–28*

(c) ESSAYS IN BOOKS

Alcock, L
'Castle-studies and the archaeological sciences: some possibilities and problems', in J R Kenyon and R Avent (eds), *Castles in Wales and the Marches: essays in honour of D J Cathcart King*, 5–22. Cardiff: University of Wales Press, 1987

ap Hywel, E
'Castles and contradictions: versions of a Welsh "heritage"', in F Baker and J Thomas (eds), *Writing the past in the present*, 178–87. Lampeter: St David's University College, 1990*

Avent, R
'The presentation of Welsh castles', in E Southworth (ed), *The interpretation of archaeological sites and monuments: proceedings of the annual conference, Salisbury, 1985*, 23–25. Liverpool: Society of Museum Archaeologists, 1988

Barber, P
'England I: pageantry, defense, and government: maps at court to 1550', in D Buisseret (ed), *Monarchs, ministers and maps: the emergence of cartography as a tool of government in early modern Europe*, 26–56. Chicago: University of Chicago Press, 1992*

Barker, N
'The building practice of the English Board of Ordnance, 1680–1720', in J Bold and E Chaney (eds), *English architecture, public and private: essays for Kerry Downes*, 199–214. London: Hambledon Press, 1993*

Barker, P A
'Timber castles of the Welsh border with reference to Hen Domen, Montgomery', in H Galinié (ed), *Les mondes normandes (VIIIe–XIIe s.)*, 135–47. Caen: Société d'Archéologie Médiévale, 1989*

Barley, M W
'Town defences in England and Wales after 1066', in M W Barley (ed), *The plans and topography of medieval towns in England and Wales*, 57–71. London: CBA, 1976* (Research report; 14)

Barry, T B

'Anglo-Norman ringwork castles: some evidence', in R Reeves-Smyth and F Hamond (eds), *Landscape archaeology in Ireland*, 295–314. Oxford: British Archaeological Reports, 1983* (British series; 116)

'The archaeology of the tower house in late medieval Ireland', in H Andersson and J Wienberg (eds), *The study of medieval archaeology: European symposium for teachers of medieval archaeology, Lund 11–15 June 1990*, 211–17. Stockholm: Almquist and Wiksell International, 1993*

'The lost frontier: defence and settlement in late medieval Ireland', in T B Barry (ed), *Colony and frontier in medieval Ireland: essays presented to J F Lydon*, 217–28. London: Hambledon Press, 1995*

'Rural settlement in medieval Ireland', in T Barry (ed), *A history of settlement in Ireland*, 110–23. London: Routledge, 2000*

'The defensive nature of Irish moated sites', in J R Kenyon and K O'Conor (eds), *The medieval castle in Ireland and Wales: essays in honour of Jeremy Knight*, 182–93. Dublin: Four Courts Press, 2003*

Blair, J

'Hall and chamber in English domestic planning 1000–1250', in G Meirion-Jones and M Jones (eds), *Manorial domestic buildings in England northern France*, 1–21. London: Society of Antiquaries, 1993* (Occasional paper; 15)

'Hall and chamber: English domestic planning 1000–1250', in R Liddiard (ed), *Anglo-Norman castles*, 307–28. Woodbridge: Boydell Press, 2003*

Bond, C J

'Anglo-Saxon and medieval defences', in J Schofield and R Leech (eds), *Urban archaeology in Britain*, 92–116. London: CBA, 1987* (Research report; 61)

'Mittelalterliche Wasserversorgung in England und Wales', in *Die Wasswever-sorgung im Mittelalter*, 147–83. Mainz: Verlag Philipp von Zabern, 1991*

Bonde, S

'Castle and church building at the time of the Norman Conquest', in K Reyerson and F Powe (eds), *The medieval castle: romance and reality*, 79–96. Dubuque: Kendall/Hunt Publishing, 1984*

Bradley, J

'Planned Anglo-Norman towns in Ireland', in H B Clarke and A Simms (eds), *The comparative history of urban origins in non-Roman Europe: Ireland, Wales, Denmark, Germany, Poland, and Russia from the ninth to the thirteenth century*, 411–67. Oxford: British Archaeological Reports, 1985* (International series; 255)

Brown, R A

'An historian's approach to the origins of the castle in England', in R A Brown, *Cas-*

tles, conquest and charters: collected papers, 1–18. Woodbridge: Boydell Press, 1989

'Royal castle-building in England', in *ibid*, 19–64

'The castles of the Conquest', in *ibid*, 65–74*

'The Norman Conquest and the genesis of English castles', in *ibid*, 75–89*

'A list of castles, 1154–1216', in *ibid*, 90–121

'Châteaux et sociétés en Angleterre du XIVe au XVIe siècle', in *ibid*, 122–37*

'Les châteaux féodaux', in *ibid*, 138–48*

'Lo studio dei castelli medievali in Inghilterra', in *ibid*, 149–57*

'Le manoir fortifié dans le Royaume d'Angleterre', in *ibid*, 158–62*

'The architecture of the Bayeux Tapestry', in *ibid*, 214–26*

'William of Malmesbury as an architectural historian', in *ibid*, 227–34

'Castle gates and garden gates', in *ibid*, 235–37

'William of Malmesbury as an architectural historian', in *Mélanges d'archéologie et d'histoire médiévales en l'honneur du doyen Michel de Boüard*, 9–16. Geneva: Librairie Droz, 1982

'Lo studio dei castelli medievali in Inghilterra', in R Comba and A A Settia (eds), *Castelli: storia e archeologia*, 29–37. Turin: [s n], 1984*

'Le manoir fortifié dans le Royaume d'Angleterre', in M Bur (ed), *La maison forte au moyen âge*, 13–16. Paris: Centre National de la Recherche Scientifique, 1986*

'Châteaux et sociétés en Angleterre du XIVe au XVIe siècle', in P Fanlac (ed), *Châteaux et sociétés du XIVe and XVIe siècle: actes des premières rencontres internationales d'archéologie et d'histoire de Commarque*, 131–47. [S l: Association Culturale de Commarque], 1986*

'The castles of the Conquest', in *Domesday Book studies*, 69–74. London: Alecto Historical Editions, 1987*

'Castle. I. Medieval', in J Turner (ed), *The dictionary of art*, **6**, 49–58. London: Macmillan, 1996*

'Royal castle-building in England, 1154–1216', in R Liddiard (ed), *Anglo-Norman castles*, 133–77. Woodbridge: Boydell Press, 2003

'The castles of the Conquest', in R W H Erskine and A Williams (eds), *The story of Domesday Book*, 104–11. Chichester: Phillimore, 2003* [first published 1987]

Burke, J
'Siege warfare in seventeenth century Ireland', in P Lenihan (ed), *Conquest and resistance: war in seventeenth-century Ireland*, 257–91. Leiden: Brill, 2001* (History of warfare; 3)

Butler, L
'Planned Anglo-Norman towns in Wales, 950–1250', in H B Clarke and A Simms (eds), *The comparative history of urban origins in non-Roman Europe: Ireland, Wales, Denmark, Germany, Poland, and Russia from the ninth to the thirteenth century*, 469–504. Oxford: British Archaeological Reports, 1985* (International series; 255)

Chibnall, M
'Orderic Vitalis on castles', in C Harper-Bill, C J Holdsworth and J L Nelson (eds), *Studies in medieval history presented to R Allen Brown*, 43–56. Woodbridge: Boydell Press, 1989

'Orderic Vitalis on castles', in R Liddiard (ed), *Anglo-Norman castles*, 119–32. Woodbridge: Boydell Press, 2003

Clack, P A G and Gosling, P F
'The later medieval period', in *Archaeology in the north: report of the Northern Archaeological Survey*, 50–52. Durham: Northern Archaeological Survey, 1976*

Coad, J
'Medieval fortifications and post-medieval artillery defences: developments in post-war research and future trends', in B Vyner (ed), *Building on the past: papers celebrating 150 years of the Royal Archaeological Institute*, 215–47. London: RAI, 1994

'Defending the realm: the changing technology of warfare', in D Gaimster and P Stamper (eds), *The age of transition: archaeology of English culture 1400–1600*, 157–69. Oxford: Oxbow Books, 1997* (Oxbow monograph; 98)

Coulson, C
'The castles of the Anarchy', in E King (ed), *The Anarchy of King Stephen's reign*, 67–92. Oxford: Clarendon Press, 1994*

'Battlements and the bourgeoisie: municipal status and the apparatus of urban defence in later-medieval England', in S Church and R Harvey (eds), *Medieval knighthood 5: papers from the sixth Strawberry Hill Conference 1994*, 119–95. Woodbridge: Boydell Press, 1995*

'Military architecture and fortification. I. Introduction. 2. Symbolism', in J Turner (ed), *The dictionary of art*, **21**, 547–50. London: Macmillan, 1996*

'Fourteenth-century castles in context: apotheosis or decline?', in N Saul (ed), *Fourteenth century England 1*, 133–51. Woodbridge: Boydell Press, 2000

'Peaceable power in English castles', in J Gillingham (ed), *Anglo-Norman studies 23: proceedings of the Battle Conference 2000*, 69–95. Woodbridge: Boydell Press, 2001*

'The castles of the Anarchy', in R Liddiard (ed), *Anglo-Norman castles*, 179–202. Woodbridge: Boydell Press, 2003*

Counihan, J

'Mrs Ella Armitage, John Horace Round, G T Clark and early Norman castles', in R A Brown (ed), *Anglo-Norman studies 8: proceedings of the Battle Conference 1985*, 73–87. Woodbridge: Boydell Press, 1986

'The growth of castle studies in England and the Continent since 1850', in R A Brown (ed), *Anglo-Norman studies 11: proceedings of the Battle Conference 1988*, 77–85. Woodbridge: Boydell Press, 1989

'Mrs Ella Armitage and Irish archaeology', in C Harper-Bill (ed), *Anglo-Norman studies 20: proceedings of the Battle Conference 1997*, 59–67. Woodbridge: Boydell Press, 1998*

Courtney, P

'The archaeology of the early-modern siege', in P W M Freeman and A Pollard (eds), *Fields of conflict: progress and prospect in battlefield archaeology*, 105–15. Oxford: Archaeopress, 2001* (BAR international series; 958)

Coutts, C

'An appraisal of the restoration of certain north east castles', in J S Smith (ed), *North east castles: castles in the landscape of north east Scotland*, 83–125. Aberdeen: Aberdeen University Press, 1990*

Creighton, O H

'Castles and castle building in town and country', in K Giles and C Dyer (eds), *Town and country in the Middle Ages: contacts, continuity and interconnections, 1100–1500*, 275–92. Leeds: Maney, 2005* (Society for Medieval Archaeology monograph; 22)

Crouch, D

'Castles and halls', in D Crouch, *The image of aristocracy in Britain, 1000–1300*, 252–80. London: Routledge, 1992*

Curnow, P E

'Some developments in military architecture *c* 1200: Le Coudray-Salbart', in R A Brown (ed), *Proceedings of the Battle Conference on Anglo-Norman studies 2, 1979*, 42–62, 172–73. Woodbridge: Boydell Press, 1980*

Dean, M A

'Early fortified houses: defenses and castle imagery between 1275 and 1350 with evidence from the southeast Midlands', in K Reyerson and F Powe (eds), *The medieval castle: romance and reality*, 147–74. Dubuque: Kendall/Hunt Publishing, 1984*

DeVries, K

'The impact of gunpowder weaponry on siege warfare in the Hundred Years War', in I V Corfis and M Wolfe (eds), *The medieval city under siege*, 227–44. Woodbridge: Boydell Press, 1995

Dixon, P

'From hall to tower: the change in seigneurial houses on the Anglo-Scottish border after *c* 1250', in P R Coss and S D Lloyd (eds), *Thirteenth century England 4: proceedings of the Newcastle upon Tyne Conference 1991*, 85–107. Woodbridge: Boydell Press, 1992*

'*Mota, aula et turris*: the manor-houses of the Anglo-Scottish border', in G Meirion-Jones and M Jones (eds), *Manorial domestic buildings in England northern France*, 22–48. London: Society of Antiquaries, 1993* (Occasional paper; 15)

'The myth of the keep', in G Meirion-Jones, E Impey and M Jones (eds), *The seigneurial residence in western Europe AD c 800–1600*, 9–13. Oxford: Archaeopress, 2002* (BAR international series; 1088)

Drage, C

'Urban castles', in J Schofield and R Leech (eds), *Urban archaeology in Britain*, 117–32. London: CBA, 1987* (Research report; 61)

Duffy, C

'Siege warfare', in J Tucker and L S Winstock (eds), *The English Civil War: a military handbook*, 65–73. London: Arms and Armour Press, 1972*

Dunbar, J G

'The medieval architecture of the Scottish Highlands', in [M MacLean (ed)], *The middle ages in the Highlands*, 38–70. [Inverness]: Inverness Field Club, 1981*

'Scottish royal residences of the late Middle Ages: some aspects of domestic planning', in G Meirion-Jones, E Impey and M Jones (eds), *The seigneurial residence in western Europe AD c 800–1600*, 51–61. Oxford: Archaeopress, 2002* (BAR international series; 1088)

Eales, R

'Castles and politics in England, 1215–1224', in P R Coss and S D Lloyd (eds), *Thirteenth century England 2: proceedings of the Newcastle upon Tyne Conference 1987*, 23–43. Woodbridge: Boydell Press, 1988

'Royal power and castles in Norman England', in C Harper-Bill and R Harvey (eds), *The ideals and practice of medieval knighthood 3: papers from the fourth Strawberry Hill Conference 1988*, 49–78. Woodbridge: Boydell Press, 1990

'Royal power and castles in Norman England', in R Liddiard (ed), *Anglo-Norman castles*, 41–67. Woodbridge: Boydell Press, 2003

'Castles and politics in England 1215–1224', in *ibid*, 367–88

Ellington, M

'Tower house restoration in Scotland', in J S Smith (ed), *North east castles: castles in the landscape of north east Scotland*, 77–82. Aberdeen: Aberdeen University Press, 1990

Emery, A
'The Hastings family: their properties and influence during the later Middle Ages', in N H Cooper (ed), *The Nottingham area: proceedings of the 135th summer meeting of the Royal Archaeological Institute, 1985*, 60–65. London: RAI, 1989

English, B
'Towns, mottes and ring-works of the Conquest', in A Ayton and J L Price (eds), *The medieval military revolution: state, society and military change in medieval and early modern Europe*, 45–61. London: Tauris Academic Studies, 1995

Everson, P
'"Delightfully surrounded with woods and ponds": field evidence for medieval gardens in England', in P Pattison (ed), *There by design: field archaeology in parks and gardens*, 32–38. Oxford: Archaeopress; Swindon: RCHME, 1998* (BAR British series; 267)

'Medieval gardens and designed landscapes', in R Wilson-North (ed), *The lie of the land: aspects of the archaeology and history of the designed landscape in the south west of England*, 24–33. Exeter: The Mint Press, 2003*

Fairclough, G
'Fortified houses and castles', in P [A G] Clack and J Ivy (eds), *The borders*, 91–99. Durham: CBA Group 3, 1983*

Faulkner, P A
'Domestic planning from the twelfth to the fourteenth centuries', in J T Smith, P A Faulkner and A Emery, *Studies in medieval domestic architecture*, 84–117. [S l]: RAI, 1975* (first published in *Archaeological Journal* 115 (1958), 150–83)

Foard, G
'The archaeology of attack: battles and sieges of the English Civil War', in P W M Freeman and A Pollard (eds), *Fields of conflict: progress and prospect in battlefield archaeology*, 87–103. Oxford: Archaeopress, 2001* (BAR international series; 958)

France, J
'Fortifications east and west', in H Kennedy (ed), *Muslim military architecture in greater Syria from the coming of Islam to the Ottoman period*, 281–94. Leiden: Brill, 2006 (History of warfare; 35)

Gaines, B
'Malory's castles in text and illustration', in K Reyerson and F Powe (eds), *The medieval castle: romance and reality*, 215–28. Dubuque: Kendall/Hunt Publishing, 1984*

Gilchrist, R
'Landscapes of the Middle Ages: churches, castles and monasteries', in J Hunter

and I Ralston (eds), *The archaeology of Britain: an introduction from the upper Palaeolithic to the industrial revolution*, 228–46. London: Routledge, 1999*

'The contested garden: gender, space and metaphor in the medieval English castle', in R Gilchrist, *Gender and archaeology: contesting the past*, 109–45. London: Routledge, 1999*

Goodall, J A A
'The architecture of war', in R Marks and P Williamson (eds), *Gothic: art for England 1400–1547*, 187–91. London: V & A Publications, 2003*

Graham, B
'Urbanisation in Ireland during the High Middle Ages, *c* 1100 to *c* 1350', in T Barry (ed), *A history of settlement in Ireland*, 110–23. London: Routledge, 2000*

Graham, B J
'The mottes of the Norman liberty of Meath', in H Murtagh (ed), *Irish midland studies: essays in commemoration of N W English*, 39–56. Athlone: Old Athlone Society, 1980*

Green, J A
'Castles, halls, and houses', in J A Green, *The aristocracy of Norman England*, 172–93. Cambridge: CUP, 1997*

Griffiths, R A
'The castle constables', in R A Griffiths, *The principality of Wales in the later middle ages: the structure and personnel of government. 1. South Wales, 1277–1536*, 193–266. Cardiff: University of Wales Press, 1972 (Board of Celtic Studies history and law series; 26)

Hale, J R
'Tudor fortifications: the defence of the realm, 1485–1558', in J R Hale, *Renaissance war studies*, 63–97. London: Hambledon Press, 1983*

Hamlin, A
'Ella Armitage, early pioneer of castle studies (1841–1931)', in A Hamlin, *Pioneers of the past*, 1–4. Cambridge: Newnham College, 2001*

Hayes-McCoy, G A (ed)
'The Blackwater Valley', in *Ulster and other Irish maps c 1600*, 14–15. Dublin: Stationery Office for the Irish Manuscripts Commission, 1964*

'The Lough Foyle expedition', in *ibid*, 26–27*

Higham, R A
'Public and private defence in the medieval south west: town, castle and fort', in R Higham (ed), *Security and defence in south-west England before 1800*, 27–49. Exeter: University of Exeter, 1987*

'Timber castles; a reassessment', in R Liddiard (ed), *Anglo-Norman castles*, 105–18. Woodbridge: Boydell Press, 2003*

'Ann Hamlin and castle studies', in I M Meek (ed), *The modern traveller to our past: Festschrift in honour of Ann Hamlin*, 259–63. [Southport]: DPK, 2006*

Hohler, C
'Kings and castles', in J Evans (ed), *The flowering of the middle ages*, 133–78. London: Thames and Hudson, 1966*

Hughes, Q
'Les tours martello', in *Forts du littoral*, 76–93. Château d'Oleron: Citadelle du Château d'Oleron, 1989*

Humphries, P
'Heritage interpretation and Cadw', in A Hems and M Blockley (eds), *Heritage interpretation*, 71–82. Abingdon: Routledge, 2006

Hunter, J R
'Maritime and military environments', in J A Atkinson, I Banks and G MacGregor (eds), *Townships to farmsteads: rural settlement studies in Scotland, England and Wales*, 178–87. Oxford: British Archaeological Reports, 2000* (British series; 293) [Scottish modern military sites]

Hutton, R and Reeves, W
'Sieges and fortifications', in J [P] Kenyon and J Ohlmeyer (eds), *The civil wars: a military history of England, Scotland, and Ireland 1638–1660*, 195–233, 349–50. Oxford: OUP, 1998*

Johnson, D N
'Later medieval castles', in M Ryan (ed), *The illustrated archaeology of Ireland*, 188–92. Dublin: Country House, 1991*

Johnson, M
'Reconstruction castles and refashioning identities in Renaissance England', in S Tarlow and S West (eds), *The familiar past? Archaeologies of later historical Britain*, 69–86. London: Routledge, 1999*

'Archaeology and social theory', in J Bintliff (ed), *A companion to archaeology*, 92–109. Oxford: Blackwell Publishing, 2004*

Kemp, A
'Deutsche Einflusse auf den britischen Festungsbau im 19. Jahrhundert', in V Schmidtchen (ed), *Festung Garnison Belvölkerung: historische Aspekte der Festungsforschung*, 81–99. Wesel: Deutsche Gesellschaft für Festungsforschung, 1982*

Kenyon, J R

'The published works of David James Cathcart King', in J R Kenyon and R Avent (eds), *Castles in Wales and the Marches: essays in honour of D J Cathcart King*, 217–21. Cardiff: University of Wales Press, 1987

'Coastal artillery fortification in England in the late fourteenth and early fifteenth century', in A Curry and M Hughes (ed), *Arms, armies and fortifications in the Hundred Years War*, 145–49. Woodbridge: Boydell Press, 1994*

'Castle studies and G T Clark, with particular reference to Wales and the Marches', in B Ll James (ed), *G T Clark, scholar ironmaster in the Victorian age*, 83–102. Cardiff: University of Wales Press, 1998*

'Fluctuating frontiers: Normanno-Welsh castle warfare c 1075 to 1240', in R Liddiard (ed), *Anglo-Norman castles*, 247–57. Woodbridge: Boydell Press, 2003*

Kerrigan, P M

'The defences of the Shannon: Portumna to Athlone, 1793–1815', in H Murtagh (ed), *Irish midland studies: essays in commemoration of N W English*, 168–92. Athlone: Old Athlone Society, 1980*

King, D J C

'Castles in England and Wales: their very varied character and purposes', in T Hoekstra [*et al*] (eds), *Liber castellorum: 40 variaties op het thema kasteel*, 81–96. Zutphen: De Walburg Pers, 1981*

King, D J C, with Kenyon, J R

'Military architecture and fortification. III. Western. 1. Medieval *c* AD 500-*c* 1450', in J Turner (ed), *The dictionary of art*, **21**, 561–65. London: Macmillan, 1996*

Klingelhöfer, E

'Castles built with air: Spenserian architecture in Ireland', in D de Boe and F Verhaeghe (eds), *Military studies in medieval Europe: papers of the 'Medieval Europe Brugge 1997' conference*, **11**, 149–54. Zellik: Institute for the Archaeological Heritage, 1997

'Proto-colonial archaeology: the case of Elizabethan Ireland', in P P A Funari, M Hall and S Jones (eds), *Historical archaeology: back from the edge*, 164–79. London: Routledge, 1999*

'The architecture of empire: Elizabethan country houses in Ireland', in S Lawrence (ed), *Archaeologies of the British: explorations of identity in Great Britain and its colonies 1600–1945*, 102–15. London: Routledge, 2003 (One world archaeology; 46)

Knight, J K

'The road to Harlech: aspects of some early thirteenth-century Welsh castles', in J R Kenyon and R Avent (eds), *Castles in Wales and the Marches: essays in honour of D J Cathcart King*, 75–88. Cardiff: University of Wales Press, 1987*

Le Patourel. J
'Fortified and semi-fortified manor houses in eastern and northern England in the later middle ages', in M Bur (ed), *La maison forte au moyen âge*, 17–29. Paris: Centre National de la Recherche Scientifique, 1986*

Loeber, R
'An architectural history of Gaelic castles and settlements, 1370–1600', in P J Duffy, D Edwards and E FitzPatrick (eds), *Gaelic Ireland c. 1250-c. 1650: land, lordship and settlement*, 271–314. Dublin: Four Courts Press, 2001*

MacIvor, I
'Artillery and major places of strength in the Lothians and the east border, 1513–1542', in D H Caldwell (ed), *Scottish weapons and fortifications 1100–1800*, 94–152. Edinburgh: John Donald, 1981*

McNeill, T E
'The great towers of early Irish castles', in M Chibnall (ed), *Anglo-Norman studies 12: proceedings of the Battle Conference 1989*, 99–117. Woodbridge: Boydell Press, 1990*

'Les limites du pouvoir Plantagenêt: les châteaux royaux d'Irlande', in M-P Baudry (ed), *Les fortifications dans les domaines Plantagenêt XIIe-XIVe siècles: actes du colloque international tenu à Poitiers du 11 au 13 novembre 1994*, 55–59. Poitiers: Centre d'Etudes Supérieures de Civilisation Médiévale, 2000* (Civilisation médiévale; 10)

'Castles', in P J Crabtree (ed), *Medieval archaeology: an encyclopedia*, 43–46. New York: Garland, 2001

'The gap below the castle in Ireland', in G Meirion-Jones, E Impey and M Jones (eds), *The seigneurial residence in western Europe AD c 800–1600*, 45–50. Oxford: Archaeopress, 2002 (BAR international series; 1088)

'Hibernia pacata et castellata', in R Liddiard (ed), *Anglo-Norman castles*, 259–71. Woodbridge: Boydell Press, 2003*

'Squaring circles: flooring round towers in Wales and Ireland', in J R Kenyon and K O'Conor (eds), *The medieval castle in Ireland and Wales: essays in honour of Jeremy Knight*, 96–106. Dublin: Four Courts Press, 2003*

'Flooring systems in the round towers of Wales and Ireland around 1200', in J-M Poisson and J-J Schwein (eds), *Le bois dans le château de pierre au moyen âge: acts du colloque de Lons-le-Saunier 23–25 octobre 1997*, 311–19. Besançon: Presses Universitaires France-Comtoises, 2003*

Marshall, P
'The great tower as residence', in G Meirion-Jones, E Impey and M Jones (eds), *The seigneurial residence in western Europe AD c 800–1600*, 27–44. Oxford: Archaeopress, 2002* (BAR international series; 1088)

Merriman, M
'Italian military engineers in Britain in the 1540's', in S Tyacke (ed), *English map-making 1500–1650: historical essays*, 57–67. London: British Library, 1983*

Moore, D
'Roman and Norman military sites in Wales: a comparison of two frontiers', in *Akten des XI internationalen Limeskongresses*, 19–34. Budapest: Akademiai Kiado, 1978*

Moore, J S
'Anglo-Norman garrisons', in C Harper-Bill (ed), *Anglo-Norman studies 22: proceedings of the Battle Conference 1999*, 205–59. Woodbridge: Boydell Press, 2000

Morley, B M
'Aspects of fourteenth-century castle design', in A Detsicas (ed), *Collectanea historica: essays in memory of Stuart Rigold*, 104–13. Maidstone: Kent Archaeological Society, 1981*

Morris, R K
'The architecture of Arthurian enthusiasm: castle symbolism in the reigns of Edward I and his successors', in M Strickland (ed), *Armies, chivalry and warfare in medieval Britain and France: proceedings of the 1995 Harlaxton Symposium*, 63–81. Stamford: Paul Watkins, 1998* (Harlaxton medieval studies; 7)

'Later Gothic architecture in south Wales', in J R Kenyon and D M Williams (eds), *Cardiff: architecture and archaeology in the medieval diocese of Llandaff*, 102–35. Leeds: British Archaeological Association and Maney Publishing, 2006 (Conference transactions; 29)

Muir, R.
'Defence in the landscape', in R Muir, *The new reading the landscape: fieldwork in landscape history*, 223–44. Exeter: Exeter University Press, 2000*

Nicolle, D
'The early trebuchet: documentation and archaeological evidence', in N Faucherre, J Mesqui and N Prouteau (eds), *Les fortifications au temps des Croisades*, 269–78. Rennes: Presses Universitaires de Rennes, 2004*

O'Conor, K
'The morphology of Gaelic lordly sites in north Connacht', in P J Duffy, D Edwards and E FitzPatrick (eds), *Gaelic Ireland c. 1250-c. 1650: land, lordship and settlement*, 329–45. Dublin: Four Courts Press, 2001*

O'Keeffe, T
'Medieval frontiers and fortifications: the pale and its evolution', in F H A Aalen and K Whelan (eds), *Dublin, city and county: from prehistory to present. Studies in honour of J H Andrews*, 57–78. Dublin: Geography Publications, 1992*

'Rural settlement and cultural identity in Gaelic Ireland, 1000–1500', in *Ruralia I, Památky Archeologické: supplement*, 5 (1996), 142–53*

'Historiography, heritage, inheritance: Irish castellology and Leask's *Irish castles*', in M Fanning and R Gillespie (eds), *Print culture and intellectual life in Ireland 1660–1941: essays in honour of Michael Adams*, 143–63. Dublin: The Woodfield Press, 2006*

O'Neil, B H St J

'The castles of Wales', in V E Nash-Williams (ed), *A hundred years of Welsh archaeology*, 129–40. [S l]: Cambrian Archaeological Association, 1949*

O'Sullivan, A

'Crannogs: places of resistance in the contested landscapes of early modern Ireland', in D Bender and M Winer (eds), *Contested landscapes: movement, exile and place*, 87–101. Oxford: Berg, 2001*

'Crannogs in late medieval Gaelic Ireland, *c.* 1350-*c.* 1650', in P J Duffy, D Edwards and E FitzPatrick (eds), *Gaelic Ireland c. 1250-c. 1650: land, lordship and settlement*, 397–417. Dublin: Four Courts Press, 2001*

Painter, S

'English castles in the early middle ages: their number, location, and legal position', in F A Cazel (ed), *Feudalism and liberty: articles and addresses by Sydney Painter*, 125–43. Baltimore: Johns Hopkins University Press, 1961 [first published in *Speculum* 10 (1935), 321–32]

'Castle guard', in *ibid*, 144–56 [first published in *American Historical Review* 40 (1934–5), 450–59]

'Castle-guard', in R Liddiard (ed), *Anglo-Norman castles*, 203–10. Woodbridge: Boydell Press, 2003

Palliser, D M

'Town defences in medieval England and Wales', in A Ayton and J L Price (eds), *The medieval military revolution: state, society and military change in medieval and early modern Europe*, 105–20. London: Tauris Academic Studies, 1995

Parsons, D

'Urban castles and late Anglo-Saxon towns', in P Lindley (ed), *The early history of Lincoln Castle*. 30–40. Lincoln: Society for Lincolnshire History and Archaeology, 2004* (Occasional papers in Lincolnshire history and archaeology; 12)

Perks, J C

The Anglo-Norman stone castle in the British Isles from its development until 1154. Unpublished typescript, MS 837 in the Library of the Society of Antiquaries of London

'David James Cathcart King: a memoir', in J R Kenyon and R Avent (eds), *Castles in Wales and the Marches: essays in honour of D J Cathcart King*, 1–3. Cardiff: University of Wales Press, 1987

Platt, C

'Architecture and the arts', in C Platt, *King death: the Black Death and its aftermath in late-medieval England*, 137–75. London: UCL Press, 1996*

Prestwich, M

'The garrisoning of English medieval castles', in R P Abels and B S Bachrach (eds), *The Normans and their adversaries: essays in memory of C Warren Hollister*, 184–200. Woodbridge: Boydell Press, 2001

Pringle, D

'Castle chapels in the Frankish east', in N Faucherre, J Mesqui and N Prouteau (eds), *Les fortifications au temps des Croisades*, 25–41. Rennes: Presses Universitaires de Rennes, 2004*

Renn, D F

'Hen Domen compared: the evidence for wooden castle building in Britain and Normandy', in A Burl (ed), *From Roman town to Norman castle: papers in honour of Philip Barker*, 56–67. Birmingham: University of Birmingham, 1988

'Burgheat and gonfanon: two sidelights from the Bayeux Tapestry', in M Chibnall (ed), *Anglo-Norman studies 16: proceedings of the Battle Conference 1993*, 177–98. Woodbridge: Boydell Press, 1994*

'Castle fortification in England and adjoining countries from 1150–1250', in A Salamagne and R Le Jan (directeurs), *Le château médiéval et la guerre dans l'Europe du nord-ouest: actes du colloque de Valenciennes 1–2–3 juin 1995*, 53–59. Lille: Revue du Nord, 1998* (Hors série. Collection art et archéologie; 5)

'Plantagenêt castle-building in England in the second half of the twelfth century', in M-P Baudry (ed), *Les fortifications dans les domaines Plantagenêt XIIe-XIVe siècles: actes du colloque international tenu à Poitiers du 11 au 13 novembre 1994*, 15–21. Poitiers: Centre d'Etudes Supérieures de Civilisation Médiévale, 2000* (Civilisation médiévale; 10)

'Burgheat and gonfanon: two sidelights from the Bayeux Tapestry', in R Liddiard (ed), *Anglo-Norman castles*, 69–90. Woodbridge: Boydell Press, 2003*

Rowley, T

'Castles and palaces of the Conquest', in T Rowley, *English Heritage book of Norman England*, 65–82. London: Batsford, in association with English Heritage, 1997*

Ryder, P F

'Fortified medieval and sub-medieval buildings in the north-east of England', in B

E Vyner (ed), *Medieval rural settlement in north-east England*, 127–39. Durham: Architectural and Archaeological Society of Durham and Northumberland, 1990*

Rynne, E
'An unnoticed constructional feature in insular church and castle building', in S M Pearce (ed), *The early church in western Britain and Ireland: studies presented to C A Ralegh Radford*, 335–50. Oxford: British Archaeological Reports, 1982* (British series; 102)

Samson, R
'The rise and fall of tower-houses in post-reformation Scotland', in R Samson (ed), *The social archaeology of houses*, 197–243. Edinburgh: Edinburgh University Press, 1990*

'Towerhouses in the sixteenth century', in S Foster, A Macinnes and R MacInnes (eds), *Scottish power centres from the early middle ages to the twentieth century*, 132–46. Glasgow: Cruithne Press, 1998*

Saunders, A D
'The defences of the Firth of Forth', in D J Breeze (ed), *Studies in Scottish antiquity presented to Stewart Cruden*, 469–80. Edinburgh: John Donald, 1984*

'Defence of the realm: medieval and later defences', in V A Maxfield (ed), *The Saxon shore: a handbook*, 96–111. Exeter: University of Exeter Press, 1989*

'Castles and fortification', in P E Szarmach, M T Tavormina and J T Rosenthal (eds), *Medieval England: an encyclopedia*, 163–65. New York; London: Garland Publishing, 1998*

Schofield, [A] J
'The role of aerial photographs in national strategic programmes: assessing recent military sites in England', in R H Bewley and W Raczkowski (eds), *Aerial archaeology: developing future practice*, 269–82. Amsterdam: IOS Press, 2002* (NATO science series 1; 337)

Simpson, G G and Webster, B
'Charter evidence and the distribution of mottes in Scotland', in K J Stringer (ed), *Essays on the nobility of medieval Scotland*, 1–24. Edinburgh: John Donald, 1985*

'Charter evidence and the distribution of mottes in Scotland', in R Liddiard (ed), *Anglo-Norman castles*, 223–46. Woodbridge: Boydell Press, 2003*

Simpson, W D
'The tower-houses of Scotland', in E M Jope (ed), *Studies in building history*, 229–42. London: Odhams, 1961*

Slater, T R
'Parks, gardens and policies: the changing landscape around the castle', in J S Smith (ed), *North east castles: castles in the landscape of north east Scotland*, 32–55. Aberdeen: Aberdeen University Press, 1990*

Smith, J S

'Room at the top: from castle to defensible residence', in *ibid*, 5–31*

Spurgeon, C J

'Mottes and castle-ringworks in Wales', in J R Kenyon and R Avent (eds), *Castles in Wales and the Marches: essays in honour of D J Cathcart King*, 23–49. Cardiff: University of Wales Press, 1987*

Stalley, R A

'A twelfth-century patron of architecture: a study of the buildings erected by Roger, bishop of Salisbury 1102–1139', in R Stalley, *Ireland and Europe in the Middle Ages: selected essays on architecture and sculpture*, 1–27. London: Pindar Press, 1994*

'William de Prene and the royal works in Ireland', in *ibid*, 54–74*

Stell, G

'Architecture: the changing needs of society', in J M Brown (ed), *Scottish society in the fifteenth century*, 153–83. London: Arnold, 1977*

'Late medieval defences in Scotland', in D H Caldwell (ed), *Scottish weapons and fortifications 1100–1800*, 21–54. Edinburgh: John Donald, 1981*

'The Scottish medieval castle: form, function and "evolution"', in K J Stringer (ed), *Essays on the nobility of medieval Scotland*, 195–209. Edinburgh: John Donald, 1985*

'Urban buildings', in M Lynch, M Spearman and G Stell (eds), *The Scottish medieval town*, 60–80. Edinburgh: John Donald, 1988*

'Kings, nobles and buildings of the later Middle Ages: Scotland', in G G Simpson (ed), *Scotland and Scandinavia 800–1800*, 60–72. Edinburgh: John Donald, 1990

'Destruction and damage: a reassessment of the historical and architectural evidence', in N Macdougall (ed), *Scotland and war AD 79–1918*, 24–35. Edinburgh: John Donald, 1991

Stenton, F

'The development of the castle in England and Wales', in G Barraclough (ed), *Social life in early England*, 96–123. London: Routledge and Kegan Paul, 1960*

Strickland, M

'Securing the north: invasion and strategy of defence in twelfth-century Anglo-Scottish warfare', in M Chibnall (ed), *Anglo-Norman studies 12: proceedings of the Battle Conference 1989*, 177–98. Woodbridge: Boydell Press, 1990

Suppe, F

'The persistence of castle-guard in the Welsh Marches and Wales: suggestions for a research agenda and methodology', in R P Abels and B S Bachrach (eds), *The Normans and their adversaries: essays in memory of C Warren Hollister*, 201–21. Woodbridge: Boydell Press, 2001

Sweetman D

'Anglo-Norman fortresses', in M Ryan (ed), *The illustrated archaeology of Ireland*, 183–88. Dublin: Country House, 1991*

'The hall-house in Ireland', in J R Kenyon and K O'Conor (eds), *The medieval castle in Ireland and Wales: essays in honour of Jeremy Knight*, 121–32. Dublin: Four Courts Press, 2003*

Talbot, E J

'The defences of earth and timber castles', in D H Caldwell (ed), *Scottish weapons and fortifications 1100–1800*, 1–9. Edinburgh: John Donald, 1981*

Taylor, A J

'Military architecture', in A L Poole (ed), *Medieval England*, **1**, 98–127. Oxford: Clarendon Press, 1958*

'Castle building in Wales in the later thirteenth century: the prelude to construction', in E M Jope (ed), *Studies in building history*, 104–33. London: Odhams, 1961*

'Castle-building in thirteenth-century Wales and Savoy', in A Taylor, *Studies in castles and castle-building*, 1–28. London: Hambledon Press, 1985*

'Master James of St George', in *ibid*, 63–97

'Castle-building in Wales in the later thirteenth century: the prelude to construction', in *ibid*, 99–128*

'Thomas de Houghton: a royal carpenter of the later thirteenth century', in *ibid*, 189–94

'Who was "John Pennardd, leader of the men of Gwynedd"?', in *ibid*, 209–27

'Master Bertram, *ingeniator regis*', in C Harper-Bill, C J Holdsworth and J L Nelson (eds), *Studies in medieval history presented to R Allen Brown*, 289–315. Woodbridge: Boydell Press, 1989*

Thomas, A

'Financing town walls in medieval Ireland', in C Thomas (ed), *Rural landscapes and communities: essays presented to Desmond McCourt*, 65–91. Blackrock: Irish Academic Press, 1986*

Thompson, M W

'The architectural significance of the building works of Ralph, Lord Cromwell (1394–1456)', in A Detsicas (ed), *Collectanea historica: essays in memory of Stuart Rigold*, 155–62. Maidstone: Kent Archaeological Society, 1981*

'The abandonment of the castle in Wales and the Marches', in J R Kenyon and R Avent (eds), *Castles in Wales and the Marches: essays in honour of D J Cathcart King*, 205–15. Cardiff: University of Wales Press, 1987

'The Green Knight's castle', in C Harper-Bill, C J Holdsworth and J L Nelson (eds), *Studies in medieval history presented to R Allen Brown*, 317–25. Woodbridge: Boydell Press, 1989*

Urquhart, A G
'The construction and restoration of the north east tower house', in J S Smith (ed), *North east castles: castles in the landscape of north east Scotland*, 56–76. Aberdeen: Aberdeen University Press, 1990*

Waterman, D M
'Some Irish seventeenth-century houses and their architectural ancestry', in E M Jope (ed), *Studies in building history*, 251–74. London: Odhams, 1961*

Watson, F
'The expression of power in a medieval kingdom: thirteenth-century Scottish castles', in S Foster, A Macinnes and R MacInnes (eds), *Scottish power centres from the early middle ages to the twentieth century*, 59–78. Glasgow: Cruithne Press, 1998

Welfare, H, Bowden, M and Blood, K
'Fieldwork and the castles of the Anglo-Scottish borders', in P Pattison, D Field and S Ainsworth (eds), *Patterns of the past: essays in landscape archaeology for Christopher Taylor*, 53–60. Oxford: Oxbow Books, 1999*

Wheatley, A
' 'King Arthur lives in merry Carleile'', in M McCarthy and D Weston (eds), *Carlisle and Cumbria: Roman and medieval architecture, art and archaeology*, 63–72. Leeds: British Archaeological Association and Maney Publishing, 2004 (Conference transactions; 27)

Williams, A
'A bell-house and a burh-geat: lordly residences in England before the Norman Conquest', in C Harper-Bill and R Harvey (eds), *Medieval knighthood 4: papers from the fifth Strawberry Hill Conference 1990*, 221–40. Woodbridge: Boydell Press, 1992

'A bell-house and a burh-geat: lordly residences in England before the Norman Conquest', in R Liddiard (ed), *Anglo-Norman castles*, 23–40. Woodbridge: Boydell Press, 2003

Williams, G
'Monuments of conquest: castle and cloister', in G Williams, *Religion, language and nationality in Wales: historical essays*, 34–70. Cardiff: University of Wales Press, 1979*

PART 2 – TOPOGRAPHICAL

ENGLAND

BEDFORDSHIRE

Baker, D. 'Mottes, moats and ringworks in Bedfordshire: Beauchamp Wadmore revisited', *Château Gaillard* 9–10 (1982), 35–54*

Dyer, J F. 'The castles: part one', *Bedfordshire Magazine* 8 (1961–3), 267–71*

Dyer, J F. 'The castles: part two', *ibid* 8 (1961–3), 345–50*

Lowerre, A. *Placing castles in the Conquest: landscape, lordship and local politics in the south-eastern midlands, 1066–1100*. Oxford: J and E Hedges, 2005* (BAR British series; 385)

Pevsner, N. *Bedfordshire and the county of Huntingdon and Peterborough (The buildings of England)*. Harmondsworth: Penguin Books, 1968*

Salter, M. *The castles of the Thames Valley and the Chilterns*. Malvern: Folly Publications, [2002]*

Ampthill
'The builder of Ampthill Castle', M S F George, *Bedfordshire Magazine* 5 (1955–7), 185–89

Bedford
'Bedford Castle, Bedford', D B Baker, *Archaeological Excavations 1970*, 24–25. London: HMSO, 1971

'Bedford Castle, Bedford', D B Baker, *Archaeological Excavations 1971*, 25–26. London: HMSO, 1972

'Bedford', D B Baker, *Archaeological Excavations 1972*, 72. London: HMSO, 1973

'Bedford Castle', J M Hassall, *Archaeological Excavations 1973*, 65–66. London: HMSO, 1974

'A regeneration issue: Bedford Castle Mound and gardens', J Oetgen, *The Archaeologist* 57 (2005), 12–14*

'Bedfordshire archaeology, 1966–69', D H Kennett, *Bedfordshire Archaeological Journal* 4 (1969), 85

'Bedfordshire archaeology, 1969–70', D H Kennett, *ibid* 5 (1970), 119

'Bedfordshire archaeology, 1970–71', D H Kennett, *ibid* 6 (1971), 81

'Bedfordshire archaeology, 1971–72', D H Kennett, *ibid* 7 (1972), 89

'Bedfordshire archaeology, 1972–1973', D H Kennett, *ibid* 8 (1973), 139

'Bedford: aspects of town origins and development', J Hassall and D Baker, *ibid* 9 (1974), 75–94*

'Excavations in Bedford 1967–1977', D Baker [*et al*], *ibid* 13 (1979), [whole issue, espec pp 7–64]*

'Archaeological recording to the rear of 29–41 High Street, Bedford', S Steadman, *Bedfordshire Archaeology* 23 (1999), 135–63*

'The siege of Bedford Castle', M F Greenshields, *Bedfordshire Magazine* 4 (1953–5), 183–90*

'Undermining a castle', anon, *ibid* 6 (1957–9), 187

'Bedford Castle: some preliminary results from rescue excavations', D Baker, *Château Gaillard* 6 (1973), 15–22*

'Bedford Castle, Beds', D Baker, *CBA Group 9 Newsletter* 1 (1971), 15

'Bedford', D Baker, *ibid* 2 (1972), 22

'Bedford, Bedfordshire', D Baker, *ibid* 3 (1973), 28

'Bedford', J Hassall, *ibid* 4 (1974), 21–22

'Besieging Bedford: military logistics in 1224', E Amt, *Journal of Medieval Military History* 1 (2002), 101–24*

'Medieval Britain in 1969', D M Wilson and D G Hurst, *Medieval Archaeology* 14 (1970), 175

'Medieval Britain in 1970', D M Wilson and S Moorhouse, *ibid* 15 (1971), 145

'Medieval Britain in 1971', L E Webster and J Cherry, *ibid* 16 (1972), 186–87

'Medieval Britain in 1972', L E Webster and J Cherry, *ibid* 17 (1973), 159

'Medieval Britain in 1973', L E Webster and J Cherry, *ibid* 18 (1974), 222–23

'Medieval Britain in 1980', S M Youngs and J Clark, *ibid* 25 (1981), 200

'Medieval Britain and Ireland in 1995', B S Nenk, S Margeson and M Hurley, *ibid* 40 (1996), 242

'Medieval Britain and Ireland in 1997', M Gaimster, C Haith and J Bradley, *ibid* 42 (1998), 114

'Bedford, castle mound and lime kiln', J Oetgen, *South Midlands Archaeology* 33 (2003), 1

Biggleswade

'Air reconnaissance: recent results, 7', J K St Joseph, *Antiquity* 40 (1966), 142–44*

'A ringwork and bailey at Biggleswade, Bedfordshire', P V Addyman, *Bedfordshire Archaeological Journal* 3 (1966), 15–18*

Cainhoe

'Cainhoe Castle, Clophill', A Taylor and P Woodward, *Archaeological Excavations 1973*, 66. London: HMSO, 1974

'Cainhoe Castle', B Baker, *Archaeological Journal* 139 (1982), 32–34*

'Bedfordshire archaeology, 1972–1973', *Bedfordshire Archaeological Journal* 8 (1973), 140

'Cainhoe Castle excavations, Clophill, Bedfordshire', A Taylor and P Woodward, *CBA Group 9 Newsletter* 4 (1974), 14

Chalgrave

'Chalgrave', B K Davison, *Archaeological Excavations 1970*, 25. London: HMSO, 1971

'Bedfordshire archaeology, 1970–71', D H Kennett, *Bedfordshire Archaeological Journal* 6 (1971), 83–84

'Chalgrave Manor', anon, *Bedfordshire Archaeologist* 1.2 (1955), 43–45

'The excavation of a motte and bailey castle at Chalgrave, Bedfordshire, 1970', A Pinder and B Davison, *Bedfordshire Archaeology* 18 (1988), 33–56*

'Chalgrave, Beds', B K Davison, *CBA Group 9 Newsletter* 1 (1971), 16–17

'Medieval Britain in 1970', D M Wilson and S Moorhouse, *ibid* 15 (1971), 145

Eaton Socon

'Excavations on the castle site known as "The Hillings" at Eaton Socon, Bedfordshire', T C Lethbridge and C F Tebbutt, *Proceedings of the Cambridge Antiquarian Society* 45 (1951), 48–60*

'Late Saxon settlements in the St Neots area: 1. The Saxon settlement and the Norman castle at Eaton Socon, Bedfordshire', P V Addyman, *ibid* 58 (1965), 38–73*

Luton

'Excavation at Castle Street, Luton: the site of Robert de Waudari's castle?', S Coles, *Bedfordshire Archaeology* 25 (2004), 201–7*

'Medieval Britain and Ireland in 2003', J Bradley and M Gaimster, *Medieval Archaeology* 48 (2004), 251–52

'Luton, former bus depot, Castle Street', S Coles, *South Midlands Archaeology* 33 (2003), 17–20*

Ridgmont

'Where was Rugemont Castle?', R Cotchin, *Bedfordshire Magazine* 22.169 (1989), 1–5*

Thurleigh

'Thurleigh Castle', E Baker and A Simco, *Archaeological Excavations 1976*, 105. London: HMSO, 1977

'Thurleigh Castle, Thurleigh, Bedfordshire', E Baker, *CBA Group 9 Newsletter* 7 (1977), 20–22*

'Medieval Britain in 1976', L E Webster and J Cherry, *Medieval Archaeology* 21 (1977), 233

Tilsworth

'[Report]', Manshead Archaeological Society, *CBA Group 9 Newsletter* 3 (1973), 42–43*

'Excavations at Warren Knoll, Tilsworth', anon, *Manshead Magazine: Journal of the Manshead Archaeological Society of Dunstable* 22 (1973), 17–18

Toddington

'Conger Hill, Toddington', J Hitchcock, *ibid* 32 (1992), 10*

Totternhoe

'Bedfordshire archaeology, 1970–71', D Kennett, *Bedfordshire Archaeological Journal* 6 (1971), 88

'Totternhoe Castle, Beds', Manshead Archaeological Society, *CBA Group 9 Newsletter* 1 (1971), 15

Yielden

'Yielden Castle', D Baker, *Archaeological Journal* 139 (1982), 17–18*

BERKSHIRE

Anon. *Bastions of Berkshire: eighteenth century redoubts in Crowthorne Woods*. Reading: Berkshire County Council, 1994*

Anon. *Bastions of Berkshire: medieval castles*. Reading: Berkshire County Council, 1995*

Anon. *Bastions of Berkshire: pillboxes of World War II*. Reading: Berkshire County Council, [1993]*

Elliott, J (ed). *Heritage unlocked: guide to free sites in London and the south east*. London; English Heritage, 2005*

Pevsner, N. *Berkshire (Buildings of England)*. Harmondsworth: Penguin Books, 1966*

Salter, M. *The castles of the Thames Valley and the Chilterns*. Malvern: Folly Publications, [2002]*

Donnington

Donnington Castle, Berkshire. M Wood. London: HMSO, 1964*

Hamstead Marshall

'Earthwork castles and settlement at Hamstead Marshall, Berkshire', D J Bonney and C J Dunn, in M Bowden, D Mackay and P Topping (eds), *From Cornwall to Caith-*

ness: some aspects of British field archaeology. Papers presented to Norman V Quinnell, 173–82. Oxford: British Archaeological Reports, 1989* (British series; 209)

'Landscape with gardens: aerial, topographical and geophysical survey at Hamstead Marshall, Berkshire', G D Keevill and N Linford, in P Pattison (ed), *There by design: field archaeology in parks and gardens*, 13–22. Oxford: Archaeopress; Swindon: RCHME, 1998* (BAR British series; 267)

'Is Newbury's medieval castle at Hamstead Marshall?', T Higgitt, *Transactions of the Newbury District Field Club* 14.2/3 (1998), 28–29

'The mystery of the Hamstead Marshal [*sic*] castles', D M Edwards, *Postern* 11 (2000), 22–23*

Long Wittenham

'Long Wittenham pillbox and Bampton pillbox', L Brown and J Steane, *CBA Group 9 Newsletter* 10 (1980), 98–99*

Newbury

'Medieval Britain and Ireland in 1990', B S Nenk, S Margeson and M Hurley, *Medieval Archaeology* 35 (1991), 133

Reading

'Reading', C F Slade, in M D Lobel (ed), *Historic towns*, **1**. Oxford: Lovell Johnson-Cook, Hammond and Kell Organization, 1969*

'Post-medieval Britain and Ireland in 2001', M Ponsford, *Post-Medieval Archaeology* 36 (2002), 182

'Post-medieval Britain and Ireland in 2002', M Ponsford, *ibid* 37 (2003), 230

Wallingford

Wallingford Castle: a brief guide. J and S Dewey. Wallingford: Wallingford Historical and Archaeological Society, 1978*

'The battle of Wallingford Castle 1971–1977', T Hassall, in R T Rowley and M Breakell (eds), *Planning and the historic environment II*, 156–68. Oxford: Oxford University Department for External Studies, 1977*

'Wallingford', R D Carr, *Archaeological Excavations 1972*, 73. London: HMSO, 1973*

'Wallingford Castle', T G Hassall, *Archaeological Journal* 135 (1978), 292–93

'Wallingford Castle in the reign of Stephen', C F Slade, *Berkshire Archaeological Journal* 58 (1960), 33–43*

'Excavations at Wallingford Castle, 1965: an interim report', N P Brooks, *ibid* 62 (1965–6), 17–21*

'Wallingford Castle', R Carr, *CBA Group 9 Newsletter* 3 (1973), 18

'Wallingford, Berkshire', A Oswald, *Country Life* 118 (1955), 336–39*

'A medieval 'cob' building', [A Selkirk], *Current Archaeology* 3 (1971–2), 319*

'Medieval Britain in 1966', D M Wilson and D G Hurst, *Medieval Archaeology* 11 (1967), 284

'Medieval Britain in 1968', D M Wilson and D G Hurst, *ibid* 13 (1969), 255

'Medieval Britain in 1972', L E Webster and J Cherry, *ibid* 17 (1973), 159–61

'Medieval Britain and Ireland in 1986', S M Youngs, J Clark and T Barry, *ibid* 31 (1987), 156

'Medieval Britain and Ireland in 2001', J Bradley and M Gaimster, *ibid* 46 (2002), 202–3

'Medieval Britain and Ireland in 2002', J Bradley and M Gaimster, *ibid* 47 (2003), 278

'Medieval Britain and Ireland in 2003', J Bradley and M Gaimster, *ibid* 48 (2004), 284–86*

'The Wallingford Burgh to Borough Research Project', O Creighton [*et al*], *Medieval Settlement Research Group Annual Report* 17 (2002), 43–46*

'The Wallingford Burgh to Borough Research Project: 2003 fieldwork', N Christie [*et al*], *ibid* 18 (2003), 9–13*

'Containing Wallingford Castle, 1146–1153', M Spurrell, *Oxoniensia* 60 (1995), 257–70*

'Post-medieval Britain in 1972', J Cherry, *Post-Medieval Archaeology* 7 (1973), 100

'Post-medieval Britain and Ireland in 1995', M Ponsford and R Jackson, *ibid* 30 (1996), 251

'Wallingford Castle, Castle Lane House', B Durham, *South Midlands Archaeology* 20 (1990), 85–86

West Woodhay

'Norman motte at West Woodhay', E Jervoise, *Transactions of the Newbury and District Field Club* 10.2 (1954), 65–67*

Windsor

The official guide to Windsor Castle. Anon. 22nd edition. London: Lord Chamberlain's Office, 1974*

Windsor revealed: new light on the history of the castle. S Brindle and B Kerr. London: English Heritage, 1997*

A history of the stained glass of St George's Chapel, Windsor Castle. S Brown (ed). Windsor: Dean and Canons of Windsor, 2005* (Historical monographs relating to St George's Chapel, Windsor Castle; 18)

The history of Windsor Castle. M De la Noy. London: Headline, 1990*

Windsor Castle. O Morshead. London: Phaidon, 1951*

Restoration: the rebuilding of Windsor Castle. A Nicolson. London: Michael Joseph, 1997*

Views of Windsor: watercolours by Thomas and Paul Sandby from the collection of Her Majesty Queen Elizabeth II. J Roberts. London: Merrell Holberton, 1995*

Windsor Castle: the official illustrated history. J M Robinson. London: Royal Collections Enterprises, 2001*

'The constructional sequence and topography of the chapel and college buildings at St George's', T Tatton-Brown, in C Richmond and E Scarff (eds), *St George's Chapel, Windsor, in the later Middle Ages*, 3–38. Windsor: Dean and Canons of Windsor, 2001* (Historical monographs relating to St George's Chapel, Windsor Castle; 17)

'The royal lodgings of Edward III at Windsor castle: form, function, representation', C Wilson, in L Keen and E Scarff (eds), *Windsor: medieval archaeology, art and architecture of the Thames Valley*, 15–94. Leeds: British Archaeological Association and Maney Publishing, 2002* (BAA conference transactions; 25)

'Henry III's Windsor: castle-building and residence', V Jansen, in *ibid*, 95–109*

'Windsor Castle: the 1992 fire, the restoration, archaeology and history', S Brindle, in *ibid*, 110–24*

'Henry III's wall paintings of the zodiac in the lower ward of Windsor Castle', D Park and R Pender, in *ibid*, 125–31*

St George's Chapel, Windsor, in the fourteenth century. N Saul (ed). Woodbridge: Boydell Press, 2005*

'The Aerary porch and its influence on late medieval English vaulting', J A A Goodall, in *ibid*, 165–202*

'Edward III's building campaigns at Windsor and the employment of masons, 1346–1377', S Brindle and S Priestley, in *ibid*, 203–23*

'Carpentry works for Edward III at Windsor Castle', J Munby, in *ibid*, 225–37*

'The chantry chapel of John Oxenbridge in St George's Chapel, Windsor Castle', P J Begent, *Antiquaries Journal* 81 (2001), 337–50*

'The Vicar's Hall, St George's Chapel, Windsor Castle, Berkshire: excavation and standing fabric recording, 1997–98', K Blockley, *Archaeological Journal* 157 (2000), 354–74*

'Monarchs & meals: food provisioning and consumption at Windsor Castle', P Baker, *The Archaeologist* 59 (2006), 26–27*

'Master Jordan, who made the king's trébuchet', D Renn, *Arms & Armour: Journal of the Royal Armouries* 1.1 (2004), 25–32*

'Windsor Castle Round Tower: results of rescue excavation and recording, 1989–90', B Kerr, *Castle Studies Group Newsletter* 4 (1990), 6–10

'Windsor Castle fire project', B Kerr, *ibid* 9 (1995–6), 28–31*

'Windsor Castle Hill, Windsor, Berkshire', J Hawke, *CBA Group 2 Newsletter* April (1990), 13–14

'Windsor Castle Governor's House floor: reading a medieval floor', T Cromwell and I Betts, *CfA News* 4 (2002–3), 10–11*

'The medieval constables of Windsor Castle', S Bond, *English Historical Review* 82 (1967), 225–49

'A carriage and cast-iron cannon at Windsor Castle', R D Smith, *Journal of the Ordnance Society* 13 (2001), 25–38*

'Medieval Britain and Ireland in 1988', D R M Gaimster, S Margeson and T Barry, *Medieval Archaeology* 33 (1989), 171

'Medieval Britain and Ireland in 1989', D R M Gaimster, S Margeson and M Hurley, *ibid* 34 (1990), 169–70

'Medieval Britain and Ireland in 1990', B S Nenk, S Margeson and M Hurley, *ibid* 35 (1991), 133

'Medieval Britain and Ireland in 1991', B S Nenk, S Margeson and M Hurley, *ibid* 36 (1992), 195

'Medieval Britain and Ireland in 1995', B S Nenk, S Margeson and M Hurley, *ibid* 40 (1996), 244–45

'Medieval Britain and Ireland in 1999', J Bradley and M Gaimster, *ibid* 44 (2000), 251

'Medieval Britain and Ireland in 2001', J Bradley and M Gaimster, *ibid* 46 (2002), 154

'Medieval Britain and Ireland in 2002', J Bradley and M Gaimster, *ibid* 47 (2003), 221

'Post-medieval Britain and Ireland in 1989', G Egan, *Post-Medieval Archaeology* 24 (1990), 160–61

'Post-medieval Britain and Ireland in 1990', M Ponsford, *ibid* 25 (1991), 119–20

'Post-medieval Britain and Ireland in 1991', M Ponsford, *ibid* 26 (1992), 102–5*

'Post-medieval Britain and Ireland in 2001', M Ponsford, *ibid* 36 (2002), 182

'Post-medieval Britain and Ireland in 2003', M Ponsford, *ibid* 38 (2004), 325–26

'A newly discovered well in the Deanery, Windsor Castle', M F Bond, *Report of the Society of the Friends of St George's and the Descendants of the Knights of the Garter* 4 (1960–72), 136–37*

'The sally-port', M F Bond, *ibid* 4 (1960–72), 182–83

'The recent discoveries in the Lower Ward, Windsor Castle', P E Curnow, *ibid* 4 (1960–72), 218–28*

'A minor discovery in the Henry VIII's Gatehouse', P E Curnow, *ibid* 5.6 (1974–5), 248–50*

'The Curfew Tower', T Tatton-Brown, *ibid* 7.4 (1992–3), 150–54*

'Destruction of St George's Chapel in the 1640's', T Tatton-Brown, *ibid* 7.7 (1995–6), 295–98

'The canons' houses and cloister at Windsor', T Tatton-Brown, *ibid* 8.3 (2001–2), 121–25*

BUCKINGHAMSHIRE

Pevsner, N and Williamson, E. *Buckinghamshire (The buildings of England)*. 2nd edition. London: Penguin Books, 1994*

Pike, A. 'The castles of Buckinghamshire', *Buckinghamshire Archaeological Society Newsletter* autumn (1982), 15–16

Salter, M. *The castles of the Thames Valley and the Chilterns*. Malvern: Folly Publications, [2002]*

Aylesbury
'Aylesbury', source: M Farley, *Current Archaeology* 9.6 (1986), 187–89*

'Aylesbury in the Civil War', G Lamb, *Records of Buckinghamshire* 41 (2001), 183–89

Boarstall
'The Civil War destruction of Boarstall', S Porter, *ibid* 26 (1984), 86–91*

Bradwell
'Bradwell motte', D C Mynard, *CBA Group 9 Newsletter* 7 (1977), 92–93*

Castlethorpe
'Archaeological investigations of the medieval earthworks at Castlethorpe, Buckinghamshire', D Bonner, J Parkhouse and N Smith, *Records of Buckinghamshire* 35 (1995), 79–99*

'Milton Keynes, Castlethorpe, 7b North Street', T Upson-Smith, *South Midlands Archaeology* 35 (2005), 18

Desborough
'Excavations at Desborough Castle, High Wycombe, 1987', M Collard, *Records of Buckinghamshire* 30 (1988), 15–41*

'Desborough Castle, High Wycombe', M Collard, *South Midlands Archaeology* 18 (1988), 28–29

Frith Hill
'A survey of the earthworks at Frith Hill, Great Missenden, Buckinghamshire', D Cater, *Records of Buckinghamshire* 38 (1996), 241–43* [possible ringwork]

Great Kimble
'Archaeological notes from the Buckinghamshire County Museum', C N G[owing], *ibid* 19 (1971–4), 95

Lavendon
'Medieval Britain in 1968', D M Wilson and D G Hurst, *Medieval Archaeology* 13 (1969), 255

'Archaeological notes from the Buckinghamshire County Museum', C N G[owing], *Records of Buckinghamshire* 18 (1966–70), 333

'Earthworks at Lavendon', T Brown and P Everson, *ibid* 45 (2005), 45–64*

Little Kimble
'Medieval Britain and Ireland in 1996', B S Nenk, C Haith and J Bradley, *Medieval Archaeology* 41 (1997), 247–48

Little Missenden
'Castle Tower, Little Missenden', S P O'Connor, *Records of Buckinghamshire* 22 (1980), 140–41*

Newton Longville
'Newton Longville', D C Mynard, *Wolverton and District Archaeological Society News Letter* 11 (1967), 14

Princes Risborough
'The Mount, Princes Risborough, Buckinghamshire', F H Pavry and G M Knocker, *Records of Buckinghamshire* 16.3 (1957–8), 131–78*

Sherington
'Archaeology in north Bucks 1973', anon, *Milton Keynes Journal of Archaeology and History* 3 (1974), 6

Weston Turville
'Excavations at the motte, Weston Turville Manor, 1985', P A St J Yeoman, *ibid* 28 (1986), 169–78*

'The Turvilles and the castle of Weston Turville', R P Hagerty, *ibid* 28 (1986), 179–81

'Excavations at the Manor House, Weston Turville', P A Yeoman, *South Midlands Archaeology* 16 (1986), 41–42

West Wycombe
'Archaeological notes from the Buckinghamshire County Museum', C N G[owing], *Records of Buckinghamshire* 18 (1966–70), 335

CAMBRIDGESHIRE

Lowerre, A. *Placing castles in the Conquest: landscape, lordship and local politics in the south-eastern midlands, 1066–1100*. Oxford: J and E Hedges, 2005* (BAR British series; 385)

Osborne, M. *Cromwellian fortifications in Cambridgeshire*. Huntingdon: Cromwell Museum, 1990*

Osborne, M. *20th century defences in Britain: Cambridgeshire*. Market Deeping: Concrete Publications, [2001]*

Pevsner, N. *Cambridgeshire (The buildings of England)*. 2nd edition. Harmondsworth: Penguin Books, 1970*

Phillips, C W. 'Ancient earthworks', in L F Salzman (ed), *The Victoria history of the county of Cambridge and the isle of Ely*, **2**, 1–47. Oxford: OUP, 1948*

Salter, M. *The castles of East Anglia*. Malvern: Folly Publications, 2001*

Taylor, A. *Castles of Cambridgeshire*. [Cambridge]: Cambridgeshire County Council, [1986?]*

Burwell

'Burwell Castle', in RCHME, *An inventory of the historical monuments in the county of Cambridge. 1. North-east Cambridgeshire*, 41–42. London: HMSO, 1972*

'Burwell Castle', B K Davison, *Archaeological Journal* 124 (1967), 255

Cambridge

Cambridge Castle. W M Palmer. Cambridge: Oleander Press, 1976* [original edition 1928]

'Cambridge', M D Lobel, in M D Lobel (ed), *The atlas of historic towns*, **2**. London: Scolar Press, 1975*

'Cambridge Castle' and 'King's ditch', in RCHME, *An inventory of the historical monuments in the city of Cambridge*, **2**, 304–7. London: HMSO, 1959*

'The castle', in A Taylor, *Cambridge: the hidden history*, 51–59. Stroud: Tempus, 1999*

'Early Cambridge: an interim report on the excavations at Castle Hill, Cambridge, 1956–1962', J Alexander, *Archaeological News Letter* 7 (1961–5), 222–26*

'Medieval Cambridge: recent finds and excavations', P V Addyman and M Biddle, *Proceedings of the Cambridge Antiquarian Society* 58 (1965), 74–137*

'Stone at Cambridge Castle: an early use of Collyweston stone slate', H B Sharp, *ibid* 72 (1982–3), 62–78*

'Cambridge Castle ditch', T Malim and A Taylor, *ibid* 80 (1991), 1–6*

'Cambridge', anon, *CBA Group 7 Bulletin* 3 (1956), 1

'Medieval Britain in 1956', D M Wilson and J G Hurst, *Medieval Archaeology* 1 (1957), 156

'Medieval Britain in 1960', D M Wilson and J G Hurst, *ibid* 5 (1961), 322

'Medieval Britain and Ireland in 1988', D R M Gaimster, S Margeson and T Barry, *ibid* 33 (1989), 172

'Medieval Britain and Ireland in 1995', B S Nenk, S Margeson and M Hurley, *ibid* 40 (1996), 246

Castle Camps
'Cambridgeshire earthwork surveys: motte and bailey castle and deserted village, Castle Camps', C C Taylor, *Proceedings of the Cambridge Antiquarian Society* 64 (1972–3), 38–43*

'Medieval Britain and Ireland in 2000', J Bradley and M Gaimster, *Medieval Archaeology* 45 (2001), 262

Ely
Cherry Hill, Ely. R Holmes and P Blakeman. [Ely]: Ely Society, 1983*

'Ely Castle', B K Davison, *Archaeological Journal* 124 (1967), 240–41

March
The Sconce, March, Civil War fortifications. T Malim. Cambridge: Archaeology Section, Cambridgeshire County Council, [1989?]*

'Cambridgeshire earthwork surveys: IV. Seventeenth-century sconce, March', A E Brown and C C Taylor, *Proceedings of the Cambridge Antiquarian Society* 70 (1980), 113–15*

Rampton
'Cambridgeshire earthwork surveys: II. Rampton: Giant's Hill', A E Brown and C C Taylor, *ibid* 67 (1977), 97–99*

Swavesey
'Swavesey, Cambridgeshire: a fortified medieval planned market town', J R Ravensdale, *ibid* 72 (1982–3), 55–58*

Wisbech
A history of Wisbech Castle. G Anniss. Ely: EARO, 1977*

'Wisbech', Dept of Archaeology, Cambridge, *CBA Group 7 Bulletin* 2 (1955), 3

CHESHIRE

Cullen, P W and Hordern, R. *The castles of Cheshire*. [Liverpool]: Crossbow Books, 1986*

Higham, N J. *A frontier landscape: the north west in the Middle Ages*. Macclesfield: Windgather Press, 2004*

Pevsner, N and Hubbard, E. *Cheshire (The buildings of England)*. Harmondsworth: Penguin Books, 1971*

Salter, M. *The castles and tower houses of Lancashire and Cheshire*. Malvern: Folly Publications, 2001*

Yates, S (ed). *Heritage unlocked: guide to free sites in the north west*. London: English Heritage, 2002*

Aldford

'A survey of Aldford Castle', S Reynolds and G White, *Cheshire Past* 4 (1995), 14–15*

'Medieval Britain in 1959', D M Wilson and D G Hurst, *Medieval Archaeology* 4 (1960), 145

'Medieval Britain and Ireland in 1999', J Bradley and M Gaimster, *ibid* 44 (2000), 255

'Medieval Britain and Ireland in 2000', J Bradley and M Gaimster, *ibid* 45 (2001), 264–65

'Medieval Britain and Ireland in 2002', J Bradley and M Gaimster, *ibid* 47 (2003), 223–24

'Where are the Normans?', S Ward, *The Past Uncovered: Quarterly Newsletter of Chester Archaeology* winter (1999), 1*

'Digging deep at Aldford Castle', S Ward, *ibid* autumn (2000), [1]*

'Aldford's towers of stone', S Ward, *ibid* October (2002), [4]*

Beeston

Beeston Castle, Cheshire. Anon. London: HMSO, 1962*

'Civil War stronghold': Beeston Castle at war 1642–45. J Barratt. Birkenhead: J Barratt, 1995*

Beeston Castle, Cheshire: a report on the excavations 1965–85 by Laurence Keen and Peter Hough. Compiled and edited by P Ellis. London: HBMCE, 1993* (English Heritage archaeological report; 23)

Beeston Castle: information for teachers. H Moffatt [ie Moffat]. London: English Heritage, 1997*

Beeston Castle. J Weaver. London: HBMCE, 1987*

'Beeston Castle', D J C King, *128th annual meeting, Chester and north east Wales, 1981*, CAA, 1981, 12

'Beeston Castle', P Hough, *Archaeological Excavations 1975*, 20. London: HMSO, 1976

'Beeston Castle', P R Hough, *Archaeological Excavations 1976*, 4. London: HMSO, 1977

'Beeston Castle', P R Hough, *CBA Calendar of Excavations* summaries 1976 (1977), 3

'Beeston Castle', P R Hough, *CBA Newsletter and Calendar* 3 (1979–80), 127

'Beeston Castle', P R Hough, *Cheshire Archaeological Bulletin* 4 (1976), 21

'Beeston', P R Hough, *ibid* 8 (1982), 22–30*

'An introduction to the story of Beeston Castle, Cheshire', M H Ridgway, *Cheshire Historian* 7 (1957), 35–38*

'Beeston Castle', P Hough, *Current Archaeology* 8.8 (1984), 245–49*

'On the remains of a jack of plate excavated from Beeston Castle in Cheshire', I Eaves, *Journal of the Arms and Armour Society* 13.2 (1989), 81–154*

'Beeston Castle, Cheshire', M H Ridgway and D J C King, *Journal of the Chester and North Wales Architectural and Archaeological Society* 46 (1959), 1–23*

'Excavations at Beeston Castle 1975–77', P R Hough, *Journal of the Chester Archaeological Society* 61 (1978), 1–23*

'Medieval Britain in 1978', L E Webster and J Cherry, *Medieval Archaeology* 23 (1979), 260

'Medieval Britain in 1980', S M Youngs and J Clark, *ibid* 25 (1981), 200

Chester

The great siege of Chester. J Barratt. Stroud: Tempus, 2003*

Excavations at Chester. Chester Castle, the seventeenth-century armoury and mint: excavation and building recording in the inner ward 1979–82. P Ellis. Chester: Chester City Council, 1996* (Chester Archaeology: excavation and survey report; 10)

Excavations at Chester: the Roman and later defences, part 1. Investigations 1978–1990. C LeQuesne and T J Strickland. Chester: Chester City Council, 1999* (Excavation and survey report; 11)

Excavations at Chester: the Civil War siegeworks 1642–6. S Ward. Chester: Chester City Council, 1987*

The walls of Chester: a guided tour. A Whimperley and D Murphy. Clapham: Dalesman, 1977*

'The early medieval city and its buildings', A Thacker, in A Thacker (ed), *Medieval archaeology, art and architecture at Chester*, 16–30. Leeds: British Archaeological Association and Maney Publishing, 2000* (Conference transactions; 22)

'Henry III's wall paintings at Chester Castle', S Cather, D Park and R Pender, in *ibid*, 170–89*

'Castle', A T Thacker, in C P Lewis and A T Thacker (eds), *A history of the county of Chester. 5.2. The city of Chester: culture, buildings, institutions*, 204–13. Woodbridge: Boydell & Brewer, for the Institute of Historical Research, 2005*

'City walls and gates', A T Thacker, in *ibid*, 213–25*

'Foregate Street, Chester (the Eastgate)', anon, *CBA Group 5 Archaeological Newsletter* 21 (1973), 7

'Chester, Foregate Street', P J Davey, *Cheshire Archaeological Bulletin* 1 (1973), 15

'The castle: colonnade and archway', T J Strickland and J A Rutter, *ibid* 7 (1980–1), 39–40

'The castle chapel', T J Strickland and J A Rutter, *ibid* 7 (1980–1), 40–41*

'Chester Castle', P R Hough, *ibid* 8 (1982), 45–46

'Chester: the city walls II', S Ward, *ibid* 9 (1983), 49

'Medieval wall paintings in Chester Castle', D Park and C Babington, *Cheshire Past* 3 (1994), 12–13*

'The Water Tower at Chester', D F Renn, *Journal of the Chester and North Wales Architectural, Archaeological and Historic Society* 45 (1958), 56–60*

'Excavations at Woolworth's, Chester, 1959', F H Thompson, *Journal of the Chester Archaeological Society* 54 (1967), 9–19*

'The Eastgate, Chester 1972', P H Alebon [*et al*], *ibid* 59 (1976), 37–49*

'Excavations within the garden of No 1 Abbey Green, Chester, 1975–77: interim report', J C McPeake [*et al*], *ibid* 63 (1980), 13–37*

'Aspects of the topography of early medieval Chester', N J Alldridge, *ibid* 64 (1981), 5–31*

'Recent work on the medieval city wall of Chester', S Ward, *ibid* 68 (1985), 79–84*

'The Heronbbridge Archaeological Research Project: an interim report on the 2002 and 2003 seasons of the Society's new fieldwork initiative', D J P Morgan, *ibid* 78 (2003), 49–106*

'Medieval Britain in 1956', D M Wilson and J G Hurst, *Medieval Archaeology* 1 (1957), 156

'Medieval Britain in 1972', L E Webster and J Cherry, *ibid* 17 (1973), 166

'Medieval Britain in 1977', L E Webster and J Cherry, *ibid* 21 (1977), 243

'Medieval Britain and Ireland in 1988', D R M Gaimster, S Margeson and T Barry, *ibid* 33 (1989), 173

'Medieval Britain and Ireland in 1990', B S Nenk, S Margeson and M Hurley, *ibid* 35 (1991), 136

'Medieval Britain and Ireland in 1991', B S Nenk, S Margeson and M Hurley, *ibid* 36 (1992), 203–4

'Medieval Britain and Ireland in 1993', B S Nenk, S Margeson and M Hurley, *ibid* 38 (1994), 196

'Uncovering medieval wall paintings in Chester Castle', C Babington and D Park, *Minerva* 4.1 (1993), 8–9*

'Post-medieval Britain in 1975', J Cherry, *Post-Medieval Archaeology* 10 (1976), 161

'Post-medieval Britain and Ireland in 1990', M Ponsford, *ibid* 25 (1991), 120

'Post-medieval Britain and Ireland in 1991', M Ponsford, *ibid* 26 (1992), 105

'Post-medieval Britain and Ireland in 1993', M Ponsford, *ibid* 28 (1994), 126

'Post-medieval Britain and Ireland in 1994', M Ponsford and R Jackson, *ibid* 29 (1995), 122

Church Shocklach

'Church Shocklach, Castletown: the "moated" site', R Williams, *Cheshire Archaeological Bulletin* 9 (1983), 59–61*

Dodleston

'Dodleston Castle', D J C King, *The hundredth and twentieth annual meeting in Wrexham and district, 1973*, CAA, 1973, 15

Dunham Massey

'Dunham Castle', R Bailey and D Hutchinson-Lord, in M Nevell, *The archaeology of Trafford: a study of the origins of community in north west England before 1900*, 33. [Sale]: Trafford Metropolitan Borough Council, 1997*

Halton

Halton Castle: 'a visual treasure'. R McNeil and A J Jamieson (eds). Liverpool: North West Archaeological Trust, 1987*

'Medieval Britain and Ireland in 1987', S M Youngs [*et al*], *Medieval Archaeology* 32 (1988), 234–45

Macclesfield

'Macclesfield Castle', R C Turner, *Transactions of the Ancient Monuments Society* new ser 31 (1987), 134–45*

Nantwich

'Nantwich: three years of excavations and observations', R McNeil-Sale, *Cheshire Archaeological Bulletin* 7 (1980–1), 29–33*

Oldcastle

'Castle Hill, Oldcastle', F H Thompson, *Cheshire Historian* 8 (1958), 23

'Excavations at Castle Hill, Oldcastle, near Malpas', F H Thompson, *Journal of the Chester Archaeological Society* 54 (1967), 5–7*

Shotwick

'"Delightfully surrounded with woods and ponds": field evidence for medieval gardens in England', P Everson, in P Pattison (ed), *There by design: field archaeology*

in parks and gardens, 32–38. Oxford: Archaeopress; Swindon: RCHME, 1998*
(BAR British series; 267)

Stockport

'Recent excavations on the site of Stockport Castle', J S Dent, *Transactions of the Lancashire and Cheshire Antiquarian Society* 79 (1977), 1–13*

'Castle on a rock: Stockport Castle – final proof', A Phillips, *Stockport Heritage* spring (1988), 4–5*

Thurstaston

'Possible motte and bailey, Thurstaston', M Anderson, *CBA Group 5 Archaeological Newsletter* 6 (1965), 10

Watch Hill

'Watch Hill Castle', N Redhead, in M Nevell, *The archaeology of Trafford: a study of the origins of community in north west England before 1900*, 34–35. [Sale]: Trafford Metropolitan Borough Council, 1997*

'Watch Hill, Bowden', K Brown and B Johnson, *Greater Manchester Archaeological Journal* 1 (1985), 35–37*

CORNWALL

Campbell, A (ed). *Heritage unlocked: guide to free sites in Cornwall and the Isles of Scilly*. London: English Heritage, 2004*

Dickinson, R. 'The Spanish raid on Mount's bay in 1595', *Journal of the Royal Institution of Cornwall* 10.2 (1988), 178–86

Dorman, J. *The later defences of Falmouth 1895–1956*. [S l]: Kent Defence Research Group, 1990*

Duffin, A. 'The defence of Cornwall in the early seventeenth century', in R Higham (ed), *Security and defence in south-west England before 1800*, 69–77. Exeter: University of Exeter, 1987

Duffy, M. 'Coastal defences and garrisons 1480–1914', in R Kain and W Ravenhill (eds), *Historical atlas of south-west England*, 158–63. Exeter: Exeter University Press, 1999*

Finberg, H P R. 'The castle of Cornwall', *Devon and Cornwall Notes and Queries* 23 (1947–9), 123

Higham, R A. 'Castles, fortified houses and fortified towns in the Middle Ages', in R Kain and W Ravenhill (eds), *Historical atlas of south-west England*, 136–43. Exeter: Exeter University Press, 1999*

Higham, R [A]. 'The study and interpretation of British town walls: medieval urbanism and urban defences in south west England', *Europa Nostra Bulletin* 53 (200), 43–52*

Hunt, I. 'Plymouth sound? The defence of the naval station', *Fort* 11 (1983), 78–111*

Johnson, N and Rose, P. *Cornwall's archaeological heritage*. Revised edition. Truro: Twelveheads Press, 2003*

Jope, E M. 'Cornish houses, 1400–1700', in E M Jope (ed), *Studies in building history*, 192–222. London: Odhams, 1961*

Kenyon, J R. 'The defence of the fortifications in the West Country in 1623', *Fort* 16 (1988), 45–52*

Kinross, J. *The Palmerston forts of the south west: why were they built?* St Austell: BBNO, [1998]*

Kitchen, F. 'The defence of the southern coast of Cornwall against the French Revolution', *Cornwall Association of Local Historians News Magazine* April (1970), 13–17

Pevsner, N. *Cornwall (The buildings of England)*. 2nd edition, revised by E Radcliffe. Harmondsworth: Penguin Books, 1970*

Preston-Jones, A and Rose, P. 'Medieval Cornwall', *Cornish Archaeology* 25 (1986), 135–85*

Price, M and H. *Castles of Cornwall*. St Teath: Bossiney Books, 1980*

Pye, A and Woodward, F. *The historic defences of Plymouth*. Truro: Cornwall County Council, 1996*

Ratcliffe, J. *Fal Estuary historic audit*. Truro: Cornwall County Council, 1997*

Salter, M. *The castles of Devon and Cornwall and forts of the Scilly Isles*. Malvern: Folly Publications, 1999*

Saunders, A D. 'Castles and later fortifications', in A D Saunders, *Exploring England's heritage: Devon and Cornwall*, 69–77. London: HMSO, in association with English Heritage, 1991*

Saunders, A D. 'The coastal defences of Cornwall', *Archaeological Journal* 130 (1973), 232–36

Spreadbury, I D. *Castles in Cornwall and the Isles of Scilly*. Redruth: Dyllansow Truran, 1984*

Stevenson, I V. 'Some West Country defences', *Fort* 17 (1989), 11–26*

Woodward, F. *Forts or follies? The story of Plymouth's Palmerston forts*. Tiverton: Halsgrove, 1998*

Bossiney

'Bossiney Castle', P Rose, *Cornish Archaeology* 31 (1992), 138–42*

Jacobstow

'The medieval manor of Penhallam, Jacobstow, Cornwall', G Beresford, *Medieval Archaeology* 18 (1974), 90–145*

ENGLAND

Kilkhampton

'Kilkhampton Castle Farm', A Reynolds, in 'Recent work by the Cornwall Archaeological Unit, 1998', *Cornish Archaeology* 39–40 (2000–1), 176–77.

Kingsand

'The Amherst gun battery, Kingsand', D Sheppard, *ibid* 12 (1973), 75–76*

Launceston

Launceston Castle, Cornwall. T L Jones. London: HMSO, 1959*

Three shell keeps. D F Renn. London: HMSO, 1969*

Launceston Castle. A D Saunders. London: HBMCE, 1984*

Launceston Castle, Cornwall. A D Saunders. London: English Heritage, 1998*

Excavations at Launceston Castle, Cornwall. A Saunders. London: Society for Medieval Archaeology, 2006* (Society for Medieval Archaeology monograph; 24)

'A stone lamp from Launceston Castle, Cornwall', A D Saunders, *Antiquaries Journal* 58 (1978), 366–67, 385*

'Launceston Castle', A D Saunders, *Archaeological Excavations 1975*, 19. London: HMSO, 1976

'Launceston Castle', A D Saunders, *Archaeological Excavations 1976*, 24–25. London: HMSO, 1977

'Launceston Castle', A D Saunders, *Archaeological Journal* 130 (1973), 251–54*

'Launceston Castle', A D Saunders, *CBA Calendar of Excavations* summaries 1976 (1977), 3

'Launceston, Launceston Castle', A D Saunders, *CBA Groups 12 and 13 Archaeological Review* 1 (1966), 33

'Launceston, Launceston Castle', A D Saunders, *ibid* 3 (1968), 25

'Launceston, Launceston Castle', A D Saunders, *ibid* 4 (1969), 53

'Launceston, Launceston Castle', A D Saunders, *ibid* 5 (1970), 31

'Launceston, the castle', A D Saunders, *ibid* 7 (1972), 51

'Mammals and birds from Launceston Castle, Cornwall: decline in status and the rise of agriculture', U Albarella and J M Davis, *Circaea* 12.1 (1994), 1–156*

'Launceston Castle: an interim report', A D Saunders, *Cornish Archaeology* 3 (1964), 63–69*

'Launceston Castle', A D Saunders, *ibid* 6 (1967), 79–80

'Launceston Castle', A D Saunders, *ibid* 7 (1968), 83

'Launceston Castle', A D Saunders, *ibid* 8 (1969), 105

'Excavations at Launceston Castle, 1965–1969: interim report', A D Saunders, *ibid* 9 (1970), 83–92*

'Launceston Castle', A D Saunders, *ibid* 10 (1971), 95

'Launceston Castle', A D Saunders, *ibid* 11 (1972), 57

'Launceston Castle', A D Saunders, *ibid* 14 (1975), 116–17

'Launceston Castle', A D Saunders, *ibid* 15 (1976), 118

'Excavations at Launceston Castle, 1970–76: interim report', A D Saunders, *ibid* 16 (1977), 129–37*

'Launceston Castle', A D Saunders, *ibid* 18 (1979), 80

'Launceston Castle', A D Saunders, *ibid* 19 (1980), 97–98

'Launceston Castle', A D Saunders, *ibid* 20 (1981), 220–21

'Launceston Castle excavations in 1981. An interim report', A D Saunders, *ibid* 21 (1982), 187–88*

'Medieval Britain in 1960', D M Wilson and D G Hurst, *Medieval Archaeology* 5 (1961), 318

'Medieval Britain in 1961', D M Wilson and D G Hurst, *ibid* 6–7 (1962–3), 320–21

'Medieval Britain in 1962 and 1963', D M Wilson and D G Hurst, *ibid* 8 (1964), 252

'Medieval Britain in 1965', D M Wilson and D G Hurst, *ibid* 10 (1966), 190

'Medieval Britain in 1966, D M Wilson and D G Hurst, *ibid* 11 (1967), 284

'Medieval Britain in 1969', D M Wilson and D G Hurst, *ibid* 14 (1970), 175

'Medieval Britain in 1970', D M Wilson and S Moorhouse, *ibid* 15 (1971), 145

'Medieval Britain in 1971', L E Webster and J Cherry, *ibid* 16 (1972), 179

'Medieval Britain in 1972', L E Webster and J Cherry, *ibid* 17 (1973), 161

'Medieval Britain in 1973', L E Webster and J Cherry, *ibid* 18 (1974), 195

'Medieval Britain in 1974', L E Webster and J Cherry, *ibid* 19 (1975), 239

'Medieval Britain in 1976', L E Webster and J Cherry, *ibid* 21 (1977), 233–34

'Medieval Britain in 1990', B S Nenk, S Margeson and M Hurley, *ibid* 35 (1991), 137

'Medieval Britain in 1992', B S Nenk, S Margeson and M Hurley, *ibid* 37 (1993), 251

'Medieval Britain and Ireland in 2002', J Bradley and M Gaimster, *ibid* 47 (2003), 224

Maker Heights

'The duke of Richmond, James Glenie, Maker and the Fortifications Bill', D Evans, *Fort* 16 (1988), 73–82

'The duke of Richmond as designer', D Evans, *ibid* 18 (1990), 83–93

'The redoubts on Maker Heights, Cornwall, 1770–1859', D Evans, *Georgian Group Journal* 9 (1999), 44–68*

'Maker fortifications', P Sheppard, *Old Cornwall* 8.5 (1975), 236–46*

'Hawkins Battery', P Cobb, *The Redan* 36 (1996), 33–37*

'Raleigh Battery', D Moore, *ibid* 40 (1997), 21–31*

Pendennis

Pendennis and St Mawes castles. Anon. London: HMSO, 1963*

Pendennis and St Mawes castles. Anon. London: HBMCE, 1985*

Pendennis Castle. Anon. London: HMSO, 1982*

The cannon of Pendennis and St Mawes castles, Cornwall. A C Carpenter. Plymouth: printed by P D S Printers, 1984*

A teacher's handbook to the castles of Pendennis and St Mawes. R Cooper. London: English Heritage, 1994*

Pendennis Castle, Cornwall. D Drake (abridged). London: HMSO, 1947*

Pendennis headland: historical credentials, current condition and future potential of the defences 1540–1956. C Johns. Truro: Cornwall County Council, 1992*

The castles of Pendennis and St Mawes. D Linzey. London: English Heritage, 1999*

The castles of Pendennis and St Mawes. B Morley. London: HBMCE, 1988*

Pendennis and St Mawes: an historical sketch of two Cornish castles. S P Oliver. Redruth: Dyllansow Truran, 1984*[facsimile of the 1875 edition]

'Pendennis Castle', B M Morley and P R White, *Archaeological Journal* 130 (1973), 283–89*

'The re-arming of Pendennis and St Mawes castles', T Musty, *Collections Review* 2 (1999), 116–18*

'Recent work of the Cornwall Committee for Rescue Archaeology: Pendennis Castle', N Johnson and P Rose, *Cornish Archaeology* 19 (1980), 99

'An ancient wall at Pendennis Point, Falmouth', D Harris and J Andrew, *ibid* 24 (1985), 182–83*

'Recent work: excavation, Pendennis', A Sharpe, *ibid* 29 (1990), 96–97

'Pendennis Castle', C Johns, N Thomas and J Gossip, in 'Recent work by the Cornwall Archaeological Unit, 1999', *ibid* 39–40 (2000–1), 200–1.

'Pendennis Castle', S C Jenkins, *Fort* 25 (1997), 169–210*

'Activity centre', S Amos, *Heritage Today* 72 (2005), 22–25*

'Post-medieval Britain and Ireland in 1992', M Ponsford, *Post-Medieval Archaeology* 27 (1993), 209–10

'Post-medieval Britain and Ireland in 1993', M Ponsford, *ibid* 28 (1994), 127

'Post-medieval Britain and Ireland in 1994', M Ponsford and R Jackson, *ibid* 29 (1995), 122

Pengersick

'Pengersick Castle', S Schofield, *Archaeological Journal* 130 (1973), 264–65*

Poundstock

'Medieval Britain and Ireland in 1993', B S Nenk, S Margeson and M Hurley, *Medieval Archaeology* 38 (1994), 201

Restormel

Restormel Castle, Cornwall. Anon. London: English Heritage, 1996 (1999 reprint)*

Restormel Castle, Cornwall. N A D Molyneux. London: English Heritage, 2003*

Restormel Castle. C A R Radford. London: HMSO. 1947*; 2nd edition, 1980*

Restormel Castle. C A R Radford. London: HBMCE, 1986*

Three shell keeps. D F Renn. London: HMSO, 1969*

Restormel Castle: information for teachers. G Wheatley. London: English Heritage, 1995*

'Medieval Britain and Ireland in 1993', B S Nenk, S Margeson and M Hurley, *Medieval Archaeology* 38 (1994), 199

'Medieval Britain and Ireland in 1994', B S Nenk, S Margeson and M Hurley, *ibid* 39 (1995), 192–93

'Medieval Britain and Ireland in 1995', B S Nenk, S Margeson and M Hurley, *ibid* 40 (1996), 249

St Mawes

Pendennis and St Mawes castles. Anon. London: HMSO, 1963*

Pendennis and St Mawes castles. Anon. London: HBMCE, 1985*

The cannon of Pendennis and St Mawes castles, Cornwall. A C Carpenter. Plymouth: printed by P D S Printers, 1984*

A teacher's handbook to the castles of Pendennis and St Mawes. R Cooper. London: English Heritage, 1994*

St Mawe's Castle. D Drake (abridged). London: HMSO, 1947*

The castles of Pendennis and St Mawes. D Linzey. London: English Heritage, 1999*

The castles of Pendennis and St Mawes. B Morley. London: HBMCE, 1988*

Pendennis and St Mawes: an historical sketch of two Cornish castles. S P Oliver. Redruth: Dyllansow Truran, 1984* [facsimile of the 1875 edition]

St Mawes Castle: a brief guide. D Tosh. London: English Heritage, 1993*

'The re-arming of Pendennis and St Mawes castles', T Musty, *Collections Review* 2 (1999), 116–18*

ENGLAND

St Michael's Mount

An archaeological evaluation of St Michael's Mount. P Herring. Truro: Cornwall County Council, 1993*

'St Michael's Mount: recent and future work', P Herring, *Cornish Archaeology* 32 (1993), 153–59*

'"The ancient and present state of St Michaels Mount, 1762"', P A S Pool (ed), *Cornish Studies* 3 (1975), 29–47*

'Walking history: St Mawes Castle', S Amos, *Heritage Today* 74 (2006), 30–31*

'Medieval Britain and Ireland in 2001', J Bradley and M Gaimster, *Medieval Archaeology* 46 (2002), 157

Tintagel

Tintagel Castle: a brief guide. Anon. London: English Heritage, 1993*

Tintagel Castle, Cornwall. B K Davison. London: English Heritage, 1999*

The medieval pottery from Tintagel. C O'Mahoney. Redruth: Institute of Cornish Studies, 1989*

Tintagel Castle, Cornwall. C A R Radford. 2nd edition (15th impression). London: HMSO, 1971*

Tintagel Castle. C Thomas. London: HBMCE, 1986*

English Heritage book of Tintagel: Arthur and archaeology. C Thomas. London: Batsford, in association with English Heritage, 1993*

'Tintagel: a new survey of the "Island"', A C Thomas and P J Fowler, *Annual Review 1984–85*, RCHME, 1985, 16–22*

'Tintagel Castle', C Thomas, *Antiquity* 62 (1988), 421–34*

'Tintagel Castle', R G Browse, *Cornish Archaeology* 21 (1982), 189–90*

'Tintagel Castle', F M McAvoy, *ibid* 23 (1984), 184*

'The medieval garden at Tintagel Castle', P Rose, *ibid* 33 (1994), 170–82*

'Excavations in the lower ward, Tintagel Castle, 1986', S Hartgroves and R Walker, *Cornish Studies* 16 (1988), 9–30*

'Minor sites at Tintagel Castle', C Thomas, *ibid* 16 (1988), 31–48*

'The 1988 CAU excavations at Tintagel Island: discoveries and their implications', C Thomas, *ibid* 16 (1988), 49–60*

'Tintagel in the twelfth and thirteenth centuries', O J Padel, *ibid* 16 (1988), 67–68

'Incised pictorial slates from Tintagel', C M Thorpe, *ibid* 16 (1988), 69–78*

'Medieval Britain and Ireland in 1986', S M Youngs, J Clark and T Barry, *Medieval Archaeology* 31 (1987), 119

'Medieval Britain and Ireland in 1994', B S Nenk, S Margeson and M Hurley, *ibid* 39 (1995), 193

'Medieval Britain and Ireland in 1995', B S Nenk, S Margeson and M Hurley, *ibid* 40 (1996), 250

'Medieval Britain and Ireland in 2001', J Bradley and M Gaimster, *ibid* 46 (2002), 157

Tregantle
'Tregantle Down high angle battery', D Moore, *The Redan* 37 (1996), 9–14*

Trematon
'Trematon Castle, Cornwall', C Hussey, *Country Life* 104 (1948), 428–31*

Week St Mary
'Week St Mary, town and castle', A Preston-Jones, *Cornish Archaeology* 31 (1992), 143–53*

CUMBERLAND

Cope, J. *Castles in Cumbria*. Milnthorpe: Cicerone Press, 1991*

Hugill, R. *Castles and peles of Cumberland and Westmorland: a guide to the strongholds of the western English borderlands together with an account of their development and their place in border history*. Newcastle upon Tyne: F Graham, 1977*

Jackson, M J. *Castles of Cumbria*. Carlisle: Carel Press; Cumbria County Library, 1990*

Perriam, D R. 'Recent trends in the study of fortified buildings in Cumbria', in P Clack and J Ivy (eds), *Making sense of buildings*, 35–40. Durham: CBA Group 3, 1985

Perriam, D R and Robinson, J. *The medieval fortified buildings of Cumbria: an illustrated gazetteer and record guide*. [S l]: Cumberland and Westmorland Antiquarian and Archaeological Society, 1998* (Extra series; 29)

Pevsner, N. *Cumberland and Westmorland (The buildings of England)*. Harmondsworth: Penguin Books, 1967*

Salter, M. *The castles and tower houses of Cumbria*. Malvern. Folly Publications, 1998*

Weaver, J. *Exploring England's heritage: Cumbria to Northumberland*. London: HMSO, 1992* [espec ch 5]

Wood, M A. 'The fortified churches of Cumberland', *Country Life* 142 (1967), 10–11*

Bewcastle
A chronological history of the manor & castle of Bewcastle. M Jackson. Carlisle: the author, 1997*

'Bewcastle' , P Austen, *Archaeological Journal* 155 (1998), 355–58*

Bowness

'Bowness Rectory Tower', D R Perriam, *Transactions of the Cumberland and Westmorland Antiquarian and Archaeological Society* 88 (1988), 193–200*

Burgh by Sands

'The excavation of the fortified manor-house at Burgh by Sands', R Hogg, *ibid* new ser 54 (1954), 105–18*

'The manor of Burgh by Sands', R L Storey, *ibid* new ser 54 (1954), 119–30

Carlisle

Carlisle Castle, Cumbria. J Charlton. London: HBMCE, 1985*

Carlisle Castle: a survey and documentary history. M R McCarthy, H R T Summerson and R G Annis. London: HBMCE, 1990* (English Heritage archaeological report; 18)

Carlisle Castle and Cathedral: a teacher's handbook. H Moffat. London: English Heritage, 1996*

Carlisle Castle. C Platt and M McCarthy. London: English Heritage, 1992*

A narrative of the siege of Carlisle in 1644 and 1645. I Tullie. Whitehaven: Michael Moore's Bookshop, 1988 [first published 1840]

Carlisle Castle, Cumberland. G H P Watson and G Bradley. 11th impression. London: HMSO, 1970*

'De Ireby's Tower in Carlisle Castle', R Gilyard-Beer, in M R Apted, R Gilyard-Beer and A D Saunders (eds), *Ancient monuments and their interpretation: essays presented to A J Taylor*, 191–210. Chichester: Phillimore, 1977*

'The great tower of Carlisle Castle', J A A Goodall, in M McCarthy and D Weston (eds), *Carlisle and Cumbria: Roman and medieval architecture, art and archaeology*, 39–62. Leeds: British Archaeological Association and Maney Publishing, 2004* (Conference transactions; 27)

'"King Arthur lives in merry Carleile"', A Wheatley, in *ibid*, 63–72

'Carlisle', D Charlesworth, *Archaeological Excavations 1972*, 13. London: HMSO, 1973

'Carlisle Castle', J Charlton, *Archaeological Journal* 115 (1958), 228–29

'Carlisle city walls', D Perriam, *ibid* 155 (1998), 376–77

'Carlisle Castle', H Summerson, *ibid* 155 (1998), 378–79

'Carlisle, Cumberland', D Charlesworth, *CBA Group 3 Newsbulletin* 3 (1973), 8

'The diamond of Carlisle', J Cornforth, *Country Life* 163 (1978), 958–60*

'The keeping of Carlisle Castle before 1381', J L Kirby, *Transactions of the Cumberland and Westmorland Antiquarian and Archaeological Society* new ser 54 (1954), 131–39

'Medieval town wall, Carlisle', R Hogg, *ibid* new ser 62 (1962), 326–27*

'The buildings of the Courts, Carlisle, 1807–1822', J Hughes, *ibid* new ser 70 (1970), 205–20*

'The topography of medieval Carlisle', B C Jones, *ibid* new ser 76 (1976), 77–96*

'The demolition of Carlisle city walls', D R Perriam, *ibid* new ser 78 (1978), 129–40*

'Excavations on the city defences, Carlisle', M R McCarthy, *ibid* 80 (1980), 69–78*

'Documents relating to the transportation of cannon from Whitehaven to Carlisle during the Jacobite rising of 1745', D Hepburn and C Richardson, *ibid* 84 (1984), 141–66*

'The demolition of the Priory of St Mary, Carlisle', D R Perriam, *ibid* 87 (1987), 127–58*

'The last siege on English soil: Carlisle, December 1745', J Oates, *ibid* 3 ser 3 (2003), 169–84*

'The paradoxical fortunes of Carlisle Castle 1745–1850', H Summerson, *Fortress* 4 (1990), 27–38*

'Medieval Britain and Ireland in 1993', B S Nenk, S Margeson and M Hurley, *Medieval Archaeology* 38 (1994), 201

Corby

'Corby Castle', H Levin, *Archaeological Journal* 115 (1958), 251–52

Dacre

Dacre Castle. E H A Stretton. Penrith: Dalmain Estate, 1994*

'Dacre Castle', R H Leech, *129th annual meeting, Cumbria and Lake District, 1982*, CAA, 1982, 28

'Dacre Castle', Major Hasel, *Archaeological Journal* 115 (1958), 251

Drumburgh

'Medieval Britain in 1978', L E Webster and J Cherry, *Medieval Archaeology* 23 (1979), 270

Egremont

'Romanesque architecture and architectural sculpture in the diocese of Carlisle', M Thurlby, in M McCarthy and D Weston (eds), *Carlisle and Cumbria: Roman and medieval architecture, art and archaeology*, 269–90. Leeds: British Archaeological Association and Maney Publishing, 2004* (BAA conference transactions; 27) [espec pp 284, 286–87]

'Recent work at Egremont Castle', P Turnbull and D Walsh, *Transactions of the Cumberland and Westmorland Antiquarian and Archaeological Society* 94 (1994), 77–89*

ENGLAND

Harby Brow
'Harby Brow pele tower', P Turnbull, *ibid* 89 (1989), 279

Hutton-in-the-Forest
'Hutton-in-the-Forest', M Baldwin, *Archaeological Journal* 115 (1958), 247–50*

Hutton John
'Hutton John', N Hudleston, *ibid* 115 (1958), 252–53*

Lamplugh
'The old tower of Lamplugh', S Taylor, *Transactions of the Cumberland and Westmorland Antiquarian and Archaeological Society* new ser 51 (1951), 142–46*

Liddell Strength
'Liddell Strength in Cumberland', R Donaldson-Hudson, *History of the Berwickshire Naturalists' Club* 37 (1965–7), 50–53

Naworth
'Naworth Castle', R Donaldson-Hudson, *ibid* 34 (1956–8), 221–31*

'Naworth Castle, Cumberland – I', G Worsley, *Country Life* 181.7 (1987), 74–79*

Penrith
'The origins of Penrith Castle', J Petre, *The Ricardian* 6.86 (1984), 371–73

'Penrith Castle and Richard duke of Gloucester', M Craster-Chambers, *ibid* 6.86 (1984), 374–78*

Rose
'Rose Castle', T Tatton-Brown, in M McCarthy and D Weston (eds), *Carlisle and Cumbria: Roman and medieval architecture, art and archaeology*, 257–68. Leeds: British Archaeological Association and Maney Publishing, 2004* (BAA conference transactions; 27)

'Rose Castle', C G Bulmer, *Archaeological Journal* 115 (1958), 246–47

'Rose Castle, Cumberland: the seat of the bishop of Carlisle', J M Robinson, *Country Life* 183.47 (1989), 70–75*

'Rose Castle', C M L Bouch, *Transactions of the Cumberland and Westmorland Antiquarian and Archaeological Society* new ser 56 (1956), 132–41*

'Medieval Britain and Ireland in 1994', B S Nenk, S Margeson and M Hurley, *Medieval Archaeology* 39 (1995), 193–94

Shank
'Shank Castle, Cumberland', S E Rigold, *Transactions of the Cumberland and Westmorland Antiquarian and Archaeological Society* new ser 54 (1954), 144–50*

Whitehaven
'The fortifications at Whitehaven', D Hay, *ibid* new ser 65 (1965), 291–97

'Excavations at the Old Fort, Whitehaven, Cumbria: a summary', J Taylor and C Richardson, *ibid* 79 (1979), 121–24*

'Documents relating to the transportation of cannon from Whitehaven to Carlisle during the Jacobite rising of 1745', D Hepburn and C Richardson, *ibid* 84 (1984), 141–66*

'Whitehaven Old Fort: an 18th-century coastal fortification', J Taylor and C Richardson, *Post-Medieval Archaeology* 14 (1980), 127–56*

DERBYSHIRE

Crisp, J B. 'Some lesser castles', *Postern* 3 (1994), 3–6*

Osborne, M. *20th century defences in the east midlands: Derbyshire, Leicestershire, Lincolnshire, Northamptonshire, Nottinghamshire and Rutland*. Market Deeping: Concrete Publications, 2003*

Pevsner, N. *Derbyshire (The buildings of England)*. 2nd edition, revised by E Williamson. Harmondsworth: Penguin Books, 1978*

Salter, M. *The castles of the east midlands*. Malvern: Folly Publications, 2002*

Bakewell

'Castle Hill, Bakewell', M J Swanton, *Derbyshire Archaeological Journal* 92 (1972), 16–27*

'Medieval Britain in 1969', D M Wilson and D G Hurst, *Medieval Archaeology* 14 (1970), 175

Bolsover

Bolsover Castle, Derbyshire. P A Faulkner. London: HMSO, 1972*

Bolsover Castle, Derbyshire. P A Faulkner. London: HBMCE, 1985*

Bolsover Castle. L Worsley. London: English Heritage, 2000*

'Haddon Hall and Bolsover Castle', P A Faulkner, *Archaeological Journal* 118 (1961), 188–205*

'Excavation of a medieval building and a Civil War refortification at Bolsover Castle, Derbyshire', R Sheppard, *Derbyshire Archaeological Journal* 123 (2003), 11–45*

'Bolsover Castle', R Sheppard, in G Guilbert, 'Some fieldwork in Derbyshire by Trent & Peak Archaeological Unit: 2000–2001', *ibid* 124 (2004), 220–22*

'Medieval Britain in 1977', L E Webster and J Cherry, *Medieval Archaeology* 22 (1978), 168

'Medieval Britain and Ireland in 1994', B S Nenk, S Margeson and M Hurley, *ibid* 39 (1995), 194

'Bolsover Castle: a review of the 17th century buildings', F W C Gregory, *Transactions of the Thoroton Society of Nottinghamshire* 51 (1947), 4–49*

Chesterfield

'Chesterfield, Station Road', T W Courtney, *Archaeological Excavations 1976*, 112. London: HMSO, 1977

Duffield

'Duffield Castle, Derbyshire', B Crisp, *Castle Studies Group Newsletter* 10 (1996–7), 38–39

'Duffield Castle excavations 1957', T G Manby, *Derbyshire Archaeological Journal* 79 (1959), 1–21*

'Medieval Britain in 1957', D M Wilson and J G Hurst, *Medieval Archaeology* 2 (1958), 195

Hathersage

'Excavations at Camp Green, Hathersage (1976–77): a Norman ringwork', R Hodges, *Derbyshire Archaeological Journal* 100 (1980), 25–34*

'Medieval Britain in 1977', L E Webster and J Cherry, *Medieval Archaeology* 22 (1978), 186

Melbourne

'Medieval Britain and Ireland in 1989', D R M Gaimster, S Margeson and M Hurley, *ibid* 34 (1990), 172–73

Morley

'Morley mounds, the Horsley connection', C Pritchard, *Derbyshire Archaeological Journal* 118 (1998), 139–41*

Peveril

Peveril Castle. M Apted. London: HBMCE, 1985*

Peveril Castle. R Eales. London: English Heritage, 2006*

Peveril Castle, Derbyshire. B Morley. London: English Heritage, 1990*

Peveril Castle, Derbyshire. B H St J O'Neil. London: HMSO, 1970*

Peveril Castle. B H St J O'Neil and P R White. 2nd edition. London: HMSO, 1979*

Peveril Castle. B H St J O'Neil and P R White. London: HBMCE, 1979*

A teacher's handbook to Peveril Castle. S Spicer. London: English Heritage, 1994*

'Peveril Castle stones, Castleton', J B Himsworth, *Derbyshire Archaeological Journal* 76 (1956), 66

Pilsbury

'Pilsbury: a forgotten castle', N Landon, P Ash and A Payne, *ibid* 126 (2006), 82–102*

Pinxton

'Excavation at Castle Wood, Pinxton', G E Monk, *ibid* 71 (1951), 68–69

South Wingfield

'The construction of the manor at South Wingfield, Derbyshire', M W Thompson, in D de G Sieveking [*et al*] (eds), *Problems in economic and social archaeology*, 417–38. London: Duckworth, 1976*

'The architectural significance of the building works of Ralph, Lord Cromwell (1394–1456)', M W Thompson, in A Detsicas (ed), *Collectanea historica: essays in memory of Stuart Rigold*, 155–62. Maidstone: Kent Archaeological Society, 1981*

'Ralph, Lord Cromwell's manor at Wingfield (1439–*c* 1450): its construction, design and influence', A Emery, *Archaeological Journal* 142 (1985), 279–339*

'Wingfield Manor, Derbyshire', A Emery and M Binney, *Country Life* 171 (1982), 946–49, 1042–45*

DEVON

Carter, K (ed). *Heritage unlocked: guide to free sites in Devon, Dorset and Somerset*. London: English Heritage, 2004*

Cherry, B and Pevsner, N. *Devon (The buildings of Ireland)*. 2nd edition. London: Penguin Books, 1989*

Duffy, M. 'Coastal defences and garrisons 1480–1914', in R Kain and W Ravenhill (eds), *Historical atlas of south-west England*, 158–63. Exeter: Exeter University Press, 1999*

Erskine, R A. 'The military coast defences of Devon, 1500–1956', in M Duffy [*et al*] (eds), *The new maritime history of Devon. 1: from early times to the late eighteenth century*, 119–29. London: Conway Maritime Press, in association with the University of Exeter, 1992*

Francis, E. 'CBA Southwest on the home front', *Devon Archaeological Society Newsletter* 85 (2003), 10–12*

Higham, R A. 'Castles in Devon', in *Archaeology of the Devon landscape*, 70–80. Exeter: Devon County Council, 1980*

Higham, R A. 'Castles, fortified houses and fortified towns in the Middle Ages', in R Kain and W Ravenhill (eds), *Historical atlas of south-west England*, 136–43. Exeter: Exeter University Press, 1999*

Higham, R A. 'Early castles in Devon, 1068–1201', *Château Gaillard* 9–10 (1982), 101–16*

Higham, R A. 'Devon castles: an annotated list', *Proceedings of the Devon Archaeological Society* 46 (1988), 142–49

Higham, R A. 'A knight to remember: the building enterprises of Hugh Courtenay (1276–1340)', *Report and Transactions of the Devonshire Association for the Advancement of Science, Literature and the Arts* 121 (1989), 153–58

Higham, R [A]. 'The study and interpretation of British town walls: medieval urbanism and urban defences in south west England', *Europa Nostra Bulletin* 53 (200), 43–52*

Hunt, I. 'Plymouth sound? The defences of the naval station', *Fort* 11 (1983), 78–111*

Kenyon, J R. 'The state of the fortifications in the West Country in 1623', *ibid* 16 (1988), 45–52*

Kinross, J. *The Palmerston forts of the south west: why were they built?* St Austell: BBNO, [1998]*

Mildren, J. *Castles of Devon*. St Teath: Bossiney Books, 1987*

Pye, A and Woodward, F. *The historic defences of Plymouth*. Truro: Cornwall County Council, 1996*

Salter, M. *The castles of Devon and Cornwall and forts of the Scilly Isles*. Malvern: Folly Publications, 1999*

Saunders, A D. 'Castles and later fortifications', in A D Saunders, *Exploring England's heritage: Devon and Cornwall*, 69–77. London: HMSO, 1991*

Woodward, F. *Forts or follies? The story of Plymouth's Palmerston forts*. Tiverton: Halsgrove, 1998*

Axminster
'Was there a castle at Axminster?', R A Higham, *Proceedings of the Devon Archaeological Society* 44 (1986), 182–83

Bampton
Bampton Castle. R A Higham. Exeter: Devon Archaeological Society, 1994* (Field guide; 10)

'Bampton Castle', A Hamlin, *Archaeological Excavations 1969*, 27. London: HMSO, 1970

'Bampton Castle, Devon: history and archaeology', R A Higham and A Hamlin, *Proceedings of the Devon Archaeological Society* 48 (1990), 101–10*

'Bampton Castle: an earthwork survey by the Royal Commission on the Historical Monuments of England', W R Wilson-North, *ibid* 49 (1991), 115–19*

'Castle, a king besieged', anon, *Devon Archaeological Society Newsletter* 57 (1994), 1–2*

'Medieval Britain in 1969', D M Wilson and D G Hurst, *Medieval Archaeology* 14 (1970), 176

'Bampton mote, or mount', H St G Gray, *Proceedings of the Somersetshire Archaeological and Natural History Society* 93 (1947), 14–16

Barnstaple
'Barnstaple', T Miles, *Archaeological Excavations 1973*, 72. London: HMSO, 1974

'Barnstaple, the castle', T J Miles, *Archaeological Excavations 1975*, 87. London: HMSO, 1976

'Barnstaple', K Markuson, *Archaeology in Devon* [3] (1980), 19*

'Barnstaple: an example of the case for urban archaeology', T J Miles, *CBA Groups 12 and 13 Archaeological Review* 7 (1972), 51–52

'Barnstaple, North Walk', T J Miles, *ibid* 7 (1972), 52

'Excavations on the Green Lane access site, Barnstaple, 1979', K W Markuson, *Proceedings of the Devon Archaeological Society* 38 (1980), 67–90*

'Barnstaple, North Gate, east abutment', M Wood, *ibid* 38 (1980), 123–24

'The excavation of a Saxon cemetery and part of the Norman castle at North Walk, Barnstaple', T J Miles, *ibid* 44 (1986), 59–84*

'Barnstaple Castle', R Higham, *Devon Archaeology* 2 (1984), 7–9*

'Medieval Britain in 1979', L E Webster and J Cherry, *Medieval Archaeology* 24 (1980), 250

'Medieval Britain and Ireland in 1986', S M Youngs, J Clark and T Barry, *ibid* 31 (1987), 120

'Medieval Britain and Ireland in 1987', S M Youngs [*et al*], *ibid* 32 (1988), 238

Berry Head

Berry Head: official guide book. Anon. Torbay: Torbay County Borough, n d*

Berry Head Fort, Brixham: an archaeological assessment. A R Pye. Exeter: Exeter Museums Archaeological Field Unit, 1989

Berry Head Fort, Brixham: an archaeological survey. A R Pye and W D Slater. Exeter: Exeter Museums Archaeological Field Unit, 1990

'More buttons, bullets & bones', P L Armitage, *Archaeology South-West* 18 (2006), 11–15*

Berry Pomeroy

Berry Pomeroy Castle, Devon. S Brown. London: English Heritage, 1997*

Berry Pomeroy Castle. E B Powley. Privately published, 1966*

Berry Pomeroy Castle. D Seymour. Torquay: D Seymour, 1982*

Berry Pomeroy Castle, Devon. H Gordon Slade. London: English Heritage, 1990*

'Berry Pomeroy Castle', H Gordon Slade, in N H Cooper (ed), *The Exeter area: proceedings of the 136th summer meeting of the Royal Archaeological Institute, 1990*, 66–70. London: RAI, 1990*

'Berry Pomeroy Castle', S Brown, *Proceedings of the Devon Archaeological Society* 54 (1996), pp [4], 1–335* [i e, the whole issue]

'Post-medieval Britain and Ireland in 1991', M Ponsford, *Post-Medieval Archaeology* 26 (1992), 105–6

Brixham

'An emergency coast artillery battery at Battery Gardens, Brixham, Torbay', P Newman and J P Salvatore', *Proceedings of the Devon Archaeological Society* 61 (2003), 209–33*

Compton

Compton Castle, Devon. Anon. London: National Trust, 1979*

Compton Castle, Devon. [W R Gilbert and O Garnett]. London: National Trust, 2005*

'Compton Castle', W R Gilbert, *Archaeological Journal* 114 (1957), 171

'The castle in the hills', C Doyle, *Heritage* 127 (2006), 56–62*

Dartmouth

The cannon of Dartmouth Castle, Devon. A C Carpenter. Plymouth: printed by P D S Printers, 1984*

Dartmouth Castle, Devon. B K Davison. London: English Heritage, 2000*

Hawley's fortalice: Dartmouth's first castle. T Edwards. Dartmouth: Dartmouth History Research Group, 1998* (Papers; 24)

Dartmouth Castle, Devonshire. B H St J O'Neil. London: HMSO, 1951*

Dartmouth Castle. A D Saunders. London: HBMCE, 1986*

Dartmouth Castle. A D Saunders. 2nd edition. London: English Heritage, 1988*; 3rd edition, 1991*; 4th edition, 1995*

'The defences of Dartmouth haven', A Saunders, in N H Cooper (ed), *The Exeter area: proceedings of the 136th summer meeting of the Royal Archaeological Institute, 1990*, 64–66. London: RAI, 1990*

'Gallants Bower, Dartmouth: a Civil War fort, revealed', S Blaylock [*et al*], *Council for British Archaeology South West Journal* 3 (1999), 7–11*

'Gallants Bower, Dartmouth', the Editor, *Devon Archaeological Society Newsletter* 70 (1998), 10*

'Medieval Britain and Ireland in 1998', J Bradley, M Gaimster and C Haith, *Medieval Archaeology* 43 (1999), 238

'Gallants Bower, Dartmouth: a Civil War fort, revealed', S Blaylock [*et al*], *National Trust Annual Archaeological Review* 6 (1997–8), 7–11*

Devonport

'Historic splendour revealed at Mount Wise', M A Watts, *Devon Archaeological Society Newsletter* 66 (1997), 1*

'Historic architecture of H M Naval Base Devonport', J Coad, *Mariner's Mirror* 69 (1983), 341–92*

Durpley

'Some notes on Shebbear and Durpley Castle', B W Oliver, *Report and Transactions of the Devonshire Association for the Advancement of Science, Literature and the Arts* 80 (1948), 159–66*

Eggesford

'Eggesford and Heywood castles', E T Vachell, *ibid* 95 (1963), 197–207*

Exeter

Danes Castle. Anon. Exeter: South West Water, [1995?]*

Exeter Castle gatehouse architectural survey, 1985. Preliminary report. S R Blaylock. Exeter: Exeter Museums Archaeological Field Unit, 1985*

Exeter Castle gatehouse: architectural survey, 1985. S R Blaylock. Revised edition. Exeter: Exeter Museums Archaeological Field Unit, 1987*

Exeter city wall survey. S R Blaylock. Exeter: Exeter Archaeology, 1995*

Exeter city wall. S Blaylock. Exeter: Devon Archaeological Society, 1998* (Devon Archaeological Society field guide; 12)

Exeter city defences: expenditure on the walls and gates recorded in the Receivers' Accounts 1600–1650. J Z Juddery, M Stoyle and P Thomas. Exeter: Exeter Museums Archaeological Field Unit, 1988

Exeter city defences project: documentary evidence for the Civil War defences of Exeter, 1642–3. M Stoyle. Exeter: Exeter Museums Archaeological Field Unit, 1988*

Exeter in the Civil War. M Stoyle. Exeter: Devon Archaeological Society, 1995*

Circled with stone: Exeter's city walls 1485–1660. M Stoyle. Exeter: University of Exeter Press, 2003*

'Exeter Castle', S R Blaylock and R A Higham, in N H Cooper (ed), *The Exeter area: proceedings of the 136th summer meeting of the Royal Archaeological Institute, 1990*, 35–39. London: RAI, 1990*

'Exeter Castle gatehouse', S R Blaylock, in C G Henderson (ed), *Archaeology in Exeter 1984/5*, 18–24. Exeter: Exeter Museums Archaeological Field Unit, 1985*

'The outer ward of Exeter Castle', P J Weddell, N Holbrook and C G Henderson, in S R Blaylock and C G Henderson (ed), *Archaeology in Exeter 1985/6*, 51–52. Exeter: Exeter Museums Archaeological Field Unit, 1987*

'Exeter', C G Henderson [*et al*], *Archaeological Excavations 1976*, 112–14. London: HMSO, 1977

'Danes Castle, Exeter', C G Henderson, *Castle Studies Group Newsletter* 7 (1993–4), 19–21*

'Exeter', I Hope, *Current Archaeology* 12.9 (1994–5), 348* [Danes Castle]

'Danes Castle: a update', C Henderson, *Devon Archaeological Society Newsletter* 57 (1994), 6*

'The development of the South Gate of Exeter and its role in the city's defences', C G Henderson, *Proceedings of the Devon Archaeological Society* 59 (2001), 45–123*

'Exeter Castle: its background, origin and history', E T Vachell, *Report and Transactions of the Devonshire Association for the Advancement of Science, Literature and the Arts* 98 (1966), 327–48*

'The town defences of Exeter', I Burrow, *ibid* 109 (1977), 13–40*

'Medieval Britain and Ireland in 1983', S M Youngs, J Clark and T Barry, *Medieval Archaeology* 28 (1984), 216

'Medieval Britain and Ireland in 1985', S M Youngs, J Clark and T Barry, *ibid* 30 (1986), 129, 131

'Medieval Britain and Ireland in 1986', S M Youngs, J Clark and T Barry, *ibid* 31 (1987), 120–21

'Medieval Britain and Ireland in 1987', S M Youngs [*et al*], *ibid* 32 (1988), 239

'Medieval Britain and Ireland in 1990', B S Nenk, S Margeson and M Hurley, *ibid* 35 (1991), 141

'Medieval Britain and Ireland in 1991', B S Nenk, S Margeson and M Hurley, *ibid* 36 (1992), 209, 211

'Medieval Britain and Ireland in 1992', B S Nenk, S Margeson and M Hurley, *ibid* 37 (1993), 252–54*

'Medieval Britain and Ireland in 1993', B S Nenk, S Margeson and M Hurley, *ibid* 38 (1994), 203–4*

'Medieval Britain and Ireland in 1994', B S Nenk, S Margeson and M Hurley, *ibid* 39 (1995), 195–96

'Medieval Britain and Ireland in 1998', J Bradley, M Gaimster and C Haith, *ibid* 43 (1999), 238

'Medieval Britain and Ireland in 2003', J Bradley and M Gaimster, *ibid* 48 (2004), 253

'Post-medieval Britain and Ireland in 1988', G Egan, *Post-Medieval Archaeology* 23 (1989), 29–32*

'Post-medieval Britain and Ireland in 1989', G Egan, *ibid* 24 (1990), 161–3*

'Post-medieval Britain and Ireland in 1992', M Ponsford, *ibid* 27 (1993), 210–14*

'Post-medieval Britain and Ireland in 1994', M Ponsford and R Jackson, *ibid* 29 (1995), 122–23

'Post-medieval Britain and Ireland in 2003', M Ponsford, *ibid* 38 (2004), 248, 250*

Gidleigh

'Medieval Britain and Ireland in 1992', B S Nenk, S Margeson and M Hurley, *Medieval Archaeology* 37 (1993), 255–57*

'Medieval Britain and Ireland in 2003', J Bradley and M Gaimster, *ibid* 48 (2004), 254

Great Torrington

'Great Torrington Castle', R A Higham and S Goddard, *Proceedings of the Devon Archaeological Society* 45 (1987), 97–103*

Hemyock

'Medieval Britain and Ireland in 1991', B S Nenk, S Margeson and M Hurley, *Medieval Archaeology* 36 (1992), 212, 214–15*

'Medieval Britain and Ireland in 1998', J Bradley, M Gaimster and C Haith, *ibid* 43 (1999), 240

Heywood

'Eggesford and Heywood castles', E T Vachell, *Report and Transactions of the Devonshire Association for the Advancement of Science, Literature and the Arts* 95 (1963), 197–207*

'Medieval Britain and Ireland in 1996', B S Nenk, C Haith and J Bradley, *Medieval Archaeology* 41 (1997), 251

Highweek

'The motte at Castle Dyke, Highweek, Newton Abbot, Devon', D and A Woolner, *Report and Transactions of the Devonshire Association for the Advancement of Science, Literature and the Arts* 85 (1953), 133–38*

Holwell

'Castles', in H Riley and R Wilson-North, *The field archaeology of Exmoor*, 102–6. Swindon: English Heritage, 2001*

'Myrtlebury North', R S Carver, *Devon Archaeological Society News Bulletin* 36 (1971), 1

Kingswear

'A Second World War emergency coastal battery at Inner Froward Point, Kingswear', W R Wilson-North, *Proceedings of the Devon Archaeological Society* 51 (1993), 199–205*

'Medieval Britain and Ireland in 1998', J Bradley, M Gaimster and C Haith, *Medieval Archaeology* 43 (1999), 241 [Gomerock Castle]

Loddiswell

'"The Rings", Loddiswell: a new survey by the Royal Commission on the Historical Monuments of England', W R Wilson-North and C J Dunn, *Proceedings of the Devon Archaeological Society* 48 (1990), 87–100*

ENGLAND

Lundy

The archaeology of Lundy: a field guide. K S Gardner. [S l]: Landmark Trust, n d*

The castle on the island of Lundy: 750 years, 1244–1994. M Ternstrom. Cheltenham: the author, 1994*

'Lundy Island, Bull's Paradise', K S Gardner, in N H Cooper (ed), *The Exeter area: proceedings of the 136th summer meeting of the Royal Archaeological Institute, 1990*, 35–39. London: RAI, 1990*

'Lundy Island, Bull's Paradise', K S Gardner, *CBA Groups 12 and 13 Archaeological Review* 1 (1966), 33

'Lundy Island, Benson's Cave', K S Gardner, *ibid* 1 (1966), 42

'Lundy Island', K S Gardner, *ibid* 2 (1967), 21

'A 17th-century fort on Lundy', M Bouquet, *Country Life* 135 (1965), 351–52*

'Lundy', [A Selkirk], *Current Archaeology* 1 (1967–8), 196–202*

'The castle in the isle of Lundy', S Dunmore, *Proceedings of the Devon Archaeological Society* 40 (1982), 153–62*

'Medieval Britain in 1966', D M Wilson and D G Hurst, *Medieval Archaeology* 11 (1967), 284

'Post-medieval Britain in 1967', D G Hurst, *Post-Medieval Archaeology* 2 (1968), 175–76*

Lydford

Lydford Castle, Devonshire. Anon. London: HMSO, 1964*

Lydford Saxon town and castle. A D Saunders. 2nd edition. London: HMSO, 1982*

'Lydford: Saxon burh and Stannary prison', A Saunders, in N H Cooper (ed), *The Exeter area: proceedings of the 136th summer meeting of the Royal Archaeological Institute, 1990*, 61–64. London: RAI, 1990*

'Lydford', P V Addyman, *CBA Groups 12 and 13 Archaeological Review* 1 (1966), 29

'Lydford Castle', A D Saunders, *Report and Transactions of the Devonshire Association for the Advancement of Science, Literature and the Arts* 91 (1959), 176–77

'Medieval Britain in 1957', D M Wilson and J G Hurst, *Medieval Archaeology* 2 (1958), 195

'Medieval Britain in 1958', D M Wilson and J G Hurst, *ibid* 3 (1959), 307

'Medieval Britain in 1962 and 1963', D M Wilson and D G Hurst, *ibid* 8 (1964), 252

'Medieval Britain in 1964', D M Wilson and D G Hurst, *ibid* 9 (1965), 188, 194

'Medieval Britain in 1965', D M Wilson and D G Hurst, *ibid* 10 (1966), 196–97*

'Lydford Castle, Devon', A D Saunders, *ibid* 24 (1980), 123–86*

Okehampton

Okehampton Castle, Devonshire. Anon. London: HMSO, 1969*

Okehampton Castle, Devon. A Endacott. London: English Heritage, 2003*

Okehampton Castle, Devon. R A Higham. London: HMSO, 1984*

Okehampton Castle, Devon. R A Higham. London: English Heritage, 1988*

Okehampton Castle: a handbook for teachers. P Planel. London; English Heritage, 1992*

'Dating in medieval archaeology: problems and possibilities', R Higham, in B Orme (ed), *Problems and case studies in archaeological dating*, 83–107. Exeter: University of Exeter, 1982

'Okehampton Castle', R A Higham, in N H Cooper (ed), *The Exeter area: proceedings of the 136th summer meeting of the Royal Archaeological Institute, 1990*, 58–61. London: RAI, 1990*

'Aspects of fourteenth-century castle design', B M Morley, in A Detsicas (ed), *Collectanea historica: essays in memory of Stuart Rigold*, 104–13. Maidstone: Kent Archaeological Society, 1981*

'Okehampton Castle', R A Higham, *Archaeological Excavations 1975*, 20. London: HMSO, 1976

'Okehampton Castle', R A Higham, *Archaeological Excavations 1976*, 25–26. London: HMSO, 1977

'Okehampton', R A Higham, *Archaeology in Devon* [2] (1979), 15

'Okehampton', R A Higham and J P Allan, *ibid* [3] (1980), 21

'Okehampton', R A Higham and J P Allan, *ibid* 4 (1981), 25

'Okehampton', R A Higham, *ibid* 5 (1982), 26–27

'Okehampton, the castle', R A Higham, *CBA Groups 12 and 13 Archaeological Review* 7 (1972), 52

'Okehampton, Devon', R A Higham and J P Allan, *CBA Newsletter and Calendar* 3 (1979–80), 129

'Okehampton, Devon', R A Higham and J P Allan, *CBA Newsletter and Calendar* 4 (1980–1), 121

'Excavations at Okehampton Castle, Devon: part I: the motte and keep', R A Higham, *Proceedings of the Devon Archaeological Society* 35 (1977), 3–42*

'Excavations at Okehampton Castle, Devon: part II: the bailey, a preliminary report', R A Higham and J P Allan, *ibid* 38 (1980), 49–51*

'Excavations at Okehampton Castle, Devon. Part 2 – the bailey', R A Higham, J P Allan and S R Blaylock, *ibid* 40 (1982), 19–151*

'Okehampton and the Norman conquest of Devon', R Higham, *Devon Archaeology* 4 (1991), 16–19*

'Okehampton Castle, Devon: interpretation, conservation, presentation and restoration from circa 1895 to circa 1995', R Higham, *Europa Nostra Bulletin* 55 (2001), 129–42, 151–52*

'Medieval Britain in 1972', L E Webster and J Cherry, *Medieval Archaeology* 17 (1973), 161

'Medieval Britain in 1973', L E Webster and J Cherry, *ibid* 18 (1974), 195

'Medieval Britain in 1974', L E Webster and J Cherry, *ibid* 19 (1975), 239

'Medieval Britain in 1975', L E Webster and J Cherry, *ibid* 20 (1976), 184

'Medieval Britain in 1976', L E Webster and J Cherry, *ibid* 21 (1977), 234

'Medieval Britain in 1977', L E Webster and J Cherry, *ibid* 22 (1978), 168–69*

'Medieval Britain in 1980', S M Youngs and J Clark, *ibid* 25 (1981), 200

'Medieval Britain and Ireland in 1991', B S Nenk, S Margeson and M Hurley, *ibid* 36 (1992), 215–17*

'Medieval Britain and Ireland in 1999', J Bradley and M Gaimster, *ibid* 44 (2000), 259

Plymouth

Drake's Island: once a fortress, now an adventure centre. Anon. Plymouth: Mayflower Centre Trust, 1978*

Guns and carriages: the construction of the world's first reproduction Moncrieff depression mounting. A C Carpenter. Tiverton: Halsgrove, 1999*

Crownhill Fort, Plymouth. P Cobb and D Moore. Fareham: Palmerston Forts Society, 1990*

Crownhill Fort. D Moore. Gosport: D Moore, 1994* (Plymouth papers; 1)

Gorges of Plymouth Fort. R A Preston. Toronto: University of Toronto Press, 1953*

The historic defences of Plymouth. A Pye and F Woodward. Truro: Cornwall County Council, 1996*

The siege of Plymouth. W Scutt. Plymouth: Plymouth City Museum and Art Gallery, 1980*

Plymouth in the Civil War. M Stoyle. Exeter: Devon Archaeological Society, 1998* (Devon Archaeology; 7)

Lost landscapes of Plymouth: maps, charts and plans to 1800. E Stuart. Stroud: Alan Sutton, 1991*

The Royal Citadel. F W Woodward. [S l: s n]: n d*

Citadel: the story of the Royal Citadel, Plymouth. F W Woodward. Exeter: Devon Books, 1987*

Plymouth's defences: a short history. F W Woodward. Cornwood: the author, 1990*

Plymouth's Palmerston forts. F Woodward. Plymouth: Old Plymouth Society, [1994?]*

Forts or follies? The story of Plymouth's Palmerston forts. F W Woodward. Tiverton: Halsgrove, 1998*

'The later history of Mount Batten', C Gaskell Brown, in B Cunliffe, *Mount Batten, Plymouth: a prehistoric and Roman port*, 206. Oxford: University Committee for Archaeology, 1988*

'The Royal Citadel, Plymouth: a possible Stowe connection', A Saunders, *Archaeological Journal* 153 (1996), 290–94*

'Crownhill Fort', T Hitchins, *Casemate* 19 (1986), 4

'Pilchards and Plymouth Fort', E Welch, *Devon and Cornwall Notes and Queries* 30 (1965–7), 260–62

'A major Plymouth find', anon, *Devon Archaeological Society Newsletter* 52 (1992), 4*

'White friars lived in fear of French', anon, *ibid* 52 (1992), 5*

'A archaeological survey of Mount Pleasant Redoubt, Plymouth', A Pye, *Proceedings of the Devon Archaeological Society* 50 (1992), 137–61*

'The Royal Citadel, Plymouth', F Woodward, *Devon Archaeology* 2 (1984), 9–12*

'Drake's Island, Plymouth', F W Woodward, *ibid* 5 (1991), 1–32* [whole issue]

'Tudor artillery towers and their role in the defence of Plymouth in 1588', M Brayshay, *Devon Historian* 35 (1987), 3–14*

'Plymouth's coastal defences in the year of the Spanish Armada', M Brayshay, *Report and Transactions of the Devonshire Association for the Advancement of Science, Literature and the Arts* 119 (1987), 169–96*

'Armada maps of Plymouth', E A Stuart, *Map Collector* 42 (1988), 2–8*

'Medieval Britain in 1959', D M Wilson and J G Hurst, *Medieval Archaeology* 4 (1960), 145

'Medieval Britain and Ireland in 1993', B S Nenk, S Margeson and M Hurley, *ibid* 38 (1994), 205–6*

'New light on old Plymouth', J Barber, *Proceedings of the Plymouth Athenaeum* 4 (1973–9), 55–66*

'Post-medieval Britain and Ireland in 1989', G Egan, *Post-Medieval Archaeology* 24 (1990), 163–64

'Post-medieval Britain and Ireland in 1992', M Ponsford, *ibid* 27 (1993), 214–17*

'Post-medieval Britain and Ireland in 1994', M Ponsford and R Jackson, *ibid* 29 (1995), 123–30*

'Post-medieval Britain and Ireland in 1995', M Ponsford and R Jackson, *ibid* 30 (1996), 249–50

'Crownhill Fort, Plymouth', P Cobb and D Moore, *The Redan* 19 (1990), 21–32*

'Crownhill Fort: part 2', P Cobb and D Moore, *ibid* 20 (1990), 12–23*

'Expense magazines at Crownhill', D Moore, *ibid* 21 (1991), 27–28*

'32pr SBBL guns at Crownhill Fort', D Moore, *ibid* 34 (1995), 27–28*

'The construction of Plymouth and Portland breakwaters', P Cobb, *ibid* 39 (1997), 16–21*

'Plymouth Breakwater Fort', D Moore, *ibid* 52 (2001), 3–18*

'The great house of Stowe - an addendum', G M Trinick, *Journal of the Royal Institution of Cornwall* 10.1 (1986–7), 58–61*

Plympton

Plympton Castle. R A Higham. Exeter: Devon Archaeological Society, 1987* (Field guide; 3)

'Plympton Castle, Devon', R A Higham, S Goddard and M Rouillard, *Proceedings of the Devon Archaeological Society* 43 (1985), 59–75*

Salcombe

'Archaeological recording at Fort Charles, Salcombe', the Editor, *Devon Archaeological Society Newsletter* 70 (1998), 7*

'Fort Charles, Salcombe: a coastal artillery fort of Henry VIII, refortified in the Civil War', R Parker, A Passmore and M Stoyle, *Proceedings of the Devon Archaeological Society* 63 (2005), 115–37*

Tiverton

'Medieval Britain and Ireland in 1988', D R M Gaimster, S Margeson and T Barry, *Medieval Archaeology* 33 (1989), 175

'The underground passages of Tiverton Castle, Devon', S Campbell, *Tiverton Civic Society Newsletter* March (1981), reprinted in *Subterranea Britannica Bulletin* 16 (1982), 19–20*

Totnes

Totnes Castle, Devon. S Brown. London: English Heritage, 1998*

Three shell keeps. D F Renn. London: HMSO, 1969*

Totnes Castle, Devon. S E Rigold. London: HMSO, 1970*; 2nd edition, 1979*

Totnes Castle. S E Rigold. London: HBMCE, 1987*; 2nd edition, 1990*

Totnes Castle: a handbook for teachers. S Brown and R Clutterbuck. London: HBMCE, 1988*

'Totnes Castle', R A Higham, in N H Cooper (ed), *The Exeter area: proceedings of the 136th summer meeting of the Royal Archaeological Institute, 1990*, 56–58. London: RAI, 1990*

'Totnes, Devon. The Saxon town, the castle and the church', A Oswald, *Country Life* 107 (1950), 302–6*

'An excavation on the defences of the Anglo-Saxon *burh* and medieval town of Totnes', M J Dyer and J Allan, *Proceedings of the Devon Archaeological Society* 62 (2004), 53–77*

'Totnes Castle: recent excavation by the Ancient Monuments Department, Ministry of Works', S E Rigold, *Report and Transactions of the Devonshire Association for the Advancement of Science, Literature and the Arts* 119 (1987), 169–96*

'Medieval Britain and Ireland in 1991', B S Nenk, S Margeson and M Hurley, *Medieval Archaeology* 36 (1992), 220

'Medieval Britain and Ireland in 1993', B S Nenk, S Margeson and M Hurley, *ibid* 38 (1994), 206

'Medieval Britain and Ireland in 1996', B S Nenk, C Haith and J Bradley, *ibid* 41 (1997), 251

'Medieval Britain and Ireland in 1998', J Bradley, M Gaimster and C Haith, *ibid* 43 (1999), 242

Woodbury
'An artillery emplacement of the Napoleonic Wars at Woodbury Castle', M Todd, *Proceedings of the Devon Archaeological Society* 63 (2005), 211

DORSET

Beavis, J. *Dorset's World Heritage Coast: an archaeological guide*. Stroud: Tempus, 2004*

Carter, K (ed). *Heritage unlocked: guide to free sites in Devon, Dorset and Somerset*. London: English Heritage, 2004*

Davies, G J. 'Dorset's coastal defences, 1715', *Somerset and Dorset Notes and Queries* 30.303 (1976), 155–57

Kenyon, J R. 'The state of the fortifications in the West Country in 1623', *Fort* 16 (1988), 45–52*

Newman, J and Pevsner, N. *Dorset (The buildings of England)*. Harmondsworth: Penguin Books, 1972*

Robertson, M. *Exploring England's heritage: Dorset to Gloucestershire*. London: HMSO, in association with English Heritage, 1992* [espec ch 2]

Salter, M. *The castles of Wessex*. Malvern: Folly Publications, 2002*

Wilton, P. *Castles of Dorset*. Wimborne: Phil Wilton Publishing, 1995*

Blandford Forum
The defences of Blandford Forum: a short history of the Second World War defences. E H R Schmidt. Blandford Forum: Blandford Forum Museum, 1987*

Bow and Arrow

'Rufus or Bow and Arrow Castle, Portland', A Hunt, *Archaeological Journal* 140 (1983), 74

'Bow and Arrow Castle, Portland', D J C King, *Proceedings of the Dorset Natural History and Archaeological Society* 69 (1947), 65–67*

Bridport

'Medieval Britain and Ireland in 1999', J Bradley and M Gaimster, *Medieval Archaeology* 44 (2000), 260

Brownsea

The antiquities of Brownsea Island. Anon. London: National Trust, 1963*

Corfe

The story of Corfe Castle: collected from ancient chronicles and records. G Bankes, edited and abridged by E Hardy. London: Regency Press, [1983]*; paperback, Dovecote Press, Wimborne, 1988*

The siege: the story of the defence of Corfe Castle in the years 1643–46. E Hardy. Sherborne: Dorset Publishing, 1984*

Corfe Castle, Dorset. D Thackray. Revised edition. London: National Trust, 1987*

Corfe Castle, Dorset: an illustrated souvenir. D Thackray. London: National Trust, 1991*

Corfe Castle: 1000 years of history. A Tinniswood. London: National Trust, 1987*

Corfe Castle. A Yarrow. London: National Trust, 2003*; reprinted with corrections, 2005*

'Corfe Castle' and 'The Rings', in RCHME, *An inventory of the historical monuments in the county of Dorset. 2. South-east: 1*, 57–78, 96–98. London: HMSO, 1970*

'A "marginal economy"? The Isle of Purbeck from the Norman Conquest to the Black Death', D A Hinton, in D A Hinton (ed), *Purbeck papers*, 84–117. Oxford: Oxbow Books, 2002* (University of Southampton, Department of Archaeology monographs; 4)

'Corfe Castle', B M Morley, *Archaeological Journal* 140 (1983), 55–57*

'"The chamber called *Gloriette*": living at leisure in thirteenth- and fourteenth-century castles', J Ashbee, *Journal of the British Archaeological Association* 157 (2004), 17–40*

'Corfe Castle, Dorset', M Papworth, *CBA Group 12 Newsletter* October (1991), 12

'A note on the excavations at Corfe Castle, 1949', G E Chambers, *Proceedings of the Dorset Natural History and Archaeological Society* 71 (1949), 58–59

'Excavations in the middle ward of Corfe Castle', R A H Farrar, *ibid* 72 (1950), 82

'The development of Corfe Castle', W D Simpson, *ibid* 73 (1951), 71–84*

'Excavations in the middle ward of Corfe Castle', RCHM, *ibid* 73 (1951), 91

'The development of Corfe Castle in the 13th century', J C Perks, *ibid* 76 (1954), 62–66

'Corfe Castle, outer gatehouse excavations 1986. Interim report', D Thackray and M Papworth, in 'Dorset archaeology in 1987, *ibid* 109 (1987), 136

'Corfe Castle, west bailey excavations 1987. Interim report', D Thackray and M Papworth, in 'Dorset archaeology in 1987', *ibid* 109 (1987), 136

'Corfe Castle, outer gatehouse excavations 1988 – interim report', D Thackray and M Papworth, in 'Dorset archaeology in 1988', *ibid* 110 (1988), 156

'Corfe Castle, west bailey excavations 1988 - interim report', D Thackray and M Papworth, in 'Dorset archaeology in 1988', *ibid* 110 (1988), 156–57

'Corfe Castle excavations 1990. Interim report', D Thackray and M Papworth, in 'Dorset archaeology in 1990', *ibid* 112 (1990), 125

'Excavations at Corfe Castle 1991: interim report', D Thackray and M Papworth, in 'Dorset archaeology in 1991', *ibid* 113 (1991), 175

'Excavations at Corfe Castle 1992', D Thackray and M Papworth, in 'Dorset archaeology in 1992', *ibid* 114 (1992), 238–39

'Excavations at Corfe Castle 1993', D Thackray and M Papworth, in 'Dorset archaeology in 1993', *ibid* 115 (1993), 151–52

'Excavations at Corfe Castle 1994', D Thackray and M Papworth, in 'Dorset archaeology in 1994', *ibid* 116 (1994), 123

'Excavations at Corfe Castle 1995', D Thackray and M Papworth, in 'Dorset archaeology in 1995', *ibid* 117 (1995), 128

'Excavations at Corfe Castle 1996', N Grace and M Papworth, in 'Dorset archaeology in 1996', *ibid* 118 (1996), 138–39

'Corfe Castle, inner ward, interim report 1997', N Grace and M Papworth, in 'Dorset archaeology in 1997', *ibid* 119 (1997), 164–65

'Excavations in the west bailey at Corfe Castle', RCHM, *Medieval Archaeology* 4 (1960), 29–55*

'King John's Gloriette at Corfe Castle', M M Reeve and M Thurlby, *Journal of the Society of Architectural Historians* 64 (2005), 168–85*

'Corfe Castle: some evidence on the second siege', J A Casada, *Somerset and Dorset Notes and Queries* 29 (1973), 296–300

'William de Thweyt, Esquire: deputy constable of Corfe Castle in the 1340s', A Ayton, *ibid* 32 (1989), 731–78

Dorchester

Dorchester excavations, **1**. J Draper and C Chaplin. Dorchester: Dorset Natural

History and Archaeological Society, 1982*

'Maumbury Rings, Dorchester: the excavations of 1908–1913', R Bradley, *Archaeologia* 105 (1976), 1–97*

East Chelborough

'Paired mottes in East Chelborough, Dorset', C Lewis, in M Bowden, D Mackay and P Topping (eds), *From Cornwall to Caithness: some aspects of British field archaeology. Papers presented to Norman Quinnell*, 159–71. Oxford: British Archaeological Reports, 1989* (British series; 209)

Poole

Excavations in Poole 1973–1983. I P Horsey, edited by K S Jarvis. Dorchester: Dorset Natural History and Archaeological Society, 1992*

Portland

Portland Castle. Anon. London: HMSO, 1965*; 2nd edition, 1979*

Portland Castle. Anon. London: English Heritage, 1989*

Portland Castle, Dorset. Anon. London: English Heritage, 2000*

Dorset coastal fortifications – Portland and Weymouth district: report on historical fortifications. P D Cobb and W E J Parker. Privately published, [1972]*

A teacher's handbook to Portland Castle. G Wheatley. London: English Heritage, 1994*

'Portland Castle', in RCHME, *An inventory of the historical monuments in the county of Dorset. 2. South-east: 2*, 250–52. London: HMSO, 1970*

'Portland Castle', B M Morley, *Archaeological Journal* 140 (1983), 72–73*

'"Imperial works and worthy kings" – the building of Portland breakwaters', M Boddy and J West, in F M Langford (ed), *The Dorset year book for 1981*, 39–43. [S l]: The Society of Dorset Men, 1981*

'Proposed new Barrackmaster's workshop, R.N.A.S. Portland', A Woodward and D Tyler, *Proceedings of the Dorset Natural History and Archaeological Society* 117 (1995), 137–40*

'The coastal defences of Portland and Weymouth', E A Andrews and M L Pinsent, supplement to *Fort* 9 (1981), 4–43*

'War Office letters about Portland', W F Jervois, *ibid*, 44–53

'The Portland breakwaters – a Victorian achievement', M Boddy and J West, *Industrial Archaeology* 16 (1981), 238–54*

'The Verne', P Cobb, *Palmerston Forts Society Newsletter* 12 (1988), 11, 14–17

'The construction of Plymouth and Portland breakwaters', P Cobb, *The Redan* 39 (1997), 16–21*

'The Verne Citadel, Portland, Cornwall', P Cobb, *ibid* 46 (1999), 21–27*

Rufus

See Bow and Arrow

Sandsfoot

'Sandsfoot Castle', in RCHME, *An inventory of the historical monuments in the county of Dorset. 2. South-east: 2*, 336–38. London: HMSO, 1970*

'Sandsfoot Castle', B M Morley, *Archaeological Journal* 140 (1983), 71–72*

Shaftesbury

'Excavations by the Shaftesbury Historical Society at Castle Hill, Shaftesbury, 1947–1949', S E Rigold, *Proceedings of the Dorset Natural History and Archaeological Society* 71 (1949), 54–57*

Sherborne

Sherborne Old Castle, Dorset. B K Davison. London: English Heritage, 2001*

Sherborne Old Castle: information for teachers. G Wheatley. London: English Heritage, 1997*

Sherborne Old Castle. P White. London: HMSO, 1971*

Sherborne Old Castle. P White. London: HBMCE, 1986*

'Sherborne Old Castle', in RCHM, *An inventory of the historical monuments in Dorset. 1. West*, 64–66. London: HMSO, 1952*

'Sherborne Old Castle, Castleton', P R White, *Archaeological Excavations 1975*, 21. London: HMSO, 1976

'Sherborne Old Castle, Castleton', P R White, *Archaeological Excavations 1976*, 26. London: HMSO, 1977

'Sherborne Old Castle', P R White, *Archaeological Journal* 140 (1983), 67–70*

'Palatial but vulnerable in Dorset', P White, *Country Life* 167 (1980), 218*

'Sherborne', E T Vachell, *Devon Archaeological Society News Bulletin* 36 (1971), 2–3

'Excavations at Sherborne Old Castle', C E Bean, *Proceedings of the Dorset Natural History and Archaeological Society* 72 (1950), 93–94

'Excavations at Sherborne Old Castle', C E Bean, *ibid* 73 (1951), 106–9*

'Excavations at Sherborne Old Castle', C E Bean, *ibid* 74 (1952), 107–8

'Excavations at Sherborne Old Castle', C E Bean, *ibid* 77 (1955), 141–42

'Sherborne Old Castle, Dorset: medieval pottery fabrics', B P Harrison and D F Williams, *ibid* 101 (1979), 91–102*

'A group of early 13th-century pottery from Sherborne Old Castle and its wider context', J Allan, *ibid* 125 (2003), 71–82*

'Sherborne Castle', R Ollard, *History Today* 44.3 (1994), 62–63*

'Medieval Britain in 1973', L E Webster and J Cherry, *Medieval Archaeology* 18 (1974), 195

'Medieval Britain in 1978', L E Webster and J Cherry, *ibid* 23 (1979), 260

Wareham

'Town defences' and 'Wareham Castle', in RCHME, *An inventory of the historical monuments in the county of Dorset. 2. South-east: 2*, 322–26. London: HMSO, 1970*

'Excavations at Castle Close, Wareham', R A H Farrar, *Proceedings of the Dorset Natural History and Archaeological Society* 72 (1950), 82

'The excavation of Wareham town walls', R A H Farrar, *ibid* 76 (1954), 86

'Some recent cuttings through Wareham walls and the dyke on Wareham Common', R A H Farrar, *ibid* 78 (1956), 77–78

'Excavations in Wareham, 1974–5', D A Hinton and R Hodges, *ibid* 99 (1977), 42–83*

'Wareham west walls: excavations by the Royal Commission on Historical Monuments (England)', RCHM, *Medieval Archaeology* 3 (1959), 120–38*

'The keep of Wareham Castle', D F Renn, *ibid* 4 (1960), 56–68*

Weymouth

Guide to the Nothe Fort. Anon. 2nd edition. Weymouth: Weymouth Civic Society, [1982]*

A short history of the Nothe Fort, Weymouth. J A C West. 2nd edition. Weymouth: Borough of Portland and Weymouth, 1981*

'The Nothe Fort, Weymouth', A Saunders, *Archaeological Journal* 140 (1983), 71

'The coastal defences of Portland and Weymouth', E A Andrews and M L Pinsent, supplement to *Fort* 9 (1981), 4–43*

DURHAM

Hugill, R. *The castles and towers of the county of Durham: a guide to the ancient palatinate of Durham*. Newcastle upon Tyne: F Graham, 1979*

Jackson, M J. *Castles of Durham and Cleveland: a gazetteer of the medieval castles of two northern counties*. Carlisle: Barmkin Books, 1996*

Pevsner, N. *County Durham (The buildings of England)*. 2nd edition, revised by E Williamson. Harmondsworth: Penguin Books, 1983, reprinted with amendments 1985*

Salter, M. *The castles and tower houses of County Durham*. Malvern: Folly Publications, 2002*

Stevenson, I. 'Tees and Hartlepool defences', *The Redan* 51 (2001), 31–47*

Stevenson, I. 'The defences of the Tyne and the Wear', *ibid* 67 (2006), 3–18*

Weaver, J. *Exploring England's heritage: Cumbria to Northumberland*. London: HMSO, in association with English Heritage, 1992* [espec ch 5]

Woodhouse, R. *Castles of Cleveland*. Redcar: A A Sotheran, 1975*

Yates, S (ed). *Heritage unlocked: guide to free sites in Yorkshire and the north east*. London: English Heritage, 2004*

Barnard

Barnard Castle, Durham. D Austin. London: English Heritage, 1988*

Barnard Castle, County Durham; Egglestone Abbey, North Yorkshire; Bowes Castle, North Yorkshire. K Kenyon. London: English Heritage, 1999*

Barnard Castle, Co Durham. A D Saunders. London: HMSO, 1971*

Barnard Castle. A D Saunders. 2nd edition. London: HMSO, 1978*; 3rd edition, 1982*

Barnard Castle: information for teachers. M Vasey. London: English Heritage, 1998*

'Barnard Castle', D Austin, *Archaeological Excavations 1975*, 21. London: HMSO, 1976

'Barnard Castle, Co Durham. First interim report: excavations in the town ward, 1974–6', D Austin, *Journal of the British Archaeological Association* 132 (1979), 50–72*

'Barnard Castle, Co Durham. 2nd interim report: excavation in the inner ward 1976–8', D Austin, *ibid* 133 (1980), 74–96*

'Barnard Castle, County Durham', D Austin, *CBA Newsletter and Calendar* 2 (1978–9), 126

'Barnard Castle, County Durham', D Austin, *CBA Newsletter and Calendar* 4 (1980–1), 122

'Barnard Castle, Co Durham', D Austin, *Château Gaillard* 9–10 (1982), 294–300*

'The castle and the landscape: annual lecture to the Society for Landscape Studies, 1984', D Austin, *Landscape History* 6 (1984), 69–81*

'Medieval Britain in 1956', D M Wilson and J G Hurst, *Medieval Archaeology* 1 (1957), 156

'Medieval Britain in 1962 and 1963', D M Wilson and D G Hurst, *ibid* 8 (1964), 252

'Medieval Britain in 1976', L E Webster and J Cherry, *ibid* 21 (1977), 234

Bowes

'Bowes Castle', R S Simms, *Archaeological Journal* 111 (1954), 218

'Medieval Britain and Ireland in 1993', B S Nenk, S Margeson and M Hurley, *Medieval Archaeology* 38 (1994), 207

Durham

Durham Castle. D Bythell. Norwich: Jarrold, 1974*

Durham Castle. University College, Durham. D Bythell. Durham: University College, 1985*

English Heritage book of Durham. M Roberts. London: Batsford, in association with English Heritage, 1994* [espec ch 2]

Durham: 1000 years of history. M Roberts. Stroud: Tempus, 2003* [espec ch 2] [new edition of the above book]

'The origins and development of Durham Castle', M Leyland, in D Rollason, M Harvey and M Prestwich (eds), *Anglo-Norman Durham 1093–1193*, 407–24. Woodbridge: Boydell Press, 1994*

'The place of Durham among Norman episcopal palaces and castles', M W Thompson, *ibid*, 425–36*

'The site and stones of Durham', K Dunham and G A L Johnson, *Fifty-second Annual Report of the Friends of Durham Cathedral* (1986), 15–21*

'An excavation below Bishop Tunstal's chapel, Durham Castle', G Simpson and V Hatley, *Antiquaries Journal* 33 (1953), 56–64*

'Back Silver Street, Durham, 1975–6 excavations', J Clipson, *Archaeologia Aeliana* 5 ser 8 (1980), 109–26*

'Durham City: Back Silver Street', J Clipson, *Archaeological Excavations 1976*, 11. London: HMSO, 1977

'Durham Castle', J Charlton, *Archaeological Journal* 111 (1954), 202–3

'Restoration of the Norman chapel in Durham Castle', B Colgrave, *Transactions of the Architectural and Archaeological Society of Durham and Northumberland* 10 (1946–54), 380–81

'The great north gate of Durham Castle', M Johnson, *ibid* new ser 4 (1978), 105–18*

'Rescue excavations in Co Durham, 1976–1978: 3. An excavation at Queen's Court, 2 North Bailey, Durham City', P A G Clack, *ibid* new ser 5 (1980), 56–70*

'Durham Castle', M Binney, *Country Life* 183.39 (1989), 134–39*

'The City of Durham: an archaeological survey', P Lowther [*et al*], *Durham Archaeological Journal* 9 (1993), 27–119*

'Medieval Britain in 1978', L E Webster and J Cherry, *Medieval Archaeology* 23 (1979), 260

Hartlepool

'Archaeology in Hartlepool', G A B Young, in *Recent excavations in Cleveland*, 45–54. Middlesborough: Cleveland County Council, 1983*

'The medieval defences of Hartlepool, Cleveland: the results of excavation and survey', R Daniels, *Durham Archaeological Journal* 2 (1986), 63–72*

'Medieval Britain and Ireland in 1983', S M Youngs, J Clark and T B Barry, *Medieval Archaeology* 28 (1984), 212

'The anonymous gunners of Hartlepool', S Bull, *Military Chest* June (1986), 38–41*

Hylton

Hylton Castle, Tyne and Wear. B M Morley. London: HMSO, 1979*

'Hylton Castle, Co Durham', T Nicholson, *Antiquities of Sunderland* 22 (1960), 11–24*

'Hylton Castle', B M Morley, *Archaeological Journal* 133 (1976), 118–34*

'Hylton Castle', B M Morley, *ibid* 133 (1976), 237–38

'Excavation and survey at Hylton Castle, Sunderland' B Morley and S Speak, *ibid* 159 (2002), 258–65*

'Medieval Britain in 1956', D M Wilson and J G Hurst, *Medieval Archaeology* 1 (1957), 156

Lumley

'Lumley Castle, its antecedents and its architect', M Hislop, *Archaeologia Aeliana* 5 ser 24 (1996), 83–98*

Raby

'The castle of Ralph fourth Baron Neville at Raby', M Hislop, *ibid* 5 ser 20 (1991), 91–97*

'Raby Castle, Co Durham', A Rowan, *Country Life* 146 (1969), 78–81, 150–53*

Westgate

'Westgate Castle in Weardale – the last 500 years', J L Drury, *Transactions of the Architectural and Archaeological Society of Durham and Northumberland* new ser 4 (1978), 31–33

ESSEX

Campbell, A (ed). *Heritage unlocked: a guide to free sites in the east of England*. London: English Heritage, 2004*

Claro, F Z. 'The Thames defences', *Thurrock Historical Society Journal* 4 (1959), 44–50

Cligman, J and Crowe, N. *Exploring England's heritage: Hertfordshire to Norfolk*. London: HMSO, in association with English Heritage, 1994* [espec ch 2]

Gifford, P R. *Resist the invader: the story of Essex forts and castles*. Chelmsford: Essex Libraries, 1982*

Gilman, P and Nash, F. *Fortress Essex*. Chelmsford: Essex County Council, 1995*

Hamilton-Baillie, J. 'Strategic safeguard or military folly? London's Victorian forts', *Country Life* 180 (1986), 1560, 1562*

Hollwey, C. 'Four Essex giants', *Postern* 10 (2000), 4–11* [Pleshey, Ongar, Stebbing and Great Canfield]

Kent, P. *Fortifications of East Anglia*. Lavenham: Dalton, 1988*

Kent, P. 'East Anglian fortifications in the twentieth century', *Fortress* 3 (1989), 43–57*

Nash, F. 'World War II defences', in P J Gilman (ed), 'Archaeology in Essex, 1993', *Essex Archaeology and History* 25 (1994), 256–57*

Nash, F. 'World War II defences survey', in A Bennett (ed), 'Work of the Essex County Council Archaeology Section, 1998', *ibid* 30 (1999), 206–8*

Nash, F. 'World War Two defences in Essex', *Essex Journal* 29.2 (1994), 40–45*

Neville, D. *Lost castles of Essex*. Romford: Ian Henry Publications, 2003*

Pawsey, J T. *Castles of East Anglia*. Ipswich: F W Pawsey, 1973*

Pevsner, N. *Essex (The buildings of England)*. 2nd edition, revised by E Radcliffe. Harmondsworth: Penguin Books, 1965*

Ponsford, M. 'Post-medieval Britain and Ireland in 1993', *Post-Medieval Archaeology* 28 (1994), 126

Salter, M. *The castles of East Anglia*. Malvern: Folly Publications, 2001*

Saunders, A. 'Thames fortifications during the 16th to 19th centuries', in *Thames gateway: recording historic buildings and landscapes in the Thames estuary*, 124–34. Swindon: RCHME, 1995*

Smith, V T C. *Defending London's river*. Rochester: North Kent Books, 1985*

Smith, V T C. 'The defences of the 20th century', in *Thames gateway: recording historic buildings and landscapes in the Thames estuary*, 135–43. Swindon: RCHME, 1995*

Wilson, J D. 'Later nineteenth century defences of the Thames, including Grain Fort', *Journal of the Society for Army Historical Research* 41 (1963), 141–58, 182–99*

Wood, R G E. *Essex and the French wars 1793–1815*. Chelmsford: Essex County Council, 1977*

Berden

'The Rookery: a ringwork at Berden, Essex', G M Knocker, *Transactions of the Essex Archaeological Society* new ser 25 (1949–60), 257–62*

Bulmer

'Surveys of two small earthwork castles at Elmdon and Bulmer', B Milton and D Priddy, in D Priddy (ed), 'Work of the Essex County Council Archaeology Section 1983–84', *Essex Archaeology and History* 16 (1984–5), 116–18*

Chelmsford

'The defences of Chelmsford', A C Wright, *Essex Journal* 8 (1974), 15–21*

Chipping Ongar

'Chipping Ongar, Banson's Yard', M R Eddy, in D Priddy (ed), 'Excavations in Essex, 1981', *Essex Archaeology and History* 14 (1982), 136

'Medieval Britain in 1981', S M Youngs, and J Clark, *Medieval Archaeology* 26 (1982), 181–82

'Medieval Britain and Ireland in 1982', S M Youngs, J Clark and T B Barry, *ibid* 27 (1983), 175

'Medieval Britain and Ireland in 1987', S M Youngs [*et al*], *ibid* 32 (1988), 240–41

Coalhouse

Coalhouse Fort and artillery defences at East Tilbury: a history and guide. V T C Smith. [S l]: Coalhouse Fort Project, 1985*

'Coalhouse', V Smith, *Casemate* 14 (1984),, 9–10*

'East Tilbury, Coalhouse Fort', J Catton, in D Priddy (ed), 'Excavations in Essex, 1983–4', *Essex Archaeology and History* 16 (1984–5), 127

'East Tilbury, Coalhouse Fort', J Catton, in D Priddy (ed), 'Excavations in Essex 1987', *ibid* 19 (1988), 264

'Coalhouse Fort, East Tilbury – 1861 folly? – 1985 museum', A Saunders, *Essex Journal* 20 (1985), 3–7*

'Post-medieval Britain and Ireland in 1989', G Egan, *Post-Medieval Archaeology* 24 (1990), 164

'Post-medieval Britain and Ireland in 1991', M Ponsford, *ibid* 26 (1992), 107

'The degaussing range at Coalhouse Fort', E Smith and T Wilson, *The Redan* 65 (2005), 2–20*

'East Tilbury fortifications and Coalhouse Fort', I G Sparkes, *Thurrock Local History Society Journal* 7 (1962), 3–12

Colchester

Colchester Castle. D T-D Clarke. 5th edition. Colchester: Colchester Borough Council, 1980*

Colchester Castle: a history, description and guide. D T-D Clarke. 6th edition. Colchester: Colchester Borough Council, 1985*; 6th edition, 1989*

The siege of Colchester 1648. D T-D Clarke. Colchester: Colchester Borough Council, n d*

Aspects of Anglo-Saxon Colchester. P Crummy. London: CBA, 1981* (Research report; 39)

Excavations at Lion Walk, Balkerne Lane, and Middleborough, Colchester, Essex. P Crummy. Colchester: Colchester Archaeological Trust, 1984*

Roman Colchester. M R Hull. London: Society of Antiquaries, 1958* (Research report; 20) [espec pp 160–91]

The siege of Colchester 1648. P Jones. Stroud: Tempus, 2003*

The siege of Colchester 1648: a history and bibliography. D Woodward and C Cockerill. Colchester: Essex County Library, 1979*

'Colchester Castle', N J G Pounds, in N J G Pounds (ed), *The Colchester area: proceedings of the 139th summer meeting of the Royal Archaeological Institute, 1992*, 14, 16. London: RAI, 1992

'The Norman bank at Colchester Castle', M A Cotton, *Antiquaries Journal* 42 (1962), 57–61*

'Colchester, Lion Walk', P Crummy, *Archaeological Excavations 1972*, 78–79. London: HMSO, 1973

'Aspects of the origins and development of Colchester Castle', P J Drury, *Archaeological Journal* 139 (1982), 302–419*

'The old castle', anon, *Colchester Archaeological Group Bulletin* 1.4 (1958), 39–41*

'The castle that Eudo built', anon, *Colchester Archaeologist* 7 (1993–4), 1–7*

'Colchester Castle well, an unusual excavation', S R Bacon, *Transactions of the Essex Archaeological Society* 3 ser 5 (1973), 237–39*

'A valiant constable of Colchester Castle, AD 1155', C L Sinclair Williams, *Essex Archaeology and History* 20 (1989), 30–33*

'The excavation of a lift-shaft at Colchester Castle', J Partridge, *ibid* 24 (1993), 234–36*

'Medieval Britain in 1969', D M Wilson and D G Hurst, *Medieval Archaeology* 14 (1970), 181

'Medieval Britain and Ireland in 1986', S M Youngs, J Clark and T Barry, *ibid* 31 (1987), 123

'Post-medieval Britain and Ireland in 1998 and 1999', M Ponsford, *Post-Medieval Archaeology* 34 (2000), 226

East Mersea

'East Mersea, Tudor blockhouse at Cudmore Grove', M R Eddy, in D Priddy (ed), 'Work of Essex County Council Archaeology Section 1982', *Essex Archaeology and History* 15 (1983), 145, 147–49*

East Tilbury

'Twydall redoubts: East Tilbury battery', T Wilson, *The Redan* 64 (2005), 30–34*

Elmdon

'Surveys of two small earthwork castles at Elmdon and Bulmer', B Milton and D Priddy, in D Priddy (ed), 'Work of the Essex County Council Archaeology Section 1983–84', *Essex Archaeology and History* 16 (1984–5), 116–18*

Great Easton

'Great Easton Castle', E Sellers, *Archaeological Excavations 1964*, 13. London: HMSO, 1965

'Great Easton', E Sellers, *Archaeological Excavations 1965*, 13. London: HMSO, 1966

'Great Easton Castle', E Sellers, *Archaeological Excavations 1966*, 13. London: HMSO, 1967

'Great Easton: brief interim report', E E Sellers and J E Sellers, *Transactions of the Essex Archaeological Society* 3 ser 1 (1961–5), 265

'Excavations at Great Easton, second interim report', J E Sellers and E E Sellers, *ibid* 3 ser 2 (1966–70), 97

'Great Easton', J E Sellers and E E Sellers, *ibid* 3 ser 2 (1966–70), 159–60

'Medieval Britain in 1964', D M Wilson and D G Hurst, *Medieval Archaeology* 9 (1965), 188–89

'Medieval Britain in 1965', D M Wilson and D G Hurst, ibid 10 (1966), 190

'Medieval Britain in 1966', D M Wilson and D G Hurst, ibid 11 (1967), 284–85

'Interim report on excavations at Great Easton, Essex', E E Sellers and J E Sellers, *Thames Basin Archaeological Observers' Group Newsletter* new ser 26 (1965), 15–16

Great Wakering

'Medieval Britain in 1969', D M Wilson and D G Hurst, *Medieval Archaeology* 14 (1970), 176

Hadleigh

Hadleigh Castle, Essex. Anon. London: HMSO, 1971*; 2nd edition, 1978*

The Thames and its buildings: a handbook for teachers. A Tinniswood. London: English Heritage, 1990*

'Excavations at Hadleigh Castle, Essex, 1971–1972', P L Drewett, *Journal of the British Archaeological Association* 3 ser 38 (1975), 90–154*

'Medieval pot quern from Hadleigh Castle', D G Buckley and H Major, *Essex Archaeology and History* 15 (1983), 175–76*

'Excavations at Hadleigh Castle, 1971: an interim report', P L Drewett, *Essex Journal* 7.2 (1972), 37–44*

'Hadleigh Castle: a second interim report', P L Drewett, *ibid* 8.3 (1973), 79–87*

'Medieval Britain in 1971', L E Webster and J Cherry, *Medieval Archaeology* 16 (1972), 179–81*

'Medieval Britain in 1972', L E Webster and J Cherry, *ibid* 17 (1973), 161–62*

'Medieval Britain and Ireland in 2004', M Gaimster and K O'Conor, *ibid* 49 (2005), 361–62

'The development of an abandoned cliff in London clay at Hadleigh Castle, Essex', J N Hutchinson and T P Gostelow, *Proceedings of the Royal Society of London* A 283 (1976), 557–604*

Harwich

Harwich Redoubt. Anon. [Harwich]: Harwich Society, n d*

Harwich Redoubt. Anon. [Harwich]: Harwich Society, [c 1987]*

Beacon Hill Fort, Harwich, Essex. M Brown and P Pattison. Cambridge: RCHME, 1997*

Beacon Hill ancient monument: draft action and management plan. Tendering District Council. Clacton-on-Sea: Tendering District Council, 1989*

'The Redoubt, Harwich', R G W Prescott, in N J G Pounds (ed), *The Colchester area: proceedings of the 139th summer meeting of the Royal Archaeological Institute, 1992*, 54–55. London: RAI, 1992

'Dovercourt, Bathside Bay', S Godbold, in P J Gilman (ed), 'Archaeology in Essex 1991', *Essex Archaeology and History* 23 (1992), 104–5*

'A Napoleonic coastal gun battery: excavations at Bathside Bay, Harwich 1990–91', S Godbold, *ibid* 25 (1994), 193–218*

'The defences of Harwich', C Trollope, *Fort* 11 (1983), 5–30*

'Post-medieval Britain and Ireland in 1990', M Ponsford, *Post-Medieval Archaeology* 25 (1991), 120

'Post-medieval Britain and Ireland in 1991', M Ponsford, *ibid* 26 (1992), 106

Hedingham

Hedingham Castle. Anon. Derby: English Life Publications, 1983*

Hedingham Castle, Castle Hedingham, Essex. M Brown. Cambridge: RCHME, 1995*

'Castle Hedingham', D Andrews, in N J G Pounds (ed), *The Colchester area: proceedings of the 139th summer meeting of the Royal Archaeological Institute, 1992*, 16–17. London: RAI, 1992

'The great tower at Hedingham Castle: a reassessment', P Dixon and P Marshall, in R Liddiard (ed), *Anglo-Norman castles*, 297–306. Woodbridge: Boydell Press, 2003*

'The great tower at Hedingham Castle: a reassessment', P Dixon and P Marshall, *Fortress* 18 (1993), 16–23*

Jaywick

'Martello tower 'C', Lion Point, Jaywick, near Clacton-on-Sea', D Went, *Essex Archaeology and History* 31 (2000), 306–7*

Lower Hope Point

'Thames defences: Lower Hope Point battery', T Wilson, *The Redan* 64 (2005), 28–29

Mount Bures

'A medieval excavation at Mount Bures, 1969', I MacMaster, *Colchester Archaeological Group Bulletin* 12.3 (1969), 30–39*

'A rescue excavation at Mount Bures, autumn, 1970', I MacMaster, *ibid* 15 (1972), 16–18*

'The investigation of a mound at Mount Bures, Essex, 1972', P R Holbert, *ibid* 16 (1973), 3–8*

'Contour survey of Mount Bures', R Clarke, *Essex Archaeology and History* 33 (2002), 378–80*

'A medieval excavation at Mount Bures', I MacMaster, *Essex Journal* 5.2 (1970), 62–69*

Mountfichet

'The castle time forgot: Mountfichet Castle', anon, *Heritage Interpretation* 33 (1986), 5*

North Weald Redoubt

North Weald Redoubt, Essex: an archaeological survey of the late 19th-century mobilisation centre. L Barker and P Pattison. Cambridge: RCHME, 2000*

Pleshey

Pleshey Castle: first interim report. P A Rahtz. Colchester: Essex Archaeological Society, 1960*

Pleshey Castle, Essex (XII-XVI century): excavations in the bailey, 1959–1963. F Williams. Oxford: British Archaeological Reports, 1977 (British series; 42)

'Utrecht between Pleshey Castle (Essex) and the Hasker Convent (Friesland): the origin and distribution of late thirteenth- and early fourteenth-century decorated floor tiles in the Netherlands', C A M Van Rooijen and T J Hoekstra, in E de Bièvre (ed), *Utrecht: Britain and the Continent: archaeology, art and architecture*, 209–15. Leeds: British Archaeological Association and Maney Publishing, 1996* (Conference transactions; 18)

'Two medieval drawings', J A Goodall, *Antiquaries Journal* 58 (1978), 159–62*

'Pleshey', anon, *The Archaeologist in Essex, Hertfordshire, London and Middlesex* (1959), 10

'Pleshey Castle', anon, *ibid* (1960), 9–10

'An Englishman's home: Pleshey Castle, Essex', E Macdonnell, *Country Life* 170 (1981), 718–19*

'Pleshey Castle – the northern bailey: excavations at the village hall site', D Priddy, *Essex Archaeology and History* 19 (1988), 166–75*

'Pleshey, The Street', D Priddy, in A Bennett and P Gilman (eds), 'The work of the Essex County Council Section 1988', *ibid* 20 (1989), 151

'Moat Cottage, The Street, Pleshey: excavations 1988', C P Clarke and N J Lavender, *ibid* 30 (1999), 266–72*

'Medieval Britain in 1959', D M Wilson and J G Hurst, *Medieval Archaeology* 4 (1960), 145–46

'Medieval Britain in 1962 and 1963', D M Wilson and D G Hurst, *ibid* 8 (1964), 252–53

'Medieval Britain in 1968', D M Wilson and D G Hurst, *ibid* 13 (1969), 255

'Medieval Britain in 1973', L E Webster and J Cherry, *ibid* 18 (1974), 196

'Medieval Britain in 1976', L E Webster and J Cherry, *ibid* 21 (1977), 235

'Medieval Britain in 1977', L E Webster and J Cherry, *ibid* 22 (1978), 169–70*

'Medieval Britain in 1979', L E Webster and J Cherry, *ibid* 24 (1980), 247

'Medieval Britain in 1980', S M Youngs and J Clark, *ibid* 25 (1981), 200

'Medieval Britain in 1981', S M Youngs and J Clark, *ibid* 26 (1982), 183

'Medieval Britain and Ireland in 1985', S M Youngs, J Clark and T Barry, *ibid* 30 (1986), 134

'Medieval Britain and Ireland in 1987', S M Youngs [*et al*], *ibid* 32 (1988), 241

'Pleshey', anon, *Thames Basin Archaeological Observers' Group Newsletter* new ser 5 (1961), 19

Purleigh
'Work of the County Council Archaeology Section, 1981: sixth annual report. 16. Purleigh', D Priddy (ed), *Essex Archaeology and History* 14 (1982), 125–27*

'Purleigh, Purleigh Mount', D Andrews, in A Bennett and P Gilman (eds), 'The work of the Essex County Council Archaeology Section 1988', *ibid* 20 (1989), 151*

Rayleigh
Rayleigh Mount. L Helliwell and D G Macleod. 2nd edition. Rayleigh: Rayleigh Mount Committee of the National Trust, 1965*

Documentary evidence and report on excavations 1959–1961 and report on ex-

cavations 1969–1970. L Helliwell and D G Macleod. Rayleigh: Rayleigh Mount Committee of the National Trust, 1981*

'Rayleigh, mill site', L Helliwell and D G Macleod, *Archaeological Excavations 1970*, 76. London: HMSO, 1971

'Rayleigh', *The Archaeologist in Essex, Hertfordshire, London and Middlesex* (1959), 10–11

'Rayleigh', anon, *ibid* (1960), 10

'A find of Stephen coins at Rayleigh Mount', R Seaman with S E Rigold, *British Numismatic Journal* 38 (1969), 186–88*

'Excavations at Bellingham Lane, Rayleigh, Essex', B Milton, *Essex Archaeology and History* 18 (1987), 39–44*

'The outer bailey ditch at Rayleigh Castle: observations at 23 Bellingham Lane, Rayleigh, 1991', S Godbold, *ibid* 28 (1997), 290–92*

'Rayleigh Castle', D G Macleod, *Essex Journal* 5.3 (1970), 112–15

'Medieval Britain in 1968', D M Wilson and D G Hurst, *Medieval Archaeology* 13 (1969), 255

'Medieval Britain in 1969', D M Wilson and D G Hurst, *ibid* 14 (1970), 176

'Medieval Britain in 1970', D M Wilson and D G Hurst, *ibid* 15 (1971), 145–46

'Medieval Britain and Ireland in 1983', S M Youngs, J Clark and T B Barry, *ibid* 28 (1984), 217

'Medieval Britain and Ireland in 1985', S M Youngs, J Clark and T Barry, *ibid* 30 (1986), 134–35

'Medieval Britain and Ireland in 1997', M Gaimster, C Haith and J Bradley, *ibid* 42 (1998), 125

Saffron Walden

Saffron Walden: excavations and research 1972–80. S R Bassett. London: CBA, 1982* (Research report; 45)

'Saffron Walden', S R Bassett, *Archaeological Excavations 1972*, 84–85. London: HMSO, 1973

'Saffron Walden, Barnard's Yard, High Street/Church Street', M Petchey, *Archaeological Excavations 1975*, 91. London: HMSO, 1976

'Excavations at Fairycroft House, Saffron Walden, 1990', H Brooks, *Essex Archaeology and History* 27 (1991), 183–87*

'Chepying Walden 1381–1420: a study from court rolls', D Cromarty, *Essex Journal* 2 (1967), 104–13*

'Medieval Britain in 1972', L E Webster and J Cherry, *Medieval Archaeology* 17 (1973), 161

'Medieval Britain in 1973', L E Webster and J Cherry, *ibid* 18 (1974), 196

'Medieval Britain in 1975', L E Webster and J Cherry, *ibid* 20 (1976), 184

'Medieval Britain and Ireland in 1986', S M Youngs, J Clark and T Barry, *ibid* 31 (1987), 124

'Medieval Britain and Ireland in 1992', B S Nenk, S Margeson and M Hurley, *ibid* 37 (1993), 258

'Medieval Britain and Ireland in 1994', B S Nenk, S Margeson and M Hurley, *ibid* 39 (1995), 201

'Medieval Britain and Ireland in 2002', J Bradley and M Gaimster, *ibid* 47 (2003), 235

'Medieval Britain and Ireland in 2005', M Gaimster and K O'Conor, *ibid* 50 (2006), 309

Springfield

'Post-medieval Britain and Ireland in 1998 and 1999', M Ponsford, *Post-Medieval Archaeology* 34 (2000), 229

Stifford

'Post-medieval Britain and Ireland in 1988', G Egan, *ibid* 23 (1989), 32

Tilbury

Tilbury Fort, Essex. P. Pattison. London: English Heritage, 2004*

Tilbury Fort, Essex. A D Saunders. London: HMSO, 1960*

Tilbury Fort, Essex. A D Saunders. London: HBMCE, 1985*

Tilbury Fort: a handbook for teachers. F Dale. London: English Heritage, 1989*

'Tilbury Fort and the development of artillery fortifications in the Thames estuary', A D Saunders, *Antiquaries Journal* 40 (1960), 152–74*

'Excavations in Essex, 1980. 27. West Tilbury, Tilbury Fort', M R Eddy (ed), *Essex Archaeology and History* 13 (1981), 54–55

'The medieval hospitals at East Tilbury and West Tilbury and Henry VIII's forts', W R Powell, *ibid* 19 (1988), 154–58*

'West Tilbury, Tilbury Fort', P J Moore, in A Bennett and P Gilman (eds), 'The work of the Essex County Council Archaeology Section 1988', *ibid* 20 (1989), 169

'Tilbury Fort', R Duncan, *Essex Journal* 9 (1974–5), 131–36*

'Tilbury Fort, Essex', P Wilkinson, *ibid* 19 (1984), 64*

'"Speed bonny boat …". Tilbury Fort and the '45 rebellion', R Binsley, *ibid* 31.2 (1996), 43–47, 53*

'Tilbury Fort – England', K Van Doninck, *Mededelingenblad van de Simon Steven-stichting* 1.4 (1986), 27–32*

'East Tilbury fortifications and Coalhouse Fort', I G Sparkes, *Thurrock Local History Society Journal* 7 (1962), 3–12

'Tilbury Fort and the rebellion of 1745', M K Southern, *Panorama: Journal of the Thurrock Local History Society* 15 (1971–2),, 44–58*

'Tilbury blockhouse and fort', anon, *ibid* 22 (1979), 57

'Excavations at Tilbury Fort, Essex, 1980', P M Wilkinson, *ibid* 24 (1980), 43–44

'Excavations at Tilbury Fort, Essex', P M Wilkinson, *Post-Medieval Archaeology* 17 (1983), 111–62*

'Post-medieval Britain and Ireland in 1988', G Egan, *ibid* 23 (1989), 32–33

'Post-medieval Britain and Ireland in 1989', G Egan, *ibid* 24 (1990), 165–66

'Post-medieval Britain and Ireland in 1990', G Egan, *ibid* 25 (1991), 120–22*

'Post-medieval Britain and Ireland in 2003', M Ponsford, *ibid* 38 (2004), 317

'A tale of two forts', I Stevenson, *The Redan* 58 (2003), 18–31*

'Integrating research and outreach at Tilbury Fort, Essex', P Pattison, *Research News: Newsletter of the English Heritage Research Department* 1 (2005), 25–27*

GLOUCESTERSHIRE

Dean Archaeological Group. *Castle sites survey 2000/1: a survey of castle sites, possible and actual, in the Forest of Dean and adjoining parishes*. [S l]: Dean Archaeological Group, [2001]*

Endacott, A and Kelleher, S (eds). *Heritage unlocked: a guide to free sites in Bristol, Gloucestershire and Wiltshire*. London: English Heritage, 2004*

Iles, R. 'Medieval castles and monasteries', in M Aston and R Iles (eds), *The archaeology of Avon: a review from the Neolithic to the Middle Ages*, 122–29. Bristol: Avon County Council, [1987]*

Rahtz, P [et al]. 'Norman castles', in *Medieval sites in the Mendip, Cotswolds, Wye Valley and Bristol region*, 14–17. Bristol: Bristol Archaeological Research Group, 1969 (Field guide; 3)

Rawes, B. 'A check list of castles and other fortified sites of medieval date in Gloucestershire', *Glevensis* 11 (1977), 39–41

Robertson, M. *Exploring England's heritage: Dorset to Gloucestershire*. London: HMSO, in association with English Heritage, 1992* [espec ch 2]

Salter, M. *The castles of Gloucestershire and Bristol*. Malvern: Folly Publications, 2002*

Stevenson, I. 'The Bristol Channel and Swansea defences', *The Redan* 50 (2000), 28–51*

Verey, D and Brooks, A. *Gloucestershire 1. The Cotswolds (The buildings of England)*. 3rd edition. London: Penguin Books, 1999*

Verey, D and Brooks, A. *Gloucestershire 2. The Vale and the Forest of Dean (The buildings of England)*. 3rd edition. London: Yale University Press, 2002*

Walker, D. 'Gloucestershire castles', *Transactions of the Bristol and Gloucester-shire Archaeological Society* 109 (1991), 5–23*

Bagpath

'Wotton-under-Edge notes: Bagpath Castle mound', E S Lindley, *ibid* 73 (1954), 234

Berkeley

Berkeley Castle. V Sackville-West. Derby: English Life Publications, n d*

'Berkeley Castle', P A Faulkner, *Archaeological Journal* 122 (1965), 197–200

'Berkeley Castle, Gloucestershire', C Hussey, *Country Life* 118 (1955), 1430–33*

'The Anglo-Norman inscriptions at Berkeley Castle', D A Trotter, *Medium Aevum* 59 (1990), 114–20*

Beverstone

'Beverstone Castle', N Pounds, in N H Cooper (ed), *The Cirencester area: proceedings of the 134th summer meeting of the Royal Archaeological Institute, 1988*, 48–50. London: RAI, 1988*

'Beverstone Castle', P A Faulkner, *Archaeological Journal* 122 (1965), 201–2

Bledisloe

'Bledisloe Castle, Awre parish', A Dornier, *Archaeological Excavations 1964*, 11. London: 1965

'Bledisloe excavations, 1964', A Dornier, *Transactions of the Bristol and Gloucestershire Archaeological Society* 85 (1966), 57–69*

'Medieval Britain in 1964', D M Wilson and D G Hurst, *Medieval Archaeology* 9 (1965), 216

Brimpsfield

'Medieval Brimpsfield: reports and reflections', R F Butler, *Proceedings of the Cotteswold Naturalist Field Club* 33 (1957–61), 113–22*

'The history of Brimpsfield Castle and the Giffard family', A Dodd and P Moss, *Glevensis* 25 (1991), 34–37*

'Map and documentary interpretation in Brimpsfield parish', J R Newbury, *ibid* 27 (1993), 33–35*

Bristol

Bristol Castle: a political history. P Fleming. Bristol: Bristol Branch of the Historical Association, 2004* (Local history pamphlet; 110)

The St Michael's Hill precinct of the University of Bristol: medieval and early modern topography. R H Leech. Bristol: Bristol Record Society, 2000* (Publication; 52) [for Fort Royal, pp 17–21]

Bristol and the Civil War. P MacGrath. Bristol: Bristol Branch of the Historical Association, 1981*

William Worcestre: the topography of medieval Bristol. F Neale (ed). Bristol: Bristol Record Society, 2000* (Publication; 51)

The storming of Bristol 1643. S Peachey. Bristol: Stuart Press, 1993*

Bristol Castle: a short summary of the recent excavations. M W Ponsford. Bristol: City Museum, [1971?]

The Civil War defences of Bristol: their archaeology and topography. J Russell. Bristol: the author, 1995*; 2nd edition, 2003*

Account of the constables of Bristol Castle in the thirteenth and early fourteenth centuries. M Sharp (ed). Bristol: Bristol Record Society, 1982 (Publication; 34)

Anglo-Saxon and Norman Bristol. D Sivier. Stroud: Tempus, 2002* [espec ch 9]

'Aspects of the medieval defences of Bristol: the town wall, the castle barbican and the Jewry', R H Leech, in M Bowden, D Mackay and P Topping (eds), *From Cornwall to Caithness: some aspects of British field archaeology. Papers presented to Norman V Quinnell*, 235–50. Oxford: British Archaeological Reports, 1989* (British series; 209)

'The medieval defences of Bristol revisited', R H Leech, in L Keen (ed), *'Almost the richest city': Bristol in the Middle Ages*, 18–30. Leeds: British Archaeological Association and Maney Publishing, 1997* (Conference transactions; 19)

'Bristol', M D Lobel and E M Carus-Wilson, in M D Lobel (ed), *The atlas of historic towns*, **2**. London: Scolar Press, 1975*

'Bristol', M Ponsford, in M Aston and R Iles (eds), *The archaeology of Avon: a review from the Neolithic to the Middle Ages*, 144–59. Bristol: Avon County Council, [1987]*

'Excavation at the town wall, Bristol, 1974', R Price, in N Thomas (ed), *Rescue archaeology in the Bristol area: 1*, 15–27. Bristol: City of Bristol Museum and Art Gallery, 1979*

'Bristol', M W Ponsford, *Archaeological Excavations 1969*, 63. London; HMSO, 1970

'Bristol', M W Ponsford, *Archaeological Excavations 1970*, 75. London; HMSO, 1971

'Bristol, Newgate', R Jones, in R Iles and A Kidd, 'Avon archaeology, 1986 & 1987', *Bristol and Avon Archaeology* 6 (1987), 49

'An excavation at Broad Quay (Watergate), Bristol, 1979', R Price, *ibid* 9 (1990–1), 24–28*

'Bristol Castle keep: a re-appraisal of the evidence and report on the excavations in 1989', G L Good, *ibid* 13 (1996), 17–45*

'Excavations on the Marsh Wall, King Street, Bristol', R Burchill, *ibid* 13 (1996), 11–16*

'Excavations in the city of Bristol, 1948–51', K Marshall, *Transactions of the Bristol and Gloucestershire Archaeological Society* 70 (1951), 5–50*

'Excavation by the town wall, Baldwin Street, Bristol, 1957', P A Rahtz, *ibid* 79 (1960), 221–50*

'A group of medieval jugs from Bristol Castle well', K J Barton, *ibid* 80 (1961), 169–74*

'Excavations on the medieval defences, Portwall Lane, Bristol, 1965', M Hebditch, *ibid* 87 (1968), 131–43*

'Archaeology in Bristol 1986–89', M Ponsford [*et al*], *ibid* 107 (1989), 243–51*

'Archaeology in Bristol 1989', M Ponsford, *ibid* 108 (1990), 175–83*

'A hidden workforce: building workers in 14th-century Bristol', S A C Penn, *ibid* 109 (1991), 171–78

'Castle Park', L Good, in B Rawes (ed), 'Archaeological review no. 18 1993', *ibid* 112 (1994), 197

'Redcliffe Way', L Good, in *ibid*, 197

'Excavations at Bristol Castle, 1969', M W Ponsford, *Bristol Archaeological Research Group Bulletin* 3.5 (1969), 121–22

'Bristol's answer to the Luftwaffe', N Roberts, *Bristol Archaeological Research Group Review* 2 (1981), 59–65*

'Bristol, Castle and Queen Sts', M G Hebditch, *CBA Groups 12 and 13 Archaeological Review* 1 (1966), 42

'Bristol, the castle', M W Ponsford, *ibid* 3 (1968), 26

'Bristol, the castle', M W Ponsford, *ibid* 4 (1969), 54–55

'Bristol, Bristol Castle', M W Ponsford, *ibid* 5 (1970), 32–34*

'Bristol, Newgate', D Dawson and R G Jackson, *ibid* 6 (1971), 40

'Bristol, Royal Fort', R H Price and R G Jackson, *ibid* 7 (1972), 62

'Bristol University digs up its own front lawn. The Royal Fort Bristol', K S Gardner, *Council for British Archaeology South West Journal* 7 (2001), 11*

'The Civil War defences of Bristol', J Russell, *ibid* 12 (2004), 19–26*

'Tower Harratz, Bristol', R Jackson, *Current Archaeology* 12.10 (1995), 387*

'Medieval Britain in 1957', D M Wilson and J G Hurst, *Medieval Archaeology* 2 (1958), 197–98

'Medieval Britain in 1960', D M Wilson and J G Hurst, *ibid* 5 (1961), 322

'The excavation of a medieval bastion at St Nicholas's Almshouses, King Street, Bristol', K J Barton, *ibid* 8 (1964), 182–212*

'Medieval Britain in 1962 and 1963', D M Wilson and D G Hurst, *ibid* 8 (1964), 265

'Medieval Britain in 1965', D M Wilson and D G Hurst, *ibid* 10 (1966), 198

'Medieval Britain in 1968', D M Wilson and D G Hurst, *ibid* 13 (1969), 255–58*

'Medieval Britain in 1969', D M Wilson and D G Hurst, *ibid* 14 (1970), 176

'Medieval Britain in 1970', D M Wilson and S Moorhouse, *ibid* 15 (1971), 146, 152

'Medieval Britain in 1971', L E Webster and J Cherry, *ibid* 16 (1972), 181

'Medieval Britain in 1974', L E Webster and J Cherry, *ibid* 19 (1975), 242–43

'Medieval Britain in 1975', L E Webster and J Cherry, *ibid* 20 (1976), 187

'Medieval Britain in 1976', L E Webster and J Cherry, *ibid* 21 (1977), 242

'Medieval Britain in 1980', S M Youngs and J Clark, *ibid* 25 (1981), 205

'Medieval Britain and Ireland in 1982', S M Youngs, J Clark and T B Barry, *ibid* 27 (1983), 164–65

'Medieval Britain and Ireland in 1983', S M Youngs, J Clark and T Barry, *ibid* 28 (1984), 207

'Medieval Britain and Ireland in 1984', S M Youngs, J Clark and T Barry, *ibid* 29 (1985), 162

'Medieval Britain and Ireland in 1987', S M Youngs [*et al*], *ibid* 32 (1988), 230

'Medieval Britain and Ireland in 1989', D R M Gaimster, S Margeson and M Hurley, *ibid* 34 (1990), 167–68*

'Medieval Britain and Ireland in 1990', B S Nenk, S Margeson and M Hurley, *ibid* 35 (1991), 132

'Medieval Britain and Ireland in 1992', B S Nenk, S Margeson and M Hurley, *ibid* 37 (1993), 246

'Medieval Britain and Ireland in 1993', B S Nenk, S Margeson and M Hurley, *ibid* 38 (1994), 191

'Medieval Britain and Ireland in 1994', B S Nenk, S Margeson and M Hurley, *ibid* 39 (1995), 186–87

'Medieval Britain and Ireland in 1995', B S Nenk, S Margeson and M Hurley, *ibid* 40 (1996), 240, 241

'Medieval Britain and Ireland in 1996', B S Nenk, C Haith and J Bradley, *ibid* 41 (1997), 247

'Medieval Britain and Ireland in 1998', J Bradley, M Gaimster and C Haith, *ibid* 43 (1999), 235

'Medieval Britain and Ireland in 1999', J Bradley and M Gaimster, *ibid* 44 (2000), 247

'Medieval Britain and Ireland in 2000', J Bradley and M Gaimster, *ibid* 45 (2001), 258–60

'Medieval Britain and Ireland in 2004', M Gaimster and K O'Conor, *ibid* 49 (2005), 353

'Post-medieval Britain in 1969', D G Hurst, *Post-Medieval Archaeology* 4 (1970), 174

'Post-medieval Britain in 1972', J Cherry, *ibid* 7 (1973), 100

'Post-medieval Britain in 1974', J Cherry, *ibid* 9 (1975), 240

'Post-medieval Britain and Ireland in 1989', G Egan, *ibid* 24 (1990), 171

'Post-medieval Britain and Ireland in 1993', G Egan, *ibid* 28 (1994), 126

'Post-medieval Britain and Ireland in 1994', M Ponsford and R Jackson, *ibid* 29 (1995), 121–22

'Post-medieval Britain and Ireland in 1995', M Ponsford and R Jackson, *ibid* 30 (1996), 248

'Post-medieval Britain and Ireland in 1996', M Ponsford and R Jackson, *ibid* 31 (1997), 261–62

'Post-medieval Britain and Ireland in 2002', M Ponsford, *ibid* 37 (2003), 231–32

'Post-medieval Britain and Ireland in 2003', M Ponsford, *ibid* 38 (2004), 244

'Exciting new discoveries at Bristol Castle', B Williams, *Rescue News* 56 (1992), 3*

'Bristol's medieval and Civil War defences', S Cox, *ibid* 73 (1997), 4*

Doynton

'Doynton, Freezing Hill, royal camp', E K Tratman, *CBA Groups 12 and 13 Archaeological Review* 7 (1972), 22

English Bicknor

'English Bicknor, castle', N P Spry, *CBA Groups 12 and 13 Archaeological Review* 6 (1971), 40

'English Bicknor Castle', N P Spry, *Glevensis* 6 (1972), 5

'English Bicknor Castle', anon, *Herefordshire Archaeological News* 50 (1988), 7–9*

Gloucester

Gloucester and the Civil War: a city under siege. M Atkin and W Laughlin. Stroud: Alan Sutton, 1992*

Garrod's Gloucester: archaeological observations 1974–81. A P Garrod and C H Heighway. [Bristol]: Western Archaeological Trust, [1984]*

Gloucester 1974. C Heighway. Bristol: Committee for Rescue Archaeology in Avon, Gloucestershire and Somerset, 1975*

The east gate of Gloucester. C Heighway. Gloucester: City Museum and Art Gallery, 1980*

FORTIFICATIONS BIBLIOGRAPHY

The east and north gates of Gloucester and associated sites: excavations 1974–81. C Heighway. [Bristol]: Western Archaeological Trust, 1983*

Gloucester: a history and guide. C Heighway. Gloucester: Alan Sutton, 1985*

Gloucester, the Roman and later defences: excavations on the E. defences and a reassessment of the defensive sequence. H R Hurst. Gloucester: Gloucester Archaeological Publications, 1986*

Historic Gloucester: an illustrated guide to the city, its buildings, the cathedral and the docks. P Moss. Moreton-in-Marsh: Windrush Press, 1993*

'Gloucester', M D Lobel and J Tann, in M D Lobel (ed), *Historic towns*, **1**. Oxford: Lovell Johns-Cook, Hammond and Kell Organization, 1969*

'Bridges, gates and walls', and 'Gloucester Castle', N M Herbert, in N M Herbert (ed), *The Victoria history of the counties of England. A history of the county of Gloucester. 4. The city of Gloucester*, 242–47. Oxford: OUP, for the Institute of Historical Research, 1988*

'Excavations at Gloucester, 1968–71: first interim report', H Hurst, *Antiquaries Journal* 52 (1972), 24–69*

'Excavations at Gloucester, 1971–1973: second interim report', H Hurst, *ibid* 54 (1974), 8–52*

'Medieval Gloucester', L E W O Fullbrook-Leggatt, *Transactions of the Bristol and Gloucestershire Archaeological Society* 66 (1945), 1–48*

'The siege of Gloucester, 1643', A R Williams, *ibid* 88 (1969), 173–83

'The archaeology of Gloucester Castle: an introduction', H Hurst, *ibid* 102 (1984), 73–128*

'Gloucester, 28–32 Commercial Road', T C Darvill, in B Rawes (ed), 'Archaeological review no 9, 1984', *ibid* 103 (1985), 232

'Gloucester Castle', A P Garrod, in B Rawes (ed), 'Archaeological review no 10', *ibid* 104 (1986), 237–38

'Archaeology in Gloucester in 1988', M Atkin and A P Garrod, *ibid* 107 (1989), 233–42*

'Archaeology in Gloucester in 1989', M Atkin and A P Garrod, *ibid* 108 (1990), 185–92*

'MEB Works, Barbican Road', M Atkin, in B Rawes (ed), 'Archaeological review no 15, 1990', *ibid* 109 (1991), 229

'Blackfriars Way (MEB oil tank)', M Atkin, in *ibid* 109 (1991), 229

'Brunswick Road sewer trench', P Greatorex, in *ibid* 109 (1991), 230

'Clarence Street sewer trench', P Greatorex, in *ibid* 109 (1991), 230

'Eastgate Street sewer renewal scheme', P Greatorex, in *ibid* 109 (1991), 230–31

'Gloucester archaeology 1900–1990: an historical review', M Atkin, *ibid* 110 (1992), 13–36*

'Gloucester's Civil War trades and industries, 1642–46', D Evans, *ibid* 110 (1992), 137–47

'David Papillon and the Civil War defences of Gloucester', M Atkin, *ibid* 111 (1993), 147–64*

'Siege!', M Atkin, *British Archaeology* 11 (1989), 6–10*

'Gloucester', [A Selkirk], *Current Archaeology* 3 (1971–2), 77–83*

'Gloucester's Norman castle rediscovered', M Atkin, *Fortress* 9 (1991), 20–23*

'The Civil War defences of Gloucester', M Atkin, *ibid* 10 (1991), 32–38*

'The north and east gates of Gloucester', C M Heighway, *Glevensis* 9 (1975), 3–6*

'Gloucester Castle: salvage brief', P Garrod, *ibid* 20 (1986), 28–29*

'Excavations in Gloucester 1988 - an interim report', M Atkin, *ibid* 23 (1989), 2–11*

'Excavations in Gloucester 1989 - an interim report', M Atkin, *ibid* 24 (1990), 2–13*

'Excavations in Gloucester 1990. Site 20/90: the MEB works, Barbican Road', M Atkin, *ibid* 25 (1991), 6–10*

'Observations on the Eastgate Street sewer renewal scheme, Gloucester, 1990 (site 4/90)', P Greatorex, *ibid* 25 (1991), 25–29*

'The medieval sieges of Gloucester, 1263–65', R Howes, *ibid* 35 (2002), 19–24*

'An eleventh-century bone *tabula* set from Gloucester', I J Stewart and M J Watkins, *Medieval Archaeology* 28 (1984), 185–90*

'Medieval Britain and Ireland in 1985', S M Youngs, J Clark and T Barry, *ibid* 30 (1986), 135–36

'Excavations on the site of the early Norman castle at Gloucester, 1983–84', T Darvill, *ibid* 32 (1988), 1–40*

'Medieval Britain and Ireland in 1990', B S Nenk, S Margeson and M Hurley, *ibid* 35 (1991), 146–48

'Medieval Britain and Ireland in 1994', B S Nenk, S Margeson and M Hurley, *ibid* 39 (1995), 202

'Medieval Britain and Ireland in 2004', M Gaimster and K O'Conor, *ibid* 49 (2005), 366

'Post-medieval archaeology in Gloucester: a review', M Atkin, *Post-Medieval Archaeology* 21 (1987), 1–24*

'Post-medieval Britain and Ireland in 1988', G Egan, *ibid* 23 (1989), 33

'Post-medieval Britain and Ireland in 1990', M Ponsford, *ibid* 25 (1991), 122–23

'The use of archaeology and documentary sources in identifying the Civil War defences of Gloucester', M Atkin and R Howes, *ibid* 27 (1993), 15–41*

Hewelsfield

'Hewelsfield Castle', P Remfry, *Herefordshire Archaeological News* 63 (1995), 45–46*

Hillesley

'Earthwork surveys of three sites in Avon', P Ellis, *Transactions of the Bristol and Gloucestershire Archaeological Society* 102 (1984), 206–10*

'Excavations of a medieval earthwork complex at Hillesley, Hawkesbury, Avon', B Williams, *ibid* 105 (1987), 147–63*

'Hillesley ringwork, Northavon', B Williams, *Bristol Archaeological Research Group Bulletin* 6.8 (1979), 204–6*

'Medieval Britain in 1979', L E Webster and J Cherry, *Medieval Archaeology* 24 (1980), 247–48*

'Medieval Britain and Ireland in 199', J Bradley and M Gaimster, *ibid* 44 (2000), 263

Holm

'Tewkesbury and the earls of Gloucester: excavations at Holm Hill, 1974–5', A Hannan, *Transactions of the Bristol and Gloucestershire Archaeological Society* 115 (1997), 79–231*

'Medieval Britain in 1974', L E Webster and J Cherry, *Medieval Archaeology* 19 (1975), 239–40*

'Medieval Britain in 1975', L E Webster and J Cherry, *ibid* 20 (1976), 184

Littledean

'Littledean Camp', C Scott-Garrett, *Transactions of the Bristol and Gloucestershire Archaeological Society* 77 (1958), 48–60*

St Briavels

The castle of St Briavels. A Clark. Chepstow: Chepstow Society, 1949*

St Briavels Castle: a handbook for teachers. R Clutterbuck. London: English Heritage, 1993*

St Briavels Castle 1066–1331. P M Remfry. Malvern Link: SCS Publishing, 1994*

A guide to St Briavels Castle in the Royal Forest of Dean. M Salter. Wolverhampton: Folly Publications, 1998*

'St Briavels Castle', D J C King, *125th annual meeting in Gwent and the Forest of Dean, 1978*, CAA, 1978, 10

'St Briavels Castle', D J C King, *Archaeological Journal* 122 (1965), 230

'St Briavels Castle', P E Curnow and E A Johnson, *Château Gaillard* 12 (1985), 91–114*

'St Briavels: the king's great arsenal', A Webb, *Dean Archaeology* 5 (1992), 18–24*

'The identification of quarrels: arrowheads from St Briavels 1223–1293 AD', A

Webb, *ibid* 6 (1993), 17*

'Medieval Britain and Ireland in 1994', B S Nenk, S Margeson and M Hurley, *Medieval Archaeology* 39 (1995), 202

Stowe
'Stowe "ringwork"', P Remfry, *Herefordshire Archaeological News* 63 (1995), 46*

Taynton
Taynton Parva deserted medieval village: its history and archaeology. S E Williams. Lydney: Dean Archaeological Group, 1996* (Occasional publication; 2)

'Taynton: Castle Hill earthwork', A F Dodd, *Glevensis* 14 (1980), 32*

'Taynton Parva', S Williams, *ibid* 30 (1997), 27–32*

Thornbury
'Thornbury Castle: Renaissance palace or stronghold of a feudal baron?', N Guy, *Castle Studies Group Journal* 19 (2006), 205–34*

'Thornbury Castle', A D K Hawkyard, *Transactions of the Bristol and Gloucestershire Archaeological Society* 95 (1977), 51–58*

Upper Slaughter
'Upper Slaughter, castle mound', J Wills, in B Rawes (ed), 'Archaeological review no 14', *Transactions of the Bristol and Gloucestershire Archaeological Society* 108 (1990), 198

'The Norman motte at Upper Slaughter, Gloucestershire', H O'Neil, *Proceedings of the Cotteswold Naturalist Field Club* 34.1–2 (1962–3), 32–36*

Winchcombe
'Winchcombe', J Hinchcliffe, *Archaeological Excavations 1972*, 13. London: HMSO, 1973

HAMPSHIRE AND THE ISLE OF WIGHT

Butchart, C B R. *Hampshire castles*. Winchester: Warren and Son, 1955*

Brading, P and Brading, W. 'William Brading (1817–1899): 3. Marchwood Magazine and the Hilsea Lines', *The Redan* 37 (1996), 2–8

Cantwell, A. 'The Needles defences', *Fort* 13 (1985), 69–88*

Cantwell, A. 'Facing the old enemy: the Victorian defence of the Isle of Wight', *Hatcher Review* 3.23 (1987), 147–56*

Cantwell, A and Sprack, P. *The Needles defences 1525–1956*. St Helens: Redoubt Consultancy, 1986* (Solent papers; 2)

Cobb, P. 'What the bird did (or did not) see of the Palmerston forts 1945–50', *The Redan* 42 (1998), 2–6

Corney, A 'The Portsmouth fortress', *Journal of the Royal Society of Arts* 131.5326 (1983), 578–86*

Elliott, J (ed). *Heritage unlocked: guide to free sites in London and the south east*. London; English Heritage, 2005*

Hughes, M. 'Settlement and landscape in medieval Hampshire', in S J Shennan and R T Schadla-Hall (eds), *The archaeology of Hampshire from the palaeolithic to the industrial revolution*, 66–77. [S l]: Hampshire Field Club and Archaeological Society, 1981*

Hughes, M. 'The fourteenth-century French raids on Hampshire and the Isle of Wight', in A Curry and M Hughes (eds), *Arms, armies and fortifications in the Hundred Years War*, 121–43. Woodbridge: Boydell Press, 1994*

Hughes, M. 'Hampshire castles and the landscape: 1066–1216', *Landscape History* 11 (1989), 27–60*

[Insole, A [et al]]. *Victoria's forts*. Newport: Isle of Wight County Council, n d*

Kenyon, J R. 'James Fergusson: a critic of early Victorian military architecture', *Fort* 8 (1980), 47–54*

Kenyon, J R. 'An aspect of the 1559 survey of the Isle of Wight: *The state of all the Quenes ma^{ties} fortresses and castelles*', *Post-Medieval Archaeology* 13 (1979), 61–77*

Kitchen, F. 'John Norden's 'Speculum Britanniae: pars – the Isle of Wight' and some Elizabethan maps of the island', *Proceedings of the Hampshire Field Club and Archaeological Society* 47 (1992), 181–89*

Lloyd, D W and Pevsner, N. *The Isle of Wight (The buildings of England)*. London: Yale University Press, 2006*

Moore, D. 'The 13-inch mortar', *The Redan* 58 (2003), 32–41*

Patterson, A T. *'Palmerston's folly': the Portsdown and Spithead forts*. Portsmouth: Portsmouth City Council, 1967* (Portsmouth Papers; 3)

Pevsner, N and Lloyd, D. *Hampshire and the Isle of Wight (The buildings of England)*. Harmondsworth: Penguin Books, 1967*

Phillips-Birt, D. 'Repelling the Solent's invaders', *Country Life* 142 (1967), 224, 226–27*

Salter, M. *The castles of Wessex*. Malvern: Folly Publications, 2002*

Saunders, A D. *Hampshire coastal defence since the introduction of artillery with a description of Fort Wallington*. [London]: RAI, 1977*

Saunders, A D. 'Hampshire coastal defence since the introduction of artillery', *Archaeological Journal* 123 (1966), 136–71*

Barley Pound

'Lidelea Castle – a suggested identification', D J C King and D F Renn, *Antiquaries*

Journal 51 (1971), 301–3*

'Castles of mystery', E Manning, *Farnham Museum Society Newsletter* 1.12 (1968), 8–10

Basing House

Basing House, Hampshire: excavations 1978–1991. D Allen and S Anderson. [S l]: Hampshire Field Club & Archaeological Society, 1999* (Monograph; 10)

'Basingstoke – Basing House, gatehouse', R T Schadla-Hall, *Archaeology in Hampshire: Annual Report for 1981*, 1982, 22–23

'Basingstoke – Basing House, gatehouse', K J Barton, *Archaeology in Hampshire: Annual Report for 1982*, 1983, 35

'Basing – Basing House', K J Barton and D Allen, *Archaeology in Hampshire: Annual Report for 1983*, 1985, 48–52*

'Basing – Basing House', D Allen, *Archaeology in Hampshire: Annual Report for 1990*, 1991, 48–51*

'Basing – Basing House', D Allen, *Archaeology in Hampshire: Annual Report for 1991*, 1992, 30–34* [illustration is a phased plan of the main gate, not the postern gate on which this is a report]

'Basingstoke, Old Basin', P C Orde-Powlett, *CBA Groups 12 and 13 Archaeological Review* 1 (1966), 36

'Basing House', K J Barton, *CBA Newsletter and Calendar* 6 (1982–3), 156

'Basing House, Hampshire', K J Barton, *ibid* 7 (1983–4), 135

'A stronghold of the Civil War', N Roskill, *Country Life* 122 (1957), 810, 813*

'Basing House', D Allen and A Turton, *Current Archaeology* 12.10 (1995), 388–92*

'Excavations near Basing House, 1962–63', H H M Pike and R C Combley, *Proceedings of the Hampshire Field Club and Archaeological Society* 23 (1964–6), 11–20*

'Medieval Britain in 1962 and 1963', D M Wilson and D G Hurst, *Medieval Archaeology* 8 (1964), 253

'Medieval Britain in 1965', D M Wilson and D G Hurst, *ibid* 10(1966), 190

'Finds from Basing House (*c* 1540–1645): part 1', S Moorhouse, *Post-Medieval Archaeology* 4 (1970), 31–91*

'Finds from Basing House (*c* 1540–1645): part 2', S Moorhouse, *ibid* 5 (1971), 35–76*

'Post-medieval Britain in 1983', G Egan, *ibid* 18 (1984), 316

Bentley

Excavations of a mid-12th century siege castle at Bentley, Hampshire: interim report 1979. P A Stamper. Winchester: County Planning Department, 1979*

'Excavations on a mid-twelfth century siege castle at Bentley, Hampshire', P A

Stamper, *Proceedings of the Hampshire Field Club and Archaeological Society* 40 (1984), 81–89*

'Medieval Britain in 1979', L E Webster and J Cherry, *Medieval Archaeology* 24 (1980), 247

'Medieval Britain in 1980', S M Youngs and J Clark, *ibid* 25 (1981), 200–1

Binstead
'A medieval earthwork at Binstead, near Alton', M A B Lyne, *Proceedings of the Hampshire Field Club and Archaeological Society* 46 (1990), 185–88*

Bishop's Waltham
Three palaces of the bishops of Winchester: Wolvesey (Old Bishop's Palace), Hampshire; Bishop's Waltham Palace, Hampshire; Farnham Castle keep, Surrey. J Wareham. London: English Heritage, 2000*

'Bishop's Waltham Palace', S E Rigold, *Archaeological Journal* 123 (1966), 217

'Bishop's Waltham Palace, Hampshire: William of Wykeham, Henry Beaufort and the transformation of a medieval episcopal palace', J N Hare, *ibid* 145 (1988), 222–54*

'Medieval Britain in 1956', D M Wilson and J G Hurst, *Medieval Archaeology* 1 (1957), 154

'Medieval Britain in 1957', D M Wilson and J G Hurst, *ibid* 2 (1958), 194

'Medieval Britain in 1960', D M Wilson and D G Hurst, *ibid* 5 (1961), 317

'Medieval Britain in 1961', D M Wilson and D G Hurst, *ibid* 6–7 (1962–3), 319

'Medieval Britain in 1962 and 1963', D M Wilson and D G Hurst, *ibid* 8 (1964), 248

'Medieval Britain in 1964', D M Wilson and D G Hurst, *ibid* 9 (1965), 184

'Medieval Britain in 1968', D M Wilson and D G Hurst, *ibid* 13 (1969), 249–50

Breamore
'Breamore Mill', N Walker, *Loopholes* 21 (198), 24–29* [pillboxes]

Calshot
Calshot Castle, Hampshire. J G Coad. London: HBMCE, 1986*; 2nd edition, 1991*

Hurst and Calshot castles: information for teachers. R Cooper. London: English Heritage, 1996*

'Calshot Castle: the later history of a Tudor fortress, 1793–1945', J Coad, *English Heritage Historical Review* 1 (2006), 102–13*

'Some lesser known Henrician castles', J Malpas, *Fort* 4 (1977), 2–3*; pp 87–91* in 1995 revised edition of *Fort* vols 4–5

'Repairs to Calshot Castle in 1612', C F Bühler, *Proceedings of the Hampshire Field Club and Archaeological Society* 17 (1952), 247–51*

ENGLAND

Carisbrooke

Carisbrooke Castle: an illustrated guide. Anon. 2nd edition. London: HMSO, 1972*

Carisbrooke Castle. R Chamberlain. London: HBMCE, 1985*

Carisbrooke Castle: teacher's resource book. R Cooper. London: English Heritage, 1988*

Carisbrooke Castle: a teacher's handbook. R Cooper. London: English Heritage, 2002*

Carisbrooke Castle, Isle of Wight. C Peers. London: HMSO, 1948*; 2nd edition, 1982*

Visiting the past: Carisbrooke Castle. J Shuter. Oxford: Heinemann Library, 1999*

Excavations at Carisbrooke Castle, Isle of Wight, 1921–1996. C J Young. Salisbury: Trust for Wessex Archaeology, 2000* (Wessex Archaeology report; 18)

Carisbrooke Castle. C Young. London: English Heritage, 2003*

'The Lower Enclosure at Carisbrooke Castle, Isle of Wight', C J Young, in B Hartley and J Wacher (eds), *Rome and her northern provinces*, 290–301. Gloucester: Alan Sutton, 1983*

'Carisbrooke Castle', C J Young, *CBA Newsletter and Calendar* 3 (1979–80), 135

'Recent investigations into the earliest defences of Carisbrooke Castle, Isle of Wight', S E Rigold, *Château Gaillard* 3 (1969), 128–38*

'Carisbrooke Castle to 1100', C J Young, *ibid* 11 (1983), 281–88*

'Carisbrooke Castle and the lords of the Isle of Wight', C B R Butchart, *Proceedings of the Hampshire Field Club and Archaeological Society* 21 (1958–60), 98–101*

'Thirteenth-century gardens in Carisbrooke Castle', M J Jones, *Proceedings of the Isle of Wight Natural History and Archaeological Society* 9 (1989), 135–36

' 'Wihtgarasbyrig' explored: a review/article considering *Excavations at Carisbrooke Castle, Isle of Wight, 1921–1996 …*', D Tomalin, *ibid* 18 (2002), 55–79*

'Medieval Britain in 1961', D M Wilson and D G Hurst, *Medieval Archaeology* 6–7 (1962–3), 321

'Medieval Britain in 1962 and 1963', D M Wilson and D G Hurst, *ibid* 8 (1964), 253

'Medieval Britain in 1965', D M Wilson and D G Hurst, *ibid* 10 (1966), 190

'Medieval Britain in 1967', D M Wilson and D G Hurst, *ibid* 12 (1968), 177

Christchurch

Christchurch Castle, Hampshire. M Wood. London: HMSO, 1956*

'Christchurch Castle', S E Rigold, *Archaeological Journal* 123 (1966), 204–5*

'Christchurch Castle, Hampshire', N Guy, *Castle Studies Group Journal* 19 (2006), 201–4*

'Christchurch', K Jarvis, *Current Archaeology* 8.6 (1983), 185–88*

'Excavations at Christchurch, Dorset, 1981 to 1983', S M Davies, *Proceedings of the Dorset Natural History and Archaeological Society* 105 (1983), 21–56*

Cowes

'Based on a Tudor bulwark: the Royal Yacht squadron, Cowes, Isle of Wight', M Binney, *Country Life* 178 (1985), 298–301*

Cumberland

Fort Cumberland 1747–1850: key to an island's defence. P A Magrath. Portsmouth: Portsmouth City Council, 1992* (Portsmouth papers; 60)

'Portsmouth – Fort Cumberland', R T Fox, *Archaeology in Hampshire: Annual Report for 1988*, 1989, 46–48*

Fareham

'Fort Fareham', G H Williams, *Fareham Past and Present* 14 (1971), 2–4

'Fort Fareham: tests in the mortar battery', anon, *The Redan* 18 (1990), 14–17*

'Fort Fareham', D Moore, *ibid* 56 (2002), 11–34*

Freshwater

Freshwater Redoubt. A R Cantwell. Privately published, 1985* [duplicated typescript]

Freshwater Redoubt. A R Cantwell. Revised edition. [S l: s n], 1986*

'The building of the Freshwater Redoubt: a personal story', P Brading, *Ravelin* 40 (1995), 20–28*

'William Brading (1817–1899): 2. Freshwater Redoubt', P Brading and W Brading, *The Redan* 36 (1996), 2–8*

Golden Hill

Golden Hill Fort, Freshwater, Isle of Wight. A R Cantwell. Privately published, 1985*

'Final battle', A Mankowski, *Building* supplement (5 September 1986), 54–55, 57, 59*

Gosport

Fort Brockhurst. J G Coad. London: HMSO, 1978*

Fort Brockhurst. J G Coad. London: HBMCE, 1987*

Fort Brockhurst and the Gomer-Elson forts. D Moore. Gosport: D Moore, 1990*; 2nd edition, 1992* (Solent papers; 6)

Fort Gilkicker. D Moore. Gosport: D Moore, 1988*; 2nd edition, 1990* (Solent papers; 5)

The earlier fortifications of Gosport. G H Williams. Gosport: Gosport Historic Records and Museum Society, 1974*

The western defences of Portsmouth Harbour 1400–1800. G H Williams.

Portsmouth: Portsmouth City Council, 1979* (Portsmouth papers; 30)

'Gosport, town moat', R Fox, *Archaeology in Hampshire: Annual Report for 1990*, 1991, 67–68*

'The Stokes Bay moat near Portsmouth', G H Williams, *Fort* 11 (1983), 57–61*

'Defence of Stokes Bay against the Spanish Armada – part I', G H and B E D Williams, *Gosport Records* 4 (1972), 21–24*

'Defence of Stokes Bay against the Spanish Armada – part II', G H and B E D Williams, *ibid* 5 (1972), 26–30*

'Defence of Stokes Bay against the Spanish Armada – part III', G H and B E D Williams, *ibid* 6 (1973), 17–21*

'Defence of Stokes Bay against the Spanish Armada – part IV', G H and B E D Williams, *ibid* 7 (1973), 8–13*

'Fort Blockhouse', R Compton-Hall, *ibid* 12 (1976), 4–8*

'The Stokes Bay moat', G H Williams, *Hampshire* 22.8 (1982), 52–54*

'Post-medieval Britain and Ireland in 1991', M Ponsford, *Post-Medieval Archaeology* 26 (1992), 107 [Gosport moat]

'Post-medieval Britain and Ireland in 1993', M Ponsford, *ibid* 28 (1994), 107 [Rowner]

'Post-medieval Britain and Ireland in 1994', M Ponsford and R Jackson, *ibid* 29 (1995), 131 [Rowner]

'Post-medieval Britain and Ireland in 1995', M Ponsford and R Jackson, *ibid* 30 (1996), 250–51 [Rowner]

'Fort Gilkicker: 1874', [D Moore], *Ravelin* 23 (1991), 32–35*

'The regular Royal Artillery garrison at the Gomer-Elson forts 1868–1890', I Maine, *The Redan* 19 (1990), 18–20

'The first Fort Gilkicker', D Moore, *ibid* 34 (1995), 17–23*

'Fort Gilkicker: the final armament', D Moore, *ibid* 39 (1997), 22–36*

'Browndown Battery', D Moore, *ibid* 60 (2004), 37–53*

Hurst

Hurst Castle. A R Cantwell and P Sprack. Privately published, 1985* [duplicated typescript]

Hurst Castle, Hampshire. J G Coad. London: HBMCE, 1985*; 2nd edition, 1990*

Hurst and Calshot castles: information for teachers. R Cooper. London: English Heritage, 1996*

Hurst Castle, Hampshire. O E Craster. London: HMSO, reprinted 1971*

Hurst Castle: an illustrated history. J James. Wimborne: Dovecote Press, 1986*

'Fortress of the Solent', A Cussans, *Country Life* 121 (1957), 1258–59*

'From monastery to castle. (Hampshire castles: 2. Hurst Castle)', F W Robins, *Proceedings of the Hampshire Field Club and Archaeological Society* 19 (1955–7), 62–65*

'Hurst Castle: the evolution of a Tudor fortress 1790–1945', J G Coad, *Post-Medieval Archaeology* 19 (1985), 62–65*

Isington

'Civil War earthworks east of Alton', M A B Lyne, *Proceedings of the Hampshire Field Club and Archaeological Society* 46 (1990), 181–84*

Merdon

Merdon Castle, Hursley – survey report. C J Webster. Southampton: University, Department of Archaeology, 1988* [duplicated typescript]

'Merdon Castle', M W Thompson, *Archaeological Journal* 123 (1966), 221

'Hursley – Merdon Castle', C J Webster, *Archaeology in Hampshire: Annual Report for 1988*, 1989, 64–69*

The Needles

The Needles batteries, Isle of Wight. A Cantwell and P Sprack. London: National Trust, 1981*; revised edition, 1984*

'The Needles Old Battery: interpretation of a Victorian fort', H Pilkington-Rowland, *Interpretation* 4.1–2 (1999), 35–37*

Netley

'Some lesser known Henrician castles', J Malpas, *Fort* 4 (1977), 2–3*; pp 87–91* in 1995 revised edition of *Fort* vols 4–5

Nodes Point

'Nodes Point Battery, Isle of Wight', I Stevenson, *The Redan* 66 (2006), 2–27*

Odiham

Odiham Castle 1200–1500: castle and community. P MacGregor, edited with additional material by P Stapleton. Gloucester: Alan Sutton, 1983*

A key to Odiham Castle. R Willoughby. Sherborne St John: R Willoughby, *c* 1998*

'Odiham – Odiham Castle', K J Barton, *Archaeology in Hampshire: Annual Report for 1981*, 1982, 25–26

'Odiham Castle', K J Barton and D Allen, *Archaeology in Hampshire: Annual Report for 1982*, 1983, 37–38, 40*

'Odiham Castle', D Allen, *Archaeology in Hampshire: Annual Report for 1983*, 1985, 52–55*

'Odiham – Odiham Castle', K J Barton and D Allen, *Archaeology and Historic Buildings in Hampshire: Annual report for 1984/5*, 1986, 39–42*

'King John at Odiham Castle', P and A A MacGregor, *Country Life* 137 (1965),

1417–19*

'Post-medieval Britain in 1983', G Egan, *Post-Medieval Archaeology* 18 (1983), 315

Portchester

Portchester. B W Cunliffe. Portsmouth: Portsmouth City Council, 1967* (Portsmouth papers; 1)

Excavations at Portchester Castle. 3. Medieval, the outer bailey and its defences. B Cunliffe. London: Society of Antiquaries, 1977* (Research report; 34)

Excavations at Portchester Castle. 4. Medieval, the inner baileys. B Cunliffe and J Munby. London: Society of Antiquaries, 1985* (Research report; 43)

Excavations at Portchester Castle. 5. Post-medieval 1609–1819. B Cunliffe and B Garratt. London: Society of Antiquaries, 1994* (Research report; 52)

Portchester Castle, Hampshire. J Goodall. London: English Heritage, 2003*

Portchester Castle, Hampshire. J T Munby. London: English Heritage, 1990*

Portchester Castle. D F Renn. London: HMSO, 1972*

Portchester Castle, Hampshire. S E Rigold. London: HMSO, 1965*

Portchester Castle, Hampshire. S E Rigold. London: HBMCE, 185*

Portchester Castle: a handbook for teachers. S Wright. London: English Heritage, 1994*

'Excavations at Portchester Castle, Hants, 1961–3: first interim report', B W Cunliffe, *Antiquaries Journal* 43 (1963), 218–27*

'Excavations at Portchester Castle, Hants, 1963–5: second interim report', B W Cunliffe, *ibid* 46 (1966), 36–49*

'Excavations at Portchester Castle, Hants, 1966–68: third interim report', B W Cunliffe, *ibid* 49 (1969), 62–74*

'Excavations at Portchester Castle, Hants, 1969–71: fourth interim report', B W Cunliffe, *ibid* 52 (1972), 70–83*

'Portchester Castle', B Cunliffe, *Archaeological Excavations 1975*, 22. London: HMSO, 1976*

'Fareham, Portchester Castle', B W Cunliffe, *CBA Groups 12 and 13 Archaeological Review* 1 (1966), 30

'Fareham, Portchester Castle', B W Cunliffe, *ibid* 2 (1967), 19

'Fareham, Portchester Castle', B W Cunliffe, *ibid* 3 (1968), 23

'Fareham, Portchester Castle', B W Cunliffe, *ibid* 4 (1969), 43–44

'Fareham, Portchester Castle', B W Cunliffe, *ibid* 5 (1970), 23

'Fareham, Portchester Castle', B W Cunliffe, *ibid* 6 (1971), 29

'Fareham, Portchester Castle', B W Cunliffe, *ibid* 7 (1972), 48–49

'Portchester', [A Selkirk], *Current Archaeology* 1.4 (1967), 100–4*

'Portchester', [A Selkirk], *ibid* 3.7 (1972), 189–96*

'The Watergate at Portchester Castle and the Anglo-Saxon porch at Titchfield: a reconsideration of the evidence', M Hare, *Proceedings of the Hampshire Field Club and Archaeological Society* 40 (1984), 71–80*

'Medieval Britain in 1961', D M Wilson and D G Hurst, *Medieval Archaeology* 6–7 (1962–3), 321

'Medieval Britain in 1962 and 1963', D M Wilson and D G Hurst, *ibid* 8 (1964), 253

'Medieval Britain in 1964', D M Wilson and D G Hurst, *ibid* 9 (1965), 189–90

'Medieval Britain in 1970', D M Wilson and S Moorhouse, *ibid* 15 (1971), 147

'Medieval Britain in 1972', L E Webster and J Cherry, *ibid* 17 (1973), 161

'Medieval Britain in 1975', L E Webster and J Cherry, *ibid* 20 (1976), 184

'The Tudor store-house at Portchester Castle, Hampshire', B W Cunliffe, *Post-Medieval Archaeology* 5 (1971), 188–90*

'Post-medieval Britain in 1970', S Moorhouse, *ibid* 5 (1971), 197

'Post-medieval Britain in 1972', J Cherry, *ibid* 7 (1973), 100

'Post-medieval fieldwork in Britain and Northern Ireland in 2004', M Ponsford, *ibid* 39 (2005), 367

Portsmouth

Portsmouth in defence of the realm: an imperial legacy. Anon. [S l]: Hampshire Field Club and Archaeological Society, 1973*

Royal Armouries: Fort Nelson. Anon. Leeds: Royal Armouries Museum, 2000*

Fortifications in old Portsmouth: a guide. A Corney. Portsmouth: Portsmouth City Museums, 1965*

Fort Widley and the great forts on Portsdown. A Corney. Portsmouth: Portsmouth City Museums, 1984*

Defence of the realm: an interpretative strategy for Portsmouth and the surrounding region. Dartington Amenity Research Trust. [Eastleigh]: Southern Tourist Board; [Portsmouth]: Portsmouth City Council, 1979*

Maps of Portsmouth before 1801: a catalogue. D Hodson. Portsmouth: City of Portsmouth, 1978* (Portsmouth records series; 4)

Hilsea Lines and Portsbridge. G Mitchell. West Wickham: G H Mitchell, 1988* (Solent papers; 4)

Fort Nelson: history and description. G Mitchell and P Cobb. West Wickham: G H Mitchell, 1986*

Fort Nelson and the Portsdown forts. G Mitchell and P Cobb. West Wickham: G H Mitchell, 1987*; 2nd edition, 1988* (Solent papers; 3)

Spit Bank Fort, Portsmouth: history and description, with a report on the restora-

tion programme. G H Mitchell and P D Cobb. Portsmouth: United Kingdom Fortifications Club, 1983*

Spit Bank Fort: history and description. G Mitchell and P Cobb. Privately published, 1984*

Spit Bank and the Spithead forts. G Mitchell [*et al*]. West Wickham: G H Mitchell, 1986*; 2nd edition, 1987* (Solent papers; 1)

A military heritage: a history of Portsmouth & Portsea town fortifications. B H Patterson. Portsmouth: Fort Cumberland & Portsmouth Militaria Society, 1985*; 2nd edition, 1987*

Spithead: the navy's anvil. M Powell. Winchester: Redan and Vedette, 1977*

The siege of Portsmouth in the Civil War. J Webb. Portsmouth: Portsmouth City Council, 1969*

'Portsmouth: approach defences', A Corney, *The Hundred and Twenty Second Annual Meeting at Winchester, 1975*, CAA, 1975, 16–18

'The Portsmouth map of 1545 and the introduction of scale maps into England', P D A Harvey, in J Webb [*et al*] (eds), *Hampshire studies*, 33–49. Portsmouth: Portsmouth City Records Office, 1981*

'Stone towers: the fortifications of Portsmouth', S Quail, in J Webb [*et al*], *The spirit of Portsmouth: a history*, 53–57. Chichester: Phillimore, 1989 (1997 printing)*

'Portsmouth', A Corney, *Archaeological Journal* 123 (1966), 179–82*

'Portsmouth – power station', R T Fox, *Archaeology and Historic Buildings in Hampshire: Annual Report for 1984/5*, 1986, 48–49*

'Portsmouth – Old Portsmouth, Camber Basin', R T Fox, *Archaeology in Hampshire: Annual Report for 1987*, 1988, 32–34*

'Portsmouth – Old Portsmouth, the Saluting Platform', R Fox, *ibid*, 34–36*

'Portsmouth – Old Portsmouth, Spur Redoubt', R T Fox, *ibid*, 36–37*

'Portsmouth – Old Portsmouth, King James Gate', R T Fox, *ibid*, 38*

'Portsmouth – Old Portsmouth, East Ravelin', R T Fox, *ibid*, 49–55*

'Portsmouth – Ten Gun Battery, Old Portsmouth', R T Fox, *Archaeology in Hampshire: Annual Report for 1989*, 1990, 60, 62*

'Portsmouth – Spur Redoubt', R Fox, *Archaeology in Hampshire: Annual Report for 1990*, 1991, 71–72*

'Old Portsmouth – King's Bastion', R T Fox, *Archaeology in Hampshire: Annual Report for 1991*, 1992, 50–53*

'Old Portsmouth – Long Curtain', R T Fox, *ibid*, 53–56*

'Portsmouth – Spur Redoubt', R Fox, *Archaeology in Hampshire: Annual Report* *for 1992*, 1993, 33–34*

'Portsmouth: Eastney Fort West', R Fox, *Archaeology in Hampshire: Annual Report for 1993*, 1994, 39–41*

'Spitbank', G Mitchell, *Casemate* 14 (1984), 8–9*

'Fort Nelson', G Mitchell, *ibid* 14 (1984), 10

'Spitbank – a Solent seafort', R Nugent, *Journal of Architectural Conservation* 7.3 (2001), 32–45*

'Portsmouth, Victoria Barracks', anon, *CBA Groups 12 and 13 Archaeological Review* 2 (1967), 25

'Fort Cumberland: recording the conversion of a Guardianship monument', D Fellows and P O'Hara, *CfA News: Newsletter of the Centre for Archaeology* (2001), 2–3*

'Spithead contrasts; the treatment of the Portsmouth sea forts', A Saunders, *Europa Nostra Bulletin* 55 (2001), 121–28*

'Portsmouth's ramparts revisited', R Fox, *Fortress* 11 (1991), 29–38*

'The defences of Southsea and Portsmouth in 1623', J R Kenyon, *Proceedings of the Hampshire Field Club and Archaeological Society* 37 (1981), 13–21*

'Historic architecture of HM Naval Base Portsmouth', J G Coad, *Mariner's Mirror* 67 (1981), 3–59*

'Nelson: armament: revised plan at terreplein level 1892/3', anon, *Palmerston Forts Society Newsletter* 12 (1988), 12–13 [plan], 24*

'Post-medieval Britain in 1967', D G Hurst, *Post-Medieval Archaeology* 2 (1968), 176

'Post-medieval Britain in 1972', J Cherry, *ibid* 7 (1973), 100

'Post-medieval Britain in 1980', J Cherry, *ibid* 15 (1981), 226–27*

'Post-medieval Britain in 1984', G Egan, *ibid* 19 (1985), 162

'Post-medieval Britain and Ireland in 1988', G Egan, *ibid* 23 (1989), 33–35

'Post-medieval Britain and Ireland in 1991', M Ponsford, *ibid* 26 (1992), 107

'Post-medieval Britain and Ireland in 2001', M Ponsford, *ibid* 36 (2002), 218–20*

'Post-medieval Britain and Ireland in 2002', M Ponsford, *ibid* 37 (2003), 272

'Post-medieval Britain and Ireland in 2003', M Ponsford, *ibid* 38 (2004), 308–9

'Post-medieval fieldwork in Britain and Northern Ireland in 2004', M Ponsford, *ibid* 39 (2005), 379

'Fort Nelson 1861: the fort that wasn't built', D Moore, *Ravelin* 23 (1991), 9–15*

'Fort Purbrook: 1940–41', A F Izett, *ibid* 23 (1991), 29–31

'The construction of the Hilsea Lines', P Brading, *ibid* 41 (1995), 2–8

'Some further considerations on the storage of gunpowder in the main magazines at Fort Nelson', D Moore, *The Redan* 16 (1989), 27–32*

'The use of mortars in the Portsmouth forts', D Moore, *ibid* 18 (1990), 11–13

'Expense magazines at Fort Nelson', D Moore, *ibid* 20 (1990), 31–32

'Howitzers in the Portsdown Hill forts', D Moore, *ibid* 21 (1991), 12

'"Fire party: close up"', P Cobb, *ibid* 21 (1991), 20–26

'Fort Southwick: the untold story', P Cobb, *ibid* 37 (1996), 38–41*

'Spitbank Fort: a history and description', D Moore, *ibid* 41 (1997), 24–36*

'Expense magazines at Fort Nelson', D Moore, *ibid* 45 (1999), 2–20*

'Gun grouping and ammunition storage at Forts Widley and Nelson: 1891', D Moore, *ibid* 48 (2000), 19–22*

'West bastion: Hilsea Lines', D Moore', *ibid* 49 (2000), 2–6*

'The Eastney batteries, Portsmouth', D Moore, *ibid* 53 (2001), 2–16*

'Restoration work in the main magazine at Fort Nelson', D Moore, *ibid* 59 (2003), 10–23*

'Keys at Fort Nelson', G Salter and D Moore, *ibid* 61 (2004), 10–18*

'The completion of the main magazine restoration project at Fort Nelson', D Moore, *ibid* 66 (2006), 34*

'The 1901 census and the Portsmouth forts', D Williams, *ibid* 66 (2006), 35–52*

'The building of the Portsdown Hill forts, with special reference to Forts Nelson, Widley and Southwick', G Salter, *ibid* 67 (2006), 19–34*

'The Portsdown Hill forts: a time-line on their construction', G Salter, *ibid* 67 (2006), 35–58

Powderham

See Barley Pound

Puckpool

Puckpool Battery. A R Cantwell and P Sprack. Rye: Redoubt Consultancy, [1987]*

Quarr Abbey

'The earliest gunports in Britain?', D F Renn, *Archaeological Journal* 125 (1968), 301–3*

'The *enceinte* wall of Quarr Abbey', D F Renn, *Fort* 8 (1980), 5–6*

'The *enceinte* wall of Quarr Abbey', D F Renn, *Proceedings of the Isle of Wight Natural History and Archaeological Society* 4 (1946–55), 350–51*

St Andrew's

'St Andrew's Castle, Hampshire, in 1623', J R Kenyon, *Fort* 6 (1978), 24–25

'St Andrew's Castle, Hamble, Hampshire', F G Aldsworth, *Proceedings of the Hampshire Field Club and Archaeological Society* 37 (1981), 5–11*

'Hamble Common', K Stubbs and F G Aldsworth, *Hampshire Newsletter* 2.3

(1972), 9–10*

St Helen's

'St Helen's Fort, Isle of Wight', D Moore, *The Redan* 61 (2004), 19–25*

Sandown

'The Sandown Bay defences', A Cantwell and P Sprack, *Fortress* 7 (1990), 51–59*

'The building of a fort at Sandown, Isle of Wight, 1632–1636', J D Jones, *Proceedings of the Isle of Wight Natural History and Archaeological Society* 6.3 (1968), 166–88*

Silchester

The Silchester amphitheatre: excavations of 1979–85. M Fulford. London: Society for the Promotion of Roman Studies, 1989* (Britannia monograph; 10) [espec pp 59–65, 193–95]

'Excavations on the sites of the amphitheatre and forum-basilica at Silchester, Hampshire: an interim report', M Fulford, *Antiquaries Journal* 65 (1985), 39–81* [espec pp 72–77]

'Round-up 1980: Silchester', [A Selkirk], *Current Archaeology* 7.4 (1981), 102–3

'Silchester', M Fulford, *ibid* 7.11 (1982), 326–31* [espec p 331]

Southampton

Mystery at God's House Tower. D V Fippard. Privately published, 1966 [duplicated typescript]

Southampton Castle. J Hodgson. Southampton: Southampton City Museums, [1986]*

Excavations at Southampton Castle. J Oxley (ed). Southampton: Southampton City Museums, 1986*

God's House Tower, Southampton. P Peberdy. Southampton: Southampton City Museums, 1972*

Excavations in medieval Southampton, 1953–1969. C Platt and R Coleman-Smith. Leicester: Leicester University Press, 1975, 2 vols*

'Southampton town wall', B H St J O'Neil, in W F Grimes (ed), *Aspects of archaeology in Britain and beyond*, 243–57. London: H W Edwards, 1951*

'The defences of Southampton in the later middle ages', A D Saunders, in L A Burgess (ed), *The Southampton terrier of 1454*, 20–34. Southampton: Southampton Records Series, **15**, 1976*

'Medieval town', anon, *Annual Report 1973–4*, Southampton Archaeological Research Committee, 1974, 13–16*

'The medieval port of Southampton', J Pallister, *Archaeological Journal* 123 (1966), 177–79

'Southampton – Winkle Street', S Hardy, *Archaeology and Historic Buildings in*

Hampshire: Annual Report 1984/5, 1986, 44–45

'Southampton – York Buildings', H Kavanagh, *Archaeology in Hampshire: Annual Report for 1986*, 1987, 26–29

'Southampton – The Arcades, Western Esplanade', T Robey, *Archaeology in Hampshire: Annual Report for 1987*, 1988, 22–23

'Southampton – York Buildings', H Kavanagh, *Archaeology in Hampshire: Annual Report for 1988*, 1989, 29

'Southampton – The Arcades', T Robey, *ibid*, 25

'Southampton – Back of the Walls', J Grace, *ibid*, 26

'Southampton – Back of the Walls', R Lindsey, *Archaeology in Hampshire: Annual Report for 1989*, 1990, 33–34

'Southampton – York Buildings, North walls', H Kavanagh, *ibid*, 36

'Southampton – Back of the Walls', M Smith, *Archaeology in Hampshire: Annual Report for 1990*, 1991, 43–44

'Southampton – Catchcold Tower', C Scott, *ibid*, 45

'Southampton – north walls', H Kavanagh, *ibid* 46

'Southampton – Bargate Street', J Vincent, *Archaeology in Hampshire: Annual Report for 1991*, 1993, 28

'Southampton: Town Quay', G Bareham and M F Garner, *Archaeology in Hampshire: Annual Report for 1993*, 1994, 33

'Southampton: the introduction of gunpowder artillery to the town's defences', A Saunders, *Europa Nostra Bulletin* 53 (2000), 53–58*

'Artillery and the defences of Southampton circa 1360–1660', J R Kenyon, *Fort* 3 (1977), 8–14*; pp 21–30* in 1993 revised edition of *Fort* vols 1–3

'Southampton excavations, 1956', J S Wacher, *Proceedings of the Hampshire Field Club and Archaeological Society* 19 (1955–7), 287–89

'Medieval Britain in 1956', D M Wilson and J G Hurst, *Medieval Archaeology* 1 (1957), 159

'Medieval Britain in 1957', D M Wilson and J G Hurst, *ibid* 2 (1958), 198–99*

'Medieval Britain in 1958', D M Wilson and J G Hurst, *ibid* 3 (1959), 310

'Medieval Britain in 1959', D M Wilson and D G Hurst, *ibid* 4 (1960), 146, 149

'Medieval Britain in 1960', D M Wilson and D G Hurst, *ibid* 5 (1961), 318

'Medieval Britain in 1961', D M Wilson and D G Hurst, *ibid* 6–7 (1962–3), 321, 328

'The Southampton Arcade', D F Renn, *ibid* 8 (1964), 226–28*

'Medieval Britain in 1975', L E Webster and J Cherry, *ibid* 20 (1976), 178

'Medieval Britain in 1977', L E Webster and J Cherry, *ibid* 22 (1978), 174

'Medieval Britain in 1980', S M Youngs and J Clark, *ibid* 25 (1981), 201

'Medieval Britain and Ireland in 1986', S M Youngs, J Clark and T Barry, *ibid* 31 (1987), 134, 136, 139

'Medieval Britain and Ireland in 1987', S M Youngs [*et al*], *ibid* 32 (1988), 254–55

'Medieval Britain and Ireland in 1988', D R M Gaimster, S Margeson and T Barry, *ibid* 33 (1989), 192–93

'Medieval Britain and Ireland in 1989', D R M Gaimster, S Margeson and M Hurley, *ibid* 34 (1990), 186–97

'Medieval Britain and Ireland in 1990', B S Nenk, S Margeson and M Hurley, *ibid* 35 (1991), 158–60

'Medieval Britain and Ireland in 1991', B S Nenk, S Margeson and M Hurley, *ibid* 36 (1992), 234

'Medieval Britain and Ireland in 1993', B S Nenk, S Margeson and M Hurley, *ibid* 38 (1994), 217–18

'Medieval Britain and Ireland in 1994', B S Nenk, S Margeson and M Hurley, *ibid* 39 (1995), 214–16

'Medieval Britain and Ireland in 1995', B S Nenk, S Margeson and M Hurley, *ibid* 40 (1996), 265

'Medieval Britain and Ireland in 2001', J Bradley and M Gaimster, *ibid* 46 (2002), 173

'Medieval Britain and Ireland in 2002', J Bradley and M Gaimster, *ibid* 47 (2003), 250

'Medieval Britain and Ireland in 2003', J Bradley and M Gaimster, *ibid* 48 (2004), 270–71

'Post-medieval Britain and Ireland in 1990', M Ponsford, *Post-Medieval Archaeology* 25 (1991), 123

'Post-medieval Britain and Ireland in 2003', M Ponsford, *ibid* 38 (2004), 314

'The building of the south wall of Southampton in the 14th century', R A Pelham, *Southampton Archaeological Society Bulletin* 4 (1963), 5–7

'Excavations in Southampton from 1956–8', J S Wacher, *ibid* 8 (1964), 1–7

'The terrier of 1454', L A Burgess, *ibid* 14 (1965), 1–7*

'The West Gate and its neighbours', L A Burgess, *ibid* 17 (1968), 10–13

'The accounts of Southampton town, 1456–1457', S D Thomson, *Southampton City Museums Archaeological Society Bulletin* 19 (1969), 1–10

'The accounts of Southampton town, 1449–1450', S D Thomson, *ibid* 20 (1969), 1–36

Southsea

Southsea Castle. S Brooks. Andover; Pitkin Guides, 1996*

Southsea Castle. A Corney. Portsmouth: Portsmouth City Museums, 1967*

'Southsea Castle', A Corney, *Archaeological Journal* 123 (1966), 196–98*

'The defences of Southsea and Portsmouth in 1623', J R Kenyon, *Proceedings of the Hampshire Field Club and Archaeological Society* 37 (1981), 13–21*

Victoria

Fort Victoria country park. Anon. [Newport]: Isle of Wight County Council, 1982*

Fort Victoria: a history. A Cantwell. Newport: Isle of Wight County Council, 1985*

Well

The Battery, Well, Long Sutton, Hants. R H Greaves. Privately published, 1972* [duplicated typescript]

'Medieval Britain in 1970', D M Wilson and S Moorhouse, *Medieval Archaeology* 15 (1971), 147

Winchester

The Westgate, Winchester. Anon. Winchester: Winchester Museum, 1971

Object and economy in medieval Winchester (Winchester studies 7. ii: artefacts from medieval Winchester). M Biddle. Oxford: Clarendon Press, 1990, 2 vols*

Wolvesey: the Old Bishop's Palace, Winchester, Hampshire. M Biddle. London: HBMCE, 1986*

Winchester Castle and the Great Hall. M Biddle and B Clayre. Winchester: Hampshire County Council, 1983*

The Castle, Winchester: Great Hall & Round Table. M Biddle and B Clayre. Winchester: Hampshire County Council, 2000*

Winchester excavations. 2. 1949–1960. Excavations in the suburbs and the western part of the town. J Collis. Winchester: City of Winchester, 1978*

Building accounts of King Henry III. H M Colvin (ed). Oxford: Clarendon Press, 1971* [espec pp 90–187]

Survey of medieval Winchester (Winchester studies 2). D Keene. Oxford: Clarendon Press, 1985, 2 vols* [the defences, vol 1, pp 42–48]

Three palaces of the bishops of Winchester: Wolvesey (Old Bishop's Palace), Hampshire; Bishop's Waltham Palace, Hampshire; Farnham Castle keep, Surrey. J Wareham. London: English Heritage, 2000*

'The setting of the Round Table: Winchester Castle and the Great Hall', M Biddle, B Clayre and M Morris, in M Biddle, *King Arthur's Round Table: an archaeological investigation*, 59–101. Woodbridge: Boydell Press, 2000*

'Excavations at Winchester, 1961–4', R N Quirk, *Transactions of the Ancient Monuments Society* new ser 12 (1964), 80–96*

'Excavations at Winchester, 1962–63: second interim report', M Biddle, *Antiquaries Journal* 44 (1964), 188–219*

'Excavations at Winchester, 1964: third interim report', M Biddle, *ibid* 45 (1965), 230–64*

'Excavations at Winchester, 1965: fourth interim report', M Biddle, *ibid* 46 (1966), 308–32*

'Excavations at Winchester, 1966: fifth interim report', M Biddle, *ibid* 47 (1967), 251–79*

'Excavations at Winchester, 1967: sixth interim report', M Biddle, *ibid* 48 (1968), 250–84*

'Excavations at Winchester, 1968; seventh interim report', M Biddle, *ibid* 49 (1969), 259–329*

'Excavations at Winchester, 1969: eighth interim report', M Biddle, *ibid* 50 (1970), 277–326*

'Excavations at Winchester, 1970: ninth interim report', M Biddle, *ibid* 52 (1972), 93–131*

'Excavations at Winchester, 1971: tenth and final interim report: part I', M Biddle, *ibid* 55 (1975), 96–126*

'Excavations at Winchester, 1971: tenth and final interim report: part II', M Biddle, *ibid* 55 (1975), 295–337*

'Winchester, Castle Yard', M Biddle, *Archaeological Excavations 1970*, 77–78. London: HMSO, 1977

'Winchester, Sussex Street', K Qualmann, *Archaeological Excavations 1976*, 122–23. London, HMSO, 1977

'Winchester – Castle Yard', K E Qualmann, *Archaeology and Historic Buildings in Hampshire: Annual Report for 1984/5*, 1986, 46*

'Winchester – Tower mound', J Bailey, *ibid*, 48

'Winchester – Peninsula Barracks', R Whinney, *Archaeology in Hampshire: Annual Report for 1987*, 1988, 26

'Winchester – Peninsula Barracks', S C Teague and P McCulloch, *Archaeology in Hampshire: Annual Report for 1990*, 1991, 26

'Winchester', M Biddle, *CBA Groups 12 and 13 Archaeological Review* 1 (1966), 30–31

'Winchester', M Biddle, *ibid* 2 (1967), 19

'Winchester', M Biddle, *ibid* 3 (1968), 23

'Winchester', M Biddle, *ibid* 4 (1969), 51

'Winchester', M Biddle, *ibid* 5 (1970), 35

'Winchester', M Biddle, *ibid* 6 (1971), 31

'Wolvesey, the *domus quasi palatium* of Henry de Blois in Winchester', M Biddle, *Château Gaillard* 3 (1969), 28–36*

'Winchester', M Biddle, *ibid* 4 (1969), 19–30*

'Winchester city wall', B W Cunliffe, *Proceedings of the Hampshire Field Club and Archaeological Society* 22 (1961–3), 51–81*

'Medieval Britain in 1962 and 1963', D M Wilson and D G Hurst, *Medieval Archaeology* 8 (1964), 248, 253–54

'Medieval Britain in 1964', D M Wilson and D G Hurst, *ibid* 9 (1965), 184, 190, 195

'Medieval Britain in 1965', D M Wilson and D G Hurst, *ibid* 10 (1966), 184–85

'Medieval Britain in 1966', D M Wilson and D G Hurst, *ibid* 11 (1967), 282

'Medieval Britain in 1967', D M Wilson and D G Hurst, *ibid* 12 (1968), 173, 177

'Medieval Britain in 1968', D M Wilson and D G Hurst, *ibid* 13 (1969), 250, 258

'Medieval Britain in 1969', D M Wilson and D G Hurst, *ibid* 14 (1970), 172–73

'Medieval Britain in 1970', D M Wilson and S Moorhouse, *ibid* 15 (1971), 143, 147

'Medieval Britain in 1972', L E Webster and J Cherry, *ibid* 17 (1973), 169

'Medieval Britain and Ireland in 1984', S M Youngs, J Clark and T Barry, *ibid* 29 (1985), 183–84

'Medieval Britain and Ireland in 1987', S M Youngs [*et al*], *ibid* 32 (1988), 256

'Medieval Britain and Ireland in 1990', B S Nenk, S Margeson and M Hurley, *ibid* 35 (1991), 162–63

'Medieval Britain and Ireland in 1994', B S Nenk, S Margeson and M Hurley, *ibid* 39 (1995), 218

'Medieval Britain and Ireland in 1996', B S Nenk, C Haith and J Bradley, *ibid* 41 (1997), 270

'Medieval Britain and Ireland in 1999', J Bradley and M Gaimster, *ibid* 44 (2000), 278

'Post-medieval Britain and Ireland in 1991', M Ponsford, *Post-medieval Archaeology* 26 (1992), 107–8

Yarmouth

Yarmouth Castle, Isle of Wight. S E Rigold. London: HMSO, reprinted with amendments 1969*; 2nd edition, 1978*

Yarmouth Castle, Isle of Wight. S E Rigold. London: HBMCE, 1985*

Yarmouth Castle: a handbook for teachers. E Newbery. London: English Heritage, 1987*

HEREFORDSHIRE

Bowden, M. *The Malvern Hills: an ancient landscape*. London: English Heritage, 2005*

Halliwell, P R. 'Castles and churches in the Erwood area', *Herefordshire Archaeological News* 64 (1995), 34–41*

Pevsner, N. *Herefordshire (The buildings of England)*. Harmondsworth: Penguin Books, 1968*

Phillips, N. *Earthwork castles of Gwent and Ergyng AD 1050–1250*. Oxford: Archaeopress, 2006* (BAR British series; 420)

Purser, T S. 'Castles of Herefordshire', *Medieval History* 4 (1994), 72–84*

Remfry, P M. *The castles of Ewias Lacy 1048 to 1403*. Malvern Link: SCS Publishing, 1998*

Remfry, P M. *Nine castles of Burford barony 1048 to 1308*. Malvern Link: SCS Publishing, 1999*

Rich, B. 'Castles and marcher lordships: report on SLS study weekend, May 2003', *Society for Landscape Studies Newsletter* autumn/winter (2003), 3–6*

Richardson, R E and Musson, C. *Herefordshire past and present: an aerial view*. Almeley: Logaston Press, 2004*

Robinson, C J. *A history of the castles of Herefordshire and their lords*. Almeley: Logaston Press, 2002* [first published 1869]

Salter, M. *The castles of Herefordshire and Worcestershire*. Wolverhampton: Folly Publications, 1989*

Salter, M. *The castles of Herefordshire and Worcestershire*. New edition. Malvern: Folly Publications, 2000*

Shoesmith, R. *A guide to the castles & moated sites in Herefordshire*. Almeley: Logaston Press, 1996* (Monuments in the landscape; 2)

Sprackling, G and Lesser, I. 'Field-names as archaeological indicators of defensive sites', *Transactions of the Woolhope Naturalists' Field Club* 48.3 (1996), 473–79*

Stirling-Brown, R. 'Field meeting at Lingen: castle investigation', *Herefordshire Archaeological News* 57 (1992), 22–28*

Stirling-Brown, R. 'Investigations in the Weobley area, 5 March 1995', *ibid* 64 (1995), 23–28*

Stirling-Brown, R. 'Mottes in the Kington area', *ibid* 69 (1998), 14–18*

Thurlby, M. *The Herefordshire School of Romanesque sculpture*. Almeley: Logaston Press, 1999*

Tonkin, J W. 'Herefordshire castles', *Transactions of the Woolhope Naturalists' Field Club* 44.1 (1982), 31–35

ENGLAND

Aston

'Notes on the Aston castles', P M Remfry, *Herefordshire Archaeological News* 67 (1997), 44–46 + illus on p 41*

Bacton

'Newcourt Farm, Bacton', R Stirling-Brown, *ibid* 53 (1990), 18–20*

Brampton Bryan

Brampton Bryan castle 1066 to 1309 and the Civil War 1642 to 1646. P M Remfry. Malvern Link: SCS Publishing, 1997*

'Brampton Bryan Castle', H Gordon Slade, *Archaeological Journal* 138 (1981), 26–29*

'Brampton Bryan', anon, *Archaeology in Hereford 1986–7*, 31*

'Brampton Bryan Castle', anon, *Archaeology in Hereford 1988–1989*, 25–26*

Bronsil

'Medieval Britain and Ireland in 1990', B S Nenk, S Margeson and M Hurley, *Medieval Archaeology* 35 (1991), 165*

'Bronsil Castle', R K Morriss, *West Midlands Archaeology* 33 (1990), 36

Castle Frome

'Castle Frome Castle: documentary evidence', B Coplestone-Crow, *Herefordshire Archaeological News* 59 (1993), 23–24

'Castle Frome Castle: a lost de Lacy caput', D Whitehead, *ibid* 59 (1993), 24–26

'Castle Frome', P Remfry, *ibid* 60 (1993), 8*

'Post-medieval Britain and Ireland in 1991', M Ponsford, *Post-Medieval Archaeology* 26 (1992), 108

'Castle Frome, medieval castle, early enclosure', P White and K Ray, *West Midlands Archaeology* 47 (2004), 26–27

'Castle Frome', I Cohen, *Transactions of the Woolhope Naturalists' Field Club* 35 (1955–7), 183

Chanstone

'Medieval Britain and Ireland in 2002', J Bradley and M Gaimster, *Medieval Archaeology* 47 (2003), 251–56*

Clifford

Clifford Castle 1066 to 1299. P M Remfry. Malvern Link: SCS Publishing, 1994*

Clifford Castle: a short guide. P M Remfry. Malvern Link: SCS Publishing, 1995*

'Clifford Castle', D J C King, *The hundred-and-twenty-first annual meeting in south Brecknock, 1974*, CAA, 1974, 36–37

'The castle of Fair Rosamund', D Iron, *The Field* 205 (1955), 576–77*

'Excavations at Clifford Castle', D Iron, *Transactions of the Woolhope Naturalists' Field Club* 34 (1952–4), 27–28, 82–84*

Croft

Croft Castle, Herefordshire. O Garnett. London: National Trust, 2004*

Croft Castle, Herefordshire. D Uhlman. London: National Trust, 1988*

'Croft Castle, Herefordshire', A Oswald, *Country Life* 107 (1950), 1206–10*

Dilwyn

'Field meeting to Dilwyn & Little Dilwyn', R Stirling-Brown, *Herefordshire Archaeological News* 76 (2005), 39–40*

Dorstone

'The Bage 'motte', Dorstone, Herefordshire', R E Kay, *Herefordshire Archaeological News* 38 (1980), 12–14*

'Dorstone, Mynydd-broeth', [R A Jackson], *ibid* 37 (1994), 28

'Medieval Britain and Ireland in 2002', J Bradley and M Gaimster, *Medieval Archaeology* 47 (2003), 256–58*

Eardisland

'Field meeting at Eardisland on 6 March 1994', R Stirling-Brown, *Herefordshire Archaeological News* 62 (1994), 14–17*

Eardisley

'Eardisley, Castle Farm', [J N Topping], *West Midlands Archaeology* 37 (1994), 29

Ewyas Harold

'The castle of Ewyas Harold and its military arrangements in the Norman period', B Coplestone-Crow, *Herefordshire Archaeological News* 57 (1992), 7–11*

'Ewyas Harold, Ewyas Harold Castle', G Dawkes, *West Midlands Archaeology* 42 (1999), 56

'The fief of Alfred of Marlborough in Herefordshire in 1986 and its descent in the Norman period', B Coplestone-Crow, *Transactions of the Woolhope Naturalists' Field Club* 45.2 (1986), 376–414*

Goodrich

Goodrich Castle. J Ashbee. London: English Heritage, 2005*

Goodrich Castle: a handbook for teachers. A Hancock. London: English Heritage, 1991*

Goodrich Castle, Herefordshire. C A R Radford. London: HMSO, 1958*

Goodrich Castle, Herefordshire. C A R Radford. London: HBMCE, 1984*

Goodrich Castle, Herefordshire. D Renn. London: English Heritage, 1993*

'Goodrich', anon, *City of Hereford Archaeology Committee Annual report 1984/5*, 20–25*

'Goodrich Castle', anon, *Archaeology in Hereford 1985/6*, 29*

'Goodrich Castle', anon, *Archaeology in Hereford 1987–88*, 33–34*

'Goodrich Castle electricity trench', anon, *Archaeology in Hereford 1988–89*, 15–16*

'Goodrich Castle: the keep', anon, *Hereford Archaeology 1989–90*, 31–33*

'Medieval Britain and Ireland in 1984', S M Youngs, J Clark and T Barry, *Medieval Archaeology* 29 (1985), 184

'Medieval Britain and Ireland in 1985', S M Youngs, J Clark and T Barry, *ibid* 30 (1986), 149

'Medieval Britain and Ireland in 1991', B S Nenk, S Margeson and M Hurley, *ibid* 36 (1992), 236

'The Goodrich bomb', R G Grey-Davies, *Severn and Wye Review* 1 (1970–2), 117–18*

Grafton

'Medieval Britain and Ireland in 1991', B S Nenk, S Margeson and M Hurley, *Medieval Archaeology* 36 (1992), 236

Hereford

Hereford city excavations. 1. Excavations at Castle Green. R Shoesmith. London: CBA, 1980* (Research report; 36)

Hereford city excavations. 2. Excavations on and close to the defences. R Shoesmith. London: CBA, 1982* (Research report; 46)

A short history of Castle Green and Hereford Castle. R Shoesmith. Hereford: Hereford City Museums, 1980*

Hereford city excavations. 4. 1976–1990: further sites & evolving interpretations. A Thomas and A Boucher (eds). Almeley: Logaston Press for Hereford City and County Archaeological Trust, 2002* (espec ch 8)

'Hereford', M D Lobel, in M D Lobel (ed), *Historic towns*, **1**. Oxford: Lovell Johns-Cook, Hammond and Kell Organization, 1969*

'Excavations in Blue School Street, 1965', F Noble, *The hundred and twelfth annual meeting at Hereford, 1965*, CAA, 1965, 13–14

'Hereford', R Shoesmith, *Archaeological Excavations 1967*, 20. London: HMSO, 1968

'Hereford', P A Rahtz and J M Gray, *Archaeological Excavations 1968*, 22–23. London, HMSO, 1969

'Hereford Castle', P J Leach, *Archaeological Excavations 1969*, 29. London: HMSO, 1970

'Castle Green, Hereford', R Shoesmith, *Archaeological Excavations 1973*, 83–84. London: HMSO, 1974

'Hereford: Wall Street', J Sawle, *Archaeological Excavations 1976*, 124. London; HMSO, 1977

'Hereford city walls', F Noble, *Archaeology in Wales* 5 (1965), 30

'Hereford', S C Stanford, *ibid* 78 (1967), 17

'Hereford', R Shoesmith, *ibid* 10 (1970), 25

'Hereford: St Nicholas' Street', R Shoesmith, *ibid* 11 (1971), 31–32

'Hereford, Castle Green', R Shoesmith, *ibid* 13 (1973), 49–51

'Hereford', R Shoesmith, *ibid* 15 (1975), 61–64

'The reconstruction of the city wall at the junction of Mill Street and St Owen Street', anon, *City of Hereford Archaeology Committee Annual report 1983/4*, 9–11*

'Hereford', P Rahtz, *Current Archaeology* 1.9 (1968), 242–46*

'Hereford', R Shoesmith, *ibid* 3.10 (1972), 256–58*

'Medieval Britain in 1958', D M Wilson and J G Hurst, *Medieval Archaeology* 3 (1959), 310

'Medieval Britain in 1965', D M Wilson and D G Hurst, *ibid* 10 (1966), 198–99

'Medieval Britain in 1966', D M Wilson and D G Hurst, *ibid* 11 (1967), 292

'Medieval Britain in 1968', D M Wilson and D G Hurst, *ibid* 13 (1969), 258, 265

'Medieval Britain in 1969', D M Wilson and D G Hurst, *ibid* 14 (1970), 176

'Medieval Britain in 1970', D M Wilson and Moorhouse, *ibid* 15 (1971), 154

'Medieval Britain in 1971', L E Webster and J Cherry, *ibid* 16 (1972), 188

'Medieval Britain in 1973', L E Webster and J Cherry, *ibid* 18 (1974), 178

'Medieval Britain in 1975', L E Webster and J Cherry, *ibid* 20 (1976), 189

'Medieval Britain in 1976', L E Webster and J Cherry, *ibid* 21 (1977), 244

'Medieval Britain and Ireland in 1984', S M Youngs, J Clark and T Barry, *ibid* 29 (1985), 186

'Medieval Britain and Ireland in 1989', D R M Gaimster, S Margeson and M Hurley, *ibid* 34 (1990), 189

'Medieval Britain and Ireland in 1989', B S Nenk, S Margeson and M Hurley, *ibid* 40 (1996), 267–68

'Post-medieval Britain and Ireland in 1992', M Ponsford, *Post-Medieval Archaeology* 27 (1993), 217

'Bastion, Hereford city wall', F Noble, *West Midlands Annual Archaeological News Sheet* 8 (1965), 8–9

'Hereford, Blue School Street and Bath Street', S C Stanford, *ibid* 9 (1966), 7

'Hereford city defences', R Shoesmith and F Noble, *ibid* 10 (1967), 13–14

'Hereford Castle', P Leach, *West Midlands Archaeological News Sheet* 12 (1969), 36

'St Nicholas' St, Hereford', R Shoesmith, *ibid* 14 (1971), 23

'Castle Green, Hereford', R Shoesmith, *ibid* 16 (1973), 31–32

'5 Cantilupe St, Hereford', R Shoesmith, *ibid* 18 (1975), 64

'Hereford, city defences', R Morriss, *West Midlands Archaeology* 32 (1989), 36

'Excavations on the supposed line of King's Ditch, Hereford, 1958', F G Heys and J F L Norwood, *Transactions of the Woolhope Naturalists' Field Club* 36 (1958–60), 117–25

'Excavations at Castle Green, 1960: a lost Hereford church', F G Heys, *ibid* 36 (1958–60), 343–57*

'Hereford city excavations 1967: introduction', F Noble and R Shoesmith, *ibid* 39 (1967–9), 44–46

'Hereford city as a defended city and the dating of the west rampart', F Noble, *ibid* 39 (1967–9), 47–50

'The western rampart', R Shoesmith, *ibid* 39 (1967–9), 51–67*

'Hereford city excavations: Kings Head site, 1968', R Shoesmith, *ibid* 39 (1967–9), 348–53

'Hereford Castle excavations, 1968–69', P J Leach, *ibid* 40 (1970–2), 225–40*

'Archaeology, 1976: City of Hereford Archaeology Committee', R Shoesmith, *ibid* 42 (1976–8), 97–100

'The post-Civil War history of the site of Hereford Castle', J C Eisel, *ibid* 51 (2003), 11–36* [published 2006]

Herefordshire Beacon

The Herefordshire Beacon 1043–1154. P M Remfry. Malvern Link: SCS Publishing, 1997*

'The Herefordshire Beacon hillfort', R E M Wheeler, *Archaeological Journal* 109 (1952), 146–48*

Howton

'Medieval Britain and Ireland in 2002', J Bradley and M Gaimster, *Medieval Archaeology* 47 (2003), 260–62*

Huntington

Huntington Castle, Herefordshire. A W Lloyd. [S l: s n], 1995*

Kington and Huntington castles 1066 to 1416. P M Remfry. Malvern Link: SCS Publishing, 1997*

'The lordship of Kington (later Huntington)', B Coplestone-Crow, *Herefordshire Archaeological News* 66 (1996), 25–29*

'The foundation and fate of Kington and Huntington castles', P M Remfry, *ibid* 66 (1996), 29–37*

Kilpeck

Excavations at Kilpeck Castle, 1982: an interim report. J Sawle. [S l]: Hereford and Worcester County Council, 1982*

'Kilpeck Castle', E J Talbot, *The hundred-and-twelfth annual meeting at Hereford, 1965*, CAA, 1965, 29

'The buildings on the motte at Kilpeck Castle, Herefordshire', E Impey, *Archaeologia Cambrensis* 146 (1997), 101–8*

'Kilpeck', C J Dunn, *Archaeology in Wales* 12 (1972), 34–35

'Medieval Britain and Ireland in 1982', S M Youngs, J Clark and T B Barry, *Medieval Archaeology* 27 (1983), 180

'Kilpeck Castle, Hereford and Worcester', J Sawle, *West Midlands Archaeology* 26 (1983), 100–2*

'Excavations at Kilpeck, Herefordshire', R Shoesmith (ed), *Transactions of the Woolhope Naturalists' Field Club* 47.2 (1992), 162–208*

King's Caple

King's Caple in Archenfield. E Taylor. Almeley: Logaston Press, 1997*

Kingsland

'Field meeting at Eardisland on 6 March 1994', R Stirling-Brown, *Herefordshire Archaeological News* 62 (1994), 14–17*

Kington

Kington and Huntington castles 1066 to 1416. P M Remfry. Malvern Link: SCS Publishing, 1997*

'The lordship of Kington (later Huntington)', B Coplestone-Crow, *Herefordshire Archaeological News* 66 (1996), 25–29*

'The foundation and fate of Kington and Huntington castles', P M Remfry, *ibid* 66 (1996), 29–37*

Lemore

'A possible castle site at Lemore', R Stirling-Brown, *ibid* 55 (1991), 28–30*

Leominster

'Leominster, Kingdom Hall', [M Napthan], *West Midlands Archaeology* 37 (1994), 36–37

'Leominster, Oldfields Close', [M J Cook], *ibid* 37 (1994), 37

Lingen

'Field trip to Lingen & Pedwardine', R Stirling-Brown, *Herefordshire Archaeological News* 76 (2005), 26–36*

ENGLAND

Llancillo

'The castle at Llancillo Court', R Stirling-Brown, *Herefordshire Archaeological News* 53 (1990), 16–18, 20*

Longtown

Longtown Castle 1048 to 1241. P M Remfry. Malvern Link: SCS Publishing, 1997*

'Longtown', M G Jarrett and G D B Jones, *Archaeology in Wales* 5 (1965), 31

'Longtown Castle', R E Kay, *Herefordshire Archaeological News* 35 (1978), 8–11*

'Longtown Castle', R Kay, *ibid* 64 (1995), 44–46* [but written in 1952]

'Longtown and Pont Hendre castles', P M Remfry, *ibid* 64 (1995), 46–48*

'Medieval Britain in 1965', D M Wilson and D G Hurst, *Medieval Archaeology* 10 (1966), 199

'Medieval Britain and Ireland in 1995', B Nenk, S Margeson and M Hurley, *ibid* 40 (1996), 266

'Longtown Castle: a report on excavations by J Nicholls, 1978', P Ellis, *Transactions of the Woolhope Naturalists' Field Club* 49.1 (1997), 64–84* [published 2000]

Lyde

'Pipe and Lyde, Herefordshire: an unrecorded castle', D Whitehead, *West Midlands Archaeological News Sheet* 22 (1979), 58–60*

'Pipe and Lyde, Herefordshire: an unrecorded castle (SO 497439)', D Whitehead, *Transactions of the Woolhope Naturalists' Field Club* 43.1 (1979), 40–43*

Moccas

'Moccas Castle', R E Kay, *Herefordshire Archaeological News* 55 (1991), 5–6*

Much Dewchurch

'Much Dewchurch castle site', R Stirling-Brown, *ibid* 50 (1988), 24–26*

Newton

'Notes on a visit to Middlewood', R Stirling-Brown, *ibid* 55 (1991), 36–38*

'Medieval Britain and Ireland in 2002', J Bradley and M Gaimster, *Medieval Archaeology* 47 (2003), 263–66*

Pedwardine

'Field trip to Lingen & Pedwardine', R Stirling-Brown, *Herefordshire Archaeological News* 76 (2005), 26–36*

Pembridge

'Pembridge Castle (formerly known as Newland Castle)', R Stirling-Brown, *Herefordshire Archaeological News* 62 (1994), 28–31*

'A visit to Pembridge Castle', P J T Templer, *Transactions of the Woolhope Naturalists' Field Club* 32 (1946–8), 13–15

Penyard

'Penyard Castle (a tentative sketch plan)', P M Remfry, *Postern* 5 (1995), 6*

'Ross Rural, Penyard Castle', [M J Cook], *West Midlands Archaeology* 37 (1994), 47

Pont Hendre

'Longtown and Pont Hendre castles', P M Remfry, *Herefordshire Archaeological News* 64 (1995), 46–48*

'Medieval Britain and Ireland in 2002', J Bradley and M Gaimster, *Medieval Archaeology* 47 (2003), 266–68*

Richard's Castle

Richard's Castle 1048 to 1219. P M Remfry. Malvern Link; SCS Publishing, 1997*

'Richard's Castle', M W Thompson, *The hundred-and-twelfth annual meeting at Hereford, 1965*, CAA, 1965, 22–24

'Excavations at Richard's Castle, Herefordshire, 1962–1964', P E Curnow and M W Thompson, *Journal of the British Archaeological Association* 3 ser 32 (1969), 105–27*

'Medieval Britain in 1962 and 1963', D M Wilson and D G Hurst, *Medieval Archaeology* 8 (1964), 254

'Medieval Britain in 1964', D M Wilson and D G Hurst, *ibid* 9 (1965), 190

'Digging at Richard's Castle', anon, *Shropshire Newsletter* 20 (1962), 2–3

Shobdon

'Shobdon, evaluation of Shobdon mound', R Edwards, *West Midlands Archaeology* 31 (1988), 7

Tretire

'Medieval Britain in 1965', D M Wilson and D G Hurst, *Medieval Archaeology* 10 (1966), 202

'Tretire', N P Bridgewater, *Transactions of the Woolhope Naturalists' Field Club* 38 (1964–6), 158–59

Upton Bishop

'An early motte and enclosure at Upton Bishop', E Taylor, *ibid* 47.1 (1991), 24–27*

Urishay

'Urishay Chapel', R Shoesmith, *ibid* 45.3 (1987), 686–720* [espec pp 689–91]

Weobley

An anatomy of a castle: the Weobley Castle project. G Nash and G Children. Almeley: Logaston Press, 2003*

Looking beyond the castle walls: the Weobley Castle project. G Nash and B Redwood (eds). Oxford: Archaeopress, 2006* (BAR British series; 415)

'Weobley Castle and borough', F Noble, *The hundred-and-twelfth annual meeting at Hereford, 1965*, CAA, 1965, 34–35

'Involving the public at Weobley Castle', G Nash, *The Archaeologist* 60 (2006), 21*

'Medieval Britain and Ireland in 2002', J Bradley and M Gaimster, *Medieval Archaeology* 47 (2003), 268

'Weobley Castle, 'An anatomy of a castle: the Weobley Castle project', Weobley', G Nash, *West Midlands Archaeology* 45 (2002), 48–55*

Wigmore

The Mortimers of Wigmore. Part 1. Wigmore Castle 1066 to 1181. P M Remfry. Malvern Link: SCS Publishing, 1995*

The Mortimers of Wigmore: a short guide of Wigmore Castle. P M Remfry. Malvern Link: SCS Publishing, 1995*

Wigmore Castle tourist guide. P M Remfry. Malvern Link: SCS Publishing, 2000*

'Setting and structure: the conservation of Wigmore Castle', G Coppack, in G Chitty and D Baker (eds), *Managing historic sites and buildings: reconciling presentation and preservation*, 61–70. London: Routledge, 1999*

'Conservation 'as found': the repair and display of Wigmore Castle, Herefordshire', G Coppack, in P M McManus (ed), *Archaeological display and the public: museology and interpretation*, 2nd edition, 145–56. London: Archetype, 2000*

'Wigmore Castle, Hereford', in A H C Oliver, *Archaeology Review 1997–98*, 41–44. London: English Heritage, 1999*

'Wigmore Castle', P E Curnow, *Archaeological Journal* 138 (1981), 23–25

'On preserving our ruins', C Stanford, *Journal of Architectural Conservation* 6.3 (2000), 28–43*

'Wigmore Castle, Herefordshire, the repair of a major monument: an alternative approach', R Tolley, *Association for Studies in the Conservation of Historic Buildings Transactions* 25 (2000), 21–49*

'Wigmore Castle', N Guy, *Castle Studies Group Newsletter* 10 (1996–7), 52–54*

'Planning for the future of a medieval castle', P Hoppen, *Conservation Bulletin* 26 (1995), 24*

'Wigmore Castle: £1m spent – and nothing to show for it!', [A Selkirk], *Current Archaeology* 14.10 (1999), 373–75*

'Wigmore Castle', R Stirling-Brown, *Herefordshire Archaeological News* 48 (1988), 30–33*

'Possible first castle site at Wigmore', P R H[alliwell], *ibid* 61 (1994), 29–30*

'Report on the excavations at Wigmore Castle', R Stone, *ibid* 69 (1998), 31

'Romancing the stone', M Palmer, *Heritage Today* 48 (1999), 12–16*

'Wigmore Castle: geophysical prospecting in the Welsh Marches', N Redhead, *Manchester Archaeological Bulletin* 5 (1990), 71–80*

'A short account of Wigmore Castle', W H Howse, *Transactions of the Radnorshire Society* 20 (1950), 19–20

'Neglect and decay: Wigmore castle – home of the Mortimers', R Shoesmith, *Rescue News* 42 (1987), 3*

'Wigmore, Wigmore Castle', R Stone, *West Midlands Archaeology* 40 (1997), 47–48

'Wigmore Castle, Herefordshire', N Appleton-Fox, *ibid* 41 (1998), 8–10*

'Wigmore Castle – a resistivity survey of the outer bailey', N Redhead, *Transactions of the Woolhope Naturalists' Field Club* 46.3 (1990), 423–31*

Wilton

Wilton Castle 1066 to 1644. P M Remfry. Malvern Link: SCS Publishing, 1998*

'Medieval Britain and Ireland in 2003', J Bradley and M Gaimster, *Medieval Archaeology* 48 (2004), 274

'Bridstow, Wilton Castle', S Fielding, *West Midlands Archaeology* 46 (2003), 50

HERTFORDSHIRE

Campbell, A (ed). *Heritage unlocked: a guide to free sites in the east of England.* London: English Heritage, 2004*

Pevsner, N. *Hertfordshire (The buildings of England)*. 2nd edition, revised by B Cherry. Harmondsworth: Penguin Books, 1977*

Renn, D F. *Medieval castles in Hertfordshire*. Chichester: Phillimore, 1971*

Salter, M. *The castles of the Thames Valley and the Chilterns*. Malvern: Folly Publications, [2002]*

Anstey

'Medieval Britain and Ireland in 1990', B S Nenk, S Margeson and M Hurley, *Medieval Archaeology* 35 (1991), 167

Benington

'The demolition of the keep at Benington', D F Renn, *Antiquaries Journal* 41 (1961), 96–97*

Berkhamsted

Berkhamsted Castle: a brief guide. R Gray. London: English Heritage, 1993*

Berkhamsted Castle, Hertfordshire. C Peers. London: HMSO, 1948*

Berkhamsted Castle 1066 to 1495. P M Remfry. Malvern Link: SCS Publishing, 1995*

Berkhamsted Castle: a short guide. P M Remfry. Malvern Link: SCS Publishing, 1995*

Berkhamsted Castle 1066 to 1495. P M Remfry. 2nd edition. Berkhamsted: Dacorum Heritage Trust, 1998*

'Support your local castle', H Catchpole, *Heritage Learning* 24 (2002), 12–13*

'Berkhamsted Castle: excavations at the south-east tower', P E Curnow, *Hertfordshire Archaeology* 2 (1970), 66–71*

'A bowstave from Berkhamsted Castle', D F Renn, *ibid* 2 (1970), 72–74*

Hertford

'The restoration of Hertford Castle gatehouse', G Moodey, *ibid* 3 (1973), 100–9*

'Excavations in Hertford 1973–4', M R Petchey, *ibid* 5 (1977), 157–75*

'Excavations within the outer bailey of Hertford Castle', R J Zeepvat and H Cooper-Reade, *ibid* 12 (1994–6), 15–40*

'Medieval Britain in 1971', L E Webster and J Cherry, *Medieval Archaeology* 19 (1975), 239

'Medieval Britain and Ireland in 1988', D R M Gaimster, S Margeson and M Hurley, *ibid* 33 (1989), 196

'Medieval Britain and Ireland in 1989', D R M Gaimster, S Margeson and M Hurley, *ibid* 34 (1990), 193

'Medieval Britain and Ireland in 2002', J Bradley and M Gaimster, *ibid* 47 (2003), 269

Pirton

'Medieval Britain and Ireland in 1988', D R M Gaimster, S Margeson and M Hurley, *ibid* 33 (1989), 197

Rickmansworth

Pillbox at the Merchant Taylors' School, Rickmansworth, Hertfordshire. M Brown. Cambridge; RCHME, 1995*

St Albans

'Excavations in the city and district of St Albans 1974–76', C Saunders and A B Havercroft, *Hertfordshire Archaeology* 6 (1978), 1–77*

'A note on the medieval defences of Saint Albans', J Hunn, *Hertfordshire's Past* 11 (1981), 2

'Medieval Britain and Ireland in 1982', S M Youngs, J Clark and T B Barry, *Medieval Archaeology* 27 (1983), 181–82

South Mimms

'South Mimms', anon, *The Archaeologist in Essex, Hertfordshire, London and Middlesex* (1960), 31–34

'South Mimms Castle', D F Renn, *Barnet and District Record Society Bulletin* 10 (1957), [whole issue]*

'Excavations at the motte and bailey of South Mimms, Herts., 1960–1967', J P C Kent, *Barnet and District Local History Society Bulletin* 16 (1968), [whole issue]*

'Medieval Britain in 1960', D M Wilson and D G Hurst, *Medieval Archaeology* 5 (1961), 318

'Medieval Britain in 1961', D M Wilson and D G Hurst, *ibid* 6–7 (1962–3), 322

'Medieval Britain in 1962 and 1963', D M Wilson and D G Hurst, *ibid* 8 (1964), 255

'South Mimms Castle', J P C Kent, *Thames Basin Archaeological Observers group Newsletter* new ser 22 (1964), 10–11

Therfield

'Therfield', anon, *The Archaeologist in Essex, Hertfordshire, London and Middlesex* (1960), 18

'The excavation of a motte and bailey castle at Therfield, Hertfordshire', M Biddle, *Journal of the British Archaeological Association* 3 ser 27 (1964), 53–91*

'Medieval Britain in 1958', D M Wilson and J G Hurst, *Medieval Archaeology* 3 (1959), 307–8

HUNTINGDONSHIRE

Lowerre, A. *Placing castles in the Conquest: landscape, lordship and local politics in the south-eastern midlands, 1066–1100*. Oxford: J and E Hedges, 2005* (BAR British series; 385)

Osborne, M. *20th century defences in Britain: Cambridgeshire*. Market Deeping: Concrete Publications, [2001]*

Pevsner, N. *Bedfordshire and the county of Huntingdon and Peterborough (The buildings of England)*. Harmondsworth: Penguin Books, 1968*

Salter, M. *The castles of East Anglia*. Malvern: Folly Publications, 2001*

Earith

'Earith bulwark', A D Saunders, *Archaeological Journal* 124 (1967), 222–23*

'The Bulwark, Earith, Cambridgeshire', C C Taylor, *proceedings of the Cambridgeshire Antiquarian Society* 87 (1998), 81–86*

Huntingdon

'Huntingdon: Huntingdon Castle', A Taylor, *Archaeological Excavations 1975*, 82. London: HMSO, 1976

'Huntingdon', P G M Dickinson, *CBA Group 7 Bulletin* 10 (1963), 2

'Huntingdon siege castle', P Dickinson, *ibid* 14 (1967), 2–3

'Medieval Britain in 1967', D M Wilson and D G Hurst, *Medieval Archaeology* 12 (1968), 175

'Medieval Britain and Ireland in 2000', J Bradley and M Gaimster, *ibid* 44 (2000), 253

'Medieval Britain and Ireland in 2005', M Gaimster and K O'Conor, *ibid* 50 (2006), 301

Kimbolton

'Cambridgeshire earthwork surveys: IV. Mound, Kimbolton', A E Brown and C C Taylor, *Proceedings of the Cambridge Antiquarian Society* 70 (1980), 124–25*

'Kimbolton', C F Tebbutt, *CBA Group 7 Bulletin* 6 (1959), 2

Maxey

'Medieval Britain and Ireland in 1999', J Bradley and M Gaimster, *Medieval Archaeology* 44 (2000), 254

Norman Cross

'Norman Cross Camp, Yaxley', A Phillips and G Barrat, *Annual Review 1984–85*, RCHME, 1985, 26*

'Das Lager für napoleonische Kriegsgefangene in Norman Cross, Huntingdonshire 1796–1816', M D Howe, in V Schmidtchen (ed), *Festung Garnison Bevolkerung: historische Aspekte der Festungsforschung*, 167–84. Wesel: Deutsche Gesellschaft für Festungsforschung, 1982*

Torpel

'Unrecorded castle discovered', anon, *Nature* 221 (1969), 905–6

Tort Hill, Sawtry

'Earthworks on Tort Hill, Sawtry, Huntingdon', C F Tebbutt and G Rudd, *Proceedings of the Cambridge Antiquarian Society* 59 (1966), 138–39

Woodwalton

'Cambridgeshire earthwork surveys. III. Woodwalton Castle', A E Brown and C C Taylor, *ibid* 68 (1978), 62–63, 65*

KENT

Barnes, D R. 'Artillery fortification in the south-east: a review', *Fort* 6 (1978), 5–12*

Beanse, A and Gill, R. *The London mobilisation centres*. Fareham: Palmerston Forts Society, 2000*

Bennett, D. *A handbook of Kent's defences*. [S l]: Kent Defence Research Group, 1977*

Bloomfield, J (ed). *Kent and the Napoleonic Wars*. Gloucester: Alan Sutton, for Kent Archives, 1987*

Bragard, P, Termote, J and Williams, J. *Walking the walls: historic town defences in Kent, Côte d'Opale and West Flanders*. Maidstone: Kent County Council, 1999*

Bragard, P [*et al*]. *The story of fortifications through the ages: ramparts and walls pre-1500*. Maidstone: Kent County Council, 2001*

Bragard, P. [*et al*]. *The story of fortifications through the ages: the rise of artillery AD 1500–1800*. Maidstone: Kent County Council, 2001*

Bragard, P. [*et al*]. *The story of fortifications through the ages: high technology & defence 1800–1945*. Maidstone: Kent County Council, 2001*

Burridge, D. *20th century defences in Britain: Kent*. London: Brassey's, 1997*

Elliott, J (ed). *Heritage unlocked: guide to free sites in London and the south east*. London: English Heritage, 2005*

Gill, R. 'Late 19th century bridge caponiers', *The Redan* 59 (2003), 2–9*

Glendinning, I H. *The hammer of Invicta, being a history of the martello towers round Romney Marsh*. Privately published, 1981*

Godwin, J E. 'Fortifications against a French invasion of the east Kent coast of England: 1750–1815', *Fort* 16 (1988), 83–96*

Greatorex, C. 'An archaeological investigation of the Royal Military Canal, near Ham Street', *Archaeologia Cantiana* 115 (1995), 231–37*

Grove, L R A. 'The repairing of the Medway forts *c* 1700', *ibid* 66 (1953), 165–70

Gulvin, K R. *The Medway forts: a short guide*. [S l]: Medway Military Research Group, 1976*

Guy, J. *Kent castles: a comprehensive guide to sixty castles and castle sites for both the visitor and the historian*. Gillingham: Meresborough Books, 1980*

Hamilton-Baillie, J. 'Strategic safeguard or military folly? London's Victorian forts', *Country Life* 180 (1986), 1560, 1562*

Lawson, T. 'Maritime Kent 1500–1700', in T Lawson and D Killingray (eds), *An historical atlas of Kent*, 91–92. Chichester: Phillimore, 2004*

MacDougall, P. *The Isle of Grain defences*. [S l]: Kent Defence Research Group, 1980*

Nelson-Singer, C. 'The Royal Military Canal and Sandgate Redoubt', *Ravelin* 51 (2001), 5–8

Newman, J. *North east and east Kent (The buildings of England)*. 3rd edition. Harmondsworth: Penguin Books, 1983*

Newman, J. *West Kent and the Weald (The buildings of England)*. 2nd edition. Harmondsworth: Penguin Books, 1976, reprinted with corrections 1980*

Rady, J. 'The Royal Military Canal, Kenardington', *Canterbury's Archaeology: 20th Annual Report 1995–1996*, Canterbury Archaeological Trust, 1997, 40–41*

Salter, M. *The castles of Kent*. Malvern: Folly Publications, 2000*

Saunders, A D. 'The coastal defences of the south-east: a reassessment', in N J G

Pounds (ed), *The Canterbury area: proceedings of the 140th summer meeting of the Royal Archaeological Institute, 1994*, 7–9. RAI, 1994

Saunders, A D. 'Thames fortifications during the 16th to 19th centuries', in *Thames gateway: recording historic buildings and landscapes in the Thames estuary*, 124–34. Swindon: RCHME, 1995*

Saunders, A D. 'The coastal defences of the south-east', *Archaeological Journal* 126 (1969), 201–5*

Saunders, A D. 'The coastal defences of the south-east: a reassessment', *Ravelin* 39 (1994), 3–7

Saunders, A D and Smith V T C. *Kent's defence heritage*. 2 vols in 3 [loose-leaf ring-binders]. Maidstone: Kent County Council, 2001* [limited circulation]

Smith, V T C. *Defending London's river*. Rochester: North Kent Books, 1985*

Smith, V T C. *Front-line Kent: defence against invasion from 1400 to the Cold war*. Maidstone: Kent County Council, 2001*

Smith, V T C. 'The defences of the 20th century', in *Thames gateway: recording historic buildings and landscapes in the Thames estuary*, 135–43. Swindon: RCHME, 1995*

Smith, V T C. 'Defence and fortifications 1700–1914', in T Lawson and D Killingray (eds), *An historical atlas of Kent*, 136–39. Chichester: Phillimore, 2004*

Smith, V T C. 'Kent's defences in the age of gunpowder. Part one: the first 500 years', *Byegone Kent* 2 (1981), 674–83*

Smith, V T C. 'Kent's defences in the age of gunpowder. Part two: the last 100 years', *ibid* 2 (1981), 716–24*

Smith, V T C. 'The London mobilisation centres', *London Archaeologist* 2.10 (1975), 244–48*

Smith, V T C. 'Chatham and London: the changing face of English land fortification, 1870–1918', *Post-Medieval Archaeology* 19 (1985), 104–49*

Smith, V T C and Killingray, D. 'Kent and the First World War', in T Lawson and D Killingray (eds), *An historical atlas of Kent*, 140–41. Chichester: Phillimore, 2004*

Smith, V T C and Killingray, D. 'Kent and the Second World War', in T Lawson and D Killingray (eds), *An historical atlas of Kent*, 142–45. Chichester: Phillimore, 2004*

Smithers, D W. *Castles in Kent*. Chatham: Hallwell, 1980*

Turner, D J. 'The nineteenth century "forts" of the North Downs', *Surrey Archaeological Society Bulletin* 92 (1972), 4–5

Vine, P A L. *The Royal Military Canal: an historical account of the waterway and military road from Shorncliffe in Kent to Cliff End in Sussex*. Newton Abbot: David and Charles, 1972*

Vine, P A L. 'In defence against the French: a history of the Royal Military Canal', *Country Life* 160 (1976), 892–94*

Ward, A. 'Castles and other defensive sites', in T Lawson and D Killingray (eds), *An historical atlas of Kent*, 53–55. Chichester: Phillimore, 2004*

Wilson, J D. 'Later nineteenth century defences of the Thames, including Grain Fort', *Journal of the Society for Army Historical Research* 41 (1963), 141–58, 182–99*

Worssam, B C and Tatton-Brown, T. 'Kentish Rag and other Kent building stones', *Archaeologia Cantiana* 112 (1993), 93–125*

Allington
The picture story of Allington Castle. D Thornton. Privately published, [1987]*

Bayford
'The enigma of Bayford Castle', J Clancy, *Kent Archaeological Society Newsletter* 57 (2003), 6*

'Bayford Castle and Bayford Court', A Ward, *ibid* 58 (2003), 12–13*

'The continuing saga of Bayford Castle', J Clancy, *ibid* 59 (2003–4), 13

Canterbury
The archaeology of Canterbury. 1. Excavations at Canterbury Castle. P Bennett, S S Frere and S Stow. Maidstone: Kent Archaeological Society for the Canterbury Archaeological Trust, 1982*

The city gates of Canterbury. C Buckingham. Canterbury: Thomas Becket Books, 1980*

The archaeology of Canterbury. 2. Excavations on the Roman and medieval defences of Canterbury. S S Frere, S Stow and P Bennett. Maidstone: Kent Archaeological Society for the Canterbury Archaeological Trust, 1982*

The archaeology of Canterbury. 8. Canterbury excavations: intra- and extramural sites. 1949–55 and 1980–84. S S Frere [et al]. Maidstone: Kent Archaeological Society for the Canterbury Archaeological Trust, 1987*

The royal castle. T Tatton-Brown. [Canterbury]: Canterbury Archaeological Trust, 1985*

The Westgate. T Tatton-Brown. Canterbury: Canterbury Archaeological Trust, 1985*

'The decoration of Canterbury Castle keep', D F Renn, in *Medieval art and architecture at Canterbury before 1220*, 125–28. [S l]: British Archaeological Association, 1982* (BAA conference transactions; 5)

'Excavations carried out at 16 Pound Lane, Canterbury', T Tatton-Brown, *Canterbury Archaeology 1975/76*, Canterbury Archaeological Trust, (?1976), 6–7*

'Excavations at Canterbury Castle 1975/76', T Tatton-Brown, *ibid*, 9*

'Building recording: West Gate, Canterbury', T Tatton-Brown, *Annual Report 1980–81*, Canterbury Archaeological Trust, 1981, 14, 16*

'Excavation. 3. Dane John site', J Rady, *Annual Report 1981–82*, Canterbury Archaeological Trust, 1982, 13–15

'The Ridingate', P Blockley, *Annual Report 1985–86*, Canterbury Archaeological Trust, [?1986], 13–14*

'Station Road East', I Anderson and J Rady, *Canterbury's Archaeology: 13th Annual Report 1988–1989*, Canterbury Archaeological Trust, 1990, 8–9*

'St Radigund's Bridge', A Ward, *Canterbury's Archaeology: 19th Annual Report 1994–1995*, Canterbury Archaeological Trust, 1996, 11–12*

'Worthgate', A Ward, *Canterbury's Archaeology: 20th Annual Report 1995–1996*, Canterbury Archaeological Trust, 1997, 21–22*

'The Dane John mound', C Jarman, *Canterbury's Archaeology: 21st Annual Report 1996–1997*, Canterbury Archaeological Trust, 1999, 7–8*

'City rampart, south of St George's Gate', J Wilson, *Canterbury's Archaeology: 24th Annual Report 1999–2000*, Canterbury Archaeological Trust, 2002, 13

'Rear of No. 89a Broad Street, Canterbury: city wall', P Seary, *Canterbury's Archaeology: 26th Annual Report 2001–2002*, Canterbury Archaeological Trust, 2003, 54

'Canterbury excavations: September – October, 1944', A Williams, *Archaeologia Cantiana* 59 (1946), 64–81*

'Interim report on the excavations at Canterbury', F Jenkins, *ibid* 86 (1971), 232–33

'A note on the excavations at Canterbury Castle, 1971', L Millard, *ibid* 87 (1972), 205–8*

'Excavations in 1976 by the Canterbury Archaeological Trust: Canterbury Castle', T Tatton-Brown, *ibid* 92 (1976), 240

'Excavations in 1976 by the Canterbury Archaeological Trust: 16 Pound Lane', T Tatton-Brown, *ibid* 92 (1976), 241–44*

'Interim report on excavations in 1981 by the Canterbury Archaeological Trust. 3. Dane John site', J Rady, *ibid* 97 (1981), 281–84*

'Interim report on work in 1983 by the Canterbury Archaeological Trust. 20. St Radigund's Street', P Bennett, *ibid* 99 (1983), 241–42

'Interim report on work in 1984 by the Canterbury Archaeological Trust. 4. Blackfriar's Gate', P Bennett, *ibid* 101 (1984), 283–84

'Interim report on work in 1984 by the Canterbury Archaeological Trust. 11. Sites along the northern city wall', P Blockley, *ibid* 101 (1984), 296–98*

'Interim report on work carried out in 1986 by the Canterbury Archaeological Trust. 8. The Ridingate', P Blockley, *ibid* 103 (1986), 205–9*

'Interim report on work carried out in 1988 by the Canterbury Archaeological Trust. 11. Westgate Chamber', P Bennett, *ibid* 106 (1988), 149–51*

'Interim report on work carried out in 1988 by the Canterbury Archaeological Trust. 12. The Westgate pavement', I Anderson, *ibid* 106 (1988), 151

'Interim report on work carried out in 1988 by the Canterbury Archaeological Trust. 13. Nos 1A-4 Pound lane', I Anderson, *ibid* 106 (1988), 151–53*

'Interim report on work carried out in 1988 by the Canterbury Archaeological Trust. 14. St George's gate', P Bennett, M Houliston and T Tatton-Brown, *ibid* 106 (1988), 153–61*

'Excavations at Riding Gate, Canterbury, 1986–87', P Blockley, *ibid* 107 (1989), 117–54*

'Interim report on work carried out in 1989 by the Canterbury Archaeological Trust. 13. Station Road East', I Anderson, *ibid* 107 (1989), 295–99*

'Interim report on work carried out in 1990 by the Canterbury Archaeological Trust. 3. Station Road East', P Bennett, *ibid* 108 (1990), 205–6

'Canterbury', L Millard, *Archaeological Excavations 1968*, 52. London: HMSO, 1969

'Canterbury', L Millard and F Jenkins, *Archaeological Excavations 1971*, 72. London: HMSO, 1972

'The defences of Canterbury', D F Renn, *Archaeological Journal* 126 (1969), 238–39*

'Station Road East', I Anderson and J Rady, *Canterbury's Archaeology 1988–1989* (1990), 8–9*

'Canterbury Castle: a case study', D F Renn, *Château Gaillard* 11 (1983), 253–55*

'Canterbury', T Tatton-Brown, *Current Archaeology* 6.3 (1978), 78–82*

'Canterbury', [A Selkirk], *ibid* 7.9 (1981), 269–75*

'Medieval Britain in 1968', D M Wilson and D G Hurst, *Medieval Archaeology* 13 (1969), 265

'Medieval Britain in 1969', D M Wilson and D G Hurst, *ibid* 14 (1970), 182

'Medieval Britain in 1971', L E Webster and J Cherry, *ibid* 16 (1972), 181

'Medieval Britain in 1972', L E Webster and J Cherry, *ibid* 17 (1973), 169

'Medieval Britain in 1981', S M Youngs and J Clark, *ibid* 26 (1982), 187–88

'Medieval Britain and Ireland in 1983', S M Youngs, J Clark and T B Barry, *ibid* 28 (1984), 224

'Medieval Britain and Ireland in 1984', S M Youngs, J Clark and T Barry, *ibid* 29 (1985), 148

'Medieval Britain and Ireland in 1988', D R M Gaimster, S Margeson and T Barry, *ibid* 34 (1990), 197

'Post-medieval archaeology in Britain and Ireland in 1990', M Ponsford, *Post-Medieval Archaeology* 25 (1991), 123

Chatham

The Napoleonic defences of Rochester and Chatham. K R Gulvin. [S l]: Medway Military Research Group, 1977*

Chatham's concrete ring. K R Gulvin. [S l]: Medway Military Research Group, 1979*

Chatham, the war years. G W Jones. Privately published, n d*

'Fort Amherst, Chatham', A Ward, *Canterbury's Archaeology: 17th Annual Report 1992–1993*, Canterbury Archaeological Trust, 1993, 39

'Fort Amherst and the Chatham Lines', A Ward, *Canterbury's Archaeology: 18th Annual Report 1993–1994*, Canterbury Archaeological Trust, 1995, 30

'Twydall profile', K Gulvin and Q Hughes, *Fort* 5 (1978), 39–43*; pp 77–85* in 1995 revised edition of *Fort* vols 4–5

'Chatham's siege operations: 1907', V T C Smith, *ibid* 5 (1978), 44–45; pp 87–93* in 1995 revised edition of *Fort* vols 4–5

'More notes on the siege exercises at Chatham, 1907', J R E Hamilton-Baillie, *ibid* 6 (1978), 34–37*

'The later nineteenth-century land defences of Chatham', V T C Smith, *Post-Medieval Archaeology* 10 (1976), 104–17*

'Chatham and London: the changing face of English land fortification', V T C Smith, *ibid* 19 (1985), 104–49*

'The fixed fortifications of the sixteenth to nineteenth centuries illustrated by the defences of Chatham', J R E Hamilton-Baillie, *Royal Engineers Journal* 88.1 (1974), 2–14*

Fort Amherst. K R Gulvin. [S l]: Medway Military Research Group, 1977*

'Gunning for Amherst', G Harvey, *Casemate* 15 (1985), 1–2*

'Napoleonic fortress breathes new life, thanks to CP', anon, *Community Programme News* 15 (1985), 8–9*

'Fort Amherst – Chatham', K R Gulvin, *Kent Archaeological Review* 50 (1977), 243–47*

'Fort Amherst', K R Gulvin, *ibid* 68 (1982), 172–74

'Fort Borstal', P Cobb, *The Redan* 17 (1989), 1–9

Fort Bridgewoods. G W Jones and M Shortland. Privately published, n d*

'Vandalism at Fort Bridgewoods', K R Gulvin and V T C Smith, *Kent Archaeological Review* 56 (1979), 137–38*

Fort Darland. G W Jones and M Shortland. Privately published, n d*

'Gillingham Fort', K R Gulvin, *Kent Archaeological Review* 62 (1980), 36–39*

Fort Horsted. G W Jones and M Shortland. Privately published, n d*

Fort Luton. G W Jones and M Shortland. Privately published, n d*

' "A bridge too far". The Fort Luton & Borstal drawbridges', D Wood, *The Redan* 35 (1995), 29–31*

'A bridge too far: part 2', D Wood, *ibid* 36 (1996), 38–39*

'The Twydall Redoubts and the 3pr QF on travelling carriage', A Beanse and R Gill, *ibid* 62 (2004), 43–46*

Fort Pitt. J Cooper. Maidstone: Kent County Library, 1976*

'Fort Pitt – Chatham', K R Gulvin, *Kent Archaeological Review* 47 (1977), 172–76*

Chilham
'Chilham Castle and Jacobean house', P E Curnow, *Archaeological Journal* 126 (1969), 266

Cliffe Fort
Cliffe Fort Brennan torpedo slipway, Medway, Kent. P Pattison. Cambridge: RCHME, 1993*

Louis Brennan CB: dirigible torpedo. R E Wilkes. Gillingham: Gillingham Public Libraries, 1973

'A Brennan torpedo station at Cliffe Fort', V T C Smith, *Kent Archaeological Review* 24 (1971), 116–18*

'Brennan', R Crowdy, *Ravelin* 26 (1991), 5–9*

Cockham Wood
'Cockham Wood Fort', V T C Smith, *Archaeologia Cantiana* 112 (1993), 55–75*

Cooling
'Cooling Castle', R Austin, *Canterbury's Archaeology: 15th Annual Report 1990–1991*, Canterbury Archaeological Trust, 1991, 37*

'Cooling Castle, near Rochester', A Ward, *Canterbury's Archaeology: 17th Annual Report 1992–1993*, Canterbury Archaeological Trust, 1993, 39*

'Interim report on work carried out in 1991 by the Canterbury Archaeological Trust. IV. Building recording. F. Cooling Castle', R Austin, *Archaeologia Cantiana* 109 (1991), 329–30

Court-at-Street
'The Holy Maid of Kent (or, I think I got it wrong again)', D Burridge, *Loopholes* 21 (1998), 6–8* [pillbox]

Darnet
Medway's island forts: the history of Fort Darnet and Fort Hoo. R Crowdy. [S l]: Medway Military Research Group, [1979]*

Medway's island forts. R Crowdy. 2nd edition. [S l]: Medway Military Research Group, 1980*

'Visits to Hoo, Darnet and Ramsgate', D Burridge, *Ravelin* 35 (1993), 19–25*

Deal

Deal and Walmer castles: the handbook for teachers. J Barnes. London: English Heritage, 1991*

Deal Castle, Kent. J Coad. London: English Heritage, 1998*

Deal Castle, Kent. B H St J O'Neil and G C Dunning. London: HMSO, 1966*

Deal Castle, Kent. B H St J O'Neil. 5th printing (reset). London: HMSO, 1983*

Deal and Walmer castles. A D Saunders. London: HMSO, 1963*; 2nd edition, 1982*

Deal and Walmer castles. A D Saunders. London: HBMCE, 1985*

'A note on two original drawings by William Stukeley depicting "The three castles which keep the downs"', J R Kenyon, *Antiquaries Journal* 58 (1978), 162–64*

'Deal Castle', A D Saunders, *Archaeological Journal* 126 (1969), 217–19*

'The siege of the Downs castles in 1648', J R Powell, *Mariner's Mirror* 51 (1965), 155–71*

Dover

Dover Castle: a brief guide. Anon. London: English Heritage, 1993*

Soldiers of the castle: Dover Castle garrisoned. G M Atherton. Dover: Triangle Publications, 2004*

Dover Castle: a handbook for teachers. J Barnes and A Harmsworth. London: English Heritage, 1991*

Dover Castle: a teacher's handbook. J Barnes and J Fordham. London: English Heritage, 2004*

Dover Castle, Kent. R A Brown. London: HMSO, 1966* 2nd edition, 1974*; 3rd edition, 1983*

Dover Castle, Kent. R A Brown. 4th edition. London: HBMCE, 1985*

The Dover Turret, Admiralty Pier Fort. D Burridge. Rochester: North Kent Books, 1987*

A guide to the Western Heights defences, Dover. D Burridge. Dover: Kent Defence Research Group, 1992* (Ravelin special no; 6); 2nd edition, 1993*

The Royal Commission defences of Dover. D Burridge. Privately published, 1989*

Dover Castle. J Coad. London: English Heritage, 1997*

English Heritage book of Dover Castle and the defences of Dover. J Coad. London: Batsford, in association with English Heritage, 1995*

Building accounts of King Henry III. H M Colvin (ed), 20–87. Oxford: Clarendon Press, 1971*

The Dover Castle story. C Nutt. Charlbury: English Heritage, in association with Thames House Books, 2005*

Dover's hidden fortress. J Peverley. Dover: Dover Society, 1996*

Dover Castle. C Platt. London: English Heritage, 1988*; reprinted with amendments, 1990*; 2nd edition, 1994*

Dover Castle. C A R Radford. London: HMSO, 1953*

The history of Archcliffe Fort, Dover, Kent. D E Welby. Dover: Polar Bear Press, 1991*

Dover's forgotten fortress. J Welby. [Maidstone]: Kent County Library, n d*

'Dover Castle 1898–1963: preservation of a monument. A postscript', J Coad, in C Harper-Bill, C J Holdsworth and J L Nelson (eds), *Studies in medieval history presented to R Allen Brown*, 57–69. Woodbridge: Boydell Press, 1989*

'Stephen de Pencestre's account as constable of Dover Castle for the years Michaelmas 1272-Michaelmas 1274', A J Taylor, in A Detsicas (ed), *Collectanea historica: essays in memory of Stuart Rigold*, 114–22. Maidstone: Kent Archaeological Society, 1981*

'Stephen de Pencestre's account as constable of Dover Castle for the years Michaelmas 1272-Michaelmas 1274', A Taylor, in A Taylor, *Studies in castles and castle-building*, 248–56. London: Hambledon Press, 1986*

'The defences of Dover Castle and Western Heights 1740–1945', J Coad, in N J G Pounds (ed), *The Canterbury area: proceedings of the 140th summer meeting of the Royal Archaeological Institute, 1994*, 34–39. London: RAI, 1994*

'Dover Castle', P Bennett, T Tatton-Brown and S Ouditt, *Canterbury's Archaeology: 14th Annual Report 1989–1990*, Canterbury Archaeological Trust, 1991, 26–29*

'A20 Dover sewers project', K Parfitt, *Canterbury's Archaeology: 16th Annual Report 1991–1992*, Canterbury Archaeological Trust, 1992, 11–16*

'H. M. Youth Custody Centre, Dover Western Heights', M Houliston, *Canterbury's Archaeology: 17th Annual Report 1992–1993*, Canterbury Archaeological Trust, 1993, 25–26*

'The Grand Shaft, Dover', B Corke and K Parfitt, *Canterbury's Archaeology: 18th Annual Report 1993–1994*, Canterbury Archaeological Trust, 1995, 22–23*

'A20 roadworks, Dover', K Parfitt, *ibid*, 23*

'The Grand Shaft, Dover', B Corke, *Canterbury's Archaeology: 20th Annual Report 1995–1996*, Canterbury Archaeological Trust, 1997, 34*

'Archcliffe Fort, Dover', K Parfitt, *Canterbury's Archaeology: 21st Annual Report 1996–1997*, Canterbury Archaeological Trust, 1999, 19*

'Archcliffe Fort, Dover', K Parfitt, *Canterbury's Archaeology: 22nd Annual Report 1997–1998*, Canterbury Archaeological Trust, 2000, 12–13

'The Citadel, Dover Western Heights', K Parfitt, *Canterbury's Archaeology: 23rd Annual Report 1998–1999*, Canterbury Archaeological Trust, 2001, 22–23*

'Broadlees Bottom, Dover Castle', K Parfitt, *ibid*, 24

'An Iron Age fort at Dover?', H M Colvin, *Antiquity* 33 (1959), 125–27*

'The Avranches traverse at Dover Castle', D F Renn, *Archaeologia Cantiana* 84 (1969), 79–92*

'The Domesday of Dover Castle – an archival history', F Hull, *ibid* 98 (1982), 67–75

'Dover Castle: key to Richard II's kingdom?', J L Gillespie, *ibid* 105 (1988), 179–95

'Interim report on work carried out in 1990 by the Canterbury Archaeological trust. 12. Dover Castle', P Bennett, T Tatton-Brown and S Ouditt, *ibid* 108 (1990), 238–44*

'Interim report on work carried out in 1993 by the Canterbury Archaeological Trust', [F Panton and P Bennett], *ibid* 112 (1993), 365–67

'Wax, stone and iron: Dover's town defences in the late Middle Ages', S Sweetinburgh, *ibid* 124 (2004), 183–207*

'Dover', B Philp, *Archaeological Excavations 1972*, 88–89. London: HMSO, 1973

'Dover Castle', R A Brown, *Archaeological Journal* 126 (1969), 205–11, 262–64*

'The earthworks around St Mary-in-Castro', M Biddle, *ibid* 126 (1969), 264–65

'Brick cliffs of Dover', J R Peverley, *Architectural Review* 125 (1959), 175–78*

'Dover Grand Shaft', L Braithwaite, *ibid* 141 (1967), 231–33*

'Master Jordan, who made the king's trébuchet', D Renn, *Arms & Armour: Journal of the Royal Armouries* 1.1 (2004), 25–32*

'Excavations at Dover Castle, 1964–1966', S E Rigold, *Journal of the British Archaeological Association* 3 ser 30 (1967), 87–121*

'Excavations at Dover Castle, principally in the inner bailey', A M Cook, D C Mynard and S E Rigold, *ibid* 3 ser 32 (1969), 54–104*

'The Grand Shaft', S Campbell, *Byegone Kent* 4.9 (1983), 540–43*

'The 18th and 19th century defences at Dover Castle', D Burridge, *ibid* 4.11 (1983), 676–83*

'Archcliff Fort: Dover', F Kitchen, *ibid* 6.7 (1985), 421–27*

'The siege of Dover Castle in 1216', M D Miriams, *ibid* 10.7 (1989), 488–90*

'Recording the keep, Dover Castle', K Booth and P Roberts, *Château Gaillard* 19 (2000), 21–23*

'Dover Castle and the great siege of 1216', J Goodall, *ibid* 19 (2000), 91–102*

'The Western Heights: Dover's *other* great fortress', P Pattison, *Conservation Bulletin* 39 (2000), 14–15*

'Dover Castle, Kent – I', M Binney, *Country Life* 174 (1983), 1902–5*

'Dover Castle, Kent – II', M Binney, *ibid* 175 (1984), 18–21*

'Saving Salvin's Mess', M Binney, *ibid* 184.46 (1990), 70*

'The key of England', J Goodall, *ibid* 193.11 (1999), 44–47*

'In the powerhouse of Kent', J Goodall, *ibid* 193.12 (1999), 110–38

'The Duke of York's pillboxes', D Burridge, *Defence Lines* 1 (1995), 7

'An introduction to the defences of Dover', N Hodgson, *Fort* 6 (1978), 38–60*

'The arming of the Dover Turret', D Burridge, *Fortress* 4 (1990), 39–52*

'The Western Heights defences, Dover', D Burridge, *ibid* 9 (1991), 35–46*

'King of castles', D Snow, *Heritage Today* 71 (2005), 20–25*

'Dover's 19th century fortifications – part 1', D Crellin, *Kent Archaeological Review* 32 (1973), 44–46*

'Dover's 19th century fortifications – part 2', D Crellin, *ibid* 33 (1973), 73–76*

'Medieval Britain in 1961', D M Wilson and D G Hurst, *Medieval Archaeology* 6–7 (1962–3), 322

'Medieval Britain in 1962 and 1963', D M Wilson and D G Hurst, *ibid* 8 (1964), 254–55

'Medieval Britain in 1964', D M Wilson and D G Hurst, *ibid* 9 (1965), 190

'Medieval Britain in 1965', D M Wilson and D G Hurst, *ibid* 10 (1966), 190–91

'Medieval Britain and Ireland in 1990', B S Nenk, S Margeson and M Hurley, *ibid* 35 (1991), 171

'The Dover Turret', K Gibbs, *Military Chest* 2.4 (1983), 47–50*

'A group of post-medieval pottery from Dover Castle', D C Mynard, *Post-Medieval Archaeology* 3 (1969), 31–46*

'Post-medieval Britain and Ireland in 1990', M Ponsford, *ibid* 25 (1991), 123

'Post-medieval Britain and Ireland in 1991', M Ponsford, *ibid* 26 (1992), 108–9

'Lighting the forts: the Dover Turret', D Burridge, *Ravelin* 23 (1991), 16–18

'Dover archaeological report', K Parfitt, *ibid* 30 (1992), 9–11

'One lost and two found: two gun batteries at Dover', K Parfitt, *ibid* 35 (1993), 26–29*

'The Duke of York's pillboxes', D Burridge, *ibid* 35 (1993), 33–35*

'Field fortifications at Dover', D Burridge, *ibid* 38 (1994), 10–12

'Lighting the Dover Turret', D Burridge, *ibid* 43 (1995), 26–28

'A military canal and the seaward defences of Dover town', K Parfitt, *ibid* 48 (1997), 17–20*

'The low-down Boys and brick', D Burridge, *ibid* 49 (1998), 2–58 [pillboxes]

'The Dover Turret: part 1', D Burridge, *The Redan* 16 (1989), 23–26

'The Dover Turret: part 2', D Burridge, *ibid* 17 (1990), 11–21*

'The Dover Turret: part 3', D Burridge, *ibid* 18 (1990), 23–26

'The Dover Turret: part 4', D Burridge, *ibid* 19 (1991), 14–17

'Dover Turret: part 5', D Burridge, *ibid* 20 (1990), 2–7

'Fort Burgoyne: "works secure in itself"', D Burridge, *ibid* 21 (1991), 7–10*

'Down into the labyrinth: Dover's Western Heights', P Cobb, *ibid* 48 (2000), 23–36*

Dungeness

'The guns of Dungeness', F Kitchen, *Byegone Kent* 10.3 (1989), 178–82*

Dymchurch

Dymchurch martello tower. M R Apted. London: HBMCE, 1985*

Dymchurch martello tower. J G Coad. London: English Heritage, 1990*

Eynsford

Eynsford Castle, Kent. S E Rigold. London: HMSO, 1964*

Eynsford Castle, Kent. S E Rigold. London: HBMCE, 1984*

'Eynsford Castle and its excavation', S E Rigold, *Archaeologia Cantiana* 86 (1971), 109–72*

'Eynsford Castle: the moat and bridge', S E Rigold and A J Fleming, *ibid* 88 (1973), 87–116*

'Eynsford Castle: a reinterpretation of its early history in the light of recent excavations', V Horsman, *ibid* 105 (1988), 39–57*

'Medieval Britain in 1956', D M Wilson and J G Hurst, *Medieval Archaeology* 1 (1957), 156–57

'Medieval Britain in 1961', D M Wilson and D G Hurst, *ibid* 6–7 (1962–3), 322

'Medieval Britain in 1964', D M Wilson and D G Hurst, *ibid* 9 (1965), 190

'Medieval Britain in 1966', D M Wilson and D G Hurst, *ibid* 11 (1967), 285

Farningham

'"Maginot-Line" at Farningham', V T C Smith, *Kent Archaeological Review* 27 (1972), 208–9*

'Excavations in the Dartford and the Darent Valley 1973: the medieval site at Farningham', A Borthwick and H Davies, *ibid* 34 (1973), 113–14

'Medieval Britain in 1972', L E Webster and J Cherry, *Medieval Archaeology* 17 (1973), 161

Folkestone

'Castle Hill, Folkestone', P Bennett, *Canterbury's Archaeology: 11th Annual Report July 1986–July 1987*, Canterbury Archaeological Trust, [?1987], 20–21*

'Discovery of masonry on Castle Hill, Folkestone', H F Bing, *Archaeologia Cantiana* 63 (1950), 147

'Interim report on work carried out in 1987 by the Canterbury Archaeological Trust. Castle Hill, Folkestone', P Bennett, *ibid* 104 (1987), 318–19*

'Interim report on work carried out in 1989 by the Canterbury Archaeological Trust. 29. Channel Tunnel excavations. 4: Excavations at Castle Hill', J Rady and S Ouditt, *ibid* 107 (1989), 352–54*

'The Bayle Fort: Folkestone', F Kitchen, *Byegone Kent* 5.5 (1984), 279–82*

'Channel Tunnel excavations. 4 Excavations at Castle Hill', J Rady, *Canterbury's Archaeology 1988–89*, Canterbury Archaeological Trust, 1990, 41–42

'Medieval Britain and Ireland in 1989', D R M Gaimster, S Margeson and M Hurley, *Medieval Archaeology* 34 (1990), 198

Grain

Coastal artillery fortifications on the Isle of Grain, Kent. M Brown, P Pattison and A Williams. Cambridge: RCHME, 1998*

'Underground at Grain', N Catford, *The Redan* 49 (2000), 7–11*

Gravesend

New Tavern Fort. V T C Smith. Gravesend: Gravesend Historical Society, 1975*

New Tavern Fort, Gravesend. V T C Smith. Gravesend: New Tavern Fort Project in association with Gravesham Leisure, 1998* (Defending London's river; 2)

'The artillery defences at Gravesend', V T C Smith, *Archaeologia Cantiana* 89 (1974), 141–68*

'Interim report on the excavations at the canal basin, Gravesend', V T C Smith, *ibid* 91 (1975), 200

'The excavation of the Gravesend blockhouse, 1975–76', D Thompson and Mrs V Smith, *ibid* 93 (1977), 153–77*

'Trinity Fort and the defences of the second Anglo-Dutch war at Gravesend in 1667', V T C Smith, *ibid* 114 (1994), 39–50*

'New Tavern Fort restored', V T C Smith, *Coast and Country* 8.4 (1979), 47–52*

'Tudor blockhouse at Gravesend', V T C Smith, *Kent Archaeological Review* 30 (1972–3), 306–7*

'The New Tavern Fort restoration project', V T C Smith, *ibid* 44 (1976), 102–4*

'The Tudor blockhouse at the Clarendon Royal Hotel, Gravesend: interim report', D G Thompson, *ibid* 45 (1976), 116–18*

'Another gun for New Tavern Fort', V Smith, *ibid* 72 (1983), 33*

'Post-medieval Britain in 1977', J Cherry, *Post-Medieval Archaeology* 12 (1978), 109–10

'More forts at Gravesend', V Smith, *Ravelin* 33 (1993), 15–18

Halstead
'Fort Halstead of the London Defence Positions', J R E Hamilton-Baillie, *Fort* 3 (1977), 15–16*; pp 31–33* in 1993 revised edition of *Fort* vols 1–3

Hever
'Hever Castle, Kent – I', P C Aslet, *Country Life* 169 (1981), 18–21*

Higham
'The Higham blockhouse hypothesis', V T C Smith, *Transactions of the Gravesend Historical Society* (1968), 13–16

'The lost Higham blockhouse', V T C Smith, *Kent Archaeological Review* 28 (1972), 251–52

Hoo
Medway's island forts: the history of Fort Darnet and Fort Hoo. R Crowdy. [S l]: Medway Military Research Group, [1979]*

Medway's island forts. R Crowdy. 2nd edition. [S l]: Medway Military Research Group, 1980*

'Visits to Hoo, Darnet and Ramsgate', D Burridge, *Ravelin* 35 (1993), 19–25*

Hythe
The martello tower – Hythe. R Ward. Privately published, 1973*

'The guns of Hythe', F Kitchen, *Byegone Kent* 10.4 (1989), 195–97

Leeds
History of Leeds Castle and its families. D A H Cleggett. Maidstone: Leeds Castle Foundation, 1990*; [revised edition], 1992*

Leeds Castle, Kent. N. McCann. Derby: English Life Publications, 2000*

'Leeds Castle', S E Rigold, *Archaeological Journal* 126 (1969), 254–55

'"The chamber called *Gloriette*": living at leisure in thirteenth- and fourteenth-century castles', J Ashbee, *Journal of the British Archaeological Association* 157 (2004), 17–40*

Leybourne
'Leybourne castle', C Jarman and J Wilson, *Canterbury's Archaeology: 22nd Annual Report 1997–1998*, Canterbury Archaeological Trust, 2000, 18–19*

Lodge Hill

'The birth of Ack-Ack: the battery at Lodge Hill, Kent', P Pattison and S Newsome, *Research News: Newsletter of the English Heritage Research Department* 3 (2006), 42–43*

Meopham

'A medieval site near Meopham', J E L Caiger, *Kent Archaeological Research Groups Council Newsletter* 4 (1966), 16–17

Milton

'The Milton blockhouse, Gravesend: research and excavation', V T C Smith, *Archaeologia Cantiana* 96 (1980), 341–62*

'Excavations on the site of the Milton blockhouse, Gravesend', V T C Smith, *Fort* 10 (1982), 127–29*

'Post-medieval Britain in 1977', J Cherry, *Post-Medieval Archaeology* 12 (1978), 110

'Milton blockhouse', V T C Smith, *Ravelin* 3 (1982), 18–20*

Newenden

'Newenden, Castle Toll', B K Davison, *Archaeological Excavations 1965*, 14. London: HMSO, 1966

'Medieval Britain in 1965', D M Wilson and D G Hurst, *Medieval Archaeology* 10 (1966), 191

Old Soar Manor

'Attack and defence at Old Soar Manor, Plaxtol', D Renn, *Archaeologia Cantiana* 121 (2001), 237–50*

Queenborough

'Queenborough Castle, Sheppey', S Pratt, *Canterbury's Archaeology: 16th Annual Report 1991–1992*, Canterbury Archaeological Trust, 1992, 19–20*

'The castles of Kent no 4: Queenborough Castle', C Hodge, *Kent Archaeological Society Newsletter* 42 (1998), 2–4*

Rochester

Fort Clarence: a case for restoration. Anon. [S l]: Medway Military Research Group, n d*

Rochester Castle, Kent. R A Brown. London: HMSO, 1969*

Rochester Castle, Kent. R A Brown. 2nd edition. London: HBMCE, 1987*

Rochester Castle: a handbook for teachers. T Copeland. London: English Heritage, 1990*

The Napoleonic defences of Rochester and Chatham. K R Gulvin. [S l]: Medway Military Research Group, 1977*

Rochester Castle. G Port. London: HBMCE, 1987*

Guide to Rochester Castle. J C Taylor. Rochester: City of Rochester, 1951*

'King John, Stephen Langton and Rochester Castle, 1213–15', I W Rowlands, in C Harper-Bill, C J Holdsworth and J L Nelson (eds), *Studies in medieval history presented to R Allen Brown*, 267–79. Woodbridge: Boydell Press, 1989

'The topography and buildings of medieval Rochester', T Tatton-Brown, in T Ayers and T Tatton-Brown (eds), *Medieval art, architecture and archaeology at Rochester*, 22–37. Leeds: British Archaeological Association and Maney Publishing, 2006* (Conference transactions; 28)

'The building stones of Rochester Castle and Cathedral', B C Worssam, with an appendix by J Ashbee, *ibid*, 238–49*

'The medieval buildings and topography of Rochester Castle', J Ashbee, *ibid*, 250–64*

'The great tower of Rochester Castle', J A A Goodall, in *ibid*, 265–99*

'Rochester town walls', A Ward and C Jarman, *Canterbury's Archaeology: 18th Annual Report 1993–1994*, Canterbury Archaeological Trust, 1995, 19–20*

'Castle wall, Rochester', A Ward, *Canterbury's Archaeology: 20th Annual Report 1995–1996*, Canterbury Archaeological Trust, 1997, 46–47*

'Rochester Castle', A Ward, *Canterbury's Archaeology: 21st Annual Report 1996–1997*, Canterbury Archaeological Trust, 1999, 24–25*

'Rochester city wall', A Ward, *ibid*, 25*

'Rochester city wall', J Wilson and A Ward, *Canterbury's Archaeology: 22nd Annual Report 1997–1998*, Canterbury Archaeological Trust, 2000, 24*

'Boley Hill repaving, Rochester', A Ward, *Canterbury's Archaeology: 23rd Annual Report 1998–1999*, Canterbury Archaeological Trust, 2001, 33–42*

'The Roman and medieval defences of Rochester in the light of recent excavations', A C Harrison and C Flight, *Archaeologia Cantiana* 83 (1968), 55–104*

'Rochester East Gate, 1969', A C Harrison, *ibid* 87 (1972), 121–57*

'Rochester Castle, 1976', C Flight and A C Harrison, *ibid* 94 (1978), 27–60*

'Rochester 1974–75', A C Harrison, *ibid* 97 (1981), 95–136*

'The southern defences of medieval Rochester', C Flight and A C Harrison, *ibid* 103 (1986), 1–26*

'Excavations at the south-east bastion, Rochester city wall', D Bacchus, *ibid* 110 (1992), 129–38*

'Refortification at Rochester in the 1220s: a public/private partnership?', D Renn, *ibid* 124 (2004), 343–63*

'Rochester, High Street', A C Harrison, *Archaeological Excavations 1969*, 30. London: HMSO, 1970

'The medieval walls of Rochester', P MacDougall, *Byegone Kent* 10.7 (1989), 466–72*

'Fort Clarence, Rochester', K R Gulvin, *Kent Archaeological Review* 53 (1978), 53–57*

'Rochester', A C Harrison, *Lower Medway Archaeological Research Group Newsletter* 37 (1965), 1

'Rochester', A C Harrison, *ibid* 46 (1966), 2

'The castles of Kent no 3: Rochester Castle', A Ward, *Kent Archaeological Society Newsletter* 40 (1998), [1–3]*

'Medieval Britain in 1965', D M Wilson and D G Hurst, *Medieval Archaeology* 10 (1966), 191

'Medieval Britain in 1969', D M Wilson and D G Hurst, *ibid* 14 (1970), 182–83

St Margaret's-at-Cliffe

'A modern site at South Foreland', J A Guy, *Kent Archaeological Society Newsletter* 6 (1984), 7*

Saltwood

'Saltwood Castle', A Emery, in N J G Pounds (ed), *The Canterbury area: proceedings of the 140th summer meeting of the Royal Archaeological Institute, 1994*, 30–34. London: RAI, 1994*

Sandgate

'Archaeological investigations at Sandgate Castle, Kent, 1976–9', E C Harris, *Post-Medieval Archaeology* 14 (1980), 53–88*

Sandown

'Sandown Castle badly damaged during seawall construction', the editor, *Kent Archaeological Review* 59 (1980), 220

Sandwich

'Mill Wall, Sandwich', B Corke, *Canterbury's Archaeology: 19th Annual Report 1994–1995*, Canterbury Archaeological Trust, 1996, 35

'The Sandown Gate at Sandwich', T Tatton-Brown, *Archaeologia Cantiana* 94 (1978), 151–56*

'Interim report on work in 1983 by the Canterbury Archaeological Trust. Sandwich Castle', T Tatton-Brown, *ibid* 99 (1983), 243–47*

'The ancient cinque port of Sandwich', E W Parkin, *ibid* 100 (1984), 189–216*

'Interim report on work carried out in 1989 by the Canterbury Archaeological Trust. 27. Sandwich watching brief', M McKenna, *ibid* 107 (1989), 340–41*

'Archaeological investigations at Sandwich Castle', I J Stewart, *ibid* 120 (2000), 51–75*

'The castles of Kent no 5: Sandwich Castle', A Ward, *Kent Archaeological Society Newsletter* 45 (1999–2000), 1–5*

'Medieval Britain in 1979', L E Webster and J Cherry, *Medieval Archaeology* 24 (1980), 253

'Medieval Britain in 1980', S M Youngs and J Cherry, *ibid* 25 (1981), 209

'Medieval Britain and Ireland in 1983', S M Youngs, J Clark and T B Barry, *ibid* 28 (1984), 225

Scotney

Scotney Castle. Anon. London: National Trust, 1979*

'A note on an excavation at Scotney Castle, 1986', F McAvoy, *Archaeologia Cantiana* 104 (1987), 377–80*

Sheerness

The Ravelin Battery, Sheerness, Kent. J Kenney. Cambridge: RCHME, 1993*

A musketry wall on the Ravelin, Sheerness, defences, Kent. P Pattison. Cambridge: RCHME, 1993*

'Sheerness: dockyard, defences and Blue Town', P Guillery, in *Thames gateway: recording historic buildings and landscapes in the Thames estuary*, 77–88. Swindon: RCHME, 1995*

'Garrison Point, Sheerness', R A Buckmaster, *Canterbury's Archaeology: 13th Annual Report 1988–1989*, Canterbury Archaeological Trust, 1990, 56*

'Government and urban development in Kent: the case of the Royal Naval dockyard town of Sheerness', T M Harris, *Archaeologia Cantiana* 101 (1984), 245–76*

'The Medway martellos', W H Clements, *Fort* 29 (2001), 75–86*

'A London tankard and the Dutch wars', R Weinstein, *Transactions of the London and Middlesex Archaeological Society* 32 (1981), 151–52*

Shornemead

Shornemead Fort. V T C Smith. [S l]: Kent Defence Research Group, 1977*

'Shornemead Fort, near Gravesend', V T C Smith, *Kent Archaeological Review* 25 (1971), 139–41*

'Shornmead [*sic*] Fort: Thames defences', D Moore, *The Redan* 45 (1999), 337–46*

Slough

'Slough Fort', D Burridge, *Ravelin* 33 (1993), 6–8, 21*

Stockbury

'Stockbury Castle, Kent', A Ward, *Castle Studies Group Newsletter* 10 (1996–7), 42–44

'Castles of Kent no 1: Stockbury Castle', A Ward, *Kent Archaeological Society Newsletter* 37 (1997), [2 pages]

Stone

'The tower of Stone Castle, Greenhithe', K W E Gravett and D F Renn, *Archaeologia Cantiana* 97 (1981), 312–18*

Sutton Valence

'Sutton Valence', L R A Grove, *ibid* 71 (1957), 227–28

Thurnham

'The castles of Kent no 2: Thurnham Castle', A Ward, *Kent Archaeological Society Newsletter* 39 (1997), [2–4]*

Tonbridge

Tonbridge Castle: a short history. J Hilton. Tonbridge: Tonbridge Design and Print Service, 1976*

Tonbridge Castle. [J Oliphant]. Tonbridge: Addax Publishing, 1992*

'Tonbridge and some other gatehouses', D Renn, in A Detsicas (ed), *Collectanea historica: essays in memory of Stuart Rigold*, 93–103. Maidstone: Kent Archaeological Society, 1981*

'Excavations at Tonbridge: interim report', C B Giles, *Archaeologia Cantiana* 87 (1972), 230

'Excavations at Lansdowne Road, Tonbridge, 1972 and 1976', A D F Streeten, *ibid* 92 (1976), 105–18*

'Tonbridge Castle: further observations on an ancient castle', S Simmons, *ibid* 116 (1996), 101–46*

'The lords and ladies of Tonbridge Castle', S Simmons, *ibid* 118 (1998), 45–61*

'Tonbridge', J Money, *Archaeological Excavations 1972*, 89–90. London: HMSO, 1973

'Tonbridge Castle', S Simmons, *Kent Archaeological Society Newsletter* 14 (1989), [1]

'Medieval Britain in 1972', L E Webster and J Cherry, *Medieval Archaeology* 17 (1973), 169

'Medieval Britain and Ireland in 2000', J Bradley and M Gaimster, *ibid* 45 (2001), 291

'Medieval Britain and Ireland in 2002', J Bradley and M Gaimster, *ibid* 47 (2003), 151–52

Upnor

Upnor: some notes on the castle and other things. S Evans. Privately published, 1951*

Upnor Castle: a handbook for teachers. C Lloyd, H Blanchard and L Edwards. London:: English Heritage, 1991*

Upnor Castle, Kent. A D Saunders. London: HMSO. 1967*

Upnor Castle, Kent. A D Saunders. London: HBMCE, 1985*

'The building of Upnor Castle, 1559–1601', A D Saunders, in M R Apted, R Gilyard-Beer and A D Saunders (eds), *Ancient monuments and their interpretation: essays presented to A J Taylor*, 263–83. Chichester: Phillimore, 1977*

'Upnor Castle near Rochester', M Hicks, *Canterbury's Archaeology: 18th Annual Report 1993–1994* Canterbury Archaeological Trust, 1995, 29*

'Upnor Castle, Kent', B H St J O'Neil and S Evans, *Archaeologia Cantiana* 65 (1952), 1–11*

'Upnor Castle', A D Saunders, *Archaeological Journal* 126 (1969), 276–78*

'Upnor Castle and gunpowder supply to the navy 1801–4', A Saunders, *Mariner's Mirror* 91 (2005), 160–74*

Walmer

Deal and Walmer castles: the handbook for teachers. J Barnes. London: English Heritage, 1991*

Walmer Castle and gardens, Kent. J G Coad and G E Hughes. London: English Heritage, 1993*

Walmer Castle, Kent. B H St J O'Neil. London: HMSO, 1949*

Deal and Walmer castles. A D Saunders. London: HMSO, 1963*; 2nd edition, 1982*

Deal and Walmer castles. A D Saunders. London: HBMCE, 1985*

Walmer Castle and gardens. R Stephens, V Hinze and J Coad. London: English Heritage, 2003*

'A note on two original drawings by William Stukeley depicting "The three castles which keep the downs"', J R Kenyon, *Antiquaries Journal* 58 (1978), 162–64*

'Walmer Castle', J Coad, in N J G Pounds (ed), *The Canterbury area: proceedings of the 140th summer meeting of the Royal Archaeological Institute, 1994*, 34–39. London: RAI, 1994*

'Walmer Castle', A D Saunders, *Archaeological Journal* 126 (1969), 215*

'Walmer Old Manor House', S E Rigold, *ibid* 126 (1969), 215, 217*

'Medieval Britain in 1974', L E Webster and J Cherry, *Medieval Archaeology* 19 (1975), 251

'Another 'proto-keep' at Walmer, Kent', M [W] Thompson, *ibid* 39 (1995), 174–76*

'Bulwarks at Walmer', R Harlow, *Ravelin* 47 (1997), 18–19*

Westenhanger

Westenhanger Castle: historical notes. B Ladley. [S l: s n], 1998*

'Westenhanger Castle – a revised interpretation', D and B Martin, *Archaeologia*

Cantiana 121 (2001), 203–36*

West Malling

St Leonard's Tower: some aspects of Anglo-Norman building design and construction', M North, *ibid* 121 (2001), 269–86*

West Wickham Common

'The causewayed earthwork and the Elizabethan redoubt on West Wickham Common', A H A Hogg, *ibid* 97 (1981), 71–78*

'An enclosure on West Wickham Common, Bromley, Greater London', A Oswald, *ibid* 115 (1995), 454–55

LANCASHIRE

Bu'lock, J D. 'Churches, crosses and mottes in the Lune Valley', *Archaeological Journal* 127 (1970), 291–92*

Freethy, R. *Lancashire 1939–1945: the secret war*. Newbury: Countryside Books, 2005*

Gibson, L I. *Lancashire castles and towers*. Clapham: Dalesman, 1977*

Higham, M C. 'The mottes of north Lancashire, Lonsdale and south Cumbria', *Transactions of the Cumberland and Westmorland Antiquarian and Archaeological Society* 91 (1991), 79–90*

Higham, N J. *A frontier landscape: the north west in the Middle Ages*. Macclesfield: Windgather Press, 2004*

Pevsner, N. *Lancashire. 1. The industrial and commercial south (The buildings of England)*. Harmondsworth: Penguin Books, 1969*

Pevsner, N. *Lancashire. 2. The rural north (The buildings of England)*. Harmondsworth: Penguin Books, 1969*

Pollard, R and Pevsner, N. *Lancashire: Liverpool and the south-west (The buildings of England)*. London: Yale University Press, 2006*

Salter, M. *The castles and tower houses of Cumbria*. Malvern: Folly Publications, 1998*

Salter, M. *The castles and tower houses of Lancashire and Cheshire*. Malvern: Folly Publications, 2001*

White, A J. *Pele towers of the Morcambe Bay area*. Lancaster: Lancaster Museum, n d*

Wood, J. 'Castles and monasteries', in R Newman (ed), *The archaeology of Lancashire: present state and future priorities*, 139–56. Lancaster: Lancaster University Archaeological Unit, 1996*

Yates, S (ed). *Heritage unlocked: guide to free sites in the north west*. London: English Heritage, 2002*

ENGLAND

Aldingham

'Moat Hill, Aldingham', B K Davison, *Archaeological excavations 1968*, 24. London: HMSO, 1969

'Aldingham motte and bailey, Lancashire north of the sands', anon, *Archaeological Newsletter for Northumberland, Cumberland and Westmorland* 5 (1969), 10

'Aldingham', B K Davison, *Current Archaeology* 2.1 (1969), 23–24*

Buckton

'Buckton Castle', in M Nevell, *A history and archaeology of Tameside: Tameside 1066–1700*, 115–17. [Ashton-under-Lyme]: Tameside Metropolitan Borough Council, 1991*

'Buckton Castle', in T Burke and M Nevell, *Buildings of Tameside*, 16. [Ashton-under-Lyme]: Tameside Metropolitan Borough Council, 1996*

'Buckton Castle: a survey of the evidence', K Booth and J Cronin, *Greater Manchester Archaeological Journal* 3 (1987–8), 61–66*

Castle Croft

'Excavations at Castle Croft, Blackrod, Lancashire, 1952', F Willett, *Transactions of the Lancashire and Cheshire Antiquarian Society* 63 (1952–3), 201–6*

Clitheroe

Clitheroe Castle: a guide. D Best. Preston: Carnegie Publishing, 1990*

'George Vertue's engravings of Clitheroe Castle', B J N Edwards, *Antiquaries Journal* 64 (1984), 366–72*

'Clitheroe Castle', P E Curnow, *Archaeological Journal* 127 (1970), 280

'Clitheroe Castle', P Adams, *Castle Studies Group Journal* 19 (2006), 179–92*

Farleton

'Medieval Britain in 1956', D M Wilson and J G Hurst, *Medieval Archaeology* 1 (1957), 157

Lancaster

Lancaster Castle: a brief history. J Champness. Preston: Lancashire County Books, 1993*

'Lancaster Castle', A D Saunders and P Fleetwood-Hesketh, *Archaeological Journal* 127 (1970), 289–90

Liverpool

'Liverpool: South Castle Street', P J Davey, *Archaeological Excavations 1976*, 138. London: HMSO, 1977

'Liverpool Castle', N Guy, *Castle Studies Group Bulletin* 18 (2004–5), 188–201*

'Liverpool, Merseyside', R M Slade, *CBA Newsletter and Calendar* 1 (1977–8), 112

'Cannon or commerce? The case of the Liverpool battery, 1824–1855', M S Partridge, *Transactions of the Historic Society of Lancashire and Cheshire* 135 (1985), 83–98

'South Castle Street 1976: interim report', P Davey, *Journal of the Merseyside Archaeological Society* 1 (1977), 13–16*

'Excavations in South Castle Street, Liverpool, 1976 and 1977', P J Davey and R McNeil, *ibid* 4 (1980–1) [whole issue]*

'Liverpool Castle: gone … but not forgotten', P E Presford, *Postern* 8 (1998), 15*

Newton-le-Willows

'Medieval Britain and Ireland in 1987', S M Youngs [*et al*], *Medieval Archaeology* 32 (1988), 261–62

Perch Rock

Notes on Fort Perch Rock, New Brighton, Merseyside, and its garrison from 1826–1956. C J Cocks. Privately published, 1978*

Fort Perch Rock. N Kingham. Privately published, 1978*

Fort Perch Rock and the defence of the Mersey. K McCarron. Birkenhead: Merseyside Portfolios for the National Museums and Galleries on Merseyside, 1991*

Piel

Furness Abbey, Cumbria. Piel Castle. S Harrison and J Wood [abbey], and R Newman [castle]. London: English Heritage, 1998*

'Excavation at Piel Castle, Cumbria, 1983', R Newman, *CBA Group 3 Newsbulletin* (1984?), 18–19

'Excavations at survey at Piel Castle, near Barrow-in-Furness, Cumbria', R Newman, *Transactions of the Cumberland and Westmorland Antiquarian and Archaeological Society* 87 (1987), 101–16*

'Further structural analysis at Piel Castle, 1987–94', R Newman, *ibid* 96 (1996), 121–378

'Medieval Britain and Ireland in 1984', S M Youngs, J Clark and T Barry, *Medieval Archaeology* 29 (1985), 168

'Medieval Britain and Ireland in 1989', D R M Gaimster, S Margeson and M Hurley, *ibid* 34 (1990), 172

'Medieval Britain and Ireland in 1990', B S Nenk, S Margeson and M Hurley, *ibid* 35 (1991), 138

'Medieval Britain and Ireland in 1990', B S Nenk, S Margeson and M Hurley, *ibid* 36 (1992), 205–6

Salwick Hall

'Medieval Britain and Ireland in 1991', B S Nenk, S Margeson and M Hurley, *Medieval Archaeology* 36 (1992), 248 [possible castle]

Samlesbury

'Medieval Britain and Ireland in 1991', B S Nenk, S Margeson and M Hurley, *ibid* 36 (1992), 248

Warrington

'Warrington', D H Hill, *Archaeological Excavations 1972*, 90. London: HMSO, 1973

West Derby

'West Derby Castle', P J Davey, in P J Davey (ed), *Medieval pottery from excavations in the north-west*, 68–69. [Liverpool]: Institute of Extension Studies, 1977

'Medieval Britain and Ireland in 1989', D R M Gaimster, S Margeson and M Hurley, *Medieval Archaeology* 34 (1990), 202

Wraysholme

'Wraysholme Tower', R W McDowall, *Transactions of the Cumberland and Westmorland Antiquarian and Archaeological Society* new ser 76 (1976), 216–19*

LEICESTERSHIRE

Cantor, L M. 'The medieval castles of Leicestershire', *Transactions of the Leicestershire Archaeological and Historical Society* 53 (1977–8), 30–41*

Creighton, O. 'Early Leicestershire castles: archaeology and landscape history', *ibid* 71 (1997), 21–36*

Hartley, R F. *The medieval earthworks of north-east Leicestershire*. Leicester: Leicestershire Museums, 1984*

Liddle, P. *Leicestershire archaeology – the present state of knowledge. 2. Anglo-Saxon and medieval periods*. Leicester: Leicestershire Museums, 1982*

McWhirr, A D and Winter, M J. 'Medieval castles: additional information', *Transactions of the Leicestershire Archaeological and Historical Society* 54 (1978–9), 74–75

Osborne, M. *20th century defences in the east midlands: Derbyshire, Leicestershire, Lincolnshire, Northamptonshire, Nottinghamshire and Rutland*. Market Deeping: Concrete Publications, 2003*

Pevsner, N. *Leicestershire and Rutland (The buildings of England)*. 2nd edition, revised by E Williamson and G K Brandwood. Harmondsworth: Penguin Books, 1984*

Salter, M. *The castles of the east midlands*. Malvern: Folly Publications, 2002*

Ashby de la Zouch

Ashby de la Zouch Castle, Leicestershire. T L Jones. London: HMSO, 1953*

Ashby de la Zouch Castle, Leicestershire. T L Jones. London: HBMCE, 1984*; 2nd edition, 1993*

Ashby de la Zouch Castle: information for teachers. V Pearson. London: English Heritage, 1996*

'Ashby de la Zouch Castle', A Emery, in N H Cooper (ed), *The Nottingham area: proceedings of the 135th summer meeting of the Royal Archaeological Institute, 1989*, 65–71. London: RAI, 1989*

Castle Donington

'Castle Donington', D T-D Clarke, *Transactions of the Leicestershire Archaeological Society* 28 (1952), 42

Groby

'Groby Castle', B K Davison, *Archaeological Excavations 1962*, 9. London: HMSO, 1963

'Archaeology in Leicestershire and Rutland', anon, *Transactions of the Leicestershire Archaeological and Historical Society* 39 (1963–4), 51

'Medieval Britain in 1962 and 1963', D M Wilson and D G Hurst, *Medieval Archaeology* 8 (1964), 8 (1964), 255

Kirby Muxloe

Kirby Muxloe Castle, Leicestershire. C Peers. 2nd edition. London: HMSO, 1957*

Kirby Muxloe Castle, Leicestershire. C Peers. London: HBMCE, 1986*

'Kirby Muxloe Castle', A Emery, in N H Cooper (ed), *The Nottingham area: proceedings of the 135th summer meeting of the Royal Archaeological Institute, 1989*, 71–77. London: RAI, 1989*

Leicester

Leicester town defences: excavations 1958–1974. R Buckley and J Lucas. Leicester: Leicestershire Museums, 1987*

Leicester Castle and the Newarke. G A Chinnery. Leicester: Leicestershire Museums, 1981*

An account of Leicester Castle. J Thompson. Melton Mowbray: Sycamore Press, 1977* [first published 1859]

The siege of Leicester – 1645. J Wilshere and S Green. Leicester: Leicester Research Society, 1970*

The siege of Leicester – 1645: a 325th anniversary history. J Wilshere and S Green. 2nd edition (new impression). Leicester: Leicester Research Department of Chamberlain Music and Books, 1984* [original 2nd edition published 1972]

The town gates and bridges of mediaeval Leicester. J Wilshere. 2nd edition. Leicester: Leicester Research Department of Chamberlain Music and Books, 1982* [first edition published 1978]

'Leicester Castle', L Fox, in A E Brown (ed), *The growth of Leicester*, 19–25. Leicester: Leicester University Press, 1972*

'The potential and limitations of radiocarbon dating in the middle ages: the art historian's view', W Horn, in R Berger (ed), *Scientific methods in medieval archaeology*, 23–87. Berkeley: University of California Press, 1970*

'Castle view', in R A McKinley (ed), *The Victoria history of the counties of England: a history of the county of Leicester*, **4**, 344–51. Oxford: OUP, 1958*

'Leicester Castle', L Fox, *Transactions of the Leicestershire Archaeological Society* 22 (1944–5), 127–70*

'The city of Leicester: town walls and castle', D T-D Clarke, *ibid* 28 (1952), 17–29*

'Leicester city wall in Sanvey Gate: excavations in 1952', R G Goodchild, *ibid* 29 (1953), 15–29*

'The town walls of Leicester: evidence for a west wall', J N Lucas, *ibid* 54 (1978–9), 61–66*

'Mill Lane', N Finn, in 'Archaeology in Leicestershire and Rutland 2001', *ibid* 76 (2002), 94–97*

'Sanvey Gate, Corella Works', W Jarvis, in N J Cooper (ed), 'Archaeology in Leicestershire and Rutland 2004', *ibid* 79 (2005), 144–45

'Leicester Castle: the Great Hall', N W Alcock and R J Buckley, *Medieval Archaeology* 31 (1987), 73–79*

'Medieval Britain and Ireland in 1990', B S Nenk, S Margeson and M Hurley, *ibid* 35 (1991), 174

'Medieval Britain and Ireland in 1991', B S Nenk, S Margeson and M Hurley, *ibid* 36 (1992), 249

'Medieval Britain and Ireland in 1992', B S Nenk, S Margeson and M Hurley, *ibid* 37 (1993), 271

'Medieval Britain and Ireland in 1993', B S Nenk, S Margeson and M Hurley, *ibid* 38 (1994), 232

'Medieval Britain and Ireland in 1994', B S Nenk, S Margeson and M Hurley, *ibid* 39 (1995), 224

'Medieval Britain and Ireland in 1999', J Bradley and M Gaimster, *ibid* 44 (2000), 287–88

'Medieval Britain and Ireland in 2005', M Gaimster and K O'Conor, *ibid* 50 (2006), 331, 333

'A siege examined: the Civil War archaeology of Leicester', P and Y Courtney, *Post-Medieval Archaeology* 26 (1992), 47–90*

Mountsorrel

'Trial excavation at Mountsorrel Castle in 1952', anon, *Bulletin of the Loughborough and District Archaeological Society* 1 (1958), 9–10

Sapcote

'Medieval Britain and Ireland in 1999', J Bradley and M Gaimster, *Medieval Archaeology* 44 (2000), 290

LINCOLNSHIRE

Osborne, M. *20th century defences in Britain: Lincolnshire*. London: Brassey's, 1997*

Osborne, M. *20th century defences in the east midlands: Derbyshire, Leicestershire, Lincolnshire, Northamptonshire, Nottinghamshire and Rutland*. Market Deeping: Concrete Publications, 2003*

Pevsner, N and Harris, J. *Lincolnshire (The buildings of England)*. 2nd edition, revised by N Antram. London: Penguin Books, 1989*

Salter, M. *The castles of the east midlands*. Malvern: Folly Publications, 2002*

White, A. *Six Lincolnshire castles*. Lincoln: Lincolnshire Museums, 1983*

Barrow

' "The castles", Barrow-on-Humber', C Atkins, *Lincolnshire History and Archaeology* 18 (1983), 91–93*

'Medieval Britain and Ireland in 1982', S M Youngs, J Clark and T B Barry, *Medieval Archaeology* 27 (1983), 183–84

Barton-upon-Humber

'Medieval Britain and Ireland in 1983', S M Youngs, J Clark and T B Barry, *ibid* 28 (1984), 223

Bolingbroke

'Old Bolingbroke Castle', M W Thompson, *Archaeological Journal* 131 (1974), 314–17*

'An alert in 1318 to the constable of Bolingbroke Castle, Lincolnshire', M W Thompson, *Medieval Archaeology* 9 (1965), 167–68

'The origins of Bolingbroke Castle, Lincolnshire', M W Thompson, *ibid* 10 (1966), 152–58*

'Further work at Bolingbroke Castle, Lincolnshire', M W Thompson, *ibid* 13 (1969), 216–17*

'The great hall at Bolingbroke Castle, Lincolnshire', P L Drewett and D J Freke, *ibid* 18 (1974), 163–65*

'Medieval Britain and Ireland in 2004', M Gaimster and K O'Conor, *ibid* 49 (2005), 387

'The excavation of the great hall at Bolingbroke Castle, Lincolnshire, 1973', P Drewett, *Post-Medieval Archaeology* 10 (1976), 1–33*

ENGLAND

Boston

'Medieval Britain in 1957', D M Wilson and J G Hurst, *Medieval Archaeology* 2 (1958), 200

'Medieval Britain in 1960', D M Wilson and J G Hurst, *ibid* 5 (1961), 323

'Medieval Britain and Ireland in 2001', J Bradley and M Gaimster, *ibid* 46 (2002), 185

Bourne

'Archaeological notes', J B Whitwell, *Lincolnshire History and Archaeology* 1 (1966), 39

'Medieval Britain and Ireland in 2001', J Bradley and M Gaimster, *Medieval Archaeology* 46 (2002), 185–86

Castle Carlton

'Castle Carlton: the origin of a medieval new town', A E Bowen, *Lincolnshire History and Archaeology* 27 (1992), 17–22*

Fleet

'Medieval Britain and Ireland in 2000', J Bradley and M Gaimster, *Medieval Archaeology* 45 (2001), 294

Goltho

Goltho: the development of an early medieval manor c 850–1150. G Beresford. London: HBMCE, 1987* (English Heritage archaeological report; 4)

'Goltho manor, Lincolnshire: the buildings and their surrounding defences c 850–1150', G Beresford, in R A Brown (ed), *Proceedings of the Battle Conference on Anglo-Norman Studies IV*, 13–36, 171–74. Woodbridge: Boydell Press, 1982*

'The Danish contribution to the origin of the English castle', R Hodges, *Acta Archaeologica* 59 (1988), 169–72*

'Goltho', G T M Beresford, *Archaeological Excavations 1972*, 91–92. London: HMSO, 1973

'Goltho', G Beresford, *Archaeological Excavations 1973*, 86–87. London: HMSO, 1974

'The excavation of a deserted medieval village of Goltho, Lincolnshire', G Beresford, *Château Gaillard* 8 (1977), 47–68*

'Goltho, a deserted medieval village and its manor house', [A Selkirk], *Current Archaeology* 5 (1975–7), 262–70*

'What's in a name? "Goltho", Goltho and Bullington', P Everson, *Lincolnshire History and Archaeology* 23 (1988), 93–99*

'Medieval Britain in 1971', L E Webster and J Cherry, *Medieval Archaeology* 16 (1972), 201–2

215

'Medieval Britain in 1972', L E Webster and J Cherry, *ibid* 17 (1973), 181–82*

'Medieval Britain in 1973', L E Webster and J Cherry, *ibid* 18 (1974), 210–11*

'The problem of Goltho', P Everson, *Medieval Settlement Research Group Annual Report* 5 (1990), 9–14*

'Goltho', G Beresford, *Medieval Village Research Group Report* 20/21 (1972–3), 32–33*

'Origins of the English castle', R Hodges, *Nature* 333 (1988), 112–13*

Hough-on-the-Hill
'Medieval Britain and Ireland in 2000', J Bradley and M Gaimster, *Medieval Archaeology* 45 (2001), 295

Hussey Tower
'Hussey Tower, Boston: a late medieval tower-house of brick', T P Smith, *Lincolnshire History and Archaeology* 14 (1979), 31–37*

Killingholme
'Post-medieval Britain and Ireland in 1997', M Ponsford and R Jackson, *Post-Medieval Archaeology* 32 (1998), 149–50

Kyme
'Kyme Castle: the tower', A W Clapham, *Archaeological Journal* 103 (1946), 189–90

Lincoln
Lincoln Castle. Anon. Lincoln: Lincolnshire County Council, n d*

Lincoln Castle in the Middle Ages: a guide for children. H Elliott. [S l]: FLARE Education Group, 1980*

Lincoln Castle. H Elliott and D Stocker. Lincoln: Lincolnshire County Council, 1984*

Lincoln Castle: official guide. F Hill. [S l: s n], n d*

The early history of Lincoln Castle. P Lindley (ed). Lincoln: Society for Lincolnshire History and Archaeology, 2004* (Occasional papers in Lincolnshire history and archaeology; 12)

'The two early castles of Lincoln', D Stocker, in *ibid*, 9–22*

'The early topography of Lincoln Castle', M Thompson, in *ibid*, 23–29*

'Urban castles and late Anglo-Saxon towns', D Parsons, in *ibid*, 30–40*

'Archaeology at Lincoln Castle: before and after 1068', L Donel and M J Jones, 41–52*

'Lincoln Castle: the architectural context of the medieval defences', P Marshall, in *ibid*, 53–65*

'Lincoln Castle and its occupants in the reign of King Stephen', P Dalton, in *ibid*, 66–78

'Cobb Hall Tower', D Renn, in *ibid*, 79–86*

Lincoln Castle: the medieval story. S Sancha. Lincoln: Lincolnshire County Council, 1985*

The archaeology of Wigford and the Brayford Pool. K Steane. Oxford: Oxbow Books, 2001* (Lincoln archaeological studies; 2)

'Excavations at Lincoln 1970–1972: the western defences of the lower town: an interim report', C Colyer, *Antiquaries Journal* 55 (1975), 227–66*

'Saltergate', N M Reynolds, in C Colyer and M J Jones (eds), 'Excavations at Lincoln: second interim report: excavations in the lower town 1972–8', *ibid* 59 (1979), 84–89*

'The gates of Roman Lincoln', F H Thompson and B Whitwell, *Archaeologia* 104 (1973), 129–207*

'Lincoln', C Colyer, *Archaeological Journal* 103 (1946), 157–59*

'Lincoln Castle', F T Baker, *ibid* 131 (1974), 378–80*

'Lincoln Castle', D Stocker, *Archaeology in Lincoln 1982–1983: Eleventh Annual Report of the Lincoln Archaeological Trust* (1983), 18–27*

'Three urban castles and their communities in the east midlands: Lincoln, Nottingham and Newark', P Marshall, *Château Gaillard* 22 (2006), 259–65*

'Lincoln Castle', [A Selkirk], source L Donel, *Current Archaeology* 11.9 (1992), 380–81*

'Lincoln Cathedral', P Miles, *ibid* 11.9 (1992), 396–97*

'Lincoln Castle, West Gate', M Otter, *Lincoln Archaeology 1988–1989* (1989), 13–16*

'Lincoln Castle: stability investigation', L Donel, *Lincoln Archaeology 1990–1991* (1991), 9–12*

'Investigations at Lincoln Castle', L Donel, *Lincoln Archaeology 1991–1992* (1992), 9–12*

'Lincoln Castle', L Donel, *Lincoln Archaeology 1992–1993* (1993), 11–14*

'Lincoln Castle', L Donel, *Lincoln Archaeology 6* (1993–4), 10–12*

'Lincoln, castle', R H Jones, *Lincolnshire History and Archaeology* 15 (1980), 73

'The South Bail gates of Lincoln', C Johnson and A Vince, *ibid* 27 (1992), 12–16*

'Medieval Britain in 1972', L E Webster and J Cherry, *Medieval Archaeology* 17 (1973), 169

'Investigations in the Observatory Tower, Lincoln Castle', N Reynolds, *ibid* 19 (1975), 201–5*

'Medieval Britain and Ireland in 1984', S M Youngs, J Clark and T Barry, *ibid* 29 (1985), 191

'Medieval Britain and Ireland in 1986', S M Youngs, J Clark and T Barry, *ibid* 31 (1987), 150

'Medieval Britain and Ireland in 1987', S M Youngs [*et al*], *ibid* 32 (1988), 261*

'Medieval Britain and Ireland in 1988', D R M Gaimster, S Margeson and T Barry, *ibid* 33 (1989), 201–2

'Medieval Britain and Ireland in 1989', D R M Gaimster, S Margeson and T Barry, *ibid* 34 (1990), 201

'Medieval Britain and Ireland in 1990', B S Nenk, S Margeson and M Hurley, *ibid* 35 (1991), 175

'Medieval Britain and Ireland in 1992', B S Nenk, S Margeson and M Hurley, *ibid* 37 (1993), 272–73

'Medieval Britain and Ireland in 1993', B S Nenk, S Margeson and M Hurley, *ibid* 38 (1994), 234

'The early Norman castle at Lincoln and a re-evaluation of the original west tower of Lincoln Cathedral', D Stocker and A Vince, *ibid* 41 (1997), 223–33*

Sleaford

'Medieval Britain and Ireland in 2000', J Bradley and M Gaimster, *Medieval Archaeology* 45 (2001), 298

'Sleaford', C Mahany and D Roffe, *South Lincolnshire Archaeology* 3 (1979), 1–33 [whole issue]

Stamford

The medieval buildings of Stamford. A Rodgers. Stamford: Stamford Survey Group, 1970*

Stamford in the thirteenth century. Two inquisitions from the reign of Edward I. D Roffe. Stamford: Paul Watkins, 1994

'Castle' and 'Town walls', in RCHME, *An inventory of historical monuments: the town of Stamford*, 3–5. London: HMSO, 1977*

'Stamford', C Mahany, *Archaeological Excavations 1972*, 94–95. London: HMSO, 1973

'Stamford Castle', C M Mahany, *Archaeological Excavations 1973*, 88. London: HMSO, 1974

'Stamford Castle', C M Mahany, *Archaeological Excavations 1974*, 97. London: HMSO, 1975

'Stamford Castle', C M Mahany, *Archaeological Excavations 1975*, 104. London: HMSO, 1976

'Stamford Castle', C M Mahany, *Archaeological Excavations 1976*, 131. London: HMSO, 1977

'Stamford Castle', C M Mahany, *Archaeology in Lincolnshire 1984–1985* (1985), 27–29*

'Excavations at Stamford Castle, 1971–6', C Mahany, *Château Gaillard* 8 (1977), 223–45*

'Stamford Castle', [A Selkirk], *Current Archaeology* 5 (1975–7), 53

'Stamford', W G Simpson, *East Midlands Archaeological Bulletin* 7 (1964), 19

'Stamford Castle', C M Mahany, *ibid* 12 (1978), 35

'Excavations at Stamford Castle 1974', C M Mahany, *Lincolnshire History and Archaeology* 10 (1975), 61

'Stamford (castle)', C M Mahany, *ibid* 11 (1976), 61

'Stamford and the Norman Conquest', D Roffe and C Mahany, *ibid* 21 (1986), 5–9*

'Medieval Britain in 1967', D M Wilson and D G Hurst, *Medieval Archaeology* 12 (1968), 177

'Medieval Britain in 1971', L E Webster and J Cherry, *ibid* 16 (1972), 188–89

'Medieval Britain in 1972', L E Webster and J Cherry, *ibid* 17 (1973), 161–62

'Medieval Britain in 1976', L E Webster and J Cherry, *ibid* 21 (1977), 235–37*

'Stamford Castle and town', C Mahany, *South Lincolnshire Archaeology* 2 (1978), 1–32* [whole issue]

Swineshead
'Swineshead', H Healey, *East Midlands Archaeological Bulletin* 4 (1961), 12

Tattershall
Tattershall Castle, Lincolnshire. T Avery. London: National Trust, 1997*

The building accounts of Tattershall Castle, 1434–1472. W D Simpson. [S l]: Lincoln Record Society, 1960* (vol 55)

Tattershall Castle, Lincolnshire. M W Thompson. London: National Trust, 1974*

'The architectural significance of the building works of Ralph, Lord Cromwell (1394–1456)', M W Thompson, in A Detsicas (ed), *Collectanea historica: essays in memory of Stuart Rigold*, 155–62. Maidstone: Kent Archaeological Society, 1981*

'Tattershall Castle', M W Thompson, *Archaeological Journal* 131 (1974), 334*

'Tattershall Castle, Lincolnshire', J Goodall, *Country Life* 190.41 (1996), 50–55*

'To me the past is sacred', J Musson, *ibid* 192.2 (1998), 34–37*

'The Tattershall household book, 1475–76', E M Byatt-Price, *Reports and Papers of the Lincolnshire Architectural and Archaeological Society* 7 (1957–8), 126–56*

'Medieval Britain and Ireland in 2004', M Gaimster and K O'Conor, *Medieval Archaeology* 49 (2005), 388

Thonock

'Thonock: ring and baileys', in P L Everson, C C Taylor and C J Dunn, *Change and continuity: rural settlement in north-east Lincolnshire*, 193–94. London: HMSO for RCHME, 1991*

Welbourn

'Medieval Britain and Ireland in 2000', J Bradley and M Gaimster, *Medieval Archaeology* 45 (2001), 300

LONDON AND MIDDLESEX

Bradley, S and Pevsner, N. *London. 1. The City of London (The buildings of England)*. London: Penguin Books, 1997*

Grimes, W F. *The excavation of Roman and medieval London*. London: Routledge and Kegan Paul, 1968*

Lobel, M D (ed). *The British atlas of historic towns. 3. The City of London from prehistoric times to c 1520*. Oxford: OUP, 1989*

Salter, M. *The castles of the Thames Valley and the Chilterns*. Malvern: Folly Publications, [2002]*

Thomas, C. *The archaeology of medieval London*. Stroud: Sutton Publishing, 2002*

Baynard's

Castle Baynard. Anon. Duplicated typescript, 1972

Baynard's Castle excavations, summer 1972. Anon. Duplicated typescript, 1972

'Baynard's Castle', P Marsden, *Archaeological Excavations 1972*, 95. London: HMSO, 1973

'A medieval armorial brooch or pendant from Baynard's Castle', T Wilmott, *Transactions of the London and Middlesex Archaeological Society* 33 (1982), 299–302*

'The 'western stream' reconsidered. Excavations at the medieval Great Wardrobe: Wardrobe Place, City of London', K Tyler, *ibid* 51 (2000), 21–44*

'Baynard's Castle', P Marsden, *London Archaeologist* 1.14 (1972), 162–64*

'Medieval Britain in 1972', L E Webster and J Cherry, *Medieval Archaeology* 17 (1973), 162–64*

'Medieval Britain in 1973', L E Webster and J Cherry, *ibid* 18 (1974), 196

'Medieval Britain in 1981', S M Youngs and J Clark, *ibid* 26 (1982), 192*

'Medieval Britain in 1984', S M Youngs, J Clark and T Barry, *ibid* 29 (1985), 176

City Defences (London Wall & Bridge)

The Thames and its buildings: a handbook for teachers. A Tinniswood. London: English Heritage, 1990*

London Bridge: 2000 years of a river crossing. B Watson, T Brigham and T Dyson. London: MoLAS, 2001* (MoLAS monograph; 8)

Excavations at medieval Cripplegate, London; archaeology after the Blitz, 1946–68. G Milne. London: English Heritage, 2002* [espec ch 2]

The medieval postern gate by the Tower of London. D Whipp. London: MoLAS, 2006 (MoLAS monograph; 29)

'The London Wall Walk', H Chapman, in E Southworth (ed), *The interpretation of archaeological sites and monuments: proceedings of the annual conference, Salisbury, 1985*, 5–7. Liverpool: Society of Museum Archaeologists, 1988*

'London: buildings and defences 1200–1600', J Schofield, in I Haynes, H Sheldon and L Hannigan (eds), *London under ground: the archaeology of a city*, 223–38. Oxford: Oxbow Books, 2000*

'Excavations in the City of London: first interim report, 1974–1975', B Hobley and J Schofield, *Antiquaries Journal* 57 (1977), 31–66*

'London Wall, EC3', anon, *The Archaeologist in Essex, Hertfordshire, London and Middlesex* (1960), 20

'London Wall, EC2', anon, *ibid* (1960), 23

'In defence of the City: the gates of London and Temple Bar in the seventeenth century', E Mann, *Architectural History* 49 (2006), 75–99*

'London Wall by St Alphage's churchyard: exposure and preservation of Roman and medieval work in the town wall of London', F J Forty, *Guildhall Miscellany* 1.5 (1955), [whole issue]*

'Archaeological finds in the City of London, 1966–68 – medieval', Guildhall Museum, *Transactions of the London and Middlesex Archaeological Society* 22.2 (1969), 23–26*

'Archaeological finds in the City of London, 1966–69 – medieval', Guildhall Museum, *ibid* 22.3 (1970), 6–9*

'Bastion 10A: a newly identified bastion in the City of London', J Schofield, *ibid* 29 (1978), 91–98*

'The discovery of bastion 4a in the City of London and its implications', J Maloney, *ibid* 31 (1980), 68–76*

'Excavations in the City of London: second interim report, 1974–1978', T Dyson and J Schofield, *ibid* 32 (1981), 24–81*

'Excavation of the Roman city wall at the Tower of London and Tower Hill, 1954–76', G Parnell, *ibid* 33 (1982), 85–133*

'Medieval London Bridge and its role in the defence of the realm', B Watson, *ibid* 50 (1999), 17–22*

'London Bridge and the identity of the medieval city', D Keene, *ibid* 51 (2000), 143–56*

'The city defences at Aldersgate', J Butler, *ibid* 52 (2001), 41–111*

'Duke's Place and Houndsditch: the medieval defences', J Maloney and C Harding, *London Archaeologist* 3.13 (1979), 347–54*

'A keyhole through the gateway: a watching brief at Aldgate', B Bishop, *ibid* 9.7 (2000), 179–84*

'1600 years of the City defences at Aldersgate', J Butler, *ibid* 9.9 (2001), 235–44*

'The late medieval bricks and brickwork of London Wall in Saint Alphage Garden, EC2', T P Smith, *ibid* 10.10 (2004), 255–63*

'The archaeology of London Wall', B Hobley, *London Journal* 7.1 (1981), 3–14*

'The ancient wall of the City of London: recent preservation work in Cripplegate by the Corporation of London', F J Forty, *Journal of the London Society* 333 (1956), 22–33*

'Medieval Britain in 1967', D M Wilson and D G Hurst, *Medieval Archaeology* 12 (1968), 184

'Medieval Britain in 1978', L E Webster and J Cherry, *ibid* 23 (1979), 267

'Medieval Britain in 1980', S M Youngs and J Clark, *ibid* 25 (1981), 211

'Medieval Britain and Ireland in 1982', S M Youngs, J Clark and T B Barry, *ibid* 27 (1983), 194

'Medieval Britain and Ireland in 1983', S M Youngs, J Clark and T B Barry, *ibid* 28 (1984), 227, 229

'Medieval Britain and Ireland in 1984', S M Youngs, J Clark and T B Barry, *ibid* 29 (1985), 173, 175

'Medieval Britain and Ireland in 1985', S M Youngs, J Clark and T Barry, *ibid* 30 (1986), 137, 139

'Medieval Britain and Ireland in 1986', S M Youngs, J Clark and T Barry, *ibid* 31 (1987), 128–29

'Medieval Britain and Ireland in 1987', S M Youngs [*et* al], *ibid* 32 (1988), 248

'Medieval Britain and Ireland in 1988', D R M Gaimster, S Margeson and T Barry, *ibid* 33 (1989), 183

'Medieval Britain and Ireland in 1989', D R M Gaimster, S Margeson and M Hurley, *ibid* 34 (1990), 176–79 [*passim*]

'Medieval Britain and Ireland in 1990', B S Nenk, S Margeson and M Hurley, *ibid* 35 (1991), 149–50

'Medieval Britain and Ireland in 1991', B S Nenk, S Margeson and M Hurley, *ibid* 36 (1992), 229

'Medieval Britain and Ireland in 1992', B S Nenk, S Margeson and M Hurley, *ibid* 37 (1993), 259, 260

'Medieval Britain and Ireland in 1993', B S Nenk, S Margeson and M Hurley, *ibid* 38 (1994), 213

'Medieval Britain and Ireland in 1995', B S Nenk, S Margeson and M Hurley, *ibid* 40 (1996), 258

'Medieval Britain and Ireland in 1997', M Gaimster, C Haith and J Bradley, *ibid* 42 (1998), 130–31

'Medieval Britain and Ireland in 1998', J Bradley, M Gaimster and C Haith, *ibid* 43 (1999), 247

'Medieval Britain and Ireland in 1999', J Bradley and M Gaimster, *ibid* 44 (2000), 266–67, 268

'Medieval Britain and Ireland in 2000', J Bradley and M Gaimster, *ibid* 45 (2001), 273

'Medieval Britain and Ireland in 2001', J Bradley and M Gaimster, *ibid* 46 (2002), 164

'Medieval Britain and Ireland in 2002', J Bradley and M Gaimster, *ibid* 47 (2003), 241–41

'Medieval Britain and Ireland in 2005', M Gaimster and K O'Conor, *ibid* 50 (2006), 312

'Post-medieval Britain in 1978', J Cherry, *Post-Medieval Archaeology* 13 (1979), 274

'Post-medieval Britain and Ireland in 1989', G Egan, *ibid* 24 (1990), 180–81

'Post-medieval Britain and Ireland in 1991', M Ponsford, *ibid* 26 (1992), 109

'Post-medieval Britain and Ireland in 1992', M Ponsford, *ibid* 27 (1993), 217–18

'Post-medieval Britain and Ireland in 1998 and 1999', M Ponsford, *ibid* 34 (2000), 234, 239, 271

Civil War Defences

The fortifications of London during the Civil War. V T C Smith. [S l]: Kent Defence Research Group, 1983*

'The lines of communication: the Civil War defences of London', V Smith and P Kelsey, in S Porter (ed), *London and the Civil War*, 117–48. London: Macmillan, 1996*

'Southampton House and the Civil War', R Weinstein, in J Bird [*et al*] (eds), *Collectanea Londiniensia: studies in London archaeology and history presented to Ralph Merrifield*, 329–45. London: London and Middlesex Archaeological Society, 1978*

'Civil War fortifications in Camden', R Weinstein, *Camden History Review* 5 (1977), 21–23*

'The defence of London during the English Civil War', V T C Smith, *Fort* 25 (1997), 61–81*

'Property destruction in Civil-War London', S Porter, *Transactions of the London and Middlesex Archaeological Society* 33 (1982), 59–62

'The Civil War defences of London', D Sturdy, *London Archaeologist* 2.13 (1975), 334–38*

'Archaeological investigations into the English Civil War defences of London', D Flintham, *ibid* 8.9 (1998), 233–35*

'Post-medieval Britain and Ireland in 1994', M Ponsford and R Jackson, *Post-Medieval Archaeology* 29 (1995), 131

'Post-medieval Britain and Ireland in 1997', M Ponsford and R Jackson, *ibid* 32 (1998), 149

'Post-medieval Britain and Ireland in 2002', M Ponsford, *ibid* 37 (2003), 264

Montfichet's

'The Norman fortress on Ludgate Hill in the City of London, England: recent excavations 1986–1990', B Watson, *Château Gaillard* 15 (1992), 335–45*

'The excavation of a Norman fortress on Ludgate Hill', B Watson, *London Archaeologist* 6.14 (1992), 371–77*

'Medieval Britain and Ireland in 1986', S M Youngs, J Clark and T Barry, *Medieval Archaeology* 31 (1987), 127

'Medieval Britain and Ireland in 1988', D R M Gaimster, S Margeson and T Barry, *ibid* 33 (1989), 180–81

'Medieval Britain and Ireland in 1990', B S Nenk, S Margeson and M Hurley, *ibid* 35 (1991), 151

Ruislip

'Medieval Britain and Ireland in 2005', M Gaimster and K O'Conor, *ibid* 50 (2006), 314

Tower of London

The Tower of London. Anon. London: HMSO, 1967*

Tower of London, Greater London. R A Brown and P E Curnow. London: HMSO, 1984*

The Tower of London. R Chamberlain. Exeter: Webb and Bower, 1989*

The riverside gardens of Thomas More's London. C P Christianson. London: Yale University Press, 2005* [espec pp 32–41]

Tales from the Tower of London. D Diehl and M P Donnelly. Stroud: Sutton Publishing, 2005*

The Tower of London: cauldron of Britain's past. P S Fry. London: Quiller Press, 1990*

Her Majesty's royal palace and fortress of the Tower of London. P Hammond. London: DoE, 1987*

Royal fortress: the Tower of London through nine centuries. P Hammond. London: HMSO, 1978*

The Tower of London young visitor's guide. P Hammond. London: HMSO, 1981*

The Tower of London. C Hibbert. London: Reader's Digest Association, 1971*

The Tower of London: the official illustrated history. E Impey and G Parnell. London: Merrell, 2000*

The Elizabethan Tower of London: the Haiward and Gascoyne plan of 1597. A Keay. London: London Topographical Society, 2001* (Publication; 158) (published in association with Historic Royal Palaces and the Society of Antiquaries of London)

The Tower of London moat: archaeological excavations 1995–9. G Keevill. Oxford: Oxford Archaeology, on behalf of Historic Royal Palaces, 2004* (Historic Royal Palaces monograph; 1)

The Tower of London New Armouries project: archaeological investigations of the New Armouries building and the former Irish barracks, 1997–2000. G Keevill and S Kelly. Oxford: Oxford Archaeology, in association with Historic Royal Palaces, 2006* (Oxford Archaeology occasional paper; 12)

The Tower of London: a 2000-year history. I Lapper and G Parnell. Oxford: Osprey for the Royal Armouries, 2000*

The Tower of London: 900 years of English history. K J Mears. Oxford: Phaidon, 1988*

The Tower of London. R J Minney. London: Cassell, 1970*

A plan for the Tower of London in 1682. G Parnell. London: London Topographical Society, 1983*

English Heritage book of the Tower of London. G Parnell. London: Batsford, in association with English Heritage, 1993*

The Tower of London past and present. G Parnell. Stroud: Sutton Publishing, 1998*

The Tower of London. A L Rowse. London: Joseph, 1977*

The Tower of London. S Thurley, E Impey and P Hammond. London: Historic Royal Palaces, 1996*

The Tower, 1078–1978. D Wilson. London: Hamish Hamilton, 1978*; reprinted by Constable as *The Tower of London*, 1990*

'Architectural history and development to *c* 1547', R A Brown, in J Charlton (ed), *The Tower of London: its buildings and institutions*, 24–37. London: HMSO, 1978*

'Architectural description', R A Brown, in *ibid*, 38–54*

'Some observations on the Tower of London', R A Brown, in R A Brown, *Castles, conquest and charters: collected papers*, 163–76. Woodbridge: Boydell Press, 1989*

'The White Tower of London', R A Brown, in *ibid*, 177–86*

'The White Tower of London', R A Brown, in B Ford (ed), *The Cambridge guide to the arts in Britain. 1. Prehistoric, Roman and early medieval*, 254–63. Cambridge: CUP, 1988*

'King Henry III and the Tower of London', D A Carpenter, in D A Carpenter, *The reign of Henry III*, 199–218. London: Hambledon Press, 1996

'The Wakefield Tower, Tower of London, P E Curnow, in M R Apted, R Gilyard-Beer and A D Saunders (eds), *Ancient monuments and their interpretation: essays presented to A J Taylor*, 155–89. Chichester: Phillimore, 1977*

'The Bloody Tower', P E Curnow, in J Charlton (ed), *The Tower of London: its buildings and institutions*, 55–61. London: HMSO, 1978*

'Some observations on the planning and construction of the west curtain at the Tower of London', P Curnow, in *Mélanges d'archéologie et d'histoire médiévales en l'honneur de doyen Michel de Boüard*, 65–74. Geneva: Librairie Droz, 1982*

'HM Tower of London', W D M Raeburn, *Transactions of the Ancient Monuments Society* new ser 19 (1972), 21–26

'The refortification of the Tower of London 1679–86', G Parnell, *Antiquaries Journal* 63 (1983), 337–52*

'Tower of London', K Hardy, *Archaeological Excavations 1975*, 23. London: HMSO, 1976

'Tower of London', G Parnell, *Archaeological Excavations 1976*, 28. London: HMSO, 1977

'Some observations on the Tower of London', R A Brown, *Archaeological Journal* 136 (1979), 99–108*

'City (Tower of London)', anon, *The Archaeologist in Essex, Hertfordshire, London and Middlesex* (1959), 30

'Royal lodgings at the Tower of London 1216–1327', S Thurley, *Architectural History* 38 (1995), 36–57*

'The Great Storehouse in the Tower', N Blackiston, *Architectural Review* 121 (1957), 453*

'Tower of London', G Parnell, *CBA Calendar of Excavations* summaries 1976 (1977), 9

'Excavations in the Tower of London, 1964', in 'Three eleventh century earthworks in England', B K Davison, *Château Gaillard* 2 (1967), 39–48*

'The Wakefield Tower, Tower of London', P E Curnow, *ibid* 8 (1977), 87–101*

'Ordnance storehouses at the Tower of London, 1450–1700', G Parnell, *ibid* 18 (1998), 171–80*

'Conservation of Reigate stone at Hampton Court Palace and HM Tower of London', R Sanderson and K Garner, *Journal of Architectural Conservation* 7.3 (2001), 7–23*

'An Irish inscription in the Tower of London', N Buttimer, *Journal of the Cork Historical and Archaeological Society* 107 (2002), 211–16*

'The Tower of London', G Worsley, *Country Life* 187.14 (1993), 48–51*

'A moat too far?', M Hall, *ibid* 190.37 (1996), 110–13*

'The king's bedchamber', M Miers, *ibid* 200.45 (2006), 74–77*

'The Tower of London', G Keevill, *Current Archaeology* 13.10 (1997), 384–87*

'Ordnance building at the Tower of London', H Tomlinson, *History Today* 32 (April, 1982), 43–47*

'The rise and fall of the Tower of London', G Parnell, *ibid* 42 (March, 1992), 13–19*

'Medieval big cat remains from the Royal Menagerie at the Tower of London', H O'Regan, A Turner and R Sabin, *International Journal of Osteoarchaeology* 16 (2006), 385–94*

'The western entrance of the Tower', J H Harvey, *Transactions of the London and Middlesex Archaeological Society* 15 (1948), 20–35*

'The Tower of London: the reconstruction of the inmost ward during the reign of Charles II', G Parnell, *ibid* 31 (1980), 147–56*

'Excavations at the Salt Tower, Tower of London, 1976', G Parnell, *ibid* 34 (1983), 95–106*

'The western defences of the inmost ward, Tower of London, 1955–77', G Parnell, *ibid* 34 (1983), 107–50*

'The Roman and medieval defences and the later development of the inmost ward, Tower of London: excavations 1955–77', G Parnell, *ibid* 36 (1985), 1–79*

'Recent archaeological work at the Tower of London', J Hiller and G D Keevill, *ibid* 45 (1994), 147–81*

'Edward IV's bulwark: excavations at Tower Hill, London, 1985', M Hutchinson, *ibid* 47 (1996), 103–44*

'The western entrance to the Tower of London, 1240–1241', E Impey, *ibid* 48 (1997), 59–75*

'The Tower of London and the Jewish expulsion of 1290', J Ashbee, *ibid* 55 (2004), 35–37

'Excavations at the Tower of London, 1976/7', G Parnell, *London Archaeologist* 3.4 (1977), 97–99*

'Nine hundred years of the Tower', D Sturdy, *ibid* 3.12 (1979), 320–26*

'A carpenter's mark from the Martin Tower, Tower of London', G Parnell, *ibid* 4.11 (1983), 397–98*

'Medieval building stone at the Tower of London', T. Tatton-Brown, *ibid* 6.13 (1991), 361–66*

'Getting into deep water: proposals to re-flood Tower moat attracts Lottery grant', G Parnell, *ibid* 7.15 (1995), 387–90*

'King Henry III and the Tower of London', D A Carpenter, *London Journal* 19 (1994), 95–107

'Five seventeenth-century plans of the Tower of London', G Parnell, *London Topographical Record* 25 (1985), 63–82*

'Medieval Britain in 1962 and 1963', D M Wilson and D G Hurst, *Medieval Archaeology* 8 (1964), 255–56*

'Medieval Britain in 1980', S M Youngs and J Clark, *ibid* 25 (1981), 201

'Medieval Britain in 1981', S M Youngs and J Clark, *ibid* 26 (1982), 194

'Medieval Britain and Ireland in 1983', S M Youngs, J Clark and T B Barry, *ibid* 28 (1984), 233

'Medieval Britain and Ireland in 1993', B S Nenk, S Margeson and M Hurley, *ibid* 38 (1994), 215

'Medieval Britain and Ireland in 1996', B S Nenk, C Haith and J Bradley, *ibid* 41 (1997), 264–68*

'Gender and space in English royal palaces c 1160–c 1547: a study in access analysis and imagery', A Richardson, *ibid* 47 (2003), 131–65*

'Medieval Britain and Ireland in 2004', M Gaimster and K O'Conor, *ibid* 49 (2005), 368–69

'Post-medieval Britain in 1983', G Egan, *Post-Medieval Archaeology* 18 (1984), 308

'The White Tower reconsidered', G Parnell, *Royal Armouries Yearbook* 3 (1998), 162–67*

'The Tower of London and the *garderobae armorum*', R Storey, *ibid* 3 (1998), 176–83*

'"Epitome of England's history": the transformation of the Tower of London as visitor attraction in the 19th century', P Hammond, *ibid* 4 (1999), 144–74*

'The Tower of London through the eyes of Polish travellers in the 17th and 18th centuries', B M Puchalska, *ibid* 4 (1999), 175–78

'The castle at war: the Tower of London in World War II', R Chester, *ibid* 5 (2000), 172–77*

NORFOLK

Barnes, J. *The defence of Norfolk, 1793–1815: Norfolk during the Napoleonic Wars*. [S l]: Mintaka, 2000*

Bird, C. *Silent sentinels: the story of Norfolk's fixed defences during the twentieth century*. Dereham: Larks Press, 1999*

Bird, C. 'The fixed defences of north and east Norfolk in the two world wars: a modern survey. Part 1', *Journal of the Norfolk Industrial Archaeology Society* 5.1 (1991), 5–33*

Bird, C. 'The fixed defences of north and east Norfolk in the two world wars: a modern survey. Part 2', *ibid* 5.2 (1992), 57–93*

Campbell, A (ed). *Heritage unlocked: guide to free sites in the east of England*. London: English Heritage, 2004*

Cligman, J and Crowe, N. *Exploring England's heritage: Hertfordshire to Norfolk*. London: HMSO, in association with English Heritage, 1994* [ch 2]

Cushion, B and Davison, A. *Earthworks of Norfolk*. Dereham: Norfolk Museums and Archaeology Service, 2003* (East Anglian archaeology; 104)

Iosson, E. 'North west Norfolk coastal defences: a study of selected post-medieval sites', *Journal of the Norfolk Industrial Archaeology Society* 4.5 (1990), 187–97*

Kent, P. *Fortifications of East Anglia*. Lavenham: Dalton, 1988*

Kent, P. 'East Anglian fortifications in the twentieth century', *Fortress* 3 (1989), 43–57*

Liddiard, R. *'Landscapes of lordship': Norman castles and the countryside in medieval Norfolk, 1066–1200*. Oxford: John and Erica Hedges, 2000* (BAR British series; 309)

Liddiard, R. 'Early castles in the medieval landscape of East Anglia', *Château Gaillard* 22 (2006), 243–50*

Liddiard, R. 'Population density and Norman castle building: some evidence from East Anglia', *Landscape History* 22 (2000), 37–46*

Margeson, S, Seillier, F and Rogerson, A. *The Normans in Norfolk*. Norwich: Norfolk Museums Service, 1994* [espec pp 22–39]

Pawsey, J T. *Castles of East Anglia*. Ipswich: F W Pawsey, 1973*

Pevsner, N and Wilson, B. *Norfolk 1: Norwich and north-east (The buildings of England)*. 2nd edition. London: Penguin Books, 1997*

Pevsner, N and Wilson, B. *Norfolk 2: north-west and south (The buildings of England)*. 2nd edition. London: Penguin Books, 1999*

Salter, M. *The castles of East Anglia*. Malvern: Folly Publications, 2001*

Wilton, J W. *Earthworks and fortifications of Norfolk*. Lowestoft: Weathercock Press, 1979*

Baconsthorpe

Baconsthorpe Castle, excavation and finds, 1951–18972. C Dallas and D Sherlock. Dereham: Norfolk Museums and Archaeology Service, 2002* (East Anglian archaeology; 102)

Baconsthorpe Castle, Norfolk. S E Rigold. London: HMSO, 1966*

'Baconsthorpe Castle', S E Rigold, *Archaeological Journal* 137 (1980), 331–32

'Baconsthorpe Castle', S E Rigold, *Norfolk Research Committee Bulletin* 6 (1953), 3

'Post-medieval Britain in 1972', J Cherry, *Post-Medieval Archaeology* 7 (1973), 101

Caister

'Caister Castle', H D Barnes and W D Simpson, *Antiquaries Journal* 32 (1952), 35–51*

'Caister Castle', H Gordon Slade, *Archaeological Journal* 137 (1980), 295–98*

'The building accounts of Caister Castle A D 1432–1435', H D Barnes and W D Simpson, *Norfolk Archaeology* 30 (1949–52), 178–86*

'Caister Castle, Norfolk. Notes on the bricks and workmanship of the castle walls', S E Glendenning, *ibid* 30 (1949–52), 186–88

Castle Acre

Castle Acre: fortress village. T Bevis. March: the author, 1990*

Castle Acre Castle, Norfolk. J G Coad. London: HBMCE, 1984*; reset reprint, 1988*

Castle Acre Castle and Priory, Norfolk. J Coad and G Coppack. London: English Heritage, 1998*

A teacher's guide to Castle Acre Priory and Castle. L Staszewska and H Cocksedge. London: English Heritage, 1994*

'Castle Acre: castle', J G Coad, *Archaeological Excavations 1976*, 28–29. London: HMSO, 1977

'Castle Acre: the castle', P K Baillie Reynolds, *Archaeological Journal* 106 (1949), 111

'Excavations at Castle Acre Castle, Norfolk, 1972–77: country house and castle of the Norman earls of Surrey', J G Coad and A D F Streeten, *ibid* 139 (1982), 138–301*

'Excavations at Castle Acre Castle, Norfolk, 1975–1982. The bridges, lime kilns, and eastern gatehouse', J G Coad, A D F Streeten and R Warmington, *ibid* 144 (1987), 256–307*

'Excavation at Castle Acre, Norfolk, 1972–1976. An interim report', J G Coad, *Château Gaillard* 8 (1977), 79–86*

'Recent work at Castle Acre Castle', J G Coad, *ibid* 11 (1983), 55–67*

'Walking history: Castle Acre Priory, Castle and Bailey Gate', M Morris, *Heritage Today* 75 (2006), 36–39*

'Excavations and watching brief at Castle Acre 1985–86', M Leah, *Norfolk Archaeology* 41.4 (1993), 494–507*

'Castle Acre', H Sutermeister, *Norfolk Research Committee Newsletter and Bulletin* 9 (1972), 15

'Castle Acre Castle', H Sutermeister, *ibid* 12 (1973), 11

Castle Rising

Castle Rising, Norfolk. R A Brown. London: HMSO, 1978*; 2nd printing (reset), 1983*

Castle Rising, Norfolk. R A Brown. London: HBMCE, 1987*

Castle Rising, King's Lynn, Norfolk: a short history of Castle Rising and its owners. R Liddiard. [Castle Rising: Castle Rising Holdings, 2000]*

Castle Rising Castle, Norfolk. B M Morley and D Gurney. Dereham: Field Archaeology Division (Norfolk Museums Service), 1997* (East Anglian archaeology; 81)

'Castle Rising, Norfolk: a 'landscape of lordship'?', R Liddiard, in C Harper-Bill (ed), *Anglo-Norman studies 22: proceedings of the Battle Conference 1999*, 169–86. Woodbridge: Boydell Press, 2000*

'Castle Rising, the castle', B M Morley, *Archaeological Excavations 1975*, 25. London: HMSO, 1976

'Castle Rising, the castle', B M Morley, *Archaeological Excavations 1976*, 29–30. London: HMSO, 1977

'Medieval Britain in 1970', D M Wilson and S Moorhouse, *Medieval Archaeology* 15 (1971), 147

'Medieval Britain in 1972', L E Webster and J Cherry, *ibid* 17 (1973), 163

'Medieval Britain in 1973', L E Webster and J Cherry, *ibid* 18 (1974), 196

'Medieval Britain in 1974', L E Webster and J Cherry, *ibid* 19 (1975), 239

'Medieval Britain in 1975', L E Webster and J Cherry, *ibid* 20 (1976), 185

'Medieval Britain in 1976', L E Webster and J Cherry, *ibid* 21 (1977), 235

'Medieval Britain and Ireland in 1987', S M Youngs [*et al*], *ibid* 32 (1988), 262

'Castle Rising, Norfolk: a 'landscape of lordship'?', R Liddiard, *Medieval Settlement Research Group Annual Report* 15 (2000), 8–9 [shortened version of the 'Battle' paper cited above]

'The settlement pattern of Castle Rising', P Rutledge, *Norfolk Research Committee Bulletin* 18 (1969), 6–7

'Castle Rising', H Sutermeister, *Norfolk Research Committee Newsletter and Bulletin* 12 (1973), 10–11

Claxton

'Medieval Britain and Ireland in 2004', M Gaimster and K O'Conor, *Medieval Archaeology* 49 (2005), 390

Denton

'Medieval Britain and Ireland in 1993', B S Nenk, S Margeson and M Hurley, *ibid* 38 (1994), 234

Great Yarmouth

Great Yarmouth town wall. Anon. 2nd edition. Great Yarmouth: Great Yarmouth and District Archaeological Society, 1971*

'Yarmouth – the defences', C Green, *CBA Group 7 Bulletin* 2 (1955), 7

'Medieval Britain and Ireland in 1996', B S Nenk, C Haith and J Bradley, *Medieval Archaeology* 41 (1997), 279

'Excavations on the town wall, Great Yarmouth, Norfolk, 1955', C Green, *Norfolk Archaeology* 35 (1970–3), 109–17*

'The East Mount, Great Yarmouth, in the light of recent observations', E J Rose, *ibid* 41.2 (1991), 196–202*

'Yarmouth, Great', R R Clarke, *Norfolk Research Committee Bulletin* 8 (1955), 2

'Yarmouth, Great', C G Rye, *ibid* 15 (1963), 12

'Great Yarmouth – town moat', G Rye, *Norfolk Research Committee Newsletter and Bulletin* 9 (1972), 16

'Post-medieval Britain in 1986', G Egan, *Post-Medieval Archaeology* 21 (1987), 269

'Great Yarmouth: the fortifications – 1750', G Rye, *Yarmouth Archaeology* 2.1 (1984), 9–12*

'Great Yarmouth fortifications, *c* 1781-*c* 1850', G Rye, *ibid* 2.2 (1985), 26–32*

'Great Yarmouth: the fortified town post', G Rye, *ibid* 2.3 (1986), 88–98*

'Great Yarmouth: the fortified town – 1880–1914', G Rye, *ibid* 2.4 (1987), 133–45*

Hunworth

'Hunworth', anon, *CBA Group 7 Bulletin* 12 (1965), 4

'Hunworth', anon, *Norfolk Research Committee Bulletin* 16 (1966), 12

King's Lynn

'The defences', A Carter, in H Clarke and A Carter, *Excavations in King's Lynn 1963–1970*, 432–38. London: Society for Medieval Archaeology, 1977* (Monograph series; 7)

'The medieval town defences of King's Lynn', T P Smith, *Journal of the British Archaeological Association* 3 ser 33 (1970), 57–88*

'King's Lynn', P Kent, *Fort* 13 (1985), 49–60*

'Medieval Britain in 1970', D M Wilson and S Moorhouse, *Medieval Archaeology* 15 (1971), 155

'Re-used bedrock ballast in King's Lynn's 'town wall' and the Norfolk port's medieval trading links', P G Hoare [*et al*], *ibid* 46 (2002), 91–105*

'The date of the King's Lynn South Gate', T P Smith, *Norfolk Archaeology* 36 (1974–7), 224–32*

'A fresh study of the South Gate at King's Lynn in the light of recent restoration work', E M James, *ibid* 40.1 (1987), 55–72*

'Post-medieval Britain in 1967', D G Hurst, *Post-Medieval Archaeology* 2 (1968), 176–77

Middleton

'Middleton Mount: excavations in and around the castle bailey of Middleton castle by Andrew Rogerson, 1987', T Ashwin, *Norfolk Archaeology* 43.4 (2001), 646–56*

Mileham

'Mileham', M C Taylor, *CBA Group 7 Bulletin* 15 (1968), 8–9

'Medieval Britain in 1968', D M Wilson and D G Hurst, *Medieval Archaeology* 13 (1969), 258–60

'Excavations at Mileham Castle', anon, *Norfolk Research Committee Bulletin* 18 (1969), 7

New Buckenham

Buckenham castles 1066 to 1649. P M Remfry. Malvern Link: SCS Publishing, 1997*

'New Buckenham Castle', S Rigold, *Archaeological Journal* 137 (1980), 353–55*

'Medieval Britain and Ireland in 1996', B S Nenk, C Haith and J Bradley, *Medieval Archaeology* 41 (1997), 278

'The keep at New Buckenham', D F Renn, *Norfolk Archaeology* 32 (1958–61), 232–35*

Norwich

Report on the city walls of Norwich. Anon. Norwich: Norfolk and Norwich Archaeological Society, 1964*

Excavations within the north-east bailey of Norwich Castle, 1979. B Ayers. Dereham: Norfolk Archaeological Unit, 1985* (East Anglian archaeology; 28)

Digging deeper: recent archaeology in Norwich. B Ayers. Norwich: Norfolk Museums Service, 1987* [espec pp 14–23, Cow Tower and castle keep]

Digging ditches: archaeology and development in Norwich. B Ayers, J Bown and J Reeve. Norwich: Norfolk Museums Service, 1992* [espec pp 17–27]

Norwich Castle Mall excavation: the trial work 1988. B Ayers. Norwich: Norfolk Museums Service, 1988*

English Heritage book of Norwich. B Ayers. London: Batsford, in association with English Heritage, 1994*

Norwich: 'a fine city'. B Ayers. Stroud: Tempus, 2003* [new edition of the above]

Norwich Castle: a fortress for nine centuries. B Green. Norwich: Jarrold, 1962*

Norwich Castle: a guide to the castle as it was about AD 1200. B Green. Norwich: Norfolk Museums Service, 1990*

Norwich Castle keep: Romanesque architecture and social context. T A Heslop. Norwich: Centre of East Anglian Studies, 1994*

Medieval Norwich. C Rawcliffe and R Wilson (eds). London: Hambledon and London, 2004*

Norwich Castle: a basic guide to Norwich Castle about AD 1200. R Teather. Norwich: Norfolk Museums Service, reprinted 1985*

'Norwich', J Campbell, in M D Lobel (ed), *The atlas of historic towns*, **2**. London: Scolar Press, 1975*

'Recent excavations at Norwich Castle', E Shepherd, in G De Boe and F Verhaeghe (eds), *Military studies in medieval Europe: papers of the 'Medieval Europe Brugge 1997' conference*, **11**, 187–90. Zellik: Institute for the Archaeological Heritage, 1997

'Norwich Castle keep', P Drury, in G Meirion-Jones, E Impey and M Jones (eds), *The seigneurial residence in western Europe AD c 800–1600*, 210–34. Oxford: Archaeopress, 2002* (BAR international series; 1088)

'Norwich Castle and its analogues', P Dixon and P Marshall, in *ibid*, 235–43*

'Norwich Castle Mall', in G J Wainwright, *Archaeology Review 1990–91*, 39–40. London: English Heritage, 1991*

'Norwich Castle', A B Whittingham, *Archaeological Journal* 106 (1949), 77

'Norwich Castle', B Green, *ibid* 137 (1980), 358–59

'Note on Norwich Castle', A B Whittingham, *ibid* 137 (1980), 359–60

'Norwich Castle excavations', L Shepherd, *Castle Studies Group Newsletter* 9 (1995–6), 25–28*

'Norwich', D R Howlett, *CBA Group 7 Bulletin* 2 (1955), 5

'Norwich', anon, *ibid* 8 (1961), 4

'Norwich', anon, *ibid* 10 (1963), 4

'Norwich', anon, *ibid* 17 (1970), 12

'Norwich Castle', E Shepherd, *Current Archaeology* 15.2 (2000), 52–59*

'The Norwich Castle flagon', R Brownsword and R F Homer, *Journal of the Pewter Society* 8.2 (1991), 62–65*

'John Bolton's cinder oven: an eighteenth century re-use of a medieval tower', M Day, *Industrial Archaeology Review* 6.3 (1982), 235–40*

'Medieval Britain in 1961', D M Wilson and D G Hurst, *Medieval Archaeology* 6–7 (1962–3), 322

'Medieval Britain in 1962 and 1963', D M Wilson and D G Hurst, *ibid* 8 (1964), 255–57

'Medieval Britain in 1972', L E Webster and J Cherry, *ibid* 17 (1973), 163

'Medieval Britain in 1979', L E Webster and J Cherry, *ibid* 24 (1980), 228–29

'The Cow Tower, Norwich: an East Anglian bastille?', A D Saunders, *ibid* 29 (1985), 109–19*

'Medieval Britain and Ireland in 1985', S M Youngs, J Clark and T Barry, *ibid* 30 (1986), 158–59

'Medieval Britain and Ireland in 1986', S M Youngs, J Clark and T Barry, *ibid* 31 (1987), 151–52

'The Cow Tower, Norwich: a detailed survey and partial reinterpretation', B S Ayers, R Smith and M Tillyard, *ibid* 32 (1988), 184–207*

'Medieval Britain and Ireland in 1987', S M Youngs [*et al*], *ibid* 32 (1988), 263–64

'Medieval Britain and Ireland in 1988', D R M Gaimster, S Margeson and T Barry, *ibid* 33 (1989), 202

'Medieval Britain and Ireland in 1989', D R M Gaimster, S Margeson and M Hurley, *ibid* 34 (1990), 202–3

'Medieval Britain and Ireland in 1990', B S Nenk, S Margeson and M Hurley, *ibid* 35 (1991), 175, 177

'Medieval Britain and Ireland in 1991', B S Nenk, S Margeson and M Hurley, *ibid* 36 (1992), 253*

'Medieval Britain and Ireland in 1994', B S Nenk, S Margeson and M Hurley, *ibid* 39 (1995), 233

'Norwich Castle bridge', A Shelley, *ibid* 40 (1996), 217–26*

'Medieval Britain and Ireland in 1995', B S Nenk, S Margeson and M Hurley, *ibid* 40 (1996), 273

'Medieval Britain and Ireland in 1998', J Bradley, M Gaimster and C Haith, *ibid* 43 (1999), 269

'Medieval Britain and Ireland in 1999', J Bradley and M Gaimster, *ibid* 44 (2000), 295–96

'Medieval Britain and Ireland in 2000', J Bradley and M Gaimster, *ibid* 45 (2001), 304

'Medieval Britain and Ireland in 2001', J Bradley and M Gaimster, *ibid* 46 (2002), 195

'Medieval Britain and Ireland in 2005', M Gaimster and K O'Conor, *ibid* 50 (2006), 340

'Norwich Castle Fee', E Shepherd Popescu, *ibid* 48 (2004), 209–19*

'Excavations in the city of Norwich, 1948', E M Jope, *Norfolk Archaeology* 30 (1949–52), 287–323*

'Excavations at St Benedict's Gates, Norwich, 1951 and 1953', J G Hurst and J Golson, *ibid* 31 (1953–7), 1–112*

'Excavations at Barn Road, Norwich, 1954–55', J G Hurst, *ibid* 33 (1962–5), 131–79*

'Excavations in Norwich – 1973. The Norwich Survey: third interim report', A Carter, P J Roberts and H Sutermeister, *ibid* 36 (1974–7), 39–71*

'Excavations in Norwich – 1975/6. The Norwich Survey: fifth interim report', M W Atkin and A Carter, *ibid* 36 (1974–7), 191–201*

'Excavations and surveys in Norfolk 1989', D Gurney (ed), *ibid* 41.1 (1990), 110

'Norwich, Old Cattle Market car park ('Castle Mall') site', J Reeve, *ibid* 41.2 (1991), 243

'Norwich', anon, *Norfolk Research Committee Bulletin* 1 (1949), 2

'Norwich', anon, *ibid* 3 (1951), [4]

'Norwich', anon, *ibid* 4 (1951), 3–4

'Norwich', anon, *ibid* 14 (1961–2), 3

'Norwich', anon, *ibid* 15 (1963), 10–11

Old Buckenham

Buckenham castles 1066 to 1649. P M Remfry. Malvern Link: SCS Publishing, 1997*

Red Castle, Thetford

'Thetford, Red Castle', G M Knocker, *CBA Group 7 Bulletin* 4 (1957), 4

'Excavations at Red Castle, Thetford', G M Knocker, *Norfolk Archaeology* 34 (1966–9), 119–86*

'Excavations and surveys in Norfolk 1989', D Gurney (ed), *ibid* 41.1 (1990), 111–12

'Thetford, Red Castle', anon, *Norfolk Research Committee Bulletin* 10 (1957), 1–2

Thetford

'Excavations at Thetford Castle, 1962 and 1985–6', J A Davies and T Gregory, in J A Davies [*et al*], *The Iron Age forts of Norfolk*, 1–30. Dereham: Norfolk Field Archaeology Division, 1991* (East Anglian archaeology; 54) [cover has 1992 as date of publication]

'Castle Hill and the early medieval development of Thetford in Norfolk', P Everson and M Jecock, in P Pattison, D Field and S Ainsworth (eds), *Patterns of the past: essays in landscape archaeology for Christopher Taylor*, 97–106. Oxford: Oxbow Books, 1999*

'Thetford Castle', S Rigold, *Archaeological Journal* 137 (1980), 355

'Thetford', G M Knocker, *CBA Group 7 Bulletin* 6 (1959), 5

'Thetford', R R Clarke, *ibid* 8 (1961), 5

'Thetford', anon, *ibid* 9 (1962), 5

'Medieval Britain in 1961', D M Wilson and D G Hurst, *Medieval Archaeology* 6–7 (1962–3), 322

'Medieval Britain in 1962 and 1963', D M Wilson and D G Hurst, *ibid* 8 (1964), 257

'Medieval Britain and Ireland in 1998', J Bradley, M Gaimster and C Haith, *ibid* 43 (1999), 271

'Thetford', anon, *Norfolk Research Committee Bulletin* 12 (1959), 2

'Excavations at Thetford Castle', R R Clarke and E B Green, *ibid* 14 (1961–2), 7–9

Walpole St Peter

'Walpole St Peter', E Talbot, *CBA Group 7 Bulletin* 14 (1967), 9

'Medieval Britain in 1967', D M Wilson and D G Hurst, *Medieval Archaeology* 12 (1968), 177

Weeting

'Weeting "Castle", a 12th-century hall house in Norfolk', T A Heslop, in D Pitte and B Ayers (eds), *The medieval house in Normandy and England*, 131–41. Rouen: La Société libre d'Emulation de la Seine-Maritime, 2002*

'Weeting "Castle", a twelfth-century hall house in Norfolk', T A Heslop, *Architectural History* 43 (2000), 42–57*

'Medieval Britain in 1964', D M Wilson and D G Hurst, *Medieval Archaeology* 9 (1965), 190–91

Wormegay

'Wormegay', J P Smallwood, *CBA Group 7 Bulletin* 16 (1969), 11

NORTHAMPTONSHIRE

Cadman, G. 'Northamptonshire's bombing decoys', *Northamptonshire Archaeology* 28 (1998–9), 139–42*

Lanning, K and Pearson, V. *Castles in Northamptonshire: a resource pack for teachers*. Northampton: Northampton County Council, 1995* [a folder with three A4 booklets + sheets]

Lowerre, A. *Placing castles in the Conquest: landscape, lordship and local politics in the south-eastern midlands, 1066–1100*. Oxford: J and E Hedges, 2005* (BAR British series; 385)

Osborne, M. *20th century defences in the east midlands: Derbyshire, Leicestershire, Lincolnshire, Northamptonshire, Nottinghamshire and Rutland*. Market Deeping: Concrete Publications, 2003*

Pevsner, N. *Northamptonshire (The buildings of England)*. 2nd edition, revised by B Cherry. Harmondsworth: Penguin Books, 1973*

Salter, M. *The castles of the east midlands*. Malvern: Folly Publications, 2002*

Barby
'Barby', G Cadman, *South Midlands Archaeology* 19 (1989), 23–24*

Barnwell
'Barnwell Castle, Barnwell St Andrew', in J Heward and R Taylor, *The country houses of Northamptonshire*, 79–81. Swindon: RCHME, 1996*

'Barnwell Castle', M Audouy, *CBA Group 9 Newsletter* 11 (1981), 19–20

'Barnwell Manor, Northamptonshire', C Hussey, *Country Life* 126 (1959), 238–41*

'Medieval Britain in 1980', S M Youngs and J Clark, *Medieval Archaeology* 25 (1981), 201

'Excavations at Barnwell Castle, Northants, 1980', M Audouy, *Northamptonshire Archaeology* 25 (1993–4), 123–26*

'Barnwell Castle survey 1980–85', B L Giggins, *South Midlands Archaeology* 16 (1986), 79–84*

Brackley
'Medieval Britain and Ireland in 1982', S M Youngs, J Clark and T B Barry, *Medieval Archaeology* 27 (1983), 197

'Brackley Castle', D Jennings, *South Midlands Archaeology* 22 (1992), 41–42

Braybrooke
'Braybrooke Castle', in RCHME, *An inventory of the historical monuments in the county of Northampton. 2. Archaeological sites in central Northamptonshire*, 11, 13. London: HMSO, 1979*

Cransley
'Motte?', in *ibid*, 28–29*

Culworth
'Ringwork', in RCHME, *An inventory of the historical monuments in the county of Northampton. 4. Archaeological sites in south-west Northamptonshire*, 39. London: HMSO, 1982*

Earls Barton
'Mound and ditch', in RCHME, *An inventory of the historical monuments in the county of Northampton. 2. Archaeological sites in central Northamptonshire*, 40, 42. London: HMSO, 1979*

Farthingstone
'Motte and bailey', in RCHME, *An inventory of the historical monuments in the county of Northampton. 3. Archaeological sites in north-west Northamptonshire*, 86–88. London: HMSO, 1981*

Fineshade

'Medieval Britain and Ireland in 1987', S M Youngs [*et al*], *Medieval Archaeology* 32 (1988), 264

Fotheringhay

'The Civil War siege of Grafton Regis', G Foard, in C FitzRoy and K Harry (eds), *Grafton Regis: the history of a Northamptonshire village*, 49–63. Cardiff: Merton Priory Press, 2000*

'Fotheringhay Castle', in RCHME, *An inventory of the historical monuments in the county of Northampton. 1. Archaeological sites in north-east Northampton-shire*, 43–46. London: HMSO, 1975*

'Fotheringhay Castle', J Oetgen, *South Midlands Archaeology* 33 (2003), 37–38*

Grafton Regis

'Motte or ringwork', in RCHME, *An inventory of the historical monuments in the county of Northampton. 4. Archaeological sites in south-west Northamptonshire*, 61–62. London: HMSO, 1982*

Higham Ferrers

'Medieval Britain and Ireland in 1991', B S Nenk, S Margeson and M Hurley, *Medieval Archaeology* 36 (1992), 255–56

'Higham Ferrers Castle – or otherwise', A E Brown, *Northamptonshire Past and Present* 5.2 (1974), 79–84*

Lilbourne

'Motte' and 'Motte and bailey', in RCHME, *An inventory of the historical monuments in the county of Northampton. 3. Archaeological sites in north-west Northamptonshire*, 125–27. London: HMSO, 1981*

Little Houghton

'Motte', in RCHME, *An inventory of the historical monuments in the county of Northampton. 2. Archaeological sites in central Northamptonshire*, 87–88. London: HMSO, 1979*

Long Buckby

'Ring and bailey', in RCHME, *An inventory of the historical monuments in the county of Northampton. 3. Archaeological sites in north-west Northamptonshire*, 133–35. London: HMSO, 1981*

'Long Buckby', anon, *Coventry and District Archaeological Society Bulletin* 327 (1996), 6*

'Trial excavation on the west bailey of a ring motte and bailey at Long Buckby, Northants', M W Thompson, *Journal of the Northamptonshire Natural History Society and Field Club* 33 (1955–9), 55–66*

Longthorpe

Longthorpe Tower, Peterborough, Northamptonshire. E C Rouse. London: HMSO, 1964*

Moor End

'The hamlet and castle of Moor End in Yardley Gobio', D Warren, *Wolverton and District Archaeological Society News Letter* 8 (1964), 7–12

Northampton

'Medieval defences' and Northampton Castle', in RCHME, *An inventory of the historical monuments in the county of Northampton. 5. Archaeological sites and churches in Northampton*, 50–51, 327–30, 332–35. London: HMSO, 1985* [the main entries are on microfiche]

'Northampton Castle', J Alexander, *Archaeological Excavations 1961*, 11. London: HMSO, 1962

'Northampton Castle, Chalk Lane', J Williams, *Archaeological Excavations 1975*, 108–9. London: HMSO, 1976

'Northampton Castle', J H Williams, *Archaeological Excavations 1976*, 141. London: HMSO, 1977

'Northampton Castle', B L Giggins, *Castle Studies Group Bulletin* 18 (2004–5), 185–87*

'Northampton Castle', J H Williams, *CBA Calendar of Excavations* summaries 1976 (1977), 10

'Northampton Castle', D C Mynard, *CBA Group 9 Newsletter* 2 (1972), 19

'Chalk Lane', J H Williams, R Hunter and F Williams, *CBA Newsletter and Calendar* 1 (1977–8), 112

'Northampton', M Shaw, A Chapman and I Soden, *Current Archaeology* 13.11 (1997), 408–15*

'Medieval Britain in 1961', D M Wilson and D G Hurst, *Medieval Archaeology* 6–7 (1962–3), 322–23

'Medieval Britain in 1962 and 1963', D M Wilson and D G Hurst, *ibid* 8 (1964), 257–58

'Medieval Britain in 1964', D M Wilson and D G Hurst, *ibid* 9 (1965), 191

'Medieval Britain in 1971', L E Webster and J Cherry, *ibid* 16 (1972), 181

'Medieval Britain in 1975', L E Webster and J Cherry, *ibid* 20 (1976), 185

'Medieval Britain and Ireland in 1987', S M Youngs [*et al*], *ibid* 32 (1988), 265

'Medieval Britain and Ireland in 1988', D R M Gaimster, S Margeson and T Barry, *ibid* 33 (1989), 204

'Medieval Britain and Ireland in 1992', B S Nenk, S Margeson and M Hurley, *ibid* 37 (1993), 278

'Socketed bowls from Northampton Castle', D H Kennet, *Journal of the Northampton Museum and Art Gallery* 6 (1969), 50*

'Northampton, the castle', J Williams, *Northamptonshire Archaeology* 8 (1973), 21

'Northampton', R Hunter, M McCarthy and J Williams, in 'Archaeology in Northamptonshire, 1975', *ibid* 11 (1976), 199

'Northampton, castle', W R G Moore and B L Giggins, in 'Archaeology in Northamptonshire, 1976', *ibid* 12 (1977), 226

'Four small excavations on Northampton's medieval defences and elsewhere', J H Williams, *ibid* 17 (1982), 60–73*

'Observations on Northampton medieval walls, Albion Place to Abington Street', T C Welsh, *ibid* 25 (1993–4), 181–82

'Excavation of the town defences at Green Street, Northampton, 1995–6', A Chapman, *ibid* 28 (1998–9), 25–60*

'Defending the heart of England: Northampton 1940–44', S R Hollowell, *ibid* 28 (1998–9), 143–52*

'Documentary sources for the course of the medieval town wall, Northampton', T C Webb, *ibid* 29 (2000–1), 193–201

'Northampton Castle', D C Mynard, *Bulletin of the Northamptonshire Federation of Archaeological Societies* 7 (1972), 44–45

'Excavations in Northampton 1961–2', J Alexander, *Journal of the Northamptonshire Natural History Society and Field Club* 34 (1960–4), 127

'The demolition of Northampton's walls, July 1662', R L Greenall, *Northamptonshire Past and Present* 6.2 (1979), 83–84

'The Civil War defences of Northampton', G Foard, *ibid* 9.1 (1994–5), 4–44*

Peterborough
'Peterborough', [A Selkirk], *Current Archaeology* 8.6 (1983), 182–83*

Preston Capes
'Motte' and 'Manor House or castle site', in RCHME, *An inventory of the historical monuments in the county of Northampton. 3. Archaeological sites in north-west Northamptonshire*, 163–65. London: HMSO, 1981*

Rockingham
Rockingham Castle. T Stock. [S l: s n], n d*

'Rockingham Castle, Rockingham', in J Heward and R Taylor, *The country houses of Northamptonshire*, 290–95. Swindon: RCHME, 1996*

'Motte', in RCHME, *An inventory of the historical monuments in the county of Northampton. 2. Archaeological sites in central Northamptonshire*, 126–27. London: HMSO, 1979*

'Rockingham Castle, Northants', M Hall, *Country Life* 188.15 (1994), 62–65*

'Rockingham', G Isham, *Reports and Papers of the Northamptonshire Antiquarian Society* 67 (1975), 9–15*

'The earthworks of Rockingham and its neighbourhood', A E Brown and C C Taylor, *Northamptonshire Archaeology* 9 (1974), 68–79*

'Rockingham Castle in 1250: form and function of a royal castle under Henry III', E Klingelhöfer, *Northamptonshire Past and Present* 7.1 (1983–4), 11–25*

Sibbertoft

'Motte and bailey', in RCHME, *An inventory of the historical monuments in the county of Northampton. 3. Archaeological sites in north-west Northamptonshire*, 170–72. London: HMSO, 1981*

Sulgrave

'Ringwork', in RCHME, *An inventory of the historical monuments in the county of Northampton. 4. Archaeological sites in south-west Northamptonshire*, 139–40. London: HMSO, 1982*

'Excavations at Sulgrave, Northamptonshire, 1968', B K Davison, *Archaeological Journal* 125 (1968), 305–7*

'Five castle excavations: reports on the Institute's research project into the origins of the castle in England. Excavations at Sulgrave, Northamptonshire, 1960–76: an interim report', B K Davison, *ibid* 134 (1977), 105–14*

'Sulgrave Castle', anon, *Cake and Cockhorse* 2.6 (1963), 99

'Sulgrave, Northants', B Davison, *CBA Group 9 Newsletter* 3 (1973), 20

'Earthworks in England: their excavation and implication', B K Davison, *Château Gaillard* 2 (1967), 39–48*

'Sulgrave', B Davison, *Current Archaeology* 2.1 (1969), 19–22*

'Medieval Britain in 1960', D M Wilson and D G Hurst, *Medieval Archaeology* 5 (1961), 328

'Medieval Britain in 1961', D M Wilson and D G Hurst, *ibid* 6–7 (1962–3), 333

'Medieval Britain in 1972', L E Webster and J Cherry, *ibid* 17 (1973), 147

'Medieval Britain and Ireland in 1987', S M Youngs [*et al*], *ibid* 32 (1988), 267

'Sulgrave', B K Davison, *Bulletin of the Northamptonshire Federation of Archaeological Societies* 3 (1969), 27–29

'Sulgrave', B K Davison, *Northamptonshire Archaeology* 8 (1973), 19

Thrapston

'Thrapston, Northamptonshire', D Hall and D Jackson, *CBA Group 9 Newsletter* 8 (1978), 18–19*

Towcester

'Motte', in RCHME, *An inventory of the historical monuments in the county of Northampton. 4. Archaeological sites in south-west Northamptonshire*, 158–59. London: HMSO, 1982*

'Towcester Mote (or Bury Mount)', R S Simms, *Archaeological Journal* 110 (1953), 211–12*

'Medieval Britain and Ireland in 1999', J Bradley and M Gaimster, *Medieval Archaeology* 44 (2000), 297

'Excavations at Towcester 1954: the Grammar School site', A E Brown and J A Alexander, *Northamptonshire Archaeology* 17 (1982), 24–59*

Weedon Bec

'Redoubt', in RCHME, *An inventory of the historical monuments in the county of Northampton. 3. Archaeological sites in north-west Northamptonshire*, 194–95. London: HMSO, 1981*

Weedon Lois

'Motte or ringwork', in RCHME, *An inventory of the historical monuments in the county of Northampton. 4. Archaeological sites in south-west Northamptonshire*, 163–64. London: HMSO, 1982*

'Medieval Britain and Ireland in 1987', S M Youngs [*et al*], *Medieval Archaeology* 32 (1988), 267

'Archaeology in Northamptonshire 1985–6', B Dix (ed), *Northamptonshire Archaeology* 21 (1986–7), 158

Wollaston

'Motte', in RCHME, *An inventory of the historical monuments in the county of Northampton. 2. Archaeological sites in central Northamptonshire*, 180–81. London: HMSO, 1979*

'Medieval Britain in 1969', D M Wilson and D G Hurst, *Medieval Archaeology* 14 (1970), 176

NORTHUMBERLAND

Beckensall, S. *Northumberland: the power of place*. Stroud: Tempus, 2001* [espec ch 3]

Clarke, D and Rudd, A. 'Tyneside in the breech loading era', *Fortress* 3 (1989), 33–42*

Clarke, D and Rudd, A. 'Northumbrian pillboxes', *Ravelin* 26 (1991), 14–21*

Dixon, P. 'From hall to tower: the change in seigneurial houses on the Anglo-Scottish border after *c* 1250', in P R Coss and S D Lloyd (eds), *Thirteenth century England IV: proceedings of the Newcastle upon Tyne conference, 1991*, 85–107. Woodbridge: Boydell Press, 1992*

Dodds, J F. *Bastions and belligerents: medieval strongholds in Northumberland*. Newcastle: Keepdate, 1999*

Foster, J. *Guns of the north-east: coastal defences from the Tyne to the Humber*. Barnsley: Pen & Sword Military, 2004*

Frodsham, P. 'From castles to bastles: the medieval period (1066–1603)', in P Frodsham, *Archaeology in Northumberland National Park*, 78–110. York: CBA, 2004* (Research report; 136)

Goodman, A. 'The defences of Northumberland: a preliminary survey', in M Strickland (ed), *Armies, chivalry and warfare in medieval Britain and France: proceedings of the 1995 Harlaxton Symposium*, 161–72. Stamford: Paul Watkins, 1998* (Harlaxton medieval studies; 7)

Graham, A. 'Notes on some Northumbrian "peles"', *Proceedings of the Society of Antiquaries of Scotland* 80 (1945–6), 37–43*

Graham, F. *The castles of Northumberland*. Newcastle: F Graham, 1976*

Graham, F. *Northumbrian castles: series 1, the coast*. Newcastle: F Graham, 1972* (Northern history booklet; 20)

Graham, F. *Northumbrian castles: series 2, Tyne, south Tyne and Allen*. Newcastle: F Graham, 1972* (Northern history booklet; 24)

Graham, F. *Northumbrian castles: series 3, Wansbeck and Coquet*. Newcastle: F Graham, 1974* (Northern history booklet; 31)

Graham, F. *Northumbrian castles: series 4, Tweed and Alan*. Newcastle: F Graham, 1974* (Northern history booklet; 61)

Grundy, J [*et al*] and Pevsner, N. *Northumberland (The buildings of England)*. 2nd edition. London: Penguin Books, 1992*

Heritage Site and Landscape Surveys. 'Anti-glider defensive ditch systems in Northumberland and Tyne and Wear', *Archaeology in Northumberland 1994–1995* (1995), 10–11*

Hogg, R. 'The Tyne turrets: coastal defence in the First World War', *Fort* 12 (1984), 97–104*

Jackson, M J. *Castles of Northumberland: a gazetteer of the medieval castles of Northumberland and Tyne and Wear*. Carlisle: Barmkin Books, 1992*

Long, B. *Castles of Northumberland: the medieval fortifications of the county*. Newcastle: H Hill, 1967*

Milner, L. 'Northumberland pele towers', *Archaeological Journal* 133 (1976), 168–69*

Ramm, H G [*et al*]. *Sheilings and bastles*. London: HMSO for RCHME, 1970*

Rowland, T H. *Medieval castles of Northumberland*. Newcastle: F Graham, 1969*

Rudd, A and Clarke, D. 'Northumberland stop lines 2: Wooler to Alnwick', *Loop-holes* 21 (1998), 9–11

Rudd, A and Clarke, D H. 'The pillbox defences of Northumberland', *Archaeology in Northumberland 1993–1994* (1994), 14–15*

Ryder, P. 'Towers and bastles survey', *Archaeology in Northumberland 1995–1996* (1996), 28–29*

Ryder, P. 'Change and decay: the disappearing towers and bastles of Northumberland', *Archaeology in Northumberland 1995–1996* (1996), 49–50*

Ryder, P. 'Towers and bastles in Northumberland National Park', in P Frodsham, *Archaeology in Northumberland National Park*, 262–71. York: CBA, 2004* (Research report; 136)

St Joseph, J K S. 'Castles of Northumberland from the air', *Archaeologia Aeliana* 4 ser 28 (1950), 7–17*

Salter, M. *The castles and tower houses of Northumberland*. Malvern: Folly Publications, 1997*

Stevenson, I. 'The defences of the Tyne and the Wear', *ibid* 67 (2006), 3–18*

Weaver, J. *Exploring England's heritage: Cumbria to Northumberland*. London: HMSO, in association with English Heritage, 1992* [espec ch 5]

Welfare, H. 'Early castles in Northumberland', *Archaeology North* 9 (1995), 35–37

Welfare, H, Bowden, M and Blood, K. 'Fieldwork and the castles of the Anglo-Scottish borders', in P Pattison, D Field and S Ainsworth (eds), *Patterns of the past: essays in landscape archaeology for Christopher Taylor*, 53–60. Oxford: Oxbow Books, 1999*

Alnwick

Alnwick Castle, home of the duke of Northumberland. C Shrimpton. Derby: English Life Publications, 1999*

'The state of Alnwick Castle, 1557–1632', G R Batho, *Archaeologia Aeliana* 4 ser 36 (1958), 129–45*

'Alnwick Castle', J Allibone, *Archaeological Journal* 133 (1976), 148–54*

'Alnwick Castle, Northumberland', A C S Dixon, *Archaeological Newsletter for Northumberland, Cumberland and Westmorland* 2 (1968), 12

'Medieval Britain and Ireland in 2001', J Bradley and M Gaimster, *Medieval Archaeology* 46 (2002), 198

Aydon

Aydon Castle, Northumberland. P Dixon. London: HBMCE, 1988*

Aydon Castle, Northumberland. H Summerson. London: English Heritage, 2004*

'Excavation at Aydon Castle, Northumberland, 1975', A Ellison, *Archaeologia Aeliana* 5 ser 4 (1976), 133–38*

'Aydon Castle', O J Weaver, *Archaeological Excavations 1975*, 25–26. London: HMSO, 1976

'Aydon Castle', O J Weaver, *Archaeological Journal* 133 (1976), 193–95*

'Barnston Manor, Dorset, and Aydon Castle, Northumberland: a re-assessment of two late thirteenth-century houses', R Machin, *ibid* 134 (1977), 297–302*

'Coparcenary and Aydon Castle', P Dixon and P Borne, *ibid* 135 (1978), 234–38*

'Aydon Castle and its roof', D Sherlock, *Archaeologia Aeliana* 5 ser 25 (1997), 71–86*

Bamburgh

Bamburgh Castle: 'the finest castle in England'. B Cleary. Derby: Heritage House Group, [c 2005]*

Bamburgh Castle: the archaeology of the fortress of Bamburgh AD 500 to AD 1500. G Young; edited by P Gething. [S l]: Bamburgh Research Project, 2003*

'The great tower of Carlisle Castle', J A A Goodall, in M McCarthy and D Weston (eds), *Carlisle and Cumbria: Roman and medieval architecture, art and archaeology*, 39–62. Leeds: British Archaeological Association and Maney Publishing, 2004* (Conference transactions; 27) [has much on Bamburgh]

'Bamburgh Castle research project', G Young and P Wood, *Castle Studies Group Newsletter* 15 (2001–2), 40–41*

'Bamburgh Castle, Northumberland', G Worsley, *Country Life* 186.35 (1992), 46–49*

'Medieval Britain and Ireland in 2003', J Bradley and M Gaimster, *Medieval Archaeology* 48 (2004), 281–82

'Geophysical survey at Bamburgh Castle, Northumberland', P N Wood, *ibid* 49 (2005), 305–10*

'Medieval Britain and Ireland in 2004', M Gaimster and K O'Conor, *ibid* 49 (2005), 396

Bellister

'Bellister Castle survey 1999', P F Ryder, *Archaeology in Northumberland 1999–2000* (2000), 29*

Belsay

Belsay Hall, garden and castle, Northumberland. R Hewlings and S Anderton. London: English Heritage, 1994*

Belsay Hall, castle and gardens. S Johnson. London: HBMCE, 1984*

An account of Belsay Castle in the county of Northumberland. A E Middleton.

Stocksfield: Spredden, 1990* [first published 1910]

Belsay Hall and castle: information for teachers. E Newbery. London: English Heritage, 1997*

Belsay Hall, castle and gardens. R White. London: English Heritage, 2005*

Berwick-upon-Tweed

Berwick-upon-Tweed and the east march. L Gordon. Chichester: Phillimore, 1985*

Berwick Barracks and fortifications, Northumberland. D Grove. London: English Heritage, 1999*

The fortifications of Berwick-upon-Tweed. I MacIvor. Edinburgh: HMSO, 1967*

The fortifications of Berwick-upon-Tweed. I MacIvor. London: English Heritage, 1990*

The fortifications of Berwick-upon-Tweed: information for teachers. D Walmsley. London: English Heritage, 1998*

'An archaeological survey of Berwick-upon-Tweed', M Ellison, in P A G Clack and P F Gosling, *Archaeology in the north: report of the Northern Archaeological Survey*, 147–64. Durham: Northern Archaeological Survey, 1976*

'Artillery and major places of strength in the Lothians and the east border, 1513–1542', I MacIvor, in D H Caldwell (ed), *Scottish weapons and fortifications*, 94–152. Edinburgh: John Donald, 1981*

'Jacopo Aconcio as an engineer', L White, *American Historical Review* 72 (1966–7), 425–44

'The Elizabethan fortifications of Berwick-upon-Tweed', I MacIvor, *Antiquaries Journal* 45 (1965), 64–96*

'The Cow Port at Berwick-upon-Tweed', P Ryder, *Archaeologia Aeliana* 5 ser 20 (1992), 99–116*

'The White Wall, Berwick-upon-Tweed', M C Bishop, *ibid* 5 ser 20 (1992), 117–19*

'From border stronghold to railway station: the fortunes of Berwick Castle 1560–1850', H Summerson, *ibid* 5 ser 23 (1995), 235–48*

'Excavations at the New Quay, Berwick-upon-Tweed, 1996', W B Griffiths, *ibid* 5 ser 27 (1999), 75–108* [see p 82]

'The Bell Tower at Berwick-upon-Tweed', C Paterson, *ibid* 5 ser 28 (2000), 163–75*

'The location of the siege camp at Berwick-upon-Tweed, 1333', C Shenton, *ibid* 5 ser 29 (2001), 253–55

'The fortifications, Berwick-upon-Tweed', I MacIvor, *Archaeological Journal* 133 (1976), 182–84*

'Ravensdowne Barracks, Berwick-upon-Tweed', I MacIvor, *ibid* 133 (1976), 184–85

'Berwick Castle', R E Young, *Archaeology in Northumberland 1999–2000* (2000), 27

'The individuality of Berwick', J Fleming, *Country Life* 105 (1949), 358–61, 422–25*

'Opportunities for history: Berwick-upon-Tweed, Northumberland – II', J Cornforth, *ibid* 167 (1980), 1198–1200*

'Elizabethan ramparts, Berwick upon Tweed', S H Cruden, *Discovery and Excavation in Scotland 1961* (1962), 54

'Medieval Britain in 1961', D M Wilson and D G Hurst, *Medieval Archaeology* 6–7 (1962–3), 347

'Medieval Britain and Ireland in 1999', J Bradley and M Gaimster, *ibid* 44 (2000), 298

'Medieval Britain and Ireland in 2001', J Bradley and M Gaimster, *ibid* 46 (2002), 198

'Medieval Britain and Ireland in 2003', J Bradley and M Gaimster, *ibid* 48 (2004), 282–83

'The siege of Berwick, 1333', R Nicholson, *Scottish Historical Review* 40 (1961), 19–42

'The Spades Mire, Berwick upon Tweed', K G White, *Proceedings of the Society of Antiquaries of Scotland* 96 (1962–3), 355–60*

Biddlestone
'Biddlestone Chapel: a tower, chapel, & air-raid shelter', P F Ryder, *Archaeology in Northumberland 1999–2000* (2000), 21*

Bywell
'Bywell Castle', L Milner, *Archaeological Journal* 133 (1976), 205

Chillingham
'Chillingham Castle, Northumberland', J Musson, *Country Life* 198.17 (2004), 130–35*

Chipchase
'Chipchase Castle', P Leach, *Achaeological Journal* 133 (1976), 177, 179

'Chipchase Castle, Northumberland', G Nares, *Country Life* 119 (1956), 1292–95*

'Medieval Britain and Ireland in 1999', J Bradley and M Gaimster, *Medieval Archaeology* 44 (2000), 299

Clifford's Fort
'Clifford's Fort and the defence of the Tyne', D Kear, *Archaeologia Aeliana* 5 ser 14 (1986), 99–134*

'Seventeenth century accounts relating to forts on Holy Island and at the mouth of the Tyne 1675–1681/2', A J Lilburn, *ibid* 5 ser 14 (1986), 135–42

'Post-medieval Britain and Ireland in 2003', M Ponsford, *Post-Medieval Archaeology* 38 (2004), 317

Corbridge

'Corbridge, the Vicar's Pele', L Milner, *Archaeological Journal* 133 (1976), 197

Craster

'Craster Tower', J Craster, *History of the Berwickshire Naturalists' Club* 36 (1962–4), 136–42

Cresswell

'Cresswell Tower', P Ryder, *Archaeologia Aeliana* 5 ser 32 (2003), 73–90*

'A tower built against border raids', C R Denton, *Country Life* 133 (1963), 531*

Dally

'Dally Castle: some tales from the country', Heritage Site and Landscape Surveys, *Archaeology in Northumberland 1995–1996* (1996), 45–46*

'Dally Castle', P F[rodsham], *Archaeology in Northumberland 1997–1998* (1998), 16*

Dunstanburgh

Dunstanburgh Castle, Northumberland. C H Hunter Blair and H L Honeyman. 2nd edition. London: HMSO, 1955*; 3rd edition, 1982*

Dunstanburgh Castle, Northumberland. C H Hunter Blair and H L Honeyman. London: HBMCE, 1986*

Dunstanburgh Castle, Northumberland. C H Hunter Blair. London: HBMCE, 1988*

Dunstanburgh Castle: information for teachers. H Moffat. London: English Heritage, 1997*

Dunstanburgh Castle, Northumberland. H Summerson. London: English Heritage, 1993*

'Further notes on Dunstanburgh Castle', W D Simpson, *Archaeologia Aeliana* 4 ser 27 (1949), 1–28*

'John of Gaunt's building works at Dunstanburgh Castle', M Hislop, *ibid* 5 ser 23 (1995), 139–44*

'Lordship, castles and locality: Thomas of Lancaster, Dunstanburgh Castle and the Lancastrian affinity in Northumberland, 1296–1322', A King, *ibid* 5 ser 29 (2001), 223–34

'Thomas, earl of Lancaster, and the great gatehouse of Dunstanburgh Castle', J Ashbee, *English Heritage Historical Review* 1 (2006), 28–35*

'Dunstanburgh Castle – Northumberland's own Camelot?', A Oswald and J Ashbee, *Research News: Newsletter of the English Heritage Research Department* 4 (2006), 34–37*

Edlingham

'Edlingham Castle, Northumberland: an interim account of excavations, 1978–82', G Fairclough, *Transactions of the Ancient Monuments Society* new ser 28 (1984), 40–60*

'Meaningful constructions: spatial and functional analysis of medieval buildings', G Fairclough, *Antiquity* 66 (1992), 348–66*

'Edlingham Castle', G J Fairclough, *CBA Newsletter and Calendar* 3 (1979–80), 135036

'Edlingham Castle: the military and domestic development of a Northumbrian manor. Excavations 1978–80: interim report', G Fairclough, *Château Gaillard* 9–10 (1982), 373–87*

'Medieval Britain in 1978', L E Webster and J Cherry, *Medieval Archaeology* 23 (1979), 260–61*

'Medieval Britain in 1979', L E Webster and J Cherry, *ibid* 24 (1980), 247–49

'Medieval Britain in 1980', S M Youngs and J Clark , *ibid* 25 (1981), 201–2

'Medieval Britain in 1981', S M Youngs and J Clark , *ibid* 26 (1982), 201

'Medieval Britain and Ireland in 1982', S M Youngs, J Clark and T B Barry, *ibid* 27 (1983), 199–200*

Elsdon

'Elsdon', A Quiney, *Archaeological Journal* 133 (1976), 173–78*

'Elsdon Tower', A J W[eir], *Archaeology in Northumberland 1994–1995* (1995), 15*

'Puzzling new evidence at Elsdon', P Ryder, *Archaeology in Northumberland 1995–1996* (1996), 38–39*

'Elsden' [*sic*], C H Hunter Blair, *History of the Berwickshire Naturalists' Club* 31 (1947–9), 40–47*

'The Mote Hills, Elsdon', A Welfare, *Northern Archaeology* 12 (1995), 45–50*

Etal

Etal Castle, Northumberland. I S Nelson. London: English Heritage, 1998*

'An excavation at Etal Castle, Northumberland, in 1978', B Harbottle and A Ellison, *Archaeologia Aeliana* 5 ser 29 (2001), 235–52*

'Medieval Britain in 1978', L E Webster and J Cherry, *Medieval Archaeology* 23 (1979), 262

'Medieval Britain and Ireland in 1994', B S Nenk, S Margeson and M Hurley, *ibid* 39 (1995), 235

ENGLAND

Featherstone
'Featherstone Castle', J Cornforth, *Country Life* 154 (1973), 1246–49*

Ford
'Ford Castle', R Fawcett, *Archaeological Journal* 133 (1976), 190–92*

'Ford, Parson's Tower', R Fawcett, *ibid* 133 (1976), 192

Halton
'Halton Castle reconsidered', P Borne and P Dixon, *Archaeologia Aeliana* 5 ser 6 (1978), 131–39*

Haltwhistle
'Two fortified houses in Haltwhistle', P Campbell and P W Dixon, *ibid* 4 ser 48 (1970), 169–81*

Harbottle
'Harbottle Castle: excavation and survey 1997–99', J Crow, in P Frodsham, *Archaeology in Northumberland National Park*, 246–61. York: CBA, 2004* (Research report; 136)

'Harbottle Castle', A W[eir], *Archaeology in Northumberland 1994–1995* (1995), 17*

'Harbottle Castle', P F[rodsham], *Archaeology in Northumberland 1996–1997* (1997), 22*

'Harbottle Castle', A W[eir], *Archaeology in Northumberland 1997–1998* (1998), 28–29*

'Harbottle Castle', J Crow, *Archaeology in Northumberland 1999–2000* (2000), 33*

'Harbottle Castle', R H Walton, *History of the Berwickshire Naturalists' Club* 38 (1968–70), 34–36

'Medieval Britain and Ireland in 1997', M Gaimster, C Haith and J Bradley, *Medieval Archaeology* 42 (1998), 148–49

Haughton
'Haughton Castle', W D Simpson, *Archaeologia Aeliana* 4 ser 29 (1951), 118–34*

Hexham
'The two towers of Hexham', P Ryder, *ibid* 5 ser 22 (1994), 185–217*

'Hexham Prison and Moot Hall', L Milner, *Archaeological Journal* 133 (1976), 202–3

Hirst
'Hirst Castle, Ashington, Northumberland', D Moffat, *Archaeological Newsletter for Northumberland, Cumberland and Westmorland* 3 (1968), 4–5

'Medieval Britain in 1968', D M Wilson and D G Hurst, *Medieval Archaeology* 13 (1969), 273

Holy Island

Lindisfarne Castle, Northumberland. [Various authors]. London: National Trust, 1999*

English Heritage book of Lindisfarne Holy Island. D O'Sullivan and R Young. London: Batsford in association with English Heritage, 1995*

Lindisfarne Priory. J Story. London: English heritage, 2005*

'Seventeenth century accounts relating to forts on Holy Island and at the mouth of the Tyne 1675–1681/2', A J Lilburn, *Archaeologia Aeliana* 5 ser 14 (1986), 135–42

'The fort on the Heugh, Holy Island', C H[ardie], *Archaeology in Northumberland 1994–1995* (1995), 8–9*

Melkridge

'Melkridge Castle, Northumberland', T L Jones and C W Field, *Archaeologia Aeliana* 4 ser 34 (1956), 138–41*

Mitford

'Mitford Castle', H L Honeyman, *ibid* 4 ser 33 (1955), 27–34*

'Notes on Mitford Castle', C H Hunter Blair and H L Honeyman, *History of the Berwickshire Naturalists' Club* 33 (1953–5), 202–6*

Morpeth

'The gatehouse of Morpeth Castle, Northumberland', P F Ryder, *Archaeologia Aeliana* 5 ser 20 (1992), 63–77*

'Haw Hill, Morpeth', J Quartermaine and J Bell, *Archaeology in Northumberland 1999–2000* (2000), 17*

'Medieval Britain and Ireland in 2001', J Bradley and M Gaimster, *Medieval Archaeology* 46 (2002), 199

Nafferton

'Nafferton Castle, Northumberland. Interim report', B Harbottle and P Salway, *Archaeologia Aeliana* 4 ser 38 (1960), 129–44

'Nafferton Castle, Northumberland. Second report', B Harbottle, P Salway and B J N Edwards, *ibid* 4 ser 39 (1961), 165–78*

'History older than legend: the story of Nafferton Castle', P Ryder, *Archaeology in Northumberland 1994–1995* (1995), 16

'Medieval Britain in 1959', D M Wilson and J G Hurst, *Medieval Archaeology* 4 (1960), 146

Newcastle upon Tyne

A guide to the royal castle of Newcastle upon Tyne. P Brewis. Newcastle: Society of Antiquaries of Newcastle upon Tyne, 1963* [previous editions date from the early 20th century]

The royal castle of Newcastle upon Tyne: a short history. W Bulmer. Newcastle: Society of Antiquaries of Newcastle upon Tyne, 1945*

The castle and town walls of Newcastle. F Graham. Newcastle: F Graham, 1972* (Northern history booklet; 21)

The castle of Newcastle upon Tyne. B Harbottle. Newcastle: Society of Antiquaries of Newcastle upon Tyne, 1977*

'Newcastle upon Tyne: archaeology and development', B Harbottle, in P A G Clack and P F Gosling (eds), *Archaeology in the north: report of the Northern Archaeological Survey*, 111–31. Durham: Northern Archaeological Survey, 1976*

'Wall Knoll, Sallyport or Carpenter's Tower', C H Hunter Blair, *Archaeologia Aeliana* 4 ser 36 (1958), 61–72*

'The town ditch of Newcastle upon Tyne', C M Fraser, *ibid* 4 ser 39 (1961), 381–83

'Excavation at the south curtain wall of the castle, Newcastle upon Tyne, 1960–61', R B Harbottle, *ibid* 4 ser 44 (1966), 79–145*

'An excavation at the Gunner Tower, Newcastle upon Tyne, 1964', B Harbottle, *ibid* 4 ser 45 (1967), 123–37*

'The town wall of Newcastle upon Tyne: consolidation and excavation 1968', R B Harbottle, *ibid* 4 ser 47 (1969), 71–95*

'Excavations and survey in Newcastle upon Tyne, 1972–1973', B Harbottle, *ibid* 5 ser 2 (1974), 57–89*

'An excavation in the castle ditch, Newcastle upon Tyne, 1974–6', B Harbottle and M Ellison, *ibid* 5 ser 9 (1981), 75–250*

'The excavation of a 17th-century bastion in the castle of Newcastle upon Tyne, 1976–81', M Ellison and B Harbottle, *ibid* 5 ser 11 (1983), 135–263*

'A cannon-ball from the town wall, Newcastle upon Tyne', J Nolan, *ibid* 5 ser 13 (1985), 216, 219

'The medieval town defences of Newcastle upon Tyne: excavation and survey 1986–87', J Nolan [*et al*], *ibid* 5 ser 17 (1989), 29–78*

'The castle of Newcastle upon Tyne after *c* 1600', J Nolan, *ibid* 5 ser 18 (1990), 79–126*

'The town wall, Newcastle upon Tyne. Excavations at Orchard Street and Croft Street, 1987–89', J Nolan, *ibid* 5 ser 21 (1993), 93–149*

'Excavation adjacent to Close Gate, Newcastle, 1988–9'. R Fraser, R Maxwell and J E Vaughan, *ibid* 5 ser 22 (1994), 85–151*

'Excavation on the Westgate Road, Newcastle, 1991', D H Heslop, L Truman and J E Vaughan, *ibid* 5 ser 22 (1994), 153–84*

'Excavation of the town wall in the Milk Market, Newcastle upon Tyne', D H Heslop, L Truman and J E Vaughan, *ibid* 5 ser 23 (1995), 215–34*

'An archaeological investigation of the town wall between St Andrew's Street and St Andrew's churchyard, Newcastle upon Tyne', J A Teasdale, *ibid* 5 ser 27 (1999), 29–43*

'The town wall, Newcastle upon Tyne', B Harbottle, *Archaeological Newsletter for Northumberland, Cumberland and Westmorland* 5 (1969), 11

'South curtain wall of the castle, Newcastle upon Tyne', R B Harbottle, *ibid* 5 (1969), 11–12

'South curtain wall of the castle, Newcastle upon Tyne', R B Harbottle, *ibid* 8 (1970), 13

'South curtain wall of the castle, Newcastle upon Tyne', R B Harbottle, *ibid* 11 (1971), 6–7

'The keep and Black Gate, Newcastle upon Tyne', A P Quiney, *Archaeological Journal* 133 (1976), 244–45

'The castle of Newcastle upon Tyne: excavations 1973–1979', B Harbottle, *Château Gaillard* 9–10 (1982), 407–18*

'Medieval Britain in 1960', D M Wilson and D G Hurst, *Medieval Archaeology* 5 (1961), 318–19

'Medieval Britain in 1961', D M Wilson and D G Hurst, *ibid* 6–7 (1962–3), 323

'Medieval Britain in 1964', D M Wilson and D G Hurst, *ibid* 9 (1965), 196

'Medieval Britain in 1966', D M Wilson and D G Hurst, *ibid* 11 (1967), 285

'Medieval Britain in 1968', D M Wilson and D G Hurst, *ibid* 13 (1969), 260, 266

'Medieval Britain in 1973', L E Webster and J Cherry, *ibid* 18 (1974), 196

'Medieval Britain in 1974', L E Webster and J Cherry, *ibid* 19 (1975), 241

'Medieval Britain in 1977', L E Webster and J Cherry, *ibid* 22 (1978), 169

'Medieval Britain in 1978', L E Webster and J Cherry, *ibid* 23 (1979), 246, 269

'Medieval Britain in 1981', S M Youngs and J Clark, *ibid* 26 (1982), 211

'Medieval Britain and Ireland in 1982', S M Youngs, J Clark and T B Barry, *ibid* 27 (1983), 206

'Medieval Britain and Ireland in 1984', S M Youngs, J Clark and T Barry, *ibid* 29 (1985), 202–3

'Medieval Britain and Ireland in 1985', S M Youngs, J Clark and T Barry, *ibid* 30 (1986), 170

'Medieval Britain and Ireland in 1987', S M Youngs [*et al*], *ibid* 32 (1988), 281–82

'Medieval Britain and Ireland in 1988', D R M Gaimster, S Margeson and T Barry, *ibid* 33 (1989), 215

'Medieval Britain and Ireland in 1989', D R M Gaimster, S Margeson and M Hurley, *ibid* 34 (1990), 216

'Medieval Britain and Ireland in 1990', B S Nenk, S Margeson and M Hurley, *ibid* 35 (1991), 194–95

'Medieval Britain and Ireland in 1992', B S Nenk, S Margeson and M Hurley, *ibid* 37 (1993), 285–86

'Post-medieval Britain in 1977', J Cherry, *Post-Medieval Archaeology* 12 (1978), 110

'The excavation of a 17th-century pit at the Black Gate, Newcastle-upon-Tyne, 1975', M Ellison, M Finch and B Harbottle, *ibid* 13 (1979), 153–81*

'Post-medieval Britain in 1983', G Egan, *ibid* 18 (1984), 313–14

'Post-medieval Britain and Ireland in 1988', G Egan, *ibid* 23 (1989), 47

'Post-medieval Britain in 1992', M Ponsford, *ibid* 27 (1993), 218

'Post-medieval Britain in 1993', M Ponsford, *ibid* 28 (1994), 127–28

'The repair of the Newcastle town wall', J E Hutchinson, *Proceedings of the Society of Antiquaries of Newcastle upon Tyne* 5 ser 1 (1951–6), 105–7*

Norham

Norham Castle, Northumberland. C H Hunter Blair and H L Honeyman. London: HMSO, 1966*

Norham Castle, Northumberland. C H Hunter Blair and H L Honeyman. London: HBMCE, 1985*

Norham Castle, Northumberland. A Saunders. London: English Heritage, 1998*

'Norham Castle', R Fawcett, *Archaeological Journal* 133 (1976), 187–88*

'The great tower in the twelfth century: the case of Norham Castle', P Dixon and P Marshall, *ibid* 150 (1993), 410–32*

'Norham Castle', G A C Binnie, *History of the Berwickshire Naturalists' Club* 39.3 (1973), 181–83

'Norham Castle and early artillery defences', A Saunders, *Fort* 25 (1997), 37–59*

Ponteland

'A jigsaw spanning six centuries: the Vicar's Tower at Ponteland', P Ryder, *Archaeology in Northumberland 1994–1995* (1995), 47

Prudhoe

Prudhoe Castle. Anon. London: HBMCE, 1986*

Prudhoe Castle, Northumberland. A Saunders. London: English Heritage, 1993*

Prudhoe Castle. S West. London: English Heritage, 2006*

'The Umfravilles, the castle and the barony of Prudhoe, Northumberland', L Keen, in R A Brown (ed), *Anglo-Norman studies 5: proceedings of the Battle Conference 1982*, 165–84. Woodbridge: Boydell Press, 1983*

'The gates of Prudhoe Castle', R Dower, J Geddes and D Sherlock, *Archaeologia Aeliana* 5 ser 33 (2004), 77–88*

'Prudhoe Castle', L Keen and D Thackray, *Archaeological Excavations 1976*, 30. London: HMSO, 1977*

'Prudhoe Castle', L Keen, *Archaeological Journal* 133 (1976), 206–8*

Thirlwall

'Thirlwall Castle: a gentry residence in medieval Tynedale', A Rushworth and R Carlton, in P Frodsham, *Archaeology in Northumberland National Park*, 272–94. York: CBA, 2004* (Research report; 136)

'Thirlwall Castle', P F[rodsham] and P Ryder, *Archaeology in Northumberland 1993–1994* (1994), 8*

'Thirlwall Castle', A W[eir], *Archaeology in Northumberland 1996–1997* (1997), 36*

'Thirlwall Castle', A W[eir], *Archaeology in Northumberland 1997–1998* (1998), 26*

'Medieval Britain and Ireland in 1993', B S Nenk, S Margeson and M Hurley, *Medieval Archaeology* 38 (1994), 239

Tynemouth

Tynemouth Priory and castle, Northumberland. R N Hadcock. London: HMSO, 1952*

Tynemouth Priory and castle, Tyne and Wear. R N Hadcock. London: HBMCE, 1986*

Tynemouth Priory, castle and twentieth-century fortifications, Tyne and Wear. A Saunders London: English Heritage, 1993*

'Excavation at Tynemouth Priory and castle', G Jobey, *Archaeologia Aeliana* 4 ser 45 (1967), 33–104*

'Tynemouth Priory and castle: excavation in the outer court, 1980', G Fairclough, *ibid* 5 ser 11 (1983), 101–33*

'Tynemouth Priory', E Cambridge, *Archaeological Journal* 133 (1976), 217–20*

Wark

'Conservation continues at Wark Castle', S R[ushton], *Archaeology in Northumberland 1996–1997* (1997), 43

'The hunt for the castle of Wark-on-Tweed', J Nolan, *Archaeology in Northumberland 1997–1998* (1998), 41–42*

'Wark Castle: "the stay and key of all this country"', C H[ardie], *ibid*, 43*

'Wark Castle', G W Bennett, *History of the Berwickshire Naturalists' Club* 37 (1965–7), 29–34*

'Wark Castle and Coldstream', H Nivet, *Transactions of the Hawick Archaeological Society* (1976), 24–25

'Wark Castle and its artillery defences in the reign of Henry VIII', J R Kenyon, *Post-Medieval Archaeology* 11 (1977), 50–60*

Warkworth

Warkworth Castle and Hermitage. J Goodall. London: English Heritage, 2006*

Warkworth Castle, Northumberland. C H Hunter Blair and H L Honeyman. London: HMSO, 1954*

Warkworth Castle, Northumberland. C H Hunter Blair and H L Honeyman. 2nd edition. London: HBMCE, 1986*

Warkworth Castle: a teacher's handbook. H Moffat. London: English Heritage, 1998*

Warkworth Castle, Northumberland. H Summerson. London: English Heritage, 1995*

'Warkworth keep, Northumberland: a reassessment of its plan and date', L Milner, in E Fernie and P Crossley (eds), *Medieval architecture and its intellectual context: essays in honour of Peter Kidson*, 219–28. London: Hambledon Press, 1990*

'An excavation at Warkworth Castle, Northumberland', B Harbottle, *Archaeologia Aeliana* 4 ser 45 (1967), 105–21*

'The date of the Warkworth donjon', M J B Hislop, *ibid* 5 ser 19 (1991), 79–92*

'Warkworth Castle', P Curnow, *Archaeological Journal* 133 (1976), 154–59*

'Warkworth Castle, Northumberland', J Goodall, *Country Life* 189.18 (1995), 82–87*

'Medieval Britain in 1966', D M Wilson and D G Hurst, *Medieval Archaeology* 11 (1967), 285

Widdrington

'Report on excavation at Widdrington Castle site by National Coal Board, August, 1954', J R Bibby, *Proceedings of the Society of Antiquaries of Newcastle upon Tyne* 5 ser 1 (1951–6), 336–42*

NOTTINGHAMSHIRE

Osborne, M. *20th century defences in the east midlands: Derbyshire, Leicestershire, Lincolnshire, Northamptonshire, Nottinghamshire and Rutland*. Market Deeping: Concrete Publications, 2003*

Pevsner, N. *Nottinghamshire (The buildings of England)*. 2nd edition, revised by

E Williamson. Harmondsworth: Penguin Books, 1979*

Salter, M. *The castles of the east midlands*. Malvern: Folly Publications, 2002*

Speight, S. 'Early medieval castles in Nottinghamshire', *Transactions of the Thoroton Society of Nottinghamshire* 98 (1994), 58–70*

Speight, S. 'Four more early medieval 'castle' sites in Nottinghamshire', *ibid* 99 (1995), 65–72*

Clipstone
'Clipstone peel: fortification and politics from Bannockburn to the Treaty of Leake, 1314–1318', D Crook, in M Prestwich, R Britnell and R Frame (eds), *Thirteenth century England 10: proceedings of the Durham conference 2003*, 187–95. Woodbridge: Boydell Press, 2005

'Clipstone park and 'peel'', D Crook, *Transactions of the Thoroton Society of Nottinghamshire* 80 (1976), 35–46*

Cuckney
'Cuckney church and castle', M W Barley, *ibid* 55 (1951), 26–29

Egmanton
'Castles and settlement in rural Nottinghamshire: Laxton, Egmanton and Greasley', S Speight, *Château Gaillard* 22 (2006), 325–34*

'Egmanton, near Laxton: Nottinghamshire's second finest motte and bailey castle?', S Speight and G Franklin, *Transactions of the Thoroton Society of Nottinghamshire* 107 (2003), 68–81*

Greasley
'Castles and settlement in rural Nottinghamshire: Laxton, Egmanton and Greasley', S Speight, *Château Gaillard* 22 (2006), 325–34*

Laxton
'Castles and settlement in rural Nottinghamshire: Laxton, Egmanton and Greasley', S Speight, *ibid* 22 (2006), 325–34*

'Settlement morphology and medieval village planning: a case study at Laxton, Nottinghamshire', K Challis, *Transactions of the Thoroton Society of Nottinghamshire* 106 (2002), 61–69*

'Laxton, the castle', K Challis and S Speight, in S Speight (ed), 'Archaeology in Nottinghamshire: 2004–2005', *ibid* 109 (2005), 157–60*

Newark
Newark Castle studies: excavations 1994. F Coupland, P Marshall and J Samuels. [S l: s n, 1995]*

Newark Castle studies: excavations 1992–1993. P Dixon [*et al*]. Newark: Newark Castle Trust, 1994*

Guardian of the Trent: the story of Newark Castle. P Marshall and J Samuels. Nottingham: Nottingham County Council [*et al*], 1997*

Newark on Trent: the Civil War siegeworks. RCHME. London: HMSO, 1964*

Newark in the Civil War. J Samuels (ed). Newark: Newark and Sherwood District Council, n d*

Newark: Civil War and siegeworks. T Warner. Nottingham: Nottinghamshire County Council, 1992*

'The twelfth-century castle at Newark', P Marshall, in J S Alexander (ed), *Southwell and Nottinghamshire: medieval art, architecture, and industry*, 110–25. Leeds: British Archaeological Association and Maney Publishing, 1998* (Conference transactions; 21)

'Newark Town Hall, Lombard Street', M Todd, *Archaeological Excavations 1972*, 100. London: HMSO, 1973

'The castle, Newark', T W Courtney, *Archaeological Excavations 1973*, 94. London: HMSO, 1974

'Newark-on-Trent', M Todd, *Archaeological Excavations 1976*, 144. London: HMSO, 1977

'Recent work at Newark Castle', P Marshall, *Castle Studies Group Newsletter* 7 (1993–4), 21–23

'Improving the image: the transformation of the bailey into courtyard at the 12th-century bishop's castle at Newark, Nottinghamshire', P Marshall, *Château Gaillard* 21 (2004), 203–14*

'Three urban castles and their communities in the east midlands; Lincoln, Nottingham and Newark', P Marshall, *ibid* 22 (2006), 259–65*

'Newark Castle', [A Selkirk; source J Samuels], *Current Archaeology* 13.12 (1998), 458–61*

'Newark', W Manning, *East Midlands Archaeological Bulletin* 1 (1958), 10

'Newark', H G Ramm, *ibid* 1 (1958), 10

'Newark', in 'Recent archaeology in Nottinghamshire, Staffordshire and Derbyshire', anon, *East Midlands Archaeology* 1 (1985), 23–24*

'Medieval Britain in 1960', D M Wilson and D G Hurst, *Medieval Archaeology* 5 (1961), 232–34

'Medieval Britain in 1972', L E Webster and J Cherry, *ibid* 17 (1973), 170

'Medieval Britain and Ireland in 1988', D R M Gaimster, S Margeson and T Barry, *ibid* 33 (1989), 206

'Medieval Britain and Ireland in 1998', J Bradley, M Gaimster and C Haith, *ibid* 43 (1999), 273

'Medieval Britain and Ireland in 2001', J Bradley and M Gaimster, *ibid* 46 (2002), 201

'Newark Castle excavations', M W Barley and F Waters, *Transactions of the Thoroton Society of Nottinghamshire* 60 (1956), 20–33*

'The Queen's Sconce, Newark', M W Barley, *ibid* 61 (1957), 26–32*

'Excavations at Colonel Greye's Sconce, near Newark, in July 1958', W H Manning, *ibid* 62 (1958), 36–42*

'Excavation of the borough ditch, Slaughterhouse Lane, Newark, 1961', M W Barley, *ibid* 65 (1961), 10–18*

'The Civil War defences, Millgate, Newark', M J Dean, *ibid* 72 (1968), 68–70*

'Newark Castle excavations 1972', T W Courtney, *ibid* 77 (1973), 34–40*

'Excavations on the medieval defences of Newark, 1872', M Todd, *ibid* 78 (1974), 27–53*

'Excavations on the medieval defences of Newark, 1976', M Todd, *ibid* 81 (1977), 41–54*

'An excavation of the royalist town ditch at Victoria Street, Newark, Nottinghamshire, 1988', C Drage, *ibid* 91 (1987), 127–32*

'Excavation on the supposed site of the Civil War redoubt 11b, Newark-on-Trent, Nottinghamshire', G Kinsley, *ibid* 92 (1988), 78

'Excavations on the Saxo-Norman town defences at Slaughter House Lane, Newark-on-Trent, Nottinghamshire', A G Kinsley, *ibid* 97 (1993), 14–63*

'Recent excavations at Newark Castle, Nottinghamshire', P Marshall and J Samuels, *ibid* 98 (1994), 49–57*

'Civil War Monuments Project, Newark-on-Trent, Nottinghamshire: rediscovery of Civil War redoubt '2'', V Holyoak, *ibid* 101 (1997), 119–24*

'Newark, the castle', S Malone, in C Allen (ed), 'Archaeology in Nottinghamshire 1999', *ibid* 104 (2000), 156–57*

'The excavation of Roman, medieval and Civil War remains at Trent Lane, Newark, Nottinghamshire', R Cuttler and E Ramsey, *ibid* 109 (2005), 47–67*

Nottingham

Nottingham Castle: a place full royal. C Drage. Nottingham: Nottingham Civil Society; Thoroton Society of Nottinghamshire, 1990* (=*Transactions of the Thoroton Society of Nottinghamshire* vol 93 for 1989)

Nottingham's royal castle. A Hamilton. Nottingham: Nottingham Civic Society, [198–?]*; 4th edition, n d*

Nottingham's royal castle and ducal palace. A Hamilton. Nottingham: Nottingham Civic Society, 1999*

Nottingham Castle. J Sheffield. Privately published, 1984*

'Nottingham', M W Barley, in M D Lobel (ed), *Historic towns*, **1**. Oxford: Lovell Johns Cook, Hammond and Kell Organization, 1969*

'The medieval town', T Foulds, in J Beckett [*et al*] (eds), *A centenary history of Nottingham*, 56–71. Manchester: Manchester University Press, 1997*

'The royal castle', P Marshall and T Foulds, in *ibid*, 43–55*

'Nottingham Castle: architecture as tyranny', in S Thurley, *Lost buildings of Britain*, 111–40. London: Penguin (Viking), 2004*

'Nottingham', M W Barley, *Archaeological Excavations 1964*, 12. London: HMSO, 1965

'Nottingham, Park Row', M Ponsford, *Archaeological Excavations 1967*, 23. London: HMSO, 1968

'Nottingham, Park Row', A Carter, *Archaeological Excavations 1968*, 27. London: HMSO, 1969

'Nottingham (city)', C S B Young, *Archaeological Excavations 1970*, 81. London: HMSO, 1971

'Nottingham Castle', C J Drage, *CBA Newsletter and Calendar* 1 (1977–8), 116

'Nottingham Castle', C J Drage, *ibid* 3 (1979–80), 136

'Nottingham Castle', C Drage, *Château Gaillard* 11 (1983), 117–27*

'Three urban castles and their communities in the east midlands; Lincoln, Nottingham and Newark', P Marshall, *ibid* 22 (2006), 259–65*

'Nottingham', C S B Young, *East Midlands Archaeological Bulletin* 12 (1978), 44–46

'Nottingham Castle', C J Drage, *ibid* 12 (1978), 46*

'Nottingham medieval town wall, Chapel Bar', M W Barley, *Medieval Archaeology* 3 (1959), 290–92*

'Medieval Britain in 1961', D M Wilson and D G Hurst, *ibid* 6–7 (1962–3), 330

'Medieval town wall, Park Row, Nottingham', M W Barley, *ibid* 9 (1965), 164–67*

'Medieval Britain in 1965', D M Wilson and D G Hurst, *ibid* 10 (1966), 199

'Medieval Britain in 1967', D M Wilson and D G Hurst, *ibid* 12 (1968), 185

'Medieval Britain in 1968', D M Wilson and D G Hurst, *ibid* 13 (1969), 266

'Medieval Britain in 1976', L E Webster and J Cherry, *ibid* 21 (1977), 235, 238

'Medieval Britain in 1977', L E Webster and J Cherry, *ibid* 22 (1978), 169

'Medieval Britain in 1978', L E Webster and J Cherry, *ibid* 23 (1979), 262

'Medieval Britain in 1981', S M Youngs and J Clark, *ibid* 26 (1982), 202–3

'Medieval Britain and Ireland in 1994', B S Nenk, S Margeson and M Hurley, *ibid* 39 (1995), 235–36

'The Civil War defences of Nottingham', R M Butler, *Transactions of the Thoroton Society of Nottinghamshire* 53 (1949), 26–33*

'Nottingham town wall: Park Row excavations, 1964', M W Barley, *ibid* 69 (1965), 50–65*

'Nottingham town wall: Park Row excavations, 1967', M W Ponsford, *ibid* 75 (1971), 5–32*

'Nottingham town wall: Park Row excavations, 1968', A Carter, *ibid* 75 (1971), 33–40*

'Nottingham Castle: the gatehouse of the outer bailey', C Drage, *ibid* 85 (1981), 48–55*

'Excavations at Nottingham Castle, 1976–8: an interim report', C Drage, *ibid* 82 (1978), 72–73*

'Recent archaeological work in Nottingham', A MacCormick, *ibid* 82 (1978), 74–75

'The siege of Nottingham Castle in 1194', T Foulds, *ibid* 95 (1991), 20–28

'Nottingham Castle', G A B Young, in S Speight (ed), 'Archaeology in Nottinghamshire 2000', *ibid* 105 (2001), 195

'"This greate house, so lately begun, and all of freestone": William Cavendish's Italianate *palazzo* called Nottingham Castle', T Foulds, *ibid* 106 (2002), 81–102*

'Recent archaeological work on the medieval castle at Nottingham', G Kinsley, *ibid* 107 (2003), 83–94*

'Nottingham, Standard Hill', G A B Young, in S Speight (ed), 'Archaeology in Nottinghamshire 2002', *ibid* 107 (2003), 199

'"Old road into the park": Nottingham Castle, Standard Hill and William Stretton', T Foulds, *ibid* 108 (2004), 125–42*

Radcliffe on Trent

'Notes on an excavation at Radcliffe on Trent', H O Houldsworth, *ibid* 55 (1951), 23–25*

OXFORDSHIRE

Bond, J. 'The Oxford region in the middle ages', in G Briggs, J Cook and T Rowley (eds), *The archaeology of the Oxford region*, 135–59. Oxford: Oxford University Department for External Studies, 1986* [espec pp 147–50 + map 17, p 168]

Elliott, J (ed). *Heritage unlocked: guide to free sites in London and the south east*. London: English Heritage, 2005*

Kerr, A W J G. 'Pillboxes in Oxfordshire', *South Midlands Archaeology* 20 (1990), 89*

Salter, M. *The castles of the Thames Valley and the Chilterns*. Malvern: Folly Publications, [2002]*

Sherwood, J and Pevsner, N. *Oxfordshire (The buildings of England)*. Harmondsworth: Penguin Books, 1974*

Ascot Doilly

'The twelfth-century castle at Ascot Doilly, Oxfordshire', E M Jope and R I Threlfall, *Antiquaries Journal* 39 (1959), 219–73*

'Medieval Britain in 1957', D M Wilson and J G Hurst, *Medieval Archaeology* 2 (1958), 195

'Recent mediaeval finds in the Oxford district. 1. Excavations at the 12th-century castle at Ascot-Doilly, Oxon, 1946', E M Jope and R I Threlfall, *Oxoniensia* 11–12 (1946–7), 165–67*

'Earthen castles, outer enclosures and the earthworks at Ascott d'Oilly Castle, Oxfordshire', J Bond, *ibid* 66 (2001), 43–69*

'A survey of the earthworks at Ascott d'Oilly Castle, Ascott under Wychwood, Oxfordshire', J Bond, *Wychwoods History: the Journal of the Wychwoods Local History Society* 15 (200), 4–35*

Ascott Earl

'Ascott Earl', anon, *CBA Group 9 Newsletter* 2 (1972), 30, 32*

'Medieval Britain in 1972', L E Webster and J Cherry, *Medieval Archaeology* 17 (1973), 163

Bampton

Bampton Castle. J Blair. Oxford: J Blair, 1988*

'Long Wittenham pillbox and Bampton pillbox', L Brown and J Steane, *CBA Group 9 Newsletter* 10 (1980), 98–99*

'Medieval Britain and Ireland in 1987', S M Youngs [*et al*], *Medieval Archaeology* 32 (1988), 268–69*

'The Bampton research project: second report, 1986–8', J Blair, *South Midlands Archaeology* 18 (1988), 89–93*

Banbury

Excavations on the site of Banbury Castle: April 1972. A preliminary report. P J Fasham. Privately published [duplicated typescript]

'Banbury', P D A Harvey, in M D Lobel (ed), *Historic towns*, **1**. Oxford: Lovell Johns Cook, Hammond and Kell Organization, 1969*

'Castle', in A Crossley (ed), *The Victoria history of the counties of England: a history of the county of Oxford*, **10**, 39–42. Oxford: OUP, 1972

'Banbury', P J Fasham, *Archaeological Excavations 1972*, 101. London: HMSO, 1973

'Banbury Castle', K A Rodwell, *Archaeological Excavations 1974*, 106. London: HMSO, 1975

'Banbury Castle – interim report', V Bromley, *Cake and Cockhorse* 1.2 (1959), 6–7

'Banbury Castle', R K Gilkes, *ibid* 1.5 (1960), 52–57

'Banbury Castle', anon, *ibid* 2.6 (1963), 99

'Banbury Castle excavations – April, 1972', anon, *ibid* 5.3 (1972), 48

'The archaeological implications of redevelopment in Banbury', P J Fasham, *ibid* 5.3 (1972), 49–56*

'Banbury Castle: a summary of excavations in 1972', P J Fasham, *ibid* 5.6 (1973), 109–16*

'Excavations at Banbury Castle 1973–74: an interim report', K A Rodwell, *ibid* 5.9 (1974), 177–81*

'Banbury, Oxon 1972', P J Fasham, *CBA Group 9 Newsletter* 3 (1973), 28

'Banbury Castle', K Rodwell, *ibid* 4 (1974), 21

'Banbury', [A Selkirk], *Current Archaeology* 3.12 (1972), 333

'Medieval Britain in 1972', L E Webster and J Cherry, *Medieval Archaeology* 17 (1973), 163

'Medieval Britain in 1973', L E Webster and J Cherry, *ibid* 18 (1974), 196

'Medieval Britain in 1974', L E Webster and J Cherry, *ibid* 19 (1975), 239

'Excavations in Banbury, 1972: first report', P J Fasham, *Oxoniensia* 38 (1973), 312–38*

'Excavations on the site of Banbury Castle, 1973–4'. K A Rodwell, *ibid* 41 (1976), 90–147*

'Excavations in Banbury, 1972: second and final report', P J Fasham, *ibid* 48 (1983), 71–118*

'Post-medieval Britain in 1974', J Cherry, *Post-Medieval Archaeology* 9 (1975), 241

Barford

'Medieval Britain and Ireland in 1993', B S Nenk, S Margeson and M Hurley, *Medieval Archaeology* 38 (1994), 240

Broughton

'Broughton Castle, Oxfordshire', H Gordon Slade, *Archaeological Journal* 135 (1978), 138–94*

'Medieval Britain and Ireland in 1995', B S Nenk, S Margeson and M Hurley, *Medieval Archaeology* 40 (1996), 277

Cornbury

'A Civil War battery at Cornbury, Oxfordshire', B H St J O'Neil, *Oxoniensia* 10 (1945), 73–78*

Deddington

'Recent mediaeval finds in the Oxford district. 2. Excavations at Deddington Castle, Oxon, 1947', E M Jope and R I Threlfall, *ibid* 11–12 (1946–7), 167–68

'Deddington Castle, Oxfordshire, and the English honour of Bayeux', R Ivens, *ibid* 49 (1984), 101–19*

'Deddington Castle, Oxfordshire. A summary of excavations 1977–1979', R J Ivens, *South Midlands Archaeology* 13 (1983), 34–41*

Grey's Court

'Grey's Court – castle or fortified house?', A Emery, *Castle Studies Group Journal* 19 (2006), 193–200*

Middleton Stoney

Excavations at Middleton Stoney, Oxfordshire, including a brief history of the parish of Middleton Stoney. R T Rowley. Oxford: Oxford University Department for External Studies, 1977*

Middleton Stoney: excavation and survey in a north Oxfordshire parish 1970–1982. S Rahtz and T Rowley. Oxford: Oxford University Department for External Studies, 1984*

'Middleton Stoney, Oxon', T Rowley and D Benson, *CBA Group 9 Newsletter* 1 (1971), 17–18

'Middleton Stoney Castle, Oxfordshire', T Rowley, *ibid* 2 (1972), 10–12*

'Middleton Stoney, Oxon', T Rowley, *ibid* 3 (1973), 22

'Middleton Stoney, Oxon', T Rowley, *ibid* 5 (1975), 23

'Medieval Britain in 1970', D M Wilson and S Moorhouse, *Medieval Archaeology* 15 (1971), 147

'Medieval Britain in 1971', L E Webster and J Cherry, *ibid* 16 (1972), 181–83*

'Recent mediaeval finds in the Oxford region. Middleton Stoney', E M Jope, *Oxoniensia* 13 (1948), 69–70

'First report on the excavations at Middleton Stoney Castle, Oxfordshire, 1970–71', T Rowley, *ibid* 37 (1972), 109–36*

Mixbury

'Beaumont Castle, Mixbury', J Steane, *CBA Group 9 Newsletter* 9 (1979), 83

Oxford

Oxford before the university: the late Saxon and Norman archaeology of the Thames crossing, the defences and the town. A Dodd (ed). Oxford: Oxford University School of Archaeology for Oxford Archaeology, 2003* (Thames Valley landscapes monograph; 17)

Oxford Castle. T G Hassall. Oxford: Oxford Archaeological Excavation Committee, 1971*

Oxford: the city beneath your feet. Archaeological excavations in the city of Oxford 1967–1972. T G Hassall. Oxford: Oxford Archaeological Excavation Committee, 1972*

Oxford buildings from medieval to modern: exteriors. D Hinton. Oxford: Oxford Archaeological Excavation Committee, 1972*

Historic Oxford. D Sturdy. Stroud: Tempus, 2004*

'Castle', J Cooper, in A Crossley (ed), *A history of the county of Oxford. 4. The city of Oxford*, 296–300. Oxford: OUP for the Institute of Historical Research, 1979*

'City walls, gates, and posterns', T G Hassall, in *ibid*, 300–4

'Archaeology of Oxford city', T Hassall, in G Briggs, J Cook and T Rowley (eds), *The archaeology of the Oxford region*, 115–34. Oxford: Oxford University Department for External Studies, 1986*

'Oxford', T Hassall, *Archaeological Excavations 1968*, 53. London: HMSO, 1969

'Oxford', T Hassall, *Archaeological Excavations 1969*, 68–69. London: HMSO, 1970

'Oxford', T G Hassall, *Archaeological Excavations 1970*, 81–82. London: HMSO, 1971

'Oxford', T G Hassall, *Archaeological Excavations 1971*, 95–96. London: HMSO, 1972

'Oxford, the city walls', T G Hassall, *Archaeological Journal* 135 (1978, 258–62

'Oxford Castle', T G Hassall, *ibid* 135 (1978), 268–69

'Oxford Castle', N Guy, *Castle Studies Group Journal* 19 (2006), 152–78*

'Oxford', T Hassall, *CBA Group 9 Newsletter* 1 (1971), 22–24

'Oxford', T G Hassall, *ibid* 2 (1972), 33–34

'Oxford 1971–1972', T Hassall, *ibid* 3 (1973), 30–31

'Oxford 1973', T G Hassall, *ibid* 4 (1974), 23

'Oxford', R Chambers, *ibid* 9 (1979), 130, 132–33*

'Oxford – 51–55 Holywell Street/St Helen's Passage', N Palmer and B Durham, *ibid* 11 (1981), 131

'Oxford: Corpus Christi College', B Durham, *ibid* 12 (1982), 156–57, 159*

'Medieval Britain in 1958', D M Wilson and J G Hurst, *Medieval Archaeology* 3 (1959), 311–12

'Medieval Britain in 1970', D M Wilson and S Moorhouse, *ibid* 15 (1971), 148

'Medieval Britain in 1971', L E Webster and J Cherry, *ibid* 16 (1972), 190

'Medieval Britain in 1972', L E Webster and J Cherry, *ibid* 17 (1973), 170

'Medieval Britain in 1974', L E Webster and J Cherry, *ibid* 19 (1975), 247

'Medieval Britain in 1980', S M Youngs and J Clark, *ibid* 25 (1981), 212

'Medieval Britain in 1981', S M Youngs and J Clark, *ibid* 26 (1982), 204

'Medieval Britain and Ireland in 1984', S M Youngs, J Clark and T Barry, *ibid* 29 (1985), 196

'Medieval Britain and Ireland in 1986', S M Youngs, J Clark and T Barry, *ibid* 31 (1987), 154–56

'Medieval Britain and Ireland in 1993', B S Nenk, S Margeson and M Hurley, *ibid* 38 (1994), 244

'Medieval Britain and Ireland in 1998', J Bradley, M Gaimster and C Haith, *ibid* 43 (1999), 274–75

'Medieval Britain and Ireland in 2004', M Gaimster and K O'Conor, *ibid* 49 (2005), 400-01

'Medieval Britain and Ireland in 2005', M Gaimster and K O'Conor, *ibid* 50 (2006), 346

'Medieval notes, 2. Oxford (New Road)', J R Kirk and H Case, *Oxoniensia* 15 (1950), 109

'Excavations on the city defences in New College, Oxford, 1949', A G Hunter and E M Jope, *ibid* 16 (1951), 28–41*

'Late Saxon pits under Oxford Castle mound: excavations in 1942', E M Jope, *ibid* 17–18 (1952–3), 77–111*

'Archaeological notes, 1953, B. Medieval and later. Oxford, Nuffield College', H Case and J R Kirk, *ibid* 17–18 (1952–3), 228

'Archaeological notes, 1955, B. Medieval and later. Oxford, Nuffield College', J R Kirk and H Case, *ibid* 20 (1955), 92

'Archaeological notes, Oxford, Jowett Walk', H Case and D Sturdy, *ibid* 25 (1960), 134

'Excavations at Oxford 1968: first interim report', T G Hassall, *ibid* 34 (1969), 5–20*

'Excavations at Oxford 1969: second interim report', T G Hassall, *ibid* 35 (1970), 5–18*

'Excavations at Oxford 1970: third interim report', T G Hassall, *ibid* 36 (1971), 1–14*

'Excavations in Merton College, Oxford, 1970', T G Hassall, *ibid* 36 (1971), 34–48*

'Excavations at Oxford 1971: fourth interim report', T G Hassall, *ibid* 37 (1972), 137–49*

'Excavations at Oxford 1972: fifth interim report', T G Hassall, *ibid* 38 (1973), 268–98*

'Excavations on the outer city wall of Oxford in St Helen's Passage and Hertford College', N Palmer, *ibid* 41 (1976), 148–60*

'Excavations at Oxford Castle, 1965–1973'. T G Hassall, *ibid* 41 (1976), 232–308*

'The fortifications of Oxford during the Civil War', A Kemp, *ibid* 42 (1977), 237–46

'A balance arm from Oxford Castle', anon, *ibid* 45 (1980), 311*

'Oxford's northern defences: archaeological studies 1971–1982', B Durham, C Halpin and N Palmer, *ibid* 48 (1983), 13–40*

'The siege of Oxford and the revolution of 1688', J Munby, *ibid* 53 (1988), 346–47

'Excavations in St Ebbe's, Oxford, 1967–1976: part 1: late Saxon and medieval domestic occupation and tenements, and the medieval Greyfriars', T G Hassall, C E Halpin and M Mellor, *ibid* 54 (1989), 71–277* [espec pp 130–40]

'The mural mansions of Oxford: attempted identifications', H L Turner, *ibid* 55 (1990), 73–79*

'Excavations on the line of the city defences at New College, Oxford, 1993', P M Booth, *ibid* 60 (1995), 205–24*

'Archaeological investigations on the site of a medieval and post-medieval watermill at Holywell Ford, Magdalen College, Oxford', C Bell, *ibid* 61 (1996), 275–95* [part of Civil War defences located]

'Archaeological investigations at Longwall Quad, Magdalen College, Oxford', M R Roberts, *ibid* 64 (1999), 275–84*

'Medieval Oxfordshire 1100–1540 (The Tom Hassall Lecture for 2000)', J Steane, *ibid* 66 (2001), 1–12

'Post-medieval Oxfordshire, 1540–2000 (The Tom Hassall Lecture for 2001)', J Munby, *ibid* 68 (2003), 1–14

'The west gate of Oxford Castle: excavations at Boreham's Yard, Tidmarsh Lane, Oxford, 1994–1995', P Booth, *ibid* 68 (2003), 363–422*

'Prehistoric and Roman activity and a Civil War ditch: excavations at the Chemistry Research Laboratory, 2–4 South parks Road, Oxford', P Bradley [*et al*], *ibid* 70 (2005), 141–202*

'Post-medieval Britain in 1980', J Cherry, *Post-Medieval Archaeology* 15 (1981), 226

'Post-medieval Britain and Ireland in 1998 and 1999', M Ponsford, *ibid* 34 (2000), 298, 299

'Oxford, Oxford Castle', A Norton, *South Midlands Archaeology* 33 (2003), 77

'Oxford, Oxford Castle', A Norton, *ibid* 35 (2005), 83

Somerton

'Somerton, Oxon', M Aston, *CBA Group 9 Newsletter* 4 (1974), 16–17*

Swerford

'Medieval Britain in 1957', D M Wilson and J G Hurst, *Medieval Archaeology* 2 (1958), 195

RUTLAND

Creighton, O H. 'Early castles in the medieval landscape of Rutland', *Transactions of the Leicestershire Archaeological and Historical Society* 73 (1999), 19–33*

Creighton, O H. 'The medieval castles of Rutland: field archaeology and landscape history', *Rutland Record* 20 (2000), 415–24*

Hartley, R F. *The medieval earthworks of Rutland: a survey*. Leicester: Leicestershire Museums, 1983*

Osborne, M. *20th century defences in the east midlands: Derbyshire, Leicestershire, Lincolnshire, Northamptonshire, Nottinghamshire and Rutland*. Market Deeping: Concrete Publications, 2003*

Pevsner, N. *Leicestershire and Rutland. (The buildings of England)*. 2nd edition, revised by E Williamson and G K Brandwood. Harmondsworth: Penguin Books, 1984*

Oakham

Oakham Castle: a guide and history. T H McK Clough. Leicester: Leicestershire Museums for the Friends of Rutland County Museum, 1981* [2nd edition 1987]

Oakham Castle: a guide and history. T H McK Clough. [3rd edition]. Oakham: Rutland County Council, 1999*

'Oakham Castle', B. Waites (ed), *A celebration of Rutland*, 28–29. Oakham: Multum in Parvo Press, 1994*

'Oakham Castle', C A R Radford, *Archaeological Journal* 112 (1955), 181–84*

'Excavations at Oakham Castle, Rutland', P W Gathercole, *Transactions of the Leicestershire Archaeological and Historical Society* 34 (1958), 17–38*

'Medieval Britain in 1956', D M Wilson and J G Hurst, *Medieval Archaeology* 1 (1957), 157

'Medieval Britain in 1957', D M Wilson and J G Hurst, *ibid* 2 (1958), 195

'Medieval Britain in 1958', D M Wilson and J G Hurst, *ibid* 3 (1959), 308

'Medieval Britain and Ireland in 1987', S M Youngs [*et al*], *ibid* 32 (1988), 260

'Medieval Britain and Ireland in 1989', D R M Gaimster, S Margeson and M Hurley, *ibid* 34 (1990), 201

SHROPSHIRE

Ascot-Symms, J. *Castles of Shropshire*. Broseley: Artscape, [1988?]*

Barker, P A. *The medieval pottery of Shropshire from the Conquest to 1400*. Shrewsbury: Shropshire Archaeological Society, 1970*

Chitty, L F. 'Interim notes on subsidiary castle sites west of Shrewsbury', *Transactions of the Shropshire Archaeological Society* 53 (1949–50), 83–90*

Chitty, L F. 'Three unrecognised castle sites in north Shropshire', *ibid* 53 (1949–50), 91–93*

Coplestone-Crow, B. 'Castles and knights' fees in the castlery of Clun', *Herefordshire Archaeological News* 63 (1995), 20–33*

Duckers, P and A. *Castles of Shropshire*. Stroud: Tempus, 2006*

Jackson, M. *Castles of Shropshire*. Shrewsbury: Shropshire Libraries, 1988*

King, D J C and Spurgeon, C J. 'The mottes in the Vale of Montgomery', *Archaeologia Cambrensis* 114 (1965), 69–86*

Lowry, B. 'Two RAF strongpoints in Shropshire', *Loopholes* 20 (1997), 25–27*

Mercer, E. *English architecture to 1900: the Shropshire experience*. Almeley: Logaston Press, 2003*

Moran, M. *Vernacular buildings of Shropshire*. Almeley: Logaston Press, 2003*

Newman, J and Pevsner, N. *Shropshire (The buildings of England)*. London: Yale University Press, 2006*

Pevsner, N. *Shropshire (The buildings of England)*. Harmondsworth: Penguin Books, 1958*

Pratt, D. '"Eggelawe" and "Ruffin"', *Clwyd Historian* 11 (1982), 21–27*

Remfry, P. 'Five castles in Clun lordship', *Herefordshire Archaeological News* 61 (1994), 15–23*

Salter, M. *The castles and moated mansions of Shropshire*. Wolverhampton: Folly Publications, 1988*

Salter, M. *The castles and moated mansions of Shropshire*. [New edition]. Malvern: Folly Publications, 2001*

Smyth, J. 'Mottes and baileys', in J Leonard [*et al*] (eds), *The gale of life: two thousand years in south-west Shropshire*, 87–97. Almeley: Logaston Press, 2000*

Suppe, F C. *Military institutions on the Welsh Marches: Shropshire, AD 1066–1300*. Woodbridge: Boydell Press, 1994*

Suppe, F C. 'Castle guard and the castlery of Clun', in R Liddiard (ed), *Anglo-Norman castles*, 211–21. Woodbridge: Boydell Press, 2003*

Suppe, F C. 'Castle guard and the castlery of Clun', *Haskins Society Journal* 1 (1989), 123–34*

Watson, M. *Shropshire: an archaeological guide*. Shrewsbury: Shropshire Books, 2002*

Watson, M and Musson, C. *Shropshire from the air: man and the landscape*. Shrewsbury: Shropshire Books, 1993*

Adderley

'Medieval pottery from sites in Shropshire: II. A group from the motte at Adderley', P A Barker, *Transactions of the Shropshire Archaeological Society* 56 (1957–60), 258–62*

Bishop's Castle

'Bishop's Castle: a medieval planned town', S Chappell and A Lawrence, in J Leonard [et al] (eds), *The gale of life: two thousand years in south-west Shropshire*, 109–17. Almeley: Logaston Press, 2000*

Bridgnorth

'A valiant constable of Colchester Castle, AD 1155', C L Sinclair Williams, *Essex Archaeology and History* 20 (1989), 30–33* [his death at the siege of Bridgnorth]

'Bridgnorth, Shropshire', A Roe, *West Midlands Archaeology* 26 (1983), 86–87*

'Bridgnorth, The Green', S Crawford, *ibid* 38 (1995), 49–52*

Brockhurst

'Brockhurst Castle, Church Stretton', P A Barker, *CBA Group 8 News Sheet* 2 (1959), 6

'A pottery sequence from Brockhurst Castle', P A Barker, *Transactions of the Shropshire Archaeological Society* 57 (1961–4), 63–80*

'Excavations at Brockhurst Castle, Church Stretton', P A Barker, *Shropshire News Letter* 9 (1959), 1

Bryn Amlwg

'Castell Bryn Amlwg', L Alcock, W G Putnam and C J Spurgeon, *Archaeology in Wales* 3 (1963), 21

'Excavations at Castell Bryn Amlwg', L Alcock [et al], *Montgomeryshire Collections* 60 (1967–8), 8–27*

'Castell Coch/Castell Hychoet: a possible identification', D Stephenson, *Shropshire History and Archaeology: Transactions of the Shropshire Archaeological and Historical Society* 77 (2002), 120–22

'Bryn Amlwg Castle, Newcastle, Clun', anon, *Shropshire News Letter* 24 (1963), 1

Callow

'Callow Castle, Hawcocks Mount and Brerelawe', J Lawson, *ibid* 28 (1965), 2–3

Caus

'Caus Castle', L F Chitty, *The hundred-and-first annual meeting: programme 1954*, CAA, 1954, 19–21

'Caus Castle', A J Taylor, *Archaeologia Cambrensis* 104 (1955), 199–201

'Caus Castle and Hawcocks Mount', P A Barker, *Archaeological Journal* 138 (1981), 34

'Caus Castle, Alretone and Trewerne', J Lawson, *Shropshire News Letter* 28 (1965), 2

Clun

Stokesay Castle, Shropshire. J Munby and H Summerson. London: English Heritage, 2002* [see pp 35–36 for Clun]

Clun Castle 1066 to 1282. P M Remfry. Malvern Link: SCS Publishing, 1994*

Clun Castle 1066 to 1282: a short guide. P M Remfry. Malvern Link: SCS Publishing, 1995*

'Norman buildings in Clun', M Young, in J Leonard [*et al*] (eds), *The gale of life: two thousand years in south-west Shropshire*, 99–107. Almeley: Logaston Press, 2000*

'Castle guard and the castlery of Clun', F C Suppe, in R Liddiard (ed), *Anglo-Norman castles*, 211–21. Woodbridge: Boydell Press, 2003*

'Clun Castle', W Rees, *Archaeologia Cambrensis* 108 (1959), 154–55

'Clun Castle reappraised', R K Morriss, *Castle Studies Group Newsletter* 7 (1993–4), 23–24

'Castle guard and the castlery of Clun', F C Suppe, *Haskins Society Journal* 1 (1989), 123–34*

'Medieval Britain and Ireland in 1992', B S Nenk., S Margeson and M Hurley, *Medieval Archaeology* 37 (1993), 279–80

'Medieval Britain and Ireland in 1993', B S Nenk, S Margeson and M Hurley, *ibid* 38 (1994),

'Clun, Clun Castle', R K Morriss, *West Midlands Archaeology* 33 (1990), 62

Dothill

'Medieval Britain in 1960', D M Wilson and D G Hurst, *Medieval Archaeology* 5 (1961), 319

Hawcocks Mount

'Caus Castle and Hawcocks Mount', P A Barker, *Archaeological Journal* 138 (1981), 34

'Callow Castle, Hawcocks Mount and Brerelawe', J Lawson, *Shropshire News Letter* 28 (1965), 2–3

Hawkstone

'Hawkstone Park and the Red Castle', A Arrol and A Snell, *Archaeological Journal* 138 (1981), 43–44

High Ercall

'High Ercall, Shropshire', in T Taylor, *Digging the dirt with Time Team*, 98–125. London: Channel 4 Books, 2001*

Hopton

Hopton Castle 1066 to 1305. P M Remfry. Malvern Link: SCS Publishing, 1994* + revised edition 1994* [taking into account the next entry]

'The tower house at Hopton Castle and its affinities', P E Curnow, in C Harper-Bill, C J Holdsworth and J L Nelson (eds), *Studies in medieval history presented to R Allen Brown*, 81–102. Woodbridge: Boydell Press, 1989*

'Medieval Britain and Ireland in 2005', M Gaimster and K O'Conor, *Medieval Archaeology* 50 (2006), 346–47

'Hopton Castle, Shropshire', M Bowden, *Research News: Newsletter of the English Heritage Research Department* 3 (2006), 18–19*

Little Ness
'The mound at Little Ness, Shropshire', L F Chitty, *Transactions of the Shropshire Archaeological Society* 52 (1947–8), 248–49

Ludlow
Ludlow Castle: a guide. Anon. Rhostryfan: Historic Tours (Wales), 1987*

Ludlow Castle: a guided tour. C Hampton. Leominster: Orphans Press, 1977*

Ludlow Castle: a history and a guide. D Lloyd. [S l: s n, 1993/4?]*

Ludlow Castle: its history & buildings. R Shoesmith and A Johnson (eds). Almeley: Logaston Press, 2000*

'Geology, building stone and water supply, N Ruckley and A Johnson, in *ibid*, 1–4*

'The town of Ludlow', R Shoesmith, in *ibid*, 5–14*

'Ludlow Castle', R Shoesmith, in *ibid*, 15–18*

'From foundation to the Anarchy', B Coplestone-Crow, 21–34*

'The end of the Anarchy to the de Genevilles', B Coplestone-Crow, in *ibid*, 35–44*

'The Mortimer lordship', D Harding, in *ibid*, 45–56*

'Ludlow during the Wars of the Roses', R A Griffiths, in *ibid*, 57–68*

'The Council in the Marches of Wales', M Faraday, in *ibid*, 69–82*

'The Civil War', J Knight, in *ibid*, 83–88*

'The castle in decline', P Hughes, in *ibid*, 89–98*

'Symbolism and assimilation', D Whitehead, in *ibid*, 99–116*

'Monument preservation, management & display', A D F Streeten, in *ibid*, 117–22*

'The Norman military works', D Renn, in *ibid*, 125–38*

'Changes to the castle keep', P White, in *bid*, 139–44*

'The round chapel of St. Mary Magdalene', G Coppack, in *ibid*, 145–54*

'The solar block', R K Morriss, in *ibid*, 155–66*

'The great hall & great chamber block', M Thompson, in *ibid*, 167–74*

'The Tudor lodgings & use of the north-east range', R Shoesmith, in *ibid*, 175–84*

'The Judges' Lodgings', A Fleming, in *ibid*, 185–90*

'The outer bailey', D Renn and R Shoesmith, in *ibid*, 191–94*

'Mortimer's Tower', P E Curnow and J R Kenyon, in *ibid*, 195–200*

'St. Peter's Chapel and the Court House', P Remfry and P Halliwell, in *ibid*, 201–4*

'The porter's lodge, prison and stable block', R Stone, in *ibid*, 205–12*

Ludlow Castle: its history & buildings. Extended edition. R Shoesmith and A Johnson (eds). Almeley: Logaston Press, 2006*

'Geology, building stone and water supply, N Ruckley and A Johnson, in *ibid*, 1–4*

'The town of Ludlow', R Shoesmith, in *ibid*, 5–14*

'Ludlow Castle', R Shoesmith, in *ibid*, 15–18*

'From foundation to the Anarchy', B Coplestone-Crow, 21–34*

'The end of the Anarchy to the de Genevilles', B Coplestone-Crow, in *ibid*, 35–44*

'The Mortimer lordship', D Harding, in *ibid*, 45–56*

'Ludlow during the Wars of the Roses', R A Griffiths, in *ibid*, 57–68*

'The Council in the Marches of Wales', M Faraday, in *ibid*, 69–82*

'The Civil War', J Knight, in *ibid*, 83–88*

'The castle in decline', P Hughes, in *ibid*, 89–98*

'Symbolism and assimilation', D Whitehead, in *ibid*, 99–116*

'Monument preservation, management & display', A D F Streeten, in *ibid*, 117–22*

'The Norman military works', D Renn, in *ibid*, 125–38*

'Changes to the castle keep', P White, in *bid*, 139–44*

'The round chapel of St. Mary Magdalene', G Coppack, in *ibid*, 145–54*

'The solar block', R K Morriss, in *ibid*, 155–66*

'The great hall & great chamber block', M Thompson, in *ibid*, 167–74*

'The Tudor lodgings & use of the north-east range', R Shoesmith, in *ibid*, 175–84*

'The Judges' Lodgings', A Fleming, in *ibid*, 185–90*

'The outer bailey', D Renn and R Shoesmith, in *ibid*, 191–94*

'Mortimer's Tower', P E Curnow and J R Kenyon, in *ibid*, 195–200*

'St. Peter's Chapel and the Court House', P Remfry and P Halliwell, in *ibid*, 201–4*

'The porter's lodge, prison and stable block', R Stone, in *ibid*, 205–12*

'The story of Castle House', R Shoesmith, in *ibid*, 213–28*

The walls and gates of Ludlow: their origins and early days. C J Train. Ludlow: Ludlow Historical Research Group, 1999*

'"Chastel de Dynan": the first phases of Ludlow', D Renn, in J R Kenyon and R Avent (eds), *Castles in Wales and the Marches: essays in honour of D J Cathcart King*, 55–73. Cardiff: University of Wales Press, 1987*

'Ludlow Castle', P E Curnow, *Archaeological Journal* 138 (1981), 12, 14

'Ludlow, Shropshire', C Hussey, *Country Life* 98 (1945), 1094–97*

'Ludlow Castle', C Hussey, *ibid* 99 (1946), 72–75, 118–21*

'Ludlow Castle, Shropshire', J Goodall, *ibid* 191.17 (1997), 46–51*

'Ludlow Castle: the outer defences', P R Halliwell and P M Remfry, *Herefordshire Archaeological News* 64 (1995), 16–19*

'Ludlow Castle: outer bailey moat', P Halliwell, *ibid* 71 (2000), 29*

'Medieval Britain and Ireland in 1989', D R M Gaimster, S Margeson and M Hurley, *Medieval Archaeology* 34 (1990), 208

'Medieval Britain and Ireland in 1990', B S Nenk, S Margeson and M Hurley, *ibid* 35 (1991), 183–84

'Medieval Britain and Ireland in 1991', B S Nenk, S Margeson and M Hurley, *ibid* 36 (1992), 258–59*

'Medieval Britain and Ireland in 1993', B S Nenk, S Margeson and M Hurley, *ibid* 38 (1994), 246

'Medieval Britain and Ireland in 2000', J Bradley and M Gaimster, *ibid* 45 (2001), 313

'Payn fitzJohn and Ludlow Castle', B Coplestone-Crow, *Shropshire History and Archaeology* 70 (1995), 171–83*

'Ludlow, Ludlow Castle', R K Morriss, *West Midlands Archaeology* 33 (1990), 63

'Ludlow, Ludlow Castle', R K Morriss, *ibid* 34 (1991), 56–58*

Marton

'Marton motte, Chirbury', C J Spurgeon, *Archaeology in Wales* 8 (1968), 27

'The destruction of Marton motte, Chirbury', C J Spurgeon, *Montgomeryshire Collections* 60 (1967–8), 165–68*

More

'More, Shropshire', anon, *CBA Group 8 News Sheet* 2 (1959), 7

Moreton Corbet

Haughmond Abbey, Lilleshall Abbey, Moreton Corbet Castle, Shropshire. I Ferris. London: English Heritage, 2000*

Moreton Corbet Castle 1066 to 1700: an open day special. P M Remfry. Malvern Link: SCS Publishing, 1999*

'Moreton Corbet Castle', O J Weaver, *Archaeological Journal* 138 (1981), 44–46*

'Moreton Corbet Castle', E Harwood, *English Heritage Historical Review* 1 (2006), 36–45*

'Moreton Corbet Castle: a house and its family', B Coulton, *Shropshire History and Archaeology: Transactions of the Shropshire Archaeological Society* 70 (1995), 184–90

Oswestry

Oswestry town wall. Border Counties Archaeological Group. Oswestry: BCAG, [1981]*

'The garrisoning of Oswestry, a baronial castle on the Welsh Marches', F Suppe, in K Reyerson and F Powe (eds), *The medieval castle: romance and reality*, 63–78. Dubuque: Kendall/Hunt Publishing, 1984* (Medieval studies at Minnesota; 1)

'Medieval Britain in 1980', S M Youngs and J Clark, *Medieval Archaeology* 25 (1981), 213

'Medieval Britain and Ireland in 1997', M Gaimster, C Haith and J Bradley, *ibid* 42 (1998), 221

'Medieval Britain and Ireland in 2002', J Bradley and M Gaimster, *ibid* 47 (2003), 278

'Oswestry town walls', W Day, *Transactions of the Shropshire Archaeological Society* 59 (1969–74), 278–79*

'Oswestry town wall', P N Reynolds', *Shropshire Archaeological Society Newsletter* 20 (1984), 11–12

'The town walls, Oswestry', C James, *Shropshire News Sheet* 10 (1979), 10

'Search for town wall', D Pratt, *West Midlands Archaeology* 23 (1980), 105–8*

'Oswestry, Oswestry Castle', I Grant, *ibid* 45 (2002), 58

Pontesbury

'Pontesbury', P V Addyman and P A Barker, *Archaeological Excavations 1961*, 11. London: HMSO, 1962

'Pontesbury', P A Barker, *Archaeological Excavations 1964*, 13. London: HMSO, 1965

'Pontesbury Castle', P A Barker, *Archaeology in Wales* 4 (1964), 21–22

'Castle Mound, Pontesbury', P A Barker, *CBA Group 8 News Sheet* 4 (1961), 8

'Pontesbury Castle', P A Barker, *ibid* 7 (1964), 10

'Medieval Britain in 1961', D M Wilson and D G Hurst, *Medieval Archaeology* 6–7 (1962–3), 323

'Medieval Britain in 1964', D M Wilson and D G Hurst, *ibid* 9 (1965), 191

'Pontesbury castle mound emergency excavation 1961 and 1964', P A Barker, *Transactions of the Shropshire Archaeological Society* 57 (1961–4), 206–23*

'Excavations on the castle mound at Pontesbury', anon, *Shropshire News Letter* 17 (1962), 2–3

'Excavations at Pontesbury Castle, Shropshire, 1964', PA Barker, *ibid* 27 (1964), 1

Quatford

'Quatford', P A Barker, *CBA Group 8 News Sheet* 3 (1960), 7

'Medieval Britain in 1960', D M Wilson and D G Hurst, *Medieval Archaeology* 5 (1961), 319

'Quatford, motte and bailey castle', P A Barker, *Transactions of the Shropshire Archaeological Society* 56 (1957–60), 346

'The Norman castle at Quatford', J F A Mason and P A Barker, *ibid* 57 (1961–4), 37–62*

'Motte and bailey castle at Quatford', P A Barker, *Shropshire News Letter* 13 (1960), 1

Ryton
'Excavation of a motte and bailey at Ryton, Shifnal, Shropshire, 1962', J W Snape, *Transactions of the Shropshire Archaeological Society* 57 (1961–4), 191–93*

Shrawardine
'Archaeological surveys at Shrawardine Castle', N W Jones, *Shropshire History and Archaeology: Transactions of the Shropshire Archaeological and Historical Society* 77 (2002), 15–25*

'Shrawardine, Shrawardine Farm', H Hannaford, *West Midlands Archaeology* 36 (1993), 63

Shrewsbury
Shrewsbury: archaeological discoveries from a medieval town. N Baker. Shrewsbury: Shropshire Books, 2003*

'Shrewsbury Castle', H Beaumont, *Archaeological Journal* 113 (1956), 191

'Shrewsbury town and defences', M O H Carver, *ibid* 138 (1981), 42

'Town defences, Shrewsbury', anon, *CBA Group 8 News Sheet* 1 (1958), 6

'Shrewsbury', G Toms, *ibid* 12 (1969), 34

'Pride Hill, Shrewsbury', G Toms, *ibid* 15 (1972), 26

'Pride Hill, Shrewsbury', M Carver, *ibid* 17 (1974), 67

'Medieval Britain in 1958', D M Wilson and J G Hurst, *Medieval Archaeology* 3 (1959), 312–14

'Excavations on the town wall, Roushill, Shrewsbury', P A Barker, *ibid* 5 (1961), 181–210*

'Medieval Britain in 1969', D M Wilson and D G Hurst, *ibid* 14 (1970), 185

'Medieval Britain in 1974', L E Webster and J Cherry, *ibid* 19 (1975), 247–48

'Medieval Britain and Ireland in 1986', S M Youngs, J Clark and T Barry, *ibid* 31 (1987), 158

'Medieval Britain and Ireland in 1993', B S Nenk, S Margeson and M Hurley, *ibid* 38 (1994), 246

'Medieval Britain and Ireland in 2000', J Bradley and M Gaimster, *ibid* 45 (2001), 313

'The medieval defences of Shrewsbury', C A R Radford, *Transactions of the Shropshire Archaeological Society* 56 (1957–60), 15–20

'Two town houses in medieval Shrewsbury: the excavation and analysis of two medieval and later houses built on the town wall at Shrewsbury', M O H Carver (ed), *ibid* 61 (1977–8), [whole issue]* [published 1983]

'The Civil War Roushill wall, Shrewsbury', T M Brown, *ibid* 66 (1989), 85–89*

'Excavations at Roushill, Shrewsbury, 1958', P A Barker, *Shropshire News Letter* 6 (1959), 1–2

'Roushill wall, Shrewsbury', P A Barker, *ibid* 16 (1961), 2–3

'The Raven site, Shrewsbury', P A Barker, *ibid* 21 (1963), 4

'Shrewsbury, Blackfriars and town wall', S Buteux, *West Midlands Archaeology* 32 (1989), 72

'Geophysical surveys at Shrewsbury Castle', M Stoke, *ibid* 43 (2000), 25–26

'Shrewsbury, 58–59 Mardol', R Stone, *ibid* 43 (2000), 72

Smethcott

'Smethcott', anon, *CBA Group 8 News Sheet* 1 (1958), 7

'Medieval Britain in 1956', D M Wilson and J G Hurst, *Medieval Archaeology* 1 (1957), 157

'Medieval Britain in 1957', D M Wilson and J G Hurst, *ibid* 2 (1958), 195

'Excavations at Smethcott', G S Gamble, *Shropshire News Letter* 6 (1959), 3

Stoke on Tern

'Stoke on Tern Castle', P A Barker, *ibid* 25 (1964), 3

Stokesay

Stokesay Castle, Shropshire. J F A Mason. Derby: English Life Publications, 1971*

Stokesay Castle, Shropshire. J Munby. London: English Heritage, 1993*

Stokesay Castle, Shropshire. J Munby and H Summerson. London: English Heritage, 2002*

'The tradition of historical consciousness: the case of Stokesay Castle', G Chitty, in G Chitty and D Baker (eds), *Managing historic sites and buildings: reconciling presentation and preservation*, 85–97. London: Routledge, 1999*

'Two views from the roof: design and defence at Conwy and Stokesay', D Renn, in J R Kenyon and K O'Conor (eds), *The medieval castle in Ireland and Wales: essays in honour of Jeremy Knight*, 163–75. Dublin: Four Court Press, 2003*

'Stokesay Castle', J T Smith, *Archaeological Journal* 113 (1956), 211–14*

'Stokesay Castle', J Blair, *ibid* 138 (1981), 11–12

'Stokesay Castle, Shropshire: the chronology of its buildings', R A Cordingley, *Art Bulletin* 45 (1963), 91–107*

'Stokesay Castle, Shropshire: the repair of a major monument', R J Tolley, *Transactions of the Association for Studies in the Conservation of Historic Buildings* 15 (1990), 3–24* [also offprinted and bound specially for English Heritage, 1991]

'Stokesay Castle, Shropshire', M Hall, *Country Life* 188.13 (1994), 72–77*

"Most renowned of merchants': the life and occupations of Laurence of Ludlow (d. 1294)', H Summerson, *Midland History* 30 (2005), 20–36

Tong

'Seventeenth and eighteenth century clay tobacco pipes excavated from Tong Castle, Shropshire', A Wharton, in P Davey (ed), *The archaeology of the clay tobacco pipe. III. Britain: the north and west*, 287–91. Oxford: British Archaeological Reports, 1980* (British series; 78)

'Tong Castle excavation – 1978–1979: interim report', A Wharton, *Shropshire News Sheet* 10 (1979), 7–8

'Tong Castle', A Wharton, *ibid* 14 (1981), 15–16

'Tong Castle excavation', A Wharton, *West Midlands Archaeological News Sheet* 19 (1976), 55–59*

'Tong Castle excavation interim report 1976/77', A Wharton, *ibid* 20 (1977), 73–78*

'Tong Castle excavation 1977/78', A Wharton, *ibid* 21 (1978), 84–89*

'Tong Castle excavation – 1978 to 1979', A Wharton, *ibid* 22 (1979), 66–75*

'Excavation and survey', A Wharton, *West Midlands Archaeology* 23 (1980), 122–23*

'Tong, Shropshire: survey and salvage recorded on line of M54 construction', A Wharton, *ibid* 24 (1981), 115–17*

Wattlesborough

'Wattlesborough Tower, Alberbury', J J West, *Archaeological Journal* 138 (1981), 33–34

Westbury

'Westbury', C J Spurgeon, *Archaeology in Wales* 3 (1963), 21

Whitchurch

'Medieval Britain and Ireland in 1997', M Gaimster, C Haith and J Bradley, *Medieval Archaeology* 42 (1998), 151

'Sir John Talbot's castle at Whitchurch', anon, *Shropshire News Letter* 23 (1963), 2

'Excavations at Blakemere Castle, Whitchurch', R W Griffiths, *ibid* 24 (1963), 2

'Primary report on the excavation at Castle Hill, Whitchurch – April 1979', R W Griffiths, *Shropshire News Sheet* 10 (1979), 5–7

Whittington

Whittington Castle, Shropshire. P Brown. Whittington: Whittington Castle Preservation Trust, 2003*

Whittington Castle and its story: a stronghold which has guarded the border for a thousand years. E Collins. Whittington: M Morris, n d* [1991? reprint of an earlier undated edition]

'Whittington Castle', D J C King, *The hundred and twentieth annual meeting in Wrexham and district, 1973*, CAA, 1973, 24–25

'Medieval water garden at Whittington Castle', anon, *Current Archaeology* 16.2 (2002), 52*

'Medieval Britain in 1970', D M Wilson and S Moorhouse, *Medieval Archaeology* 15 (1971), 148

'Medieval Britain in 1976', L E Webster and J Cherry, *ibid* 21 (1977), 238

'Medieval Britain and Ireland in 1999', J Bradley and M Gaimster, *ibid* 44 (2000), 304

'Medieval Britain and Ireland in 2003', J Bradley and M Gaimster, *ibid* 48 (2004), 287–88

'*Fouke le Fitz Waryn* and Llywelyn ap Gruffydd's claim to Whittington', D Stephenson, *Shropshire History and Archaeology: Transactions of the Shropshire Archaeological and Historical Society* 77 (2002), 26–31

'Whittington Castle: the Marcher fortress of the Fitz Warin family', P Brown, P King and P Remfry, *ibid* 79 (2004), 106–27

Wilmington

'Wilmington motte, Chirbury', C J Spurgeon, *Archaeology in Wales* 3 (1963), 21

Winsbury

'Winsbury, Chirbury', P V Addyman, *Archaeological Excavations 1961*, 11. London: HMSO, 1962

'Medieval Britain in 1961', D M Wilson and D G Hurst, *Medieval Archaeology* 6–7 (1962–3), 323

'Excavation of a motte at Winsbury, near Chirbury', P V Addyman, *Shropshire News Letter* 17 (1962), 1

Woolstaston

'Wollstaston' [*sic*], T Rowley, *Archaeological Excavations 1965*, 16. London: HMSO, 1966

'Medieval Britain in 1965', D M Wilson and D G Hurst, *Medieval Archaeology* 10 (1966), 191

'Excavations at Woolstaston motte-and-bailey castle, 1965', T Rowley, *Transactions of the Shropshire Archaeological Society* 60 (1975–6), 75–79*

SOMERSET

Barrett, J H. *A history of the maritime forts in the Bristol Channel 1866–1900*. Privately published, 1978*; 2nd edition, 1993*

Carter, K (ed). *Heritage unlocked: guide to free sites in Devon, Dorset and Somerset*. London: English Heritage, 2004*

Dunning, R. *Somerset castles*. Tiverton: Somerset Books, 1995*

Hellis, J. 'The Somerset stop-line', *Fortress* 14 (1992), 39–47*

Iles, R. 'Medieval castles and monasteries', in M Aston and R Iles (eds), *The archaeology of Avon: a review from the Neolithic to the Middle Ages*, 122–29. Bristol: Avon County Council, [1987]*

Pevsner, N. *North Somerset and Bristol (The buildings of England)*. Harmondsworth: Penguin Books, 1958*

Pevsner, N. *South and west Somerset (The buildings of England)*. Harmondsworth: Penguin Books, 1958*

Prior, S. *A few well-positioned castles: the Norman art of war*. Stroud: Tempus, 2006*

Rahtz, P [et al]. 'Norman castles', in *Medieval sites in the Mendip, Cotswold, Wye Valley and Bristol region*, 14–17. Bristol: Bristol Archaeological Research Group, 1969 (Field guide; 3)

Robertson, M. *Exploring England's heritage: Dorset to Gloucester*. London: HMSO, in association with English Heritage, 1992* [espec ch 2]

Salter, M. *The castles of Wessex*. Malvern: Folly Publications, 2002*

Stevenson, I. 'The Bristol Channel and Swansea defences', *The Redan* 50 (2000), 28–51*

Bath

Medieval Bath uncovered. P Davenport. Stroud: Tempus, 2002* [city walls, pp 126–31]

'Bath, New Orchard Street', M B Owen, *CBA Groups 12 and 13 Archaeological Review* 6 (1971), 41

'Excavations at Upper Borough Walls, Bath, 1980', T J O'Leary, *Medieval Archaeology* 25 (1981), 1–30*

'Medieval Britain and Ireland in 1990', B S Nenk, S Margeson and M Hurley, *ibid* 35 (1991), 131–32

'Medieval Britain and Ireland in 1991', B S Nenk, S Margeson and M Hurley, *ibid* 36 (1992), 190

'Medieval Britain and Ireland in 1995', B S Nenk, S Margeson and M Hurley, *ibid* 40 (1996), 238–39

'Medieval Britain and Ireland in 1996', B S Nenk, C Haith and J Bradley, *ibid* 41 (1997), 246

'Post-medieval Britain and Ireland in 1995', M Ponsford and R Jackson, *Post-Medieval Archaeology* 30 (1996), 255–56

'The city walls of Bath, the church of St James South Gate, and the area east of the church of St James', W J Wedlake, *Proceedings of the Somersetshire Archaeological and Natural History Society* 110 (1965–6), 85–107*

Black Down
'Second World War remains on Black Down: a reinterpretation', A J Schofield, C J Webster and M J Anderton, *Somerset Archaeology and Natural History* 142 (1998), 271–86*

Brean Down
Images of Brean Down Fort, 1870–1945: a report to the National Trust on the possibilities for the restoration and presentation to the public of the 19th-20th century artillery fort. V T C Smith. Northfleet: V T C Smith, 1989*

'Brean Down, Somerset: interim report on a new survey by the Royal Commission on the Historical Monuments of England', H Riley, *Archaeology in the Severn Estuary* 6 (1995), 13–21*

'Somerset archaeology 1974–75', M Aston (ed), *Somerset Archaeology and Natural History* 120 (1976), 75

'The Victorian and Second World War artillery batteries on Brean Down', C J Webster, *ibid* 145 (2001), 89–115*

Bridgwater
'Castle Moat, King Square, Bridgwater', M Langdon and F Richardson, *Bridgwater and District Archaeological Society Annual Report* (1981), 23–48*

'Bridgwater, Head Post Office', R R Nesbitt, *CBA Groups 12 and 13 Archaeological Review* 2 (1967), 23

'Bridgwater', M Langdon, *ibid* 7 (1972), 57

'Somerset archaeology 1974–75', M Aston (ed), *Somerset Archaeology and Natural History* 120 (1976), 73

'Excavations at Friarn Street and West Quay, Bridgwater, 1983/84', P Ellis, *ibid* 129 (1984–5), 69–80*

'Somerset archaeology 1986', E Dennison (ed), *ibid* 130 (1985–6), 152

'Bridgwater, Castle Moat and King Square', R A Croft, in E Dennison (ed), 'Somerset archaeology 1988', *ibid* 132 (1988), 225

'Bridgwater Castle, West Quay', C Sidaway, *ibid* 135 (1991), 169–70*

Bury
'Castles', in H Riley and R Wilson-North, *The field archaeology of Exmoor*, 102–6. Swindon: English Heritage, 2001*

Castle Batch

'Somerset archaeology, 1978', S Minnitt and B J Murless (eds), *Somerset Archaeology and Natural History* 123 (1978–9), 104

Castle Cary

The castles of Cary. C P Hershon. Bristol: Pavallas Press, 1990*

'Medieval Britain and Ireland in 1999', J Bradley and M Gaimster, *Medieval Archaeology* 44 (2000), 304–5

'Manor Farm, Castle Cary', J and R Keynes, in M A Aston and B J Murless (eds), 'Somerset archaeology 1977', *Somerset Archaeology and Natural History* 122 (1978), 128–29*

'Manor Farm, Castle Cary', J and R Keynes, in S Minnitt and B J Murless (eds), 'Somerset archaeology 1978', *ibid* 123 (1979), 90

'Roman and medieval remains at Manor Farm, Castle Cary', P Leach and P Ellis, *ibid* 147 (2004), 80–128*

Castle Neroche

'Castle Neroche', B K Davison, *Archaeological Excavations 1964*, 13. London: HMSO, 1965

'Castle Neroche', H St G Gray, *Archaeological Journal* 107 (1950), 122

'Excavations at Castle Neroche, Somerset, 1961–64', in 'Three eleventh-century earthworks in England: their excavation and implication', B K Davison, *Château Gaillard* 2 (1967), 39–48*

'Castle Neroche reconsidered', B K Davison, *Council for British Archaeology South West Journal* 8 (2002), 12–15*

'Medieval Britain in 1961', D M Wilson and D G Hurst, *Medieval Archaeology* 6–7 (1962–3), 323

'Medieval Britain in 1962 and 1963', D M Wilson and D G Hurst, *ibid* 8 (1964), 258–59*

'Medieval Britain in 1964', D M Wilson and D G Hurst, *ibid* 9 (1965), 191

'Excavations at Castle Neroche, 1961', B K Davison, *Somerset and Dorset Notes and Queries* 28 (1961–7), 49–52*

'Castle Neroche: an abandoned Norman fortress in south Somerset', B K Davison, *Proceedings of the Somersetshire Archaeological and Natural History Society* 116 (1971–2), 16–58*

Croft

'Croft Castle', R W Dunning, *Somerset Archaeology and Natural History* 121 (1977), 129–30

Culverhay

'Englishcombe, Culverhay Castle', R Iles and M Stacey, in R Iles, 'Avon archaeology 1982', *Bristol and Avon Archaeology* 2 (1983), 54*

Dunster

Dunster Castle, Somerset. Anon. London: National Trust, 2003*

'Castles', in H Riley and R Wilson-North, *The field archaeology of Exmoor*, 102–6. Swindon: English Heritage, 2001*

'Dunster Castle', M Whinney, *Archaeological Journal* 107 (1950), 123

'Dunster Castle, Somerset – I: a property of the National Trust', R Haslam, *Country Life* 181.29 (1987), 124–27*

'The medieval castle at Dunster', J H P Gibb, *Somerset Archaeology and Natural History* 125 (1981), 1–15*

Farleigh Hungerford

Farleigh Hungerford Castle, Somerset. Anon. London: HMSO, reprinted 1971*

Farleigh Hungerford Castle. Anon. London: HBMCE, 1986*

Farleigh Hungerford Castle. C Kightly. London: English Heritage, 2006*

Farleigh Hungerford Castle: information for teachers. P Planel. London: English Heritage, 1995*

'Late medieval wall painting techniques at Farleigh Hungerford Castle and their context', H Howard, T Manning and S Stewart, in A Roy and P Smith (eds), *Painting techniques: history, materials and studio practice*, 59–64. London: International Institute for Conservation of Historic and Artistic Works, 1998*

'Farleigh Hungerford, Farleigh Castle', R Wilcox, *Archaeological Excavations 1975*, 26–27. London: HMSO, 1976

'Farleigh Hungerford, Farleigh Castle', R Wilcox, *Archaeological Excavations 1976*, 31. London: HMSO, 1977

'Farleigh Hungerford Castle, Somerset', B M Morley, *Archaeological Journal* 134 (1977), 356–58*

'The chantry priests' house at Farleigh Hungerford Castle', T J Miles and A D Saunders, *Medieval Archaeology* 19 (1975), 165–94*

'Excavations at Farleigh Hungerford Castle, Somerset, 1973–76', R Wilcox, *Somerset Archaeology and Natural History* 124 (1980), 87–109*

Ilchester

'Ilchester, the rectory garden', P J Casey, *CBA Groups 12 and 13 Archaeological Review* 4 (1969), 46

'Medieval Britain in 1981', S M Youngs and J Clark, *Medieval Archaeology* 26 (1982), 206

'Ilchester archaeology: excavation on the western defences and suburbs, 1985', P Leach and P Ellis, *Somerset Archaeology and Natural History* 135 (1991), 11–84*

Locking

'Locking, Locking Head. Motte and bailey', M W Ponsford and R Iles, in R Iles, 'Avon archaeology 1981', *Bristol and Avon Archaeology* 1 (1982), 53–55*

Newton St Loe

'Medieval Britain in 1976', L E Webster and J Cherry, *Medieval Archaeology* 21 (1977), 233

'Medieval Britain in 1980', S M Youngs and J Clark, *ibid* 25 (1981), 200

'Medieval Britain in 1981', S M Youngs and J Clark, *ibid* 26 (1982), 170

'The fortified manor house at Newton St Loe: interim report on the excavations', C J Arnold, *Somerset Archaeology and Natural History* 124 (1980), 77–86*

'Excavations at Newton St Loe Castle, 1975–1984', C J Arnold, *ibid* 143 (1999), 57–115*

Nunney

Nunney Castle, Somerset. S E Rigold. London: HMSO, 1957*

'Nunney Castle', D J C King, *133rd annual meeting: Avon, 1986. Rhaglen/Programme*, CAA, 1986, 35–36

'Nunney Castle, Somerset', B M Morley, *Archaeological Journal* 134 (1977), 353–54*

'Nunney Castle', C Peers, *Proceedings of the Somersetshire Archaeological and Natural History Society* 94 (1948–9), 39–40

Penselwood

'The Pen Pits and Castle Orchard', H St G Gray, *ibid* 96 (1951), 8–11

Richmont

'East Harptree, Richmont Castle', J R Russell, in R Iles, 'Avon archaeology 1983', *Bristol and Avon Archaeology* 3 (1984), 61–62*

Steep Holm

Steep Holm: an investigation into the island's history. S D and J N Rendell. Privately published, 1978*

Steep Holm: a survey. Anon. Taunton: Somerset Archaeological and Natural History Society, 1981*

'The Palmerston follies', R Legg, in J Fowles (ed), *Steep Holm: a case history in the study of evolution*, 99–118. Milborne Port: Kenneth Allsop Memorial Trust, 1978*

'Hitler's war', R Legg, in *ibid*, 119–32*

'Steepholm', anon, *133rd annual meeting: Avon, 16 August-23 August 1986. Rhaglen/Programme*, CAA, 1986, 36–38

Sticklynch

'West Pennard: evidence for a motte and bailey castle at Sticklynch', S Rands, *Notes and Queries for Somerset and Dorset* 33.341 (1995), 353–55

Stogursey

'Somerset archaeology 1974–75', M Aston (ed), *Somerset Archaeology and History* 120 (1976), 73

Stoke sub Hamdon

'Stoke sub Hamdon Castle', R H Leech, *Archaeological Excavations 1976*, 146. London: HMSO, 1977

'Medieval Britain in 1976', L E Webster and J Cherry, *Medieval Archaeology* 21 (1977), 238

'Excavations at Stoke sub Hamdon Castle, Somerset, 1976', P J Leach, *Somerset Archaeology and Natural History* 124 (1980), 61–76*

Stoney Littleton

'Stoney Littleton', E K Tratman, *Somerset and Dorset Notes and Queries* 27 (1955–60), 204

Taunton

Taunton: the borough defences. R Bush and P Leach. Bristol: Bristol Committee for Rescue Archaeology in Avon, Gloucestershire and Somerset, 1977

A brief history of Taunton Castle. T J Hunt. Taunton: Somerset County Museum, 1964*

The archaeology of Taunton: excavations and fieldwork to 1980. P Leach (ed). [Bristol]: Western Archaeological Trust, 1984*

'Taunton Castle', W A Seaby, *Archaeological Journal* 107 (1950), 98–100*

'Taunton, Silver St – Mansfield Road', C F Clements, *CBA Groups 12 and 13 Archaeological Review* 7 (1972), 64

'Medieval Britain in 1978', L E Webster and J Cherry, *Medieval Archaeology* 23 (1979), 262, 268–69

'Medieval Britain and Ireland in 1987', S M Youngs [*et al*], *ibid* 32 (1988), 272–73

'Medieval Britain and Ireland in 1992', B S Nenk, S Margeson and M Hurley, *ibid* 37 (1993), 282

'Medieval Britain and Ireland in 1993', B S Nenk, S Margeson and M Hurley, *ibid* 38 (1994), 248

'Medieval Britain and Ireland in 1994', B S Nenk, S Margeson and M Hurley, *ibid* 39 (1995), 240

'Post-medieval archaeology in Britain in 1977', J Cherry, *Post-Medieval Archaeology* 12 (1978), 110

'Post-medieval Britain and Ireland in 1994', M Ponsford and R Jackson, *ibid* 29 (1995), 131

Post-medieval Britain and Ireland in 1996', M Ponsford and R Jackson, *ibid* 31 (1997), 263

'Post-medieval fieldwork in Britain and Northern Ireland in 2004', M Ponsford, *ibid* 39 (2005), 388

'The history of Taunton Castle in the light of recent excavations', C A R Radford, *Proceedings of the Somersetshire Archaeological and Natural History Society* 98 (1953), 55–96*

'Further excavations at Taunton Castle, 1964', A D Hallam, *ibid* 109 (1964–5), 98–103*

'Some 13th century building accounts for Taunton Castle', T J Hunt, *ibid* 115 (1970), 39–44

'Castle House, Taunton Castle', R Taylor, *ibid* 118 (1973–4), 25–27*

'Somerset archaeology 1976', M Aston (ed), *Somerset Archaeology and Natural History* 121 (1977), 121

'Taunton, Mill Lane', I Burrow, in I Burrow, S Minnitt and B Murless (eds), 'Somerset archaeology, 1980', *ibid* 125 (1981), 99

'Somerset archaeology 1987', E Dennison (ed), *ibid* 131 (1987), 221, 223

'Taunton, Taunton Castle', J Hawkes [*et al*], in C J Webster and R A Croft (eds), 'Somerset archaeology 1992', *ibid* 136 (1992), 175–76

Wells
'The Bishop's Palace, Wells, Somerset', M Binney, *Country Life* 158 (1975), 1666–69, 1738–41*

Yeovil
Yeovil: the hidden history. B and M Gittos. Stroud: Tempus, 2004*

STAFFORDSHIRE

Cantor, L M. 'The medieval castles of Staffordshire', *North Staffordshire Journal of Field Studies* 6 (1966), 38–46*

Graham-Kerr, A. 'The Tamworth to Burton-on-Trent stopline', *West Midlands Archaeology* 36 (1993), 35–36

Hunt, J. *Lordship and landscape: a documentary and archaeological study of the honor of Dudley c 1066–1322*. Oxford: J & E Hedges, 1997* (BAR British series; 264)

Palliser, D M. 'Staffordshire castles: a provisional list', *Staffordshire Archaeology* 1 (1972), 5–8*

Pevsner, N. *Staffordshire (The buildings of England)*. Harmondsworth: Penguin Books, 1974*

Salter, M. *The castles and moated mansions of Staffordshire and the West Midlands county*. Wolverhampton: Folly Publications, 1989*

Salter, M. *The castles and moated mansions of Staffordshire*. Malvern: Folly Publications, 1997* [2nd edition of the above entry]

Alton
'Medieval Britain and Ireland in 1988', D R M Gaimster, S Margeson and T Barry, *Medieval Archaeology* 33 (1989), 207

'Alton Castle, recording of castle structure', A Simpson, *West Midlands Archaeology* 31 (1988), 19

Biddulph
'Excavations at Lea Forge, Biddulph, 1967: interim survey', J D Bestwick, *Biddulph Historical Society Publication* 1 (1968), 6–9*

Chartley
'Medieval Britain and Ireland in 1998', J Bradley, M Gaimster and C Haith, *Medieval Archaeology* 43 (1999), 279

'Chartley, Chartley Castle', I Soden, A Thorne and T Baker, *West Midlands Archaeology* 41 (1998), 72–73*

Dudley
Dudley Castle Archaeological Project: an introduction and summary of excavations 1983–1985. P Boland (ed). Dudley: Dudley Castle Archaeological Project, 1985*

Dudley as it was and as it is today. G Chandler and I C Hannah. London: Batsford, 1949*

Dudley Castle guide & commemoration brochure to celebrate the visit of Her Majesty Queen Elizabeth II 24 June 1994. B Moore and A Guest. Dudley: Dudley Metropolitan Borough Council, 1994*

Animals, economy and status: integrating zooarchaeological and historical data in the study of Dudley Castle, West Midlands (c 1100–1750). R Thomas. Oxford: Archaeopress, 2005* (BAR British series; 392)

'Food for dogs? The consumption of horseflesh at Dudley Castle in the eighteenth century', R Thomas and M Locock, *Environmental Archaeology* 5 (2000), 83–91*

'Medieval Britain and Ireland in 1984', S M Youngs, J Clark and T Barry, *Medieval Archaeology* 29 (1985), 203–5*

'Medieval Britain and Ireland in 1985', S M Youngs, J Clark and T Barry, *ibid* 30 (1986), 172

'Medieval Britain and Ireland in 1986', S M Youngs, J Clark and T Barry, *ibid* 31 (1987), 166–67

'Medieval Britain and Ireland in 1987', S M Youngs [*et al*], *ibid* 32 (1988), 286

'Medieval Britain and Ireland in 1994', B S Nenk, S Margeson and M Hurley, *ibid* 39 (1995), 258

'Post-medieval Britain in 1984', G Egan, *Post-medieval Archaeology* 19 (1985), 162–63*

'Post-medieval Britain in 1986', G Egan, *ibid* 21 (1987), 269–70

'The archaeology of private life: the Dudley Castle condoms', D Gaimster [*et al*], *ibid* 30 (1996), 129–42*

'The use of video cameras for archaeological recording: a practical evaluation at Dudley Castle, West Midlands', M Locock, *Scottish Archaeological Review* 7 (1990), 146–49

'The post-medieval coarsewares from the motte and keep of Dudley Castle', S Rátkai, *Staffordshire Archaeological Studies* 4 (1987), 1–11* [published 1990]

'Dudley Castle archaeological project: first interim report (1983–1984)', P Boland, *West Midlands Archaeology* 27 (1984), 1–20*

'Dudley Castle archaeological project: summary report 1984–1985', P Boland, *ibid* 28 (1985), 23–30*

'Dudley, Dudley Castle archaeological project', M Locock, *ibid* 31 (1988), 45–47*

'Dudley, Dudley Castle, a recently conserved small find', anon, *ibid* 31 (1988), 47*

'Dudley, Dudley Castle archaeological project', S J Linnane, *ibid* 32 (1989), 98

'Dudley, watching brief at Green man Entry', P Boland, *ibid* 32 (1989), 98–101*

'Dudley, Dudley Castle archaeological project', S J Linnane, *ibid* 34 (1991), 89–91*

'Dudley, Dudley Castle: a note on some excavated window glass', S J Linnane, *ibid* 34 (1991), 91–92*

'Dudley, castle', C Mould, *ibid* 37 (1994), 105–8*

'Flights of fancy over Dudley Castle', A Durkin, *ibid* 41 (1998), 13–15*

Eccleshall
'Post-medieval Britain in 1974', J Cherry, *Post-Medieval Archaeology* 9 (1975), 241

Gailey
'Gailey, Staffs', I Newcomb, *CBA Group 8 News Sheet* 9 (1966), 8

Lichfield
'Boundaries and gates', N J Tringham, in M W Greenslade (ed), *The Victoria history of the counties of England. A history of the county of Stafford*, **14**, 39–40. Oxford: OUP, for the Institute of Historical Research, 1990

'Medieval Britain and Ireland in 1986', S M Youngs, J Clark and T Barry, *Medieval Archaeology* 31 (1987), 159

'Medieval Britain and Ireland in 1987', S M Youngs [*et al*], *ibid* 32 (1988), 274–75

Newcastle-under-Lyme
'Castle', in J G Jenkins (ed), *The Victoria history of the counties of England. A history of the county of Stafford*, **8**, 11–15. Oxford: OUP, 1967

'Newcastle, castle site', S H Beaver, *Archaeological Journal* 120 (1963), 289

Stafford

Stafford Castle: a brief history. Anon. [Stafford]: Stafford Borough Council, [*c* 1989]*

Stafford Castle: survey, excavation and research 1978–98. 1. The surveys. J Darlington (ed). Stafford: Stafford Borough Council, 2001*

'Castle', in L M Midgley (ed), *The Victoria history of the counties of England. A history of the county of Stafford*, **5**, 84–86. Oxford: OUP, 1959*

'The Stafford Castle project', J Darlington, *Castle Studies Group Newsletter* 10 (1996–7), 37

'Stafford, Staffordshire', C Hill, *CBA Newsletter and Calendar* 4 (1980–1), 129

'Stafford Castle', C Hill, *ibid* 5 (1981–2), 149

'Stafford, Tenterbanks', P H Robinson, *CBA Group 8 News Sheet* 12 (1969), 32

'Medieval Britain in 1978', L E Webster and J Cherry, *Medieval Archaeology* 23 (1979), 262

'Medieval Britain in 1980', S M Youngs and J Clark, *ibid* 25 (1981), 202

'Medieval Britain and Ireland in 1984', S M Youngs, J Clark and T Barry, *ibid* 29 (1985), 198–99*

'Medieval Britain and Ireland in 1986', S M Youngs, J Clark and T Barry, *ibid* 31 (1987), 159

'Medieval Britain and Ireland in 1990', B S Nenk, S Margeson and M Hurley, *ibid* 35 (1991), 185

'Medieval Britain and Ireland in 1991', B S Nenk, S Margeson and M Hurley, *ibid* 36 (1992), 261

'Medieval Britain and Ireland in 1993', B S Nenk, S Margeson and M Hurley, *ibid* 38 (1994), 250

'Master John of Burcestre and the castles of Stafford and Maxstoke', M J B Hislop, *Transactions of the South Staffordshire Archaeological and Historical Society* 33 (1991–2), 14–20

'Stafford Castle', P A Barker, *West Midlands Archaeological News Sheet* 21 (1978), 93–94

'Stafford Castle, Staffordshire: excavation and survey at castle and DMV', C Hill, *West Midlands Archaeology* 23 (1980), 113

'Stafford Castle, Staffordshire', C Moffett, *ibid* 26 (1983), 117–19

'Stafford Castle: the development of an amenity', anon, *ibid* 27 (1984), 122–23

'Stafford Castle 1985', W D Klemperer, *ibid* 28 (1985), 15–17*

'Stafford Castle 1986', W D Klemperer, *ibid* 29 (1986), 38–39

'Stafford Castle', J Gale, *ibid* 31 (1988), 23–24*

'Stafford, castle', S Tomson, *ibid* 32 (1989), 79

'Stafford, Stafford Castle', S J N Tomson, *ibid* 33 (1990), 78

'Stafford, excavation at Stafford Castle', J Darlington, *ibid* 34 (1991), 65

'Stafford, geophysical survey at Stafford Castle', J Darlington, *ibid* 34 (1991), 65–68*

'Stafford, excavation at Stafford Castle', J Darlington, *ibid* 35 (1992), 46–47*

'Stafford, Stafford Castle', C Hewitson, *ibid* 46 (2003), 102–3

Tamworth

Tamworth Castle Museum. Anon. Tamworth: Tamworth Borough Council, 1987*

'Tamworth', J Gould, *Archaeological Excavations 1967*, 23. London: HMSO, 1968

'Tamworth, the castle', T E McNeill, *Archaeological Excavations 1972*, 104–5. London: HMSO, 1973

'Tamworth Castle', C A R Radford, *Archaeological Journal* 120 (1963), 296–97*

'The timber frame of the hall at Tamworth Castle, Staffordshire, and its context', R Meeson, *ibid* 140 (1983), 329–40*

'Tamworth', anon, *CBA Group 8 News Sheet* 3 (1960), 8

'Tamworth, town defences', J Gould, *ibid* 10 (1967), 16

'Tamworth', [A Selkirk], *Current Archaeology* 3.6 (1971), 164–68*

'First report of the excavations at Tamworth, Staffs, 1967: the Saxon defences', J Gould, *Transactions of the Lichfield and South Staffordshire Archaeological and Historical Society* 9 (1967–8), 17–29*

'Medieval Britain in 1960', D M Wilson and D G Hurst, *Medieval Archaeology* 5 (1961), 319

'Medieval Britain in 1967', D M Wilson and D G Hurst, *ibid* 12 (1968), 185

'Medieval Britain in 1968', D M Wilson and D G Hurst, *ibid* 13 (1969), 239

'Medieval Britain in 1970', D M Wilson and D G Hurst, *ibid* 15 (1971), 156

'Medieval Britain in 1971', L E Webster and J Cherry, *ibid* 16 (1972), 161, 190

'Medieval Britain in 1972', L E Webster and J Cherry, *ibid* 17 (1973), 163

'Medieval defences, Albert Road', K Sheridan, *Transactions of the South Staffordshire Archaeological and Historical Society* 14 (1972–3), 32–37*

'Seventh report of excavations at Tamworth, Staffs: a section through the northern defences excavated by Dr F T Wainwright in 1960', K Sheridan, *ibid* 14 (1972–3), 38–44*

'Ninth report of excavations at Tamworth, Staffs, 1972. A section through the north defences at Bell Inn Corner', K W Sheridan, *ibid* 16 (1975), 54–57*

'Tenth Tamworth excavation report, 1977: the Norman bailey defences of the castle', R A Meeson, *ibid* 20 (1978–9), 15–28*

'Excavations at Tamworth Castle, 1972 and 1974', T E McNeill, *ibid* 29 (1987–8), 1–54* [whole issue]

'Albert Road, Tamworth, Staffs', K W Sheridan, *West Midlands Archaeological News Sheet* 14 (1971), 23

'Tamworth Castle, Staffs', T E McNeill, *ibid* 15 (1972), 27–28*

'Tamworth, castle', J Cane, *West Midlands Archaeology* 32 (1989), 80

Tutbury

A guide to Tutbury Castle, Staffordshire. [Text based on 1960 version by R Somerville]. Revised edition. London: Duchy of Lancaster, 1990*

Tutbury Castle. Anon. [Tour by R Somerville]. Tutbury: Tutbury Castle, 2000*

'Tutbury Castle', R Somerville, *Archaeological Journal* 120 (1963), 276–78*

'Tutbury Castle', M Hislop, *Castle Studies Group Journal* 19 (2006), 150–51*

'Tutbury Castle', G Williams, *Current Archaeology* 17.11 (2006), 586–91*

'Medieval Britain and Ireland in 1988', D R M Gaimster, S Margeson and T Barry, *Medieval Archaeology* 33 (1989), 207

'Tutbury, Tutbury Castle', M Neil and A Simpson, *West Midlands Archaeology* 31 (1988), 25–26

'Tutbury, Tutbury Castle', G Barratt and M Hislop, *ibid* 47 (2004), 58–60*

SUFFOLK

Cligman, J and Crowe, N. *Exploring England's heritage: Hertfordshire to Norfolk*. London: HMSO, in association with English Heritage, 1994* [ch 2]

Kedney, R J. 'Castles in Suffolk', *Lowestoft Archaeological and Local History Society Annual Report* (1967–8), 33–36*

Kent, P. *Fortifications of East Anglia*. Lavenham: Dalton, 1988*

Kent, P. 'Coastal fortifications, 1500–1900', in D Dymond and E Martin (eds), *An historical atlas of Suffolk*, 3rd edition, 184–85, 217–18. Ipswich: Suffolk County Council, 1999*

Kent, P. Fortifications of the two world wars', in *ibid*, 186–87, 218*

Kent, P. 'East Anglian fortifications in the twentieth century', *Fortress* 3 (1989), 43–57*

Liddiard, R. 'Early castles in the medieval landscape of East Anglia', *Château Gaillard* 22 (2006), 243–50*

Marten-Holden, L. 'Dominion in the landscape: early Norman castles in Suffolk', *History Today* 51.4 (2001), 46–52*

Martin, E. 'Medieval castles', in D Dymond and E Martin (eds), *An historical atlas of Suffolk*, 3rd edition, 58–59, 198–99. Ipswich: Suffolk County Council, 1999*

Newsome, S. 'The coastal landscapes of Suffolk during the Second World War', *Landscapes* 4.2 (2003), 42–58*

Pawsey, J T. *Castles of East Anglia*. Ipswich: F W Pawsey, 1973*

Pevsner, N. *Suffolk (The buildings of England)*. 2nd edition, revised by E Radcliffe. Harmondsworth: Penguin Books, 1974*

Salter, M. *The castles of East Anglia*. Malvern: Folly Publications, 2001*

Bawdsey

'The defences of RAF Bawdsey', S Purcell, *Loopholes: Journal of the Pillbox Study Group* 19 (1997), 2–8*

Bungay

Bungay Castle: historical notes and account of the excavations. H Braun. Bungay: Morrow & Co for the Bungay Castle Trust, 1991* [first published in *Procs Suffolk Inst Archaeol & Nat Hist* for 1934 and 1935]

Bungay Castle guide. H Cane. Bungay: Bungay Castle Trust, 1988*

'Medieval Britain and Ireland in 1982', S M Youngs, J Clark and T B Barry, *Medieval Archaeology* 27 (1983), 204

'Medieval Britain and Ireland in 1983', S M Youngs, J Clark and T B Barry, *ibid* 28 (1984), 241

'Archaeology in Suffolk 1983', E Martin, J Plouviez and H Ross, *Proceedings of the Suffolk Institute of Archaeology and History* 35 (1981–4), 327

Burgh

Burgh Castle, Suffolk. Anon. London: HMSO, 1967*

Burgh Castle. J S Johnson. London: HMSO, 1978*

Burgh Castle, excavations by Charles Green, 1958–61. S Johnson. Dereham: Norfolk Archaeological Unit, 1983* (East Anglian Archaeology; 20)

'Burgh Castle', C Green, *Archaeological Excavations 1961*, 11. London: HMSO, 1962

'Medieval Britain in 1960', D M Wilson and D G Hurst, *Medieval Archaeology* 5 (1961), 319

Bury St Edmunds

'Medieval Britain in 1968', D M Wilson and D G Hurst, *Medieval Archaeology* 13 (1969), 267

'Medieval Britain and Ireland in 1993', B S Nenk, S Margeson and M Hurley, *ibid* 38 (1994), 250

'Medieval Britain and Ireland in 2000', J Bradley and M Gaimster, *ibid* 45 (2001), 319

'The excavation of the town defences at Tayfen Road, Bury St Edmunds, 1968', S E West, *Proceedings of the Suffolk Institute of Archaeology* 32 (1970–2), 17–24*

Clare

'Clare Castle', N J G Pounds, in N J G Pounds (ed), *The Colchester area: proceedings of the 139th summer meeting of the Royal Archaeological Institute, 1992*, 14–15. London: RAI, 1992*

'A find from the other Clare castle', P Holland, *North Munster Antiquarian Journal* 30 (1988), 54–55

Dunwich

'Dunwich', S E West, *Archaeological Excavations 1970*, 37. London: HMSO, 1971

'Dunwich', S E West, *CBA Group 7 Bulletin* 17 (1970), 19

'Medieval Britain in 1970', D M Wilson and S Moorhouse, *Medieval Archaeology* 15 (1971), 156

'Medieval Britain and Ireland in 1996', B S Nenk, C Haith and J Bradley, *ibid* 41 (1997), 287

'The excavation of Dunwich town defences, 1970', S E West, *Proceedings of the Suffolk Institute of Archaeology* 32 (1970–2), 25–37, 95*

Eye

An archaeological survey at Eye Castle, Suffolk. A Oswald. Cambridge: RCHME, 1994*

The history of Eye. C Paine. [S l]: Benyon de Beauvoir, 1993* [espec pp 4–5]

'Norman walls at Eye Castle', anon, *Ipswich Archaeological Trust News* 22 (1987), 1*

'Medieval Britain in 1979', L E Webster and J Cherry, *Medieval Archaeology* 24 (1980), 249

'Medieval Britain and Ireland in 1987', S M Youngs [*et al*], *ibid* 32 (1988), 275

'Medieval Britain and Ireland in 1990', B S Nenk, S Margeson and M Hurley, *ibid* 35 (1991), 186–87

'Medieval Britain and Ireland in 1996', B S Nenk, C Haith and J Bradley, *ibid* 41 (1997), 287

'Suffolk Archaeological Unit excavations, 1978', E A Martin, *Proceedings of the Suffolk Institute of Archaeology and History* 34 (1977–80), 218

'Eye, the castle motte and Kerrison's Folly', T Loader, in E Martin, C Pendleton and J Plouviez, 'Archaeology in Suffolk 1990', *ibid* 37.3 (1991), 267

Framlingham

Framlingham Castle, Suffolk. M Brown. London: English Heritage, 2003*

Framlingham and Orford castles: a handbook for teachers. J Fairclough. London: English Heritage, 1990*

Framlingham Castle, Suffolk. F J E Raby and P K Baillie Reynolds. London: HMSO, 1959*

Framlingham Castle, Suffolk. F J E Raby and P K Baillie Reynolds. London: HBMCE, 1987*

Framlingham and Orford castles. D Renn. London: HBMCE, 1988*

'Framlingham Castle and Bigod 1154–1216', R A Brown, in R A Brown, *Castles, conquest and charters: collected papers*, 187–208. Woodbridge: Boydell Press, 1989

'Framlingham Castle', J G Coad, *CBA Group 7 Bulletin* 17 (1970), 20

'An Englishman's home', M Morris, *Heritage Today* 74 (2006), 24–27*

'Medieval Britain in 1970', D M Wilson and S Moorhouse, *Medieval Archaeology* 15 (1971), 148

'Medieval Britain in 1974', L E Webster and J Cherry, *ibid* 19 (1975), 241

'Medieval Britain and Ireland in 1993', B S Nenk. S Margeson and M Hurley, *ibid* 38 (1994), 251

'The Framlingham Castle, Suffolk, hoard of *Cross-and-crosslets (Tealby)* and short cross coins, 1850', M Cross, *Numismatic Chronicle* 164 (2004), 282–85

'Framlingham Castle and Bigod, 1154–1216', R A Brown, *Proceedings of the Suffolk Institute of Archaeology* 25 (1949–51), 127–48*

'Excavations at Framlingham Castle, 1854', G M Knocker, *ibid* 27 (1956–8), 65–88*

'Recent excavations within Framlingham Castle', J G Coad, *ibid* 32 (1970–2), 152–63*

'Defending Framlingham Castle', D F Renn, *ibid* 33 (1973–6), 58–67*

'Archaeology in Suffolk, 1974', E J Owles, *ibid* 33 (1973–6), 215

Haughley

Haughley Crauford's CEVC Primary School (HGH015): archaeological excavations November 1999. J Meredith. Ipswich: Suffolk County Council, 2000*

'Medieval Britain and Ireland in 2004', M Gaimster and K O'Conor, *Medieval Archaeology* 49 (2005), 410

'Haughley Castle', S E West, *Proceedings of the Suffolk Institute of Archaeology and History* 34 (1977–80), 65–66*

Icklingham

'Icklingham', [Civil War sconce], in C J Balkwill, 'Archaeology in Suffolk: archaeological finds, 1978', *Proceedings of the Suffolk Institute of Archaeology and History* 34 (1977–80), 215

Ipswich

'Ipswich', S E West, *CBA Group 7 Bulletin* 6 (1959), 7

'Ipswich, Westgate Street', anon, *ibid* 14 (1967), 12

'Ipswich archaeological survey: second interim report', S Dunmore, T Loader and K Wade, *East Anglian Archaeology Suffolk* 3 (1976), 135–40*

'Medieval Britain in 1959', D M Wilson and J G Hurst, *Medieval Archaeology* 4 (1960), 150

'Medieval Britain in 1967', D M Wilson and D G Hurst, *ibid* 12 (1968), 185

'Medieval Britain in 1974', L E Webster and J Cherry, *ibid* 19 (1975), 248

'Medieval Britain and Ireland in 1982', S M Youngs, J Clark and T B Barry, *ibid* 27 (1983), 204

'Medieval Britain and Ireland in 2002', J Bradley and M Gaimster, *ibid* 47 (2003), 283

'Excavations at Cox Lane (1958), and at the town defences, Shire Hall Yard, Ipswich, (1959), S E West, *Proceedings of the Suffolk Institute of Archaeology* 28 (1961–3), 233–303*

'The West Gate of Ipswich', E Owles, *ibid* 32 (1970–2), 164–67*

'Archaeology in Suffolk, 1975', E J Owles, *ibid* 33 (1973–6), 325–26

Landguard

Suffolk invasion: the Dutch attack on Landguard Fort, 1667. F Hussey. Lavenham: Dalton, 1983*

Landguard Fort. P Pattison. London: English Heritage, 2006*

Landguard Fort, Felixstowe. D Rayner. Felixstowe: Felixstowe History and Museum Society, 1983*

An update on Landguard Fort, Felixstowe in Suffolk. D Rayner. Felixstowe: the author, [c 1995]*

Landguard Fort, Felixstowe. D A Wood. Privately published, 1983*; 3rd edition, 199?*

'Landguard Fort and batteries: conservation and management', R Linzey, *Conservation Bulletin* 44 (2003), 15–17*

'Thomas Hyde Page and Landguard Fort, 1778–1803', P Pattison, *English Heritage Historical Review* 1 (2006), 92–101*

'Left Battery at Landguard Fort', D Wood, *The Redan* 51 (2001), 9–16*

Orford

Orford Castle, Suffolk. R A Brown. London: HMSO, 1964*

Orford Castle, Suffolk. R A Brown. London: HBMCE, 1988*

Aerial photography. M Corbishley. London: English Heritage, 2004* (Education on site)

Framlingham and Orford castles: a handbook for teachers. J Fairclough. London: English Heritage, 1990*

The building of Orford Castle: a translation from the Pipe Rolls 1163–78. V Potter, M Poulter and J Allen. Orford: Orford Museum, 2002*

Framlingham and Orford castles. D Renn. London: HBMCE, 1988*

Orford Castle, Suffolk. J Rhodes. London: English Heritage, 2003*

'Orford Castle, nostalgia and sophisticated living', T A Heslop, in R Liddiard (ed), *Anglo-Norman castles*, 273–96. Woodbridge: Boydell Press, 2003*

'Orford Castle, nostalgia and sophisticated living', T A Heslop, *Architectural History* 34 (1991), 36–58*

'Medieval Britain and Ireland in 1995', B S Nenk, S Margeson and M Hurley, *Medieval Archaeology* 40 (1996), 284

'Suffolk Archaeological Unit excavations, 1978', E A Martin, *Proceedings of the Suffolk Institute of Archaeology and History* 34 (1977–80), 220

'Twelfth-century floor- and roof-tiles at Orford Castle', P J Drury and E C Norton, *ibid* 36.1 (1985), 1–7*

Sudbury

'Medieval Britain and Ireland in 1993', B S Nenk, S Margeson and M Hurley, *Medieval Archaeology* 38 (1994), 255

SURREY

Beanse, A and Gill, R. *The London mobilisation centres*. Fareham: Palmerston Forts Society, 2000*

Hamilton-Baillie, J. 'Strategic safeguard or military folly? London's Victorian forts', *Country Life* 180 (1986), 1560, 1562*

Nairn, I and Pevsner, N. *Surrey (The buildings of England)*. 2nd edition, revised by B Cherry. Harmondsworth: Penguin Books, 1971*

Salter, M. *The castles of Surrey*. Malvern: Folly Publications, 2001*

Smith, V T C. 'The London mobilisation centres', *London Archaeologist* 2.10 (1975), 244–48*

Smith, V T C. 'Chatham and London: the changing face of English land fortification, 1870–1918', *Post-Medieval Archaeology* 19 (1985), 105–49*

Turner, D J. 'Archaeology of Surrey, 1066–1540', in J Bird and D G Bird (eds), *The archaeology of Surrey to 1540*, 222–61. Guildford: Surrey Archaeological Society, 1987*

Turner, D J. 'The nineteenth century "forts" of the North Downs', *Surrey Archaeological Society Bulletin* 92 (1972), 4–5

Abinger

'The Norman motte at Abinger, Surrey, and its wooden castle', B Hope-Taylor, in R L S Bruce-Mitford (ed), *Recent archaeological excavations in Britain*, 223–49. London: Routledge and Kegan Paul, 1956*

'The excavation of a motte at Abinger in Surrey', B Hope-Taylor, *Archaeological Journal* 107 (1950), 15–43*

'William fitz Ansculf and the Abinger motte', J Blair, *ibid* 138 (1981), 146–48*

'The excavation of a motte at Abinger, Surrey, B Hope-Taylor, *Archaeological Newsletter* 3 (1950–1), 195–96

'New light on mottes', B Hope-Taylor, *Country Life* 109 (1951), 1528–30*

Ash Ranges
'Two late nineteenth-century military earthworks on Ash Ranges, near Aldershot, Surrey', J English, *Landscape History* 26 (2004), 87–93*

Banstead
'The earthworks on Banstead Heath: some fresh evidence as to their date', A W G Lowther, *Surrey Archaeological Collections* 50 (1946–7), 170

'Investigation on Walton Heath and Banstead Common', J M Prest and E J Parrish, *ibid* 51 (1949), 57–64* [espec pp 63–64]

Blechingley
'The Norman owners of Blechingley Castle: a review', D Turner, *ibid* 83 (1996), 37–56

'Bletchingley [*sic*] Castle excavation. Part I', D J Turner, *Surrey Archaeological Society Bulletin* 214 (1986), [4]

'Bletchingley Castle excavation. Part II', D J Turner, *ibid* 215 (1986), [3–5]

'Bletchingley Castle excavation. Part III', D J Turner, *ibid* 216 (1986–7), [3–4]

Chilworth
'The development of the Chilworth gunpowder works, Surrey, from the mid-19th century', W D Cocroft and C Tuck, *Industrial Archaeology Review* 27 (2005), 217–34*

Crawley
'A Bofors tower at Crawley', R Martin, *Loopholes* 23 (2002), [11–14]*

Farnham
Farnham Castle: the forgotten years. P D Brooks. Farnham: Farnham and District Museum Society, 1985*

Farnham Castle: a short history and guide. [H Holland]. [Farnham]: Centre for International Briefing, 1973*

Excavations at Borelli Yard, Farnham, Surrey, 1985–86. N Riall and V Shelton-Bunn. Farnham: Farnham and District Museum Society, 1989*

Farnham Castle keep, Surrey. M W Thompson. London: HMSO, 1961*

Farnham Castle keep, Surrey. M W Thompson. London: HBMCE, 1987*

Three palaces of the bishops of Winchester: Wolvesey (Old Bishop's Palace), Hampshire; Bishop's Waltham Palace, Hampshire; Farnham Castle keep, Surrey. J Wareham. London: English Heritage, 2000*

'Excavations at Farnham Castle', B Hope-Taylor, *Antiquity* 33 (1959), 124–25, 217

'Excavations at Farnham Castle keep, Surrey, England', M W Thompson, *Château Gaillard* 2 (1967), 100–5*

'Farnham Castle "grate chapel" investigation report', D Graham, *Farnham Museum Society Newsletter* 3.3 (1972), 11*

'Medieval Britain in 1958', D M Wilson and J G Hurst, *Medieval Archaeology* 3 (1959), 308

'Recent investigations in the keep of Farnham Castle, Surrey', M W Thompson, *ibid* 4 (1960), 81–94*

'Medieval Britain and Ireland in 1985', S M Youngs, J Clark and T Barry, *ibid* 30 (1986), 164–65

'Medieval Britain and Ireland in 1988', D R M Gaimster, S Margeson and T Barry, *ibid* 33 (1989), 210–11

'The new castles of Henry de Blois as bishop of Winchester: the case against Farnham, Surrey', N Riall, *ibid* 47 (2003), 115–29*

'Some late 12th- and early 13th-century great brick at Farnham Castle', N Riall, *Medieval Ceramics* 25 (2001), 22–26*

'The date of "Fox's Tower", Farnham Castle, Surrey', M W Thompson, *Surrey Archaeological Collections* 57 (1960), 85–92*

'Two late and post-medieval pottery groups from Farnham Castle, Surrey', S Moorhouse, *ibid* 68 (1971), 39–55*

'Archaeology in Surrey 1987', D G Bird, G Crocker and J S MacCracken, *ibid* 79 (1989), 182, 184*

'The town ditch and the early development of Farnham town and *borough*', P Parks, *ibid* 85 (1998), 114–18*

'Excavation at Borelli Yard, Farnham: the town ditch', N Riall, *ibid* 85 (1998), 120–32*

'Excavation between Castle Street and Bear lane, Farnham', R Poulton, *ibid* 85 (1998), 133–43*

'Discussion: the town ditch and the origins and early development of Farnham', R Poulton and N Riall, *ibid* 85 (1998), 145–51

'Farnham Park – a minor battlefield?', D Graham, *Surrey Archaeological Society Bulletin* 367 (2003), 12–13*

'Farnham Castle', D Graham, *ibid* 378 (2004), 1–3*

'Farnham Castle', D Graham, *ibid* 396 (2006), 3–4*

Godstone

'An excavation at Castle Hill, Godstone', M O'Connell and R Poulton, *Surrey Archaeological Collections* 74 (1983), 213–15* [possible castle]

Guildford

Guildford Castle. M Alexander. Guildford: Guildford Borough Council, 1999*

"With ramparts crown'd": the early history of Guildford Castle. M Alexander. Guildford: Guildford Museum, 2006*

The royal palace and castle at Guildford: its story as revealed by archaeological excavation. R Poulton. Guildford: Surrey Archaeological Society, [1998]*

A medieval royal complex at Guildford: excavations at the castle and palace. R Poulton. Guildford: Surrey Archaeological Society, 2005*

'Tracing the royals at home, in Guildford Castle and palace', R Poulton, *The Archaeologist* 60 (2006), 22–23*

'Medieval Britain and Ireland in 1990', B S Nenk, S Margeson and M Hurley, *Medieval Archaeology* 35 (1991), 191

'Medieval Britain and Ireland in 1991', B S Nenk, S Margeson and M Hurley, *ibid* 36 (1992), 267

'Medieval Britain and Ireland in 1992', B S Nenk, S Margeson and M Hurley, *ibid* 37 (1993), 283

'Medieval Britain and Ireland in 1993', B S Nenk, S Margeson and M Hurley, *ibid* 38 (1994), 255–56

'Medieval Britain and Ireland in 1994', B S Nenk, S Margeson and M Hurley, *ibid* 39 (1995), 250

'Guildford Castle', D J Turner, *Medieval Archaeology Newsletter* 3 (1990), 7

'The decoration of Guildford Castle keep', D F Renn, *Surrey Archaeological Collections* 55 (1958), 4–6*

'Conservation work at Guildford Castle keep', M Alexander, *Surrey Archaeological Society Bulletin* 371 (2003), 3–4*

Hungry Hill

'Survey of a post-medieval 'squatter' occupation site and 19th century military earthworks at Hungry Hill, Upper Hale, near Farnham', J English, *Surrey Archaeological Collections* 92 (2005), 245–53*

Reigate

'Medieval Britain and Ireland in 1988', D R M Gaimster, S Margeson and T Barry, *Medieval Archaeology* 33 (1989), 212

'Medieval Britain and Ireland in 1990', B S Nenk, S Margeson and M Hurley, *ibid* 35 (1991), 192

'Medieval Britain and Ireland in 1992', B S Nenk, S Margeson and M Hurley, *ibid* 37 (1993), 283–84

'Medieval Britain and Ireland in 1994', B S Nenk, S Margeson and M Hurley, *ibid* 39 (1995), 251

'Three sites in Reigate: 12–14 London Road, 20–22 and 74–76 High Street', D Williams, *Surrey Archaeological Collections* 92 (2005), 125–46*

Westcott

'A suggested location of Black Hawes 'castle' at Westcott', G Rapson, *Surrey Archaeological Society Bulletin* 357 (2002), 11–12*

'Castles at Westcott – some corrections', G Rapson, *ibid* 367 (2003), 13

SUSSEX

Beswick, M. 'Bricks for the martello towers in Sussex', *Sussex Industrial History* 17 (1987), 20–27*

Beswick, M. 'Bricks for the martello towers: further details', *ibid* 19 (1989), 36–37

Brown, M. 'War and rumour of war: the defences of Sussex 1530–1990', in D Rudling (ed), *The archaeology of Sussex to AD 2000*, 191–202. Great Dunham: Heritage Marketing Publications, 2003*

Goodwin, J. *Fortification of the south coast: the Pevensey, Eastbourne and Newhaven defences 1750–1945*. Goring-by-Sea: the author, 1994*

Goodwin, J. *The military defence of West Sussex*. Midhurst: Middleton Press, 1985*

Goodwin, J. 'Naval and military co-operation and control over invasion warnings, 1803', *Fortress* 15 (1992), 31–36*

Guy, J. *Castles in Sussex*. Chichester: Phillimore, 1984*

Holden, E W. 'Slate roofing in medieval Sussex: a reappraisal', *Sussex Archaeological Collections* 127 (1989), 73–88 + microfiche*

Jones, R. 'Castles and other defensive sites', in K Leslie and B Short (eds), *An historical atlas of Sussex*, 50–51. Chichester: Phillimore, 1999*

Jones, R. 'Hastings to Herstmonceux: the castles of Sussex', in D Rudling (ed), *The archaeology of Sussex to AD 2000*, 171–78. Great Dunham: Heritage Marketing Publications, 2003*

Kitchen, F. 'The building of the coastal towns' batteries', *Sussex Archaeological Society Newsletter* 45 (1985), 417 + illus on p 409*

Kitchen, F. 'The towers Twiss didn't build', *Sussex History* 2.10 (1986), 49–51

Kitchen, F. 'The defence of Sussex against Napoleon', *ibid* 22 (1986), 17–20

Leslie, K and Mace, M. 'Sussex defences in the Second World War', in K Leslie and B Short (eds), *An historical atlas of Sussex*, 118–19. Chichester: Phillimore, 1999*

Longstaff-Tyrrell, P. *Front-line Sussex: Napoleon Bonaparte to the Cold War*. Stroud: Tempus, 2000*

Lovegrove, H. 'The martello towers of England', *Mariner's Mirror* 52 (1966), 52

Mace, M F. *Frontline Sussex: the defence lines of West Sussex 1939–1945*. Storrington: Historic Military Press, 1996*

Mace, M F. *Sussex wartime relics and memorials: wrecks, relics & memorials from Sussex at war 1939–1945*. Storrington: Military Press, 1998*

Nairn, I and Pevsner, I. *Sussex (The buildings of England)*. Harmondsworth: Penguin Books, 1965*

Salter, M. *Castles of Sussex*. Wolverhampton: Folly Publications, 2000*

Saunders, A D. 'The coastal defences of the south-east', *Archaeological Journal* 126 (1969), 201–5*

Saunders, A D. 'The coastal defences of the south-east: a reassessment', *Ravelin* 39 (1994), 3–7

Vine, P A L. *The Royal Military Canal: an historical account of the waterway and military road from Shornecliffe in Kent to Cliff End in Sussex*. Newton Abbot: David and Charles, 1972*

Vine, P A L. 'In defence against the French: a history of the Royal Military Canal', *Country Life* 160 (1976), 892–94*

Woodburn, C W. 'Fortifications and defensive works 1500–1900', in K Leslie and B Short (eds), *An historical atlas of Sussex*, 102–3. Chichester: Phillimore, 1999*

Woodburn, C W and Guy, N. 'The Castle Studies Group conference – Worthing April 2005', *Castle Studies Group Journal* 19 (2006), 4–85*

Aldingbourne

'Aldingbourne', T C M Brewster, *Archaeological Excavations 1961*, 12. London: HMSO, 1962

'Aldingbourne', T C M Brewster, *Archaeological Excavations 1962*, 10. London: HMSO, 1963

'Medieval Britain in 1961', D M Wilson and D G Hurst, *Medieval Archaeology* 6–7 (1962–3), 323

'Medieval Britain in 1962 and 1963', D M Wilson and D G Hurst, *ibid* 8 (1964), 259

'Tote Copse Castle, Aldingbourne', T C M and A Brewster, *Sussex Archaeological Collections* 107 (1969), 141–79*

'Aldingbourne. Excavations at Tote Copse Castle', E W Holden, *Sussex Notes and Queries* 15 (1958–62), 332–33

ENGLAND

Amberley

Amberley Castle: hunting lodge, fortified manor, country castle hotel. D Arscott, historical research by A Hughes. Wimborne: Dovecote Press, 2002*

'Amberley Castle', K Gravett, *Archaeological Journal* 142 (1985), 60–61*

Arundel

Arundel Castle. J M Robinson. Arundel: Arundel Castle Trustees, n d*

Arundel Castle, a seat of the Duke of Norfolk EM: a short history and guide. J M Robinson. Chichester: Phillimore, 1994*

Plans elevations and particular measurements of Arundel Castle in Sussex belonging to His Grace Charles Howard Duke of Norfolk, Earl of Arundel, &c. &c. &c. F W Steer (ed). Arundel: His Grace the Duke of Norfolk, 1976*

'Arundel Castle and its owners', F Steer, *Connoisseur* 197 (1978), 155–61*

'Medieval Britain and Ireland in 1988', D R M Gaimster, S Margeson and T Barry, *Medieval Archaeology* 33 (1989), 213

'The siege castles at Arundel', P Purton, *Postern* 8 (1998), 13–14*

'A medieval gate in the earthworks surrounding the 'Little Park', Arundel, West Sussex', C Place, *Sussex Archaeological Collections* 130 (1992), 130–39*

Bodiam

Bodiam Castle, East Sussex. J Goodall. London: National Trust, 2001*; reprinted with corrections, 2005*

Bodiam Castle medieval bridges. D Martin. Robertsbridge: Robertsbridge and District Archaeological Society, 1973*

Bodiam Castle, Sussex. C Morton. London: National Trust, 1973*; new edition, 1979*

Bodiam Castle, Sussex. W D Simpson. London: National Trust, 1971*

Bodiam Castle, East Sussex. D Thackray. London: National Trust, 1991*

Bodiam Castle: an activity book for children. A Yarrow. Bodiam: Local Committee of Management for Bodiam Castle, 1982*

Bodiam Castle. A Yarrow. London: National Trust, 1985*

'Bodiam Castle, East Sussex: a fourteenth-century designed landscape', P Everson, in D M Evans, P Salway and D Thackray (eds), *'The remains of distant times': archaeology and the National Trust*, 66–72. Woodbridge: Boydell Press, 1996*

'Bodiam, Sussex: true castle or old soldier's dream house?', D J Turner, in W M Ormrod (ed), *England in the fourteenth century: proceedings of the 1985 Harlaxton Symposium*, 267–77. Woodbridge: Boydell Press, 1986*

'Some analysis of the castle of Bodiam, East Sussex', C Coulson, in C Harper-Bill and R Harvey (eds), *Medieval knighthood IV: papers from the fifth Strawberry Hill conference 1990*, 51–107. Woodbridge: Boydell Press, 1992*

'Bodiam Castle, East Sussex: castle and its designed landscape', P Everson, *Château Gaillard* 17 (1996), 79–84*

'To me the past is sacred', J Musson, *Country Life* 192.2 (1998), 34–37*

'The battle for Bodiam Castle', J Goodall, *ibid* 192.16 (1998), 58–63*

'Bodiam Castle: truth and tradition', C Coulson, *Fortress* 10 (1991), 3–15*

'Bodiam Castle', N Saul, *History Today* 45.1 (1995), 16–21*

'An English landscape garden before "The English landscape garden"?', M Leslie, *Journal of Garden History* 13 (1993), 3–15*

'The Bodiam mortar', R D Smith and R R Brown, *Journal of the Ordnance Society* 1 (1989), 3–22*

'Medieval Britain in 1970', D M Wilson and S Moorhouse, *Medieval Archaeology* 15 (1971), 148

'Bodiam Castle, Sussex', C Taylor, P Everson and R Wilson-North, *ibid* 34 (1990), 155–57*

'Medieval Britain and Ireland in 1990', B S Nenk, S Margeson and M Hurley, *ibid* 35 (1991), 193

'Medieval Britain and Ireland in 2001', J Bradley and M Gaimster, *ibid* 46 (2002), 158–59

'Dallingridge's bay and Bodiam Castle millpond: elements of a medieval landscape', C Whittick, *Sussex Archaeological Collections* 131 (1993), 119–23*

'A section through the moat bank at Bodiam Castle', S Stevens, *ibid* 137 (1999), 182–83*

'Bodiam Castle', D Martin, *Sussex Archaeological Society Newsletter* 2 (1971), 2

'Recovery of a missing gift', G Barker, *ibid* 52 (1987), 18

Bramber

'Castle', in T P Hudson (ed), *The Victoria history of the counties of England. A history of the county of Sussex. 6.1. Bramber rape (southern part)*, 204–6. Oxford: OUP, for the Institute of Historical Research, 1980*

'Five castle excavations: reports on the Institute's research into the origins of the castle in England. Excavations at Bramber Castle, Sussex, 1966–67', K J Barton and E W Holden, *ibid* 134 (1977), 11–79*

'Bramber Castle', E W Holden, *Archaeological Journal* 142 (1985), 27

'Bramber castle: excavations 1966 & 1967', [A Selkirk], *Current Archaeology* 1.5 (1967), 131–32*

'Medieval Britain in 1966', D M Wilson and D G Hurst, *Medieval Archaeology* 11 (1967), 285–86

'Medieval Britain in 1967', D M Wilson and D G Hurst, *ibid* 12 (1968), 178

'Medieval Britain and Ireland in 1987', S M Youngs [*et al*], *ibid* 32 (1988), 278

'Excavations at Bramber Castle, 1966', K J Barton and E W Holden, *Sussex Notes and Queries* 16 (1963–7), 256–58

'Excavations at Bramber Castle, 1967', K J Barton and E W Holden, *ibid* 16 (1963–7), 333–35

Brighton

'The making of Francis Grose's *Antiquities*: evidence from Sussex', J H Farrant, *Sussex Archaeological Collections* 131 (1993), 152–58*

'Brighton's batteries', F Kitchen, *Sussex History* 21 (1986), 2–13*

Burlough

'Burlough Castle or Middleton Castle', R Musson, *Sussex Notes and Queries* 14 (1954–7), 10–22

Camber

Henry VIII's coastal artillery fort at Camber Castle, Rye, East Sussex: an archaeological, structural and historical investigation. M Biddle, J Hiller, I Scott and A Streeten. Oxford: Oxford Archaeological Unit for English Heritage, 2001*

'Medieval Britain in 1962 and 1963', D M Wilson and D G Hurst, *Medieval Archaeology* 8 (1964), 259–60

'A note on the results of recent excavations at Camber Castle, Sussex', H S Ames, *Post-Medieval Archaeology* 9 (1975), 233–36*

'Post-medieval Britain in 1982', G Egan, *ibid* 17 (1983), 186

'Interim report on excavations at Camber Castle, East Sussex, 1982', A Streeten, *Sussex Archaeological Society Newsletter* 39 (1983), 316*

Chichester

Chichester excavations 1. A Down and M Rule. Chichester: Phillimore, 1971*

The archaeology of Chichester city walls. A E Wilson. Chichester: Chichester Papers, 1957*

'Medieval Britain and Ireland in 1984', S M Youngs, J Clark and T Barry, *Medieval Archaeology* 29 (1985), 202

'Medieval Britain and Ireland in 1990', B S Nenk, S Margeson and M Hurley, *ibid* 35 (1991), 193–94

'Medieval Britain and Ireland in 2000', J Bradley and M Gaimster, *ibid* 45 (2001), 331

'Medieval Britain and Ireland in 2005', M Gaimster and K O'Conor, *ibid* 50 (2006), 352

'Post-medieval Britain and Ireland in 1998 and 1999', M Ponsford, *Post-Medieval Archaeology* 34 (2000), 307

Church Norton

' "The Mound" at Church Norton, Selsey, and the site of St Wilfrid's Church', F G Aldsworth, *Sussex Archaeological Collections* 117 (1979), 103–7*

'Excavations on "The Mound" at Church Norton, Selsey, in 1911 and 1965', F G Aldsworth and E D Garnett, *ibid* 119 (1981), 217–21*

Clay Hill

'Anarchy in Sussex', R Jones, *Sussex Past & Present* 89 (1999), 6*

Eastbourne

Tower 73: the Wish Tower, Eastbourne. D Galer. Eastbourne: Borough of Eastbourne, n d

The Great Redoubt, Eastbourne. S Guise. Eastbourne: Eastbourne Borough Council, 1979

The Redoubt fortress and Martello towers of Eastbourne 1804–2004. R Milton and R Callaghan. Eastbourne: Eastbourne Local History Society, 2005*

'Fortress to museum of defence: the Great Redoubt, Eastbourne, Sussex', J N P Watson, *Country Life* 166 (1979), 860, 862*

'Circular masonry redoubt', J E Goodwin, *Fort* 2 (1976), 5–6*

Hartfield

'Medieval Britain in 1975', L E Webster and J Cherry, *Medieval Archaeology* 20 (1976), 185

'Castle Field, Hartfield', C F Tebbutt, *Sussex Archaeological Collections* 118 (1980), 377–78

Hastings

The story of Hastings Castle. W H Dyer. Hastings: Hastings Tourism and Recreation Department, [?1979]*

'Evidence for a pre-Conquest origin for the chapels in Hastings and Pevensey castles', A Taylor, in A Taylor, *Studies in castles and castle-building*, 233–40. London: Hambledon Press, 1986*

'Excavations at Hastings Castle, 1968', P A Barker, *Archaeological Journal* 125 (1968), 303–5

'Five castle excavations: report on the Institute's research into the origins of the castle in England. Excavations at Hastings Castle, 1968', P A Barker and K J Barton, *ibid* 134 (1977), 80–100*

'Evidence for a pre-Conquest origin for the chapels in Hastings and Pevensey castles', A J Taylor, *Château Gaillard* 3 (1969), 144–51*

'Medieval Britain in 1968', D M Wilson and D G Hurst, *Medieval Archaeology* 13 (1969), 260

'Medieval Britain and Ireland in 1985', S M Youngs, J Clark and T Barry, *ibid* 30 (1986), 167

'Medieval Britain and Ireland in 1992', B S Nenk, S Margeson and M Hurley, *ibid* 37 (1993), 284

Herstmonceux

A history of Herstmonceux Castle. D Calvert and R Martin. Kingston, Ontario: Queen's University; Hailsham: Herstmonceux Castle, 1994*

'A medieval masterpiece: Herstmonceux Castle, Sussex', J A A Goodall, *Burlington Magazine* 146 (2004), 516–25*

'How meaningful were the defences of Herstmonceux Castle?', A Emery, *Castle Studies Group Bulletin* 18 (2004–5), 169–82*

Isfield

'Recent work on the earthworks at Isfield, East Sussex', M Gardiner, *Sussex Archaeological Collections* 130 (1992), 140–46*

Lewes

Lewes Castle. W H Godfrey. Lewes: Sussex Archaeological Society, 1972*

Lewes Castle & Barbican House Museum. H Poole. Lewes: Sussex Archaeological Society, 1997*

Lewes Castle. A Yarrow. Lewes: Sussex Archaeological Society, 1983*

'Rich man, poor man: an archaeological comparison of the economy of a castles and a farm in East Sussex, England, *c* 1100–1500 AD', P Drewett, in J Kubková [*et al*] (eds), *Life in the archaeology of the Middle Ages*, 160–68. Prague: Peres, 1997*

'Lewes', D Thomson, *Archaeological Excavations 1967*, 24. London: HMSO, 1968

'Excavations at Lewes, East Sussex', D Freke, in P Drewett (ed), 'Rescue archaeology in Sussex, 1974: a progress report on the Sussex Archaeological Field Unit', *Bulletin of the Institute of Archaeology* 12 (1975), 52–58*

'Digging in to defend Lewes', anon, *Sussex Past and Present* 75 (1995), 7*

'Medieval Britain in 1962 and 1963', D M Wilson and D G Hurst, *Medieval Archaeology* 8 (1964), 260

'Medieval Britain in 1970', D M Wilson and S Moorhouse, *ibid* 15 (1971), 148

'Medieval Britain and Ireland in 1986', S M Youngs, J Clark and T Barry, *ibid* 31 (1987), 162

'Medieval Britain and Ireland in 1987', S M Youngs [*et al*], *ibid* 32 (1988), 278

'Excavations in Lewes, 1974', D J Freke, *Sussex Archaeological Collections* 113 (1975), 66–84*

'The archaeology of Lewes: some recent research', D R Rudling, *ibid* 121 (1983), 45–77*

'A trial excavation in Castle Ditch Lane, Lewes, East Sussex', D Rudling, *ibid* 122 (1984), 222

'Excavations at Lewes Castle, East Sussex 1985–1988', P L Drewett, *ibid* 130 (1992), 69–106 + microfiche*

' "A garden in a desert place and a palace among the ruins": Lewes Castle transformed, 1600–1850', J H Farrant, *ibid* 134 (1996), 169–77*

'A Romano-British (?) barrow cemetery and the origins of Lewes', J Bleach, *ibid* 135 (1997), 131–42* [espec sites 6 & 8]

'An archaeological discovery on Brack Mount, Lewes, East Sussex', G Thomas, *ibid* 139 (2001), 224–27*

'Town defences, Lewes: rear of 11 Keere Street', R Lewis, *Sussex Archaeological Society Newsletter* 8 (1972), 2

'Lewes Castle excavations', P Drewett, *ibid* 50 (1986), 501–3*

'A palace among the ruins …', J H Farrant, *ibid* 52 (1987), 12–13*

'Excavations of the south-west motte 1985–88', P Drewett, *ibid* 56 (1988), 3–6*

'Lewes Castle', E W Holden, *Sussex Notes and Queries* 17 (1968–71), 184–88*

Lindfield
'Medieval Britain in 1968', D M Wilson and D G Hurst, *Medieval Archaeology* 13 (1969), 260

Littlehampton
'A description of the mid nineteenth century forts at Littlehampton and Shoreham, West Sussex', F G Aldsworth, *Sussex Archaeological Collections* 119 (1981), 181–93*

Lodsbridge
'Medieval Britain in 1964', D M Wilson and D G Hurst, *Medieval Archaeology* 9 (1965), 192

'The excavation of a motte at Lodsbridge Mill, Lodsworth', E W Holden, *Sussex Archaeological Collections* 105 (1967), 103–25*

Middleton
See Burlough

Midhurst
Midhurst. J Magilton and S Thomas. Chichester: Chichester District Council, 2001* (Chichester district archaeology; 1)

'Midhurst town and castle', M Hallam, *Archaeological Journal* 142 (1985), 57–58

Newhaven
Fort Newhaven. Anon. Derby: English Life, [?1983]

Newhaven and Seaford coastal fortifications. R J Goulden and A Kemp. Privately published, 1974*

'The guns that disappeared (part 4): the 9–inch RML of 12 tons', D Moore, *The Redan* 48 (2000), 9–18*

Old Erringham

'Excavations at Old Erringham, Shoreham, West Sussex, part II: the "chapel" and ringwork', E W Holden, *Sussex Archaeological Collections* 118 (1980), 257–97*

Pevensey

Pevensey Castle, East Sussex. J Goodall. London: English Heritage, 1999*

Pevensey Castle: a handbook for teachers. D Meades. London: English Heritage, 1991*

Pevensey Castle. C Peers (abridged). London: HMSO, 1946*

Pevensey Castle, Sussex. D F Renn. London: HMSO, 1970*

'Evidence for a pre-Conquest origin for the chapels in Hastings and Pevensey castles', A Taylor, in A Taylor, *Studies in castles and castle-building*, 233–40. London: Hambledon Press, 1986*

'A Norman pit at Pevensey Castle and its contents', G C Dunning, *Antiquaries Journal* 38 (1958), 205–17*

'Evidence for a pre-Conquest origin for the chapels in Hastings and Pevensey castles', A J Taylor, *Château Gaillard* 3 (1969), 144–51*

'Medieval Britain in 1961', D M Wilson and D G Hurst, *Medieval Archaeology* 6–7 (1962–3), 323–24

'Medieval Britain in 1964', D M Wilson and D G Hurst, *ibid* 9 (1965), 192

'Medieval Britain and Ireland in 1993', B S Nenk, S Margeson and M Hurley, *ibid* 38 (1994), 257–58*

'Medieval Britain and Ireland in 1994', B S Nenk, S Margeson and M Hurley, *ibid* 39 (1995), 252

'Medieval Britain and Ireland in 1995', B S Nenk, S Margeson and M Hurley, *ibid* 40 (1996), 288

'The *turris de Penuesel*: a reappraisal and a theory', D F Renn, *Sussex Archaeological Collections* 109 (1971), 55–64*

'Lords, castellans, constables and dowagers: the rape of Pevensey from the 11th to the 13th century', K Thompson, *ibid* 135 (1997), 209–20

'Early motte evidence at Pevensey', [based on report by M Fulford], *Sussex Past and Present* 72 (1994), 7*

'The Romans in Pevensey', M Fulford, *ibid* 74 (1994), 8–9*

Pevensey Bay

'Martello tower no 60, Pevensey Bay', S E Rigold, *Archaeological Journal* 116 (1959), 236

Pulborough

'Park mound, Pulborough', K M E Murray, *Sussex Notes and Queries* 15 (1958–62), 145–47

Rye

The story of the Ypres Tower and Rye Museum. Anon. Rye: Rye Museum, 1978*

'The castles of Rye and Winchelsea', D F Renn, *Archaeological Journal* 136 (1979), 193–202*

'Rye, Sussex – 1. The medieval town', A Oswald, *Country Life* 117 (1955), 36–39*

'Medieval Britain and Ireland in 1993', B S Nenk, S Margeson and M Hurley, *Medieval Archaeology* 38 (1994), 257, 259

'Medieval Britain and Ireland in 1994', B S Nenk, S Margeson and M Hurley, *ibid* 39 (1995), 253

'Medieval Britain and Ireland in 1999', J Bradley and M Gaimster, *ibid* 44 (2000), 306

'Medieval Britain and Ireland in 2001', J Bradley and M Gaimster, *ibid* 46 (2002), 159

'An excavation at 1–3 Tower Street, Rye, East Sussex', J Hadfield, *Sussex Archaeological Collections* 119 (1981), 222–25*

'Rye and the defence of the narrow seas: a 16th-century town at war', G J Mayhew, *ibid* 122 (1984), 107–26*

Seaford

Newhaven and Seaford coastal fortifications. R J Goulden and A Kemp. Privately published, 1974*

Shoreham

'Shoreham Fort', F G Aldsworth, *Archaeological Journal* 142 (1985), 23–24*

'Excavations in Southdown Road, Shoreham-by-sea', F H Witten, *Sussex Archaeological Collections* 116 (1978), 393–96*

'A description of the mid nineteenth century forts at Littlehampton and Shoreham, West Sussex', F G Aldsworth, *ibid* 119 (1981), 181–93*

Tottingworth

'An earthwork at Tottingworth, Heathfield', M Gardiner, *ibid* 131 (1993), 68–72*

Winchelsea

New Winchelsea, Sussex: a medieval port town. D and B Martin. Great Dunham: Heritage Marketing and Publications, 2004* (Institute of Archaeology, University College London, Field Archaeology Unit monograph; 2)

Excavations in Winchelsea, Sussex, 1974–2000. D Martin and D Rudling (eds). Great Dunham: Heritage Marketing and Publications, 2004* (Institute of Archaeology, University College London, Field Archaeology Unit monograph; 3)

'Winchelsea: a medieval new town', D Martin, in K Leslie and B Short (eds), *An historical atlas of Sussex*, 44–45. Chichester: Phillimore, 1999*

'The castles of Rye and Winchelsea', D F Renn, *Archaeological Journal* 136 (1979), 193–202*

'Further fieldwork at Winchelsea, East Sussex', D R Rudling and P Leach, in O Bedwin (ed), 'Rescue archaeology in Sussex, 1982: a ninth progress report on the Sussex Archaeological Field Unit', *Bulletin of the Institute of Archaeology* 20 (1983), 95–98*

'Medieval Britain in 1980', S M Youngs and J Clark, *Medieval Archaeology* 25 (1981), 213

'Medieval Britain and Ireland in 1982', S M Youngs, J Clark and T B Barry, *ibid* 27 (1983), 205

'Medieval Britain and Ireland in 1983', S M Youngs, J Clark and T B Barry, *ibid* 28 (1984), 242

'Medieval Britain and Ireland in 2001', J Bradley and M Gaimster, *ibid* 46 (2002), 160

'Winchelsea', D Rudling, *Sussex Archaeological Society Newsletter* 39 (1983), 323

WARWICKSHIRE

Chatwin, P B. 'Castles in Warwickshire', *Transactions and Proceedings of the Birmingham Archaeological Society* 67 (1947–8), 1–34*

Pevsner, N and Wedgwood, A. *Warwickshire (The Buildings of England)*. Harmondsworth: Penguin Books, 1966*

Salter, M. *The castles and moated mansions of Warwickshire*. Malvern: Folly Publications, 1992*

Baginton

'Baginton Castle excavations, 1933–48', J H Edwards, *Transactions and Proceedings of the Birmingham Archaeological Society* 69 (1951), 44–49

'Medieval Britain in 1959', D M Wilson and J G Hurst, *Medieval Archaeology* 4 (1960), 146

'Medieval Britain and Ireland in 1994', B S Nenk, S Margeson and M Hurley, *ibid* 39 (1995), 256

'Baginton, Baginton Castle', P Moore and N Palmer, *West Midlands Archaeology* 37 (1994), 71–72

Beaudesert

'Henley in Arden (Warwickshire)', P B Chatwin, *Transactions and Proceedings of the Birmingham Archaeological Society* 73 (1955), 63–83*

Boteler's

'Excavations in the outer enclosure of Boteler's Castle, Oversley, Alcester, 1992–93', C Jones [*et al*], *Transactions of the Birmingham and Warwickshire Archaeological Society* 101 (1997), 1–99* [whole issue]

'Medieval Britain and Ireland in 1993', B S Nenk, S Margeson and M Hurley, *ibid* 38 (1994), 259–60

'Alcester, Oversley, Boteler's Castle', G Eyre-Morgan, *West Midlands Archaeology* 36 (1993), 80–81

Brandon

'Brandon Castle, Warwickshire', P B Chatwin, *Transactions and Proceedings of the Birmingham Archaeological Society* 73 (1955), 63–83*

Caludon

'Caludon Castle', V A Singer, *CBA Group 8 News Sheet* 9 (1966), 5

Castle Bromwich

'Castle Bromwich, the castle', W J Ford, *Archaeological Journal* 128 (1971), 214–15

'Castle Bromwich, Birmingham, motte and bailey', B Ford, *CBA Group 8 News Sheet* 12 (1969), 34–35

'Medieval Britain in 1970', D M Wilson and S Moorhouse, *Medieval Archaeology* 15 (1971), 148–49

Cheswick Green

'Excavations at the Mount, Cheswick Green, Shirley, Birmingham', T L Jones, *Transactions and Proceedings of the Birmingham Archaeological Society* 71 (1953), 80–95*

'The Mount, Cheswick Green', S J Taylor, *CBA Group 8 News Sheet* 16 (1973), 27

Coventry

Coventry: excavations on the town wall 1976–1978. J Bateman and M Redknap. Coventry: Coventry City Council, 1986*

Coventry's town wall. E Gooder. Coventry: Coventry and North Warwickshire History Pamphlets, 1971*

The excavations at Broadgate East, Coventry 1974–5. M Rylatt and M A Stokes. Coventry: Coventry Museums & Galleries, [1996]*

'The castle' and 'City walls and gates', in W B Stephens (ed), *The Victoria history of the counties of England: a history of the county of Warwick*, **8**, 18, 21–23. Oxford: OUP, 1969*

'Coventry', J C Lancaster, in M D Lobel (ed), *The atlas of historic towns*, **2**. London: Scolar Press, 1975*

'The walls of Coventry', E Gooder, C Woodfield and R E Chaplin, *Transactions and Proceedings of the Birmingham Archaeological Society* 81 (1963–4), 88–138*

'Medieval town defences', C Woodfield, *CBA Group 8 News Sheet* 3 (1960), 4

'Medieval town defences', C Woodfield, *ibid* 4 (1961), 4

'The city wall, Coventry', anon, *ibid* 8 (1965), 7

'Medieval Britain in 1960', D M Wilson and D G Hurst, *Medieval Archaeology* 5 (1961), 324–25*

'Medieval Britain in 1961', D M Wilson and D G Hurst, *ibid* 6–7 (1962–3), 330

'Medieval Britain in 1965', D M Wilson and D G Hurst, *ibid* 10 (1966), 200–1

'Medieval Britain in 1971', L E Webster and J Cherry, *ibid* 16 (1972), 183

'Medieval Britain in 1972', L E Webster and J Cherry, *ibid* 17 (1973), 171

'Medieval Britain in 1974', L E Webster and J Cherry, *ibid* 19 (1975), 241

'Medieval Britain in 1980', S M Youngs and J Clark, *ibid* 25 (1981), 214

'Medieval Britain in 1981', S M Youngs and J Clark, *ibid* 26 (1982), 212

'Medieval Britain and Ireland in 1986', S M Youngs, J Clark and T Barry, *ibid* 31 (1987), 166

'Medieval Britain and Ireland in 1987', S M Youngs [*et al*], *ibid* 32 (1988), 285

'Medieval Britain and Ireland in 1991', B S Nenk, S Margeson and M Hurley, *ibid* 36 (1992), 270–71

'Medieval Britain and Ireland in 2002', J Bradley and M Gaimster, *ibid* 47 (2003), 288

'Medieval Britain and Ireland in 2003', J Bradley and M Gaimster, *ibid* 48 (2004), 294

'Medieval Britain and Ireland in 2005', M Gaimster and K O'Conor, *ibid* 50 (2006), 350–51

'Post-medieval Britain and Ireland in 2002', M Ponsford, *Post-Medieval Archaeology* 37 (2003), 298

'Post-medieval Britain and Ireland in 2003', M Ponsford, *ibid* 38 (2004), 246

'Medieval town wall (Godiva Street), Coventry, 1970 and 1972', W Ford and B Hobley, *West Midlands Archaeological News Sheet* 15 (1972), 30

'Late medieval town defences, Coventry', J Bateman, *ibid* 21 (1978), 90–92*

'Excavation of medieval defensive ditch at New Law Courts, Earl Street', M A Stokes, *West Midlands Archaeology* 23 (1980), 83–84*

'Salvage recording of medieval defensive ditch at Kirby House', M Rylatt, *ibid* 23 (1980), 83

'Coventry: excavation of medieval defensive ditch at New Law Courts, Earl Street', M A Stokes, *ibid* 24 (1981), 63–64*

'Coventry, Fleet Street', M Rylatt and R Wallwork, *ibid* 30 (1987), 64

'Coventry, Parkside', M Rylatt and R Wallwork, *ibid* 30 (1987), 65

'Coventry, Hay Lane', M Rylatt and I Soden, *ibid* 33 (1990), 92–94*

'Coventry, Spon Street/Corporation Street', M Rylatt and I Soden, *ibid* 33 (1990), 95

'Coventry, the Cheylesmore', M Rylatt and I Soden, *ibid* 34 (1991), 88

'Coventry, Gosford Street', M Rylatt, I Soden and E Dickinson, *ibid* 34 (1991), 88

'Coventry, Shelton Square', anon, *ibid* 37 (1994), 105

'A Civil War redoubt at Coventry?', K D Lilley, *ibid* 38 (1995), 11–15*

'Coventry, town wall, Hill Street', C Coutts, *ibid* 46 (2003), 159–60

Hartshill

'Hartshill Castle and an issue of trust', M Wilson, *The Archaeologist* 60 (2006), 24–25*

'Medieval Britain and Ireland in 2004', M Gaimster and K O'Conor, *Medieval Archaeology* 49 (2005), 414

Kenilworth

Kenilworth Castle: an illustrated guide. Anon. London: HMSO, reprinted 1969*

Kenilworth Castle, Warwickshire. P K Baillie Reynolds. London: HMSO, reprinted 1969*

Kenilworth Castle illustrated. J Brandard; introduction by J H Drew. Buckingham: Barracuda, [*c* 1982]* [first published *c* 1865]

Kenilworth Castle: a handbook for teachers. T Copeland. London: English Heritage, 1990*

Kenilworth Castle. R K Morris. London: English Heritage, 2006*

Kenilworth Castle. D F Renn. London: HMSO, 1973*

Kenilworth Castle. D Renn. London: English Heritage, 1991*

Kenilworth Castle, Warwickshire. M W Thompson. London: HMSO, 1977*

Kenilworth Castle, Warwickshire. M W Thompson. London: HBMCE, 1985*

'Warwickshire fishponds', M Aston and C J Bond, in M Aston (ed), *Medieval fish, fisheries and fishponds*, 417–34. Oxford: BAR, 1988* (BAR British series; 182) [espec pp 420–23]

'A note on Kenilworth Castle: the change to royal ownership', R A Brown, in R A Brown, *Castles, conquest and charters: collected papers*, 209–13. Woodbridge: Boydell Press, 1989

'Three stages in the construction of the hall at Kenilworth Castle, Warwickshire', M W Thompson, in M R Apted, R Gilyard-Beer and A D Saunders (eds), *Ancient* *monuments and their interpretation: essays presented to A J Taylor*, 211–18. Chichester: Phillimore, 1977*

'Kenilworth Castle', P J Brown, *Archaeological Excavations 1975*, 27–28. London: HMSO, 1976

'Kenilworth Castle', D A L Cranstone, *Archaeological Excavations 1976*, 32. London: HMSO, 1977

'A note on Kenilworth Castle: the change to royal ownership', R A Brown, *Archaeological Journal* 110 (1953), 120–24

'Kenilworth Castle', M W Thompson, *ibid* 128 (1971), 204–7*

'Kenilworth Castle, 1960', P Rahtz, *Transactions and Proceedings of the Birmingham and Warwickshire Archaeological Society* 81 (1963–4), 55–73*

'Notes on the water system at Kenilworth Castle', J H Drew, *ibid* 81 (1963–4), 74–77*

'Kenilworth Castle: a discussion of its entrances', J H Drew, *Transactions of the Birmingham and Warwickshire Archaeological Society* 84 (1967–70), 148–58*

'Kenilworth Castle and the country weavers', J H Drew, *ibid* 85 (1971–3), 214–16

'The Elizabethan gardens and Leicester's stables at Kenilworth Castle', P Ellis (ed), *ibid* 99 (1995), 81–116*

'Kenilworth Castle', P A Rahtz, *CBA Group 8 News Sheet* 3 (1960), 6

'Kenilworth Castle', H L G Sunley, *ibid* 8 (1965), 9

'The meres of Kenilworth', C R Denton, *Country Life* 126 (1959), 714–15*

'A fragment of architecture at Kenilworth Castle, and its implications', M J Johnson, *Durham Archaeological Journal* 14–15 (1999), 173–76*

'Kenilworth, the earl of Leicester's pleasure grounds following Robert Laneham's letter', E Woodhouse, *Garden History* 27 (1999), 127–44*

'An English landscape garden before 'The English landscape garden'?', M Leslie, *Journal of Garden History* 13 (1993), 3–15*

'Medieval Britain in 1960', D M Wilson and D G Hurst, *Medieval Archaeology* 5 (1961), 319–21*

'Medieval Britain in 1961', D M Wilson and D G Hurst, *ibid*, 6–7 (1962–3), 324

'The reclamation of waste ground for the Pleasance at Kenilworth Castle, Warwickshire', M W Thompson, *ibid* 8 (1964), 222–23

'Medieval Britain in 1962 and 1963, D M Wilson and D G Hurst, *ibid* 8 (1964), 260

'Two levels of the mere at Kenilworth Castle, Warwickshire', M W Thompson, *ibid* 9 (1965), 156–61*

'Medieval Britain in 1965', D M Wilson and D G Hurst, *ibid* 10 (1966), 191

'Kenilworth Castle since 1962', M W Thompson, *ibid* 13 (1969), 218–20*

'Medieval Britain in 1976', L E Webster and J Cherry, *ibid* 21 (1977), 238

'Medieval Britain and Ireland in 1991', B S Nenk, S Margeson and M Hurley, *ibid* 36 (1992), 269

'Medieval Britain and Ireland in 1998', J Bradley, M Gaimster and C Haith, *ibid* 43 (1999), 281

'Medieval Britain and Ireland in 2001', J Bradley and M Gaimster, *ibid* 46 (2002), 207–8

'Medieval Britain and Ireland in 2002', J Bradley and M Gaimster, *ibid* 47 (2003), 286

'Medieval Britain and Ireland in 2003', J Bradley and M Gaimster, *ibid* 48 (2004), 290

'Medieval Britain and Ireland in 2004', M Gaimster and K O'Conor, *ibid* 49 (2005), 414

'Post-medieval fieldwork in Britain and Northern Ireland in 2004', M Ponsford, *Post-Medieval Archaeology* 39 (2005), 392

'Kenilworth, Kenilworth Castle', T J Crump, *West Midlands Archaeology* 28 (1985), 60

'Kenilworth, Kenilworth Castle', M Jones, *ibid* 34 (1991), 81–82

'Kenilworth, Kenilworth Castle, Lunns Tower', C Coutts, *ibid* 46 (2003), 129–30

Maxstoke

A short history of Maxstoke Castle. C B Fetherston-Dilke and M C Fetherston-Dilke. [S l: s n], 2000

'Maxstoke Castle', C B Fetherston-Dilke, *Archaeological Journal* 128 (1971), 244–45*

'Maxstoke Castle, Warwickshire', N W Alcock, P A Faulkner and S R Jones, *ibid* 135 (1978), 195–233*

'Medieval Britain and Ireland in 1997', M Gaimster, C Haith and J Bradley, *Medieval Archaeology* 42 (1998), 152–53

'Master John of Burcestre and the castles of Stafford and Maxstoke', M J B Hislop, *Transactions of the South Staffordshire Archaeological and Historical Society* 33 (1991–2), 14–20*

Ratley

'Excavations at Ratley Castle, 1968–73', K Steane, *Transactions of the Birmingham and Warwickshire Archaeological Society* 96 (1989–90), 5–26*

'Ratley, Warks', F Radcliffe, *CBA Group 8 News Sheet* 11 (1968), 29–30

'Ratley and Upton, Warws', F Radcliffe, *ibid* 14 (1971), 32

'Ratley and Upton, Warws', F Radcliffe, *ibid* 15 (1972), 29

'Ratley and Upton, Warks', F Radcliffe, *ibid* 16 (1973), 28

'Medieval Britain in 1968', D M Wilson and D G Hurst, *Medieval Archaeology* 13

(1969), 260

'Medieval Britain in 1971', L E Webster and J Cherry, *ibid* 16 (1972), 183

'Medieval Britain in 1972', L E Webster and J Cherry, *ibid* 17 (1973), 163, 165

'Medieval Britain in 1973', L E Webster and J Cherry, *ibid* 18 (1974), 196–97

Warwick

Warwick Castle: a thousand years of history in your hands. Anon. Warwick: Warwick Castle, 2002*

Warwick Castle. [P A Barker *et al*]. Warwick: Warwick Castle Ltd, 1987*

Canaletto and Warwick Castle. D Buttery. Chichester: Phillimore, 1992*

Warwick Castle. P E Curnow. [Unpublished typescript prepared for the Royal Archaeological Institute's summer meeting at Warwick in 1971. A copy is in the Library of the Society of Antiquaries of London]

An historical and descriptive account of the town and castle of Warwick. W Field. Wakefield: E P Publishing, 1970* [first published 1815]

'The castle and castle estate of Warwick', in W B Stephens (ed), *The Victoria history of the counties of England: a history of the county of Warwick*, **8**, 452–64. Oxford: OUP, 1969*

'The architecture of the earls of Warwick in the fourteenth century', R K Morris, in W M Ormrod (ed), *England in the fourteenth century: proceedings of the 1985 Harlaxton Symposium*, 161–74. Woodbridge: Boydell Press, 1986*

'Barrack Street excavations, Warwick, 1972', E Klingelhöfer, *Transactions of the Birmingham and Warwickshire Archaeological Society* 88 (1976–7), 87–104*

'Warwick Castle revisited', M Binney, *Country Life* 172 (1982), 1746–49, 1882–85, 1952–55, 2023–26*

'Medieval Britain in 1967', D M Wilson and D G Hurst, *Medieval Archaeology* 12 (1968), 185–86

'Medieval Britain in 1972', D M Wilson and D G Hurst, *ibid* 17 (1973), 171

'Medieval Britain and Ireland in 1991', B S Nenk, S Margeson and M Hurley, *ibid* 36 (1992), 270

'Medieval Britain and Ireland in 1993', B S Nenk, S Margeson and M Hurley, *ibid* 38 (1994), 261–62

'Medieval Britain and Ireland in 1994', B S Nenk, S Margeson and M Hurley, *ibid* 39 (1995), 258

'Medieval Britain and Ireland in 1995', B S Nenk, S Margeson and M Hurley, *ibid* 40 (1996), 289

'Medieval Britain and Ireland in 1996', B S Nenk, C Haith and J Bradley, *ibid* 41 (1997), 293–94

'Medieval Britain and Ireland in 1997', M Gaimster, C Haith and J Bradley, *ibid* 42 (1998), 153–54

'Medieval Britain and Ireland in 1998', J Bradley, M Gaimster and C Haith, *ibid* 43 (1999), 282–83

'Medieval Britain and Ireland in 2000', J Bradley and M Gaimster, *ibid* 45 (2001), 331

'Medieval Britain and Ireland in 2002', J Bradley and M Gaimster, *ibid* 47 (2003), 287

'Medieval Britain and Ireland in 2003', J Bradley and M Gaimster, *ibid* 48 (2004), 293–94

'Medieval Britain and Ireland in 2004', M Gaimster and K O'Conor, *ibid* 49 (2005), 416, 417

'Medieval Britain and Ireland in 2005', M Gaimster and K O'Conor, *ibid* 50 (2006), 349–50

'The 'Kingmaker': a look at Richard Neville and his magnificent castle at Warwick', M Watson Brown, *Medieval History Magazine* 2.5 (2004), 52–61*

'Post-medieval Britain and Ireland in 2003', M Ponsford, *Post-Medieval Archaeology* 38 (2004), 322–23

'Post-medieval fieldwork in Britain and Northern Ireland in 2004', M Ponsford, *ibid* 39 (2005), 393

'Warwick, Warwick Castle', M Jones, *West Midlands Archaeology* 30 (1987), 54

'Warwick, Warwick Castle', N Palmer, *ibid* 36 (1993), 102–3

'Warwick, Warwick Castle', N Palmer, *ibid* 37 (1994), 101

'Warwick, Warwick Castle', N Palmer, *ibid* 38 (1995), 103–4

'Warwick, Warwick Castle', N Palmer, *ibid* 39 (1996), 97

'Warwick, King's High School for Girls', N Palmer, *ibid* 40 (1997), 92–93

'Warwick, castle', N Palmer, *ibid* 41 (1998), 99–100

'Warwick, town wall adjacent to Lord Leycester's Hospital', N Palmer, *ibid* 41 (1998), 101

'Warwick, Warwick Castle', N Palmer, *ibid* 43 (2000), 103–4*

Weoley

Weoley Castle. Anon. Birmingham: Birmingham Museums and Art Gallery, 1974*

Birmingham: the hidden history. M Hodder. Stroud: Tempus, 2004*

'Weoley Castle: progress of excavations', A H Oswald, *Archaeological News Letter* 7 (1961–5), 65

'Interim report on excavations at Weoley Castle, 1955–60', A H Oswald, *Transactions and Proceedings of the Birmingham Archaeological Society* 78 (1962), 61–85*

'Analysis of some metal objects from Weoley Castle', R Brownsword, E Pitt and D Symons, *Transactions of the Birmingham and Warwickshire Archaeological Society* 93 (1983–4), 33–43*

'Weoley Castle and Northfield in 1424', D Symons, *ibid* 93 (1983–4), 45–55*

'Weoley Castle', A Oswald, *CBA Group 8 News Sheet* 2 (1959), 3

'Weoley Castle', A Oswald, *ibid* 3 (1960), 3

'Weoley Castle', A Oswald, *ibid* 4 (1961), 3

'Weoley Castle', A Oswald, *ibid* 5 (1962), 3

'The wooden pipe from Weoley Castle', A Raines, *Galpin Society Journal* 26 (1973), 144–45*

'Medieval Britain in 1956', D M Wilson and J G Hurst, *Medieval Archaeology* 1 (1957), 157

'Medieval Britain in 1957', D M Wilson and J G Hurst, *ibid* 2 (1958), 195–96

'Excavations of a thirteenth century wooden building at Weoley Castle, Birmingham, 1960–61. An interim report', A H Oswald, *ibid* 6–7 (1962–3), 109–34*

'Medieval Britain in 1962 and 1963', D M Wilson and J G Hurst, *ibid* 8 (1964), 260

'The structure of the timber kitchen at Weoley Castle, Birmingham', J T Smith, *ibid* 9 (1965), 82–93*

'Weoley Castle, stone recording', anon, *West Midlands Archaeology* 43 (2000), 123–24*

WESTMORLAND

Bowden, M. 'Recent archaeological fieldwork in the Howgill Fells by the Royal Commission on the Historical Monuments of England', *Transactions of the Cumberland and Westmorland Antiquarian and Archaeological Society* 96 (1996), 1–11*

Cope, J. *Castles in Cumbria*. Milnthorpe: Cicerone Press, 1991*

Higham, M C. 'The mottes of north Lancashire, Lonsdale and south Cumbria', *Transactions of the Cumberland and Westmorland Antiquarian and Archaeological Society* 91 (1991), 79–90*

Hugill, R. *Castles and peles of Cumberland and Westmorland: a guide to the strongholds of the western English borderlands together with an account of their development and their place in border history*. Newcastle upon Tyne: F Graham, 1977*

Jackson, M J. *Castles of Cumbria*. Carlisle: Carel Press; Cumbria County Library, 1990*

Lott, B. 'Seigneurial hierarchy and medieval buildings in Westmorland', in G Meirion-Jones, E Impey and M Jones (eds), *The seigneurial residence in western*

Europe AD c 800–1600, 101–11. Oxford: Archaeopress, 2002* (BAR international series; 1088)

Perriam, D R. 'Recent trends in the study of fortified buildings in Cumbria', in P Clack and J Ivy (eds), *Making sense of buildings*, 35–40. Durham: CBA Group 3, 1985

Perriam, D R and Robinson, J. *The medieval fortified buildings of Cumbria: an illustrated gazetteer and record guide*. [S l]: Cumberland and Westmorland Antiquarian and Archaeological Society, 1998* (Extra series; 29)

Pevsner, N. *Cumberland and Westmorland (The buildings of England)*. Harmondsworth: Penguin Books, 1967*

Salter, M. *The castles and tower houses of Cumbria*. Malvern: Folly Publications, 1998*

Yates, S (ed). *Heritage unlocked: guide to free sites in the north west*. London: English Heritage, 2002*

Weaver, J. *Exploring England's heritage: Cumbria to Northumberland*. London: HMSO, 1992* [espec ch 5]

Appleby

Appleby Castle. M Holmes. Appleby: Ferguson Industrial Holdings, 1974*

'Appleby Castle', R Simms, *Archaeological Journal* 115 (1958), 239

'The town and castle of Appleby: a morphological study', W D Simpson, *Transactions of the Cumberland and Westmorland Antiquarian and Archaeological Society* new ser 49 (1949), 118–33*

Brough

Brough Castle, Cumbria. J Charlton. London: English Heritage, 1986*

Brough Castle, Westmorland. W D Simpson. London: HMSO, reprinted 1969*; 2nd edition, 1982*

Brougham and Brough castles, Cumbria. H Summerson. London: English Heritage, 1999*

'Brough Castle', P Turnbull, *Archaeological Journal* 155 (1998), 365–66*

'Brough-under-Stainmore: the castle and the church', W D Simpson, *Transactions of the Cumberland and Westmorland Antiquarian and Archaeological Society* new ser 46 (1946), 223–83*

'Medieval Britain and Ireland in 1993', B S Nenk, S Margeson and M Hurley, *Medieval Archaeology* 38 (1994), 201

Brougham

Brougham Castle, Westmorland. J Charlton. London: HMSO, 1950*

Brougham Castle. J Charlton. London: HBMCE, 1985*

Brougham Castle: information for teachers. R David. London: English Heritage, 1997*

Brougham and Brough castles, Cumbria. H Summerson. London: English Heritage, 1999*

Brougham Castle, Cumbria. A survey and documentary history. H Summerson, M Trueman and S Harrison. Kendal: Cumberland and Westmorland Antiquarian and Archaeological Society, 1998* (Research series; 8)

'Brougham Castle', F Lynch, *127th annual meeting, Cumbria and Lake District 1982*, CAA, 1982, 28*

'Brougham Castle', H Summerson, *Archaeological Journal* 155 (1998), 361–63*

'Brough Castle and early communications in the Eden Valley', P A Wilson, *Transactions of the Cumberland and Westmorland Antiquarian and Archaeological Society* new ser 76 (1976), 67–76

'Excavations at Brougham Castle, 1987', J H Williams, *ibid* 92 (1992), 105–21 + microfiche*

'An excavation at Brougham Castle', J M Zant, *ibid* 3 ser 1 (2001), 31–37*

'Medieval Britain and Ireland in 1990', B S Nenk, S Margeson and M Hurley, *Medieval Archaeology* 35 (1991), 139

'Medieval Britain and Ireland in 1991', B S Nenk, S Margeson and M Hurley, *ibid* 36 (1992), 207

Clifton

'Clifton Hall, Cumbria: excavations 1977–79', G Fairclough, *Transactions of the Cumberland and Westmorland Antiquarian and Archaeological Society* 80 (1980), 45–68*

Kendal

'Kendal Castle', R H Leech, *125th annual meeting, Cumbria and Lake District, 1982*, CAA, 1982, 27

'Kendal Castle, Westmorland', B Harbottle, *Archaeological Newsletter for Northumberland, Cumberland and Westmorland* 2 (1968), 9

'Kendal Castle, Westmoreland', B Harbottle, *ibid* 5 (1969), 10–11

'Kendal Castle, Westmoreland', B Harbottle, *ibid* 8 (1970), 13

'Kendal Castle, Westmorland: the sources of its building stone', R M Haworth, *ibid* 11 (1971), 11–12

'Kendal Castle, Westmoreland', B Harbottle, *CBA Group 3 Newsbulletin* 1 (1972), 7

'Excavations at Kendal Castle', K E Spence, *Transactions of the Cumberland and Westmorland Antiquarian and Archaeological Society* new ser 51 (1951), 185–86*

'Medieval Britain in 1967', D M Wilson and D G Hurst, *Medieval Archaeology* 12 (1968), 183

'Medieval Britain in 1968', D M Wilson and D G Hurst, *ibid* 13 (1969), 260–61

'Medieval Britain in 1971', L E Webster and J Cherry, *ibid* 16 (1972), 183

'Excavations at Kendal Castle, Westmorland, 1967', R B Harbottle, *Quarto: Quarterly Bulletin of the Abbot Hall Art Gallery* 5.4 (1968), [6pp, unpaginated]*

'Excavations at Kendal Castle, Westmorland, 1968', R B Harbottle, *ibid* 6.4 (1969), 14–20*

'Excavations at Kendal Castle, Westmorland, 1969', R B Harbottle, *ibid* 7.4 (1970), 13–18*

'Excavations at Kendal Castle, Westmorland', R B Harbottle, *ibid* 10.1 (1972), 12–16*

Pendragon

'Survey data enhancement and interpretative work for the recording and conservation of Pendragon Castle', C Binney [*et al*], in J Wilcock and K Lockyear (eds), *Computer applications and quantitative methods in archaeology 1993*, 237–44. Oxford: Tempus Reparatum, 1995* (BAR international series; 598)

'Medieval Britain and Ireland in 1991', B S Nenk, S Margeson and M Hurley, *Medieval Archaeology* 36 (1992), 207

Sizergh

'Sizergh Castle', F Lynch, *125th annual meeting, Cumbria and Lake District, 1982*, CAA, 1982, 29–30*

'Sizergh Castle', H Hornyold-Strickland, *Archaeological Journal* 127 (1970), 260

'Sizergh Castle, Westmorland', G Nares, *Country Life* 106 (1949), 1216–18*

WILTSHIRE

Creighton, O H. 'Early castles in the medieval landscape of Wiltshire', *Wiltshire Archaeological and Natural History Magazine* 93 (2000), 105–19*

Endacott, A and Kelleher, S (eds). *Heritage unlocked: guide to free sites in Bristol, Gloucestershire and Wiltshire*. London: English Heritage, 2004*

Pevsner, N. *Wiltshire (The buildings of England)*. 2nd edition, revised by B Cherry. Harmondsworth: Penguin Books, 1975*

Rahtz, P [*et al*]. 'Norman castles', in *Medieval sites in the Mendip, Cotswold, Wye Valley and Bristol region*, 14–17. Bristol: Bristol Archaeological Research Group, 1969 (Field guide; 3)

Robertson, M. *Exploring England's heritage: Dorset to Gloucestershire*. London: HMSO, in association with English Heritage, 1992* [espec ch 2]

Salter, M. *The castles of Wessex*. Malvern: Folly Publications, 2002*

ENGLAND

Ashton Keynes

'Hall's Close, Ashton Keynes', G M Knocker, *Wiltshire Archaeological and Natural History Magazine* 57 (1958–60), 241–42

Castle Combe

'Castle Combe: castle', in anon, 'Excavation and fieldwork in Wiltshire 1990', *ibid* 85 (1992), 158

Clack Mount

'Clack Mount', S Hobb, *ibid* 96 (2003), 219–20

Devizes

'Castle and lordship to *c* 1550, in E Crittal (ed), *The Victoria history of the counties of England: a history of Wiltshire*, **10**, 237–45. Oxford: OUP, 1975*

'Medieval Britain and Ireland in 1986', S M Youngs, J Clark and T Barry, *Medieval Archaeology* 31 (1987), 167

'Medieval Britain and Ireland in 2000', J Bradley and M Gaimster, *ibid* 45 (2001), 332

'Devizes Castle: a suggested reconstruction', R H Cunningham, *Wiltshire Archaeological and Natural History Magazine* 51 (1945–7), 496–99*

'The excavation of the defences of Devizes, Wilts, 1974', J Haslam, *ibid* 72–3 (1977–8), 59–65*

'Excavations at Vale's Lane, Devizes, 1996–7', P Andrews and L Mepham, *ibid* 93 (2000), 241–48*

Downton

'The Moot, Downton', H Shortt, *Archaeological Journal* 104 (1947), 166

'Medieval Britain and Ireland in 1991', B S Nenk, S Margeson and M Hurley, *Medieval Archaeology* 36 (1992), 271–72

'Medieval Britain and Ireland in 1992', B S Nenk, S Margeson and M Hurley, *ibid* 37 (1993), 287

'Medieval Britain and Ireland in 1995', B S Nenk, S Margeson and M Hurley, *ibid* 40 (1996), 290

'Saxon and medieval features at Downton, Salisbury', P A Rahtz, *Wiltshire Archaeological and Natural History Magazine* 59 (1964), 124–29*

'Old Court, Downton, and the Moot earthwork', J Musty, *ibid* 61 (1966), 98–99

Lewisham

'Aldbourne, Stock Lane, Lewisham Castle', B and R Phillips, *CBA Groups 12 and 13 Archaeological Review* 4 (1969), 58

'Lewisham Castle', H C Brentall, *Wiltshire Archaeological and Natural History Magazine* 51 (1945–7), 472–73

Ludgershall

Ludgershall Castle, Wiltshire: a report on the excavations by Peter Addyman, 1964–1972. P Ellis (ed). Devizes: Wiltshire Archaeological and Natural History Society, 2000* (Monograph series; 2)

'Excavations at Ludgershall Castle, Wilts 1966', R W Emery, *Andover Archaeological Society* spring (1967), 16–17*

'Excavations at Ludgershall Castle, Wiltshire', P V Addyman, *Château Gaillard* 4 (1969), 9–12*

Excavations at Ludgershall Castle, Wiltshire, England (1964–1972)', P V Addyman, *ibid* 6 (1973), 7–13*

'Ludgershall, Ludgershall Castle', P V Addyman, *CBA Groups 12 and 13 Archaeological Review* 1 (1966), 40

'Ludgershall, Ludgershall Castle', P V Addyman, *ibid* 3 (1968), 30

'Ludgershall, Ludgershall Castle', P V Addyman, *ibid* 4 (1969), 59

'Ludgershall, Ludgershall Castle', P V Addyman, *ibid* 6 (1971), 44

'Ludgershall Castle, Wiltshire: public access to research', P Everson, *Conservation Bulletin* 39 (2000), 18–19*

'The royal hunting lodge at Ludgershall', [A Selkirk], *Current Archaeology* 1.1 (1967), 14*

'Medieval Britain in 1964', D M Wilson and D G Hurst, *Medieval Archaeology* 9 (1965), 192

'Medieval Britain in 1965', D M Wilson and D G Hurst, *ibid* 10 (1966), 191–92

'Medieval Britain in 1966', D M Wilson and D G Hurst, *ibid* 11 (1967), 286–88*

'Medieval Britain in 1967', D M Wilson and D G Hurst, *ibid* 12 (1968), 179–80*

'Medieval Britain in 1968', D M Wilson and D G Hurst, *ibid* 13 (1969), 261*

'Medieval Britain in 1969', D M Wilson and D G Hurst, *ibid* 14 (1970), 176–77

'Medieval Britain in 1971', L E Webster and J Cherry, *ibid* 16 (1972), 183–84

'Ludgershall', anon, *Wiltshire Archaeological and Natural History Magazine* 61 (1966), 104–5*

'Ludgershall', anon, *ibid* 62 (1967), 127–28

'Ludgershall', anon, *ibid* 63 (1968), 111–12

'Ludgershall', anon, *ibid* 64 (1969), 124–26*

'Ludgershall', anon, *ibid* 65 (1970), 205

'Ludgershall, Ludgershall Castle', P V Addyman, *ibid* 67 (1972), 176

'The castles of Marlborough and Ludgershall in the middle ages', J H Stevenson, *ibid* 85 (1992), 70–79*

'Ludgershall Castle: two addenda', J Cherry and B Ellis, *ibid* 94 (2001), 234–35*

Malmesbury

'Medieval Britain and Ireland in 1997', M Gaimster, C Haith and J Bradley, *Medieval Archaeology* 42 (1998), 155

'Malmesbury, its castle and walls', H Rees, *Wiltshire Archaeological and Natural History Magazine* 51 (1945–7), 184–92*

'Iron Age and later defences at Malmesbury: excavations 1998–2000', T Longman, *ibid* 99 (2006), 104–64*

Marlborough

'Marlborough Castle', in D A Crowley (ed), *The Victoria history of the counties of counties of England: a history of Wiltshire*, **12**, 165–68. Oxford: OUP, for the Institute of Historical Research, 1983*

'Accounts for works on the royal mills and castle at Marlborough, 1237–8 and 1238–9', S Challenger (ed), in N J Williams (ed), *Collectanea*, 1–49. Devizes: Wiltshire Archaeological and Natural History Society, Records Branch, vol 12, 1956

'Medieval Britain in 1956', D M Wilson and D G Hurst, *Medieval Archaeology* 1 (1957), 157

'Medieval Britain and Ireland in 2000', J Bradley and M Gaimster, *ibid* 45 (2001), 333

'Marlborough Castle', J H P Pafford, *Wiltshire Archaeological and Natural History Magazine* 60 (1965), 129

'The castles of Marlborough and Ludgershall in the middle ages', J H Stevenson, *ibid* 85 (1992), 70–79*

'The Marlborough mount revisited', D Field, G Brown and A Crockett, *ibid* 94 (2001), 195–204*

'A possible outer bailey ditch to Marlborough Castle: excavations at Marlborough College pool', M Heaton and B Moffat, *ibid* 95 (2002), 100–6*

Mere

'The silent past of Castle Hill', B Berry, *Country Life* 144 (1968), 180–81*

Old Sarum

Old Sarum, Wiltshire. Anon. London: HMSO, 1950*

Old Sarum. J McNeill. London: English Heritage, 2006*

Old Sarum: a handbook for teachers. P Planel. London: English Heritage, 1991*

Old Sarum, Wiltshire. D Renn. London: English Heritage, 1994*

Old Sarum. H de S Shortt. London: HMSO, 1965*

'The castle', in E Crittall (ed), *The Victoria history of the counties of counties of England: a history of Wiltshire*, **6**, 53–60. Oxford: OUP, 1962*

'Old Sarum', in RCHME, *Ancient and historical monuments in the city of Salisbury*, **1**, 1–15, 173–74. London: HMSO, 1980*

'Old Sarum', D H Montgomerie, *Archaeological Journal* 104 (1947), 129–42*

'Medieval Britain in 1957', D M Wilson and J G Hurst, *Medieval Archaeology* 2 (1958), 196

'Medieval Britain in 1961', D M Wilson and D G Hurst, *ibid* 6–7 (1962–3), 324

'Medieval Britain in 1964', D M Wilson and D G Hurst, *ibid* 9 (1965), 192

'Medieval Britain in 1967', D M Wilson and D G Hurst, *ibid* 12 (1968), 289

'Excavations at Old Sarum', P A Rahtz, *Wiltshire Archaeological and Natural History Magazine* 57 (1958–60), 352–70*

'The earthworks of Old Sarum', H Braun, *ibid* 57 (1958–60), 406–7*

'The site of the borough at Old Sarum 1066–1226: an examination of some of the documentary evidences', D Stroud, *ibid* 80 (1986), 120–26*

Old Wardour

Old Wardour Castle, Wiltshire. B K Davison. London: English Heritage, 1999*

Old Wardour Castle, Wiltshire. R B Pugh and A D Saunders. London: HMSO, 1968*

Old Wardour Castle, Wiltshire. 2nd edition. A D Saunders and R B Pugh. London: English Heritage, 1991*

'Aspects of fourteenth-century castle design', B M Morley, in A Detsicas (ed) *Collectanea historica: essays in memory of Stuart Rigold*, 104–13. Maidstone: Kent Archaeological Society, 1981*

'Old Wardour Castle', A D Saunders, *Archaeological Journal* 140 (1983), 70–71

'Wardour Old Castle – I', M Girouard, *Country Life* 185.7 (1991), 44–49*

'Wardour Old Castle – II', M Girouard, *ibid* 185.8 (1991), 76–79*

'Old Wardour Castle, Wiltshire', J Goodall, *ibid* 199.17 (2005), 94–99*

'Medieval Britain and Ireland in 1990', B S Nenk, S Margeson and M Hurley, *Medieval Archaeology* 35 (1991), 196

'Post-medieval Britain and Ireland in 1990', M Ponsford, *Post-Medieval Archaeology* 25 (1991), 123–24

'Excavations at Old Wardour Castle', L Keen, *Wiltshire Archaeological and Natural History Magazine* 62 (1967), 67–78*

'Excavation at Old Wardour Castle, 1983', G Smith, *ibid* 80 (1986), 223–24

Salisbury

'Salisbury', K H Rogers, in M D Lobel (ed), *Historic towns*, **1**. Oxford: Lovell Johns-Cook, Hammond and Kell Organization, 1969*

'City defences', in RCHME, *Ancient and historical monuments in the city of Salisbury*, **1**, 50–51. London: HMSO, 1980*

'Brief introduction to the history of Salisbury and to the city rampart, hall of John

Halle, Council House and other buildings', F Stevens, *Archaeological Journal* 104 (1947), x-xii

'Salisbury', C N Moore, *CBA Groups 12 and 13 Archaeological Review* 4 (1969), 59

'New Sarum, Salisbury', D J Algar, *ibid* 7 (1972), 59–60

'Medieval Britain in 1960', D M Wilson and D G Hurst, *Medieval Archaeology* 5 (1961), 326

'Medieval Britain and Ireland in 1984', S M Youngs, J Clark and T Barry, *ibid* 29 (1985), 205

'Medieval Britain and Ireland in 1988', D R M Gaimster, S Margeson and T Barry, *ibid* 33 (1989), 219–20

Trowbridge

Excavations in the town centre of Trowbridge, Wiltshire, 1977 and 1986–1988: the prehistoric and Saxon settlements, the Saxo-Norman manorial settlement and the anarchy period castle. A H Graham and S M Davies. Salisbury: Trust for Wessex Archaeology, 1993*

'Medieval Britain in 1977', L E Webster and J Cherry, *Medieval Archaeology* 22 (1978), 169

'Medieval Britain and Ireland in 1986', S M Youngs, J Clark and T Barry, *ibid* 31 (1987), 168

'Medieval Britain and Ireland in 1987', S M Youngs [*et al*], *ibid* 32 (1988), 289–90

'Medieval Britain and Ireland in 1988', D R M Gaimster, S Margeson and T Barry, *ibid* 33 (1989), 220

'Excavations and fieldwork in Wiltshire 1987', anon, *Wiltshire Archaeological and Natural History Magazine* 82 (1988), 178–80*

'Trowbridge Castle excavations 1988: an interim report', S M Davies and A H Graham, *ibid* 83 (1990), 50–56*

WORCESTERSHIRE

Bond, C J. 'Field work notes 1. Castles', *Worcestershire Archaeology Newsletter* 5 (1970), 7–8

Bowden, M. *The Malvern Hills: an ancient landscape*. London: English Heritage, 2005*

County Museum. 'Worcestershire archaeological inventory – checklist no 2. Medieval castles', *Worcestershire Archaeology Newsletter* 8 (1971), 17–18

Remfry, P M. *Nine castles of the Burford barony 1048 to 1308*. Malvern Link: SCS Publishing, 1999*

Salter, M. *The castles of Herefordshire and Worcestershire*. Wolverhampton: Folly Publications, 1989*

Salter, M. *The castles of Herefordshire and Worcestershire*. New edition. Malvern: Folly Publications, 2000*

Beoley

'The Mount, Beoley: hillfort or castle?', D Whitehead, *CBA Group 8 News Sheet* 13 (1970), 4–7

Castlemorton

'Castlemorton, sewage works, Castle Tump', Archaeological Service, Worcester, *West Midlands Archaeology* 41 (1998), 126

'Castle Morton. Motte and bailey', A Wilson, *Worcestershire Archaeology and Local History Newsletter* 15 (1974–5), 7

Elmley

'Elmley Castle, Worcs', J Bond and M Aston', *CBA Group 8 News Sheet* 13 (1970), 25*

'Building accounts of Elmley Castle, Worcestershire, 1345–6', R H Hilton, *University of Birmingham Historical Journal* 10 (1965–6), 78–87

'A note on pottery and other objects from Elmley Castle', C C Dyer, *ibid* 10 (1965–6), 88–89

'Elmley Castle', [M Napthan], *West Midlands Archaeology* 37 (1994), 29–30*

'The Beauchamp earls of Warwick and the castle at Elmley', R K Field, *Transactions of the Worcestershire Archaeological Society* 3 ser 15 (1996), 135–46*

'Elmley Castle', C J Bond and M A Aston, *Worcestershire Archaeology Newsletter* 6 (1970), 3

Hanley

'Hanley Castle', C J Bond, *Worcestershire Archaeology and Local History Newsletter* 14 (1974), 3–4

Inkberrow

'The site of Inkberrow Castle and park', E Ruth and C Jackson, *ibid* 18 (1976), 3–6*

Kidderminster

'Excavations at Caldwall Hall, Kidderminster 1961–69', C I Walker, *Transactions of the Worcestershire Archaeological Society* 3 ser 13 (1992), 135–65*

Pershore

'The defense of Pershore bridges, 1940–1944', M Wilkes, *Defence Lines* 12 (1999), 13–14*

Redditch

'Post-medieval Britain and Ireland in 1994', M Ponsford and R Jackson, *Post-Medieval Archaeology* 29 (1995), 131

'Redditch, Brockhill', K Nichol, *West Midlands Archaeology* 40 (1997), 40–42

Severn Stoke
'Medieval Britain and Ireland in 1991', B S Nenk, S Margeson and M Hurley, *Medieval Archaeology* 32 (1992), 239

Worcester
'Worcester, Fort Royal', P J Reynolds, *Archaeological Excavations 1969*, 69. London: HMSO, 1970

'Worcester, city wall', P Barker, *Archaeological Excavations 1973*, 101. London: HMSO, 1974

'Town defences, Worcester', D Macnair, *CBA Group 8 News Sheet* 2 (1959), 7

'Worcester, King School site', P A Barker, *ibid* 9 (1966), 17

'Worcester, city walls', P A Barker, *ibid* 10 (1967), 9

'Worcester: medieval city wall', P Reynolds, *ibid* 12 (1969), 32

'Worcester: Fort Royal', P Reynolds, *ibid* 12 (1969), 40

'Recent archaeological research in Worcester', P A Barker, *Château Gaillard* 4 (1969), 13–18*

'Medieval Britain in 1959', D M Wilson and J G Hurst, *Medieval Archaeology* 4 (1960), 150

'Medieval Britain in 1968', D M Wilson and D G Hurst, *ibid* 13 (1969), 267

'Medieval Britain in 1969', D M Wilson and D G Hurst, *ibid* 14 (1970), 186

'Medieval Britain in 1980', S M Youngs and J Clark, *ibid* 25 (1981), 208

'Medieval Britain and Ireland in 1992', B S Nenk, S Margeson and M Hurley, *ibid* 37 (1993), 268

'Medieval Britain and Ireland in 1998', J Bradley, M Gaimster and C Haith, *ibid* 43 (1999), 283, 284

'Medieval Britain and Ireland in 2003', J Bradley and M Gaimster, *ibid* 48 (2004), 274

'Post-medieval Britain in 1966', D G Hurst, *Post-Medieval Archaeology* 1 (1967), 108

'Post-medieval Britain in 1966', D G Hurst, *ibid* 4 (1970), 175

'Post-medieval Britain and Ireland in 1991', M Ponsford, *ibid* 26 (1992), 108

'Post-medieval Britain and Ireland in 1998 and 1999', M Ponsford, *Post-Medieval Archaeology* 34 (2000), 309, 310

'Excavations on the city wall, Sidbury', J Sawle, *West Midlands Archaeology* 23 (1980), 132–35*

'Worcester archaeological project 1985/86', C Mundy, *ibid* 28 (1985), 7–14*

'Worcester, 3–5 The Butts', Archaeological Service, Worcester, *ibid* 41 (1998), 141

'Worcester, Sidbury Gate, 73–75 Sidbury', J Dinn, *ibid* 41 (1998), 145

'Worcester, former cattle market site, Croft Road and Dolday', M Napthan, *ibid* 44 (2001), 241

'Worcester, 1 The Butts', M Napthan, *ibid* 46 (2003), 193–94

'Worcester, castle site, College Green and Castle Place', M Napthan, *ibid* 46 (2003), 194.

'Worcester, 4–5 Cornmarket', M Napthan, *ibid* 46 (2003), 196–97

'Worcester, 4–5 Cornmarket', M Napthan, *ibid* 46 (2003), 197–98

'Worcester, 16–18 Sansome Street', M Napthan, *ibid* 46 (2003), 2203

'Worcester, Kings School, School House', M Napthan, *ibid* 47 (2004), 139–40*

'Dating the city wall by excavation', D R Shearer, *Transactions of the Worcestershire Archaeological Society* new ser 36 (1959), 60–64*

'Worcester Castle', P A Barker, *ibid* 3 ser 2 (1968–9), 36–37*

'Documentary evidence for the history of Worcester's city defences', C Beardsmore, *ibid* 3 ser 7 (1980), 53–64

'Excavation and survey on the medieval city wall, 1973', J Bennett, *ibid* 3 ser 7 (1980), 65–85*

'Excavation behind the city wall at Talbot Street, 1975', S Hirst, *ibid* 3 ser 7 (1980), 87–106*

'Excavation and salvage recording at Friars Gate, Union Street, 1976', J Wills, *ibid* 3 ser 7 (1980), 107–14*

'Archaeology in the City of Worcester 1997–99', J Dinn, *ibid* 3 ser 17 (2000), 321–31* [espec pp 325–27]

'Excavation, survey and watching brief at Warner Village Cinemas, Driar Street, Worcester', R Jackson [*et al*], *ibid* 3 ser 18 (2002), 53–101*

'City wall excavation – Bowling Green Terrace, Worcester', M Wise, *Worcestershire Archaeology Newsletter* 1 (1967), 3–4

'City wall, Worcester', anon, *ibid* 3 (1969), 8

'Worcester city wall – Friars Gate, Union Street, 1976', J Wills, *Worcestershire Archaeology and Local History Newsletter* 19 (1976–7), 4–5*

'Medieval trans-riparian defences at Worcester?', D Whitehead, *ibid* 23 (1979), 2–3

'The ancient walls and ditches of Worcester', L Richardson, *Transactions of the Worcestershire Naturalists' Club* 11.2 (1956–7), 100–22*

'The city wall, Worcester: a possible source of the building stone', L Richardson, *ibid* 11.4 (1960–1), 209–11

YORKSHIRE

Birch, J. 'The castles and fortified houses of South Yorkshire', *Archaeological Journal* 137 (1980), 374–76*

Bowden, M. 'Recent archaeological fieldwork in the Howgill Fells by the Royal Commission on the Historical Monuments of England', *Transactions of the Cumberland and Westmorland Antiquarian and Archaeological Society* 96 (1996), 1–11*

Butler, L. 'The origins of the honour of Richmond and its castles', in R Liddiard (ed), *Anglo-Norman castles*, 91–103. Woodbridge: Boydell Press, 2003*

Butler, L. 'The origins of the honour of Richmond and its castles', *Château Gaillard* 16 (1994), 69–80*

DoE. *Yorkshire castles picture book*. 2nd edition. London: HMSO, 1973*

Dorman, J E. *Guardians of the Humber: a history of the Humber defences 1856–1956*. Hull: Humberside Leisure Services, 1990*

Garlick, T. *Yorkshire castles*. Clapham: Dalesman, 1972*

Garlick, T. *Exploring Yorkshire castles*. New edition. Clapham: Dalesman, 1979*

Hatcher, J. *Exploring England's heritage: Yorkshire to Humberside*. London: HMSO, in association with English Heritage, 1994* [espec chs 4 & 5]

Hey, D. *A history of Yorkshire: 'county of broad acres'*. Lancaster: Carnegie Publishing, 2005* [espec ch 4]

Illingworth, J L. *Yorkshire's ruined castles*. Wakefield: S R Publishers, 1970* [first published 1938]

Ingham, B. *Bernard Ingham's Yorkshire castles*. Skipton: Dalesman Publishing, 2001*

Jackson, M J. *Castles of Durham and Cleveland: a gazetteer of the medieval castles of two northern counties*. Carlisle: Barmkin Books, 1996*

Jackson, M J. *Castles of North Yorkshire: a gazetteer of medieval castles*. Carlisle: Barmkin Books, 2001* (Medieval castles of England; 5)

Muir, R. 'Yorkshire's castles', in R Muir, *The Yorkshire countryside: a landscape history*, 169–84. Edinburgh: Keele University Press, 1997*

Pevsner, N. *Yorkshire: the North Riding (The buildings of England)*. Harmondsworth: Penguin Books, 1966*

Pevsner, N. *Yorkshire: the West Riding (The buildings of England)*. 2nd edition, revised by E Radcliffe. Harmondsworth: Penguin Books, 1967*

Pevsner, N and Neave, D. *Yorkshire: York and the East Riding (The buildings of England)*. 2nd edition. London: Penguin Books, 1995*

Ryder, P F. *Medieval buildings of Yorkshire*. Ashbourne: Moorland, 1982*

Salter, M. *The castles and tower houses of Yorkshire*. Malvern: Folly Publications, 2001*

Sneyd, S. *The devil's logbooks: castles and fortified sites around South Yorkshire*. Almondbury: Hilltop Press, 1995*

Speight, S. 'Violence and the creation of socio-political order in post-Conquest Yorkshire', in G Halsall (ed), *Violence and society in the early medieval west*, 157–74. Woodbridge: Boydell Press, 1998

Thomas, R J C. 'Coastal defence: monitoring military sites on the Yorkshire coast', *Conservation Bulletin* 44 (2003), 12–14*

Whitworth, A. *Northern strongholds. 1. North Yorkshire*. Whitby: Culva House Publications, 2004*

Whitworth, A. *Northern strongholds. 2. York & East Yorkshire*. Whitby: Culva House Publications, 2004*

Williamson, P R. *Castle walks in Yorkshire*. Lancaster: Palatine Books, 2006*

Woodhouse, R. *Castles of Cleveland*. Redcar: A A Sotheran, 1975*

Almondbury

Castle Hill, Almondbury: a brief guide to the excavations 1939–1972. W J Varley. Huddersfield: Tolson Memorial Museum, 1973*

'Almondbury Castle and hill fort', T G Manby, *Archaeological Journal* 125 (1968), 352–54*

'Medieval Britain in 1970', D M Wilson and S Moorhouse, *Medieval Archaeology* 15 (1971), 149

Ayton

Ayton Castle: its history and excavation. F C Rimington and J G Rutter. Scarborough: Scarborough and District Archaeological Society, 1967* (Research report; 5)

'Medieval Britain in 1961', D M Wilson and D G Hurst, *Medieval Archaeology* 6–7 (1962–3), 336, 338

'A resistivity survey at Ayton Castle', C P Evans, *Transactions of the Scarborough and District Archaeological Society* 2.11 (1968), 64–71*

Baynards

'Medieval Britain and Ireland in 1991', B S Nenk, S Margeson and M Hurley, *Medieval Archaeology* 36 (1992), 243

'Medieval Britain and Ireland in 1996', B S Nenk, C Haith and J Bradley, *ibid* 41 (1997), 299

Beverley

Beverley: an archaeological and architectural study. K Miller [*et al*]. London: HMSO, 1982*

'Fortifications', G H R Kent, in K Allison (ed), *A history of the county of York: East Riding. 6. The borough and liberty of Beverley*, 178–80. Oxford: OUP, for the Institute of Historical Research, 1989* (The Victoria County History of England)

'Beverley town defences', K Miller, *Archaeological Journal* 141 (1984), 21–22

'Beverley, North Bar', K Miller, *ibid* 141 (1984), 23–25

'Medieval Britain and Ireland in 1985', S M Youngs, J Clark and T Barry, *Medieval Archaeology* 30 (1986), 154

'Medieval Britain and Ireland in 1989', D R M Gaimster, S Margeson and M Hurley, *ibid* 34 (1990), 193–94

Bolton

Bolton Castle, Wensleydale. Anon. Leyburn: Bolton Castle, [*c* 2000]*

The story of Bolton Castle: an introduction to the Wensleydale fortress of the Scropes. G Jackson. Clapham: Dalesman, 1956* + later impressions

'Bolton Castle and the practice of architecture in the middle ages', M Hislop, *Journal of the British Archaeological Association* 149 (1996), 10–22*

'Bolton Castle, Yorkshire', M Binney, *Country Life* 186.21 (1992), 60–63*

'Medieval Britain and Ireland in 1990', B S Nenk, S Margeson and M Hurley, *Medieval Archaeology* 35 (1991), 197–98

Medieval Britain and Ireland in 1991', B S Nenk, S Margeson and M Hurley, *ibid* 36 (1992), 273

Bowes

Barnard Castle, County Durham; Egglestone Abbey, North Yorkshire; Bowes Castle, North Yorkshire. K Kenyon. London: English Heritage, 1999*

Bradfield

'Bailey Hill, Bradfield', J Birch, *Archaeological Journal* 137 (1980), 457–58*

'Castle Hill, Bradfield', J Birch, *ibid* 137 (1980), 458–59*

Bull Sand Fort

'Bull Sand Fort – Humber estuary', C A Waters, *Ships Monthly* November (1981), 41*

Burton-in-Lonsdale

'Excavations at Burton-in-Lonsdale: a reconsideration', S Moorhouse, *Yorkshire Archaeological Journal* 43 (1971), 85–98*

Castlehaw

'Combating erosion in the Yorkshire Dales National Park', R White, in A Q Berry and I W Brown (eds), *Erosion on archaeological earthworks: its prevention, control and repair*, 93–101. Mold: Clwyd County Council, 1994*

FORTIFICATIONS BIBLIOGRAPHY

Castleton
'Excavations at Castle Hill, Castleton, North Yorkshire', S J Sherlock, *Yorkshire Archaeological Journal* 64 (1992), 41–47*

Catterick
'Medieval Britain and Ireland in 1983', S M Youngs, J Clark and T B Barry, *Medieval Archaeology* 28 (1984), 248

Cawood
'Medieval Britain and Ireland in 1986', S M Youngs, J Clark and T Barry, *ibid* 31 (1987), 168

'Medieval Britain and Ireland in 1987', S M Youngs [*et al*], *ibid* 32 (1988), 290

Conisbrough
Conisbrough Castle, South Yorkshire. S Johnson. London: HBMCE, 1984*

Conisbrough Castle. S Johnson. London: HBMCE, 1985*

Conisbrough Castle, Yorkshire. M W Thompson. London: HMSO, 1959*

'The donjons of Conisborough [sic] and Bothwell', W D Simpson, *Archaeologia Aeliana* 4 ser 32 (1954), 100–15*

'Conisbrough Castle', J S Johnson, *Archaeological Excavations 1975*, 28–29. London: HMSO, 1976

'Conisbrough Castle', J S Johnson, *Archaeological Excavations 1976*, 33–34. London: HMSO, 1977

'Conisbrough Castle', M W Thompson, *Archaeological Journal* 137 (1980), 416*

'Conisbrough Castle', C Young, *Conservation Bulletin* 19 (1993), 22–23*

'A single-aisled hall at Conisbrough Castle, Yorkshire', M W Thompson, *Medieval Archaeology* 12 (1968), 153

'Medieval Britain in 1975', L E Webster and J Cherry, *ibid* 20 (1976), 185

'Excavations at Conisbrough Castle 1973–77', J S Johnson, *Yorkshire Archaeological Journal* 52 (1980), 59–88*

Dalton
'Dalton Castle', J Melville, *Archaeological Journal* 127 (1970), 266–67*

Doncaster
'Doncaster', P C Buckland, *Archaeological Excavations 1971*, 37. London: HMSO, 1972

'Doncaster', P C Buckland and M J Dolby, *Archaeological Excavations 1972*, 113. London: HMSO, 1973

'Yorkshire archaeological register: 1972', S Moorhouse, *CBA Group 4, Yorkshire Archaeology 1972*, (1972), 8

'Doncaster', [A Selkirk], *Current Archaeology* 3.10 (1972), 273–77*

'Medieval Britain in 1970', D M Wilson and S Moorhouse, *Medieval Archaeology* 15 (1971), 135–46

'The Yorkshire archaeological register: 1986', anon, *Yorkshire Archaeological Journal* 59 (1987), 197

Flamborough

'Medieval Britain and Ireland in 1996', B S Nenk, C Haith and J Bradley, *Medieval Archaeology* 41 (1997), 299

Great Driffield

'A Roman settlement and early medieval motte at Moot Hill, Great Driffield, North Humberside', M R Eddy, *East Riding Archaeologist* 7 (1983), 40–51*

'Medieval Britain in 1975', L E Webster and J Cherry, *Medieval Archaeology* 20 (1976), 184

Harewood

'Harewood Castle', D Black, *Archaeological Journal* 125 (1968), 339–41*

Harpham

'Post-medieval Britain in 1970', S Moorhouse, *Post-Medieval Archaeology* 5 (1971), 198

Hellifield

'Hellifield Peel: a North Yorkshire tower-house', P Ryder and J Birch, *Yorkshire Archaeological Journal* 55 (1983), 73–94*

Helmsley

Helmsley Castle, North Yorkshire. J Clark. London: English Heritage, 2004*

Helmsley Castle, North Yorkshire. G Coppack. London: English Heritage, 1990*; 2nd edition, 1997*

Helmsley Castle: a handbook for teachers. J E Hassid. London: English Heritage, 1991*

Helmsley Castle, Yorkshire. C Peers. London: HMSO, 1966*

'The development of Helmsley Castle', W D Simpson, in A Small (ed), *The fourth Viking congress*, 166–74. Edinburgh: Oliver and Boyd, 1965*

'Helmsley Castle', G Coppack, *Archaeological Journal* 154 (1997), 286–88*

'Medieval Britain in 1957', D M Wilson and J G Hurst, *Medieval Archaeology* 2 (1958), 196

'Medieval Britain and Ireland in 1985', S M Youngs, J Clark and T Barry, *ibid* 30 (1986), 173

'Medieval Britain and Ireland in 1995', B S Nenk, S Margeson and M Hurley, *ibid* 40 (1996), 291

'The Yorkshire archaeological register: 1985', anon, *Yorkshire Archaeological Journal* 58 (1986), 203

'Excavations at Helmsley Castle', P R Wilson, *ibid* 61 (1989), 29–33*

Hickleton
Hickleton Castle: a desktop study. J A Dabell. Hickleton: Hickleton Heritage Trust, 2001*

Hood
'Hood Castle', A H Whitaker, *Ryedale Historian* 5 (1970), 36–40*

'A survey of Hood Hill Castle', E Dennison, *ibid* 21 (2002–4), 26–29*

Huddersfield
'Mysterious Ark Hill', S Sneyd, *Northern Earth* 104 (1995), 10–13*

'Who put the ark in Ark Hill?', S Sneyd, *Postern* 1 (1993), 4–6*

Hull
Beverley Gate: the birthplace of the English Civil War. D Evans and B Sitch. Hull: City Council; Beverley: Hutton Press, 1990*

An investigation of the archaeological potential of the Hull Citadel. M Foreman. Beverley: Humberside County Council, [1987]*

Hull Citadel 1988. M Foreman. Beverley: Humberside County Council, 1988*

Trial excavations in Tower Street, Hull. M Foreman. Hull: Humberside Archaeology Unit, 1995*

Trial excavations at Sammy's Point, Kingston upon Hull, March 1997. M Foreman. Kingston upon Hull: Humber Archaeology, 1997* (Humber Archaeology report; 16)

Town and gun: the 17th-century defences of Hull. A Howes and M Foreman. Kingston upon Hull: Kingston Press, 1999*

'Fortifications', in K J Allison (ed), *The Victoria history of the counties of England: a history of the county of York – East Riding*, **1**, 412–18. Oxford: OUP, 1969*

'Kingston upon Hull, old town', J B Whitwell, *Archaeological Excavations 1976*, 127. London: HMSO, 1977

'Kingston upon Hull', J B[artlett], *CBA Group 4 Annual News-Sheet* (1969), [10–11]

'Hull, Beverley Gate, Humberside', P Armstrong, *CBA Forum: Annual Newsletter of CBA Group 4* (1986), 36–37

'The Beverley Gate and the medieval walls of Hull', anon, *ibid* (1987), 15–16

'Remains of the Myton Gate in Hull', B S Ayers and D H Evans, *East Riding Archaeologist* 10 (2001), 42–46*

'Recent archaeological work in the East Riding', D H Evans and K Steedman, *ibid* 10 (2001), 67–156 [espec pp 138–45]*

'The defences of Hull', M Foreman, *Fortress* 2 (1989), 36–45*

'Inventories of bows and arrows in store in the magazine at Hull, East Yorkshire', A M Howes, *Journal of the Society of Archer-Antiquaries* 45 (2002), 82–83*

'North walls excavation, Kingston upon Hull', J Bartlett, *Kingston upon Hull Museums Bulletin* 4 (1970), 1–23*

'Hull Castle: excavation 1970', A Cook, *ibid* 6 (1971), 16–17*

'Medieval Britain in 1964', D M Wilson and D G Hurst, *Medieval Archaeology* 9 (1965), 197

'Medieval Britain in 1969', D M Wilson and D G Hurst, *ibid* 14 (1970), 186

'Medieval Britain and Ireland in 1986', S M Youngs, J Clark and T Barry, *ibid* 31 (1987), 147

'Medieval Britain and Ireland in 1988', D R M Gaimster, S Margeson and T Barry, *ibid* 33 (1989), 197

'Post-medieval Britain in 1970', S Moorhouse, *Post-Medieval Archaeology* 5 (1971), 198–201*

'The two earliest maps of Hull', G de Boer, *ibid* 7 (1973), 79–87*

'Post-medieval Britain in 1976', J Cherry, *ibid* 11 (1977), 87

'Post-medieval Britain and Ireland in 1988', G Egan, *ibid* 23 (1989), 35

'The construction of Hull Citadel', M Foreman and S Goodhand, *ibid* 30 (1996), 143–85*

'Post-medieval Britain and Ireland in 1996', M Ponsford and R Jackson, *ibid* 31 (1997), 262–63

'Post-medieval Britain and Ireland in 1997', M Ponsford and R Jackson, *ibid* 32 (1998), 148–49

'Post-medieval Britain and Ireland in 2002', M Ponsford, *ibid* 37 (2003), 281–82

'Post-medieval Britain and Ireland in 2003', M Ponsford, *ibid* 38 (2004), 299–300

'The Yorkshire archaeological register: 1986', *Yorkshire Archaeological Journal* 59 (1987), 197–98

'The Yorkshire archaeological register: 1987', *ibid* 60 (1988), 186–87

'The seizure of Hull and its magazine, January 1642', I E Ryder, *ibid* 61 (1989), 139–48

Hutton Colswain

'Excavation of the fortified medieval hall of Hutton Colswain at Huttons Ambo, near Malton, Yorkshire', M W Thompson, *Archaeological Journal* 114 (1957), 69–91*

Keld

'The Yorkshire archaeological register: 1976', S Moorhouse, *Yorkshire Archaeological Journal* 49 (1977), 11

Kilton

'A bronze, eagle-shaped spout from Kilton Castle, Cleveland', A Aberg, *Antiquaries Journal* 59 (1979), 411–12, 424*

'The Yorkshire archaeological register: 1971', S Moorhouse, *CBA Group 4 Annual Newsletter* (1971), 8

'The Yorkshire archaeological register: 1972', S Moorhouse, *CBA Group 4, Yorkshire Archaeology 1972* (1972), 9

'Medieval Britain in 1965', D M Wilson and D G Hurst, *Medieval Archaeology* 10 (1966), 192

'Medieval Britain in 1966', D M Wilson and D G Hurst, *ibid* 11 (1967), 288

'Medieval Britain in 1967', D M Wilson and D G Hurst, *ibid* 12 (1968), 181

'Medieval Britain in 1968', D M Wilson and D G Hurst, *ibid* 13 (1969), 262–63*

'Medieval Britain in 1970', D M Wilson and S Moorhouse, *ibid* 15 (1971), 149

'Medieval Britain in 1971', L E Webster and J Cherry, *ibid* 16 (1972), 184

'Medieval Britain in 1972', L E Webster and J Cherry, *ibid* 17 (1973), 165

'Medieval Britain in 1973', L E Webster and J Cherry, *ibid* 18 (1974), 197

'Medieval Britain in 1974', L E Webster and J Cherry, *ibid* 19 (1975), 241

'Medieval Britain and Ireland in 1986', S M Youngs, J Clark and T Barry, *ibid* 31 (1987), 119

'The Yorkshire archaeological register: 1975', F Thorp, *Yorkshire Archaeological Journal* 48 (1976), 8

'Brotton: Kilton Castle', in 'Yorkshire archaeological register: 1985', *ibid* 58 (1986), 203

Knaresborough

'A group of twelfth-century pottery and other finds from Knaresborough Castle', D Waterman, *Antiquaries Journal* 33 (1953), 211–13*

'Knaresborough Castle', J Le Patourel, *Archaeological Excavations 1961*, 12. London: HMSO, 1962

'The donjon at Knaresborough: the castle as theatre', P Dixon, *Château Gaillard* 14 (1990), 121–39*

'Medieval Britain in 1961', D M Wilson and D G Hurst, *Medieval Archaeology* 6–7 (1962–3), 324

'Knaresborough Castle: a turbulent passage through time', L Kelly, *Old Yorkshire* autumn (1998), 2–9*

'A note on Knaresborough Castle', W A Atkinson, *Yorkshire Archaeological Journal* 36 (1944–7), 198–208*

'Knaresborough Castle', J Le Patourel, *ibid* 41 (1963–6), 591–607*

'The Yorkshire archaeological register: 1986', anon, *ibid* 59 (1987), 200

'King John at Knaresborough: the first known Royal Maundy', A Kellett, *ibid* 62 (1990), 69–90* [espec pp 70–74]

Laughton-en-le-Morthen
'Castle Yard or Thurcroft Castle Hill, Laughton-en-le-Morthen', J Birch, *Archaeological Journal* 137 (1980), 429–30*

Lowe Hill
Excavations at Lowe Hill, Wakefield, Yorkshire, 1953. B Hope-Taylor. Wakefield: Wakefield Historical Society, n d*

Malton
The archaeology of Malton and Norton. J F Robinson. Leeds: Yorkshire Archaeological Society, 1978*

Middleham
Middleham Castle, Yorkshire. C Peers. London: HMSO, 1965*; 2nd edition, 1978*

Middleham Castle: information for teachers. M Vasey. London: English Heritage, 1997*

Middleham Castle, Yorkshire. J Weaver. London: English Heritage, 1993*

'Aspects of fourteenth-century castle design', B M Morley, in A Detsicas (ed), *Collectanea historica: essays in memory of Stuart Rigold*, 104–13. Maidstone: Kent Archaeological Society, 1981*

Mortham
'Mortham Tower, Yorkshire', C Hussey, *Country Life* 98 (1945), 24–27*

Neville
'Neville Castle, Kirkbymoorside: excavations 1963 and 1965', A M Dornier, *Yorkshire Archaeological Journal* 42 (1967–70), 98–102*

Paull Holme
'Paull Holme Tower', P F Ryder and S Coleman, *East Riding Archaeologist* 7 (1983), 85–90*

Peasholm
'Post-medieval Britain and Ireland in 1991', M Ponsford, *Post-Medieval Archaeology* 26 (1992), 109

Pickering
Pickering Castle, North Yorkshire. L Butler. London: English Heritage, 1993*

Pickering Castle: information for teachers. L Goddard. London: English Heritage, 1998*

Pickering Castle, Yorkshire. M W Thompson. London: HMSO, 1958*

Pickering Castle, North Yorkshire. M W Thompson. London: HBMCE, 1985*

'Pickering Castle', J Clark, *Archaeological Journal* 154 (1997), 255–60*

'Medieval Britain in 1961', D M Wilson and D G Hurst, *Medieval Archaeology* 6–7 (1962–3), 324

'Medieval Britain in 1962 and 1963', D M Wilson and D G Hurst, *ibid* 8 (1964), 260

Pontefract

Pontefract Castle. I Roberts. Wakefield: West Yorkshire Archaeology Service, 1990*

Pontefract Castle: the archaeology of the Civil War. [I Roberts]. Wakefield: West Yorkshire Archaeology Service, 1988*

The third siege of Pontefract Castle. I Roberts. Wakefield: West Yorkshire Archaeology Service, 1988*

Pontefract Castle: archaeological excavations 1982–86. I Roberts. Leeds: West Yorkshire Archaeology Service, 2002*

The medieval cellar at Pontefract Castle with details of the Civil war inscriptions. I Roberts. Morley: Archaeological Services WYAS, 2005*

'A resistivity survey at Pontefract Castle, West Yorkshire', S J Dockrill, J A Gater and J J Hill, in L A Pocock (ed), *Geophysical surveys 1982*, 197–94. Bradford: Bradford University, School of Archaeological Sciences, 1983*

'Pontefract castle – Albarrana towers and influences from castles in Spain', P A Burton, *Castle Studies Group Journal* 19 (2006), 239–44*

'The Yorkshire archaeological register: 1972', S Moorhouse, *CBA Group 4, Yorkshire Archaeology 1972* (1972), 11

'Pontefract Castle', S Moorhouse, *CBA Forum: Annual Newsletter of CBA Group 4*, (1984–5), 38–41*

'Pontefract, Pontefract Castle, West Yorkshire', I Roberts, *ibid* (1986), 38

'Back to reality: Pontefract Castle, West Yorkshire', E Macdonnell, *Country Life* 172 (1982), 1356, 1358*

'Pontefract', T Wilmott, *Current Archaeology* 9.11 (1987), 340–44*

'Medieval Britain in 1981', S M Youngs and J Clark, *Medieval Archaeology* 26 (1982), 216–17

'Medieval Britain and Ireland in 1982', S M Youngs, J Clark and T Barry, *ibid* 27 (1983), 213–14*

'Medieval Britain and Ireland in 1984', S M Youngs, J Clark and T Barry, *ibid* 29 (1985), 208–9

'Medieval Britain and Ireland in 1986', S M Youngs, J Clark and T Barry, *ibid* 31 (1987), 172–73

'Medieval Britain and Ireland in 2004', M Gaimster and K O'Conor, *ibid* 49 (2005), 424

'Post-medieval Britain in 1982', G Egan, *Post-Medieval Archaeology* 17 (1983), 187

'Post-medieval Britain in 1986', G Egan, *ibid* 21 (1987), 270

'Post-medieval Britain and Ireland in 2000', M Ponsford, *ibid* 35 (2001), 185

'Post-medieval fieldwork in Britain and Northern Ireland in 2004', M Ponsford, *ibid* 39 (2005), 395

'Pontefract Castle', in P Turnbull, 'The Yorkshire archaeological register: 1981', *Yorkshire Archaeological Journal* 54 (1982), 181

'Eighteenth- and nineteenth-century clay tobacco pipes from Pontefract Castle', S D White and P J Davey, *ibid* 75 (2003), 129–44*

'Coins from the Pontefract Castle excavations', I Roberts and P Seaby, *Yorkshire Numismatist* 2 (1992), 101–4*

Ravensworth

'Ravensworth Castle, North Yorkshire', P F Ryder, *Yorkshire Archaeological Journal* 51 (1979), 81–100*

Redcar

'World War One coastal defences', E W Sockett, *CBA Group 3 Newsbulletin* 3.9 (1988), [18–20]*

Richmond

Richmond Castle, North Yorkshire. St Agatha's Abbey, Easby, North Yorkshire. J Goodall. London: English Heritage, 2001*

Richmond Castle, Yorkshire. C Peers. London: HMSO, 1953*

Richmond Castle, Yorkshire. C Peers. London: HBMCE, 1985*

Richmond Castle: information for teachers. M Vasey. London: English Heritage, 1997*

Richmond Castle and Easby Abbey. J Weaver. London: English Heritage, 1989*

'The great tower of Carlisle Castle', J A A Goodall, in M McCarthy and D Weston (eds), *Carlisle and Cumbria: Roman and medieval architecture, art and archaeology*, 39–62. Leeds: British Archaeological Association and Maney Publishing, 2004* (Conference transactions; 27) [has much on Richmond]

'Richmond Castle, Yorkshire', J Goodall, *Country Life* 197.20 (2003), 148–51*

Sandal

Sandal Castle. R Bell. Wakefield: Willow Island Editions, 2001*

Sandal Castle, Wakefield: the history and archaeology of a medieval castle. L Butler. Wakefield: Wakefield Historical Publications, 1991*

Sandal Castle: a short account of the history of the site and the 1964 excavations. P Mayes. Wakefield: Wakefield Historical Society, 1965*

Sandal Castle: a short account of the history of the site and the 1965 excavations. P Mayes. Wakefield: Wakefield Historical Society, 1966*

Sandal Castle: excavations 1966. P Mayes. Wakefield: Wakefield Historical Society, 1967*

Sandal Castle: excavations 1967. P Mayes. Wakefield: Wakefield Historical Society, 1968*

Sandal Castle, Wakefield, Yorkshire: excavations 1968. L A S Butler, 1969 [duplicated typescript]

Sandal Castle, Wakefield, Yorkshire: excavations 1969. L A S Butler, 1970 [duplicated typescript]

Sandal Castle, Wakefield, Yorkshire: excavations 1970. L A S Butler, 1971 [duplicated typescript]

Sandal Castle, Wakefield, Yorkshire: excavations 1971. L A S Butler and K Stubbs, 1972 [duplicated typescript]

Sandal Castle: excavations, 1972. P Mayes, 1972 [duplicated typescript]

Sandal Castle, Wakefield: excavations 1964–72. P Mayes. Wakefield: Wakefield Corporation, 1973*

Sandal Castle excavations 1964–1973: a detailed archaeological report. P Mayes and L Butler. Wakefield: Wakefield Historical Publications, 1983*

'Sandal Castle, Wakefield, West Yorkshire', P Mayes, *Archaeological Journal* 137 (1980), 401–2*

'Wakefield, Sandal magna', P Mayes, *CBA Group 4 Annual Newsheet* (1964), [10–11]

'Sandal Magna', L A S Butler, *ibid* (1969), [12]

'The Yorkshire archaeological register: 1971', S Moorhouse, *CBA Group 4 Annual Newsletter* (1971), 8

'The Yorkshire archaeological register: 1972', S Moorhouse, *CBA Group 4, Yorkshire Archaeology 1972* (1972), 10

'A stronghold regained: Sandal Castle, West Yorkshire', E Macdonnell, *Country Life* 170 (1981), 1802*

'Medieval Britain in 1964', D M Wilson and D G Hurst, *Medieval Archaeology* 9 (1965), 192

'Medieval Britain in 1965', D M Wilson and D G Hurst, *ibid* 10 (1966), 196

'Medieval Britain in 1966', D M Wilson and D G Hurst, *ibid* 11 (1967), 288

'Medieval Britain in 1969', D M Wilson and D G Hurst, *ibid* 14 (1970), 177–78*

'Medieval Britain in 1970', D M Wilson and S Moorhouse, *ibid* 15 (1971), 149

'Medieval Britain in 1971', L E Webster and J Cherry, *ibid* 16 (1972), 184–85*

'Medieval Britain in 1972', L E Webster and J Cherry, *ibid* 17 (1973), 165

'Medieval Britain in 1973', L E Webster and J Cherry, *ibid* 18 (1974), 197

'Paleopathology of a royalist garrison', K Manchester, *Ossa* 5 (1978), 25–33*

'Post-medieval Britain in 1966', D G Hurst, *Post-Medieval Archaeology* 1 (1967), 109

'Post-medieval Britain in 1967', D G Hurst, *ibid* 2 (1968), 177

'Post-medieval Britain in 1968', D G Hurst, *ibid* 3 (1969), 193

Sand-le-Mere
'The defence of a coastal outlet: Sand-le-Mere, East Yorkshire', A Ruddy, *Loopholes* 20 (1997), 15–24*

Scarborough
Scarborough Castle: an illustrated guide. Anon. London: HMSO, 1960*

Scarborough Castle. Anon. London: HMSO, 1980*

Scarborough Castle. Anon. London: HMSO, 1981*

'A place of great importance': Scarborough in the Civil Wars, 1640–1660. J Binns. Preston: Carnegie Publishing, 1996*

Scarborough Castle and headland. S J Garton. London: HMSO, 1946*

Scarborough Castle, North Yorkshire. J A A Goodall. London: English Heritage, 2000*

The archaeology of medieval Scarborough: excavation and research 1987–2004. T Pearson. Scarborough: Scarborough Archaeological and Historical Society, 2005*

Scarborough Castle. G Port. London: English Heritage, 1989*

Scarborough Castle: information for teachers. D Walmsley. London: English Heritage, 1998*

'Scarborough Castle', J Clark, *Archaeological Journal* 154 (1997), 241–48*

'Scarborough', T Pearson, *Current Archaeology* 11.5 (1991), 208–9*

'Beside the seaside', T Pearson, *Interim* 14.4 (1989), 24–29*

'Medieval Britain and Ireland in 1989', D R M Gaimster, S Margeson and M Hurley, *Medieval Archaeology* 34 (1990), 218

'Medieval Britain and Ireland in 1991', B S Nenk, S Margeson and M Hurley, *ibid* 36 (1992), 274

'Medieval Britain and Ireland in 2000', J Bradley and M Gaimster, *ibid* 45 (2001), 336

'Scarborough and the Civil Wars 1642–1651', J Binns, *Northern History* 22 (1986), 95–122

'Post-medieval Britain and Ireland in 2000', M Ponsford, *Post-Medieval Archaeology* 35 (2001), 172

'Excavations on the 'Balmoral site', in Scarborough during 1973: interim report', P G Farmer, *Transactions of the Scarborough and District Archaeological Society* 2.16 (1973), 27–36, 44

'Excavations in Scarborough old town – 1989 and 1990', T Pearson and C Hall, *Transactions of the Scarborough Archaeological and Historical Society* 28 (1990), 4–12*

'Excavations in Scarborough 1987–1997', T Pearson, *ibid* 33 (1997), 14–22*

'The Yorkshire archaeological register: 1976', S Moorhouse, *Yorkshire Archaeological Journal* 49 (1977), 11

'Excavation of the great hall or 'Kyngeshalle' at Scarborough Castle, North Yorkshire', C Hayfield and T Pacitto, *ibid* 77 (2005), 31–92*

Sheffield

'Sheffield Castle', N Guy, *Castle Studies Group Bulletin* 18 (2004–5), 202–21*

'Medieval Britain in 1958', D M Wilson and J G Hurst, *Medieval Archaeology* 3 (1959), 308

'Medieval Britain and Ireland in 2001', J Bradley and M Gaimster, *ibid* 46 (2002), 211

Sheriff Hutton

Within the pale: the story of Sheriff Hutton park. Sheriff Hutton Women's Institute Community Pale Project, edited by E Dennison . York: William Sessions, 2005*

Castellum Huttonicum: some notes on the castle at Sheriff Hutton. R W Howarth. Sheriff Hutton: the author, 1993*

'Sheriff Hutton Castle', E Dennison, *Archaeological Journal* 154 (1997), 291, 293–96*

'The Yorkshire archaeological register: 1971', S Moorhouse, *CBA Group 4 Annual Newsletter* (1971), 8

Skipsea

'Skipsea Brough', R Butler, *Archaeological Journal* 141 (1984), 45–46

'Medieval Britain and Ireland in 1987', S M Youngs [*et al*], *Medieval Archaeology* 32 (1988), 259

Skipton

Skipton Castle. Anon. [S l: s n], 1986*

Skipton Castle. Anon. Norwich: printed by Jarrold, 1989*

Skipton Castle in the Great Civil War, 1642–1645. R T Spence. Skipton: Skipton Castle, 1991*

Skipton Castle and its builders. R T Spence. Skipton: Skipton Castle, 2002*

'Skipton Castle', E A Gee, *Archaeological Journal* 125 (1968), 333–35*

'An Angevin gatehouse at Skipton Castle (Yorkshire, West Riding)', D F Renn, *Château Gaillard* 7 (1975), 173–82*

Spofforth

Spofforth Castle, Yorkshire. R J A Burnett, O J Weaver and R Gilyard-Beer. London: HMSO, 1965*

Stainborough

'Stainborough Castle', J Birch, *Archaeological Journal* 137 (1980), 448–49*

Thirsk

'Medieval Britain and Ireland in 1999', J Bradley and M Gaimster, *ibid* 44 (2000), 314–15

Tickhill

'Robert de Bellême and the castle of Tickhill', M Chibnall, in *Droit privé et institutions régionales: études historiques offertes à Jean Yver*, 151–56. Paris: Presses Universitaires de France, 1976

'Tickhill Castle', South Yorkshire County Archaeology Service, *CBA Forum: Annual Newsletter of CBA Group 4* (1985), 30*

'Tickhill Castle', J Birch, *Archaeological Journal* 137 (1980), 416–17*

'On preserving our ruins', C Stanford, *Journal of Architectural Conservation* 6.3 (2000), 28–43*

'Medieval Britain in 1961', D M Wilson and D G Hurst, *Medieval Archaeology* 6–7 (1962–3), 325

'The Yorkshire archaeological register: 1987', anon, *Yorkshire Archaeological Journal* 60 (1988), 186

York

Clifford's Tower and the castles of York. Anon. London: HBMCE, 1987*

Clifford's Tower and the castles of York. L Butler. London: English Heritage, 1997*

The bars and walls of York: a handbook for visitors. R M Butler. York: Yorkshire Architectural and York Archaeological Society, 1974*

York. J Harvey. London: Batsford, 1975*

Clifford's Tower: information for teachers. A Jones. London: English Heritage, 1998*

Clifford's Tower, York Castle. B H St J O'Neil. London: HMSO, 1959*

Clifford's Tower and the castles of York. D F Renn. London: HMSO, 1971*

An inventory of the historical monuments in the city of York. 2. The defences. RCHME. London: HMSO, 1972*

York Castle: an illustrated guide. RCHME. London: HMSO, 1973* [offprinted from the above item]

The walls of York: a guided tour. W R Ward. 2nd edition. Clapham: Dalesman, 1976*

The bars and walls of York: a survey. An assessment of their condition and state of repair. R D Waterman. [York: City Engineer's Department], 1980*

The great and close siege of York. P Wenham. Kineton: Roundwood Press, 1970*

The city walls and castles of York: the pictorial evidence. B Wilson and F Mee. York: York Archaeological Trust, 2005* (The archaeology of York supplementary series; 1/3)

'The city walls, bars and postern' and 'The castle and the Old Baile', in P M Tillott (ed), *The Victoria history of the counties of England: a history of Yorkshire – the city of York*, 510–14, 521–29. Oxford: OUP, 1961*

'The date of Clifford's Tower, York', A Taylor, in A Taylor, *Studies in castles and castle-building*, 241–47. London: Hambledon Press, 1986*

'A late seventeenth-century plan of York', R M Butler, *Antiquaries Journal* 52 (1972), 320–29*

'York', B K Davison, *Archaeological Excavations 1971*, 37. London: HMSO, 1972

'The date of Clifford's Tower, York', A J Taylor, *Archaeological Journal* 111 (1954), 153–59

'Excavations at Baile Hill, York, 1968', P V Addyman, *ibid* 125 (1968), 307–8

'Excavations at Baile Hill, York, 1969', P V Addyman, *ibid* 126 (1969), 178–79

'Five castle excavations: reports on the Institute's research into the origins of the castle in England. Baile Hill, York: a report on the Institute's excavations', P V Addyman and J Priestley, *ibid* 134 (1977), 115–56*

'York city walls', York Archaeological Trust, *CBA Forum: Annual Newsletter of CBA Group 4* (1988), 31

'York city', J Radley, *CBA Group 4 Annual Newsheet* (1969), [13]

'The Yorkshire archaeological register: 1971', S Moorhouse, *CBA Group 4 Annual Newsletter* (1971), 5

'Excavations at Baile Hill, York', P V Addyman, *Château Gaillard* 5 (1972), 7–12*

'Baile Hill, York', P Addyman, *Current Archaeology* 2.1 (1969), 25–26*

'York defences', [A Selkirk], *ibid* 2.6 (1969), 167*

'City walls tower 11', N Pearson, *Interim* 8.3 (1982), 16–20*

'The hole in the wall', R Kemp, *ibid* 10.2 (1985), 15–17*

'Medieval Britain in 1969', D M Wilson and D G Hurst, *Medieval Archaeology* 14 (1970), 177

'Medieval Britain in 1970', D M Wilson and S Moorhouse, *ibid* 15 (1971), 157

'Medieval Britain in 1971', L E Webster and J Cherry, *ibid* 16 (1972), 191–92

'Medieval Britain in 1981', S M Youngs and J Clark, *ibid* 26 (1982), 214–15

'Medieval Britain and Ireland in 1985', S M Youngs, S Margeson and T Barry, *ibid* 30 (1986), 174–76

'Medieval Britain and Ireland in 1989', D R M Gaimster, S Margeson and M Hurley, *ibid* 34 (1990), 220

'Medieval Britain and Ireland in 1990', B S Nenk, S Margeson and M Hurley, *ibid* 35 (1991), 198

'Medieval Britain and Ireland in 1991', B S Nenk, S Margeson and M Hurley, *ibid* 36 (1992), 275

'Medieval Britain and Ireland in 2002', J Bradley and M Gaimster, *ibid* 47 (2003), 294

'Post-medieval Britain in 1985', G Egan, *Post-Medieval Archaeology* 20 (1986), 336

'A Bootham mystery: Galmanho, Kenningdike, Werkdike', J H Harvey, *York Historian* 1 (1976), 13–17*

'Who saved York walls? The roles of William Etty and the Corporation of York', G G Curr, *ibid* 5 (1984), 25–38*

'Excavations in the defences of the city of York: an early medieval stone tower and the successive earth ramparts', J Radley, *Yorkshire Archaeological Journal* 44 (1972), 38–64*

'The Yorkshire archaeological register: 1985', anon, *ibid* 58 (1986), 204–5

'The excavation of the earthwork on Holgate Hill, York, 1936', P Corder, *Yorkshire Architectural and York Archaeological Society Annual Report* (1951–2), 31–35*

'Romano-British cemetery and 17th-century gun emplacement on the Mount, York', L P Wenham, *ibid* (1952–3), 18–34*

WALES

ANGLESEY

Carr, A D and Carr, G. *Cestyll Gwynedd*. Cardiff: Cadw: Welsh Historic Monuments, 1985*

Harding, J. ' 'The mini castles of Wales': pillboxes in Anglesey', *Transactions of the Anglesey Antiquarian Society and Field Club* (2001), 59–70*

Lynch, F. *A guide to ancient and historic Wales: Gwynedd*. London: HMSO, for Cadw: Welsh Historic Monuments, 1995* [espec ch 7]; revised edition, 2001*

Salter, M. *The castles of north Wales*. Wolverhampton: Folly Publications, 1997*

Aberlleiniog

'Aber Lleiniog', D J C King, *Programme of the hundred-and-eleventh annual meeting at Llangefni, 1964*, CAA, 1964, 18–19

Beaumaris

Beaumaris Castle, Anglesey. Anon. London: HMSO, reprinted 1968*

Anglesey: a guide to ancient and historic sites on the Isle of Anglesey. L Macinnes. Cardiff: Cadw: Welsh Historic Monuments, 1989*

Beaumaris Castle: an illustrated souvenir. A Phillips. London: HMSO, 1961*

Beaumaris Castle/Castell Biwmares, Gwynedd. A J Taylor. Cardiff: HMSO, 1980*

Beaumaris Castle. A J Taylor. Revised edition. Cardiff: Cadw: Welsh Historic Monuments, 1985*; reprinted with amendments, 1988*; 4th edition, 1999*; 5th edition, 2004*

'Beaumaris Castle', in RCAHMW, *an inventory of the ancient monuments in Anglesey*, 8–13. London: HMSO, 1937, reprinted 1960*

'Beaumaris Castle', G C Dunning, in P J Davey (ed), *Medieval pottery from excavations in the north west*, 8–9. [Liverpool]: Institute of Extension Studies, 1977*

'Beaumaris Castle, A J Taylor, *131st annual meeting, Anglesey, 1984: programme*, CAA, 1984, 35

'Building at Caernarvon and Beaumaris in 1295–6', A Taylor, in A Taylor, *Studies in castles and castle-building*, 139–44. London: Hambledon Press, 1986

'The Beaumaris Castle building account of 1295–1298', A Taylor, in J R Kenyon and R Avent (eds), *Castles in Wales and the Marches: essays in honour of D J Cathcart King*, 125–42. Cardiff: University of Wales Press, 1987*

'Investigations in 1985 by R B White at Castle Meadows, Beaumaris', P J Fasham, *Transactions of the Anglesey Antiquarian Society and Field Club* (1992), 123–30*

'Beaumaris', R B White, *Archaeological Excavations 1975*, 147. London: HMSO, 1976

'Beaumaris Castle', A J Taylor, *Archaeological Journal* 132 (1975), 279–81*

'Beaumaris', R B White, *Archaeology in Wales* 15 (1975), 53

'Building at Caernarvon and Beaumaris in 1295–6', A J Taylor, *Bulletin of the Board of Celtic Studies* 15 (1952–4), 61–66

'The "mill" at Beaumaris Castle', A J Parkinson, *Melin: Journal of the Welsh Mills Group* 4 (1988), 58–61*

Castell

'The excavation of Castell, Porth Trefadog, a coastal promontory fort in north Wales', D Longley, *Medieval Archaeology* 35 (1991), 64–85*

BRECONSHIRE

Burnham, H. *A guide to ancient and historic Wales: Clwyd and Powys*. London: HMSO, for Cadw: Welsh Historic Monuments, 1995*

Coplestone-Crow, B. 'Trewalkin and its Anglo-Norman lords', *Brycheiniog* 26 (1992–3), 43–51*

Haslam, R. *Powys (The buildings of Wales)*. Harmondsworth: Penguin Books, 1979*

King, D J C. 'The castles of Breconshire', *Brycheiniog* 7 (1961), 711–94*

King, D J C. 'Two further castles in Breconshire', *ibid* 13 (1968–9), 155–57*

Remfry, P M. *Four castles of the middle reaches of the river Wye, 1066–1282*. Malvern Link: SCS Publishing, 1995*

Remfry, P M. *The castles of Breconshire*. Almeley: Logaston Press, 1999* (Monuments in the landscape; 8)

Renn, D F. 'The round keeps of the Brecon region', *Archaeologia Cambrensis* 110 (1961), 129–43*

Salter, M. *The castles of mid Wales*. Wolverhampton: Folly Publications, 1991*

Salter, M. *The castles of mid Wales*. New edition. Malvern: Folly Publications, 2001*

Walker, D. 'The lordship of Builth', *Brycheiniog* 20 (1984–5), 9–11

Aberllynfi

'A motte and bailey and an ancient church site at Aberllynfi', R E Kay, *Herefordshire Archaeological News* 61 (1994), 26–27*

'Some additional notes on Aberllynfi Castle', P M Remfry, *ibid* 62 (1994), 11–12

Blaenllynfi

'Castell Blaenllynfi, Brecknock: a marcher castle and its landscape', R J Silvester, P Courtney and S E Rees, *Archaeologia Cambrensis* 153 (2004), 75–103*

'Medieval Britain and Ireland in 1990', B S Nenk, S Margeson and M Hurley, *Medieval Archaeology* 35 (1991), 233

Brecon

'Brecon Castle', J K Knight, *The hundred-and-twenty-first annual meeting in south Brecknock, 1974*, CAA, 1974, 12–14

'The castle', in G C Boon (ed), *137th annual meeting, north and west Brecknock ... 1990*, CAA, 1990, 32–33

'Brecon Castle', A J Taylor, *Archaeologia Cambrensis* 101 (1950–1), 173

'Brecon, Bethel Square', M Locock and A G Marvell, *Archaeology in Wales* 35 (1995), 59–60

'Towards a topography of early Brecon', D R Morgan, *Brycheiniog* 23 (1988–9), 23–41*

'Bethel Square, Brecon: excavations in the medieval town', M Locock, *ibid* 28 (1995–6), 35–79*

'Bishop Morton and the Ely Tower at Brecon: documenting intrigue', R A Griffiths, *ibid* 34 (2002), 13–30*

'Brecon tower research project, Watergate, Brecon', G Cruse, S Priestley and G Children, *ibid* 36 (2004), 15–50*

'Priory, friary and castle', B Little, *Country Life* 137 (1965), 1518–20*

'Medieval Britain and Ireland in 1989', D R M Gaimster, S Margeson and M Hurley, *Medieval Archaeology* 34 (1990), 250

'Medieval Britain and Ireland in 1995', B S Nenk, S Margeson and M Hurley, *ibid* 40 (1996), 316

'Medieval Britain and Ireland in 1997', M Gaimster, C Haith and J Bradley, *ibid* 42 (1998), 188–89

'Post-medieval Britain and Ireland in 1997', M Ponsford and R Jackson, *Post-Medieval Archaeology* 32 (1998), 154–55

Bronllys

Bronllys Castle/Castell Bronllys, Powys. J B Smith and J K Knight. Cardiff: HMSO, 1981*

'Bronllys Castle', J K Knight, *The hundred-and-twenty-first annual meeting in south Brecknock, 1974*, CAA, 1974, 27–28

'Bronllys Castle', A J Taylor, *Archaeologia Cambrensis* 101 (1950–1), 174

Builth

'Builth Castle', C J Spurgeon, *124th annual meeting in Aberystwyth, south Montgomery and north Radnor, 1977*, CAA, 1977, 29–30

'Builth Castle', A J Taylor, *Archaeologia Cambrensis* 101 (1950–1), 174–75

'Builth Castle', C J Spurgeon, *Brycheiniog* 18 (1978–9), 47–59*

Bwlchyddinas

'Castell Dinas', R E Kay, *ibid* 10 (1964), 15–27*

'Bwlchyddinas Castle, Breconshire, and the survey of 1337', R F Walker, *ibid* 31 (1998–9), 19–30*

Camlais

'A castle of Llywelyn ap Gruffydd in Brycheiniog', D J C King, *ibid* 11 (1965), 151–53

'Camlais and Sennybridge castles', D J C King, *ibid* 21 (1984–5), 9–11

Coch

'Castell Coch – Mellte Castle', in G C Boon (ed), *137th annual meeting, north and west Brecknock … 1990*, CAA, 1990, 27–28*

'Castell Coch, parish of Ystradfellte, Breconshire', R E Kay, *Brycheiniog* 13 (1968–9), 87–94*

Crickhowell

'Crickhowell, Bwthyn y Castell', G A Makepeace, *Archaeology in Wales* 40 (2000), 125

'Crwcws'

'Brecon, Crwcws Castle', A Marvell and M Locock, *ibid* 36 (1996), 82–83

Hay on Wye

Hay on Wye Castle 1066–1298. P M Remfry. Malvern Link: SCS Publishing, 1995*

Hay on Wye Castle 1066–1298: a short guide. P M Remfry. Malvern Link: SCS Publishing, 1995*

'Hay Castle', A J Taylor, *Archaeologia Cambrensis* 101 (1950–1), 174

'Medieval Britain and Ireland in 2004', M Gaimster and K O'Conor, *Medieval Archaeology* 49 (2005), 470

'Post-medieval Britain and Ireland in 2001', M Ponsford, *Post-Medieval Archaeology* 36 (2002), 285–86

Llangattock

'Hen Castell, Llangattock', A Lewis, *Archaeology in Wales* 42 (2002), 152–53*

Llanthomas

'Llanthomas motte, Llanigon', P Dorling, *ibid* 28 (1988), 68*

Madoc

'Castell Madoc', E J Talbot, *ibid* 7 (1967), 15

'The excavation of Castell Madoc ringwork, Lower Chapel, Breconshire', E J Talbot and B V Field, *Brycheiniog* 12 (1966–7), 131–32

'Medieval Britain in 1967', D M Wilson and D G Hurst, *Medieval Archaeology* 12 (1968), 181

Maescelyn
'Maescelyn motte, Crickhowell', A Phillips, *Archaeology in Wales* 43 (2003), 149–50*

Pont Estyll, Llanspyddid
'Llanspyddid', E J Talbot, *ibid* 4 (1964), 17

'Pont Estyll, Llanspyddyd', D M Browne, *ibid* 26 (1986), 49*

'Medieval Britain in 1964', D M Wilson and D G Hurst, *Medieval Archaeology* 9 (1965), 193

Sennybridge
'Camlais and Sennybridge castles', D J C King, *Brycheiniog* 21 (1984–5), 9–11

Sgethrog
'The houses of Breconshire. Part III. The Brecon district', S R Jones and J T Smith, *ibid* 11 (1965), 1–149* [espec pp 5–10]

Talgarth
'The houses of Breconshire. Part II. The Hay and Talgarth district', S R Jones and J T Smith, *ibid* 10 (1964), 69–183* [espec pp 74–75]

Trecastle
'Trecastle motte and bailey', in G C Boon (ed), *137th annual meeting, north and west Brecknock … 1990*, CAA, 1990, 18

Tretower
Tretower Castle. D W Humphreys. [S l: s n], n d*

Tretower Court and Castle, Breconshire. C A R Radford. London: HMSO, 1957*

Tretower Court and Castle. C A R Radford, revised by D M Robinson. Cardiff: Cadw: Welsh Historic Monuments, 1985*

Tretower Court and Castle. C A R Radford. 3rd edition, revised and edited by D M Robinson. Cardiff: Cadw: Welsh Historic Monuments, 1986*

'Tretower Court & Castle', in G C Boon (ed), *137th annual meeting, north and west Brecknock … 1990*, CAA, 1990, 36

'Tretower: the castle and the court', C A R Radford, *Brycheiniog* 6 (1960), 1–50*

'A manor of the Welsh Marches', H J Massingham, *Country Life* 112 (1952), 331–32*

CAERNARVONSHIRE

Carr, A D and Carr, G. *Cestyll Gwynedd*. Cardiff: Cadw: Welsh Historic Monuments, 1985*

Johnstone, N. 'An investigation into the location of the royal courts of thirteenth-century Gwynedd', in N Edwards (ed), *Landscape and settlement in medieval Wales*, 55–69. Oxford: Oxbow Books, 1997* (Oxbow monograph; 81)

Jones, G R J. 'The defence of Gwynedd in the thirteenth century', *Transactions of the Caernarvonshire Historical Society* 30 (1969), 29–43*

Longley, D. 'The royal courts of the Welsh princes AD 400–1283', in N Edwards (ed), *Landscape and settlement in medieval Wales*, 41–54. Oxford: Oxbow Books, 1997* (Oxbow monograph; 81)

Lynch, F. *A guide to ancient and historic Wales: Gwynedd*. London: HMSO, for Cadw: Welsh Historic Monuments, 1995* [espec ch 7]; revised edition, 2001*

Salter, M. *The castles of north Wales*. Wolverhampton: Folly Publications, 1997*

Williams-Jones, K. 'Twelfth and thirteenth century mottes and trackways', in T M Bassett and B L Davies (eds), *Atlas of Caernarvonshire*, 78–81. Caernarfon: Gwynedd Rural Council, 1977*

Williams-Jones, K. 'Edwardian castles and boroughs', in *ibid*, 82–88*

Aber

'Medieval Britain and Ireland in 1993', B S Nenk, S Margeson and M Hurley, *Medieval Archaeology* 38 (1994), 288

Belan

Fort Belan. I W Jones. Caernarfon: Arfon Air, 1979*

A maritime fortress: the collections of the Wynn family at Belan Fort, c. 1750–1950. M Stammers. Cardiff: University of Wales Press, 2001*

'Belan Fort', in RCAHMW, *An inventory of the ancient monuments in Caernarvonshire. 2. Central*, 220–21. London: HMSO, 1960*

'Belan Fort', D B Hague, *126th annual meeting, Lleyn and Snowdonia, 1979*, CAA, 1979, 36–37*

Caernarfon

Les châteaux forts: le siècle de grands Capétiens 1180–1328. S W Gondoin. Apt: Editions Harnois, 2002* [pp. 90–95]

A royal palace in Wales: Caernarfon. C Kightly. Cardiff: Cadw: Welsh Historic Monuments, 1991*

Caernarfon Castle and town: an educational resource pack. R M Morris. Cardiff: Cadw: Welsh Historic Monuments, 1991*

Caernarfon Castle: an illustrated souvenir. A Phillips. London: HMSO, 1961*

Caernarvon Castle and town wall, Caernarvonshire. A J Taylor. London: HMSO, 1953*

Caernarvon Castle and town walls, Caernarvonshire. A J Taylor. London: HMSO, reprinted with amendments, 1969*

Caernarfon Castle. A J Taylor. Revised edition, edited by M R Apted. Cardiff: Cadw: Welsh Historic Monuments, 1986*

Caernarfon Castle and town walls. A Taylor. Revised edition, edited by M R Apted, reprinted with revisions. Cardiff: Cadw: Welsh Historic Monuments, 1989*; 3rd edition, 1993*; 4th edition, 1997*; 5th edition, 2001*; 6th edition, 2004*

'Caernarvon Castle', and 'Caernarvon town walls', in RCAHMW, *An inventory of the ancient monuments in Caernarvonshire. 2. Central*, 124–56. London: HMSO, 1960*

'Caernarfon', H Carter, in M D Lobel (ed), *Historic towns*, **1**. Oxford: Lovell Johns-Cook, Hammond and Kell Organization, 1969*

'The castle builders: Harlech and Caernarfon', N Coldstream, in 'Architecture', in B Ford (ed), *The Cambridge guide to the arts in Britain. 2. The Middle Ages*, 81–87. Cambridge: CUP, 1988*

'Geological provenance of Caernarfon Castle and town walls', D Nichol, in M G Bassett, V K Deisler and D Nichol (eds), *Urban geology in Wales: 2*, 204–8. Cardiff: National Museum of Wales, 2005*

'The conservation and restoration of Caernarfon Castle 1845–1912', R Avent, in M Meek (ed), *The modern traveller to our past: Festschrift in honour of Ann Hamlin*, 344–52. [Southport]: DPK, 2006*

'Caernarfon Castle and town walls', A J Taylor, *131st annual meeting, Anglesey, 1984: programme*, CAA, 1984, 33–34

'Caernarfon Castle', R Avent, *Programme of the 149th annual meeting 2002, Caernarfon*, CAA, 2002, 2–5*

'The date of Caernarvon Castle', A Taylor, in A Taylor, *Studies in castles and castle-building*, 129–38. London: Hambledon Press, 1986*

'Building at Caernarvon and Beaumaris in 1295–6', A Taylor, in *ibid*, 139–44

'Caernarfon Castle', M W Thompson, *126th annual meeting, Lleyn and Snowdonia, 1979*, CAA, 1979, 27–29

'The date of Caernarvon Castle', A J Taylor, *Antiquity* 26 (1952), 25–34*

'Caernarvon', C N Johns, *Archaeological Excavations 1961*, 14–15. London: HMSO, 1962

'Caernarvon Castle and town walls', A J Taylor, *Archaeological Journal* 132 (1975), 287–89*

'Caernarvon', C N Johns, *Archaeology in Wales* 2 (1962), 12

'Caernarvon Castle', D M Evans, *ibid* 9 (1969), 23

'Caernarfon, Eastgate Street evaluation', A Davidson, *ibid* 39 (1999), 109–10

'Building at Caernarvon and Beaumaris in 1295–96', A J Taylor, *Bulletin of the Board of Celtic Studies* 15 (1952–4), 61–66

'A note on Walter of Hereford, builder of Caernarvon Castle', A J Taylor, *Transactions of the Caernarvonshire Historical Society* 9 (1948), 16–19

'Dau arolwg o Gastell Caernarfon 1622 a 1624', G Parry, *ibid* 48 (1987), 7–15

'Caernarfon's princely castle', D B Hague, *Country Life* 145 (1969), 1650–52*

'Datgelu gwaith trwsio Caernarfon', R Avent, *Etifeddiaeth y Cymry* 26 (2003), 11–13*

'Uncovering repairs at Caernarfon', R Avent, *Heritage in Wales* 26 (2003), 11–13*

'The birth of Edward of Caernarfon and the beginnings of Caernarfon Castle', A J Taylor, *History* new ser 35 (1950), 256–61

'Seventeenth-century finds from Caernarfon Castle', P J Davey and D O'Hanlon, *Medieval and Later Pottery in Wales* 8 (1985), 81

'Medieval Britain in 1959', D M Wilson and J G Hurst, *Medieval Archaeology* 4 (1960), 147, 151

'Medieval Britain in 1969', D M Wilson and D G Hurst, *ibid* 14 (1970), 179

'Space and structure at Caernarfon Castle', M Fradley, *ibid* 50 (2006), 165–78*

'A new interpretation of Caernarfon Castle', J R Mathieu, *Medieval Life* 9 (1998), 11–15*

Carn Fadrun

'Carn Fadrun', in RCAHMW, *An inventory of the ancient monuments in Caernarvonshire. 3. West*, 69–71. London: HMSO, 1964*

Conwy

Conwy Castle: an illustrated souvenir. A Phillips. London: HMSO, 1961*

Conway Castle and town walls, Caernarvonshire. A J Taylor. London: HMSO, 1956*

Conwy Castle and town walls, Caernarvonshire. A J Taylor. London: HMSO, reprinted with amendments, 1969*

Conwy Castle and town walls. A J Taylor. Revised edition. Cardiff: Cadw: Welsh Historic Monuments, 1986*; 3rd edition, 1990*; 4th edition, 1998*; 5th edition, 2003*

Conwy Castle. R White and D Owen. Cardiff: Cadw: Welsh Historic Monuments, 1987* (Cadw cartoon series)

'Conway Castle' and Conway town walls and gates', in RCAHMW, *An inventory of the ancient monuments in Caernarvonshire. 1. East*, 46–57. London: HMSO, 1956*

'"Changing rooms": interpreting form and function in the inner ward at Conwy Castle', J Ashbee, in P Draper (ed), *Current work in architectural history: papers read at the annual symposium of the Society of Architectural Historians of Great Britain 2004*, 6–10. London: Society of Architectural Historians of Great Britain, 2005*

'Conwy', L A S Butler and D H Evans, in P J Davey (ed), *Medieval pottery from excavations in the north west*, 24–29. [Liverpool]: Institute of Extension Studies, 1977*

'Two views from the roof: design and defence at Conwy and Stokesay', D Renn, in J R Kenyon and K O'Conor (eds), *The medieval castle in Ireland and Wales: essays in honour of Jeremy Knight*, 163–75. Dublin: Four Court Press, 2003*

'The Conwy particulars accounts for Nov 1285 – Sept 1286', A Taylor, in A Taylor, *Studies in castles and castle-building*, 145–54. London: Hambledon Press, 1986*

'The dismantling of Conwy Castle', A Taylor, in *ibid*, 155–54*

'Conway Castle and town walls', A J Taylor, *131st annual meeting, Anglesey, 1984: programme*, CAA, 1984, 32–33

'Conway', J Swarbrick, *Transactions of the Ancient Monuments Society* new ser 1 (1953), 41–48*

'The dismantling of Conwy Castle', A J Taylor, *ibid* new ser 29 (1985), 81–89*

'The town and castle of Conwy: preservation and interpretation', A J Taylor, *Antiquaries Journal* 75 (1995), 339–63*

'The walls of Conway', A J Taylor, *Archaeologia Cambrensis* 119 (1970), 1–9*

'The Old Vicarage, Conway: excavations, 1963–64', L A S Butler and D H Evans, *ibid* 128 (1979), 40–103*

'Excavation on two sites in Conway, 1975', R S Kelly, *ibid* 128 (1979), 104–18*

'The royal apartments in the inner ward at Conwy Castle', J Ashbee, *ibid* 153 (2004), 51–72*

'Conwy: Old Railway Station', R S Kelly, *Archaeological Excavations 1975*, 147. London: HMSO, 1976

'Conway Castle and town walls', A J Taylor, *Archaeological Journal* 132 (1975), 245–47*

'The Conwy particulars accounts for Nov 1285 – Sept 1286', A J Taylor, *Bulletin of the Board of Celtic Studies* 30 (1982–3), 134–43

'Excavations in Conway, 1961–64', L A S Butler, *Transactions of the Caernarvonshire Historical Society* 26 (1965), 20–30*

'The taking of Conwy Castle, 1401', K Williams-Jones, *ibid* 39 (1978), 7–43*

'Llywelyn's Hall, Conwy: an excavation in 1984 by R B White', M A Mason, *ibid* 56 (1995), 11–35*

'Battles for Wales: Castell Conwy', anon, *Cambria* 3.3 (2000), 39–40*

'Conway, Caernarvonshire', W J Hemp, *Country Life* 104 (1948), 678–81*

'Conwy Castle in the 20th century', A Taylor, *Current Archaeology* 13.6 (1996), 222–25*

'Medieval Britain in 1956', D M Wilson and J G Hurst, *Medieval Archaeology* 1 (1957), 158

'Medieval Britain in 1957', D M Wilson and J G Hurst, *ibid* 2 (1958), 197

'Medieval Britain in 1959', D M Wilson and J G Hurst, *ibid* 4 (1960), 147, 151

'Medieval Britain in 1961', D M Wilson and D G Hurst, *ibid* 6–7 (1962–3), 325

'The master builders: 6', A J Taylor, *Sunday Times Magazine* 5 September (1971), 20–21, 23–24, 27–28*

Criccieth

Criccieth Castle, Gwynedd. Anon. [Cardiff: HMSO], n d* [c 1970s]

Criccieth Castle. R Avent. Cardiff: Cadw: Welsh Historic Monuments, 1987*

Criccieth Castle, Penarth Fawr medieval hall-house, St Cybi's Well. R Avent. Cardiff: Cadw: Welsh Historic Monuments, 1989*

Criccieth Castle, Caernarvonshire. C N Johns. London: HMSO, 1970*

Criccieth Castle/Castell Cricieth, Gwynedd. C N Johns. 2nd edition. Cardiff: HMSO, 1984*

Criccieth Castle, Caernarvonshire. B H St J O'Neil. London: HMSO, 1947*

'Cricieth Castle', in RCAHMW, *An inventory of the ancient monuments in Caernarvonshire. 2. Central*, 59–62. London: HMSO, 1960*

'Criccieth Castle', M de Levandowicz, *Programme of the 149th annual meeting 2002, Caernarfon*, CAA, 2002, 15–17*

'Criccieth Castle, Caernarvonshire', B H St J O'Neil, *Archaeologia Cambrensis* 98 (1944–5), 1–51*

'Criccieth Castle: corrections', B H St J O'Neil, *ibid* 98 (1944–5), 258

'Criccieth Castle', R Flook, *Archaeology in Wales* 32 (1992), 77

'The development of Criccieth Castle', C A Gresham, *Transactions of the Caernarvonshire Historical Society* 34 (1973), 14–22*

'Some problems about the origin of Criccieth Castle', D Turnbull, *Fort* 7 (1979), 52–68*

Degannwy

'Degannwy Castle', in RCAHMW, *An inventory of the ancient monuments in Caernarvonshire. 1. East*, 152–55. London: HMSO, 1956*

'Deganwy Castle', D J C King, *Programme of the 116th annual meeting at the Vale of Conway, 1969*, CAA, 1969, 13–15

'A crowned head from Degannwy Castle, Caernarvonshire', L Alcock, *Antiquaries Journal* 47 (1967), 112*

'Excavations at Degannwy Castle, Caernarvonshire, 1961–6', L Alcock, *Archaeological Journal* 124 (1967), 190–201*

'Deganwy Castle', L Alcock, *Archaeology in Wales* 1 (1961), 10

'Deganwy Castle', L Alcock and R G Livens, *ibid* 2 (1962), 13

'Deganwy Castle', L Alcock and R G Livens, *ibid* 3 (1963), 15–16

'Castell Degannwy', L Alcock, *ibid* 5 (1965), 16–17

'Castell Degannwy', L Alcock, *ibid* 6 (1966), 18

'Deganwy Castle', J L Davies, *ibid* 8 (1968), 20

'Medieval Britain in 1961', D M Wilson and D G Hurst, *Medieval Archaeology* 6–7 (1962–3), 313

'Medieval Britain in 1962 and 1963', D M Wilson and D G Hurst, *ibid* 8 (1964), 261

'Medieval Britain in 1965', D M Wilson and D G Hurst, *ibid* 10 (1966), 193–94

'Medieval Britain in 1966', D M Wilson and D G Hurst, *ibid* 11 (1967), 289

Dinas Emrys

Castell Dinas Emrys. P M Remfry. Malvern Link: SCS Publishing, 1995*

'Dinas Emrys', D Longley, *Programme of the 149th annual meeting 2002, Caernarfon*, CAA, 2002, 9–10*

'Dinas Emrys', W J Hemp, *Archaeologia Cambrensis* 100 (1949), 309–10

'Excavations at Dinas Emrys, Beddgelert (Caern), 1954–56', H N Savory, *ibid* 109 (1960), 13–77* [espec pp 15, 30]

Dolbadarn

Dolwyddelan Castle, Dolbadarn Castle. R Avent. Cardiff: Cadw: Welsh Historic Monuments, 1994*

Dolwyddelan Castle, Dolbadarn Castle, Castell y Bere. R Avent. Cardiff: Cadw, 2004*

Castell Dolbadarn Castle: catalog yr arddangosfa/exhibition catalogue. P Joyner. Aberystwyth: National Library of Wales, 1990*

Dolbadarn Castle, Caernarvonshire. C A R Radford. London: HMSO, 1948*

Dolbadarn Castle. D Williams. Cadw: Welsh Historic Monuments, 1990*

'Dolbadarn: the castle', C J Spurgeon, in P Joyner (ed), *Dolbadarn: studies on a theme*, 65–81. Aberystwyth: National Library of Wales, 1990*

'Dolbadarn Castle', in RCAHMW, *An inventory of the ancient monuments in Caernarvonshire. 2. Central*, 165–68. London: HMSO, 1960*

'Dolbadarn Castle', D J C King, *126th annual meeting, Lleyn and Snowdonia, 1979*, CAA, 1979, 26–27

'Dolbadarn Castle', R Avent, *Programme of the 149th annual meeting 2002, Caernarfon*, CAA, 2002, 6–7*

'Dolbadarn Castle', B M Morley, *Archaeological Journal* 132 (1975), 292–94*

Dolwyddelan

Dolwyddelan Castle. R Avent. Cardiff: Cadw: Welsh Historic Monuments, 1988*

Dolwyddelan Castle, Dolbadarn Castle. R Avent. Cardiff: Cadw: Welsh Historic Monuments, 1994*

Dolwyddelan Castle, Dolbadarn Castle, Castell y Bere. R Avent. Cardiff: Cadw, 2004*

Dolwyddelan Castle, Caernarvonshire. C A R Radford. London: HMSO, reprinted 1968*

Dolwyddelan Castle, Caernarvonshire. C A R Radford. London: HMSO, 1972*

Castell Dolwyddelan, Sir Gaernarfon. C A R Radford. London: HMSO, 1972*

'Dolwyddelan Castle', in RCAHMW, *An inventory of the ancient monuments in Caernarvonshire. 1. East*, 80–82. London: HMSO, 1956*

'Dolwyddelan Castle', A J Taylor, *Archaeological Journal* 132 (1975), 260–61

Dolwyddelan, Tomen Castell

'Tomen Castell, Dolwyddelan', J E Jones, *Archaeology in Wales* 3 (1963), 16

'Tomen Castell, Dolwyddelan', J E Jones, *ibid* 4 (1964), 17

'Medieval Britain in 1961', D M Wilson and D G Hurst, *Medieval Archaeology* 9 (1965), 193

Williamsburg

'Fort Williamsburg', in RCAHMW, *An inventory of the ancient monuments in Caernarvonshire. 2. Central*, 187–88. London: HMSO, 1960*

'Fort Williamsburg', D B Hague, *126th annual meeting, Lleyn and Snowdonia, 1979*, CAA, 1979, 35–36*

CARDIGANSHIRE

ab Alun, A. *Cestyll Ceredigion*. Capel Garmon: Gwasg Carreg Gwalch, 1991*

Davis, P R. *Castles of Dyfed*. Llandysul: Gomer Press, 1987*

Davis, P R. *A company of forts: a guide to the medieval castles of west Wales*. Revised edition. Llandysul: Gomer, 2000* [1st edition = *Castles of Dyfed*]

King, D J C. 'The Norman invasion and the building of castle', in D Moore (ed), *The land of Dyfed in early times*, 23–26. [S l]: CAA, 1964*

King, D J C. 'The castles of Ceredigion', *Ceredigion* 3 (1956–9), 50–69*

Lloyd, T, Orbach, J and Scourfield, R. *Carmarthenshire and Ceredigion (The buildings of Wales)*. London: Yale University Press, 2006*

Rees, S. *A guide to ancient and historic Wales: Dyfed*. London: HMSO, for Cadw: Welsh Historic Monuments, 1992*

Roberts, T. *Castles and ancient monuments of west Wales*. Fishguard: Abercastle Publications, 1989*

Salter, M. *The castles of south-west Wales*. Malvern: Folly Publications, 1996*

Turvey, R. 'The defences of twelfth-century Deheubarth and the castle strategy of the Lord Rhys', *Archaeologia Cambrensis* 144 (1995), 103–32*

Abereinon
'Castell Abereinon, Llandysul', J Thorburn, *Archaeology in Wales* 27 (1987), 55

Aberystwyth
Aberystwyth Castle: a history and souvenir guide. I Rogers. [Aberystwyth: Ceredigion County Council/Gifford and Partners, 1997]*

Castell Aberystwyth: llyfryn hanes a swfenîr. I Rogers. [Aberystwyth: Cyngor Sir Ceredigion/Gifford a'i Bartneriaid, 1997]*

The castle and borough of Aberystwyth. C J Spurgeon. Privately published, 1973*; 2nd edition, Aberystwyth: Ceredigion District Council, 1975*

'Aberystwyth Castle', D Browne, in *Old town Aberystwyth*, [16–19]. Aberystwyth: M Harris, [1992]*

'Aberystwyth Castle and borough to 1649', C J Spurgeon, in I G Jones (ed), *Aberystwyth 1277–1977: eight lectures to celebrate the seventh centenary of the foundation of the borough*, 28–45. Llandysul: Gomer Press, 1977*

'The three castles at Aberystwyth', R A Griffiths, in R A Griffiths, *Conquerors and conquered in Wales*, 322–36. Stroud: Alan Sutton, 1994*

'Aberystwyth Castle', C J Spurgeon, *124th annual meeting in Aberystwyth, south Montgomery and north Radnor, 1977*, CAA, 1977, 10–11

'The three castles at Aberystwyth', R A Griffiths, *Archaeologia Cambrensis* 126 (1977), 74–87*

'Aberystwyth Castle', C J Spurgeon and E Whatmore, *Archaeology in Wales* 15 (1975), 54–55

'Aberystwyth Castle', D M Browne, *ibid* 16 (1976), 38

'Aberystwyth Castle', D M Browne, *ibid* 18 (1978), 54

'Aberystwyth Castle', J Thorburn, *ibid* 22 (1982), 30

'Aberystwyth Castle', J Thorburn, *ibid* 23 (1983), 51–52*

'Aberystwyth Castle', A Davis, *ibid* 24 (1984), 61–62*

'Aberystwyth Castle', A Davis, *ibid* 25 (1985), 35–36*

'Aberystwyth Castle', A Davis, *ibid* 26 (1986), 51–52*

'Aberystwyth Castle', D Stewart, *ibid* 27 (1987), 56*

'Aberystwyth Castle', D S Stewart, D M Browne and C J Spurgeon, *ibid* 28 (1988), 69

'Aberystwyth Castle', H Burnham, *ibid* 30 (1990), 63–64*

'The Aberystwyth town walls', D B Hague, *Ceredigion* 2 (1952–5), 276

'Test pits at Aberystwyth Castle, December 1989: results of archaeological recording', H Burnham, *ibid* 11.4 (1992), 337–56*

'Two fourteenth-century surveys of Aberystwyth Castle', R F Walker, *ibid* 12.3 (1995), 3–22*

'Medieval Britain in 1974', L E Webster and J Cherry, *Medieval Archaeology* 19 (1975), 249

'Medieval Britain in 1975', L E Webster and J Cherry, *ibid* 20 (1976), 186

'Medieval Britain in 1976', L E Webster and J Cherry, *ibid* 21 (1977), 240

'Medieval Britain and Ireland in 1984', S M Youngs, J Clark and T Barry, *ibid* 29 (1985), 228–29

See also R A Griffiths in Part 1(c)

Cardigan

Castle in crisis: the Tivy-Side campaign to save Cardigan Castle/Helbul y castell: ymgyrch Tivy-Side i achub Castell Aberteifi. Cardigan: Tivy-Side Advertiser, 2002*

'Cardigan Castle', in P Wilkinson, *Restoration: the story continues*, 148–55. London: English Heritage, 2004*

'Cardigan', T A James, *Archaeology in Wales* 18 (1978), 54

'Cardigan Castle', K Murphy, *ibid* 24 (1984), 62–63*

'Cardigan, castle', N Page, *ibid* 44 (2004), 165–66*

'Excavations at Woolworth's, Cardigan, 1978', T James, *Ceredigion* 9.4 (1983), 336–42*

'Excavation and survey at Cardigan Castle', K Murphy and C O'Mahoney, *ibid* 10.2 (1985), 189–218*

'The making of medieval Cardigan', R A Griffiths, *ibid* 11.2 (1990), 97–133*

See also R A Griffiths in Part 1(c)

Goginan

'Castell Goginan, Melindwr', J Thorburn, *Archaeology in Wales* 27 (1987), 55

Gwallter

'Castell Gwalter', C J Spurgeon, *124th annual meeting in Aberystwyth, south Montgomery and north Radnor, 1977*, CAA, 1977, 15–16*

'Castell Gwallter motte', B H St J O'Neil, *Archaeologia Cambrensis* 99 (1946–7), 156–57*

Gwithian

'Castell Gwithian, Blaenporth', C J Spurgeon, *Archaeology in Wales* 9 (1969), 23

'Medieval Britain in 1969', D M Wilson and D G Hurst, *Medieval Archaeology* 14 (1970), 179

Llanrhystyd

'Llanrhystyd mound', C J Spurgeon, *Archaeology in Wales* 10 (1970), 21

'Llanrhystyd mound', C J Spurgeon and H J Thomas, *ibid* 13 (1973), 44

Pistog

'Castell Pistog, Llandyfriog', S M Bishop, *ibid* 31 (1991), 40

Tan-y-bwlch

'Tanycastell ring and bailey (Old Aberystwyth)', C H Houlder, *124th annual meeting in Aberystwyth, south Montgomery and north Radnor, 1977*, CAA, 1977, 10–11 [C J Houlder printed in error]

'Recent excavations in Old Aberystwyth', C H Houlder, *Ceredigion* 3 (1956–9), 114–17

'Medieval Britain in 1956', D M Wilson and J G Hurst, *Medieval Archaeology* 1 (1957), 158

'Medieval Britain in 1958', D M Wilson and J G Hurst, *ibid* 3 (1959), 309

'Medieval Britain in 1961', D M Wilson and D G Hurst, *ibid* 6–7 (1962–3), 325

'Medieval Britain in 1962 and 1963', D M Wilson and D G Hurst, *ibid* 8 (1964), 261

Ystrad Meurig

'Ystrad Meurig', C J Spurgeon, *124th annual meeting in Aberystwyth, south Montgomery and north Radnor, 1977*, CAA, 1977, 37–38

'Ystradmeurig Castle', R O Jones, *Ceredigion* 1 (1950–1), 38–42

Ystrad Peithyll

'Castell Ystrad Peithyll, Parcel Canol', J Thorburn, *Archaeology in Wales* 27 (1987), 55*

CARMARTHENSHIRE

Anon. *Cestyll/Castles: llyfryn ar gestyll Sir Gaerfyrddin/a brief guide to the castles of Carmarthenshire*. Carmarthen: Dyfed County Council, 1983*

Davies, J D. 'The castle of Carnwyllion', *Carmarthenshire Antiquary* 18 (1982), 29–36*

Davis, P R. *Castles of Dyfed*. Llandysul: Gomer Press, 1987*

Davis, P R. *A company of forts: a guide to the medieval castles of west Wales*. Revised edition. Llandysul: Gomer, 2000* [1st edition = *Castles of Dyfed*]

Glover, D G. 'A command stop line on Rhos Llangeler, with further references to Pembrey and Burry Port', *Carmarthenshire Antiquary* 26 (1990), 81–90*

Kenyon, J R. 'Recent castle studies and Carmarthenshire', *ibid* 36 (2000), 47–57*

King, D J C. 'The Norman invasion and the building of castles', in D Moore (ed), *The land of Dyfed in early times*, 23–26. [S l]: CAA, 1964*

Lloyd, T. 'Castles and old houses', *Rural Wales* 55 (1986), 8–9*

Lloyd, T, Orbach, J and Scourfield, R. *Carmarthenshire and Ceredigion (The buildings of Wales)*. London: Yale University Press, 2006*

Murphy, K. 'Small boroughs in south-west Wales: their planning, early development and defences', in N Edwards (ed), *Landscape and settlement in medieval Wales*, 139–56. Oxford: Oxbow Books, 1997* (Oxbow monograph; 81)

Rees, D. 'The changing borders of Iscennen', *Carmarthenshire Antiquary* 24 (1988), 15–21*

Rees, S. *A guide to ancient and historic Wales: Dyfed*. London: HMSO, for Cadw: Welsh Historic Monuments, 1992*

Roberts, T. *Castles and ancient monuments of west Wales*. Fishguard: Abercastle Publications, 1989*

Salter, M. *The castles of south-west Wales*. Malvern: Folly Publications, 1996*

Turvey, R. *Cestyll ac abatai Deheubarth*. Cardiff: Cadw: Welsh Historic Monuments, 2002*

Turvey, R. 'The defences of twelfth-century Deheubarth and the castle strategy of the Lord Rhys', *Archaeologia Cambrensis* 144 (1995), 103–32*

Ammanford
'Ammanford Castle, Tir-y-dail', N Ludlow, *Archaeology in Wales* 42 (2002), 122–23

Carmarthen
Tref hynaf Cymru: Caerfyrddin/Carmarthen: the oldest town in Wales. G Hughes. Llandeilo: Cambria Archaeology, 2006*

Carmarthen: an archaeological and topographical survey. T James. Carmarthen: Carmarthenshire Antiquarian Society for the Dyfed Archaeological Trust, 1980*

'Carmarthen Castle', A J Taylor, *Archaeologia Cambrensis* 100 (1948–9), 123–24

'Carmarthen Civil War ramparts', B H St J O'Neil, *ibid* 100 (1948–9), 124–25

'Carmarthen Castle', H J James, *Archaeology in Wales* 20 (1980), 56

'Carmarthen Castle, Carmarthen', N D Ludlow, *ibid* 34 (1994), 62–64*

'Carmarthen Castle, Carmarthen', N Ludlow, *ibid* 35 (1995), 61

'Carmarthen, Dan-y-banc', N Ludlow, *ibid* 35 (1995), 61

'Carmarthen Castle, Carmarthen', N Ludlow and N Page, *ibid* 37 (1997), 85–86

'Carmarthen Castle', N Ludlow and P Crane, *ibid* 41 (2001), 142

'Carmarthen Castle', D Schlee and N Ludlow, *ibid* 43 (2003), 130–31*

'Carmarthen "mount"', J F Jones, *Carmarthen Antiquary* 4 (1962–3), 188

'Medieval Carmarthen and its burgesses: a study of town growth and burgess families in the later thirteenth century', T James, *Carmarthenshire Antiquary* 25 (1989), 9–26*

'Carmarthen's Civil War defences: discoveries at Carmarthen Greyfriars excavations 1983–1990', T James, *ibid* 27 (1991), 21–30*

'An interim review of 10 years' work at Carmarthen Castle, 1993–2003', N Ludlow, *ibid* 39 (2003), 147–51*

'Medieval Britain in 1980', S M Youngs and J Clark, *Medieval Archaeology* 25 (1981), 202–3

'Post-medieval Britain and Ireland in 1998 and 1999', M Ponsford, *Post-Medieval Archaeology* 34 (2000), 377

See also R A Griffiths in Part 1(c)

Carreg Cennen

Carreg Cennen: castle and farm. Anon. Cardiff: Cadw: Welsh Historic Monuments, 1990*

Carreg Cennen Castle. R Gittins. Llandysul: Gomer Press, 1983*

The story of Carreg Cennen Castle and farm: history, description, legends and rare breeds centre. V Isaac. Llandeilo: Hydemarket, 1985*

Carreg Cennen Castle, Carmarthenshire. J M Lewis. London: HMSO, 1960*

Carreg Cennen Castle. J M Lewis. Cardiff: Cadw: Welsh Historic Monuments, 1990*

Carreg Cennen Castle. J M Lewis. Cardiff: Cadw, 2006*

'Carreg Cennen Castle', D J C King, *132nd annual meeting, old Carmarthenshire, 1985*, CAA, 1985, 19

'Carreg Cennen Castle', J Jenkins, *Carmarthen Antiquary* 3 (1959–61), 30–31

Dinefwr

Dinefwr Castle. R Gittins. Llandysul: Gomer Press, 1984*

Dinefwr Castle, Dryslwyn Castle. S E Rees and C Caple. Cardiff: Cadw: Welsh Historic Monuments, 1999*

'Old Dynevor Castle', M R Apted, in *Dynevor Castle: guide book*, 20–23. Privately published, n d*

'A tale of two towns: Llandeilo Fawr and Dinefwr in the late Middle Ages', R A Griffiths, in H James (ed), *Sir Gâr: studies in Carmarthenshire history. Essays in memory of W H Morris and M C S Evans*, 205–26. Carmarthen: Carmarthenshire Antiquarian Society, 1991*

'A tale of two towns: Llandeilo Fawr and Dinefwr in the late Middle Ages', R A Griffiths, in R A Griffiths, *Conquerors and conquered in medieval Wales*, 254–76. Stroud: Alan Sutton, 1994*

'Dinefwr Castle', S E Rees, in D Moore and D Austin (eds), *Welsh archaeological heritage: proceedings of a conference held by the Cambrian Archaeological Association in 1985*, 159–60. Lampeter: CAA: St David's University College, 1986

'Dynevor Castle', S Rees and M Francis, *132 annual meeting, old Carmarthenshire 1985*, CAA, 1985, 23

'Dynevor Castle', A J Taylor, *Archaeologia Cambrensis* 100 (1948–9), 136–37

'Dynevor Castle and Newton House: some seventeenth-century pictures', D Moore, *ibid* 143 (1994), 204–35*

'Dinefwr Castle', K Murphy, *Archaeology in Wales* 35 (1995), 61

'Dinefwr Castle, Llandeilo', I M Darke, *ibid* 36 (1996), 84–85

'Dinefwr Castle, Llandeilo', A Manning, *ibid* 37 (1997), 86

'Artists' views of Dynevor', D Moore, *Carmarthenshire Antiquary* 30 (1994), 19–32*

'Blwyddyn fawr i Dinefwr', V Johnson, *Etifeddiaeth i Cymro* 7 (1997), 14–15*

'Mawredd lle bu mieri?', S Rees, *ibid* 11 (1998), 15–17* [issue mis-numbered 10]

'Fingers crossed for Dinefwr', V Johnson, *Heritage in Wales* 7 (1997), 14–15*

'Out of the wilderness', S Rees, *ibid* 11 (1998), 15–17* [issue mis-numbered 10]

'The castle and the landscape: annual lecture to the Society for Landscape Studies', D Austin, *Landscape History* 6 (1984), 69–81*

'Medieval Britain and Ireland in 1998', J Bradley, M Gaimster and C Haith, *Medieval Archaeology* 43 (1999), 296

'Post-medieval Britain and Ireland in 1997', M Ponsford and R Jackson, *Post-Medieval Archaeology* 32 (1998), 154

See also R A Griffiths in Part 1(c)

Dryslwyn

Interim reports on excavations at three castles in Wales 1981–1982. C Arnold [*et al*]. Cardiff: Department of Extra-Mural Studies, University College, 1983*

Interim reports of excavations at Laugharne Castle, Dyfed, 1976–1980, and Dryslwyn Castle, Dyfed, 1980. R Avent and P Webster. Privately published, 1981*

An interim guide to Dryslwyn Castle and its excavation. C Caple. [Durham: Dryslwyn Castle Excavations], 1996*

Dinefwr Castle, Dryslwyn Castle. S E Rees and C Caple. Cardiff: Cadw: Welsh Historic Monuments, 1999*

The last siege of Dryslwyn Castle. A Solomon. Carmarthen: Lodwick, 1982*

'Dryslwyn Castle', P Webster, in J R Kenyon and R Avent (eds), *Castles in Wales and the Marches: essays in honour of D J Cathcart King*, 89–104. Cardiff: University of Wales Press, 1987*

'A medieval macehead from Dryslwyn Castle, Wales', O Jessop, in M Steiner, *Approaches to archaeological illustration: a handbook*, 44–49. York: CBA, 2005* (Practical handbooks in archaeology; 18)

'Dryslwyn Castle excavations 1989', C Caple, *Archaeological Reports 1989*, 55–60. Durham: University of Durham, 1990*

'Dryslwyn Castle excavation 1990: interim report', C Caple, in P Lowther (ed), *Archaeological Reports 1990*, 53–55. Durham: University of Durham, 1991*

'Dryslwyn Castle excavation 1991', C Caple, *Archaeological Reports 1991*, 51–54. Durham: University of Durham, 1992*

'Dryslwyn Castle excavation 1992', C Caple, *Archaeological Reports 1992*, 51–55. Durham: University of Durham, 1993*

'Dryslwyn Castle excavations 1995', C Caple and O Jessop, *Archaeological Reports 1995*, 69–75. Durham: University of Durham, 1996*

'Dryslwyn Castle', D J C King, *The hundred-and-fourteenth annual meeting at Carmarthen, 1967*, CAA, 1967, 24–25

'Dryslwyn Castle', P Webster, *132 annual meeting, old Carmarthenshire 1985*, CAA, 1985, 24

'Dryslwyn Castle', P V Webster, *Archaeology in Wales* 20 (1980), 56–58

'Dryslwyn Castle', P Webster, *ibid* 21 (1981), 56–57

'Dryslwyn Castle', P Webster, *ibid* 22 (1982), 30–33*

'Dryslwyn Castle', P Webster and C Caple, *ibid* 23 (1983), 55–57*

'Dryslwyn Castle', C Caple, *ibid* 32 (1992), 79–80*

'Dryslwyn Castle', C Caple and O Jessop, *ibid* 36 (1996), 85–86*

'Rise and fall of Welsh power at Dryslwyn', anon, *British Archaeological News* new ser 15 (1994), 2*

'Dryslwyn, Dyfed', P V Webster, *CBA Newsletter and Calendar* 5 (1981–2), 144

'Dryslwyn, Dyfed', P V Webster, *ibid* 6 (1982–3), 154

'Dryslwyn, Dyfed', C Caple, *ibid* 8 (1984–5), 138

'The castle and lifestyle of a 13th-century independent Welsh lord: excavations at Dryslwyn Castle 1980–1988', C Caple, *Château Gaillard* 14 (1990), 47–59*

'Y ffordd i adfeilion y Dryslwyn', D Lewis, *Etifeddiaeth i Cymro* 9 (1996), 9–10*

'Road to Dryslwyn ruins', D Lewis, *Heritage in Wales* 6 (1996), 9–10*

'Medieval Britain in 1980', S M Youngs and J Clark, *Medieval Archaeology* 25 (1981), 203

'Medieval Britain in 1981', S M Youngs and J Clark, *ibid* 26 (1982), 223–24

'Medieval Britain and Ireland in 1983', S M Youngs, J Clark and T B Barry, *ibid* 28 (1984), 263

'Medieval Britain and Ireland in 1984', S M Youngs, J Clark and T B Barry, *ibid* 29 (1985), 229

'Medieval Britain and Ireland in 1990', B S Nenk, S Margeson and M Hurley, *ibid* 35 (1991), 230

'Medieval Britain and Ireland in 1991', B S Nenk, S Margeson and M Hurley, *ibid* 36 (1992), 300

'Medieval Britain and Ireland in 1994', B S Nenk, S Margeson and M Hurley, *ibid* 39 (1995), 281–83*

See also R A Griffiths in Part 1(c)

Gwyddgrug

'Castell Gwyddgrug', J B Smith, *Bulletin of the Board of Celtic Studies* 26.1 (1974), 74–77

Kidwelly

Kidwelly Castle, Carmarthenshire. C A R Radford. 2nd edition. London: HMSO, 1952*

Kidwelly Castle. J R Kenyon. Cardiff: Cadw: Welsh Historic Monuments, 1986*; revised edition, 1990*; 3rd edition (fully revised), 2002*

'The early development of three coastal castles', R Avent, in H James (ed), *Sir Gâr: studies in Carmarthenshire history. Essays in memory of W H Morris and M C S Evans*, 167–88. Carmarthen: Carmarthenshire Antiquarian Society, 1991*

'Kidwelly Castle, Carmarthenshire: the reinterpretation of a monument', J R Kenyon, in J R Kenyon and K O'Conor (eds), *The medieval castle in Ireland and Wales: essays in honour of Jeremy Knight*, 178–81. Dublin: Four Court Press, 2003*

'Kidwelly Castle', J R Kenyon, *132 annual meeting, old Carmarthenshire 1985*, CAA, 1985, 11–12

'The plan of Kidwelly Castle: the case for a reconsideration', J C Perks, *Archaeologia Cambrensis* 98 (1944–5), 259–62

'Kidwelly. Castle Farm car park', H James, *Archaeology in Wales* 20 (1980), 58–59

'Kidwelly Castle', J F J[ones], *Carmarthen Antiquary* 2 (1945–6), 125–26

'Cydweli (Kidwelly) and the Glyn Dŵr revolt', W H Morris, *ibid* 3 (1959–61), 4–16

'Topographical notes on the early mediaeval borough of Kidwelly', H James, *Carmarthenshire Antiquary* 16 (1980), 6–17*

'Medieval Britain in 1980', S M Youngs and J Clark, *Medieval Archaeology* 25 (1981), 203

Laugharne

Laugharne Castle News. No. 1 in an occasional series. Cardiff: Cadw: Welsh Historic Monuments, 1994*

Laugharne Castle News. No. 2 in an occasional series. Cardiff: Cadw: Welsh Historic Monuments, 1995

Interim reports on excavations at three castles in Wales 1981–1982. C Arnold [*et al*]. Cardiff: Department of Extra-Mural Studies, University College, 1983*

Laugharne Castle. R Avent. Cardiff: Cadw: Welsh Historic Monuments, 1995*

Interim reports of excavations at Laugharne Castle, Dyfed, 1976–1980, and Dryslwyn Castle, Dyfed, 1980. R Avent and P Webster. Privately published, 1981*

'The siege of Laugharne Castle from 28 October to 3 November 1644', R Avent, in J R Kenyon and R Avent (eds), *Castles in Wales and the Marches: essays in honour of D J Cathcart King*, 185–204. Cardiff: University of Wales Press, 1987*

'The early development of three coastal castles', R Avent, in H James (ed), *Sir Gâr: studies in Carmarthenshire history. Essays in memory of W H Morris and M C S Evans*, 167–88. Carmarthen: Carmarthenshire Antiquarian Society, 1991*

'Laugharne Castle, Dyfed', R Avent, *132 annual meeting, old Carmarthenshire 1985*, CAA, 1985, 17

'Laugharne Castle', R Avent, *Archaeological Excavations 1976*, 169. London: HMSO, 1977

'Laugharne Castle', R Avent, *Archaeology in Wales* 16 (1976), 38

'Laugharne Castle', R Avent, *ibid* 18 (1978), 55

'Laugharne Castle excavations, 1976–1988', R Avent, *ibid* 28 (1988), 24–27* [references on p 24]

'Laugharne Castle', R Avent and M Jones, *ibid* 33 (1993), 70–72*

'Laugharne Castle 1976: introduction, historical summary and excavations', R Avent and E Read, *Carmarthenshire Antiquary* 13 (1977), 17–41*

'Laugharne Castle 1977: second interim report', R Avent, *ibid* 14 (1978), 21–35*

'Laugharne Castle 1978: third interim report', R Avent, *ibid* 15 (1979), 39–56*

'Notes on the topography of Laugharne', K Murphy, *ibid* 23 (1987), 62–65*

'Laugharne, Dyfed', R Avent, *CBA Newsletter and Calendar* 1 (1977–8), 108

'Laugharne Castle', R Avent, *ibid* 3 (1979–80), 131

'The medieval development of Laugharne Castle, Dyfed, Wales', R Avent, *Château Gaillard* 15 (1992), 7–18*

'Castell o fewn gardd a fewn castell', R Avent, *Etifeddiaeth y Cymro* 2 (1995), 14–16*

'A castle within a garden within a castle', R Avent, *Heritage in Wales* 2 (1995), 14–16*

'Medieval Britain in 1976', L E Webster and J Cherry, *Medieval Archaeology* 21 (1977), 240

'Medieval Britain and Ireland in 1990', B S Nenk, S Margeson and M Hurley, *ibid* 35 (1991), 231

Llandovery

'Llandovery Castle', D J C King, *The hundred-and-fourteenth annual meeting at Carmarthen, 1967*, CAA, 1967, 29–30

'The old cattle market, Llandovery', K Murphy, *Archaeology in Wales* 32 (1992), 80

'Llandovery Castle and the Pipe Rolls (1159–62)', R K Turvey, *Carmarthenshire Antiquary* 26 (1990), 5–11*

Llanelli

'The castle of Carnwyllion', J D Davies *ibid* 18 (1982), 29–36*

Llansteffan

Llansteffan Castle. P H Humphries. Cardiff: Cadw: Welsh Historic Monuments, 1988*; revised edition, 1996*; 3rd edition, 2006*

Llanstephan Castle, Carmarthenshire. D J C King. London: HMSO, 1963*

'The early development of three coastal castles', R Avent, in H James (ed), *Sir Gâr: studies in Carmarthenshire history. Essays in memory of W H Morris and M C S Evans*, 167–88. Carmarthen: Carmarthenshire Antiquarian Society, 1991*

'Llanstephan Castle', D J C King, *132 annual meeting, old Carmarthenshire 1985*, CAA, 1985, 9–10

'Llanstephan castle', A J Taylor, *Archaeologia Cambrensis* 100 (1948–9), 129–31

'Llanstephan Castle', L Murray Thriepland, *Archaeology in Wales* 7 (1967), 15

'Llanstephan Castle', L Murray Thriepland, *ibid* 8 (1968), 20–21

'Llanstephan Castle', L Murray Thriepland, *ibid* 9 (1969), 23

'Llanstephan Castle', G Guilbert, *ibid* 11 (1971), 22

'Llanstephan Castle', G Guilbert, *ibid* 13 (1973), 44–45

'Llanstephan Castle', G C Guilbert, *ibid* 15 (1975), 56

'Llanstephan Castle. An interim discussion of the 1971 excavation', G C Guilbert and J J Schweiso, *Carmarthenshire Antiquary* 8 (1972), 75–90*

'Llanstephan Castle. 1973 interim report', G C Guilbert, *ibid* 10 (1974), 37–48*

'Medieval Britain in 1961', D M Wilson and D G Hurst, *Medieval Archaeology* 6–7 (1962–3), 325

'Medieval Britain in 1967', D M Wilson and D G Hurst, *ibid* 12 (1968), 181–82

'Medieval Britain in 1969', D M Wilson and D G Hurst, *ibid* 14 (1970), 179

'Medieval Britain in 1971', D M Wilson and J Cherry, *ibid* 16 (1972), 186

'Medieval Britain in 1975', L E Webster and J Cherry, *ibid* 20 (1976), 186

Newcastle Emlyn

'Newcastle Emlyn', D J C King, *The hundred-and-nineteenth annual meeting in Lampeter and district, 1972*, CAA, 1972, 42–44

'Newcastle Emlyn', C M Stenger and J Isaac, *Archaeology in Wales* 23 (1983), 58

'Newcastle Emlyn Castle', C Parry, *ibid* 25 (1985), 46

'Survey and excavation at Newcastle Emlyn Castle', C Parry, *Carmarthenshire Antiquary* 23 (1987), 11–27*

'The fourteenth-century surveys of Newcastle Emlyn and the building programme of 1347–8', R F Walker, *ibid* 28 (1992), 37–50*

Roche

'Roche Castle, Laugharne', L A S Butler, *Archaeology in Wales* 1 (1961), 12

'Roche Castle, Laugharne', L A S Butler, *Carmarthen Antiquary* 4 (1962–3), 9–15*

'Medieval Britain in 1961', D M Wilson and D G Hurst, *Medieval Archaeology* 6–7 (1962–3), 325

'A bird whistle from Roche castle, Carmarthenshire', L A S Butler, *ibid* 17 (1973), 134–5*

St Clears

'St Clears motte and bailey', D J C King, *132 annual meeting, old Carmarthenshire 1985*, CAA, 1985, 15–16

'Lower St Clears', H J James, *Archaeology in Wales* 19 (1979), 37–38

'Notes on the castle of Saint Clears', D J C King, *Carmarthenshire Antiquary* 19 (1983), 5–7

DENBIGHSHIRE

Burnham, H. *A guide to ancient and historic Wales: Clwyd and Powys*. London: HMSO, for Cadw: Welsh Historic Monuments, 1995*

Hubbard, E. *Clwyd (Denbighshire and Flintshire) (The buildings of Wales)*. Harmondsworth: Penguin Books, 1986*

Jones, F P. *The story of Denbighshire through its castles*. [S l]: Denbighshire Education Committee, 1951/2*

King, D J C. 'The stone castles', in J Manley, S Grenter and F Gale (eds), *The archaeology of Clwyd*, 173–85. Mold: Clwyd County Council, 1991*

Pratt, D. ' "Eggelawe" and "Ruffin"', *Clwyd Historian* 11 (1982), 21–27*

Pratt, D. 'Norman castles in Clwyd', *ibid* 17 (1986), 16–24*

Salter, M. *The castles of north Wales*. Wolverhampton: Folly Publications, 1997*

Spurgeon, J. 'Mottes and moated sites', in J Manley, S Grenter and F Gale (eds), *The archaeology of Clwyd*, 157–72. Mold: Clwyd County Council, 1991*

Chirk

Chirk Castle. Anon. London: National Trust, 1983*

Chirk Castle, Wrexham. Anon. London: National Trust, 2003*

Chirk Castle, Clwyd: an illustrated souvenir. R Dean. London: National Trust, 1990*

'Chirk Castle, Denbighshire', C Hussey, *Country Life* 110 (1951), 896–99, 980–83*

Denbigh

Denbigh Castle and town walls. Anon. London: HMSO, reprinted 1967*

Denbigh Castle, town walls and friary, Clwyd. L A S Butler. Cardiff: Cadw: Welsh Historic Monuments, 1988*

Denbigh Castle and town walls, Lord Leicester's Church, St Hilary's Chapel, Denbigh Friary. L A S Butler. Cardiff: Cadw: Welsh Historic Monuments, 1990*

The Exchequer Gate, Denbigh: a report on excavations in 1982 and 1983. C Smith. Newcastle upon Tyne: University, Department of Archaeology, 1988*

'The excavation of the Exchequer Gate, Denbigh, 1982–83', C Smith, *Archaeologia Cambrensis* 137 (1988), 108–12*

'The Exchequer Gate, Denbigh', C Smith, *Archaeology in Wales* 22 (1982), 33–34

'Medieval Britain in 1959', D M Wilson and J G Hurst, *Medieval Archaeology* 4 (1960), 147, 151

Dinas Brân

Castell Dinas Brân (new guides to old places). J Cole. Llangollen: J Cole, [2003]*

Castell Dinas Brân, Llangollen. S Grenter and A Berry. Mold: Clwyd Archaeology Service, [1991]*

A history of Castell Dinas Brân with notes on Valle Crucis Abbey. R S Hewitt. Privately published, 1977*

Dinas Brân Castle, Llangollen/Castell Dinas Brân, Llangollen. C Kightly. Ruthin: Denbighshire County Council, 2003*

The story of Castell Dinas Brân. K West. Ellesmere: Hardwick House, 1991*

'Two castles in northern Powys: Dinas Brân and Caergwrle', D J C King, *Archaeologia Cambrensis* 123 (1974), 113–39*

'Medieval earthworks at Dinas Brân, Llangollen', W B Jones, *ibid* 147 (1998), 234–39*

'County "captures" Castell Dinas Brân', anon, *Clwyd Archaeology News* spring (1990), [4]*

'The building of Castell Dinas Brân, Llangollen', W B Jones, *Clwyd Historian* 45 (2000), 1–8*

'Castell Dinas Brân', E P Jones, *Transactions of the Denbighshire Historical Society* 33 (1984), 69–74* [in Welsh]

Erddig
'Erddig motte and bailey', D J C King, *The hundred-and-twentieth annual meeting in Wrexham and district*, CAA, 1973, 34

'Erddig motte and bailey', N Jones, *Archaeology in Wales* 39 (1999), 131–33*

Holt
'Holt Castle: John de Warenne and Chastellion', L Butler, in J R Kenyon and R Avent (eds), *Castles in Wales and the Marches: essays in honour of D J Cathcart King*, 105–24. Cardiff: University of Wales Press, 1987*

'The corporation of Holt, the manor of Farndon, and the bridge over the Dee, Denbighshire', P H W Booth, *Archaeologia Cambrensis* 146 (1997), 109–16*

'Holt Castle', S Grenter, *Archaeology in Clwyd* 10 (1988), 6–8*

Ruthin
'Ruthin Castle', S W Patterson, *The hundred and sixth annual meeting at Ruthin: programme, 1959*, CAA, 1959, 7–13*

Sycharth
'Excavations at Sycharth Castle, Denbighshire', D B Hague and C Warhurst, *Archaeologia Cambrensis* 115 (1966), 108–27*

Sycharth', D B Hague, *Archaeology in Wales* 2 (1962), 13

'Motte and bailey at Sycharth', D B Hague, *ibid* 3 (1963), 16–17

'Report on the geophysical and historical survey at Sycharth motte and bailey', S G Smith, *Transactions of the Denbighshire Historical Society* 52 (2003), 17–36*

'Gofalu am olion Glyn Dŵr', S E Rees, *Etifeddiaeth y Cymry* 16 (2000), 15–18*

'Looking after Glyn Dŵr', S E Rees, *Heritage in Wales* 16 (2000), 15–18*

'Medieval Britain in 1962 and 1963', D M Wilson and D G Hurst, *Medieval Archaeology* 8 (1964), 261–62

Tomen y Rhodwydd
'Tomen y Rhodwydd', T Jones Pierce and A H A Hogg, *Archaeologia Cambrensis* 109 (1960), 197–98

'Tomen y Rhodwydd', D Pratt, *ibid* 127 (1978), 130–32*

FLINTSHIRE

Burnham, H. *A guide to ancient and historic Wales: Clwyd and Powys*. London: HMSO, for Cadw: Welsh Historic Monuments, 1995*

Hubbard, E. *Clwyd (Denbighshire and Flintshire) (The buildings of Wales)*. Harmondsworth: Penguin Books, 1986*

King, D J C. 'The stone castles', in J Manley, S Grenter and F Gale (eds), *The archaeology of Clwyd*, 173–85. Mold: Clwyd County Council, 1991*

Salter, M. *The castles of north Wales*. Wolverhampton: Folly Publications, 1997*

Spurgeon, J. 'Mottes and moated sites', in J Manley, S Grenter and F Gale (eds), *The archaeology of Clwyd*, 157–72. Mold: Clwyd County Council, 1991*

Broughton Park

'Post-medieval archaeology in 1997', M Ponsford and R Jackson, *Post-Medieval Archaeology* 32 (1998), 154

Caergwrle (Hope)

Caergwrle Castle. Anon. [Chester]: Cheshire County Council (Central Graphic Design) for Flintshire County Council, n d*

Caergwrle Castle: the 1988 excavations. Clwyd Archaeology Service. [S l]: Clwyd County Council, n d*

Caergwrle: an enigmatic castle. C L Harston. Rhostyllen: Ceiriog Press, 2000* (Spyglass history series; 1)

'The earliest reference to works at Hope Castle', A Taylor, in A Taylor, *Studies in castles and castle-building*, 177–78. London: Hambledon Press, 1986

'Two castles in northern Powys: Dinas Brân and Caergwrle', D J C King, *Archaeologia Cambrensis* 123 (1974), 113–39*

'Caergwrle Castle', S Grenter, *Archaeology in Clwyd* 9 (1987), 28–32*

'Caergwrle Castle', S Grenter, *Archaeology in Wales* 29 (1989), 58–59

'A medieval bread-oven from Caergwrle Castle, Clwyd', J Manley, *ibid* 30 (1990), 21–24*

'Caergwrle Castle: 1988 dig', anon, *Clwyd Archaeology News* winter (1988), 2–3*

'The 1989 excavations at Caergwrle Castle', anon, *ibid* winter (1989–90), [2–3]*

'Caergwrle Castle: the ultimate dig', anon, *ibid* autumn (1990), [2–3]*

'Caergwrle Castle: the finds', anon, *ibid* autumn (1990), [2–3]*

'Caergwrle Castle excavations', D P[ratt], *Clwyd Historian* 23 (1989), 33*

'The earliest reference to works at Hope Castle', A J Taylor, *Journal of the Flintshire Historical Society* 22 (1965–6), 76–77

'The outer enclosure on Caergwrle hill, Clwyd', J Manley, *ibid* 33 (1992), 13–20*

'The Hope castle account of 1282', A J Taylor, *ibid* 33 (1992), 21–53

'A German import from Caergwrle Castle, Clwyd', M Redknap, *Medieval and Later Pottery in Wales* 10 (1988), 54–59*

'Medieval Britain and Ireland in 1990', B S Nenk, S Margeson and M Hurley, *Medieval Archaeology* 35 (1991), 228–29

'Excavations at Caergwrle Castle, Clwyd, north Wales: 1988–1990', J Manley, *ibid* 38 (1994), 83–133*

Dyserth

'Dyserth Castle', D E M Morgan and N E Hewitt, in P J Davey (ed), *Medieval pottery from excavations in the north west*, 34–41. [Liverpool]: Institute of Extension Studies, 1977*

'Dyserth Castle', N E Hewitt, *Archaeology in Wales* 3 (1963), 17

'Dyserth Castle', anon, *ibid* 4 (1964), 17

Ewloe

Ewloe Castle, Flintshire. Anon. London: HMSO, 1946*

Ewloe Castle, Flintshire. Anon. London: HMSO, 1972*

Flint Castle, Ewloe Castle. D Renn and R Avent. Cardiff: Cadw: Welsh Historic Monuments, 1995*; revised edition, 2001*

'Ewloe Castle', D J C King, *Programme of the 113th annual meeting at Chester, 1966*, CAA, 1966, 26–27

'Ewloe Castle', B H St J O'Neil, *Archaeologia Cambrensis* 99 (1946–7), 325–26

Flint

Flint Castle, Flintshire. Anon. London: HMSO, 1946*

Flint Castle. From an original text by the late W J Hemp. Cardiff: Cadw: Welsh Historic Monuments, 1987*

Flint Castle, Ewloe Castle. D Renn and R Avent. Cardiff: Cadw: Welsh Historic Monuments, 1995*; revised edition, 2001*

'Flint Castle', T J Miles, in P J Davey (ed), *Medieval pottery from excavations in the north west*, 104. [Liverpool]: Institute of Extension Studies, 1977*

'Flint Castle', D J C King, *128th annual meeting, Chester and north east Wales, 1981*, CAA, 1981, 10–11

'The building of Flint: a postscript', A Taylor, in A Taylor, *Studies in castles and castle-building*, 165–72. London: Hambledon Press, 1986

'Flint Castle', A J Taylor, *Archaeologia Cambrensis* 99 (1946–7), 323–25

'Flint: excavations at the castle and on the town defences 1971–1974', T J Miles, *ibid* 145 (1996), 67–151* [published spring 2000]

'Flint borough defences', T J Miles, *Archaeological Excavations 1971*, 42. London: HMSO, 1972

'Flint', T J Miles, *Archaeology in Wales* 11 (1971), 23

'Flint', T J Miles, *ibid* 12 (1972), 28

'Flint Castle', H R Hannaford, *ibid* 28 (1988), 70–71*

'Flint Castle, Clwyd: excavations to the west of the castle', H R Hannaford, *ibid* 33 (1993), 30–33*

'Flint, Flint Castle moat', G Wait, *ibid* 35 (1995), 62

'Flint Castle', D Morgan, *ibid* 36 (1996), 87

'The donjon of Flint', D J C King, *Journal of the Chester and North Wales Architectural, Archaeological and Historic Society* 45 (1958), 61–69*

'Flint Castle saved', anon, *Clwyd Archaeology News* autumn (1990), [4]*

'The building of Flint', J G Edwards, *Flintshire Historical Society Publications* 12 (1951–2), 5–20*

'The building of Flint: a postscript', A J Taylor, *Journal of the Flintshire Historical Society* 17 (1957), 34–41

'The supposed outer ditch of Flint Castle', O E Craster, *ibid* 22 (1965–6), 71–72*

'Early 18th-century pottery from Flint Castle', J G Hurst, *ibid* 22 (1965–6), 73–74*

'The final sieges of Flint', N Tucker, *ibid* 24 (1969–70), 44–55

'A letter from Henry Taylor', A J Taylor, *ibid* 28 (1977–8), 85–87

'Medieval Britain in 1971', L E Webster and J Cherry, *Medieval Archaeology* 16 (1972), 186, 192

'Medieval Britain in 1972', L E Webster and J Cherry, *ibid* 17 (1973), 165–66

Hawarden

Hawarden old castle. Anon. [S l: s n], 1964*

My firelocks use not to parley: Hawarden Castle in the English Civil War. P Francis-Wemyss. Newtown: Jacobus Publications, 1994*

Hawarden old castle. E W Gladstone. Privately published, 1974*

'Hawarden Castle', D J C King, *Programme of the 113th annual meeting at Chester, 1966*, CAA, 1966, 28–29

'The sieges of Hawarden Castle during the First Civil War, 1642–6', K Ll Gruffydd, *Buckley* 28 (2004), 3–16*

Hen Blas

'Hen Blas', P J Davey and D E M Morgan, in P J Davey (ed), *Medieval pottery from excavations in the north west*, 42–47. [Liverpool]: Institute of Extension Studies, 1977*

'Excavations at Hen Blas, Coleshill Fawr, near Flint: first report', G B Leach, *Journal of the Flintshire Historical Society* 17 (1957), 1–15*

'Excavations at Hen Blas, Coleshill Fawr, near Flint: second report', G B Leach, *ibid* 18 (1960), 13–60*

Hope

See Caergwrle

Llys Edwin

'The lost palace of Llys Edwin', S Griffiths, *Clwyd Historian* 55 (2006), 5–8

Llyseurgain

'Llyseurgain and the Tower', P Smith and P Hayes, *Journal of the Flintshire Historical Society* 22 (1965–6), 1–8*

Mold, the Tower

'Llyseurgain and the Tower', P Smith and P Hayes, *ibid* 22 (1965–6), 1–8*

Rhosesmor

'Castell, Rhosesmor', D Wayne, *Archaeology in Wales* 32 (1992), 80

Rhuddlan

Excavations at Rhuddlan, Clwyd: 1969–73. Mesolithic to medieval. H Quinnell and M R Blockley. York: CBA, 1994* (Research report; 95)

Rhuddlan Castle, Flintshire. A J Taylor. London: HMSO, 1949*; 2nd edition, 1955*

Rhuddlan Castle/Castell Rhuddlan, Clwyd. A J Taylor. 3rd edition. Cardiff: HMSO, 1982*

Rhuddlan Castle. A Taylor. 4th revised edition. Cardiff: Cadw: Welsh Historic Monuments, 1987*

Rhuddlan Castle. A Taylor (abridged). Cardiff: Cadw, 2004*

'Rhuddlan', H Miles, in P J Davey (ed), *Medieval pottery from excavations in the north west*, 60–61. [Liverpool]: Institute of Extension Studies, 1977*

'Rhuddlan Castle', R Avent, *128th annual meeting, Chester and north east Wales, 1981*, CAA, 1981, 10

'Rhuddlan town ditch', in *Review of Projects*, Clwyd-Powys Archaeological Trust, 1979, 12*

'Salvage excavations at Lon Hylas, Rhuddlan, Clwyd: ditches of the roman and medieval periods', J Manley, *Archaeologia Cambrensis* 134 (1985), 230–35*

'Rhuddlan', H Miles, *Archaeological Excavations 1969*, 38. London: HMSO, 1970

'Rhuddlan Norman borough', H Miles, *Archaeological Excavations 1970*, 42–43. London: HMSO, 1971

'Rhuddlan', H Miles, *Archaeological Excavations 1973*, 116–17. London: HMSO, 1974

'Excavations at Rhuddlan, Clwyd, 1979–80', J F Manley, *Archaeology in Clwyd 1980*, 9–10

'Rhuddlan', H Miles, *Archaeology in Wales* 9 (1969), 24

'Rhuddlan', H Miles, *ibid* 10 (1970), 21

'Rhuddlan', H Miles, *ibid* 11 (1971), 23

'Rhuddlan', H Miles, *ibid* 12 (1972), 28

'Rhuddlan', H Miles, *ibid* 13 (1973), 46

'Rhuddlan', J F Manley, *ibid* 19 (1979), 39

'Rhuddlan', J F Manley, *ibid* 20 (1980), 59–62*

'Rhuddlan', J Manley, *ibid* 23 (1983), 58

'Rhuddlan, Gwindy Street', I Rogers, *ibid* 35 (1995), 62

'A fortress shaken by wind and war: Rhuddlan Castle, Flintshire', M C Harris, *Country Life* 132 (1962), 1656–57*

'Rhuddlan', H Miles, *Current Archaeology* 3.9 (1972), 245–48*

'Excavations at Rhuddlan, 1969–71: interim report', H Miles, *Journal of the Flintshire Historical Society* 25 (1971–2), 1–8*

'Henry Conewey, knight, constable of the castle of Rhuddlan, 1390–1407', J E Messham, *ibid* 35 (1999), 11–55

'Medieval Britain in 1969', D M Wilson and D G Hurst, *Medieval Archaeology* 14 (1970), 186–88

'Medieval Britain in 1970', D M Wilson and S Moorhouse, *ibid* 15 (1971), 158

'Medieval Britain in 1971', L E Webster and J Cherry, *ibid* 16 (1972), 192

'Medieval Britain in 1972', L E Webster and J Cherry, *ibid* 17 (1973), 173

'Medieval Britain and Ireland in 1983', S M Youngs, J Clark and T B Barry, *ibid* 28 (1984), 263

GLAMORGAN

Barrett, J H. *A history of maritime forts in the Bristol Channel 1866–1900*. Privately published, 1978*; 2nd edition, 1993*

Davis, P R. *Castles of Glamorgan*. Port Talbot: Alun Books, 1983*

Davis, P R. *Historic Gower: an illustrated guide to the prehistoric, dark age and medieval monuments of the Gower peninsular*. Swansea: C Davies, 1986*

Hague, D B. 'The castles of Glamorgan and Gower', in T B Pugh (ed), *Glamorgan county history*, **3**, 417–48. Cardiff: University of Wales Press, 1971*

Harrison, P. 'The tower churches of Gower', *Gower* 46 (1995), 15–23*

Homfray, J. *The castles of the lordship of Glamorgan*. Barry: S Williams, 1972* [first published 1828]

Moore, D and Moore, P. 'Buck's engravings of Glamorgan antiquities', *Glamorgan Historian* 5 (1968), 133–51*

Morris, B. *The castles of Gower*. Swansea: Gower Society, 1970*; revised edition, 1985*

Morris, B. 'The castles of Gower', in D Strawbridge and P J Thomas (eds), *A guide to Gower*, 6th edition, 55–61. Swansea: Gower Society, 1999*

Morris, B. 'The castles of Gower', *Gower* 20 (1969), 39–51*

Newman, J. *Glamorgan (Mid Glamorgan, South Glamorgan and West Glamorgan) (The buildings of Wales)*. London: Penguin, 1995*

Randall, H J. 'Sites of early castles', in H J Randall, *The Vale of Glamorgan: studies in landscape and history*, 74–79. Newport: Johns, 1961*

RCAHMW. *An inventory of the ancient monuments in Glamorgan. 3. 1a: medieval secular monuments. The early castles from the Norman Conquest to 1217*. London: HMSO, 1991*

RCAHMW. *An inventory of the ancient monuments in Glamorgan. 3. 1b: medieval secular monuments. The later castles from 1217 to the present*. Aberystwyth: RCAHMW, 2000*

RCAHMW. *An inventory of the ancient monuments in Glamorgan. 4. Domestic architecture from the Reformation to the Industrial Revolution, part 1. The greater houses*. Cardiff: HMSO, 1981*

Richard, A J. 'The castles of Glamorgan: an introductory study', *Glamorgan Historian* 1 (1963), 37–43*

Salter, M. *The castles of Gwent, Glamorgan & Gower*. Malvern: Folly Publications, 1991*; revised edition, 2002*

Spurgeon, C J. 'The castles of Glamorgan: some sites and theories of general interest', *Château Gaillard* 13 (1987), 203–26*

Spurgeon, C J. 'Glamorgan's first castles', *Fortress* 8 (1991), 3–14*

Spurgeon, C J. 'The medieval town defences of Glamorgan', *Studia Celtica* 35 (2001), 161–212*

Spurgeon, C J and Thomas, H J. 'Glamorgan castles (general): early castles in Glamorgan', *Archaeology in Wales* 20 (1980), 64–69*

Spurgeon, C J and Thomas, H J. 'Medieval Glamorgan: an interim report on recent fieldwork', *Morgannwg* 22 (1978), 14–41

Spurgeon, C J, Roberts, D J and Thomas, H J. 'Supposed castles in Glamorgan: a review', *Archaeology in Wales* 39 (1999), 27–40

Stevenson, I. 'The Bristol Channel and Swansea defences', *The Redan* 50 (2000), 28–51*

Traherne, C G. 'The conquest of Glamorgan', *Archaeologia Cambrensis* 133 (1984), 1–7*

Walker, R F and Spurgeon, C J. 'The custody of the de Clare castles in Glamorgan and Gwent, 1262–1263', *Studia Celtica* 37 (2003), 43–73*

Whittle, E. *A guide to ancient and historic Wales: Glamorgan and Gwent*. London: HMSO, for Cadw: Welsh Historic Monuments, 1992* [espec ch 7]

Williams, D. *Gower: a guide to ancient and historic monuments on the Gower peninsula*. Cardiff: Cadw: Welsh Historic Monuments, 1998* [Weobley, Loughor and Swansea castles]

Aberafan

'Averavon Castle', C J Spurgeon and H J Thomas, *Archaeology in Wales* 14 (1974), 29

'Aberafan Castle', C J Spurgeon and H J Thomas, *ibid* 20 (1980), 69

Baglan

'Plas Baglan, Baglan', C J Spurgeon and H J Thomas, *ibid* 20 (1980), 77–78

Barry

'Castle, church and village: medieval Barry, 1100–1500', H J Thomas, in D Moore (ed), *Barry: the centenary book*, 56–99. Barry: Barry Centenary Association, 1984*; 2nd revised edition, 1988*

'Barry Castle', H J Thomas, *130th annual meeting, Vale of Glamorgan, 1983: programme*, CAA, 1983, 17–18

'Medieval Britain in 1965', D M Wilson and D G Hurst, *Medieval Archaeology* 10 (1966), 194

Beauville

'Beauville', G Dowdell, *Archaeology in Wales* 11 (1971), 23–24

Blaengwrach

'Blaengwrach', M Locock, *ibid* 33 (1993), 88 [pillboxes]

'Post-medieval Britain and Ireland in 1993', M Ponsford, *Post-Medieval Archaeology* 28 (1994), 131–32

Bolan

'Castle Bolan, Port Talbot', C J Spurgeon and H J Thomas, *Archaeology in Wales* 20 (1980), 73

Bonvilston

'Bonvilston', T F R Jones, *ibid* 5 (1965), 25

'Bonvilston ring', C J Spurgeon and H J Thomas, *ibid* 20 (1980), 70

Bridgend

Coity Castle, Ogmore Castle, Newcastle (Bridgend). J R Kenyon and C J Spurgeon. Cardiff: Cadw: Welsh Historic Monuments, 2001*

Newcastle, Bridgend, Glamorgan. B H St J O'Neil and H J Randall. London: HMSO, reprinted 1971*

'Newcastle Bridgend', J K Knight, *130th annual meeting, Vale of Glamorgan, 1983: programme*, CAA, 1983, 19

'Old Castle Bridgend', C J Spurgeon and H J Thomas, *Archaeology in Wales* 13 (1973), 48

Caerphilly

Caerphilly Castle, Glamorgan. Anon. London: HMSO, 1958*

Caerphilly Castle. Anon. Cardiff: Cadw: Welsh Historic Monuments, 1988*

Engines of war: replica medieval siege weapons at Caerphilly Castle. P H Humphries. Cardiff: Cadw: Welsh Historic Monuments, 1992*; 2nd edition, 1996*

Caerphilly Castle, Mid Glamorgan. C N Johns. Cardiff: HMSO, 1978*

Caerphilly Castle and its place in the annals of Glamorgan. W Rees. New enlarged edition. Cowbridge: D Brown, 1974*

Caerphilly Castle. D F Renn. Cardiff: Cadw: Welsh Historic Monuments, 1989*; revised edition, 1997*

'Heritage interpretation and Cadw', P Humphries, in A Hems and M Blockley (eds), *Heritage interpretation*, 71–82. Abingdon: Routledge, 2006

'Caerphilly Castle', J Knight, in N J G Pounds (ed), *The Cardiff area: proceedings of the 139th summer meeting of the Royal Archaeological Institute, 1993*, 26–28. London: RAI, 1993*

'Caerphilly Castle', V A Williams, in *Selected lectures and visits, 1961–1964*, 27–28. Gelligaer: Gelligaer Historical Society, [1964]

'Caerphilly Castle', D J C King, *130th annual meeting, Vale of Glamorgan, 1983: programme*, CAA, 1983, 19

'Caerphilly and its illustrators', G G Jones, in G G Jones, *Cronicl Caerffili: a collection of notes relating to Caerphilly's past*, [**1**], 32–34. Privately published, 1973*

'Caerphilly and its illustrators, part 2', G G Jones, *ibid* **2**, 9–10. Privately published, 1974*

'Caerphilly and its illustrators, part 3', G G Jones, *ibid* **3**, 11. Privately published, 1976*

'Caerphilly and its illustrators, part 4', G G Jones, *ibid* **4**, 44–44b. Privately published, 1977*

'Caerphilly and its illustrators, part 5', G G Jones, *ibid* **5**, 28. Privately published, 1977*

'The pillars of the great hall and the inscribed stones of Caerphilly Castle', G G Jones, *ibid* **6**, 59–64. Privately published, 1979*

'The Roman fort and Civil War earthwork at Caerphilly Castle, Glamorgan', J M Lewis, *Archaeologia Cambrensis* 115 (1966), 67–87*

'A limestone mortar from Caerphilly Castle', J K Knight, *ibid* 124 (1975), 114–16*

'Caerphilly Castle: the Civil War redoubt', C J Spurgeon and H J Thomas, *ibid* 147 (1998), 181–93*

'A plan of Caerphilly Castle, 1782', P Moore and H M Thomas, *ibid* 147 (1998), 194–98*

'Caerphilly Castle', J M Lewis, *Archaeology in Wales* 8 (1968), 23

'Caerphilly Castle', H Milne, *ibid* 41 (2001), 140

'Caerphilly Castle', H Milne, *ibid* 42 (2002), 121

'Building at Caerphilly in 1326', A J Taylor, *Bulletin of the Board of Celtic Studies* 14 (1950–2), 299–300

'The restoration of Caerphilly Castle', C N Johns, *Caerphilly: Journal of the Caerphilly Local History Society* 3 (1971), 20–25

'Medieval chapels of the town and castle', J R Guy, *ibid* 4 (1977), 22024

'Caerphilly Castle: a modified plan', J Owen, *ibid* 5 (1995), 36–40*

'Peiriannau dinistrio', P Humphries, *Etifeddiaeth y Cymro* 6 (1996), 19–21*

'Destruction engines', P Humphries, *Heritage in Wales* 6 (1996), 19–21*

'Medieval Britain in 1957', D M Wilson and J G Hurst, *Medieval Archaeology* 2 (1958), 197

'Medieval Britain in 1959', D M Wilson and J G Hurst, *ibid* 4 (1960), 147

'Medieval Britain in 1961', D M Wilson and D G Hurst, *ibid* 6–7 (1962–3), 325–26

'Medieval Britain and Ireland in 2001', J Bradley and M Gaimster, *ibid* 46 (2002), 256

'Recent archaeological excavation and discovery in Glamorgan. II. Roman and medieval periods', L Alcock, *Morgannwg* 7 (1963), 125

'Archaeological notes: Caerphilly Castle', J K Knight, *ibid* 21 (1977), 96–97

'Caerphilly Castle: its construction and defences', J Owen, *Postern* 11 (2000), 13–21*

'Records of the lordship of Senghenydd with the castle of Caerphilly (from the time of Edward I to Henry VIII)', W Rees, *South Wales and Monmouthshire Record Society Publications* 4 (1957), 33–41

'The mystery of the "leaning tower"', D Robinson, *Welsh Style* 17 (1989), 34–35*

Candleston

'Candleston Castle', J K Knight, *130th annual meeting, Vale of Glamorgan, 1983: programme*, CAA, 1983, 20

'Candelston [*sic*] Castle: the sad site', R Morgan, *Postern* 9 (1999). 16–17*

Cardiff

Cardiff Castle. Anon. [Cardiff: Cardiff City Council], n d*

The lords of Cardiff Castle. C Glenn. Swansea: Davies, 1976*

The Norman keep, Cardiff Castle. K Banks. Cardiff: Cardiff City Council, 1984*

Cardiff: a history of the city. W Rees. 2nd edition. Cardiff: Cardiff Corporation, 1969*

'Cardiff Castle', J Hilling, in N J G Pounds (ed), *The Cardiff area: proceedings of the 139th summer meeting of the Royal Archaeological Institute, 1993*, 28–29. London: RAI, 1993*

'Cardiff Castle: the excavation of a crop mark site', P Webster, *Aerial Archaeology* 2 (1978), 56–57*

'Cardiff Castle', *Annual Report 1977–78*, Glamorgan-Gwent Archaeological Trust, 1978, 10–12

'Cardiff', J and P Webster, *Archaeology in Wales* 14 (1974), 30

'Cardiff Castle', J and P Webster, *ibid* 15 (1975), 44–45

'Cardiff Castle', J and P Webster, *ibid* 16 (1976), 33–34

'Cardiff Castle', J and P Webster, *ibid* 18 (1978), 50

'Cardiff Castle', J and P Webster, *ibid* 19 (1979), 29–30

'Cardiff Castle', P Webster, *ibid* 23 (1983), 58

'Queen Street Centre, Cardiff, South Glamorgan', N Maylan, *ibid* 31 (1991), 43

'Cardiff, Cardiff Castle', P Evans, *ibid* 43 (2003), 129

'Cardiff, Cardiff Castle', P Evans, *ibid* 43 (2003), 153

'Excavations in Cardiff Castle 2003', P Evans, *ibid* 44 (2004), 43–60*

'Conserving Cardiff Castle', J Edwards, *Journal of Architectural Conservation* 8.1 (2002), 7–22*

'Cardiff Castle, Glamorganshire', M Girouard, *Country Life* 129 (1961), 760–63*

'Post-medieval pottery from the castle ditch, Kingsway, Cardiff', P V Webster, *Medieval and Later Pottery in Wales* 11 (1989), 10–35*

'A salt curl from Cardiff Castle?', P V Webster, *ibid* 12 (1990–1), 110–12*

'Medieval Britain in 1974', L E Webster and J Cherry, *Medieval Archaeology* 19 (1975), 242

'Medieval Britain in 1976', L E Webster and J Cherry, *ibid* 21 (1977), 240–41

'Medieval Britain and Ireland in 1991', B S Nenk, S Margeson and M Hurley, *ibid* 36 (1992), 300–1

'Medieval Britain and Ireland in 2003', J Bradley and M Gaimster, *ibid* 48 (2004), 338

'Cardiff Castle', J and P Webster, *Morgannwg* 18 (1974), 74–75

'Rose & Crown site, Cardiff', J M Lewis, *ibid* 18 (1974), 76–77

'Archaeological notes: Cardiff Castle', P and J Webster, *ibid* 19 (1975), 75–76

'Archaeological notes: Cardiff Castle', J and P Webster, *ibid* 20 (1976), 73–74

'Archaeological notes: Cardiff Castle', J and P Webster, *ibid* 21 (1977), 97–98

'Archaeological notes: Cardiff Castle', J and P Webster, *ibid* 22 (1978), 88

'Archaeological notes: Cardiff Castle', J and P Webster, *ibid* 23 (1979), 88–89

'Archaeological notes: Cardiff Castle excavations 1974–81', P Webster, *ibid* 25 (1981), 201–11*

'Archaeological notes: Queen Street, Cardiff', N M Maylan, *ibid* 35 (1991), 90

'Archaeological notes: Cardiff Castle, Cardiff', P Evans, *ibid* 48 (2004), 86–87

'Post-medieval Britain and Ireland in 2003', M Ponsford, *Post-Medieval Archaeology* 38 (2004), 396

Coch

Castell Coch, Glamorgan. P Floud. London: HMSO, 1954*

Castell Coch. D McLees. Cardiff: Cadw: Welsh Historic Monuments, 1998*; revised edition, 2005*

Castell Coch. S Rousham. Cardiff: Cadw: Welsh Historic Monuments, 1988*

'Castell Coch before Burges and Bute', R L Brown, in R L Brown, (ed), *More about Ton*, 1–15. Tongwynlais: Eglwys Press, 1983*

'Castell Coch', J Knight, in N J G Pounds (ed), *The Cardiff area: proceedings of the 139th summer meeting of the Royal Archaeological Institute, 1993*, 29–32. London: RAI, 1993*

'Castell Coch, Glamorgan', M Girouard, *Country Life* 131 (1962), 1092–95*

'Mwy na chastell tegan', D Iorwerth, *Etifeddiaeth y Cymro* 11 (1998), 6–10* [issue misnumbered 10]

'More than a fairytale castle', D Iorwerth, *Heritage in Wales* 11 (1998), 6–10* [issue misnumbered 10]

Coed-y-cwm

'Coed-y-cwm', J B Akerman, *Archaeology in Wales* 3 (1963), 17

'Coed-y-cwm ringwork', E J Talbot, *ibid* 4 (964), 17–18

'Coed-y-cwm, St Nicholas', E J Talbot, *ibid* 5 (1965), 30

'Medieval Britain in 1964', D M Wilson and D G Hurst, *Medieval Archaeology* 9 (1965), 193

'Medieval Britain in 1965', D M Wilson and D G Hurst, *ibid* 10 (1966), 194

'Recent archaeological excavation and discovery in Glamorgan. III. Medieval and industrial archaeology', L Alcock, *Morgannwg* 8 (1964), 69–70

'Recent archaeological excavation and discovery in Glamorgan. III. Medieval period', L Alcock, *ibid* 9 (1965), 95

Coity

Coity Castle, Ogmore Castle, Newcastle (Bridgend). J R Kenyon and C J Spurgeon. Cardiff: Cadw: Welsh Historic Monuments, 2001*

Owain Glyndwr and the siege of Coety Castle 1404–1405. R A Griffiths. Coity: Coity Village Association, n d*

A history of Coety Castle, its occupants and families. D J Pearce. Coity: Coity Village Association, n d*

Coity Castle, Glamorgan. C A R Radford. London: HMSO, 1946*

'Coity Castle: a stronghold of the Vale', T Bevan, in S Williams (ed), *The garden of Wales*, 35–46. [Barry]: S Williams, 1961*

'Coity Castle', C J Spurgeon, *130th annual meeting, Vale of Glamorgan, 1983: programme*, CAA, 1983, 18–19

'Coity Castle', J Spurgeon, in N J G Pounds (ed), *The Cardiff area: proceedings of the 139th summer meeting of the Royal Archaeological Institute, 1993*, 34–38. London: RAI, 1993*

'A medieval brass mortar from south Wales and its affinities', J M Lewis, *Antiquaries Journal* 64 (1984), 326–36*

'Battles for Wales: Coety castle 1404', R A Griffiths, *Cambria* 6.3 (2004), 46–47*

'Owain Glyndŵr and the siege of Coity Castle, 1404–1405', R A Griffiths, *Morgannwg* 45 (2001), 5–28*

Cowbridge

Cowbridge: the archaeology and topography of a small market town in the Vale of Glamorgan. D M Robinson. Swansea: Glamorgan-Gwent Archaeological Trust, 1980*

'Bear Hotel, Cowbridge: some evidence for the medieval town defences and Romano-British occupation', *Annual Report 1978–79*, Glamorgan-Gwent Archaeological Trust, 1979, 27–28*

'Excavations in Cowbridge', J Parkhouse, *Annual Report 1981–82*, Glamorgan-Gwent Archaeological Trust, 1982, 7–21*

'Bear Hotel, Cowbridge', A Davidson, *Archaeology in Wales* 19 (1979), 40

'Cowbridge', J Parkhouse, *ibid* 21 (1981), 62–64

'Cowbridge', J Parkhouse, *ibid* 22 (1982), 35

'Medieval Britain in 1980', S M Youngs and J Clark, *Medieval Archaeology* 25 (1981), 215

'Medieval Britain in 1981', S M Youngs and J Clark, *ibid* 26 (1982), 224

'Medieval Britain and Ireland in 1982', S M Youngs, J Clark and T B Barry, *ibid* 27 (1983), 227

'Archaeological notes: Bear Hotel, Cowbridge', Glamorgan-Gwent Archaeological Trust, *Morgannwg* 23 (1979), 90

'Archaeological notes: Cowbridge', J Parkhouse, *ibid* 26 (1982), 76–79

Dinas Powys

Dinas Powys: an Iron Age, Dark Age and early medieval settlement in Glamorgan. L Alcock. Cardiff: University of Wales Press, 1963*

'Dinas Powys Castle', C J Spurgeon, *130th annual meeting, Vale of Glamorgan, 1983: programme*, CAA, 1983, 15–16

'Dinas Powis', G Dowdell, *Archaeology in Wales* 5 (1965), 26

'Dinas Powis Castle', C J Spurgeon and H J Thomas, *ibid* 14 (1974), 31–32

'The hill-fort in Cwrt-y-ala Park, near Dinas Powis (Glam): 1. The defences', L Alcock, *Bulletin of the Board of Celtic Studies* 16 (1954–6), 242–50*

'The Dinas Powis (Glam) hill-fort: II. A further section across the defences', L Alcock, *ibid* 17 (1965–8), 131–36*

'Medieval Britain and Ireland in 1998', J Bradley, M Gaimster and C Haith, *Medieval Archaeology* 43 (1999), 302

'Recent archaeological excavation and discovery in Glamorgan. II. Roman and post-Roman Glamorgan', L Alcock, *Morgannwg* 2 (1958), 69–71

'Recent archaeological excavation and discovery in Glamorgan. II. Dinas Powys and some other early medieval fortifications in Glamorgan', L Alcock, *ibid* 3 (1959), 103–5

East Aberthaw

'Marsh House, East Aberthaw, Penmark, South Glamorgan', M Griffiths and H J Thomas, *Annual Report 1981–82*, Glamorgan-Gwent Archaeological Trust, 1982, 63–69*

'Marsh House, East Aberthaw: a seventeenth-century fortified tobacco store in Glamorgan', C J Spurgeon and H J Thomas, *Archaeologia Cambrensis* 146 (1997), 127–37*

'Marsh House, East Aberthaw, Penmark', M Griffiths, *Archaeology in Wales* 22 (1982), 45–46*

'Archaeological notes: Marsh House, Aberthaw', M Griffiths and H Thomas, *Morgannwg* 26 (1982), 84–88*

Ewenny

Ewenny Priory, Glamorgan. C A R Radford. London: HMSO, 1952*

'Ewenny Priory', J Spurgeon, in N J G Pounds (ed), *The Cardiff area: proceedings of the 139th summer meeting of the Royal Archaeological Institute, 1993*, 46–48. London: RAI, 1993*

'Ewenny Priory, Mid Glamorgan', R Haslam, *Country Life* 180 (1986), 1270–75*

Felin Isaf

'Felin Isaf mound', C J Spurgeon and H J Thomas, *Archaeology in Wales* 16 (1976), 40

Flat Holm

Flat Holm during World War 2. J Barrett. [S l]: the author, 1992*

Flat Holm: an account of its history and ecology. D H Worrall and P R Surtees. Cardiff: South Glamorgan County Council, 1984*

Fonmon

Fonmon Castle, South Glamorgan: a residence since the thirteenth century. P Moore. 2nd edition. [Cardiff]: Glamorgan Archives Joint Committee, 1978*

'Fonmon Castle', A Oswald, *Country Life* 105 (1949), 606–9*

'The manor and castle of Fonmon, near Barry', H J Thomas, *Morgannwg* 43 (1999), 63–82*

Gelligaer

'Twyn Castell, Gelligaer', C J Spurgeon and H J Thomas, *Archaeology in Wales* 20 (1980), 81

Hen Gastell

'Hen Gastell, Briton Ferry, West Glamorgan', anon, *Annual Report 1991–1992*, Glamorgan-Gwent Archaeological Trust, 1992, 23–25*

'Briton Ferry', C J Spurgeon and H J Thomas, *Archaeology in Wales* 20 (1980), 70

'Hen Gastell, Briton Ferry, West Glamorgan', P Wilkinson, *ibid* 31 (1991), 43

'Medieval Britain and Ireland in 1991', B S Nenk, S Margeson and M Hurley, *Medieval Archaeology* 36 (1992), 301–2

'Excavations at Hen Gastell, Briton Ferry, West Glamorgan', P F Wilkinson, *ibid* 39 (1995), 1–50*

'Hen Gastell, Briton Ferry, West Glamorgan', P Wilkinson, *Morgannwg* 35 (1991), 87–88

'Briton Ferry Castle (Hen Gastell)', C Morgan, *Neath Antiquarian Society Transactions* (1996-7), 8–12*

Howe Hill

'Howe Hill enclosure, St Mary Church', C J Spurgeon and H J Thomas, *Archaeology in Wales* 20 (1980), 75–76

Kenfig

'Medieval pottery from Kenfig Castle', M Francis and J M Lewis, *Medieval and Later Pottery in Wales* 7 (1984), 1–8*

Llanblethian

St Quintin's Castle News. No 1 in an occasional series. Cardiff: Cadw: Welsh Historic Monuments, [?1994]*

St Quintin's Castle News. No 2 in an occasional series. Cardiff: Cadw: Welsh Historic Monuments, 1995

St Quentin's Castle, Llanblethian. [RCAHMW]. Cardiff: Cadw: Welsh Historic Monuments, 2000*

'Llanblethian Castle', D J C King, *130th annual meeting, Vale of Glamorgan, 1983: programme*, CAA, 1983, 27

'Llanblethian Castle, Cowbridge', K Blockley, *Archaeology in Wales* 36 (1996), 90

Llandaff

The Old Bishop's Palace, Llandaff. C N Johns. Privately published, 1972*

'Bishop's Palace, Llandaff', D McLees, in N J G Pounds (ed), *The Cardiff area: proceedings of the 139th summer meeting of the Royal Archaeological Institute, 1993*, 53–54. London: RAI, 1993

'Llandaff Castle', C N Johns, *Archaeology in Wales* 11 (1971), 25–26

'Llandaff Cathedral School', T Young, *ibid* 42 (2002), 121–22

'The castle and manor of Llandaff', C N Johns, *Glamorgan Historian* 10 (1974), 177–95*

Llandow

'Llandow, medieval ringwork', G A Makepeace, *Archaeology in Wales* 40 (2000), 135

Llangewydd

'Llangewydd: an unrecorded Glamorgan castle', F G Cowley, *Archaeologia Cambrensis* 117 (1977), 204–6*

Llangynwyd

'Llangynwyd Castle', C J Spurgeon and H J Thomas, *Archaeology in Wales* 14 (1974), 34

'Llangynwyd Castle', T C Williams, *Transactions of the Port Talbot Historical Society* 2.1 (1969), 58–64

Llanquian

'Llanquian Castle, Llanblethian', C J Spurgeon and H J Thomas, *Archaeology in Wales* 20 (1980), 76

Llantrisant

'Application of seismic refraction to archaeological prospecting', S M Ovenden, *Archaeological Prospection* 1.1 (1994), 53–63*

'Llantrisant Castle', C J Spurgeon and H J Thomas, *Archaeology in Wales* 20 (1980), 76–77

Llantrithyd

Llantrithyd: a ringwork in South Glamorgan. P Charlton, J Roberts and V Vale. [Cardiff]: Cardiff Archaeological Society, 1977*

'A medieval gold finger-ring from Llantrithyd, South Glamorgan', J M Lewis, *Antiquaries Journal* 62 (1982), 129, 131*

'Llantrithyd', T F R Jones, *Archaeology in Wales* 1 (1961), 13

'Llantrithyd', T F R Jones, *ibid* 2 (1962), 15

'Llantrithyd', T F R Jones, *ibid* 3 (1963), 18

'Llantrithyd', T F R Jones, *ibid* 4 (1964), 18

'Llantrithyd', T F R Jones, *ibid* 5 (1965), 28

'Llantrithyd', P J Green, *ibid* 7 (1967), 15–16

'The 1962 Llantrithyd treasure trove and some thoughts on the first Norman coinage of Wales', R H M Dolley, *British Numismatic Journal* 31 (1962), 74–79*

'Two further coins of Henry I from Llantrithyd', R H M Dolley, *ibid* 33 (1964), 169–71*

'Medieval Britain in 1961', D M Wilson and D G Hurst, *Medieval Archaeology* 6–7 (1962–3), 338

'Medieval Britain in 1962 and 1963', D M Wilson and D G Hurst, *ibid* 8 (1964), 276

'Medieval Britain in 1964', D M Wilson and D G Hurst, *ibid* 9 (1965), 206

'Medieval Britain in 1965', D M Wilson and D G Hurst, *ibid* 10 (1966), 207

'Recent archaeological excavation and discovery in Glamorgan. II. Excavations at three Glamorgan castles', L Alcock, *Morgannwg* 5 (1961), 79–82

'Recent archaeological excavation and discovery in Glamorgan. II. Medieval period', L Alcock, *ibid* 6 (1962), 98–100

'Recent archaeological excavation and discovery in Glamorgan. II. Roman and medieval periods', L Alcock, *ibid* 7 (1963), 126

'Recent archaeological excavation and discovery in Glamorgan. III. Medieval and industrial archaeology', L Alcock, *ibid* 8 (1964), 70–71

Loughor

'Loughor Castle', J M Lewis, *Programme of the 127th annual meeting 1980*, CAA, 1980, 33–35

'Excavations at Loughor Castle, West Glamorgan 1969–73', J M Lewis, *Archaeologia Cambrensis* 142 (1993), 99–181*

'Loughor Castle', J M Lewis, *Archaeological Excavations 1973*, 117. London: HMSO, 1974

'Loughor Castle', J M Lewis, *Archaeology in Wales* 8 (1968), 24

'Loughor Castle', J M Lewis, *ibid* 9 (1969), 26

'Loughor Castle', J M Lewis, *ibid* 10 (1970), 23

'Loughor Castle', J M Lewis, *ibid* 11 (1971), 26–27

'Loughor Castle', J M Lewis, *ibid* 13 (1973), 47

'Recent excavations at Loughor Castle (south Wales)', J M Lewis, *Château Gaillard* 7 (1975), 147–57*

'The Roman fort at Loughor, 1969', J M Lewis, *Gower* 20 (1969), 89–92*

'Medieval pottery from Loughor Castle – 1', J M Lewis and B E Vyner, *Medieval and Later Pottery in Wales* 2 (1979), 1–13*

'Medieval Britain in 1969', D M Wilson and D G Hurst, *Medieval Archaeology* 14 (1970), 180

'Medieval Britain in 1971', L E Webster and J Cherry, *ibid* 16 (1972), 186

'Archaeological notes: medieval period. Loughor Castle', J M Lewis, *Morgannwg* 17 (1973), 60–62

Morgraig

Castell Morgraig: a castle revived. A Gill, A Davies and J Greig. [Caerphilly: St Martin's Comprehensive School, 1986]*

'Castell Morgraig', C J Spurgeon, *130th annual meeting, Vale of Glamorgan, 1983: programme*, CAA, 1983, 21, 25*

'Castell Morgraig', A T Gill, *Caerphilly: Journal of the Caerphilly Local History Society* 5 (1995), 19–27*

'Castell Morgraig update', A T Gill, *ibid* 6 (2000), 81–83*

'Dirgelwch Morgraig', D Iorwerth, *Etifeddiaeth y Cymro* 7 (1997), 17–19*

'The mystery of Morgraig', D Iorwerth, *Heritage in Wales* 7 (1997), 17–19*

'Medieval Britain and Ireland in 1998', J Bradley, M Gaimster and C Haith, *Medieval Archaeology* 43 (1999), 294

Morlais

'Morlais Castle as viewed by Samuel and Nathaniel Buck', J R Kenyon, *Archaeologia Cambrensis* 134 (1985), 235–37*

'Castle Morlais', H Brooksby, C J Spurgeon and H J Thomas, *Archaeology in Wales* 12 (1972), 29–30

'An aerial survey at Morlais Castle, Merthyr Tydfil, Mid Glamorgan', D M Robinson, *Bulletin of the Board of Celtic Studies* 30.3–4 (1983), 431–40*

'Medieval Britain in 1981', S M Youngs and J Clark, *Medieval Archaeology* 26 (1982), 224

Neath

Medieval Neath: ministers' accounts 1262–1316. A D Hopkins (ed). Pontypool: Nidum Publications, 1988*

'Neath Castle', D J C King and H Brooksby, *Programme of the 127th annual meeting, 1980*, CAA, 1980, 30–33

'Neath Castle', C N Johns, *Archaeology in Wales* 5 (1965), 29–30

'Neath Castle', H Brooksby, *ibid* 10 (1970), 24

'Neath Castle', H Brooksby, *ibid* 11 (1971), 28–29

'Neath Castle', H Brooksby, *ibid* 12 (1972), 31

'Neath Castle', H Brooksby, *ibid* 13 (1973), 47–48

'Neath Castle', K Lightfoot and P F Wilkinson, *ibid* 28 (1988), 72–73

'Neath, Neath Castle', N Page, *ibid* 34 (1994), 68, 80

'Medieval Britain in 1962 and 1963', D M Wilson and D G Hurst, *Medieval Archaeology* 8 (1964), 262

'Medieval Britain in 1965', D M Wilson and D G Hurst, *ibid* 10 (1966), 194, 196

'Medieval Britain and Ireland in 1988', D R M Gaimster, S Margeson and T Barry, *ibid* 33 (1989), 239

'Medieval Britain and Ireland in 1993', B S Nenk, S Margeson and M Hurley, *ibid* 38 (1994), 290

'Medieval Britain and Ireland in 1994', B S Nenk, S Margeson and M Hurley, *ibid* 39 (1995), 288

'Archaeological notes: medieval period. Neath Castle', H Brooksby, *Morgannwg* 17 (1973), 62–64

' "Dig" at Neath Castle (1970–76)', C T Phillips, *Neath Antiquarian Society Transactions* (1977), 7–8

'Post-medieval Britain and Ireland in 1994', M Ponsford and R Jackson, *Post-Medieval Archaeology* 29 (1995), 134–35

Newcastle

See Bridgend

Nos

'Castell Nos', C J Spurgeon and H J Thomas, *Archaeology in Wales* 20 (1980), 75

Ogmore

Coity Castle, Ogmore Castle, Newcastle (Bridgend). J R Kenyon and C J Spurgeon. Cardiff: Cadw: Welsh Historic Monuments, 2001*

Ogmore Castle, Glamorgan. C A R Radford. London: HMSO, reprinted 1969*

Ogmore Castle 1066 to 1283. P M Remfry. Malvern Link: SCS Publishing, 1995*

Ogmore Castle: a short guide. P M Remfry. Malvern Link: SCS Publishing, 1995*

'Ogmore Castle', C J Spurgeon, *130th annual meeting, Vale of Glamorgan, 1983: programme*, CAA, 1983, 19–20

'A medieval limekiln at Ogmore Castle, Glamorgan', O E Craster, *Archaeologia Cambrensis* 101 (1950–1), 72–76*

Oystermouth

A brief description and history of the castle of Oystermouth. W H Jones. Swansea: City of Swansea, n d*

Oystermouth Castle, Swansea. K W B Lightfoot. Swansea: City of Swansea, n d*

Oystermouth Castle 1066 to 1326. P M Remfry. Malvern Link: SCS Publishing, 1995*

Oystermouth Castle 1066 to 1326: a short guide. P M Remfry. Malvern Link: SCS Publishing, 1995*

'Oystermouth Castle', W Rees, *The hundred and seventh annual meeting at Swansea: programme, 1960*, CAA, 1960, 33–34

'Oystermouth Castle', B Morris, *Programme of the 127th annual meeting, 1980*, CAA, 1980, 38–39*

'Oystermouth, Oystermouth Castle', E Evans, *Archaeology in Wales* 34 (1994), 68

'Oystermouth Castle', E M Evans and A G Marvell, *ibid* 35 (1995), 62

'Oystermouth Castle', A Parsons, *ibid* 43 (2003), 149

'Oystermouth: Roman settlement and medieval castle', J E R[ees] *Gower* 1 (1948), 38–42*

'The Oystermouth Castle mystery', B Morris, *ibid* 19 (1968), 79–81

'Oystermouth Castle and its gatehouse', B Morris, *ibid* 48 (1997), 33–40*

'Medieval Britain and Ireland in 1994', B S Nenk, S Margeson and M Hurley, *Medieval Archaeology* 39 (1995), 288

Pancross

'Middlecross ring-work and bailey, Llancarvan', C J Spurgeon and H J Thomas, *Archaeology in Wales* 14 (1974), 36

Pant Glas

'Archaeological notes: Pant Glas', H J Thomas and M Griffiths, *Morgannwg* 27 (1983), 73

Penlle'r Castell

'Penlle'r Castell', B Morris, *The hundred and seventh annual meeting at Swansea: programme, 1960*, CAA, 1960, 27–28*

'Penlle'r Castell', J B Smith, *Morgannwg* 9 (1965), 5–10

Penmaen

'Castle Tower, Penmaen: a Norman ringwork in Glamorgan', L Alcock, *Antiquaries Journal* 46 (1966), 178–210*

'Castle Tower, Penmaen', L Alcock, *Archaeology in Wales* 1 (1961), 13

'Excavation of Castle Tower, Penmaen', L Alcock, *Gower* 13 (1960), 62–63

'Medieval Britain in 1960', D M Wilson and D G Hurst, *Medieval Archaeology* 5 (1961), 321

'Medieval Britain in 1961', D M Wilson and D G Hurst, *ibid* 6–7 (1962–3), 326

'Recent archaeological excavation and discovery in Glamorgan. II. Excavations at Castle Tower, Penmaen, Gower', L Alcock, *Morgannwg* 4 (1960), 67–70

'Recent archaeological excavation and discovery in Glamorgan. II. Excavations at three Glamorgan castles', L Alcock, *ibid* 5 (1961), 79–82

Penmark

'Penmark Castle', C J Spurgeon, *130th annual meeting, Vale of Glamorgan, 1983: programme*, CAA, 1983, 16–17

'Penmark Castle', C J Spurgeon and H J Thomas, *Archaeology in Wales* 20 (1980), 77

Pennard

'Pennard Castle', L Alcock, *Archaeology in Wales* 1 (1961), 13

'Pennard Castle: the last two hundred years', B Morris, *Gower* 38 (1987), 6–15*

'Medieval Britain in 1961', D M Wilson and D G Hurst, *Medieval Archaeology* 6–7 (1962–3), 326

'Recent archaeological excavation and discovery in Glamorgan. II. Excavations at three Glamorgan castles', L Alcock, *Morgannwg* 5 (1961), 79–82

'Pennard Castle: Gower's familiar, neglected ruin', R Morgan, *Postern* 8 (1998), 3–4*

Penrice

'Penrice Castle, Gower', D J C King and J C Perks, *Archaeologia Cambrensis* 110 (1961), 71–101*

Pen-y-pil

'Pen-y-pill [*sic*], St Mellons', E J Talbot, *Archaeology in Wales* 5 (1965), 32

'Medieval Britain in 1965', D M Wilson and D G Hurst, *Medieval Archaeology* 10 (1966), 196

Port Eynon

'Salt House, Port Eynon: a sixteenth-century saltworks in Gower', C J Spurgeon, D J Roberts and H J Thomas, *Archaeologia Cambrensis* 146 (1997), 117–26*

'Port Eynon salt house', P Wilkinson, *Archaeology in Wales* 26 (1986), 63–64*

'Archaeological notes: Port Eynon, Gower', P Wilkinson, *Morgannwg* 32 (1988), 94

'A 16th-century saltworks at Port Eynon, Gower', P F Wilkinson, M Locock and S Sell, *Post-Medieval Archaeology* 32 (1998), 3–32*

WALES

Rhyndwyclydach

'Cae-castell, Rhyndwyclydach', C J Spurgeon and H J Thomas, *Archaeology in Wales* 20 (1980), 71, 73

Rumney

Welsh hoards 1979–1981. G C Boon. Cardiff: National Museum of Wales, 1986*

'Cae Castell, Rumney', anon, *Annual Report 1977–78*, Glamorgan-Gwent Archaeological Trust, 1978, 6–9*

'An interim report on the excavation of Cae Castell, Rumney, Cardiff', K W B Lightfoot, *Annual Report 1979–80*, Glamorgan-Gwent Archaeological Trust, 1980, 9–12*

'Cae Castell, Rumney, Cardiff', K W B Lightfoot, *Annual Report 1980–81*, Glamorgan-Gwent Archaeological Trust, 1981, 11–15*

' "Cae Castell", Rumney, Cardiff: final interim report', K W B Lightfoot, *Annual Report 1981–82*, Glamorgan-Gwent Archaeological Trust, 1982, 1–7*

'Rumney Castle', C J Spurgeon and H J Thomas, *Archaeology in Wales* 14 (1974), 37–38

'Cae Castell, Rumney', K W B Lightfoot, *ibid* 20 (1980), 71–72*

'Cae Castell, Rumney', K W B Lightfoot, *ibid* 21 (1981), 60–62*

'Medieval Britain in 1978', L E Webster and J Clark, *Medieval Archaeology* 23 (1979), 263

'Medieval Britain in 1980', S M Youngs and J Clark, *ibid* 25 (1981), 202–3

'Medieval Britain in 1981', S M Youngs and J Clark, *ibid* 26 (1982), 225

'Rumney Castle, a ringwork and manorial centre in South Glamorgan', K W B Lightfoot, *ibid* 36 (1992), 96–163*

'Archaeological notes: Rumney Castle', Glamorgan-Gwent Archaeological Trust, *Morgannwg* 22 (1978), 87

'Archaeological notes: Rumney, Cae Castell', J M Lewis and G C Boon, *ibid* 24 (1980), 91, 94–95

Ruperra

'Craig Ruperra', C J Spurgeon and H J Thomas, *Archaeology in Wales* 20 (1980), 26–27*

'Coed Craig Ruperra', S Clarke [*et al*], *ibid* 42 (2002), 121

St Donat's

St Donat's Castle: a guide and brief history. E Blackburn and R Williams. [S l: s n], n d* [post-1962]

The story of St Donat's Castle and Atlantic College. R Denning (ed). Cowbridge: Barry: D Brown with S Williams, 1983*

Hearst's other castle. E McMurry. Bridgend: Seren, 1999*

'St Donat's Castle', A Hall, *130th annual meeting, Vale of Glamorgan, 1983: programme*, CAA, 1983, 30

'St Donat's Castle', D McLees, in N J G Pounds (ed), *The Cardiff area: proceedings of the 139th summer meeting of the Royal Archaeological Institute, 1993*, 41–43. London: RAI, 1993

'St Donat's Castle: a recent revised interpretation by the RCAHM Wales', C J Spurgeon, *Archaeological Journal* 150 (1993), 498, 501–3*

'The Tudor gardens of St Donat's Castle, Glamorgan, south Wales', E Whittle, *Garden History* 27 (1999), 109–26*

Stormy

'Stormy Castle, Tythegston', C J Spurgeon and H J Thomas, *Archaeology in Wales* 20 (1980), 78–79

Sully

'Sully Castle', G Dowdell, *Archaeology in Wales* 5 (1965), 30

'Sully Castle', G Dowdell, *ibid* 6 (1966), 20

'Sully Castle', G Dowdell, *ibid* 11 (1971), 29–30

'Excavations at Sully Castle 1963–69', D Dowdell, *Bulletin of the Board of Celtic Studies* 37 (1990), 308–60*

'Medieval Britain in 1966', D M Wilson and D G Hurst, *Medieval Archaeology* 11 (1967), 289

'Recent archaeological excavation and discovery in Glamorgan. III. Medieval period. 2. Sully Castle', G Dowdell, *Morgannwg* 10 (1966), 67

Swansea

Swansea Castle and the medieval town. E Evans, with contributions by C J Spurgeon. Swansea: Swansea City Council and the Glamorgan-Gwent Archaeological Trust, 1983*

Swansea Castle. B Morris. Swansea: Swansea City Council, [1992]*; reprint with minor amendments, 2000*

'Swansea Castle', J K Knight, *Programme of the 127th annual meeting 1980*, CAA, 1980, 35–37*

'Swansea Castle', *Annual Report 1976–77*, Glamorgan-Gwent Archaeological Trust, 1977, 18

'A salvage excavation at Swansea Castle', *Annual Report 1977–78*, Glamorgan-Gwent Archaeological Trust, 1978, 33–34

'Whitewalls, Swansea: a section of the medieval town defences', *Annual Report 1978–79*, Glamorgan-Gwent Archaeological Trust, 1979, 39–53*

'Swansea, Little Wind Street', G Dowdell and S Sell, *Archaeological Excavations 1976*, 173–74. London: HMSO, 1977

'Swansea', B Morris, *Archaeology in Wales* 15 (1975), 60–61

'Swansea, Whitewalls', K Lightfoot, *ibid* 19 (1979), 42–43

'Swansea Castle', S H Sell, *ibid* 19 (1979), 43

'Rutland Street, Swansea', S H Sell and J Parkhouse, *ibid* 20 (1980), 64

'Swansea Castle', E Evans, *ibid* 28 (1988), 73

'Swansea, Worcester Place', E Evans, *ibid* 34 (1994), 68–69

'Notes on Swansea Castle', D B Hague, *Gower* 10 (1957), 3–9*

'A brief history of Swansea Castle', G Williams, *ibid* 10 (1957), 10–14

'Swansea's medieval defences: some recent discoveries', B Morris, *ibid* 26 (1975), 11–158

'Swansea Castle defences: the western ditch', B Morris, *ibid* 27 (1976), 14–19*

'The medieval town defences of Swansea: the Whitewalls excavation, 1978–79', K Lightfoot, *ibid* 30 (1979), 76–79*

'Excavations at Little Wind Street, Swansea, 1976', S H Sell, *ibid* 32 (1981), 71–83*

'Medieval Britain in 1975', L E Webster and J Cherry, *Medieval Archaeology* 20 (1976), 192

'Medieval Britain in 1978', L E Webster and J Cherry, *ibid* 23 (1979), 269

'Medieval Britain in 1980', S M Youngs and J Clark, *ibid* 25 (1981), 215

'Medieval Britain and Ireland in 1988', D R M Gaimster, S Margeson and T Barry, *ibid* 33 (1989), 239

'Medieval Britain and Ireland in 1994', B S Nenk, S Margeson and M Hurley, *ibid* 39 (1995), 288–89

'Medieval Britain and Ireland in 2005', M Gaimster and K O'Conor, *ibid* 50 (2006), 399

'Archaeological notes: Whitewalls, Swansea', Glamorgan-Gwent Archaeological Trust, *Morgannwg* 23 (1979), 89–90

Talybont
'Talybont Castle, Llandeilo Talybont', C J Spurgeon and H J Thomas, *Archaeology in Wales* 16 (1976), 42

Talyfan
'Talyfan Castle', C J Spurgeon and H J Thomas, *ibid* 20 (1980), 79

Tre Oda
'Tre Oda motte, Whitchurch, Cardiff', J K Knight, E J Talbot and I Rowlands, *Archaeological Excavations 1966*, 19. London: HMSO, 1967

'Tre Oda motte, Whitchurch, Cardiff', J K Knight, E J Talbot and I Rowlands, *Archaeology in Wales* 6 (1966), 20

'Tre Oda, Whitchurch, Cardiff', C J Spurgeon and H J Thomas, *ibid* 20 (1980), 79–81

'The excavation of a castle mound and round barrow at Tre Oda, Whitchurch', J Knight and E J Talbot, *Transactions of the Cardiff Naturalists' Society* 95 (1968–70), 9–23*

'Medieval Britain in 1966', D M Wilson and D G Hurst, *Medieval Archaeology* 11 (1967), 289

'Recent archaeological excavation and discovery in Glamorgan. III. Medieval period. 3. Tre Oda castle mound', J K Knight, *Morgannwg* 10 (1966), 68

Ty Du

'Ty Du, Pendoylan', C J Spurgeon and H J Thomas, *Archaeology in Wales* 20 (1980), 81

Walterston

'Walterston ringwork', C J Spurgeon and H J Thomas, *ibid* 14 (1974), 38

'Medieval Britain and Ireland in 1995', B S Nenk, S Margeson and M Hurley, *Medieval Archaeology* 40 (1996), 311

Weobley

Weobley Castle. D M Robinson. Cardiff: Cadw: Welsh Historic Monuments, 1987*

Weobley Castle, Glamorgan. W G Thomas. London: HMSO, 1971*

Weobley Castle. D M Williams. Cardiff: Cadw: Welsh Historic Monuments, 1995*

'Weobley Castle', W G Thomas, *Programme of the 127th annual meeting 1980*, CAA, 1980, 37–38*

Wrinstone

'The manor and township of Wrinstone, South Glamorgan', B Vyner, S Wrathmell and S Wrathmell, *Transactions of the Cardiff Naturalists' Society* 99 (1976–8), 15–27*

Ynyscrug

'Ynyscrug, Rhondda', C J Spurgeon and H J Thomas, *Archaeology in Wales* 20 (1980), 81–82

'Ynys y crug motte, Tonypandy', H J Thomas and D Clayton, *Morgannwg* 30 (1986), 74–75

Ystradowen

'Ystradowen motte', D J C King, *130th annual meeting, Vale of Glamorgan, 1983: programme*, CAA, 1983, 21

'Castle mound, Ystradowen', C J Spurgeon and H J Thomas, *Archaeology in Wales* 20 (1980), 73–75*

MERIONETH

Carr, A D and Carr, G. *Cestyll Gwynedd*. Cardiff: Cadw: Welsh Historic Monuments, 1985*

Johnstone, N. 'An investigation into the location of the royal courts of thirteenth-century Gwynedd', in N Edwards (ed), *Landscape and settlement in medieval Wales*, 55–69. Oxford: Oxbow Books, 1997* (Oxbow monograph; 81)

Jones, G R J. 'The defences of Gwynedd in the thirteenth century', *Transactions of the Caernarvonshire Historical Society* 30 (1969), 29–43*

King, D J C and Kenyon, J R. 'The castles: a study in military architecture', in J B Smith and Ll B Smith (eds), *History of Merioneth. 2. The Middle Ages*, 386–421. Cardiff: University of Wales Press on behalf of the Merioneth Historical and Record Society, 2001*

Longley, D. 'The royal courts of the Welsh princes AD 400–1283', in N Edwards (ed), *Landscape and settlement in medieval Wales*, 41–54. Oxford: Oxbow Books, 1997* (Oxbow monograph; 81)

Lynch, F. *A guide to ancient and historic Wales: Gwynedd*. London: HMSO for Cadw: Welsh Historic Monuments, 1995* [espec ch 7]; revised edition, 2001*

Salter, M. *The castles of north Wales*. Wolverhampton: Folly Publications, 1997*

Aber Ia

'Castell Aber Ia', W J Hemp, *Ninety-sixth annual meeting programme, 1949*, CAA, 1949, 21 [reprinted in the 1971 Harlech programme, pp 30–31]

'Castell Aber Ia', W J Hemp, *Archaeologia Cambrensis* 100 (1948–9), 311–12

Bala

'Medieval Bala and Llanfor', D Longley, *138th annual meeting, Dolgellau, Meirionydd, 1991: programme*, CAA, 1991, 10–11

'Bala, Tomen y Bala', I P Brooks and K Laws, *Archaeology in Wales* 45 (2005), 162

'Medieval Britain and Ireland in 1993', B S Nenk, S Margeson and M Hurley, *Medieval Archaeology* 38 (1994), 291–91

Bere

Castell y Bere. R Avent. Cardiff: Cadw: Welsh Historic Monuments, 1997*

Dolwyddelan Castle, Dolbadarn Castle, Castell y Bere. R Avent. Cardiff: Cadw, 2004*

'Medieval finds from Castell-y-Bere, Merioneth', L A S Butler, *Archaeologia Cambrensis* 123 (1974), 78–112*

'The last stronghold', R Humphreys, *Cambria* 5.5 (2003), 58–59*

'Medieval Britain in 1959', D M Wilson and J G Hurst, *Medieval Archaeology* 4 (1960), 147

'Castell y Bere', E D Evans, *Journal of the Merioneth Historical and Record Society* 3 (1957–60), 31–44, 210

Carndochan

'Castell Carndochan', A H A Hogg, *ibid* 2 (1953–6), 178–80*

Cynfal

'Castell Cynfal', R S Greenough, *Talyllyn News* 166 (1995), 25–28*

Gronw

'Castell Gronw at Pen y Bont', J Spurgeon, *152nd annual summer meeting in Bala and Penllyn: programme 2005*, CAA, 2005, 19–20

Harlech

Harlech Castle, Merioneth. Anon. London: HMSO, 1971*

Harlech Castle: an illustrated souvenir. A Phillips. London: HMSO, 1961*

Harlech Castle/Castell Harlech, Gwynedd. A J Taylor. Cardiff: HMSO, 1980*

Harlech Castle. A J Taylor. Revised edition. Cardiff: Cadw: Welsh Historic Monuments, 1985*

Harlech Castle. A Taylor. Revised edition, reprinted with amendments. Cardiff: Cadw: Welsh Historic Monuments, 1988*; 3rd edition, 1997*; 4th edition, 2002*

'The castle builders: Harlech and Caernarfon', N Coldstream, in 'Architecture', in B Ford (ed), *The Cambridge guide to the arts in Britain. 2. The middle ages*, 81–87. Cambridge: CUP, 1988*

'Harlech Castle: the dating of the outer enclosure', A Taylor, in A Taylor, *Studies in castles and castle-building*, 173–75. London: Hambledon Press, 1986*

'Harlech Castle', A J Taylor, *Archaeologia Cambrensis* 100 (1948–9), 278–80

'The building stones of Harlech Castle and Cymmer Abbey', E Neaverson, *ibid* 100 (1948–9), 280–81

'Harlech Castle', A J Taylor, *Archaeological Journal* 132 (1975), 258–60*

'Egryn sandstone: a lost and rediscovered Welsh freestone', T Palmer, *Fforwm Cerrig Cymru/Welsh Stone Forum Newsletter* 1 (2003), 7–9*

'Some notes on the Savoyards in north Wales, 1277–1300, with special reference to the Savoyard element in the construction of Harlech Castle', A J Taylor, *Genava* new ser 11 (1963), 289–315*

'Medieval Britain in 1962 and 1963', D M Wilson and D G Hurst, *Medieval Archaeology* 8 (1964), 262

'Harlech Castle: the dating of the outer enclosure', A J Taylor, *Journal of the Merioneth Historical and Record Society* 1 (1949–51), 202–3*

'The last royal flag comes down', N Tucker, *ibid* 4 (1961–4), 16–21

Owain Glyndŵr's Mount

'Counting the cost … The sequel', A Q Berry, in A Q Berry and I W Brown (eds), *Erosion on archaeological earthworks: its prevention, control and repair*, 45–56. Mold: Clwyd County Council, 1994*

'21st century motte!', anon, *Clwyd Archaeology News* summer (1991), [4]*

'Owain Glyndŵr's Mount', anon, *ibid* spring (1992), [4]*

'Gofalu am olion Glyn Dŵr', S E Rees, *Etifeddiaeth y Cymry* 16 (2000), 15–18*

'Looking after Glyn Dŵr', S E Rees, *Heritage in Wales* 16 (2000), 15–18*

Penucha'r Llan

'Penucha'r Llan', J Spurgeon, *152nd annual summer meeting in Bala and Penllyn: programme 2005*, CAA, 2005, 14–15

Prysor

'Castell Prysor', C A Gresham and W J Hemp, *Ninety-sixth annual meeting programme, 1949*, CAA, 1949, 23* [reprinted in the 1971 Harlech programme, pp 26–27]

'Castell Prysor', M de Levandowicz, *152nd annual summer meeting in Bala and Penllyn: programme 2005*, CAA, 2005, 8–10*

'Castell Prysor', C A Gresham and W J Hemp, *Archaeologia Cambrensis* 100 (1948–9), 312–13

'A survey of Castell Prysor, Meirionnydd', M de Levandowicz, *Archaeology in Wales* 38 (1998), 36–42*

Rug

'The mound at Rug', W Gardner, *Journal of the Merioneth Historical and Record Society* 4 (1961–4), 3–6*

Tomen-y-mur

'Tomen-y-mur. The motte', W J Hemp, *Ninety-sixth annual meeting programme, 1949*, CAA, 1949, 22–23

MONMOUTHSHIRE

Anon. 'Castles in Monmouthshire', *Presenting Monmouthshire* 30 (1970), 40–43

Allen, J R L. 'Roman and medieval-modern building stones in south east Wales: the Sudbrook Sandstone and Dolomitic Conglomerate (Triassic)', *Monmouthshire Antiquary* 21 (2005), 21–44*

Barber, W T. 'Castles on the Monnow', *Presenting Monmouthshire* 40 (1975), 37–43*

Coplestone-Crow, B. 'Robert de la Haye and the lordship of Gwynllwg: the Norman settlement of a Welsh cantref', *Gwent Local History* 85 (1998), 3–46*

Davies, E T. *A guide to the castles of Gwent*. Newport: Johns, 1978*

Jones, P M. 'A towering misconception?', *Gwent Local History* 98 (2005), 3–7*

Kenyon, J R. 'Early castle studies and the Association', *Monmouthshire Antiquary* 13 (1997), 22–25*

Knight, J. *Civil War & restoration in Monmouthshire*. Almeley: Logaston Press, 2005*

Knight, J. 'The mediaeval castle in Monmouthshire', *Gwent Local History* 42 (1977), 40–47

Knight, J. 'The medieval castle in Monmouthshire (part 2)', *ibid* 43 (1977), 34–39

Lewis, J M. 'The castles of Gwent', *Proceedings of the Cotteswold Naturalist Field Club* 34.4 (1965), 196–203

Locock, M. 'The archaeology of the Second World War in Gwent', *Monmouthshire Antiquary* 12 (1996), 68–72*

Meredith, J. *The iron industry of the Forest of Dean*. Stroud: Tempus, 2006* [see Appendix 5 for Grosmont, Skenfrith and White castles]

Newman, J. *Gwent/Monmouthshire (The buildings of Wales)*. London: Penguin Books, 2000*

Phillips, N. *Earthwork castles of Gwent and Ergyng AD 1050–1250*. Oxford: Archaeopress, 2006* (BAR British series; 420)

Priestley, S G and Turner, R C. 'Three castles of the Clare family in Monmouthshire during the thirteenth and fourteenth centuries', *Archaeologia Cambrensis* 152 (2003), 9–52*

Prior, S. *A few well-positioned castles: the Norman art of war*. Stroud: Tempus, 2006*

Rahtz, P [et al]. 'Norman castles', in *Medieval sites in the Mendip, Cotswold, Wye Valley and Bristol region*, 14–17. Bristol: Bristol Archaeological Research Group, 1969 (Field guide; 3)

Renn, D F. 'The round keeps of the Brecon region', *Archaeologia Cambrensis* 110 (1961), 129–43*

Salter, M. *The castles of Gwent, Glamorgan & Gower*. Wolverhampton: Folly Publications, 1991*; 2nd edition, 2002*

Thurlby, M. *The Herefordshire School of Romanesque sculpture*. Almeley: Logaston Press, 1999*

Walker, R F and Spurgeon, C J. 'The custody of the de Clare castles in Glamorgan and Gwent, 1262–1263', *Studia Celtica* 37 (2003), 43–73*

Whittle, E. *A guide to ancient and historic Wales: Glamorgan and Gwent*. London: HMSO, for Cadw: Welsh Historic Monuments, 1992* [espec ch 7]

Abergavenny

Abergavenny Castle. Anon. [S l: s n], n d* [folded typescript]

Abergavenny Castle. A L Ralphs. Abergavenny: Abergavenny Borough Council, 1956*

'Abergavenny Castle and Museum', J K Knight, *Gwent: programme for the 141st annual meeting ... 1994*, CAA, 1994, 8–9, 11

'Excavations on the Roman fort at Abergavenny, Orchard site, 1972–73', K Blockley, *Archaeological Journal* 150 (1993), 169–242*

'Abergavenny', F Radcliffe, *Archaeology in Wales* 2 (1962), 16

'Abergavenny', P J Ashmore, *ibid* 12 (1972), 37

'Abergavenny Castle, Abergavenny', N Maylan, *ibid* 30 (1990), 66*

'Abergavenny Castle', S H Sell, *ibid* 38 (1998), 129

'Abergavenny Castle', G A Makepeace, *ibid* 39 (1999), 111–12

'The Norman defences of Abergavenny: a watching brief at Cross Street', S H Clarke, *ibid* 41 (2001), 78–81*

'Abergavenny Castle 1087–1535', N Phillips, *Gwent Local History* 88 (2000), 17–31*

'Medieval Britain in 1962 and 1963', D M Wilson and D G Hurst, *Medieval Archaeology* 8 (1964), 270

'Medieval Britain in 1964', D M Wilson and D G Hurst, *ibid* 9 (1965), 198

'Medieval Britain and Ireland in 1990', B S Nenk, S Margeson and M Hurley, *ibid* 35 (1991), 232

'Medieval Britain and Ireland in 1998', J Bradley, M Gaimster and C Haith, *ibid* 43 (1999), 296

'The Norman town defences of Abergavenny', S Clarke and J Bray, *ibid* 47 (2003), 186–89*

'Excavations at Abergavenny, 1962–1969. II. Medieval and later', F Radcliffe and J Knight, *Monmouthshire Antiquary* 3.2 (1972–3), 65–103*

'Excavations at Abergavenny Orchard site, 1972', P J Ashmore and F M Ashmore, *ibid* 3.2 (1972–3), 104–10*

'Abergavenny Castle: a reinterpretation of Thomas Cocke's painting "The Castle and Mount", Caerleon, 1785', J R Kenyon, *ibid* 5.1–2 (1983–4), 62–63*

Arnallt

'Castell Arnallt survey, Lanover Fawr', N Phillips, *Archaeology in Wales* 40 (2000), 107–9*

'Castell Arnallt: a topographical survey', N Phillips, *Gwent Local History* 90 (2001), 8–11*

'Medieval Britain and Ireland in 2000', J Bradley and M Gaimster, *Medieval Archae-ology* 45 (2001), 369–71*

Caerleon

'Caerleon Castle', J K Knight, *The hundred-and-seventeenth annual meeting in the Vale of Usk, 1970*, CAA, 1970, 16–18

'Three castles of the Clare family in Monmouthshire during the thirteenth and fourteenth centuries', S G Priestley and R C Turner, *Archaeologia Cambrensis* 152 (2003), 9–52*

'The keep of Caerleon Castle', J K Knight, *Monmouthshire Antiquary* 1 (1961–4), [71–72]* [pagination misprinted 23–24]

'Abergavenny Castle: a reinterpretation of Thomas Cocke's painting "The Castle and Mount", Caerleon, 1785', J R Kenyon, *ibid* 5.1–2 (1983–4), 62–63*

Caerwent

'Caerwent Roman town: conservation, excavation and interpretation', S E Rees and M Anthony, *ibid* 22 (2006), 57–72*

Caldicot

A brief history of Caldicot Castle. Anon. [Monmouth]: Monmouth District Coun-cil, n d*

Caldicot Castle. Anon. [Cwmbran]: Monmouthshire County Council, [2005]*

Caldicot Castle. T T Birbeck. Chepstow: Chepstow Rural District Council, 1965*

Sword and ploughshare: the story of the de Bohuns and Caldicot. T T Birbeck. Chepstow: Chepstow Society, [1973]*

'Caldicot Castle', W Rees, *Programme of the hundredth annual meeting at Chep-stow, 1953*, CAA, 1953, 11–12

'Caldicot Castle', D J C King, *125th annual meeting in Gwent and the Forest of Dean, 1978*, CAA, 1978, 13–14

'Caldicot Castle', I Daintith [*et al*], *Archaeology in Wales* 42 (2002), 125–27*

'Caldicot, Caldicot Castle', S Clarke and J Bray, *ibid* 43 (2003), 135

'Ballon and Caldicot castles', P R Halliwell, *Herefordshire Archaeological News* 62 (1994), 46–48*

'Caldicot Castle', P M Remfry, *ibid* 64 (1995), 60–62*

'Medieval Britain and Ireland in 1996', B S Nenk, S Margeson and J Bradley, *Me-dieval Archaeology* 41 (1997), 325

'Caldicot Castle', T T Birbeck, *Presenting Monmouthshire* 20 (1965), 27–30*

'Medieval Caldicot', T T Birbeck, *Severn and Wye Review* 1 (1970–2), 11–16*

Cas Troggy

'The hunting preserves', R Turner and S Priestley, in R Turner and A Johnson (eds), *Chepstow Castle: its history & buildings*, 185–98. Almeley: Logaston Press, 2006*

Chepstow

Chepstow: its castle and lordship. A Clark. [Newport]: Newport and Monmouthshire Branch of the Historical Association, 1950*

Chepstow Castle. J K Knight. Cardiff: Cadw: Welsh Historic Monuments, 1986*

Chepstow Castle and Port Wall, Runston Church, Chepstow Bulwarks Camp. J K Knight. Revised edition. Cardiff: Cadw: Welsh Historic Monuments, 1991*

Chepstow Castle, Monmouthshire. J C Perks. London: HMSO, 1955*; 2nd edition, 1967*

Excavations at Chepstow 1973–1974. R Shoesmith. [S l]: CAA, 1991* (Cambrian archaeological monograph; 4)

Chepstow Castle, Chepstow Bulwarks Camp, Runston Church. R Turner. Cardiff: Cadw: Welsh Historic Monuments, 2002*; revised edition, 2006*

Chepstow Castle: its history & buildings. R Turner and A Johnson (eds). Almeley: Logaston Press, 2006*

'Introduction', R Shoesmith and J R L Allen, in *ibid*, 1–14*

'William the Conqueror, William fitz Osbern and Chepstow Castle', D Bates, in *ibid*, 15–22*

'The Norman Great Tower', R Turner, C Jones-Jenkins and S Priestley, in *ibid*, 23–42*

'Chepstow under the Marshals', D Crouch, in *ibid*, 43–50*

'The main gatehouse', R Avent and D Miles, in *ibid*, 51–62*

'The middle bailey', R Avent and R Turner, in *ibid*, 63–70*

'The upper bailey', R Turner, in *ibid*, 71–80*

'William Marshal's castle at Chepstow & its place in military architecture', R Avent, in *ibid*, 81–90*

'The Marshals' use of the Great Tower', R Turner, S Priestley and C Jones-Jenkins, in *ibid*, 91–100*

'The architecture and decoration of the Marshals' Great Tower', N Coldstream and R K Morris, in *ibid*, 101–12*

'The upper barbican', R Turner, in *ibid*, 113–18*

'The sub-tidal cistern', R Turner, in *ibid*, 119–26*

'The life of Roger Bigod, fifth earl of Norfolk', M Morris, in *ibid*, 127–34*

'The 'gloriette' in the lower bailey', R Turner [*et al*], in *ibid*, 135–50*

'The New or Marten's Tower', R Turner [*et al*], in *ibid*, 151–66*

'Roger Bigod's Great Tower', R Turner, C Jones-Jenkins and S Priestley, in *ibid*, 167–76*

'From Edward II to the later Middle Ages', S Priestley, in *ibid*, 177–84*

'The hunting preserves', R Turner and S Priestley, in *ibid*, 185–98*

'Chepstow town, priory and Port Wall', R Shoesmith, in *ibid*, 199–212*

'The Tudor period', R Turner, with contributions by D Miles and S Priestley, in *ibid*, 213–20*

'Civil War and Commonwealth', J Knight, in *ibid*, 221–28*

'After the restoration', G Geear, S Priestley and R Turner, in *ibid*, 229–42*

'Chepstow Castle as a picturesque ruin', A Rainsbury, in *ibid*, 243–52*

'The Victorian period and the 20th century', A Rainsbury and R Turner, in *ibid*, 253–70*

'William Marshal's building works at Chepstow Castle, Monmouthshire, 1189–1219', R Avent, in J R Kenyon and K O'Conor (eds), *The medieval castle in Ireland and Wales: essays in honour of Jeremy Knight*, 50–71. Dublin: Four Court Press, 2003*

'Counting the cost at Chepstow', in T Eaton, *Plundering the past: Roman stonework in medieval Britain*, 31–57. Stroud: Tempus, 2000*

'Chepstow Castle', J Knight, in N J G Pounds (ed), *The Cardiff area: proceedings of the 139th summer meeting of the Royal Archaeological Institute, 1993*, 32–34. London: RAI, 1993*

'The Romanesque sculpture of the Welsh Marches', G Zarnecki, in G R Owen-Crocker and T Graham (eds), *Medieval art: recent perspectives. A memorial tribute to C R Dodwell*, 60–88. Manchester: Manchester University Press, 1998*

'The Great Tower, Chepstow Castle, Wales', R C Turner, *Antiquaries Journal* 84 (2004), 223–318*

'Chepstow Port Wall', T J Miles, *Archaeological Excavations 1971*, 42. London: HMSO, 1972

'Chepstow Castle', A J Taylor, *Archaeological Journal* 122 (1965), 226, 228–29*

'A sub-tidal water cistern at Chepstow Castle', R Turner, *Archaeology in the Severn Estuary* 13 (2002), 123–31*

'Chepstow: the Port Wall', T J Miles, *Archaeology in Wales* 11 (1971), 33

'Chepstow: the Port Wall', R Shoesmith, *ibid* 12 (1972), 37

'Chepstow, Chepstow Castle', D N Williams, *ibid* 34 (1994), 69

'Chepstow Castle', I Halfpenny, *ibid* 38 (1998), 130

'Chepstow, Chepstow Castle', D Schlee, *ibid* 39 (1999), 112

'Chepstow. A. Chepstow Castle', K Trott, *ibid* 43 (2003), 135

'Excavation in the middle bailey, Chepstow Castle', K Trott and K Blockley, *ibid* 44 (2004), 87–93*

'The architectural history of Chepstow Castle during the middle ages', J C Perks,

Transactions of the Bristol and Gloucestershire Archaeological Society 67 (1946–8), 307–46*

'"The chamber called *Gloriette*": living at leisure in thirteenth- and fourteenth-century castles', J Ashbee, *Journal of the British Archaeological Association* 157 (2004), 17–40*

'The late twelfth century gatehouse at Chepstow Castle, Monmouthshire, Wales', R Avent, *Château Gaillard* 20 (2002), 27–40*

'A fortified town on the Wye. Chepstow, Gwent – I', R Haslam, *Country Life* 163 (1978), 510–12*

'Hen hanes drysau'r castell', R Turner, *Etifeddiaeth y Cymro* 13 (1999), 6–9*

'The oldest castle doors in Europe?', R Turner, *Heritage in Wales* 13 (1999), 6–9*

'Medieval Britain in 1959', D M Wilson and J G Hurst, *Medieval Archaeology* 4 (1960), 147, 151

'Medieval Britain in 1971', L E Webster and J Cherry, *ibid* 16 (1972), 192

'Medieval Britain in 1972', L E Webster and J Cherry, *ibid* 17 (1973), 173

'Medieval Britain and Ireland in 1994', B S Nenk, S Margeson and M Hurley, *ibid* 39 (1995), 289

'Medieval Britain and Ireland in 2003', J Bradley and M Gaimster, *ibid* 48 (2004), 339

'Chepstow Port Wall excavations', T J Miles, *Monmouthshire Antiquary* 7 (1991), 5–15*

'Chepstow Castle: excavations in the Great Gatehouse, 1991', K Booth, *ibid* 9 (1993), 19–25*

'An inventory of the contents of Chepstow Castle, 1313', W H Baker, *Presenting Monmouthshire* 7 (1959), 10–11

'Tree-ring dates 1998. List 94: Welsh dendrochronology – phase two. 2. Chepstow', D H Miles and M J Worthington, *Vernacular Architecture* 29 (1998), 127

Coed-y-fedw
'Coed-y-fe[d]w', C S Briggs, *Archaeology in Wales* 14 (1974), 42

'Coed-y-fedw, Mitchell Troy United', A G Mein, *ibid* 31 (1991), 47

Coldra Woods
'Coldra Woods anti-aircraft battery, Christchurch', M Locock, *Archaeology in Wales* 33 (1993), 89

'A Second World War anti-aircraft battery near Newport, Gwent: an archaeological survey', M Locock, *Fort* 23 (1995), 127–37*

'Post-medieval Britain and Ireland in 1994', M Ponsford, *Post-Medieval Archaeology* 28 (1994), 167

Crick

'The Berries, Crick, (Mon)', C Scott-Garrett, *Archaeologia Cambrensis* 101 (1950–1), 163–65*

'Ballon and Caldicot castles', P R Halliwell, *Herefordshire Archaeological News* 62 (1994), 46–48*

Dingestow

'Dingestow Castle', J V Leslie, *Archaeology in Wales* 9 (1969), 28

'Medieval Britain in 1969', D M Wilson and D G Hurst, *Medieval Archaeology* 14 (1970), 180

Dixton

'Monmouth, Dixton mound', S Wilson and S Clarke, *Archaeology in Wales* 37 (1997), 100

'Medieval Britain and Ireland in 1997', M Gaimster, C Haith and J Bradley, *Medieval Archaeology* 42 (1998), 185

Goytre

'"Goytre" motte and bailey earthwork', R E Kay, *Herefordshire Archaeological News* 54 (1990), 10–11*

Grosmont

Grosmont Castle, Gwent/Castell y Grysmwnt. J K Knight. Cardiff: HMSO, 1980*

The three castles: Grosmont, Skenfrith and White Castle. J K Knight. Cardiff: Cadw: Welsh Historic Monuments, 1987*

The three castles: Grosmont Castle, Skenfrith Castle, White Castle. Hen Gwrt moated site. J K Knight. Cardiff: Cadw: Welsh Historic Monuments, 1991*

The three castles: Grosmont Castle, Skenfrith Castle, White Castle. Hen Gwrt medieval moated site. J K Knight. 2nd edition. Cardiff: Cadw: Welsh Historic Monuments, 2000*

Grosmont Castle, Monmouthshire. C A R Radford. London: HMSO, 1946

Grosmont Castle 1066 to 1538. P M Remfry. Malvern Link: SCS Publishing, 2000*

'Grosmont Castle', J K Knight, *125th annual meeting in Gwent and the Forest of Dean, 1978*, CAA, 1978, 22–23

'Three border castles: Skenfrith, Grosmont and White castles', G Grigson, *Country Life* 119 (1956), 98–100*

'Medieval Britain and Ireland in 2000', J Bradley and M Gaimster, *Medieval Archaeology* 45 (2001), 369

Langstone

'Langstone castle mound', L Alcock, *Archaeological Excavations 1964*, 16. London: HMSO, 16

'Langstone Court', L Alcock, *Archaeology in Wales* 4 (1964), 20

'Langstone Court motte, Monmouthshire: excavations by Leslie Alcock', K Blockley with P Courtney, *ibid* 34 (1994), 17–25*

'Medieval Britain in 1964', D M Wilson and D G Hurst, *Medieval Archaeology* 9 (1965), 193

Llanfihangel Crucorney

'Llanfihangel Crucorney. A. Pen y Clawdd castle mound', N Phillips, *Archaeology in Wales* 42 (2002), 128–31*

'Llanfinhangel Crucorney, Pen y Clawdd, castle mound', N Phillips, *ibid* 43 (2003), 136

Llangibby

'Llangibby Castle', D J C King and J C Perks, *Archaeologia Cambrensis* 105 (1956), 96–132*

'Three castles of the Clare family in Monmouthshire during the thirteenth and fourteenth centuries', S G Priestley and R C Turner, *ibid* 152 (2003), 9–52*

'Tregrug old castle, Llangybi Fawr', A G Mein, *Archaeology in Wales* 37 (1997), 102–4

Meredydd

'An archaeological survey of the Machen Ridge, Monmouthshire', K L Dallimore, *Bulletin of the Board of Celtic Studies* 28 (1978–80), 469–503* [espec pp 483, 486–88*]

Mitchell Troy

'Artha, Mitchell-Troy United', A G Mein, *Archaeology in Wales* 29 (1989), 61–62

Monmouth

Monmouth and its buildings. K Kissack. Almeley: Logaston Press, 2003*

Monnow Bridge and Gate. M L J Rowlands. Stroud: Alan Sutton, 1994*

Monmouth Castle and Great Castle House. A J Taylor. London: HMSO, 1951*

'Monmouth Castle and bridge', K Kissack, in N J G Pounds (ed), *The Cardiff area: proceedings of the 139th summer meeting of the Royal Archaeological Institute, 1993*, 32–34. London: RAI, 1993*

'Monnow Bridge and Gate', M L J Rowlands, *Archaeologia Cambrensis* 142 (1993), 243–87*

'Castle Ditches, Monmouth', D Jemmett, *Archaeology in Wales* 6 (1966), 21

'Clawdd Du, Monmouth', S H Clarke, *ibid* 6 (1966), 21

'Castle Hill, Monmouth', S H Clarke, *ibid* 6 (1966), 21

'Castle Hill, Monmouth', P Wilson and M Griffin, *ibid* 9 (1969), 29

'Monmouth, Dixton Gate', R Shoesmith, *ibid* 13 (1973), 53–54

'Recent archaeological work in Monmouth, Gwent', S Clarke, *ibid* 30 (1990), 25–27*

'Archaeological evidence for Monmouth's Roman and early medieval defences', S Clarke and R and P Jackson, *ibid* 32 (1992), 1–2*

'Monmouth, 22–24 Monnow Street', S Clarke, *ibid* 32 (1992), 81

'Monmouth, Goldwire Lane, Overmonnow', S Clarke, *ibid* 32 (1992), 81–82

'Monmouth, 22–24 Monnow Street', S Clarke, *ibid* 33 (1993), 80

'Monmouth, Nailer's Lane', S Clarke and J Perryman, *ibid* 34 (1994), 70

'Monmouth, the Victoria Dairy, Overmonnow', S Clarke, J Bray and D Jemmett, *ibid* 39 (1999), 119

'Monmouth. K. Swift House', S Clarke [*et al*], *ibid* 42 (2002), 135

'Monmouth. B. Agincourt House, Agincourt Street', S Clarke [*et al*], *ibid* 45 (2005), 164

'Medieval Britain in 1966', D M Wilson and D G Hurst, *Medieval Archaeology* 11 (1967), 290

'Medieval Britain in 1969', D M Wilson and D G Hurst, *ibid* 14 (1970), 188

'Medieval Britain in 1973', L E Webster and J Cherry, *ibid* 18 (1974), 207

'Medieval Britain and Ireland in 1990', B S Nenk, S Margeson and M Hurley, *ibid* 35 (1991), 233

'Medieval Britain and Ireland in 1991', B S Nenk, S Margeson and M Hurley, *ibid* 36 (1992), 302–3

'Medieval Britain and Ireland in 1992', B S Nenk, S Margeson and M Hurley, *ibid* 37 (1993), 309–10

'Medieval Britain and Ireland in 1995', B S Nenk, S Margeson and M Hurley, *ibid* 40 (1996), 314–15

'Medieval Britain and Ireland in 1997', M Gaimster, C Haith and J Bradley, *ibid* 42 (1998), 185

'Medieval Britain and Ireland in 2005', M Gaimster and K O'Conor, *ibid* 50 (2006), 395

'Excavations in Monmouth, 1973', R Shoesmith, *Monmouthshire Antiquary* 6 (1990), 1–15*

'Post-medieval Britain and Ireland in 1998 and 1999', M Ponsford, *Post-Medieval Archaeology* 34 (2000), 384

'Post-medieval Britain and Ireland in 2002', M Ponsford, *ibid* 37 (2003), 371–72

Nantyglo

Nantyglo roundtowers, Gwent. Anon. [S l: s n], n d*

'Crawshay's Tower, Nantyglo', J K Knight, *Gwent: programme for the 141st annual meeting ... 1994*, CAA, 1994, 13

'Roundhouse Farm, Nantyglo', N Jones, *Archaeology in Wales* 45 (2005), 188–90*

Nash
'Nash, Pye Corner', R Young, *ibid* 45 (2005), 197

Newport
'Newport Castle', J K Knight, *ibid* 9 (1969), 29–30

'Newport Castle', [J K Knight], *Gwent: programme for the 141st annual meeting ... 1994*, CAA, 1994, 5–6

'Castell newydd ar Wysg/A new castle on the Usk', C E Smith, *Gwent Local History* 95 (2003), 3–8*

'Medieval Britain in 1969', D M Wilson and D G Hurst, *Medieval Archaeology* 14 (1970), 180

'Newport Castle', J K Knight, *Monmouthshire Antiquary* 7 (1991), 17–42*

Oldcastle
'Oldcastle', E J Talbot, *Archaeology in Wales* 7 (1967), 18–19

Pencoed
'Pencoed Castle', N Maylan, *ibid* 30 (1990), 67*

'Pencoed Castle, Llanmartin', S Clarke, *ibid* 44 (2004), 173

'Fieldwork in the Wilcrick-Pencoed area of Monmouthshire', L N Parkes and P V Webster, *Bulletin of the Board of Celtic Studies* 25 (1972–4), 512–18* [espec appendix 1]

'Medieval Britain and Ireland in 1990', B S Nenk, S Margeson and M Hurley, *Medieval Archaeology* 35 (1991), 233

'Medieval Britain and Ireland in 2004', M Gaimster and K O'Conor, *ibid* 49 (2005), 469–70

Penhow
Penhow Castle, Gwent, Wales. [S Weeks]. Penhow: Penhow Castle Publications, 1987*

'Penhow Castle', A Clark, *Programme of the hundredth annual meeting at Chepstow, 1953*, CAA, 1953, 12

'Penhow Castle', J K Knight, *The hundred-and-seventeenth annual meeting in the Vale of Usk, 1970*, CAA, 1970, 8–10

'Penhow Castle', J K Knight and S Wrathmell, *125th annual meeting in Gwent and the Forest of Dean, 1978*, CAA, 1978, 39–40

'Observations on artefacts from ditch deposits', S Wrathmell, in B Vyner and S Wrathmell (eds), *Studies in medieval and later pottery in Wales presented to J M*

Lewis, 189–97. Cardiff: University College, 1987*

'Penhow Castle', S Wrathmell, *Archaeology in Wales* 17 (1977), 44

'Penhow Castle', S Wrathmell, *ibid* 18 (1978), 57–58

'Penhow Castle, Gwent', R Haslam, *Country Life* 166 (1979), 1050–53*

'Penhow Castle', S Weeks, *Gwent Local History* 46 (1979), 20–26*

'Medieval Britain in 1978', L E Webster and J Cherry, *Medieval Archaeology* 23 (1979), 263–64

'Penhow Castle, Gwent: survey and excavation, 1976–9: part one', S Wrathmell, *Monmouthshire Antiquary* 6 (1990), 17–45*

Penrhos

'Penrhos motte and bailey castle', J K Knight, *Gwent: programme for the 141st annual meeting … 1994*, CAA, 1994, 20

'Penrhos Castle', F Olding, *Gwent Local History* 88 (2000), 3–16*

'Penrhos Castle', R E Kay, *Herefordshire Archaeological News* 42 (1983), 12–14*

Raglan

Raglan Castle. Anon. Cardiff: Cadw: Welsh Historic Monuments, 1987*

Raglan Castle and the Civil war in Monmouthshire. A Clark. [Newport]: Newport and Monmouthshire Branch of the Historical Association and Chepstow Society, 1953*

Raglan Castle. H Durant. Pontypool: Hughes, 1966*; 2nd edition, Risca: Starling Press, 1980*

Raglan Castle. J R Kenyon. Cardiff: Cadw: Welsh Historic Monuments, 1988*; 2nd edition, 1994*; revised edition, 2003*

Raglan Castle, Monmouthshire. A J Taylor. London: HMSO, 1950*

Raglan Castle, Gwent/Castell Rhaglan. A J Taylor. 14th impression. Cardiff: HMSO, 1979*

'The chapel at Raglan Castle and its paving tiles', J M Lewis, in J R Kenyon and R Avent (eds), *Castles in Wales and the Marches: essays in honour of D J Cathcart King*, 143–60. Cardiff: University of Wales Press, 1987*

'The gunloops at Raglan Castle, Gwent', J R Kenyon, in *ibid*, 161–72*

'Raglan Castle', J R Kenyon, in N J G Pounds (ed), *The Cardiff area: proceedings of the 139th summer meeting of the Royal Archaeological Institute, 1993*, 32–34. London: RAI, 1993*

'Raglan Castle', J R Kenyon, *Gwent: programme for the 141st annual meeting … 1994*, CAA, 1994, 17

'The Civil War earthworks around Raglan Castle, Gwent: an aerial view', J R Kenyon, *Archaeologia Cambrensis* 131 (1982), 139–42*

'A cannon shot mould from Raglan Castle, Gwent', J R Kenyon, *ibid* 131 (1982), 142–43*

'The development of Raglan Castle and keeps in late medieval England', A Emery, *Archaeological Journal* 132 (1975), 151–86*

'Raglan Castle', K Blockley, *Archaeology in Wales* 36 (1996), 100

'Raglan, Raglan Castle', M Anthony, *ibid* 43 (2003), 162

'Raglan, Raglan Castle', M Anthony, *ibid* 44 92004), 171

'Raglan and after: the 17th-century Welsh houses of the Beauforts', R Haslam, *Country Life* 183.45 (1989), 96–101*

'Rhaglan – palas y gerddi', E Whittle, *Etifeddiaeth y Cymry* 25 (2003), 7–9*

'The Renaissance gardens of Raglan Castle', E Whittle, *Garden History* 17.1 (1989), 83–94*

'Strongbow's grant of Raglan to Walter Bluet', B Coplestone-Crow, *Gwent Local History* 89 (2000), 3–27

'Raglan – a palace with gardens', E Whittle, *Heritage in Wales* 25 (2003), 7–9*

'Medieval Britain in 1959', D M Wilson and J G Hurst, *Medieval Archaeology* 4 (1960), 147

'The sixteenth and seventeenth century gardens at Raglan Castle', E H Whittle, *Monmouthshire Antiquary* 6 (1990), 69–75*

'Raglan Castle: a reconsideration of an aspect of the Herbert period c. 1460–69', J R Kenyon, *ibid* 12 (1996), 52–55*

'My favourite castle – Raglan', J R Kenyon, *National Museums & Galleries of Wales Friends Newsletter* September (2001), [7–8]*

'Post-medieval Britain and Ireland in 1996', M Ponsford and R Jackson, *Post-Medieval Archaeology* 31 (1997), 267

'Post-medieval Britain and Ireland in 2003', M Ponsford, *ibid* 38 (2004), 397

'Notes on White Castle and Raglan Castle', H Menken, *Transactions of the Woolhope Naturalists' Field Club* 32 (1946–8), 223–27

Risca

'Craig-y-neuadd, Risca', *Annual Report 1977–78*, Glamorgan-Gwent Archaeological Trust, 1978, 46–47

Skenfrith

Skenfrith Castle, Monmouthshire. O E Craster. London: HMSO, 1970*

The three castles: Grosmont, Skenfrith and White Castle. J K Knight. Cardiff: Cadw: Welsh Historic Monuments, 1987*

The three castles: Grosmont Castle, Skenfrith Castle, White Castle. Hen Gwrt moated site. J K Knight. Cardiff: Cadw: Welsh Historic Monuments, 1991*

The three castles: Grosmont Castle, Skenfrith Castle, White Castle. Hen Gwrt medieval moated site. J K Knight. 2nd edition. Cardiff: Cadw: Welsh Historic Monuments, 2000*

'Skenfrith Castle: when was it built?', O E Craster, *Archaeologia Cambrensis* 116 (1967), 133–58*

'Skenfrith Castle,' J K Knight, *Archaeology in Wales* 10 (1970), 26

'Skenfrith Castle, Skenfrith', A G Marvell, *ibid* 36 (1996), 93

'Skenfrith. A. Skenfrith Castle', K Trott, *ibid* 43 (2003), 136–38*

'Three border castles: Skenfrith, Grosmont and White castles', G Grigson, *Country Life* 119 (1956), 98–100*

'D r gwyllt a chei yr ynys', anon, *Etifeddiaeth y Cymry* 26 (2003), 5*

'Wild water and wharfs at Skenfrith', anon, *Heritage in Wales* 26 (2003), 5*

'Medieval Britain in 1956', D M Wilson and J G Hurst, *Medieval Archaeology* 1 (1957), 158

'Medieval Britain in 1957', D M Wilson and J G Hurst, *ibid* 2 (1958), 197

'Medieval Britain in 1972', L E Webster and J Cherry, *ibid* 17 (1973), 166

'Medieval Britain and Ireland in 1996', B S Nenk, S Margeson and J Bradley, *ibid* 41 (1997), 325

'Medieval Britain and Ireland in 2003', J Bradley and M Gaimster, *ibid* 48 (2004), 340–41*

'Post-medieval Britain and Ireland in 2002', M Ponsford, *Post-Medieval Archaeology* 37 (2003), 372

Tregate
'Tregate Castle', G Jenkins [*et al*], *Archaeology in Wales* 10 (1970), 26

Trelech
'Trelech'. C. Tump Terret', N Phillips, *ibid* 42 (2002), 143–45*

'Trelech. E. Excavations on various sites', R Howell, *ibid* 42 (2002), 145–47

'Trelech, Tump Terret', N Phillips, *ibid* 43 (2003), 138

'The decayed medieval town of Trelech', R Howell, *Medieval Settlement Research Group Annual Report* 17 (2002), 68–69

'Trelech: a decayed borough of medieval Gwent', I Soulsby, *Monmouthshire Antiquary* 4.3–4 (1981–2), 41–44*

Trostrey
'Trostrey Castle, Trostrey', A G Mein, *Archaeology in Wales* 31 (1991), 47–48

'Excavations at Trostrey Castle, Usk, Gwent', A G Mein, *ibid* 32 (1992), 11–14*

'Trostrey Castle, Trostrey, A G Mein, *ibid* 33 (1993), 79–80

'Trostrey Castle, Trostrey', A G Mein, *ibid* 39 (1999), 122–23

'Trostrey Castle, Trostrey', G Mein, *ibid* 40 (2000), 121

'Excavations at Trostrey Castle, nr Usk', A G Mein, *Monmouthshire Antiquary* 5.3 (1985–8), 98–99

'Gwent seals III. A medieval seal mould from Trostrey Castle', A G Mein, *ibid* 8 (1992), 25–28*

Twm-barlwm

'Twn-barlwm [*sic*], Caerleon', A G Mein, *Archaeology in Wales* 37 (1997), 105

Usk

Medieval and later Usk (Report on the excavations at Usk 1969–1976). P Courtney. Cardiff: University of Wales Press, 1994*

Norman Usk: the birth of a town. A G Mein. Usk: the author, 1986*

'Usk Castle and its affinities', J K Knight, in M R Apted, R Gilyard-Beer and A D Saunders, *Ancient Monuments and their interpretation: essays presented to A J Taylor*, 139–54. Chichester: Phillimore, 1977*

'Usk Castle', [J K Knight], *Gwent: programme for the 141st annual meeting … 1994*, CAA, 1994, 15–16

'Usk', *Annual Report 1976–77*, Glamorgan-Gwent Archaeological Trust, 1977, 20–21

'Old Market Street, Usk: an interim report on the post-medieval, medieval and Romano-British occupation', *Annual Report 1978–79*, Glamorgan-Gwent Archaeological Trust, 1979, 44–55*

'Usk castle and the pipe roll of 1185, with a note on an expenses account of 1289', A J Taylor, *Archaeologia Cambrensis* 99 (1946–7), 249–55

'Three castles of the Clare family in Monmouthshire during the thirteenth and fourteenth centuries', S G Priestley and R C Turner, *ibid* 152 (2003), 9–52*

'Usk', R P J Jackson and W H Manning, *Archaeology in Wales* 15 (1975), 49–50

'Usk', P and G Mein, *ibid* 17 (1977), 44

'Usk, Old Market Street', V M Metcalf, *ibid* 19 (1979), 32–33

'Usk, 3–5 Castle Street', I Dennis, *ibid* 40 (2000), 121–22

'Medieval Britain in 1975', L E Webster and J Cherry, *Medieval Archaeology* 20 (1976), 193

'Medieval Britain in 1976', L E Webster and J Cherry, *ibid* 21 (1977), 219

'Medieval Britain and Ireland in 1987', S M Youngs [*et al*], *ibid* 32 (1988), 311–12

'Medieval Britain and Ireland in 2001', J Bradley and M Gaimster, *ibid* 46 (2002), 261

'Excavations at Old Market Street, Usk', V Metcalf-Dickinson, *Monmouthshire Antiquary* 4.3–4 (1981–2), 6–40*

'Elizabeth de Burgh and Usk Castle', J C Ward, *ibid* 18 (2002), 13–22

White

The three castles: Grosmont, Skenfrith and White Castle. J K Knight. Cardiff: Cadw: Welsh Historic Monuments, 1987*

The three castles: Grosmont Castle, Skenfrith Castle, White Castle. Hen Gwrt moated site. J K Knight. Cardiff: Cadw: Welsh Historic Monuments, 1991*

The three castles: Grosmont Castle, Skenfrith Castle, White Castle. Hen Gwrt medieval moated site. J K Knight. 2nd edition. Cardiff: Cadw: Welsh Historic Monuments, 2000*

White Castle, Monmouthshire. C A R Radford. London: HMSO, 1962*

'The military effectiveness of arrow loops: some experiments at White Castle', P N Jones and D Renn, *Château Gaillard* 9–10 (1982), 445–56*

'Three border castles: Skenfrith, Grosmont and White castles', G Grigson, *Country Life* 119 (1956), 98–100*

'White Castle in the thirteenth century: a reconsideration', A J Taylor, *Medieval Archaeology* 5 (1961), 169–75*

'An end-blown flute or flageolet from White Castle', J V S Megaw, *ibid* 5 (1961), 176–80*

'White Castle and the dating of medieval pottery', J G Hurst, *ibid* 6–7 (1962–3), 135–55*

'Two pewter vessels from White Castle', J M Lewis, *Monmouthshire Antiquary* 2 (1965–8), 127–30*

'Notes on White Castle and Raglan Castle', H Menken, *Transactions of the Woolhope Naturalists' Field Club* 32 (1946–8), 223–27

MONTGOMERYSHIRE

Arnold, C J. *The archaeology of Montgomeryshire to AD 1300*. [Abermule]: the author; [Welshpool]: Powysland Club, 1990* [espec ch 7]

Burnham, H. *A guide to ancient and historic Wales: Clwyd and Powys*. London: HMSO, for Cardiff: Cadw: Welsh Historic Monuments, 1995*

Haslam, R. *Powys (The buildings of Wales)*. Harmondsworth: Penguin Books, 1979*

Richards, R. 'The mediaeval castles of north Montgomeryshire: a topical survey. IV', *Montgomeryshire Collections* 49 (1945–6), 171–78

Salter, M. *The castles of mid Wales*. Wolverhampton: Folly Publications, 1991*

Salter, M. *The castles of mid Wales*. New edition. Malvern: Folly Publications, 2001*

Spurgeon, C J. 'The castles of Montgomeryshire', in D Jenkins (ed), *The historical atlas of Montgomeryshire*, 41–43. Welshpool: Powysland Club, 1999*

Spurgeon, C J. 'The castles of Montgomeryshire', *Montgomeryshire Collections* 59 (1965–6), 1–59*

Berriew
'The Moat, Berriew', C J Spurgeon, *Archaeology in Wales* 1 (1961), 14

Cann Office
'The earthwork at Cann Office (Llangadfan)', G D B Jones and W G Putnam, *Montgomeryshire Collections* 59 (1965–6), 155–58*

Dolforwyn
Dolforwyn Castle: Llywelyn's last stronghold/Castell Dolforwyn: cadarnle olaf Llywelyn. Anon. Cardiff: Cadw: Welsh Historic Monuments, 2002* [leaflet produced for the castle's opening]

Interim report on excavations at three castles in Wales 1981–1982. C Arnold [*et al*]. Cardiff: Department of Extra-Mural Studies, University College, 1983*

Dolforwyn Castle, Montgomery Castle. L Butler and J K Knight. Cardiff: Cadw, 2004*

'Dolforwyn Castle: prospect and retrospect', L Butler, in J R Kenyon and K O'Conor (eds), *The medieval castle in Ireland and Wales: essays in honour of Jeremy Knight*, 149–62. Dublin: Four Court Press, 2003*

'Dolforwyn Castle, Montgomery, Powys. First report: the excavations 1981–1986', L Butler, *Archaeologia Cambrensis* 138 (1989), 78–98*

'Dolforwyn Castle, Montgomery, Powys. Second report: the excavations 1987–1994', L Butler, *ibid* 144 (1995), 133–203*

'Dolforwyn Castle', L Butler and C Arnold, *Archaeology in Wales* 23 (1983), 62–63*

'Dolforwyn Castle', L Butler and C Arnold, *ibid* 24 (1984), 69–70

'Dolforwyn Castle', L Butler and C Arnold, *ibid* 25 (1985), 42*

'Dolforwyn Castle', L Butler, *ibid* 29 (1989), 64*

'Excavations at Dolforwyn Castle, Powys, 1986–90', L Butler, *ibid* 30 (1990), 19–20

'Dolforwyn Castle', L Butler, *ibid* 30 (1990), 68–69*

'Dolforwyn Castle', L Butler, *ibid* 31 (1991), 48–49

'Dolforwyn Castle', L Butler, *ibid* 32 (1992), 83–84*

'Dolforwyn Castle', L Butler, *ibid* 33 (1993), 82

'Dolforwyn Castle', L Butler, *ibid* 34 (1994), 72–74*

'Dolforwyn Castle, Abermule', L Butler, *ibid* 35 (1995), 69

'Dolforwyn Castle, Abermule', L Butler, *ibid* 37 (1997), 107–8

'Dolforwyn Castle', L Butler, *ibid* 38 (1998), 140–42*

'Dolforwyn Castle, Abermule', L Butler, *ibid* 40 (2000), 127–28

'Dolforwyn Castle, Powys', L Butler, *Castle Studies Group Newsletter* 12 (1998–9), 26–27*

'Dolforwyn Castle, Powys. Interim report on excavations: July 1st-22nd, 2000', L Butler, *ibid* 14 (2000–1), 29–32

'Dolforwyn: uncovering the last of the castles', L Butler, *ibid* 16 (2002–3), 56–59* [first published in *Heritage in Wales*]

'Dolforwyn Castle, Powys, Wales: excavations 1981–4', L Butler, *Château Gaillard* 12 (1985), 167–77*

Dolforwyn Castle, Powys, Wales: excavations 1985–1990', L Butler, *ibid* 15 (1992), 73–82*

'The siege of Dolforwyn Castle in 1277', L Butler, *ibid* 19 (2000), 25–26

'Dolforwyn Castle, Powys: the last castle of the last Welsh prince of north Wales', L Butler, *Current Archaeology* 10.13 (1990), 418–23*

'Dolforwyn Castle', L Butler, *ibid* 197 (2005), 228–34*

'Cyfrinach y castell olaf', L Butler, *Etifeddiaeth y Cymry* 22 (2002), 6–9*

'Dolforwyn Castle and the Welsh castles of north Wales', L Butler, *Fortress* 8 (1991), 15–24*

'Uncovering the last of the castles', L Butler, *Heritage in Wales* 22 (2002), 6–9*

'Medieval Britain and Ireland in 1981', S M Youngs and J Clark, *Medieval Archaeology* 26 (1982), 227

'Medieval Britain and Ireland in 1982', S M Youngs, J Clark and T B Barry, *ibid* 27 (1983), 228–29

'Medieval Britain and Ireland in 1983', S M Youngs, J Clark and T B Barry, *ibid* 28 (1984), 263–64*

'Medieval Britain and Ireland in 1985', S M Youngs, J Clark and T Barry, *ibid* 30 (1986), 197

'Medieval Britain and Ireland in 1986', S M Youngs, J Clark and T Barry, *ibid* 31 (1987), 191

'Medieval Britain and Ireland in 1987', S M Youngs [*et al*], *ibid* 32 (1988), 312

'Medieval Britain and Ireland in 1991', B S Nenk, S Margeson and M Hurley, *ibid* 36 (1992), 304–5

'Medieval Britain and Ireland in 1993', B S Nenk, S Margeson and M Hurley, *ibid* 38 (1994), 292–93

'Medieval Britain and Ireland in 1994', B S Nenk, S Margeson and M Hurley, *ibid* 39 (1995), 292–93

'Medieval Britain and Ireland in 1995', B S Nenk, S Margeson and M Hurley, *ibid* 40 (1996), 316–18*

'Medieval Britain and Ireland in 1996', B S Nenk, C Haith and J Bradley, *ibid* 41 (1997), 326–27

'Medieval Britain and Ireland in 1997', M Gaimster, C Haith and J Bradley, *ibid* 42 (1998), 187–88

'Medieval Britain and Ireland in 2000', J Bradley and M Gaimster, *ibid* 45 (2001), 378–79

Hen Domen

Hen Domen, Montgomery: a timber castle on the English-Welsh border. P Barker and R Higham. [London]: Royal Archaeological Institute, 1982*

Hen Domen, Montgomery: a timber castle on the English-Welsh border. Excavations 1960–1988: a summary report. P Barker and R Higham. Worcester: Hen Domen Archaeological Project, 1988*

The Hen Domen archaeological project, Montgomery, Powys. Interim report: 1988–1990. R A Higham. Exeter: the author, 1990* [duplicated typescript]

Hen Domen, Montgomery: a timber castle on the English-Welsh border. A final report. R Higham and P Barker. Exeter: Exeter University Press, 2000*

'Hen Domen revisited', P Barker, in J R Kenyon and R Avent (eds), *Castles in Wales and the Marches: essays in honour of D J Cathcart King*, 51–54. Cardiff: University of Wales Press, 1987

'Dating in medieval archaeology: problems and possibilities', R Higham, in B Orme (ed), *Problems and case studies in archaeological dating*, 83–107. Exeter: University of Exeter, 1982

'Hen Domen, Montgomery: a case study', in R Higham and P Barker, *Timber castles*, 326–47. London: Batsford, 1992*; reissued, University of Exeter Press, 2004* [ch 9]

'Timber castles of the Welsh border with special reference to Hen Domen, Montgomery', P A Barker, in H Galinié (ed), *Les mondes Normandes (VIIIe-XIIe s)*, 135–47. Caen: Société d'Archéologie Médiévale, 1989*

'Hen Domen, Montgomery', P A Barker, *Archaeological Journal* 125 (1968), 303

'Excavations at Hen Domen, Montgomery, 1969', P A Barker, *ibid* 126 (1969), 177–78

'Hen Domen, Montgomery: excavations, 1970', P A Barker, *ibid* 127 (1970), 222

'Five castle excavations: reports on the Institute's research project into the origins of the castle in England. Hen Domen, Montgomery, 1966–77', P A Barker, *ibid* 134 (1977), 101–4

'Hen Domen, Montgomery', P A Barker, *ibid* 138 (1981), 18

'Hen Domen', P A Barker, *Archaeology in Wales* 1 (1961), 14

'Hen Domen', P A Barker, *ibid* 2 (1962), 17

'Hen Domen', P A Barker, *ibid* 3 (1963), 20

'Hen Domen, Montgomery', P A Barker, *ibid* 4 (1964), 21

'Hen Domen', P A Barker, *ibid* 5 (1965), 33

'Hen Domen, Montgomery', P A Barker, *ibid* 6 (1966), 22

'Hen Domen, Montgomery', P A Barker, *ibid* 7 (1967), 17–18

'Hen Domen, Montgomery', P A Barker, *ibid* 8 (1968), 25

'Hen Domen, Montgomery', P A Barker, *ibid* 9 (1969), 27–28

'Hen Domen, Montgomery', P Barker, *ibid* 10 (1970), 27

'Hen Domen, Montgomery', P A Barker, *ibid* 12 (1972), 39–40

'Hen Domen, Montgomery', P Barker, *ibid* 13 (1973), 54–55

'Hen Domen, Montgomery', P Barker and R A Higham, *ibid* 20 (1980), 87–89

'Hen Domen', P A Barker, *CBA Group 8 News Sheet* 3 (1960), 7

'Hen Domen', P A Barker, *ibid* 4 (1961), 7

'Hen Domen', P A Barker, *ibid* 5 (1962), 8

'Hen Domen, Montgomery', P A Barker, *ibid* 6 (1963), 8

'Hen Domen', P A Barker, *ibid* 7 (1964), 10

'Hen Domen', P A Barker, *ibid* 8 (1965), 15

'Hen Domen', P A Barker, *ibid* 9 (1966), 4

'Hen Domen, Montgomery', P A Barker, *ibid* 10 (1967), 8–9

'Hen Domen, Montgomery', P A Barker, *ibid* 11 (1968), 28–29

'Hen Domen, Montgomery', P Barker, *ibid* 12 (1969), 30–31

'Hen Domen, Montgomery', P Barker, *ibid* 13 (1970), 42–43

'Hen Domen, Montgomery', P Barker, *ibid* 14 (1971), 27

'Hen Domen, Montgomery', P Barker, *ibid* 15 (1972), 25–26

'Hen Domen, Montgomery', P Barker, *ibid* 16 (1972), 23

'Excavations at Hen Domen, Montgomery, 1974', P Barker, *ibid* 17 (1974), 60–61

'Hen Domen', P A Barker, *CBA Newsletter and Calendar* 2 (1978–9), 133

'Hen Domen, Montgomery, Powys', P A Barker, *ibid* 5 (1981–2), 148

'Hen Domen, Montgomery, Powys', P A Barker, *ibid* 6 (1982–3), 159

'Montgomery, Powys: Hen Domen', P A Barker, *ibid* 7 (1983–4), 137

'Hen Domen, Montgomery: excavations, 1960–7', P A Barker, *Château Gaillard* 3 (1969), 15–27*

'The development of a timber castle at Hen Domen, Montgomery (Powys, Wales), c. 1070–1270', R A Higham, *ibid* 21 (2004), 113–17*

'Hen Domen', P A Barker, *Current Archaeology* 1.5 (1967), 133–36*

'Hen Domen', P Barker, *ibid* 10.4 (1988), 137–42*

'Medieval Britain in 1960', D M Wilson and J G Hurst, *Medieval Archaeology* 5 (1961), 322

'Medieval Britain in 1961', D M Wilson and D G Hurst, *ibid* 6–7 (1962–3), 326–28*

'Medieval Britain in 1962 and 1963', D M Wilson and D G Hurst, *ibid* 8 (1964), 262

'Medieval Britain in 1964', D M Wilson and D G Hurst, *ibid* 9 (1965), 193

'Medieval Britain in 1965', D M Wilson and D G Hurst, *ibid* 10 (1966), 195–96*

'Medieval Britain in 1966', D M Wilson and D G Hurst, *ibid* 11 (1967), 290

'Medieval Britain in 1967', D M Wilson and D G Hurst, *ibid* 12 (1968), 182

'Medieval Britain in 1968', D M Wilson and D G Hurst, *ibid* 13 (1969), 242–43

'Medieval Britain in 1969', D M Wilson and D G Hurst, *ibid* 14 (1970), 180

'A pre-Norman field system at Hen Domen, Montgomery', P A Barker and J Lawson, *ibid* 15 (1971), 58–72*

'Medieval Britain in 1970', D M Wilson and S Moorhouse, *ibid* 15 (1971), 151–52

'Medieval Britain in 1971', L E Webster and J Cherry, *ibid* 16 (1972), 186

'Medieval Britain in 1972', L E Webster and J Cherry, *ibid* 17 (1973), 166

'Medieval Britain in 1973', L E Webster and J Cherry, *ibid* 18 (1974), 198

'Medieval Britain in 1974', L E Webster and J Cherry, *ibid* 19 (1975), 242

'Medieval Britain in 1975', L E Webster and J Cherry, *ibid* 20 (1976), 187

'Medieval Britain in 1976', L E Webster and J Cherry, *ibid* 21 (1977), 241–42*

'Medieval Britain in 1977', L E Webster and J Cherry, *ibid* 22 (1978), 171

'Medieval Britain in 1979', L E Webster and J Cherry, *ibid* 24 (1980), 249

'Medieval Britain in 1980', S M Youngs and J Clark, *ibid* 25 (1981), 204

'Medieval Britain and Ireland in 1983', S M Youngs, J Clark and T Barry, *ibid* 28 (1984), 265

'Medieval Britain and Ireland in 1985', S M Youngs, J Clark and T Barry, *ibid* 30 (1986), 197–98

'Medieval Britain and Ireland in 1990', B S Nenk, S Margeson and M Hurley, *ibid* 35 (1991), 236–38*

'Medieval Britain and Ireland in 1992', B S Nenk, S Margeson and M Hurley, *ibid* 37 (1993), 310–13*

'Hen Domen, Montgomery', P A Barker, *Transactions of the Shropshire Archaeological Society* 56 (1957–60), 346

'Hen Domen, Montgomery – 1979. Interim note', P A Barker, *Shropshire News Sheet* 10 (1979), 2

'Hen Domen 1981', P A Barker and R A Higham, *ibid* 15 (1982), 1–2

'Hen Domen, Montgomery – 1982: interim report [P A Barker and R A Higham], *ibid* 17 (1983), 2–4

'Hen Domen, Montgomery (Powys) (1983)', P A Barker and R A Higham, *Shropshire Archaeological Newsletter* 19 (1984), 1–3

'Hen Domen: interim report 1984', P A Barker and R A Higham, *ibid* 20 (1984), 8–9

'Hen Domen, Montgomery: an interim interpretation of the NE sector of the bailey', P A Barker, *West Midlands Archaeological News Sheet* 19 (1976), 66–68*

'Hen Domen, Montgomery, 1977', P A Barker, *ibid* 20 (1977), 83

'Hen Domen 1978', P A Barker, *ibid* 21 (1978), 97

'Hen Domen, Montgomery, 1979', P A Barker, *ibid* 22 (1979), 65

'Hen Domen, Montgomery. Excavations of Norman motte-and-bailey', P A Barker and R A Higham, *West Midlands Archaeology* 23 (1980), 92–93

'Hen Domen, Montgomery: excavation of motte-and-bailey castle', P A Barker and R A Higham, *ibid* 26 (1983), 93–95

'Hen Domen, Montgomery (Powys), interim report 1985', P A Barker and R A Higham, *ibid* 28 (1985), 18–19*

'Some aspects of the excavation of timber buildings 1. Hen Domen', P A Barker, *World Archaeology* 1 (1969–70), 221–28*

Hyssington
'Castle Hill, Hyssington', C J Spurgeon, *Archaeology in Wales* 3 (1963), 19

Llandrinio
'Llandrinio, Llandrinio Argae (Domen Castell)', R Hankinson, *ibid* 40 (2000), 128

Llanfechain
'Y Domen Castell', R Richards, *Montgomeryshire Collections* 51 (1951), 72–74

Lletty Field
'Earthwork in Lletty Field', C J Spurgeon and H J Thomas, *Archaeology in Wales* 13 (1973), 55

Luggy Moat
'Luggy Moat, Berriew: recording and conservation', R J Silvester, *Montgomeryshire Collections* 85 (1997), 1–12*

Mathrafal
'Mathrafal', J W Huggett and C J Arnold, *Archaeology in Wales* 25 (1985), 42–43*

'Mathrafal, Meifod', C J Arnold [*et al*], *ibid* 28 (1988), 73

'Mathrafal, Powys: a reassessment', C J Arnold and J W Huggett, *Bulletin of the Board of Celtic Studies* 33 (1986), 436–51*

'Medieval Britain and Ireland in 1985', S M Youngs, J Clark and T Barry, *Medieval Archaeology* 30 (1986), 198

'Excavations at Mathrafal, Powys, 1989', C J Arnold and J W Huggett, *Montgomeryshire Collections* 83 (1995), 59–74*

Moat Lane

'Moat Lane motte (Rhos Diarbed)', C J Spurgeon, *124th annual meeting in Aberystwyth, south Montgomery and north Radnor, 1977*, CAA, 1977, 21–22

Montgomery

Dolforwyn Castle, Montgomery Castle. L Butler and J K Knight. Cardiff: Cadw, 2004*

Montgomery 1644: the story of the castle and the Civil War battle. D E Evans. Llanidloes: St Idloes Press, [198–?]*

Montgomery Castle, Montgomeryshire. J D K Lloyd and J K Knight. London: HMSO, 1973*

Montgomery Castle, Powys/Castell Trefaldwyn. J D K Lloyd and J K Knight. 2nd edition. Cardiff: HMSO, 1981*

Bloody Montgomery, 1223 to 1295. P M Remfry. Malvern Link: SCS Publishing, 1998*

Herbert correspondence: the sixteenth and seventeenth century letters of the Herberts of Chirbury, Powis Castle and Dolguog, formerly at Powis Castle in Montgomeryshire. Edited by W J Smith. Cardiff: University of Wales Press, 1963

The story of Montgomery. A and J Welton. Almeley: Logaston Press, 2003*

'"One of the goodliest and strongest places that I ever looked upon": Montgomery and the Civil War', P Gaunt, in D Dunn (ed), *War and society in medieval and early modern Britain*, 180–203. Liverpool: Liverpool University Press, 2000*

'An incident at Montgomery Castle on New Year's day, 1288', A Taylor, in A Taylor, *Essays in castles and castle-building*, 179–84. London: Hambledon Press, 1986

'Montgomery town wall', A J Taylor, *Archaeologia Cambrensis* 99 (1946–7), 282–83

'Montgomery Castle and the Herberts', J D K Lloyd, *ibid* 104 (1955), 52–64*

'The "new building" at Montgomery Castle', J D K Lloyd, *ibid* 114 (1965), 60–68

'An incident at Montgomery Castle on New Year's day, 1288', A J Taylor, *ibid* 116 (1967), 159–64

'The excavation of the "new building" at Montgomery Castle', J M Lewis, *ibid* 117 (1968), 127–56*

'A medieval steelyard weight from Montgomery Castle', J D K Lloyd, *ibid* 121 (1972), 70–73*

'Excavations at Montgomery Castle. Part I. The documentary evidence, structures and excavated features', J K Knight, *ibid* 141 (1992), 97–180*

'Excavations at Montgomery Castle. Part II. The finds: metalwork', J K Knight, *ibid* 142 (1993), 182–242*

'Excavations at Montgomery Castle. Part III. The finds: other than metalwork', J K Knight, *ibid* 143 (1994), 139–203*

'Montgomery Castle', J K Knight, *Archaeological Journal* 138 (1981), 18–20*

'Montgomery Castle', anon, *Archaeology in Wales* 6 (1966), 22–23

'Montgomery Castle', J K Knight, *ibid* 8 (1968), 26–27

'Montgomery Castle', J K Knight, *ibid* 9 (1969), 27

'Montgomery, town walls', N Jones and W Owen, *ibid* 28 (1988), 73

'Montgomery town ditch, Montgomery', A Gibson, *ibid* 30 (1990), 69*

'Montgomery', A Gibson, *ibid* 31 (1991), 49–50*

'Montgomery, Plas Trefaldwyn', N Jones, *ibid* 32 (1992), 84

'Montgomery, Plas Du', N Jones, *ibid* 35 (1995), 69

'Montgomery, town defences', N Jones, *ibid* 38 (1998), 143

'Montgomery, Montgomery Castle', P Evans, *ibid* 44 (2004), 178

'Montgomery: a castle of the Welsh March, 1223–1649', J Knight, *Château Gaillard* 11 (1983), 169–82*

'Montgomery Castle: a provisional check-list of fabric types', J K Knight, *Medieval and Later Pottery in Wales* 5 (1982), 44–62*

'The pottery from Montgomery Castle', J Knight, *ibid* 12 (1990–1), 1–100*

'Medieval Britain in 1966', D M Wilson and D G Hurst, *Medieval Archaeology* 11 (1967), 290

'Medieval Britain in 1967', D M Wilson and D G Hurst, *ibid* 12 (1968), 182–83

'Medieval Britain in 1968', D M Wilson and D G Hurst, *ibid* 13 (1969), 263

'Medieval Britain in 1969', D M Wilson and D G Hurst, *ibid* 14 (1970), 180

'Medieval Britain and Ireland in 1990', B S Nenk, S Margeson and M Hurley, *ibid* 35 (1991), 238

'Medieval Britain and Ireland in 1993', B S Nenk, S Margeson and M Hurley, *ibid* 38 (1994), 293

'Medieval Britain and Ireland in 1994', B S Nenk, S Margeson and M Hurley, *ibid* 39 (1995), 318

'Montgomery Castle: a survey of 1592–3', J D K Lloyd, *Montgomeryshire Collections* 59 (1965–6), 140–44

'The well-tower at Montgomery Castle', J D K Lloyd, *ibid* 68 (1980), 129

'Trial excavations at Rook Cottages, Montgomery', K Brassil, *ibid* 76 (1988), 127–28*

'Montgomery town wall: excavation and recording at Plas Du, 1995–97', N W Jones and W J Britnell, *ibid* 86 (1998), 5–15*

'Post-medieval Britain in 1968', D G Hurst, *Post-Medieval Archaeology* 3 (1969), 193

'Montgomery Castle', J Knight, *West Midlands Pottery Research Group Newsletter* 9 (1986), 7–9

Nantcribba

'Nantcribba, Forden', C J Spurgeon, *Archaeology in Wales* 2 (1962), 17

'Medieval Britain in 1962 and 1963', D M Wilson and D G Hurst, *Medieval Archaeology* 8 (1964), 262

'Gwyddgrug Castle (Forden) and the Gorddwr dispute in the thirteenth century', C J Spurgeon, *Montgomeryshire Collections* 57 (1961–2), 125–36*

Newtown Hall

'Newtown Hall motte', C J Spurgeon, *Archaeology in Wales* 7 (1967), 18

Old Hall Camp

'Hubert's Folly: the abortive castle of the Kerry campaign, 1228', C J Spurgeon, in J R Kenyon and K O'Conor (eds), *The medieval castle in Ireland and Wales: essays in honour of Jeremy Knight*, 107–20. Dublin: Four Court Press, 2003*

'Old Hall Camp, Kerry', C J Spurgeon, *Archaeology in Wales* 2 (1962), 17

Powis

Powis Castle, Powys. Anon. Revised edition. London: National Trust, 1993*

Powis Castle, Powys. Anon.. London: National Trust, 2000*; revised edition, 2006*

'Powis Castle', C A R Radford, *The hundred and ninth annual meeting: programme, 1962*, CAA, 1962, 25–27

'Powis Castle, Welshpool', C J Arnold, *Archaeology in Wales* 25 (1985), 42

'Powis Castle', C J Arnold, *ibid* 27 (1987), 62

'Powis Castle, Welshpool', C J Arnold, *ibid* 28 (1988), 73–74

'Medieval Britain and Ireland in 1985', S M Youngs, J Clark and T Barry, *Medieval Archaeology* 30 (1986), 198

'A note on Powis Castle', R Morgan, *Montgomeryshire Collections* 68 (1980), 90–92

'Powis Castle: recent excavations and observations', C J Arnold, *ibid* 73 (1985), 30–37*

'Powis Castle: the outer bailey', C J Arnold, *ibid* 74 (1986), 70–72*

'Powis Castle: the outer bailey', C J Arnold, *ibid* 78 (1990), 65–71*

'Powis Castle: the development of the structure', C J Arnold, *ibid* 81 (1993), 97–109*

Rhos Ddiarbed

See Moat Lane

Rhyd yr Onen

'Rhyd yr Onen Castle: politics and possession in western Arwystli in the later twelfth century', D Stephenson, *Montgomeryshire Collections* 94 (2006), 15–22*

Symon's

'Simon's Castle, Church Stoke', C J Spurgeon, *Archaeology in Wales* 4 (1964), 22

'Symon's Castle, Churchstoke', C J Arnold and J W Huggett, *ibid* 25 (1985), 43*

'Symon's Castle, Churchstoke', J W Huggett and C J Arnold, *ibid* 26 (1986), 56

'Symon's Castle, Churchstoke', C J Arnold and J W Huggett, *ibid* 27 (1987), 62

'Symon's Castle, Churchstoke', C J Arnold and J W Huggett, *ibid* 28 (1988), 74

'Symon's Castle', J Huggett, *Castle Studies Group Newsletter* 16 (2002–3), 40–45*

'3D interpretative modelling of archaeological sites: a computer reconstruction of a medieval timber and earthwork castle', J Huggett and G-Y Chen, *Internet Archaeology* 8 (2000)*

'Medieval Britain and Ireland in 1985', S M Youngs, J Clark and T Barry, *Medieval Archaeology* 30 (1986), 198

Tomen y Maerdy

'Tomen y Maerdy', R Richards, *Montgomeryshire Collections* 50 (1948), 45–48

Welshpool

'Welshpool motte, Welshpool', A Gibson, *Archaeology in Wales* 31 (1991), 49

'Medieval Britain and Ireland in 1991', B S Nenk, S Margeson and M Hurley, *Medieval Archaeology* 36 (1992), 307–8

PEMBROKESHIRE

Davis, P R. *Castles of Dyfed*. Llandysul: Gomer, 1987*

Davis, P R. *A company of forts: a guide to the medieval castles of west Wales*. Revised edition. Llandysul: Gomer, 2000* [1st edition = *Castles of Dyfed*]

Fitzgerald, M. *Pembrokeshire castles and strongholds*. Newport: Rosedale Publications, 1991*

Hull, L. *The castles & bishops palaces of Pembrokeshire*. Almeley: Logaston Press, 2005* (Monuments in the landscape; 10)

Kenyon, J R and King, D J C. 'The castles of Pembrokeshire', in R F Walker (ed), *Pembrokeshire county history. 2. Medieval Pembrokeshire*, 522–47. Haverfordwest: Pembrokeshire Historical Society, 2002*

King, D J C. 'The Norman invasion and the building of castles', in D Moore (ed), *The land of Dyfed in early times*, 23–26. [S l]: CAA, 1964*

King, D J C. 'The castles of Pembrokeshire', *Archaeological Journal* 119 (1962), 313–16

King, D J C. 'The old earldom of Pembroke', *Pembrokeshire Historian* 7 (1981), 6–15*

Knight, J. 'Amddiddynfeydd Sir Benfro', *Etifeddiaeth y Cymro* 1 (1995), 18–19*

Knight, J. 'Pembrokeshire's defences', *Heritage in Wales* 1 (1995), 18–19*

Lloyd, T, Orbach, J and Scourfield, R. *Pembrokeshire (The buildings of Wales)*. London: Yale University Press, 2004*

Miles, D. *Castles of Pembrokeshire*. Newport: Greencroft Books, 1979*

Miles, D. *Castles of Pembrokeshire*. Revised edition. Haverfordwest: Pembrokeshire Coast National Park Authority, 1983*

Murphy, K. 'Small boroughs in south-west Wales: their planning, early development and defences', in N Edwards (ed), *Landscape and settlement in medieval Wales*, 139–56. Oxford: Oxbow Books, 1997* (Oxbow monograph; 81)

Rees, S. *A guide to ancient and historic Wales; Dyfed*. London: HMSO, for Cadw: Welsh Historic Monuments, 1992*

Roberts, T. *Castles and ancient monuments of west Wales*. Fishguard: Abercastle Publications, 1989*

Salter, M. *The castles of south-west Wales*. Malvern: Folly Publications, 1996*

Stickings, T G. *Stories of the castles and strongholds of Pembrokeshire*. Tenby: H G Walters, 1972*

Thomas R J C. *Survey of 19th- and 20th-century military buildings of Pembrokeshire*. Haverfordwest: Pembrokeshire Coast National Park, 1994*

Turner, R C. 'The medieval palaces of the bishops of St Davids, Wales', in G De Boe and F Verhaeghe (eds), *Military studies in medieval Europe: papers of the 'Medieval Europe Brugge 1997' conference*, **11**, 217–25. Zellick: Institute for the Archaeological Heritage, 1997*

Turvey, R. 'The defences of twelfth-century Deheubarth and the castle strategy of the Lord Rhys', *Archaeologia Cambrensis* 144 (1995), 103–32*

Angle

'East Blockhouse, Angle', M Locock and M Lawler, *Archaeology in Wales* 33 (1993), 87

'Angle, the Old Rectory', K Blockley, *ibid* 36 (1996), 96

'Angle, the windmill', N D Ludlow, D H Wilson and M Trethowen, *ibid* 40 (2000), 145

'Post-medieval Britain and Ireland in 1993', M Ponsford, *Post-Medieval Archaeology* 28 (1994), 131

'Post-medieval Britain and Ireland in 2000', M Ponsford, *ibid* 35 (2001), 285

Camrose
'Camrose Castle', R Ramsey, *Archaeology in Wales* 36 (1996), 96

Carew
Carew Castle archaeological project: 1992 season interim report. D Austin (ed). Lampeter: University of Wales, Lampeter, Department of Archaeology, 1993*

Carew Castle archaeological project: 1993 season interim report. D Austin (ed). Lampeter: University of Wales, Lampeter, Department of Archaeology, 1995*

Carew Castle archaeological project: 1994 season interim report. D Austin (ed). Lampeter: University of Wales, Lampeter, Department of Archaeology, 1995*

Carew Castle. P R Davis. Haverfordwest: Pembrokeshire Coast National Park Authority, 1987*

Bastion: Carew Castle Archaeological Project Newsletter 1. Haverfordwest: Pembrokeshire Coast National Park Authority, [1988]*

Bastion: Carew Castle Archaeological Project Newsletter 2. Haverfordwest: Pembrokeshire Coast National Park Authority, [1989]*

Bastion: Carew Castle Archaeological Project Newsletter 3. Haverfordwest: Pembrokeshire Coast National Park Authority, [?1990]*

'Carew Castle, Pembrokeshire Coast National Park', S Gerrard, in R F White and R Iles, *Archaeology in national parks*, 47–54. Leyburn: National Parks Staff Association, 1991*

'Carew Castle', R F Walker, *Archaeologia Cambrensis* 105 (1956), 81–95*

'Carew Castle, Pembrokeshire', D J C King and J C Perks, *Archaeological Journal* 119 (1962), 270–307*

'Carew Castle, Carew', K Murphy, *Archaeology in Wales* 24 (1984), 70–72*

'Carew Castle', S Gerrard, *ibid* 27 (1987), 62–64*

'Carew Castle', S Gerrard, *ibid* 28 (1988), 74–75*

'The Carew Castle project 1986–1990', S Gerrard, *Fortress* 6 (1990), 45–50*

'Little England beyond Wales: re-defining the myth', D Austin, *Landscapes* 6 (2005), 30–62*

'Medieval Britain and Ireland in 1986', S M Youngs, J Clark and T Barry, *Medieval Archaeology* 31 (1987), 189–90

'Medieval Britain and Ireland in 1987', S M Youngs [*et al*], *ibid* 32 (1988), 310

'Medieval Britain and Ireland in 1989', D R M Gaimster, S Margeson and M Hurley, *ibid* 34 (1990), 249

Castle Hendre
'Castle Hendre, Henry's Moat', E J Talbot, *Archaeology in Wales* 6 (1966), 23

Castlemartin
'Castlemartin's little piece of Tobruk', R J C Thomas, *Sanctuary* 24 (1995), 42–43*

Cilgerran
Cilgerran Castle, Pembrokeshire. O E Craster. London: HMSO, 1957*

Cilgerran Castle, St Dogmael's Abbey, Pentre Ifan burial chamber, Carreg Coetan Arthur burial chamber. J B Hilling. Cardiff: Cadw: Welsh Historic Monuments, 1992*; 2nd edition, 2000*

Cilgerran Castle, north Pembrokeshire: descriptive and historical sketch. O Ll Jones. Cardigan: printed by E L Jones [*c* 1953]*

Cilgerran Castle. R Turner. Cardiff: Cadw: Welsh Historic Monuments, 1990*

'Cilgerran Castle', O E Craster, *Archaeological Journal* 119 (1962), 337–38*

'Cilgerran Castle', L Lane and P Crane, *Archaeology in Wales* 27 (1987), 64–65*

'Medieval Britain in 1957', D M Wilson and J G Hurst, *Medieval Archaeology* 2 (1958), 197

'Medieval Britain in 1959', D M Wilson and J G Hurst, *ibid* 4 (1960), 147

'Medieval Britain in 1962 and 1963', D M Wilson and D G Hurst, *ibid* 8 (1964), 262

Dale
'Iron Age promontory fort to medieval castle? Excavations at Great Castle Camp, Dale, Pembrokeshire 1999', P Crane, *Archaeologia Cambrensis* 148 (1999), 86–145*

'Post-medieval Britain and Ireland in 1998 and 1999', M Ponsford, *Post-Medieval Archaeology* 34 (2000), 386

Fishguard
The building of Fishguard Fort. P Horn. Fishguard: Preseli Printers, 1982*

Haverfordwest
'Haverfordwest Castle c 1110–1577', D J C King, in D Miles (ed), *A history of the town and county of Haverfordwest*, 34–41. Llandysul: Gomer, 1999*

'Haverfordwest Castle 1577–1964', M Freeman, in *ibid*, 42–54*

'Haverfordwest Castle', D J C King, *The hundred-and-twenty-third annual meeting in south Pembrokeshire, 1976*, CAA, 1976, 37–38

'Haverfordwest Castle', M Freeman, in D Moore (ed), *Excursions in north Pembrokeshire: programme for the Association's 139th summer meeting 1992*, CAA, 1992, 35–37*

'Excavation at Hayguard Lane, Haverfordwest, 1978 and 2003', P Crane, *Archaeology in Wales* 44 (2004), 61–68*

Hubberston

'The open battery at Hubberston', J Tomkinson, *Fort* 5 (1978), 35–38*; pp 67–76* in 1995 revised edition of *Fort* vols 4–5

'The main magazine of Fort Hubberston at Milford Haven', J Tomkinson, *ibid* 12 (1984), 83–86*

Little Newcastle

'Little Newcastle', E J Talbot, *Archaeology in Wales* 6 (1966), 23

Llangwathen

'Llangwathen', J W Evans, M G R Roberts and G H Williams, *ibid* 21 (1981), 65

Llawhaden

Llawhaden Castle, Pembrokeshire. C A R Radford. London: HMSO, 1947*

Lamphey Bishop's Palace, Llawhaden Castle, Carswell medieval house, Carew cross. R Turner. Cardiff: Cadw: Welsh Historic Monuments, 1991*; 2nd edition (revised), 2000*

Manorbier

Manorbier Castle, Pembrokeshire. C Dashwood. [S l: s n, *c* 2003]*

Manorbier Castle: a brief guide to Manorbier Castle in the county of Pembroke. F Dashwood. Narberth: H G Walters (printers), n d*

Manorbier Castle & Gerald of Wales. R Vlitos. [S l: s n], n d*

'Manorbier Castle, Pembrokeshire', D J C King and J C Perks, *Archaeologia Cambrensis* 119 (1970), 83–118*

'Manorbier Castle, Pembrokeshire', D J C King, *Archaeological Journal* 119 (1962), 319–20

'The wall paintings of Manorbier Castle, Pembrokeshire', J Roche, *Postern* 2 (1993), 10–11*

Milford Haven

Milford Haven waterway. B John. Newport: B John for the Pembrokeshire Coast National Park Authority, 1981*

The fortifications of Milford Haven and Pembroke Dock. N J Wheeler. Haverfordwest: Pembrokeshire Coast National Park Authority, n d*

'Harbour fortresses of a century ago', A D Saunders, *Country Life* 129 (1961), 1040, 1042*

'Milford Haven's harbour fortress', E Beazley, *ibid* 160 (1976), 732–34*

'Gynnau a grym yn yr aber', D Iorwerth, *Etifeddiaeth y Cymry* 34 (20060, 14–18*

'Military might in the haven', D Iorwerth, *Heritage in Wales* 34 (2006), 14–18*

'Milford Haven', I Stevenson, *The Redan* 62 (2004), 2–42*

Minwear

'Minwear', E J Talbot, *Archaeology in Wales* 6 (1966), 23

Nanhyfer

See Nevern

Narberth

The story of Narberth. M G R Morris (ed). Narberth: Narberth Society, 1990*

'Narberth Castle', D J C King, *The hundred-and-twenty-third annual meeting in south Pembrokeshire, 1976*, CAA, 1976, 13–14

'Narberth Castle', W Harrison, *Archaeological Journal* 119 (1962), 328–30*

'Narberth Castle', N Ludlow and T Jamieson, *Archaeology in Wales* 43 (2003), 143*

'Adfeilion I'r dyfodol', D Iorwerth, *Etifeddiaeth y Cymry* 31 (2005), 10–13*

'A ruin for the future', D Iorwerth, *Heritage in Wales* 31 (2005), 10–13*

'The castle and lordship of Narberth', N Ludlow, *Journal of the Pembrokeshire Historical Society* 12 (2003), 5–43*

Nevern

'Castell Nanhyfer, Nevern (Pemb.)', D J C King and J C Perks, *Archaeologia Cambrensis* 101 (1950–1), 123–28*

'Nevern Castle: a new interpretation', R Turvey, *Journal of the Pembrokeshire Historical Society* 3 (1989), 57–66*

Newport

Newport Castle (Pembrokeshire): an architectural study. D M Browne and D Percival. Aberystwyth: RCAHMW, 1992*

'Newport Castle (Castell Trefdraeth)', D Miles, in D Moore (ed), *Excursions in north Pembrokeshire: programme for the Association's 139th summer meeting 1992*, CAA, 1992, 20–22*

'Newport Castle', D Miles, *Archaeological Journal* 119 (1962), 340

Parc-y-castell

'Parc-y-castell ringwork & bailey', C J Spurgeon, in D Moore (ed), *Excursions in north Pembrokeshire: programme for the Association's 139th summer meeting 1992*, CAA, 1992, 13

Pembroke

Pembroke Castle: a young visitor's guide and history. G M Candler. Derby: Pilgrim Press, 1989*

Pembroke Castle. R Innes-Smith. Derby: Pilgrim Press, [?1996]*

Pembroke Castle. The town walls of Pembroke. D J C King and M Cheshire. [S l: s n], n d* (first published in *Archaeologia Cambrensis*, vols 127 & 131)

Pembroke Castle. N Ludlow. Pembroke: Pembroke Castle Trust, 2001*

'The donjon at Pembroke Castle', D F Renn, *Transactions of the Ancient Monuments Society* new ser 15 (1967–8), 35–47*

'Pembroke Castle', D J C King, *Archaeologia Cambrensis* 127 (1978), 75–121*

'The town walls of Pembroke', D J C King and M Cheshire, *ibid* 131 (1982), 77–84*

'Investigation of the town wall and burgage plots at South Quay and Castle terrace, Pembroke', M Lawler, *ibid* 147 (1998), 158–80*

'Pembroke Castle', A J Taylor, *Archaeological Journal* 119 (1962), 343–44

'Pembroke town walls', N Ludlow, *Archaeology in Wales* 41 (2001), 154

'Henry II's charter to Pembroke', R F Walker, *Bulletin of the Board of Celtic Studies* 36 (1989), 132–46*

'Pembroke Castle', N Ludlow, *Castle Studies Group Newsletter* 12 (1998–9), 21–23*

'Pembroke Castle: derivations and relationships of the domed vault of the donjon and of the Horseshoe Gate', D J C King, *Château Gaillard* 8 (1977), 159–69*

'William Marshal, Pembroke Castle and the historians', I W Rowlands, *ibid* 17 (1966), 151–55

'Pembroke Castle and town walls', N Ludlow, *Fortress* 8 (1991), 25–30*

'Medieval Britain in 1959', D M Wilson and J G Hurst, *Medieval Archaeology* 4 (1960), 148

'Medieval Pembroke', B P Hindle, *Pembrokeshire Historian* 6 (1979), 76–80*

'Post-medieval Britain and Ireland in 1994', M Ponsford and R Jackson, *Post-Medieval Archaeology* 29 (1995), 134

Pembroke Dock

Pembroke Dock: the town built to build ships. P Carradice. Pembroke Dock: Accent Press, 2006*

'The gun towers of Pembroke Dock', R Thomas, *Casemate* 11 (1983), 3, 6*

Pen-yr-allt

'Castell Pen-yr-allt, Llantood', E J Talbot, *Archaeology in Wales* 6 (1966), 23

Picton

'Picton Castle', D J C King, *The hundred-and-twenty-third annual meeting in south Pembrokeshire, 1976*, CAA, 1976, 39–40

'Picton Castle', B Howells, in D Moore (ed), *Excursions in north Pembrokeshire: programme for the Association's 139th summer meeting 1992*, CAA, 1992, 32–33

'Picton Castle', D B Hague, *Archaeological Journal* 119 (1962), 341

'Picton Castle, Pembrokeshire', M Girouard, *Country Life* 127 (1960), 18–21*

Popton

'Popton Fort', A D Saunders, *Archaeological Journal* 119 (1962), 345–47*

Puncheston

'Puncheston', E J Talbot, *Archaeology in Wales* 6 (1966), 24

Roch

'Roch Castle', W G Thomas, *Archaeological Journal* 119 (1962), 336

St Davids

'Porth-y-twr, St David's', A D R Caroe, *Archaeologia Cambrensis* 103 (1954), 1–17*

Scoveston

'Fort Scoveston', K Phillips, *The Redan* 38 (1996), 32–33*

Sentence

The Landsker borderlands: Templeton. Anon. [S l: s n], n d* [post-1987]

Tenby

The story of Tenby. M Davies. Tenby: Tenby Museum, 1979*

'Tenby Castle' and 'Tenby town walls', W G Thomas, *The hundred-and-twenty-third annual meeting in south Pembrokeshire, 1976*, CAA, 1976, 26–28

'The walls of Tenby', W G Thomas, *Archaeologia Cambrensis* 142 (1993), 1–39*

'Town walls', W G Thomas, *Archaeological Journal* 119 (1962), 336

'Tenby Castle', W G Thomas, *ibid* 119 (1962), 325–26

'Tenby, Brechmaenchine Tower', R Jones, *Archaeology in Wales* 44 (2004), 174–75*

'Jasper Tudor and the town of Tenby', R F Walker, *National Library of Wales Journal* 16 (1969–70), 1–22*

'St Catherine's Fort', P Cobb, *Palmerston Forts Society Newsletter* 13 (1988), 3–11*

Upton

'Upton Castle and chapel', D J C King, *The hundred-and-twenty-third annual meeting in south Pembrokeshire, 1976*, CAA, 1976, 33–34

Walwyn's

'Walwyn's Castle', W F Grimes, *ibid*, 45

Wiston

Wiston Castle. R Turner. Cardiff: Cadw: Welsh Historic Monuments, 1996*

'Wiston Castle', D J C King, *The hundred-and-twenty-third annual meeting in south Pembrokeshire, 1976*, CAA, 1976, 38–39

'The castle and borough of Wiston, Pembrokeshire', K Murphy, *Archaeologia Cambrensis* 144 (1995), 71–102*

'Wiston Castle', D J C King, *Archaeological Journal* 119 (1962), 326, 328

'Wiston, Wiston Castle', K Murphy, *Archaeology in Wales* 34 (1994), 76

'Wizo Flandrensis and the Flemish settlement in Pembrokeshire', L Toorians, *Cambridge Medieval Celtic Studies* 20 (1990), 99–118

Wolfcastle
'Wolfcastle, St Dogwell's', M D Freeman, *Archaeology in Wales* 17 (1977), 45

RADNORSHIRE

Burnham, H. *A guide to ancient and historic Wales: Clwyd and Powys*. London: HMSO, for Cardiff: Cadw: Welsh Historic Monuments, 1995*

Cole, E J L. 'The castles of Maelienydd', *Transactions of the Radnorshire Society* 16 (1946), 33–19

Cole, E J L. 'Border castles seized by Edward II', *ibid* 23 (1953), 49–50

Gibson, A. 'Survey in the Walton Basin (Radnor Valley), Powys', *ibid* 67 (1997), 20–62* [espec p 42, Castle Nimble and Bogs Mount]

Halliwell, P R and Kay, R E. 'Visit to south Radnorshire castles', *Herefordshire Archaeological News* 54 (1990), 13–20*

Haslam, R. *Powys (The buildings of Wales)*. Harmondsworth: Penguin Books, 1979*

Remfry, P M. *Ten castles of the Radnor lordship 1066–1304*. Malvern Link: SCS Publishing, 1995*

Remfry, P M. *Four castles of the middle reaches of the river Wye, 1066–1282*. Malvern Link: SCS Publishing, 1995*

Remfry, P M. *The borough and castles of Radnor lordship: a short guide*. Malvern Link: SCS Publishing, 1995*

Remfry, P M. *A guide to the castles of Radnorshire*. Almeley: Logaston Press, 1996* (Monuments in the landscape; 3)

Remfry, P M. *Nine castles of Burford barony 1048 to 1308*. Malvern Link: SCS Publishing, 1999*

Remfry, P M. 'Investigations of some castle sites on the Herefordshire border suggested by the late Frank Noble', *Herefordshire Archaeological News* 62 (1994), 32–34*

Rich, B. 'Castles and marcher lordships: report on SLS study weekend, May 2003', *Society for Landscape Studies Newsletter* autumn/winter (2003), 3–6*

Salter, M. *The castles of mid Wales*. Wolverhampton: Folly Publications, 1991*

Salter, M. *The castles of mid Wales*. New edition. Malvern: Folly Publications, 2001*

Aberedw
'Aberedw Castle', W R Pye, *Archaeology in Wales* 18 (1978), 59

'Aberedw Castle', N Jones and P Frost, *ibid* 34 (1994), 76–78*

'Medieval Britain and Ireland in 1994', B S Nenk, S Margeson and M Hurley, *Medieval Archaeology* 39 (1995), 289–92*

'Aberedw Castle. (Some evidence on its probable foundation)', E J L Cole, *Transactions of the Radnorshire Society* 21 (1951), 53–57

Blaidd

'Castell y Blaidd, Llanbadarn Fynydd', L A Roche, *Archaeology in Wales* 2 (1962), 18

Boughrood

'Boughrood Castle', R A Brown, B V Field and E J Talbot, *ibid* 6 (1966), 24

'Medieval Britain in 1966', D M Wilson and D G Hurst, *Medieval Archaeology* 11 (1967), 290–91

'Boughrood Castle, Radnorshire (SO/132391). An interim report', R A Brown, B V Field and E J Talbot, *Transactions of the Radnorshire Society* 36 (1966), 63–64

'Boughrood in the middle ages', I W Rowlands, *ibid* 38 (1968), 68–70

Cefnllys

Cefnllys Castle, Radnorshire. D M Browne and A Pearson. Aberystwyth: RCAHMW, 2006* www.rcahmw.gov.uk/pubs/cefnllys_castle

'Castle Bank, Cefnllys', D M Browne and A W Pearson, *Archaeology in Wales* 25 (1985), 44

'Cefn Llys: Castell Glan Ithon', anon, *Transactions of the Radnorshire Society* 15 (1945), 50–51

'Cefn-y-llys', C H Stanford, *ibid* 16 (1946), 55–56

'The castle, borough and park of Cefnllys', A E Brown, *ibid* 42 (1972), 11–22*

'Cefnllys and the Hereford Map', A Breeze, *ibid* 69 (1999), 173–75

Colwyn

'Castell Colwyn', C J Spurgeon, *124th annual meeting in Aberystwyth, south Montgomery and north Radnor, 1977*, CAA, 1977, 30–32

'Colwyn Castle', C J Spurgeon, *Archaeology in Wales* 14 (1974), 20–21

'The Roman fort at Colwyn Castle, Powys (Radnorshire)', S Frere, *Britannia* 35 (2004), 115–20*

Crug Eryr

'Castell Crug Eryr', W Rees, *Archaeologia Cambrensis* 108 (1959), 157–58

Cwm Aran

'Resurvey of a Welsh castle', P M Remfry, *Herefordshire Archaeological News* 57 (1992), 48*

'Resurvey of a Norman castle in Wales', P M Remfry, *Postern* 3 (1994), 13*

Glasbury

'Glasbury', E J Talbot, *Archaeology in Wales* 6 (1966), 24

'Medieval Britain in 1967', D M Wilson and D G Hurst, *Medieval Archaeology* 12 (1968), 183

'Notes on two newly identified castle sites in southern Radnorshire', E J Talbot, *Transactions of the Radnorshire Society* 37 (1967), 66–68

New Radnor

'New Radnor: the topography of a medieval planned town in mid-Wales', R Silvester, in N Edwards (ed), *Landscape and settlement in medieval Wales*, 157–64. Oxford: Oxbow Books, 1997* (Oxbow monograph; 81)

'The last royal visit to Radnor Castle', W H Howse, *Transactions of the Radnorshire Society* 24 (1954), 18–19

'The last royal visit to Radnor Castle', W H Howse, *ibid* 70 (2000), 61–62 [reprint of the above]

'New Radnor murage grant, 1283', E J L Cole, *ibid* 27 (1957), 25–26

'New Radnor Castle', E J L Cole, *ibid* 28 (1958), 24–26

'Account of the keeper of Radnor Castle, 9–10 Edward III', E J L Cole, *ibid* 33 (1963), 36–42

'New Radnor on old maps', R J Silvester, *ibid* 64 (1994), 15–24*

Old Radnor

Radnor Castle 1066 to 1282. P M Remfry. Malvern Link: SCS Publishing, 1994*

Radnor Castle 1066 to 1282: a short guide. P M Remfry. Malvern Link: SCS Publishing, 1995*

Painscastle

Painscastle 1066 to 1405. P M Remfry. Malvern Link: SCS Publishing, 1999*

'Painscastle, or Castle Maud', W Rees, *Archaeologia Cambrensis* 108 (1959), 159–60

'Painscastle Castle', P R Halliwell, *Herefordshire Archaeological News* 50 (1988), 37–38*

'Castle Matilda', E J L Cole, *Transactions of the Radnorshire Society* 24 (1954), 30–32

Rhayader

'The structure of an early castle', anon, *Review of Projects*, Clwyd-Powys Archaeological Trust, 1982, 11*

'Tomen Llansantffraid, Cwmdeuddwr, Rhayader', C R Musson and R Cain, *Archaeology in Wales* 22 (1982), 41

'Llansantffraid Cwmdeuddwr, Tomen Llansantffraid', B [i e R] Silvester, *ibid* 30 (1990), 69

'Tomen Llansantffraid: a motte near Rhaeadr, Powys', R J Silvester, *Medieval Archaeology* 35 (1991), 109–14*

'Medieval Britain and Ireland in 1990', B S Nenk, S Margeson and M Hurley, *ibid* 35 (1991), 236

Tinboeth

'Castell Tynboeth', R Kay and P Remfry, *Herefordshire Archaeological News* 60 (1993), 27–30*

Twyn-y-garth

'Tywyn-y-garth, Llandeilo Graban', E J Talbot, *Archaeology in Wales* 6 (1966), 25

'Tywyn-y-garth, Llandeilo Graban', E J Talbot, *ibid* 7 (1967), 19

'Medieval Britain in 1967', D M Wilson and D G Hurst, *Medieval Archaeology* 12 (1968), 183

'Notes on two newly identified castle sites in southern Radnorshire', E J Talbot, *Transactions of the Radnorshire Society* 37 (1967), 66–68

SCOTLAND

ABERDEENSHIRE

Barclay, G J. 'The Cowie line: a Second World War "stop line" west of Stonehaven, Aberdeenshire', *Proceedings of the Society of Antiquaries of Scotland* 135 (2005), 119–61*

Bogdan, N and Bryce, I B D. 'Castles, manors, and "town houses" survey', *Discovery and Excavation in Scotland 1991* (1991), 23–24, 25–27, 28–31, 35–37 [arranged by districts]

Graham, C. *Grampian: the castle country*. Aberdeen: Grampian Regional Council, 1981*

Salter, M. *The castles of Grampian and Angus*. Wolverhampton: Folly Publications, 1995*

Scott, S. *The castles of Mar*. Edinburgh: National Trust for Scotland, 1977*

Scott, S. 'The castles of Mar', in A A Tait (ed), *Treasures in trust*, 21–29. Edinburgh: HMSO, 1981*

Shepherd, I A G. *Exploring Scotland's heritage: Grampian*. Edinburgh: HMSO, 1986*

Shepherd, I A G. *Exploring Scotland's heritage: Aberdeen and north-east Scotland*. 2nd edition. Edinburgh: HMSO, 1996*

Simpson, W D. 'The castles of Mar and the Garioch', in W D Simpson, *The earldom of Mar*, 117–43. Aberdeen: Aberdeen University Press, 1949*

Aberdeen
'Robert Gordon's College', A Cameron, *Discovery and Excavation in Scotland* new ser 1 (2000), 7

'Torry Battery', A Cameron, *ibid* new ser 5 (2004), 9

'Post-medieval Britain and Ireland in 2000', M Ponsford, *Post-Medieval Archaeology* 35 (2001), 189

Abergeldie
'Abergeldie Castle', W D Simpson, *Archaeological Journal* 110 (1953), 125–34*

Auchleven
'Auchleven, Castle Hillock', P Yeoman, *Discovery and Excavation in Scotland 1987* (1988), 21

Barra
Barra Castle. N Q Bogdan. Privately published, 1993*

Beldorney

'Beldorney Castle, Aberdeenshire: an early Z-plan tower house', H Gordon Slade, *Proceedings of the Society of Antiquaries of Scotland* 105 (1972–4), 262–80*

Benholm's Tower

'Benholm's Tower, Nether Kirkgate, Aberdeen', E Meldrum, *ibid* 95 (1961–2), 249–61*

Cairnbulg

'Cairnbulg Castle', W D Simpson, *ibid* 83 (1948–9), 32–44*

Castle Fraser

Castle Fraser. M Ash. Edinburgh: National Trust for Scotland, 1994*

'The development of Castle Fraser', W D Simpson, in *Miscellany 3*, 101–22. Aberdeen: Third Spalding Club, 1960*

'The Aberdeenshire tower house with particular reference to Castle Fraser', J S Smith, *Aberdeen University Review* 47.2 (1977), 113–21*

'Castle Fraser', H Gordon Slade, *Archaeological Journal* 129 (1972), 190–92*

'Castle Fraser, Aberdeenshire', J Cornforth, *Country Life* 164 (1978), 370–73, 442–45*

'Post-medieval Britain and Ireland in 2003', M Ponsford, *Post-Medieval Archaeology* 38 (2004), 335

Castle Hill, Aberdeen

'Medieval Britain in 1970', D M Wilson and S Moorhouse, *Medieval Archaeology* 15 (1971), 149

Castle of Wardhouse

'Castle of Wardhouse', P Yeoman, *Discovery and Excavation in Scotland 1987* (1988), 21

'Castle of Wardhouse', P Yeoman, *Discovery and Excavation in Scotland 1988* (1989), 14

'Medieval Britain and Ireland in 1987', S M Youngs [*et al*], *Medieval Archaeology* 32 (1988), 303

'Medieval Britain and Ireland in 1988', D R M Gaimster, S Margeson and T Barry, *ibid* 33 (1989), 232

'Excavations at Castle of Wardhouse, Aberdeenshire', P A Yeoman, *Proceedings of the Society of Antiquaries of Scotland* 128 (1998), 581–617*

Cluny

'Cluny Castle, Aberdeenshire', H Gordon Slade, *ibid* 111 (1981), 454–92*

Corgarff

Corgarff Castle. I MacIvor and C Tabraham. Edinburgh: Historic Scotland, 1993*

'Corgarff Castle', in W D Simpson, *The earldom of Mar*, 117–43. Aberdeen: Aberdeen University Press, 1949*

'Corgarff Castle', S Cruden, *Archaeological Journal* 129 (1972), 189–90

Craigievar

Craigievar Castle, the rock of Mar: an illustrated account. W D Simpson. New edition. Edinburgh: National Trust for Scotland, 1978*

'Craigievar Castle', N Q Bogdan, *Archaeological Journal* 129 (1972), 187–88

'Craigievar: a fresh look at Scotland's premier tower-house', I D B Bryce, *Architectural Heritage* 11 (2000), 1–11*

'Craigievar Castle', M K Greig, *Discovery and Excavation in Scotland 1988* (1989), 14

'Craigievar Castle', M K Greig, *Discovery and Excavation in Scotland 1990* (1990), 18

'Craigievar Castle', J C Murray, *Discovery and Excavation in Scotland* new ser 3 (2002), 10

'Medieval Britain and Ireland in 2003', J Bradley and M Gaimster, *Medieval Archaeology* 48 (2004), 251–52

'Post-medieval Britain and Ireland in 2002', M Ponsford, *Post-Medieval Archaeology* 37 (2003), 309

'Post-medieval Britain and Ireland in 2003', M Ponsford, *ibid* 38 (2004), 338

'Excavations at Craigievar Castle, Aberdeenshire', M Greig, *Proceedings of the Society of Antiquaries of Scotland* 123 (1993), 381–93* + microfiche

Drum

Drum Castle, Aberdeenshire. C Graham and D Learmont. Edinburgh: National Trust for Scotland, 1977*

Drum Castle. O Thomson. Edinburgh: National Trust for Scotland, 1996*

'Drum Castle', N Q Bogdan, *Archaeological Journal* 129 (1972), 186–87

'Drum Castle', M Greig, *Discovery and Excavation in Scotland 1991* (1991), 34

'Drum Castle', J C Murray, *Discovery and Excavation in Scotland* new ser 3 (2002), 9

'Medieval Britain and Ireland in 1991', B S Nenk, S Margeson and M Hurley, *Medieval Archaeology* 36 (1992), 294–95

'Post-medieval Britain and Ireland in 1996', M Ponsford and R Jackson, *Post-Medieval Archaeology* 31 (1997), 264

'The tower and house of Drum, Aberdeenshire', H Gordon Slade, *Proceedings of the Society of Antiquaries of Scotland* 115 (1985), 297–356*

'Excavations in the Lord's Hall, Drum Castle, Aberdeenshire', M K Greig, *ibid* 134 (2004), 423–56*

Druminnor

'Druminnor Castle', H Gordon Slade, *Archaeological Journal* 129 (1972), 193–96*

'Drumminor [*sic*] Castle, Castlehill', P Yeoman, *Discovery and Excavation in Scotland 1987* (1988), 21–22

'Druminnor Castle, Rhynie', J Lewis, *Discovery and Excavation in Scotland* new ser 5 (2004), 10–11

'Medieval Britain and Ireland in 2004', M Gaimster and K O'Conor, *Medieval Archaeology* 49 (2005), 436

'Druminnor, formerly Castle Forbes: an investigation into the original building of a mid-fifteenth century palace house', H Gordon Slade, *Proceedings of the Society of Antiquaries of Scotland* 99 (1966–67), 148–66*

Dundarg

Dundarg Castle: a history of the site and a record of the excavations in 1950 and 1951. W D Simpson. Edinburgh: Oliver & Boyd, 1954*

'Dundarg: castle and fort', N Fojut and P Love, *Discovery and Excavation in Scotland 1981* (1982), 12

Dunnideer

Dunnideer. Anon. Aberdeen: Grampian Regional Council, n d*

Fetternear

The Bishop's Palace, Fetternear, Aberdeenshire, Scotland. P Z Dransart and N Q Bogdan. Lampeter: Scottish Episcopal Palaces Project in association with the Department of Archaeology, University of Wales, Lampeter, 1996*

'Fetternear', P Z Dransart and N Q Bogdan, *Discovery and Excavation in Scotland 1996* (1997), 7

'Fetternear', P Z Dransart and N Q Bogdan, *Discovery and Excavation in Scotland 1998* (1999), 6–7

'Fetternear', P Z Dransart and N Q Bogdan, *Discovery and Excavation in Scotland* new ser 1 (2000), 9

'Fetternear', P Z Dransart, *ibid* new ser 5 (2004), 12

'Medieval Britain and Ireland in 1995', B S Nenk, S Margeson and M Hurley, *Medieval Archaeology* 40 (1996), 308

'Medieval Britain and Ireland in 1996', B S Nenk, C Haith and J Bradley, *ibid* 41 (1997), 312–13

'Medieval Britain and Ireland in 1997', M Gaimster, C Haith and J Bradley, *ibid* 42 (1998), 171

'Medieval Britain and Ireland in 1999', J Bradley and M Gaimster, *ibid* 44 (2000), 320–22

'Medieval Britain and Ireland in 2001', J Bradley and M Gaimster, *ibid* 46 (2002), 223–24

'Post-medieval Britain and Ireland in 1998 and 1999', M Ponsford, *Post-Medieval Archaeology* 34 (2000), 321–22

'Post-medieval Britain and Ireland in 2003', M Ponsford, *ibid* 38 (2004), 337

'Post-medieval fieldwork in Britain and Northern Ireland in 2004', M Ponsford, *ibid* 39 (2005), 399

Fyvie

'Fyvie Castle, Aberdeenshire, Scotland', H Gordon Slade, *Château Gaillard* 12 (1985), 151–66*

'Fyvie Castle', I A G Shepherd, *Discovery and Excavation in Scotland 1985* (1986), 17

'Fyvie Castle', I A G Shepherd, *Discovery and Excavation in Scotland 1988* (1989), 13

'Fyvie Castle', T Addyman, *Discovery and Excavation in Scotland* new ser 4 (2003), 18

'Fyvie Castle', S M Fraser and L Hesketh-Campbell, *ibid*, 18

'Medieval Britain and Ireland in 1985', S M Youngs, J Clark and T Barry, *Medieval Archaeology* 30 (1986), 191

'Post-medieval Britain and Ireland in 2002', M Ponsford, *Post-Medieval Archaeology* 37 (2003), 308–9

'Post-medieval Britain and Ireland in 2003', M Ponsford, *ibid* 38 (2004), 337

Glenbuchat

Kildrummy and Glenbuchat castles, Aberdeenshire. W D Simpson. Edinburgh: HMSO, 1957*

Kildrummy and Glenbuchat castles. W D Simpson. 2nd edition. Edinburgh: HMSO, 1965*; 3rd edition, 1968*; 4th edition, 1978*

Kildrummy Castle and Glenbuchat Castle. Revised edition. C Tabraham. Edinburgh: Historic Scotland, 1995*

Huntly

Huntly Castle: ideas and information for teachers. E and N Curtis, edited by M Fry. Edinburgh: Historic Scotland, n d*

Huntly Castle. W D Simpson. Edinburgh: HMSO, 1954*; 2nd edition, 1960*; 3rd edition, 1978*

Huntly Castle. W D Simpson and C J Tabraham. 4th edition. Edinburgh: HMSO, 1985*

Huntly Castle. C Tabraham. Revised edition. Edinburgh: Historic Scotland, 1995*

'Huntly Castle', S Cruden, *Archaeological Journal* 129 (1972), 200–1

'Huntly Castle', G Ewart and A Radley, *Discovery and Excavation in Scotland 1997* (1998), 9

'Medieval Britain and Ireland in 1996', B S Nenk, C Haith and J Bradley, *Medieval Archaeology* 41 (1997), 313

'Post-medieval Britain and Ireland in 1997', M Ponsford and R Jackson, *Post-Medieval Archaeology* 32 (1998), 150–51

Kildrummy

Kildrummy and Glenbuchat castles, Aberdeenshire. W D Simpson. Edinburgh: HMSO, 1957*

Kildrummy and Glenbuchat castles. W D Simpson. 2nd edition. Edinburgh: HMSO, 1965*; 3rd edition, 1968*; 4th edition, 1978*

Kildrummy Castle. C J Tabraham. Edinburgh: HMSO, 1986*

Kildrummy Castle and Glenbuchat Castle. Revised edition. C Tabraham. Edinburgh: Historic Scotland, 1995*

'Kildrummy Castle', M R Apted, *Archaeological Journal* 129 (1972), 188–89*

'Kildrummy Castle', M R Apted, *Discovery and Excavation: Scotland 1955* (1956), 4–5

'Kildrummy Castle, Aberdeenshire', S Cruden, *Discovery and Excavation: Scotland 1956* (1957), 36

'Kildrummy Castle, Aberdeenshire', S H Cruden, *Discovery and Excavation: Scotland 1959* (1960), 37

'Kildrummy Castle, Aberdeenshire', S H Cruden, *Discovery and Excavation: Scotland 1960* (1961), 45

'Kildrummy Castle', G Ewart and S Coulter, *Discovery and Excavation in Scotland* new ser 3 (2002), 10

'Medieval Britain in 1956', D M Wilson and J G Hurst, *Medieval Archaeology* 1 (1957), 158

'Medieval Britain in 1958', D M Wilson and J G Hurst, *ibid* 3 (1959), 308

'Medieval Britain in 1959', D M Wilson and J G Hurst, *ibid* 4 (1960), 146–47

'Medieval Britain in 1960', D M Wilson and D G Hurst, *ibid* 5 (1961), 321

'Excavation at Kildrummy Castle, Aberdeenshire, 1952–62', M R Apted, *Proceedings of the Society of Antiquaries of Scotland* 96 (1962–3), 208–36*

Kinnaird Head

'Kinnaird Head Castle and lighthouse', F Baker, *Discovery and Excavation in Scotland 1998* (1999), 8

'Post-medieval Britain and Ireland in 1998 and 1999', M Ponsford, *Post-Medieval Archaeology* 34 (2000), 322

Knock

'Knock Castle', P Yeoman, *Discovery and Excavation in Scotland 1987* (1988), 22

Lethenty

'Lethenty: tower', I Shepherd, *Discovery and Excavation in Scotland 1982* (1983), 12

Migvie

'Migvie Castle', K C Cooper, D Anderson and D Irving, *Discovery and Excavation in Scotland* new ser 1 (2000), 11

'Medieval Britain and Ireland in 2001', J Bradley and M Gaimster, *Medieval Archaeology* 46 (2002), 224–25

Peel of Lumphanan

'The Peel of Lumphanan', E J Talbot, *Archaeological Excavations 1976*, 157. London: HMSO, 1977

'The Peel Ring of Lumphanan', S Cruden, *Archaeological Journal* 129 (1972), 187

'The Peel of Lumphanan', E J Talbot, *Discovery and Excavation in Scotland 1975* (1976), 6

'Peel of Lumphanan', E J Talbot, *Discovery and Excavation in Scotland 1976* (1977), 5–6

'Peel of Lumphanan', E J Talbot, *Discovery and Excavation in Scotland 1977* (1978), 4

'Peel of Lumphanan: motte', E J Talbot, *Discovery and Excavation in Scotland 1978* (1979), 10

'Peel of Lumphanan: motte', E J Talbot, *Discovery and Excavation in Scotland 1980* (1981), 11–12

'Medieval Britain in 1975', L E Webster and J Cherry, *Medieval Archaeology* 20 (1976), 185–86

'Medieval Britain in 1976', L E Webster and J Cherry, *ibid* 21 (1977), 240

'Medieval Britain in 1977', L E Webster and J Cherry, *ibid* 22 (1978), 171

'Medieval Britain in 1979', L E Webster and J Cherry, *ibid* 24 (1980), 249

'Excavations at the Peel of Lumphanan, Aberdeenshire, 1975–9', N S Newton and E J Talbot, *Proceedings of the Society of Antiquaries of Scotland* 128 (1998), 653–70*

Pitfoddel's

'Pitfoddel's Castle', CFA, *Discovery and Excavation in Scotland 1992* (1992), 34–35

Pitsligo

'Pitsligo Castle, Rosehearty, Aberdeenshire', W D Simpson, *Proceedings of the Society of Antiquaries of Scotland* 88 (1954–6), 125–29*

'The House of Pitsligo', C McKean, *ibid* 121 (1991), 369–90*

Rattray

'Old Rattray', H K and J C Murray, *Discovery and Excavation in Scotland 1986* (1987), 10

'Old Rattray', H K and J C Murray, *Discovery and Excavation in Scotland 1987* (1988), 20

'Old Rattray', H K and J C Murray, *Discovery and Excavation in Scotland 1988* (1989), 13

'Old Rattray', H K and J C Murray, *Discovery and Excavation in Scotland 1989* (1989), 20

'Medieval Britain and Ireland in 1985', S M Youngs, J Clark and T Barry, *Medieval Archaeology* 30 (1986), 191–92

'Medieval Britain and Ireland in 1986', S M Youngs, J Clark and T Barry, *ibid* 31 (1987), 186

'Medieval Britain and Ireland in 1987', S M Youngs [*et al*], *ibid* 32 (1988), 303

'Medieval Britain and Ireland in 1988', D R M Gaimster, S Margeson and T Barry, *ibid* 33 (1989), 231

'Medieval Britain and Ireland in 1989', D R M Gaimster, S Margeson and M Hurley, *ibid* 34 (1990), 243–44

'Excavations at Rattray, Aberdeenshire. A Scottish deserted burgh', H K Murray and J C Murray, *ibid* 37 (1993), 109–218*

Tillycairn

'Tillycairn Castle, Aberdeenshire', H Gordon Slade, *Proceedings of the Society of Antiquaries of Scotland* 112 (1982), 497–517*

Tillydrone

'Tillydrone motte', A Cameron, *Discovery and Excavation in Scotland* new ser 3 (2002), 7

Tolquhon

Tolquhon Castle: information for teachers. E and N Curtis, edited by M Fry. Edinburgh: Historic Scotland, 1995*

Tolquhon Castle, Aberdeenshire. W D Simpson. Edinburgh: HMSO, 1948*

Tolquhon Castle. W D Simpson and C J Tabraham. Edinburgh: HMSO, 1984*

Tolquhon Castle. C Tabraham. Revised edition. Edinburgh: Historic Scotland, 1993*

'Tolquhon Castle', A Barlow, *Discovery and Excavation in Scotland 1996* (1997), 10

'Tolquhon Castle', G Ewart, *Discovery and Excavation in Scotland* new ser 4 (2003), 23

'Medieval Britain and Ireland in 1996', B S Nenk, C Haith and J Bradley, *Medieval Archaeology* 41 (1997), 313

'Post-medieval Britain and Ireland in 2003', M Ponsford, *Post-Medieval Archaeology* 38 (2004), 339

ANGUS

Salter, M. *The castles of Grampian and Angus*. Wolverhampton: Folly Publications, 1995*

Stell, G. 'Castles and tower', in N J G Pounds (ed), *The St Andrews area: proceedings of the 137th summer meeting of the Royal Archaeological Institute, 1991*, 13–15. London, 1991

Walker, B and Ritchie, G. *Exploring Scotland's heritage: Fife and Tayside*. Edinburgh: HMSO, 1987*

Walker, B and Ritchie, G. *Exploring Scotland's heritage: Fife, Perthshire and Angus*. 2nd edition. Edinburgh: HMSO, 1996*

Black Jack's
'Black Jack's Castle, Boddin', R Benvie, *Discovery and Excavation in Scotland* new ser 1 (2000), 12

'Excavation at Black Jack Castle, Craig, Angus', J Wilson and E M Wilson, *Proceedings of the Society of Antiquaries of Scotland* 98 (1964–6), 249–53*

Broughty
Broughty Castle and its history. Anon. Dundee: Dundee Museums and Art Galleries, [1981?]*

Broughty Castle and the defence of the Tay. F Mudie, D Walker and I MacIvor. Dundee: Abertay Historical Society, 1970*

'Broughty Castle, Angus', R G W Preston, in N J G Pounds (ed), *The St Andrews area: proceedings of the 137th summer meeting of the Royal Archaeological Institute, 1991*, 22. London, 1991

'Broughty Castle', F M C Baker, *Discovery and Excavation in Scotland 1993* (1993), 97–98

'Broughty Castle, gun emplacements', G Ewart, *Discovery and Excavation in Scotland* new ser 2 (2001), 29

'Post-medieval Britain and Ireland in 2001', M Ponsford, *Post-Medieval Archaeology* 36 (2002), 253

Claypotts
Claypotts. M R Apted. Edinburgh: HMSO, 1957*

Claypotts Castle. M R Apted. 2nd edition. Edinburgh: HMSO, 1980*

'Claypotts Castle', F Stewart, in N J G Pounds (ed), *The St Andrews area: proceedings of the 137th summer meeting of the Royal Archaeological Institute, 1991*, 25–27. London, 1991*

'The lands and tower of Claypotts', M R Apted, *Proceedings of the Society of Antiquaries of Scotland* 88 (1954–6), 100–9*

Dudhope

'Post-medieval Britain and Ireland in 1992', M Ponsford, *Post-Medieval Archaeology* 27 (1993), 222

Dundee

'Dundee: Wishart Arch, Cowgate', D R Perry and D P Bowler, *Discovery and Excavation in Scotland 1989* (1989), 62

'East Port, Dundee', R Cachart, *Discovery and Excavation in Scotland 1993* (1993), 98

'Dundee city: 152–154 Nethergate', R Cachart, *Discovery and Excavation in Scotland 1997* (1998), 27

'The storming of Dundee, 1651', J Robertson, *History Scotland* 3.3 (2003), 23–27*

'Medieval Britain and Ireland in 1993', B S Nenk, S Margeson and M Hurley, *Medieval Archaeology* 38 (1994), 285–86

'Post-medieval Britain and Ireland in 1997', M Ponsford and R Jackson, *Medieval Archaeology* 32 (1998), 151

Dundee Law

'Excavations on Dundee Law, 1993', S T Driscoll, *Proceedings of the Society of Antiquaries of Scotland* 125 (1995), 1091–1108*

Edzell

Edzell Castle: information and ideas for teachers. M Fry. Edinburgh: Historic Scotland, 1994* + poster

Edzell Castle, Angus. W D Simpson. Edinburgh: HMSO, 1952*

Edzell Castle. W D Simpson, revised by R Fawcett. Edinburgh: HMSO, 1982*; 3rd edition, revised by R Fawcett, 1987*

Edzell Castle. W D Simpson. Revised edition. Edinburgh: Historic Scotland, 1994*

'Edzell Castle garden', D Stewart, *Discovery and Excavation in Scotland* new ser 5 (2004), 19

'Edzell Castle', C Tabraham, in N J G Pounds (ed), *The St Andrews area: proceedings of the 137th summer meeting of the Royal Archaeological Institute, 1991*, 27–28. London, 1991*

Finavon

'Finavon Castle', W D Simpson, *Proceedings of the Society of Antiquaries of Scotland* 89 (1955–6), 398–416*

Forfar

'Castle Hill: motte', M Spearman, *Discovery and Excavation in Scotland 1979* (1980), 41

Glamis

Glamis Castle. H Gordon Slade. London: Society of Antiquaries, 2000* (Reports of the Research Committee; 63)

'Glamis Castle 1372–1626: from medieval hunting lodge to feudal castle and Renaissance palace', H Gordon Slade, *Château Gaillard* 16 (1994), 233–39*

Hatton

'Hatton Castle', D Glenday, *Discovery and Excavation in Scotland 1985* (1986), 61

Mains

Mains Castle & the Grahams of Fintry. F Mudie and D M Walker. Dundee: Abertay Historical Society, 1964*

'Mains Castle', L M Thoms, *Discovery and Excavation in Scotland 1981* (1982), 46–47

'Medieval Britain in 1981', S M Youngs and J Clark, *Medieval Archaeology* 26 (1982), 222

Melgund

'Melgund Castle', J Lewis and R Cachart, *Discovery and Excavation in Scotland 1990* (1990), 40

'Melgund Castle', J Lewis, *Discovery and Excavation in Scotland 1991* (1991), 71

'Melgund Castle', J Lewis, *Discovery and Excavation in Scotland 1994* (1994), 80

'Medieval Britain and Ireland in 1990', B S Nenk, S Margeson and M Hurley, *Medieval Archaeology* 35 (1991), 228

'Medieval Britain and Ireland in 1991', B S Nenk, S Margeson and M Hurley, *ibid* 36 (1992), 297

'Medieval Britain and Ireland in 1994', B S Nenk, S Margeson and M Hurley, *ibid* 39 (1995), 279

'Medieval Britain and Ireland in 1996', B S Nenk, C Haith and J Bradley, *ibid* 41 (1997), 313

'Post-medieval Britain and Ireland in 1996', M Ponsford and R Jackson, *Post-Medieval Archaeology* 31 (1997), 264–65

'Excavations at Melgund Castle, Angus, 1990–96', J Lewis, *Tayside & Fife Archaeological Journal* 10 (2004), 134–51*

Montrose

'62–64 Bridge Street, Montrose', R Cachart, *Discovery and Excavation in Scotland 1996* (1997), 14

'Post-medieval Britain and Ireland in 1996', M Ponsford and R Jackson, *Post-Medieval Archaeology* 31 (1997), 265

Red

'Red Castle, Inverkeilor', J Wilson, *Discovery and Excavation in Scotland 1959* (1960), 1

'Red Castle, Inverkeilor', J Wilson, *Discovery and Excavation in Scotland 1960* (1961), 3

'Red Castle', A Gibson and D Pollock, *Discovery and Excavation in Scotland 1983* (1984), 34

'Medieval Britain in 1959', D M Wilson and J G Hurst, *Medieval Archaeology* 4 (1960), 147

'Medieval Britain in 1960', D M Wilson and D G Hurst, *ibid* 5 (1961), 321

'Medieval Britain and Ireland in 1983', S M Youngs, J Clark and T B Barry, *ibid* 28 (1984), 263

'A medieval midden at Red Castle, Inverkeilor, Angus', J Wilson, *Proceedings of the Society of Antiquaries of Scotland* 94 (1960–1), 325

'The Lunan Valley Project: medieval rural settlement in Angus', D Pollock, *ibid* 115 (1985), 357–99*

ARGYLL

Campbell, M and Sandeman, M L S. 'Mid Argyll: a field survey of the historic and prehistoric monuments', *Proceedings of the Society of Antiquaries of Scotland* 95 (1961–2), 1–125* [castles, pp 86–88]

Dalglish, C. 'An age of transition? Castles and the Scottish Highland estate in the 16th and 17th centuries', *Post-Medieval Archaeology* 29 (2005), 243–66*

McNeill, T E. 'Dunineny Castle and the Gaelic view of castle building', *Château Gaillard* 20 (2002), 153–61*

RCAHMS. *Argyll castles in the care of Historic Scotland: extracts from RCAHMS inventories of Argyll volumes 1, 2 and 7*. Edinburgh: Historic Scotland, 1997*

Ritchie, G and Harman, M. *Exploring Scotland's heritage: Argyll and the Western Isles*. Edinburgh: HMSO, 1985*; 2nd edition, 1996*

Salter, M. *The castles of western and northern Scotland*. Wolverhampton: Folly Publications, 1995*

Stell, G. *Dunstaffnage and the castles of Argyll*. Edinburgh: Historic Scotland, 1994*

Walker, F A. *Argyll and Bute (The buildings of Scotland)*. London: Penguin Books, 2000*

Achallader

'Achallader Castle', in RCAHMS, *Argyll: an inventory of the ancient monuments. 2. Lorn*, 171–75. Edinburgh: HMSO, 1975*

Achanduin

'Achanduin Castle, Lismore', in *ibid*, 168–71*

'Achanduin Castle', D J Turner, *Discovery and Excavation in Scotland 1970* (1971), 6–7

'Achanduin Castle', D J Turner, *Discovery and Excavation in Scotland 1971* (1972), 6–7

'Achanduin Castle', D J Turner, *Discovery and Excavation in Scotland 1972* (1973), 7–8

'Achanduin Castle', D J Turner, *Discovery and Excavation in Scotland 1975* (1976), 9

'Medieval Britain in 1970', D M Wilson and S Moorhouse, *Medieval Archaeology* 15 (1971), 149–50

'Medieval Britain in 1971', L E Webster and J Cherry, *ibid* 16 (1972), 185–86

'Medieval Britain in 1972', L E Webster and J Cherry, *ibid* 17 (1973), 165

'Medieval Britain in 1973', L E Webster and J Cherry, *ibid* 18 (1974), 197

'Medieval Britain in 1974', L E Webster and J Cherry, *ibid* 19 (1975), 241–42

'Medieval Britain in 1975', L E Webster and J Cherry, *ibid* 20 (1976), 186

'The bishops of Argyll and the castle of Achanduin, Lismore, AD 1180–1343', D Turner, *Proceedings of the Society of Antiquaries of Scotland* 128 (1998), 645–52*

Airds

'Airds Castle, Carradale', in RCAHMS, *Argyll: an inventory of the ancient monuments. 1. Kintyre*, 157–58. Edinburgh: HMSO, 1971*

Ardfad

'Ardfad Castle, Seil', in RCAHMS, *Argyll: an inventory of the ancient monuments. 2. Lorn*, 175. Edinburgh: HMSO, 1975*

Ardtornish

'Ardtornish Castle', in RCAHMS, *Argyll: an inventory of the monuments. 3. Mull, Tiree, Coll and northern Argyll*, 170–73. Edinburgh: HMSO, 1980*

'Ardtornish Castle', H B Millar and J Kirkhope, *Discovery and Excavation in Scotland 1969* (1970), 48

Aros

'Aros Castle, Mull', in RCAHMS, *Argyll: an inventory of the monuments. 3. Mull, Tiree, Coll and northern Argyll*, 172–77. Edinburgh: HMSO, 1980*

'Aros Castle', H B Millar and J Kirkhope, *Discovery and Excavation: Scotland 1964* (1965), 10

Barcaldine

'Barcaldine Castle', in RCAHMS, *Argyll: an inventory of the ancient monuments. 2. Lorn*, 176–80. Edinburgh: HMSO, 1975*

Breachacha

'Breachacha Castle, Coll', in RCAHMS, *Argyll: an inventory of the monuments. 3. Mull, Tiree, Coll and northern Argyll*, 177–84. Edinburgh: HMSO, 1980*

'Breachacha Castle, Coll', D J Turner, *Discovery and Excavation: Scotland 1965* (1966), 9–10

'Breachacha Castle, Coll', D J Turner, *Discovery and Excavation: Scotland 1966* (1967), 3–4

'Breachacha Castle, Coll', D J Turner, *Discovery and Excavation in Scotland 1967* (1968), 10–11

'Breachacha Castle, Coll', D J Turner, *Discovery and Excavation in Scotland 1968* (1969), 7

'Medieval Britain in 1965', D M Wilson and D G Hurst, *Medieval Archaeology* 10 (1966), 192

'Medieval Britain in 1966', D M Wilson and D G Hurst, *ibid* 11 (1967), 288

'Medieval Britain in 1967', D M Wilson and D G Hurst, *ibid* 12 (1968), 181

'Breachacha Castle, Coll: excavations and field survey, 1965–8', D J Turner and J Dunbar, *Proceedings of the Society of Antiquaries of Scotland* 102 (1969–70), 155–87*

Cairnburgh

'Cairnburgh Castle, Treshnish Isles', in RCAHMS, *Argyll: an inventory of the monuments. 3. Mull, Tiree, Coll and northern Argyll*, 184–90. Edinburgh: HMSO, 1980*

Caisteal Dubh nan Cliar

'Caisteal Dubh nan Cliar, Kilchoan', *ibid*, 190*

Caisteal na Nighinn Ruaidhe

'Caisteal na Nighinn Ruaidhe, Loch Avich', in RCAHMS, *Argyll: an inventory of the ancient monuments. 2. Lorn*, 182–84. Edinburgh: HMSO, 1975*

Caisteal nan Con, Killundine

'Caisteal nan Con, Killundine', in RCAHMS, *Argyll: an inventory of the monuments. 3. Mull, Tiree, Coll and northern Argyll*, 190–91. Edinburgh: HMSO, 1980*

Caisteal nan Con, Torsa

'Caisteal nan Con, Torsa', in RCAHMS, *Argyll: an inventory of the ancient monuments. 2. Lorn*, 181–82. Edinburgh: HMSO, 1975*

'Caisteal nan Con', H B Millar and K Kirkhope, *Discovery and Excavation: Scotland 1964* (1965), 9–10

Carnasserie

Dunstaffnage and the castles of Argyll. G Stell. Edinburgh: Historic Scotland, 1994*

'Carnasserie Castle', in RCAHMS, *Argyll: an inventory of the monuments. 7. Mid Argyll and Cowal: medieval and later monuments*, 214–26. [Edinburgh]: HMSO, 1992*

Carrick

'Carrick Castle', in *ibid*, 226–35, 237*

'Carrick Castle', J Cannell, *Discovery and Excavation in Scotland 1985* (1986), 37–38

'Carrick Castle', I Rogers, *Discovery and Excavation in Scotland 1992* (1992), 60

'Carrick Castle', F Baker, *Discovery and Excavation in Scotland 1993* (1993), 76–77

'Carrick Castle', G Ewart and A Dixon, *Discovery and Excavation in Scotland 1996* (1997), 24–25*

'Medieval Britain and Ireland in 1985', S M Youngs, J Clark and T Barry, *Medieval Archaeology* 30 (1986), 193

'Post-medieval Britain and Ireland in 1993', M Ponsford, *Post-Medieval Archaeology* 28 (1994), 130

'Post-medieval Britain and Ireland in 1996', M Ponsford and R Jackson, *ibid* 31 (1997), 265

'A still worm from excavations at Carrick Castle, Argyll', M L Haynes, F Baker and R Tipping, *ibid* 32 (1998), 33–44*

'Carrick Castle: symbol and source of Campbell power in south Argyll from the 14th to the 17th century', G Ewart and F Baker, *Proceedings of the Society of Antiquaries of Scotland* 128 (1998), 937–1016*

Castle Coeffin

'Castle Coeffin, Lismore', in RCAHMS, *Argyll: an inventory of the ancient monuments. 2. Lorn*, 184–87. Edinburgh: HMSO, 1975*

Castle Shuna

'Castle Shuna, Appin', in *ibid*, 187–88*

Castle Stalker

'Castle Stalker', in *ibid*, 188–94*

Castle Sween

Dunstaffnage and the castles of Argyll. G Stell. Edinburgh: Historic Scotland, 1994*

'Castle Sween', in RCAHMS, *Argyll: an inventory of the monuments. 7. Mid Argyll and Cowal: medieval and later monuments*, 245–59. [Edinburgh]: HMSO, 1992*

'Castle Sween', G Ewart, *Discovery and Excavation in Scotland 1989* (1989), 56

'Castle Sween', W D Simpson, *Transactions of the Glasgow Archaeological Society* new ser 15 (1960–7), 3–14*

'Medieval Britain and Ireland in 1989', D R M Gaimster, S Margeson and M Hurley, *Medieval Archaeology* 34 (1990), 246–47

'Archaeological excavations at Castle Sween, Knapdale, Argyll & Bute, 1989–90', G Ewart and J Triscott, *Proceedings of the Society of Antiquaries of Scotland* 126 (1996), 517–57*

Claig
'Claig Castle, Jura', in RCAHMS, *Argyll: an inventory of the monuments. 5. Islay, Jura, Colonsay & Oronsay*, 263–64. Edinburgh: HMSO, 1984*

Craigens
'A 'Chrannag, Craigens, Islay', in *ibid*, 263*

Du Ban
'Du Ban, Ulva', in RCAHMS, *Argyll: an inventory of the monuments. 3. Mull, Tiree, Coll and northern Argyll*, 202. Edinburgh: HMSO, 1980*

Duart
'Duart Castle, Mull', in *ibid*, 191–98, 200*

Dùn Ara
'Dùn Ara Castle, Mull', in *ibid*, 199–202*

Dùn Athad
'Fortification, Dùn Athad, Islay', in RCAHMS, *Argyll: an inventory of the monuments. 5. Islay, Jura, Colonsay & Oronsay*, 254–55. Edinburgh: HMSO, 1984*

Dun Chonaill
'Dun Chonaill Castle, Garvellachs', in *ibid*, 265–68*

Dunaverty
'Dunaverty Castle', in RCAHMS, *Argyll: an inventory of the ancient monuments. 1. Kintyre*, 157. Edinburgh: HMSO, 1971*

Dunderave
'Dunderave Castle', in RCAHMS, *Argyll: an inventory of the monuments. 7. Mid Argyll and Cowal: medieval and later monuments*, 264–73. [Edinburgh]: HMSO, 1992*

Dunivaig
'Dunivaig Castle, Islay', in RCAHMS, *Argyll: an inventory of the monuments. 5. Islay, Jura, Colonsay & Oronsay*, 268–75. Edinburgh: HMSO, 1984*

'Dunyvaig Castle', H B Millar and J Kirkhope, *Discovery and Excavation: Scotland 1964* (1965), 6

Dunollie

Excavations at Dun Ollaigh, Oban, Argyll: 1978: an interim report. L Alcock. Glasgow: University of Glasgow, n d*

Dunollie Castle and the brooch of Lorne. W D Simpson. Aberdeen: Aberdeen University Press, 1991*

'Dunollie Castle', in RCAHMS, *Argyll: an inventory of the ancient monuments. 2. Lorn*, 194–98. Edinburgh: HMSO, 1975*

'Dunollie Castle', L Alcock, *Discovery and Excavation in Scotland 1979* (1980), 29

'Medieval Britain in 1978', L E Webster and J Cherry, *Medieval Archaeology* 23 (1979), 247–48

'Reconnaissance excavation on early historic fortifications and other royal sites in Scotland, 1974–84: 2, excavations at Dunollie Castle, Oban, Argyll, 1978', L Alcock and E A Alcock, *Proceedings of the Society of Antiquaries of Scotland* 117 (1987), 119–47 + microfiche*

Dunstaffnage

Dunstaffnage Castle and chapel. D Grove. Edinburgh: Historic Scotland, 2004*

Dunstaffnage Castle and the Stone of Destiny. W D Simpson. Edinburgh: Oliver and Boyd, 1958*

Dunstaffnage Castle. W D Simpson and J G Dunbar. Edinburgh: HMSO, 1981*; 2nd edition, 1986*

Dunstaffnage and the castles of Argyll. G Stell. Edinburgh: Historic Scotland, 1994*

'Dunstaffnage Castle', in RCAHMS, *Argyll: an inventory of the ancient monuments. 2. Lorn*, 198–211. Edinburgh: HMSO, 1975*

'Dunstaffnage Castle, Kilmore and Kilbride', RCAHMS, *Discovery and Excavation in Scotland 1970* (1971), 64

'Dunstaffnage Castle', J H Lewis, *Discovery and Excavation in Scotland 1987* (1988), 38

'Dunstaffnage Castle', J H Lewis, *Discovery and Excavation in Scotland 1988* (1989), 23

'Dunstaffnage Castle', J Lewis, *Discovery and Excavation in Scotland 1989* (1989), 57–58*

'Dunstaffnage Castle', J Lewis, *Discovery and Excavation in Scotland 1992* (1992), 60

'Dunstaffnage Castle', A Radley, *Discovery and Excavation in Scotland* new ser 1 (2000), 16–17

'The early development of Dunstaffnage Castle', H B Millar, *Transactions of the Glasgow Archaeological Society* new ser 15 (1960–7), 53–57*

'Medieval Britain in 1970', D M Wilson and S Moorhouse, *Medieval Archaeology* 15 (1971), 149

'Medieval Britain and Ireland in 1987', S M Youngs [*et al*], *ibid* 32 (1988), 307

'Medieval Britain and Ireland in 1988', D R M Gaimster, S Margeson and T Barry, *ibid* 33 (1989), 236

'Medieval Britain and Ireland in 1989', D R M Gaimster, S Margeson and M Hurley, *ibid* 34 (1990), 247–48*

'Medieval Britain and Ireland in 1991', B S Nenk, S Margeson and M Hurley, *ibid* 36 (1992), 297

'Medieval Britain and Ireland in 1992', B S Nenk, S Margeson and M Hurley, *ibid* 37 (1993), 305

'Post-medieval Britain and Ireland in 1991', M Ponsford, *Post-Medieval Archaeology* 26 (1992), 113

'Post-medieval Britain and Ireland in 1992', M Ponsford, *ibid* 27 (1993), 222

'Post-medieval Britain and Ireland in 2000', M Ponsford, *ibid* 35 (2001), 194

'Dunstaffnage Castle, Argyll & Bute: excavations in the north tower and east range, 1987–94', J Lewis, *Proceedings of the Society of Antiquaries of Scotland* 126 (1996), 559–603*

Duntrune

'Duntrune Castle', in RCAHMS, *Argyll: an inventory of the monuments. 7. Mid Argyll and Cowal: medieval and later monuments*, 276–82. [Edinburgh]: HMSO, 1992*

Eilean Dearg

'Eilean Dearg', H B Millar and J Kirkhope, *Discovery and Excavation: Scotland 1964* (1965), 6–7

'Eilean Dearg', H B Millar and J Kirkhope, *Discovery and Excavation: Scotland 1965* (1966), 5–6

'Eilean Dearg', H B Millar and J Kirkhope, *Discovery and Excavation: Scotland 1966* (1967), 4–5

'Eilean Dearg', H B Millar and J Kirkhope, *Discovery and Excavation: Scotland 1967* (1968), 11

'Medieval Britain in 1964', D M Wilson and D G Hurst, *Medieval Archaeology* 9 (1965), 192–93

'Medieval Britain in 1965', D M Wilson and D G Hurst, *ibid* 10 (1966), 193

'Medieval Britain in 1966', D M Wilson and D G Hurst, *ibid* 11 (1967), 288–89

'A dig on Red Island', H Millar, *Scots Magazine* 94.5 (1971), 468–78*

'A dig on Red Island', H Millar, *ibid* 94.6 (1971), 574–82*

Fincharn

'Fincharn Castle', H B Millar and J Kirkhope, *Discovery and Excavation: Scotland 1964* (1965), 9

Finlaggan

'Castle, Finlaggan, Islay', in RCAHMS, *Argyll: an inventory of the monuments. 5. Islay, Jura, Colonsay & Oronsay*, 275–81. Edinburgh: HMSO, 1984*

'Medieval Britain and Ireland in 1994', B S Nenk, S Margeson and M Hurley, *Medieval Archaeology* 39 (1995), 277

Fraoch Eilean

'Castle, Fraoch Eilean', in RCAHMS, *Argyll: an inventory of the ancient monuments. 2. Lorn*, 212–17. Edinburgh: HMSO, 1975*

'Fraoch Eilean, Loch Awe', A R Cross, *Discovery and Excavation: Scotland 1956* (1957), 11

'The castle of Fraoch Eilean, Loch Awe, Argyll', H B Millar, *Transactions of the Glasgow Archaeological Society* new ser 15 (1960–7), 111–28*

'Medieval Britain in 1956', D M Wilson and J G Hurst, *Medieval Archaeology* 1 (1957), 158

Glendaruel

'Glendaruel', J Kirby and H B Millar, *Discovery and Excavation in Scotland 1967* (1968), 8

Glensands

'Castle, Glensands', in RCAHMS, *Argyll: an inventory of the monuments. 3. Mull, Tiree, Coll and northern Argyll*, 202–5. Edinburgh: HMSO, 1980*

Gylen

'Gylen Castle, Kerrera', in RCAHMS, *Argyll: an inventory of the ancient monuments. 2. Lorn*, 217–23. Edinburgh: HMSO, 1975*

'Gylen Castle in Kerrera', in W D Simpson, *Dunollie Castle and the brooch of Lorne*, 86–92. Aberdeen: Aberdeen University Press, 1991

'Gylen Castle, Kerrera', T Addyman, *Discovery and Excavation in Scotland 1998* (1999), 20–21

'Gylen Castle, Kerrera', T Addyman, *Discovery and Excavation in Scotland* new ser 2 (2001), 21

'Gylen Castle, Kerrera', D Connolly, *ibid* new ser 3 (2002), 20*

'Post-medieval Britain and Ireland in 1998 and 1999', M Ponsford, *Post-Medieval Archaeology* 34 (2000), 329

'Post-medieval Britain and Ireland in 2002', M Ponsford, *ibid* 37 (2003), 313

Innis Chonnell

'Innis Chonnell', in RCAHMS, *Argyll: an inventory of the ancient monuments. 2. Lorn*, 223–31. Edinburgh: HMSO, 1975*

'Inch Chonnel', H B Millar and J Kirkhope, *Discovery and Excavation: Scotland 1964* (1965), 7

'Inchonnell', H B Millar and J Kirkhope, *Discovery and Excavation: Scotland 1965* (1966), 7

'Three sites at Portinnisherrich, Loch Awe. (3). Innish Connell', W A Anderson, *Transactions of the Glasgow Archaeological Society* new ser 11 (1946–7), 24–27*

'Medieval Britain in 1965', D M Wilson and D G Hurst, *Medieval Archaeology* 10 (1966), 192–93

'Medieval Britain in 1969', D M Wilson and D G Hurst, *ibid* 14 (1970), 179

Inveraray

'Inveraray', H B Millar and J Kirkhope, *Discovery and Excavation: Scotland 1966* (1967), 12–13

Island Muller

'Castle, Island Muller', in RCAHMS, *Argyll: an inventory of the ancient monuments. 1. Kintyre*, 159–60. Edinburgh: HMSO, 1971*

Kilchurn

Dunstaffnage and the castles of Argyll. G Stell. Edinburgh: Historic Scotland, 1994*

'Kilchurn Castle', in RCAHMS, *Argyll: an inventory of the ancient monuments. 2. Lorn*, 231–40. Edinburgh: HMSO, 1975*

'Kilchurn Castle', G Ewart, *Discovery and Excavation in Scotland 1993* (1993), 72–73

'Post-medieval Britain and Ireland in 1993', M Ponsford, *Post-Medieval Archaeology* 28 (1994), 130–31

Kilkerran

'Kilkerran Castle', in RCAHMS, *Argyll: an inventory of the ancient monuments. 1. Kintyre*, 159–60. Edinburgh: HMSO, 1971*

Kilmartin

'Kilmartin Castle', R Will, *Discovery and Excavation in Scotland 1991* (1991), 57

'Post-medieval Britain and Ireland in 1991', M Ponsford, *Post-Medieval Archaeology* 26 (1992), 113

Kinlochaline

'Kinlochaline Castle', in RCAHMS, *Argyll: an inventory of the monuments. 3. Mull, Tiree, Coll and northern Argyll*, 205–8. Edinburgh: HMSO, 1980*

'Kinlochaline Castle', S Halliday, *Discovery and Excavation in Scotland 1998* (1999), 57

'Post-medieval Britain and Ireland in 1998 and 1999', M Ponsford, *Post-Medieval Archaeology* 34 (2000), 355

Loch an Eilein
'Castle, Loch an Eilein', in RCAHMS, *Argyll: an inventory of the monuments. 3. Mull, Tiree, Coll and northern Argyll*, 208–9. Edinburgh: HMSO, 1980*

Loch an Sgoltaire
'Fortification, Loch an Sgoltaire, Colonsay', in RCAHMS, *Argyll: an inventory of the monuments. 5. Islay, Jura, Colonsay & Oronsay*, 281–82. Edinburgh: HMSO, 1984*

Loch Gorm
'Castle, Loch Gorm', in *ibid*, 282–83*

Lochnell
'Lochnell', H B Millar and J Kirkhope, *Discovery and Excavation: Scotland 1964* (1965), 8

Macewen's
'McEwen's Castle, Kilfinan', anon, *Discovery and Excavation in Scotland 1969* (1970), 8–9

'Excavations at Macewen's Castle, Argyll, in 1969–69', D N Marshall, *Glasgow Archaeological Journal* 10 (1983), 131–42*

'A Romanesque crucifix from Macewen's Castle, Loch Fyne, mid Argyll', J G Scott, *ibid* 16 (1989–90), 81–83*

'Medieval Britain in 1969', D M Wilson and D G Hurst, *Medieval Archaeology* 14 (1970), 177, 179

Mingary
'Mingary Castle', in RCAHMS, *Argyll: an inventory of the monuments. 3. Mull, Tiree, Coll and northern Argyll*, 209–17. Edinburgh: HMSO, 1980*

'Castle Tioram, Moidart, Inverness-shire, and Mingary Castle, Ardnarurchan, Argyllshire', W D Simpson, *Transactions of the Glasgow Archaeological Society* new ser 13 (1954), 79–90*

Moy
'Moy Castle, Mull', in RCAHMS, *Argyll: an inventory of the monuments. 3. Mull, Tiree, Coll and northern Argyll*, 212–27. Edinburgh: HMSO, 1980*

Old Castle Lachlan
'Old Castle Lachlan', in RCAHMS, *Argyll: an inventory of the monuments. 7. Mid Argyll and Cowal: medieval and later monuments*, 236–45. [Edinburgh]: HMSO, 1992*

Saddell

'Saddell Castle', in RCAHMS, *Argyll: an inventory of the ancient monuments. 1. Kintyre*, 161–65. Edinburgh: HMSO, 1971*

'A chronology of the abbey and castle of Saddell, Kintyre', A McFerral, *Proceedings of the Society of Antiquaries of Scotland* 86 (1951–2), 115–21*

Skipness

Dunstaffnage and the castles of Argyll. G Stell. Edinburgh: Historic Scotland, 1994*

'Skipness Castle', in RCAHMS, *Argyll: an inventory of the ancient monuments. 1. Kintyre*, 165–78. Edinburgh: HMSO, 1971*

'Skipness Castle', A M Kahane, *Archaeological Excavations 1975*, 134–35. London: HMSO, 1976

'Skipness Castle (Kintyre), Argyll', K A Steer, *Discovery and Excavation: Scotland 1966* (1967), 46

'Skipness Castle', A M Kahane, *Discovery and Excavation in Scotland 1975* (1976), 11

'Skipness Castle and Kilbrannan Chapel', G Ewart, *Discovery and Excavation in Scotland 1993* (1993), 77

'Skipness Castle', G Ewart and P Sharman, *Discovery and Excavation in Scotland 1996* (1997), 25

'Skipness Castle', W D Simpson, *Transactions of the Glasgow Archaeological Society* new ser 15 (1960–7), 87–109*

'Post-medieval Britain and Ireland in 1996', M Ponsford and R Jackson, *Post-Medieval Archaeology* 31 (1997), 265

'Fragment of a medieval aquamanile from Skipness Castle, Argyll', J G Dunbar, *Proceedings of the Society of Antiquaries of Scotland* 99 (1966–7), 263–64*

Strachur

'Strachur', J Kirby and H B Millar, *Discovery and Excavation: Scotland 1966* (1967), 15

Tangy Loch

'Fortified dwelling, Tangy Loch', in RCAHMS, *Argyll: an inventory of the ancient monuments. 1. Kintyre*, 179. Edinburgh: HMSO, 1971*

Tarbert

'Tarbert Castle', in *ibid*, 179–84*

'Tarbert Castle: a contribution to the history of Argyll', J G Dunbar and A A M Duncan, *Scottish Historical Review* 50 (1971), 1–17*

Toward

'Toward Castle', in RCAHMS, *Argyll: an inventory of the monuments. 7. Mid Argyll and Cowal: medieval and later monuments*, 297–302. [Edinburgh]: HMSO, 1992*

AYRSHIRE

Linge, J. 'Re-discovering a landscape: the barrow and motte in north Ayrshire', *Proceedings of the Society of Antiquaries of Scotland* 117 (1987), 23–32*

Salter, M. *The castles of south-west Scotland*. Wolverhampton: Folly Publications, 1993*

Stell, G. 'Castles and towers in south-western Scotland: some recent surveys', *Transactions of the Dumfriesshire and Galloway Natural History and Antiquarian Society* 3 ser 57 (1982), 65–77*

Stevenson, J B. *Exploring Scotland's heritage: the Clyde estuary and Central Region*. Edinburgh: HMSO, 1985*

Stevenson, J B. *Exploring Scotland's heritage: Glasgow, Clydeside and Stirling*. 2nd edition. Edinburgh: HMSO, 1995*

Ardrossan

'Ardrossan Castle, Ayrshire: a preliminary report', D H Caldwell, *Proceedings of the Society of Antiquaries of Scotland* 104 (1971–2), 201–21*

Auldhill

'Auldhill, Portencross', G J Ewart, *Discovery and Excavation in Scotland 1987* (1988), 48

'Auldhill, Portencross', G J Ewart, *Discovery and Excavation in Scotland 1989* (1989), 60

'Medieval Britain and Ireland in 1987', S M Youngs [*et al*], *Medieval Archaeology* 32 (1988), 307–8

Ayr

'Cromwell's citadel in Ayr', H Caldwell, H Fraser and L Lyall, *Collections of the Ayrshire Archaeological and Natural History Society* 2 ser 8 (1967–9), 153–54

Baltersan

'Baltersan: a stately tower house in Ayrshire', J Brown, *Proceedings of the Society of Antiquaries of Scotland* 130 (2000), 725–42*

Courthill

'The hall and motte at Courthill, Dalry, Ayrshire', J G Scott, *Proceedings of the Society of Antiquaries of Scotland* 119 (1989), 271–78*

SCOTLAND

Culzean

'Post-medieval Britain and Ireland in 1998 and 1999', M Ponsford, *Post-Medieval Archaeology* 34 (2000), 366–67

'Post-medieval Britain and Ireland in 2000', M Ponsford, *ibid* 35 (2001), 256

Dean

'Dean Castle, Kilmarnock', J Hunter, *Archaeological Journal* 143 (1986), 43–45*

Dundonald

'Dundonald Castle', G Stell, *ibid* 143 (1986), 45

'Dundonald Castle', W D Simpson, *Collections of the Ayrshire Archaeological and Natural History Society* 2 ser 1 (1947–9), 42–51

'Dundonald Castle: recent work', G Ewart, *Château Gaillard* 16 (1994), 167–78*

'Dundonald Castle, Ayrshire', anon, *Discovery and Excavation in Scotland 1968* (1969), 49

'Dundonald', G J Ewart, *Discovery and Excavation in Scotland 1985* (1986), 68

'Dundonald Castle', G J Ewart, *Discovery and Excavation in Scotland 1986* (1987), 38

'Dundonald', G Ewart, *Discovery and Excavation in Scotland 1987* (1988), 52

'Dundonald', G J Ewart, *Discovery and Excavation in Scotland 1988* (1989), 25

'Dundonald', G Ewart, *Discovery and Excavation in Scotland 1991* (1991), 60–61

'Dundonald', G Ewart, *Discovery and Excavation in Scotland 1993* (1993), 85

'Dundonald', G Ewart and D Stewart, *Discovery and Excavation in Scotland 1997* (1998), 73

'Medieval Britain in 1968', D M Wilson and D G Hurst, *Medieval Archaeology* 13 (1969), 263

'Medieval Britain and Ireland in 1985', S M Youngs, J Clark and T Barry, *ibid* 30 (1986), 193

'Medieval Britain and Ireland in 1986', S M Youngs, J Clark and T Barry, *ibid* 31 (1987), 189

'Medieval Britain and Ireland in 1987', S M Youngs [*et al*], *ibid* 32 (1988), 307

'Medieval Britain and Ireland in 1988', D R M Gaimster, S Margeson and T Barry, *ibid* 33 (1989), 236

'Medieval Britain and Ireland in 1991', B S Nenk, S Margeson and M Hurley, *ibid* 36 (1992), 296–97

'Medieval Britain and Ireland in 1997', M Gaimster, C Haith and J Bradley *ibid* 42 (1998), 182

'Post-medieval Britain and Ireland in 1991', M Ponsford, *Post-Medieval Archaeology* 26 (1992), 112–13

'"There is a castle in the west ..."': Dundonald Castle excavations 1986–93', G Ewart and D Pringle, *Scottish Archaeological Journal* 26 (2004), [whole issue; x, 166pp]*

Dunure

'Dunure Castle', T Addyman, *Discovery and Excavation in Scotland 1998* (1999), 87–88

'Dunure Castle', T Addyman, *Discovery and Excavation in Scotland* new ser 1 (2000), 84

'Medieval Britain and Ireland in 1999', J Bradley and M Gaimster, *Medieval Archaeology* 44 (2000), 341–42

'Medieval Britain and Ireland in 2001', J Bradley and M Gaimster, *ibid* 46 (2002), 251–52

'Post-medieval Britain and Ireland in 1998 and 1999', M Ponsford, *Post-Medieval Archaeology* 34 (2000), 367

'Post-medieval Britain and Ireland in 2000', M Ponsford, *ibid* 35 (2001), 257

East Newton

'East Newton, near Newmilns', J G Scott, *Discovery and Excavation in Scotland 1969* (1970), 15

Laverock

'Laverock Castle', A Hallifax Crawford and F Newall, *Discovery and Excavation: Scotland 1958* (1959), 16

Loudoun

'Old Castle of Loudoun: motte and bailey', J Mair, *Discovery and Excavation in Scotland 1981* (1982), 40

'Old Castle of Loudoun', A Johnstone, J Mair and G Hearns, *Discovery and Excavation in Scotland 1994* (1994), 70*

'Medieval Britain in 1981', S M Youngs and J Clark, *Medieval Archaeology* 26 (1982), 222

Montfode

'Montfode Mount', H F James, *Discovery and Excavation in Scotland 1985* (1986), 42

'Excavation at Montfode Mount motte', H F James, *Glasgow Archaeological Journal* 13 (1986), 78–85*

Portencross

'Portencross Castle', in P Wilkinson, *Restoration: the story continues*, 174–79. London: English Heritage, 2004*

'Portencross Castle, Portencross', S Macleod and M Macneill, *Discovery and Excavation: Scotland 1964* (1965), 20

'Portencross Castle', E M Patterson, *Discovery and Excavation in Scotland 1987* (1988), 47–48

'Portencross Castle', E M Patterson, *Discovery and Excavation in Scotland 1988* (1989), 24

'Medieval Britain and Ireland in 1987', S M Youngs [*et al*], *Medieval Archaeology* 32 (1988), 308

Rowallan

'Rowallan old castle', D Stewart and A Duns, *Discovery and Excavation in Scotland 1999* (2000), 26

'Medieval Britain and Ireland in 2000', J Bradley and M Gaimster, *Medieval Archaeology* 45 (2001), 355–56

'Post-medieval Britain and Ireland in 1998 and 1999', M Ponsford, *Post-Medieval Archaeology* 34 (2000), 338–89

Seagate

'Seagate Castle, Irvine', A Bailey, *Discovery and Excavation in Scotland 1992* (1992), 62

'Seagate Castle, Irvine', D Lelong, *Discovery and Excavation in Scotland* new ser 1 (2000), 61

'Post-medieval Britain and Ireland in 2000', M Ponsford, *Post-Medieval Archaeology* 35 (2001), 242–43

Thomaston

'Thomaston Castle, Culzean', T Addyman, *Discovery and Excavation in Scotland 1998* (1999), 87

'Post-medieval Britain and Ireland in 1998 and 1999', M Ponsford, *Post-Medieval Archaeology* 34 (2000), 367

BANFFSHIRE

Bogdan, N and Bryce, I B D. 'Castles, manors, and "town houses" survey', *Discovery and Excavation in Scotland 1991* (1991), 23–24, 25–27, 28–31, 35–37 [arranged by districts]

Graham, C. *Grampian: the castle country*. Aberdeen: Grampian Regional Council, 1981*

Salter, M. *The castles of Grampian and Angus*. Wolverhampton: Folly Publications, 1995*

Shepherd, I A G. *Exploring Scotland's heritage: Grampian*. Edinburgh: HMSO, 1986*

Shepherd, I A G. *Exploring Scotland's heritage: Aberdeen and north-east Scotland*. 2nd edition. Edinburgh: HMSO, 1996*

Auchindoun

'Excavation at Auchindoun Castle, Moray district, in 1984', J Wordsworth, *Proceedings of the Society of Antiquaries of Scotland* 120 (1990), 169–71*

Balvenie

The castle of Balvenie, Banffshire. J S Richardson and M E B Simpson. Edinburgh: HMSO, 1947*

Balvenie Castle. J S Richardson and M E Root. Edinburgh: HMSO, 1980*

Balvenie Castle. I MacIvor and M E Root. 2nd edition. Edinburgh: HMSO, 1988*

Balvenie Castle. I MacIvor. Revised edition. Edinburgh: Historic Scotland, 1995*

'Balvenie Castle', J Lewis, *Discovery and Excavation in Scotland 1990* (1990), 19

'Balvenie Castle', R Murdoch, *Discovery and Excavation in Scotland 1993* (1993), 41

'Medieval Britain and Ireland in 1990', B S Nenk, S Margeson and M Hurley, *Medieval Archaeology* 35 (1991), 222

Banff

'Castle Hill and Deveronside, Banff', S Stronach, *Discovery and Excavation in Scotland* new ser 2 (2001), 8–9

'Banff Castle', J C Murray, *Discovery and Excavation in Scotland* new ser 4 (2003), 14

'Medieval Britain and Ireland in 2001', J Bradley and M Gaimster, *Medieval Archaeology* 46 (2002), 222–23

'Medieval Britain and Ireland in 2003', J Bradley and M Gaimster, *ihid* 48 (2004), 313

Boharm

'"Castellum meum de Bucharm": a Banffshire hall-house of *circa* 1220', I B D Bryce, *Aberdeen University Review* 54.1 (1991), 13–22*

Carnousie

'Carnousie, Banffshire', H Gordon Slade, *Archaeological Journal* 136 (1979), 229–39*

Craig O'Boyne

'Craig O'Boyne', L M Maclagan-Wedderburn, *Discovery and Excavation: Scotland 1966* (1967), 18

Cullen

'Mains of Cullen (Cullen Castle), Gamrie, Macduff', J C Murray, *Discovery and Excavation in Scotland* new ser 4 (2003), 18–19

'Medieval Britain and Ireland in 2003', J Bradley and M Gaimster, *Medieval Archaeology* 48 (2004), 315

Drumin

'Drumin Castle, Glenlivet', D Alexander, *Discovery and Excavation in Scotland 1996* (1997), 76

BERWICKSHIRE

Baldwin, J R. *Exploring Scotland's heritage: Lothian and the Borders*. Edinburgh: HMSO, 1985*

Baldwin, J R. *Exploring Scotland's heritage: Edinburgh, Lothian and the Borders*. 2nd edition. Edinburgh: TSO, 1997*

Cruft, K, Dunbar, J and Fawcett, R. *Borders (The buildings of Scotland)*. London: Yale University Press, 2006*

Dent, J and McDonald, R. *Warfare and fortifications in the Borders*. Melrose: Scottish Borders Council, 2000*

Salter, M. *The castles of Lothian and the Borders*. Wolverhampton: Folly Publications, 1994*

Borthwick

'Borthwick Castle, near Duns: excavations, 1979', A M T Maxwell-Irving, *Proceedings of the Society of Antiquaries of Scotland* 111 (1981), 430–44*

Bunkle

'Bunkle Castle and its legend', R H Johnston, *History of the Berwickshire Naturalists' Club* 33 (1953–5), 56–62

Cranshaws

'Cranshaws Castle', S E A Landale, *ibid* 36 (1962–4), 272–74

'Notes on the history of Cranshaws Castle', D B Robertson, *ibid* 41.4 (1980), 234–35

'Notes on the history of Cranshaws Castle', D B Robertson, *ibid* 42.1 (1981), 27–28

Eyemouth

Excavations at Eyemouth Fort 1980–1986: an interim report. D H Caldwell and G Ewart. Privately published, n d*

Eyemouth Fort excavations: 7th season 1987. Interim report. D H Caldwell and G Ewart. Privately published, n d*

The forts of Eyemouth 1547–1559. M H Merriman. Lancaster: the author, 1987*

'Eyemouth Fort: 16th century artillery fortalice', G J Ewart, *Discovery and Excavation in Scotland 1980* (1981), 2

'Eyemouth Fort: 16th century artillery fort', G J Ewart, *Discovery and Excavation in Scotland 1981* (1982), 2

'Eyemouth Fort', G J Ewart, *Discovery and Excavation in Scotland 1982* (1983), 1–2

'Eyemouth Fort', G J Ewart and D H Caldwell, *Discovery and Excavation in Scotland 1983* (1984), 1

'Eyemouth Fort', D H Caldwell and G J Ewart, *Discovery and Excavation in Scotland 1985* (1986), 68

'Eyemouth Fort', D H Caldwell and G J Ewart, *Discovery and Excavation in Scotland 1986* (1987), 1

'Eyemouth Fort', G J Ewart and D H Caldwell, *Discovery and Excavation in Scotland 1987* (1988), 1

'Eyemouth Fort', G J Ewart and D H Caldwell, *Discovery and Excavation in Scotland 1988* (1989), 7

'Post-medieval Britain in 1982', G Egan, *Post-Medieval Archaeology* 17 (1983), 187

'Post-medieval Britain in 1983', G Egan, *ibid* 18 (1984), 310

'Post-medieval Britain in 1985', G Egan, *ibid* 20 (1986), 336

'Post-medieval Britain in 1986', G Egan, *ibid* 21 (1987), 271

'Post-medieval Britain and Ireland in 1988', G Egan, *ibid* 23 (1989), 37

'Excavations at Eyemouth, Berwickshire, in a mid 16th-century *trace italienne* fort', D H Caldwell and G Ewart, *ibid* 31 (1997), 61–119*

'The forts of Eyemouth: anvils of British union', M H Merriman, *Scottish Historical Review* 67.2 (1988), 142–55

Fast

Fast Castle. Anon. Edinburgh: Edinburgh Archaeological Field Society, 1977*

Fast Castle: the early years. M Kennaway. Edinburgh: Edinburgh Archaeological Field Society, 1992*

Fast Castle: a history from 1602. K L Mitchell. Edinburgh: Edinburgh Archaeological Field Society, 1988*

Fast Castle: excavations 1971–86. K L Mitchell, K R Murdoch and J R Ward. Edinburgh: Edinburgh Archaeological Field Society, 2001*

Excavations at Fast Castle: the well. J Ward. Edinburgh: Edinburgh Archaeological Field Society, 1985*

'Notes on Fast Castle', W M L Home, *History of the Berwickshire Naturalists' Club* 33 (1953–5), 186–90

'Fast Castle', E Robertson, *Discovery and Excavation in Scotland 1975* (1976), 16

'Fast Castle', E Robertson, *Discovery and Excavation in Scotland 1976* (1977), 22

'Fast Castle', E Robertson, *Discovery and Excavation in Scotland 1977* (1978), 9

'Fast Castle', E Robertson, *Discovery and Excavation in Scotland 1978* (1979), 1

'Fast Castle', E Robertson, *Discovery and Excavation in Scotland 1979* (1980), 1

'Fast Castle', E Robertson, *Discovery and Excavation in Scotland 1980* (1981), 1

'Fast Castle', E Robertson, *Discovery and Excavation in Scotland 1982* (1983), 1

'Fast Castle', K L Mitchell, *Discovery and Excavation in Scotland 1984* (1985), 1

'Fast Castle', K R Murdoch, *Discovery and Excavation in Scotland 1985* (1986), 1

'Fast Castle', K L Mitchell, *Discovery and Excavation in Scotland 1986* (1987), 1

'Medieval Britain in 1972', L E Webster and J Cherry, *Medieval Archaeology* 17 (1973), 165

'Medieval Britain in 1981', S M Youngs and J Clark, *ibid* 26 (1982), 218

'Medieval Britain and Ireland in 1982', S M Youngs, J Clark and T B Barry, *ibid* 27 (1983), 222

'Medieval Britain and Ireland in 1984', S M Youngs, J Clark and T B Barry, *ibid* 29 (1985), 220

'Medieval Britain and Ireland in 1985', S M Youngs, J Clark and T B Barry, *ibid* 30 (1986), 188

'Medieval Britain and Ireland in 1986', S M Youngs, J Clark and T B Barry, *ibid* 31 (1987), 182

'The imported pottery from Fast Castle, near Dunbar, Scotland', G Haggarty and S Jennings, *Medieval Ceramics* 16 (1992), 45–54*

'Post-medieval Britain in 1975', J Cherry, *Post-Medieval Archaeology* 10 (1976), 169

'Textiles from Fast Castle, Berwickshire, Scotland', M L Ryder and T Gabra-Sanders, *Textile History* 23 (1992), 5–22*

Greenknowe

Greenknowe Tower. Anon. Edinburgh: HMSO, 1976*

'Greenknowe Tower: courtyard buildings', C J Tabraham, *Discovery and Excavation in Scotland 1979* (1980), 1

Mote Hill

'Notes on the Mote Hill and Castle Law', W R Elliot, *History of the Berwickshire Naturalists' Club* 33 (1953–5), 113–18*

Thirlestane [Lauder Fort]

'Thirlestane Castle', S Carter, *Discovery and Excavation in Scotland* new ser 1 (2000), 77

'Post-medieval Britain and Ireland in 2000', M Ponsford, *Post-Medieval Archaeology* 35 (2001), 251

BUTE

Salter, M. *The castles of western and northern Scotland*. Wolverhampton: Folly Publications, 1995*

Stevenson, J B. *Exploring Scotland's heritage: the Clyde estuary and Central Region*. Edinburgh: HMSO, 1985*

Stevenson, J B. *Exploring Scotland's heritage: Glasgow, Clydeside and Stirling*. 2nd edition. Edinburgh: HMSO, 1995*

Walker, F A. *Argyll and Bute (The buildings of Scotland)*. London: Penguin Books, 2000*

Brodick

'Brodick Castle, Arran', D Alexander and J Farrer, *Discovery and Excavation in Scotland* new ser 2 (2001), 69–70

'Post-medieval Britain and Ireland in 1993', M Ponsford, *Post-Medieval Archaeology* 28 (1994), 131

Lochranza

The ancient monuments of Arran. R McLellan. 2nd edition, revised by G Barclay and C Tabraham. Edinburgh: HMSO, 1989*

Rothesay

Rothesay Castle. J Hume. Edinburgh: HMSO, 1986*

Isle of Bute. J R Hume. Edinburgh: HMSO, 1987*

Rothesay Castle and St Mary's Church. D Pringle. Edinburgh: Historic Scotland, 1995*

Rothesay Castle, Bute. W D Simpson. Edinburgh: HMSO, 1972*

'Rothesay Castle and the Norse siege of 1230', W D Simpson, in K Falck (ed), *Annen Viking Kongress, Bergen 1953*, 73–76. Bergen: J Griegs, 1955*

'Rothesay Castle', S Cruden, *Archaeological Journal* 143 (1986), 32–33*

'Rothesay Castle', A Dunn, *Discovery and Excavation in Scotland* new ser 1 (2000), 18

'Rothesay Castle', D Stewart, *ibid* new ser 6 (2005), 38

'Rothesay Castle and the Stewarts', D Pringle, *Journal of the British Archaeological Association* 151 (1998), 149–69*

'Medieval Britain and Ireland in 2001', J Bradley and M Gaimster, *Medieval Archaeology* 46 (2002), 228

'Post-medieval Britain and Ireland in 2000', M Ponsford, *Post-Medieval Archaeology* 35 (2001), 195

'Post-medieval Britain and Ireland in 2002', M Ponsford, *ibid* 37 (2003), 314–15

'Post-medieval Britain and Ireland in 2003', M Ponsford, *ibid* 38 (2004), 345

CAITHNESS

Close-Brooks, J. *Exploring Scotland's heritage: the Highlands*. Edinburgh: HMSO, 1986*; 2nd edition, 1995*

Gifford, J. *Highlands and islands (The buildings of Scotland)*. London: Penguin, 1992*

Lamb, R G. 'The Caithness group of early promontory-sited castles', in R G Lamb, *Iron Age promontory forts in the northern isles*, 90–96. Oxford: BAR, 1980* (British series; 79)

Salter, M. *The castles of western and northern Scotland*. Wolverhampton: Folly Publications, 1995*

Castle Sinclair

'Castle Sinclair Girnigoe', N Topp and J Garner-Lahire, *Discovery and Excavation in Scotland* new ser 6 (2005), 91

'Medieval Britain and Ireland in 2005', M Gaimster and K O'Conor, *Medieval Archaeology* 50 (2006), 377–78

'Post-medieval fieldwork in Britain and Northern Ireland in 2004', M Ponsford, *Post-Medieval Archaeology* 39 (2005), 416

Dounreay

'Dounreay Castle, Caithness', H Gordon Slade, in R J Mercer (ed), *Archaeological field survey in northern Scotland. 2. 1980–81*, 99–103. Edinburgh: University of Edinburgh, 1981*

'Dounreay Castle', G Ewart and A Dunn, *Discovery and Excavation in Scotland 1998* (1999), 59–60

'Post-medieval Britain and Ireland in 1998 and 1999', M Ponsford, *Post-Medieval Archaeology* 34 (2000), 352

Freswick

'Medieval Britain in 1979', L E Webster and J Cherry, *Medieval Archaeology* 24 (1980), 235

Scrabster

'Bishop's Palace, Scrabster', E J Talbot, *Archaeological Excavations 1973*, 111. London: HMSO, 1974

'Scrabster, Bishop's Palace', P R Ritchie, *Discovery and Excavation in Scotland 1970* (1971), 60

'Medieval Britain in 1970', D M Wilson and S Moorhouse, *Medieval Archaeology* 15 (1971), 150

'Medieval Britain in 1973', L E Webster and J Cherry, *ibid* 18 (1974), 198

'A report on excavations at Bishop's Castle, Scrabster, 1973', E Talbot, *Northern Studies* 2 (1973), 37–39

CLACKMANNANSHIRE

Gifford, J and Walker, F A. *Stirlingshire and central Scotland (The buildings of Scotland)*. London: Yale University Press, 2002*

Salter, M. *The castles of the heartland of Scotland*. Wolverhampton: Folly Publications, 1994*

Stevenson, J B. *Exploring Scotland's heritage: the Clyde estuary and Central Region*. Edinburgh: HMSO, 1985*

Stevenson, J B. *Exploring Scotland's heritage: Glasgow, Clydeside and Stirling*. 2nd edition. Edinburgh: HMSO, 1995*

Alloa

'Alloa Tower, Clackmannanshire', J Cornforth, *Country Life* 197.34 (2003), 58–63*

'Alloa Tower', A Bailey, *Discovery and Excavation in Scotland 1991* (1991), 8

'Alloa Tower', G Ewart, *Discovery and Excavation in Scotland 1996* (1997), 26

'Medieval Britain and Ireland in 1989', D R M Gaimster, S Margeson and M Hurley, *Medieval Archaeology* 34 (1990), 240

'Medieval Britain and Ireland in 1991', B S Nenk, S Margeson and M Hurley, *ibid* 36 (1992), 291

'Medieval Britain and Ireland in 1996', B S Nenk, C Haith and J Bradley, *ibid* 41 (1997), 314

'Post-medieval Britain and Ireland in 1996', M Ponsford and R Jackson, *Post-Medieval Archaeology* 31 (1997), 301

Castle Campbell

Castle Campbell. S Cruden. Edinburgh: HMSO, 1953*; 8th impression, 1984*

Castle Campbell. S Cruden. Revised edition. Edinburgh: Historic Scotland, 1994*

Castle Campbell. S Cruden, revised by R Fawcett and C Tabraham. Edinburgh: Historic Scotland, 1999*

'Observations on the age of Castle Campbell tower', J Orr, *AHSS: the Magazine of the Architectural Heritage Society of Scotland* 15 (2002), 10–14*

Clackmannan

'Clackmannan Tower', G Ewart, *Discovery and Excavation in Scotland* new ser 1 (2000), 19

Sauchie

'Sauchie Tower', J Cannell, *Discovery and Excavation in Scotland 1985* (1986), 45

'Sauchie Tower, Sauchie', T Addyman, *Discovery and Excavation in Scotland* new ser 1 (2000), 19

'Sauchie Tower and Old Sauchie House', T Addyman, *ibid* new ser 6 (2005), 40–41

'Medieval Britain and Ireland in 1985', S M Youngs, J Clark and T Barry, *Medieval Archaeology* 30 (1986), 189

'Medieval Britain and Ireland in 2005', M Gaimster and K O'Conor, *Medieval Archaeology* 50 (2006), 365–66

'Excavations at Sauchie Tower, Clackmannanshire', J Cannell and J Lewis, *Proceedings of the Society of Antiquaries of Scotland* 127 (1997), 843–53*

DUMFRIESSHIRE

Feachem, R W. 'Iron Age and early medieval monuments in Galloway and Dumfriesshire. 4. Mottes and homestead moats', *Transactions of the Dumfriesshire and Galloway Natural History and Antiquarian Society* 3 ser 33 (1954–5), 64–65

Gifford, J. *Dumfries and Galloway (The buildings of Scotland)*. London: Penguin Books, 1996*

Maxwell-Irving, A M T. *The border towers of Scotland: their history and architecture. The west march (Dumfriesshire & eastern Galloway)*. Blairlogie: the author, 2000*

Maxwell-Irving, A M T. 'The tower-houses of Kirtleside', *Transactions of the Dumfriesshire and Galloway Natural History and Antiquarian Society* 72 (1997), 55–67*

Mercer, R. *Kirkpatrick Fleming, Dumfriesshire: an anatomy of a parish in south west Scotland*. Dumfries: Dumfriesshire and Galloway Natural History and Antiquarian Society, 1997* [espec pp 91–103, H Gordon Slade on towers]

RCAHMS. *Eastern Dumfriesshire: an archaeological landscape*. Edinburgh: TSO, 1997* [espec pp 186–220, 'The archaeology of lordship']

Roberts, G. *Towers of stone: the fortified buildings of Dumfries and Galloway*. Dumfries: Dumfries and Galloway Libraries, 1993*; 2nd impression, with corrections, 1993*

Salter, M. *The castles of south-west Scotland*. Wolverhampton: Folly Publications, 1993*

Stell, G. *Exploring Scotland's heritage: Dumfries and Galloway*. Edinburgh: HMSO, 1986*; 2nd edition, TSO, 1996*

Stell, G. 'Castles and towers in south-western Scotland: some recent surveys', *Transactions of the Dumfriesshire and Galloway Natural History and Antiquarian Society* 3 ser 57 (1982), 65–77*

Abbot's Tower

'Abbot's Tower, New Abbey', A Bailey, *Discovery and Excavation in Scotland 1991* (1991), 16

'An excavation at Abbot's Tower, near New Abbey, Dumfries and Galloway, 1991', A Bailey, *Transactions of the Dumfriesshire and Galloway Natural History and Antiquarian Society* 3 ser 67 (1992), 55–60*

Annan

'The burgh ditch of Annan: an excavation at Butts Street, Annan', R Toolis and C Cavanagh, *ibid* 3 ser 76 (2002), 141–58*

'Sixteenth-century town defences at Annan? A case not yet proven', C Wallace, *ibid* 3 ser 78 (2004), 141–42

'Fifteenth-century town defences at Annan? A rebuttal', R Toolis, *ibid* 3 ser 79 (2005), 183–85

Bonshaw

'A recent discovered shot-hole block at Bonshaw Tower', A M T Maxwell-Irving, *ibid* 3 ser 44 (1967), 224–46*

Breconside

'The lands and tower of Breconside', W A J Prevost, *ibid* 3 ser 55 (1980), 124–32*

Burnswark

'A military redoubt on Burnswark Hill, Dumfriesshire', G Jobey, *ibid* 3 ser 50 (1973), 72–81*

Caerlaverock

Look at Caerlaverock Castle. Anon. Doncaster: Bessacarr Prints, 1996*

Excavations at Caerlaverock Old Castle, Dumfries and Galloway 1998–9. M Brann. [S l]: Dumfriesshire and Galloway Natural History and Antiquarian Society, 2004*

Caerlaverock Castle: information and ideas for teachers. G Crompton, edited by M Fry. [2nd edition]. Edinburgh: Historic Scotland, 1997*

Caerlaverock Castle. D Grove. Edinburgh: Historic Scotland, 1994*

Caerlaverock Castle. B H St J O'Neil. Edinburgh: HMSO, 1952*; 2nd edition, with revisions by C Tabraham, 1982*; 3rd edition, with revisions by J R Hume, 1986*

'Access to the evidence. Interpretation of an excavation at a Scottish castle', A Cox, in P Frodsham (ed), *Interpreting the ambiguous: archaeology and interpretation in early 21st century Britain*, 95–104. Oxford: Archaeopress, 2004* (BAR British series; 362)

'Excavations at Caerlaverock Castle, 1955–66', I MacIvor and D Gallagher, *Archaeological Journal* 156 (1999), 143–245*

'Clamour of the Scots: the castle of Caerlaverock', G Kerr-Priest, *Country Life* 182.39 (1988), 209*

'Caerlaverock Castle, Dumfries', S Cruden, *Discovery and Excavation: Scotland 1955* (1956), 36

'Caerlaverock Castle, Dumfriesshire', S Cruden, *Discovery and Excavation: Scotland 1956* (1957), 35

'Caerlaverock Castle, Dumfriesshire: excavation of ancient bridges 1959', S H Cruden, *Discovery and Excavation: Scotland 1956* (1957), 38–39

'Caerlaverock Castle, Dumfriesshire', S H Cruden, *Discovery and Excavation: Scotland 1960* (1961), 46

'Caerlaverock Castle, Dumfriesshire', anon, *Discovery and Excavation: Scotland 1962* (1963), 55

'Caerlaverock Castle, Dumfries-shire', anon, *Discovery and Excavation: Scotland 1963* (1964), 60

'Caerlaverock old castle', M L Brann, *Discovery and Excavation in Scotland 1998* (1999), 25

'Caerlaverock old castle', M L Brann, *Discovery and Excavation in Scotland 1999* (2000), 22–23*

'Caerlaverock Castle', D Stewart and P Sharman, *Discovery and Excavation in Scotland* new ser 1 (2000), 20

'Caerlaverock Castle', G Ewart and P Sharman, *ibid* new ser 3 (2002), 28

'Medieval Britain in 1956', D M Wilson and J G Hurst, *Medieval Archaeology* 1 (1957), 158

'Medieval Britain in 1958', D M Wilson and J G Hurst, *ibid* 3 (1959), 309

'Medieval Britain in 1959', D M Wilson and J G Hurst, *ibid* 4 (1960), 147

'Medieval Britain in 1960', D M Wilson and D G Hurst, *ibid* 5 (1961), 321

'Medieval Britain in 1962 and 1963', D M Wilson and D G Hurst, *ibid* 8 (1964), 260

'Medieval Britain and Ireland in 1999', J Bradley and M Gaimster, *ibid* 44 (2000), 329

'Medieval Britain and Ireland in 2000', J Bradley and M Gaimster, *ibid* 45 (2001), 354–55

'Castle by the Solway shore: the great siege of Caerlaverock', G Irving, *Scotland's Magazine* 68 (July, 1972), 12–14*

'Caerlaverock Castle', W D Simpson, *Scottish Historical Review* 32 (1953), 123–27*

Canonbie

'Canonbie', A E Truckell, *Discovery and Excavation: Scotland 1960* (1961), 26

FORTIFICATIONS BIBLIOGRAPHY

Castledykes

'Castledykes, Dumfries', A E Truckell, *Transactions of the Dumfriesshire and Galloway Natural History and Antiquarian Society* 3 ser 32 (1953–4), 192

Castlemilk

'The plate of Castlemilk', M Merriman, *ibid* 3 ser 44 (1967), 175–81*

Comlongon

'The dating of the tower-houses at Comlongon and Elphinstone', A Maxwell-Irving, *Proceedings of the Society of Antiquaries of Scotland* 126 (1996), 871–79*

Drumlanrig

'Drumlanrig Castle, Thornhill', anon, *Discovery and Excavation in Scotland 1968* (1969), 16

Glen Cairn

'Glen Cairn Castle and Maxwelton', J Gladstone, *Transactions of the Dumfriesshire and Galloway Natural History and Antiquarian Society* 3 ser 28 (1949–50), 104–19*

Hoddom

'Hoddom Castle: a reappraisal of its architecture and place in history', A M T Maxwell-Irving, *Proceedings of the Society of Antiquaries of Scotland* 117 (1987), 183–217*

Jarbruck

'Glencairn', A E Truckell, *Discovery and Excavation: Scotland 1956* (1957), 17

Langholm

'Langholm Castle', T C Welsh, *Discovery and Excavation in Scotland* new ser 5 (2004), 37

Lochmaben

The castles of Lochmaben. J Wilson. Privately published, 1973*

'Lochmaben motte', anon, *Discovery and Excavation in Scotland 1967* (1968), 18

'Lochmaben Castle, Dumfriesshire', anon, *Discovery and Excavation in Scotland 1968* (1969), 49

'Lochmaben Castle, Dumfriesshire', anon, *Discovery and Excavation in Scotland 1969* (1970), 54

'Lochmaben Castle, Dumfriesshire', P R Ritchie, *Discovery and Excavation in Scotland 1970* (1971), 58–60

'Lochmaben', L R Laing and A D S Macdonald, *Discovery and Excavation in Scotland 1971* (1972), 54

'Castle Gardens, Mounsey's Wynd, Lochmaben', R Cachart, *Discovery and Excavation in Scotland 1993* (1993), 15

'Lochmaben Castle', D Stewart and G Ewart, *Discovery and Excavation in Scotland* new ser 2 (2001), 27

'Edward I's pele at Lochmaben', R C Reid, *Transactions of the Dumfriesshire and Galloway Natural History and Antiquarian Society* 3 ser 31 (1952–3), 58–73*

'A siege of Lochmaben Castle (1343)', A A M Duncan, *ibid* 3 ser 31 (1952–3), 74–77

'Medieval Britain in 1967', D M Wilson and D G Hurst, *Medieval Archaeology* 12 (1968), 181

'Medieval Britain in 1968', D M Wilson and D G Hurst, *ibid* 13 (1969), 262

'Medieval Britain in 1969', D M Wilson and D G Hurst, *ibid* 14 (1970), 179

'Medieval Britain in 1970', D M Wilson and D G Hurst, *ibid* 15 (1971), 150–51

'Medieval Britain and Ireland in 2004', M Gaimster and K O'Conor, *ibid* 49 (2005), 441

'Excavations at Lochmaben Castle, Dumfriesshire', A D S Macdonald and L R Laing, *Proceedings of the Society of Antiquaries of Scotland* 106 (1974–5), 124–57*

Lockerbie

'Lockerbie Tower', A M T Maxwell-Irving, *Transactions of the Dumfriesshire and Galloway Natural History and Antiquarian Society* 3 ser 67 (1992), 61–65*

'Lockerbie Tower', A M T Maxwell-Irving, *ibid* 3 ser 73 (1999), 225–26*

Lochwood

'Lochwood Tower', anon, *Discovery and Excavation in Scotland 1968* (1969), 19

'Lochwood Castle – a preliminary site survey', A M T Maxwell-Irving, *Transactions of the Dumfriesshire and Galloway Natural History and Antiquarian Society* 3 ser 45 (1968), 184–99*

'Lochwood Castle: a resumé', A M T Maxwell-Irving, *ibid* 3 ser 65 (1990), 93–99*

Morton

'Morton Castle', anon, *Discovery and Excavation in Scotland 1967* (1968), 19

'Morton Castle', anon, *Discovery and Excavation in Scotland 1968* (1969), 16

'Morton Castle', A E Truckell and J Williams, *Discovery and Excavation in Scotland 1972* (1973), 19

'The castles of Duffus, Rait, and Morton reconsidered', W D Simpson, *Proceedings of the Society of Antiquaries of Scotland* 92 (1958–9), 10–14

Mossknow

'Searching for Mossknow Tower by resistivity survey', J Williams and D Shiel, *Transactions of the Dumfriesshire and Galloway Natural History and Antiquarian Society* 3 ser 78 (2004), 142–47*

Torthorwald

'Torthorwald Castle', anon, *Discovery and excavation in Scotland 1967* (1968), 18

'Torthorwald Castle', anon, *Discovery and excavation in Scotland 1968* (1969), 16

'Torthorwald Castle', A M T Maxwell-Irving, *Transactions of the Dumfriesshire and Galloway Natural History and Antiquarian Society* 3 ser 68 (1993), 97–106*

Tynron Doon

'Tynron Doon, Dumfriesshire: a history of the site with notes on the finds 1924–67', J Williams, *ibid* 3 ser 48 (1971), 106–20*

Wauchope

'Wauchope Castle', anon, *Discovery and Excavation in Scotland 1967* (1968), 20

'Excavations at Wauchope Castle, 1966', A McCracken, *Transactions of the Dumfriesshire and Galloway Natural History and Antiquarian Society* 3 ser 47 (1970), 193–94

'Medieval Britain in 1967', D M Wilson and D G Hurst, *Medieval Archaeology* 12 (1968), 181

DUNBARTONSHIRE

Gifford, J and Walker, F A. *Stirlingshire and central Scotland (The buildings of Scotland)*. London: Yale University Press, 2002*

Mason, G W. *The castles of Glasgow and the Clyde*. Musselburgh: Goblinshead, 2000*

Salter, M. *The castles of the heartland of Scotland*. Wolverhampton: Folly Publications, 1994*

Stevenson, J B. *Exploring Scotland's heritage: the Clyde estuary and Central Region*. Edinburgh: HMSO, 1985*

Stevenson, J B. *Exploring Scotland's heritage: Glasgow, Clydeside and Stirling*. 2nd edition. Edinburgh: HMSO, 1995*

Cumbernauld

'Cumbernauld', Cumbernauld Historical Society, *Discovery and Excavation: Scotland 1962* (1963), 28

'Cumbernauld Castle: tower house', J E McCann, *Discovery and Excavation in Scotland 1981* (1982), 38

Dumbarton

Dumbarton Castle, Dunbartonshire. I MacIvor. Edinburgh: HMSO, 1958*

Dumbarton Castle. I MacIvor. Edinburgh: HMSO, 1986*

Dumbarton Castle. I MacIvor. Revised edition. Edinburgh: Historic Scotland, 1993*

Dumbarton Castle. I M M MacPhail. Edinburgh: John Donald, 1979*

'Dumbarton Castle', G Ewart and J Franklin, *Discovery and Excavation in Scotland* new ser 3 (2002), 116

'Dumbarton Castle', G Ewart and D Stewart, *ibid* new ser 4 (2003), 129

'Dumbarton Castle', C Shaw, *ibid* new ser 6 (2005), 141

'Dumbarton Castle', D Stewart, *ibid* new ser 6 (2005), 141–42

'Dumbarton Rock 1st & 2nd April 1571', H Potter, *History Scotland* 5.5 (2005), 32–36*

'Medieval Britain in 1975', L E Webster and J Cherry, *Medieval Archaeology* 20 (1976), 186

'Dumbarton Castle', J Cosh, *Medieval History Magazine* 13 (2004), 8–9*

'Post-medieval Britain and Ireland in 1997', M Ponsford and R Jackson, *Post-Medieval Archaeology* 32 (1998), 153–54

'A silver pendant cross from Dumbarton Castle', D H Caldwell, *Proceedings of the Society of Antiquaries of Scotland* 121 (1991), 329–30*

Peel Park

'Peel Park', D Swan and H F James, *Discovery and Excavation in Scotland* new ser 4 (2003), 54

'Medieval Britain and Ireland in 2003', J Bradley and M Gaimster, *Medieval Archaeology* 48 (2004), 320

Rossdhu

'Rossdhu Castle', J Lewis and R Murdoch, *Discovery and Excavation in Scotland 1996* (1997), 25

'Medieval Britain and Ireland in 1996', B S Nenk, C Haith and J Bradley, *Medieval Archaeology* 41 (1997), 322

'Post-medieval Britain and Ireland in 1996', M Ponsford and R Jackson, *Post-Medieval Archaeology* 31 (1997), 267

EAST LOTHIAN

Anon. *Looking at East Lothian castles*. Doncaster: Bessacarr Prints, 1989*

Baldwin, J R. *Exploring Scotland's heritage: Lothian and the Borders*. Edinburgh: HMSO, 1985*

Baldwin, J R. *Exploring Scotland's heritage: Edinburgh, Lothian and the Borders*. 2nd edition. Edinburgh: TSO, 1997*

Coe, G S. *Edinburgh and the Lothians*. Tavistock: COECAST, 2006* (Castle touring guides; 4)

McWilliam, C. *Lothian except Edinburgh (The buildings of Scotland)*. Harmondsworth: Penguin, 1978*

Salter, M. *The castles of Lothian and the Borders*. Wolverhampton: Folly Publications, 1994*

Black

'Black Castle, Oldhamstocks', R Conolly, *Discovery and Excavation in Scotland* new ser 2 (2001), 36

Dirleton

Dirleton Castle. D Grove. Edinburgh: Historic Scotland, 1995*

The castle of Dirleton, East Lothian. J S Richardson. 2nd edition. Edinburgh: HMSO, 1950*

Dirleton Castle. J S Richardson. 3rd edition, with amendments by C J Tabraham. Edinburgh: HMSO, 1982*

Dirleton Castle. W K Ritchie and K Traynor, edited by K Traynor. Edinburgh: Historic Scotland, 1991* + set of slides [school pack]

Dirleton Castle: information and ideas for teachers. W K Ritchie and K Traynor, edited by M Fry. 2nd edition. Edinburgh: Historic Scotland, 1997*

'Dirleton Castle', W D Simpson, *Archaeological Journal* 121 (1964), 171–73*

'Dirleton Castle', G Ewart, *Discovery and Excavation in Scotland 1997* (1998), 29

'Dirleton Castle', A Spratt, *Medieval History Magazine* 3 (2003), 12–13*

'The thirteenth century castle of Dirleton', W D Simpson, *Scottish Historical Review* 27 (1948), 48–56*

Dunbar

Archaeological excavation at Castle Park, Dunbar, March 1988 – March 1989. Anon. [S l]: Scottish Urban Archaeological Trust, 1989* [duplicated typescript]

Historic Dunbar: archaeology and development. E P Dennison, S Stronach and R Coleman. York: CBA for Historic Scotland, 2006*

Castle Park, Dunbar: two thousand years on a fortified headland. D R Perry. Edinburgh: Society of Antiquaries of Scotland, 2000* (Monograph series; 16)

'Artillery and major places of strength in the Lothians and the east border, 1513–1542', I MacIvor, in D H Caldwell (ed), *Scottish weapons and fortifications 1100–1800*, 94–152. Edinburgh: John Donald, 1981*

'Dunbar, Castle Park', D Hall and P Holdsworth, *Discovery and Excavation in Scotland 1989* (1989), 52

'Castle Park, Dunbar', R Cachart, *Discovery and Excavation in Scotland 1991* (1991), 49

'Castle Park, Dunbar', C J Maloney, *Discovery and Excavation in Scotland 1992* (1992), 50

'Medieval Britain and Ireland in 1989', D R M Gaimster, S Margeson and M Hurley, *Medieval Archaeology* 34 (1990), 321

'Medieval Britain and Ireland in 1991', B S Nenk, S Margeson and M Hurley, *ibid* 36 (1992), 295

'Post-medieval Britain and Ireland in 1989', G Egan, *Post-Medieval Archaeology* 24 (1990), 169–70

'Post-medieval Britain and Ireland in 1991', M Ponsford, *ibid* 26 (1992), 112

'Post-medieval Britain and Ireland in 1992', M Ponsford, *ibid* 27 (1993), 222

' "Bamburgh's Castle" and town wall, Dunbar', G H P Watson, *Proceedings of the Society of Antiquaries of Scotland* 84 (1949–50), 211–12

'The old harbours of Dunbar', A Graham, *ibid* 99 (1966–7), 173–90*

Elphinstone

'The dating of the tower-houses at Comlongon and Elphinstone', A M T Maxwell-Irving, *ibid* 126 (1996), 871–79*

Fenton

'Fenton Tower', M Cressey, D Alexander and I Suddaby, *Discovery and Excavation in Scotland* new ser 2 (2001), 35

Hailes

Hailes Castle, East Lothian. J S Richardson. Edinburgh: HMSO, 1950*

'Hailes Castle', Lady McEwen, *History of the Berwickshire Naturalists' Club* 41.1 (1977), 33–40

Kilspindie

'Medieval Britain and Ireland in 1999', J Bradley and M Gaimster, *Medieval Archaeology* 44 (2000), 331

Preston

'Post-medieval Britain and Ireland in 1996', M Ponsford and R Jackson, *ibid* 31 (1997), 301

Tantallon

Tantallon Castle: information and ideas for teachers. M Fry (ed). Edinburgh: Historic Scotland, 1998*

Tantallon Castle. J S Richardson. 2nd edition. Edinburgh: HMSO, 1950*; 3rd edition, 1980*

Tantallon Castle. C J Tabraham. 2nd edition. Edinburgh: HMSO, 1986*

Tantallon Castle. C Tabraham and D Grove. Edinburgh: Historic Scotland, 1994*

'Tantallon Castle', J H Lewis, *Discovery and Excavation in Scotland 1978* (1979), 15

'Tantallon Castle', N Tranter, *History of the Berwickshire Naturalists' Club* 37 (1965–7), 200–1

'Tantallon Castle', W D Simpson, *Transactions of the East Lothian Antiquarian and Field Naturalists' Society* 7 (1958), 18–26*

'Medieval Britain in 1978', L E Webster and J Cherry, *Medieval Archaeology* 23 (1979), 263

'Tantallon Castle', A Spratt, *Medieval History Magazine* 4 (2003), 8–9*

'Tantallon Castle, East Lothian: a catalogue of the finds', D H Caldwell, *Proceedings of the Society of Antiquaries of Scotland* 121 (1991), 335–57*

Yester

'Yester Castle', W D Simpson, *Transactions of the East Lothian Antiquarian and Field Naturalists' Society* 5 (1952), 52–58*

FIFE

Clark, N H. 'Twentieth century defences of the Firth of Forth', *Fort* 14 (1986), 49–54*

Coe, G S. *Coe's castles: a touring guide to the castles of Scotland. Fife region. 1. St Andrews & the East Neuk*. New edition. Sancton: the author, 1995*

Coe, G S. *Coe's castles: a touring guide to the castles of Scotland. The kingdom of Fife. 2. The Howe of Fife*. Sancton: the author, 1996*

Coe, G S. *The heart and west of Fife*. Sancton: COECAST, 1999* (Castle touring guides; 3)

Fawcett, R. *Castles of Fife: a heritage guide*. Glenrothes: Fife Regional Council, [1993]*

Gifford, J. *Fife (The buildings of Scotland)*. London: Penguin Books, 1988*

Salter, M. *The castles of the heartland of Scotland*. Wolverhampton: Folly Publications, 1994*

Saunders, A. 'The defences of the Firth of Forth', in D J Breeze (ed), *Studies in Scottish antiquity presented to Stewart Cruden*, 469–80. Edinburgh: John Donald, 1984*

Smith, V. 'Defending the Forth: 1880–1910', *Fort* 13 (1985), 89–102*

Stell, G. 'Castles and towers', in N J G Pounds (ed), *The St Andrews area: proceedings of the 137th summer meeting of the Royal Archaeological Institute, 1991*, 13–15. London: RAI, 1991

Walker, B and Ritchie, G. *Exploring Scotland's heritage: Fife and Tayside*. Edinburgh: HMSO, 1987*

Walker, B and Ritchie, G. *Exploring Scotland's heritage: Fife, Perthshire and Angus*. 2nd edition. Edinburgh: HMSO, 1996*

Aberdour

Aberdour Castle. M R Apted. Edinburgh: HMSO, 1961*; 2nd edition, 1985*

Aberdour Castle. M R Apted. Revised edition. Edinburgh: Historic Scotland, 1996*

'Aberdour Castle', C J Tabraham, in N J G Pounds (ed), *The St Andrews area: proceedings of the 137th summer meeting of the Royal Archaeological Institute, 1991*, 22–23. London: RAI, 1991

'Aberdour Castle', M R Apted, *Archaeological Journal* 121 (1964), 188–89*

'Aberdour Castle', G J Ewart, *Discovery and Excavation in Scotland 1980* (1981), 4–5

'Aberdour Castle', G Ewart, *Discovery and Excavation in Scotland 1998* (1999), 39

'Aberdour Castle', G Ewart, *Discovery and Excavation in Scotland 1999* (2000), 45

'Aberdour Castle', G Ewart, *Discovery and Excavation in Scotland* new ser 4 (2003), 76

'Medieval Britain and Ireland in 1999', J Bradley and M Gaimster, *Medieval Archaeology* 34 (2000), 346

'Post-medieval Britain in 1978', J Cherry, *Post-Medieval Archaeology* 13 (1979), 279–80

'Post-medieval Britain and Ireland in 2003', M Ponsford, *ibid* 38 (2004), 363

Balgonie

'Balgonie Castle', T N Dixon, *Discovery and Excavation in Scotland 1978* (1979), 6

'Excavations at Balgonie Castle, Markinch, Fife', R S Will and T N Dixon, *Proceedings of the Society of Antiquaries of Scotland* 125 (1995), 1109–18*

Ballinbreich

'Ballinbreich Castle', P Yeoman, *Discovery and Excavation in Scotland 1991* (1991), 22

Canmore

'Canmore's Tower, Pittencrieff Park', D Perry and D Bowler, *Discovery and Excavation in Scotland 1989* (1989), 16

'Medieval Britain and Ireland in 1989', D R M Gaimster, S Margeson and M Hurley, *Medieval Archaeology* 34 (1990), 241

Carden

'Carden Tower', A Hutchinson, *Discovery and Excavation in Scotland 1988* (1989), 11

'Carden Tower', P Yeoman, *Discovery and Excavation in Scotland 1992* (1992), 31

Charles Hill

'Charles Hill gun battery', G Heddle and R Morris, *Tayside and Fife Archaeological Journal* 3 (1997), 207–15*

Cupar

'Castle Hill', D W Hall, *Discovery and Excavation in Scotland 1987* (1988), 14

Dairsie

'Dairsie Castle', M Lind and E Proudfoot, *Discovery and Excavation in Scotland 1988* (1989), 12

'Dairsie Castle', E Proudfoot, *Discovery and Excavation in Scotland 1993* (1993), 30

'Medieval Britain and Ireland in 1992', B S Nenk, S Margeson and M Hurley, *Medieval Archaeology* 37 (1993), 300–1

'Medieval Britain and Ireland in 1993', B S Nenk, S Margeson and M Hurley, *ibid* 38 (1994), 280–81

'Post-medieval Britain and Ireland in 1993', M Ponsford, *Post-Medieval Archaeology* 28 (1994), 129

Dunfermline

'Dunfermline: from 'Saracen' castle to 'populous manufacturing royal burrow'', D Perry, *Proceedings of the Society of Antiquaries of Scotland* 129 (1999), 779–815*

Inchcolm

Inchcolm Abbey and Island. R Fawcett and D McRoberts, with a section on the 20th century defences by F Stewart. Edinburgh: HMSO, 1989*

Inchcolm Abbey and Island. R Fawcett, D McRoberts and F Stewart. Revised edition. Edinburgh: Historic Scotland, 1998*

'Inchcolm Island tunnel', D Murray, *Discovery and Excavation in Scotland 1998* (1999), 40

'Inchcolm Island coast battery', G Ewart, *Discovery and Excavation in Scotland* new ser 4 (2003), 76

'Post-medieval Britain and Ireland in 1998 and 1999', M Ponsford, *Post-Medieval Archaeology* 34 (2000), 346

Inchkeith

'Inchkeith: the water supply of an island fortress', N A Ruckley, *Fort* 12 (1984), 67–82*

Kellie

'Kellie Castle', H Smith, *Discovery and Excavation in Scotland 1995* (1995), 26

'Post-medieval Britain and Ireland in 1995', M Ponsford and R Jackson, *Post-Medieval Archaeology* 30 (1996), 253

Kirkhill

'St Mary of the Rock, Kirkhill', J Wordsworth, *Discovery and Excavation in Scotland 1980* (1981), 7

Lordscairnie

'Lordscairnie Castle', A Dunn, *Discovery and Excavation in Scotland* new ser 1 (2000), 41–42

Moat Hill

'Moat Hill', R Coleman, *Discovery and Excavation in Scotland 1996* (1997), 48

Monimail

'Monimail Castle', CFA, *Discovery and Excavation in Scotland 1993* (1993), 31

'Monimail tower', S Farrell, *Discovery and Excavation in Scotland* new ser 1 (2000), 41

'Post-medieval Britain and Ireland in 1993', M Ponsford, *Post-Medieval Archaeology* 28 (1994), 129

Newark

'Newark Castle', T Neighbour, *Discovery and Excavation in Scotland* new ser 3 (2002), 57

'Newark Castle', J Lewis, *ibid* new ser 3 (2002), 57

'Post-medieval Britain and Ireland in 2002', M Ponsford, *Post-Medieval Archaeology* 37 (2003), 333–34

Ravenscraig

Ravenscraig Castle. Anon. Edinburgh: HMSO, 1976*

'Ravenscraig Castle', C J Tabraham, in N J G Pounds (ed), *The St Andrews area: proceedings of the 137th summer meeting of the Royal Archaeological Institute, 1991*, 33. London: RAI, 1991

'Ravenscraig Castle, Fife', S Cruden, *Discovery and Excavation: Scotland 1964* (1965), 56

'Medieval Britain in 1964', D M Wilson and D G Hurst, *Medieval Archaeology* 9 (1965), 193

Rosyth

Rosyth Castle. Anon. Edinburgh: HMSO, 1975*

St Andrews

Look at St Andrews Cathedral and Castle. Anon. Doncaster: Bessacarr Prints, 1988*

St Andrews Castle, Fife. S Cruden. Edinburgh: HMSO, 1951*

St Andrews Castle. S Cruden. 2nd edition Edinburgh: HMSO, 1958*; 3rd edition, 1982*

St Andrews Castle. R Fawcett. Edinburgh: Historic Scotland, 1992*

St Andrews Castle. R Fawcett, revised by C Tabraham and D Grove. Edinburgh: Historic Scotland, 2001*

St Andrews Cathedral and Castle. M Reilly and K Traynor. Edinburgh: Historic Scotland, 1991* + set of transparencies [school pack]

'St Andrews Castle', R Fawcett, in N J G Pounds (ed), *The St Andrews area: proceedings of the 137th summer meeting of the Royal Archaeological Institute, 1991*, 33–34. London: RAI, 1991

'St Andrews Castle', J Lewis, *Discovery and Excavation in Scotland 1989* (1989), 16

'St Andrews Castle', J Lewis, *Discovery and Excavation in Scotland 1990* (1990), 14–15*

'St Andrews Castle', C Shaw, *Discovery and Excavation in Scotland* new ser 5 (2004), 64

'The recovery of St Andrew's Castle in 1547: French naval policy and diplomacy in the British Isles', E Bonner, *English Historical Review* 111 (1996), 378–98*

'Medieval Britain and Ireland in 1988', D R M Gaimster, S Margeson and T Barry, *Medieval Archaeology* 33 (1989), 230–31

'Medieval Britain and Ireland in 1989', D R M Gaimster, S Margeson and M Hurley, *ibid* 34 (1990), 242

'Medieval Britain and Ireland in 1990', B S Nenk, S Margeson and M Hurley, *ibid* 35 (1991), 221–22

'Excavations at St Andrews, Castlecliffe, 1988–90', J H Lewis, *Proceedings of the Society of Antiquaries of Scotland* 126 (1996), 605–88*

Scotstarvit

Scotstarvit Tower. Anon. Edinburgh: HMSO, 1967

Scotstarvit Tower. I MacIvor. Edinburgh: HMSO, 1985*

Tulliallan

Tulliallan Castle: a medieval fortified house. J G Dunbar. [S l: s n, 1994]*

INVERNESS-SHIRE

Close-Brooks, J. *Exploring Scotland's heritage: the Highlands*. Edinburgh: HMSO, 1986*; 2nd edition, 1995*

Dunbar, J. 'The medieval architecture of the Scottish Highlands', in [L MacLean (ed)], *The Middle Ages in the Highlands*, 38–70. [Inverness]: Inverness Field Club, 1981*

Fojut, N, Pringle, D and Walker, B. *The ancient monuments of the Western Isles*. Edinburgh: HMSO, 1994*

Gifford, J. *Highland and islands (The buildings of Scotland)*. London: Penguin, 1992*

MacGregor, A A. 'Ruined castles of Skye', *Country Life* 135 (1965), 162–64*

Meldrum, E. 'Medieval castles and towerhouses', in L MacLean (ed), *The hub of the Highlands: the book of Inverness and district*, 141–52. Edinburgh: Albyn Press for Inverness Field Club, 1975*

Miket, R and Roberts, D L. *The medieval castles of Skye & Lochalsh*. Portree: MacLean Press, 1990*

Ritchie, G and Harman, M. *Exploring Scotland's heritage: Argyll and the Western Isles*. Edinburgh: HMSO, 1985*; 2nd edition, 1996*

Salter, M. *The castles of western and northern Scotland*. Wolverhampton: Folly Publications, 1995*

Ardersier

'Assessment of a motte at Ardersier, Inverness district', S Carter, *Historic Scotland: Archaeological Operations and Conservation, Annual Report 1989* (1990), 41

Bernera

'Highland garrisons 1717–23: Bernera barracks', G Stell, *Post-Medieval Archaeology* 7 (1973), 20–30*

Castle Roy

'Nethy Bridge cemetery', J R Mackenzie, *Discovery and Excavation in Scotland 1996* (1997), 57

Castle Tioram

Castle Tioram in Moidart. C W H Aikman. Privately published, [1989?]

'Castle Tioram', D A MacCullough and M Taylor, *Discovery and Excavation in Scotland 1998* (1999), 47

'Castle Tioram and Eilean Tioram', C Evans, *ibid* (1999), 47–48*

'Castle Tioram, Moidart, Inverness-shire, and Mingary Castle, Argyllshire', W D Simpson, *Transactions of the Glasgow Archaeological Society* new ser 13 (1954), 70–90*

'Post-medieval Britain and Ireland in 1998 and 1999', M Ponsford, *Post-Medieval Archaeology* 34 (2000), 353–54

Dunvegan

Dunvegan Castle, Isle of Skye. W D Simpson. 6th edition. Aberdeen: Aberdeen University Press, 1951*

Fort George

Look at Fort George. Anon. Doncaster: Bessacarr Prints, 1989*

Fort George. I MacIvor. Edinburgh: HMSO, 1970*; 2nd edition, 1983*

FORTIFICATIONS BIBLIOGRAPHY

Fort George. I MacIvor. Edinburgh: HMSO, 1988*

Fort George. I MacIvor. New edition. Edinburgh: Historic Scotland, 2001*

Fort George: ideas and information for teachers. L Sutherland. Edinburgh: Historic Scotland, n d* + poster

'Fort George and the '45', W A Nelson and B A Stenhouse, *Casemate* 16 (1985), 7–8*

'Fort George, Inverness-shire', I MacIvor, *Country Life* 160 (1976), 410–13, 478–81*

'Defence of the realm: the restoration of Fort George', G Worsley, *ibid* 180 (1986), 498–500*

'Fort George', G Ewart, *Discovery and Excavation in Scotland 1994* (1994), 33

'Fort George', G Ewart, D Stewart and A Dunn, *Discovery and Excavation in Scotland 1995* (1995), 38–39

'Fort George', G Ewart, D Stewart and A Dunn *Discovery and Excavation in Scotland 1996* (1997), 58

'Fort George', D Murray, *Discovery and Excavation in Scotland 1998* (1999), 46

'Fort George', P Sharman, *Discovery and Excavation in Scotland 1999* (2000), 51

'Fort George', J Triscott, *Discovery and Excavation in Scotland 1999* (2000), 51

'Fort George, barrack room', P Sharman and G Ewart, *Discovery and Excavation in Scotland* new ser 2 (2001), 50

'Floreat Fort George: Hanoverian fortress', D Grove, *Popular Archaeology* 7.7 (1986), 2–9*

'Post-medieval Britain and Ireland in 1994', M Ponsford and R Jackson, *Post-Medieval Archaeology* 29 (1995), 132–33

'Post-medieval Britain and Ireland in 1995', M Ponsford and R Jackson, *ibid* 30 (1996), 253

'Post-medieval Britain and Ireland in 1996', M Ponsford and R Jackson, *ibid* 31 (1997), 266

'Post-medieval Britain and Ireland in 1997', M Ponsford and R Jackson, *ibid* 32 (1998), 151

'Post-medieval Britain and Ireland in 1998 and 1999', M Ponsford, *ibid* 34 (2000), 350

'Post-medieval Britain and Ireland in 2000', M Ponsford, *ibid* 35 (2001), 225

'Post-medieval fieldwork in Britain and Northern Ireland in 2004', M Ponsford, *ibid* 39 (2005), 413–14

'Firing quill from the Duke of Cumberland's Bastion, Fort George', J R Hume, *Proceedings of the Society of Antiquaries of Scotland* 121 (1991), 423–25*

SCOTLAND

Inverlochy

'Inverlochy Castle', J Lewis, *Discovery and Excavation in Scotland 1983* (1984), 14

'Inverlochy Castle', J Lewis, *Discovery and Excavation in Scotland 1989* (1989), 28–29*

'Inverlochy Castle', J Lewis, *Discovery and Excavation in Scotland 1994* (1994), 37

'Inverlochy Castle', H Smith, *Discovery and Excavation in Scotland 1995* (1995), 41

'Inverlochy Castle', H Smith, *Discovery and Excavation in Scotland 1996* (1997), 66

'Medieval Britain and Ireland in 1983', S M Youngs, J Clark and T B Barry, *Medieval Archaeology* 28 (1984), 260

'Medieval Britain and Ireland in 1989', D R M Gaimster, S Margeson and M Hurley, *ibid* 34 (1990), 244–45*

'Medieval Britain and Ireland in 1994', B S Nenk, S Margeson and M Hurley, *ibid* 39 (1995), 276

'Medieval Britain and Ireland in 1995', B S Nenk, S Margeson and M Hurley, *ibid* 40 (1996), 309

'Medieval Britain and Ireland in 1996', B S Nenk, C Haith and J Bradley, *ibid* 41 (1997), 320

'Post-medieval Britain and Ireland in 1994', M Ponsford and R Jackson, *Post-Medieval Archaeology* 29 (1995), 133

'Excavations at Inverlochy Castle, Inverness-shire, 1983–95', J Lewis and H Smith, *Proceedings of the Society of Antiquaries of Scotland* 128 (1998), 619–44*

Inverness

'Inverness', G Duncan, *Archaeological Excavations 1976*, 167. London: HMSO, 1977

'Inverness: Eastgate, medieval defences', W G Duncan, *Discovery and Excavation in Scotland 1976* (1977), 37

'Cromwell's Fort, Inverness', J Kendrick, *Discovery and Excavation in Scotland 1999* (2000), 54

'Cromwell's Fort, Inverness', J Wood, *Discovery and Excavation in Scotland* new ser 6 (2005), 82

'Medieval Britain in 1976', L E Webster and J Cherry, *Medieval Archaeology* 21 (1977), 250

'Medieval Britain and Ireland in 2001', J Bradley and M Gaimster, *ibid* 46 (2002), 242

'Post-medieval Britain and Ireland in 2001', M Ponsford, *Post-Medieval Archaeology* 36 (2002), 266

'Inverness: an historical and archaeological review', D Perry, *Proceedings of the Society of Antiquaries of Scotland* 128 (1998), 831–57*

'Excavation of two ditches and a medieval grain-drying kiln, Inverness, Highland', C Ellis, *ibid* 132 (2002), 425–37*

Kisimul

Castle in the sea. R L MacNeil. London: Collins, 1964*

'Barra, Kiessimul Castle', H B Millar and J Kirkhope, *Discovery and Excavation: Scotland 1965* (1966), 21–22

'Kisimul Castle, Castlebay, Barra', J Morrison, *Discovery and Excavation in Scotland* new ser 2 (2001), 99

'Kisimul Castle, Isle of Barra', J G Dunbar, *Glasgow Archaeological Journal* 5 (1978), 25–43*

Ruthven

Ruthven Barracks. G P Stell. Edinburgh: HMSO, 1983*

'Ruthven in Badenoch: the excavation of a Highland garrison', E McB Cox, *Proceedings of the Society of Antiquaries of Scotland* 128 (1998), 1105–19*

South Kinrara

'Aerial photographic surveys: South Kinrara', G Harden and J Bone, *Discovery and Excavation in Scotland 1990* (1990), 21

'Medieval Britain and Ireland in 1990', B S Nenk, S Margeson and M Hurley, *Medieval Archaeology* 35 (1991), 223

Urquhart

Excavations at Urquhart and Dunnottar castles 1983 & 1984: interim reports. S M Foster, S T Driscoll and L Alcock. Glasgow: University of Glasgow, 1985*

What's special about Urquhart Castle? M Fry and M McCluskie. Edinburgh: Historic Scotland, 2002*

Urquhart Castle, Inverness-shire. W D Simpson. Edinburgh: HMSO, 1947*

Urquhart Castle. W D Simpson, revised by C Lindsay and N Reynolds. Edinburgh: HMSO, 1983*

Urquhart Castle. C Tabraham and F Stewart. Edinburgh: Historic Scotland, 1991*

Urquhart Castle, Loch Ness. C Tabraham. Edinburgh: Historic Scotland, 2002*

'Glen Urquhart and its castle: a study in environment', W D Simpson, in W F Grimes (ed), *Aspects of archaeology in Britain and beyond*, 316–31. London: H W Edwards, 1951*

'Urquhart Castle: castle baileys', C J Tabraham, *Discovery and Excavation in Scotland 1981* (1982), 19

'Urquhart Castle', L Alcock, *Discovery and Excavation in Scotland 1985* (1986), 23–24

'Urquhart Castle', R Will, *Discovery and Excavation in Scotland 1999* (2000), 61

'Urquhart Castle', I Banks, *Discovery and Excavation in Scotland* new ser 1 (2000), 57

'Urquhart Castle', J Duncan, *ibid* new ser 2 (2001), 65

'Urquhart Castle', D Stewart and G Ewart, *ibid* new ser 2 (2001), 65

'Medieval Britain in 181', S M Youngs and J Clark, *Medieval Archaeology* 26 (1982), 219–20

'Medieval Britain and Ireland in 1984', S M Youngs, J Clark and T Barry, *ibid* 29 (1985), 224–25

'Medieval Britain and Ireland in 1997', M Gaimster, C Haith and J Bradley, *ibid* 42 (1998), 177–78

'Medieval Britain and Ireland in 2000', J Bradley and M Gaimster, *ibid* 45 (2001), 361

'Medieval Britain and Ireland in 2001', J Bradley and M Gaimster, *ibid* 46 (2002), 243

'Some medieval ironwork from Castle Urquhart, Inverness', L R Laing, in A D S Macdonald and L R Laing, 'Excavations at Lochmaben Castle, Dumfriesshire', *Proceedings of the Society of Antiquaries of Scotland* 106 (1974–5), 154–56*

'Finds from Urquhart Castle in the National Museum, Edinburgh', R Samson, *ibid* 112 (1982), 465–76*

'A copper alloy pin from Urquhart Castle, Inverness-shire', C E Batey, *ibid* 122 (1992), 351–53*

KINCARDINESHIRE

Salter, M. *The castles of Grampian and Angus*. Wolverhampton: Folly Publications, 1995*

Walker, B and Ritchie, G. *Exploring Scotland's heritage: Fife and Tayside*. Edinburgh: HMSO, 1987*

Walker, B and Ritchie, G. *Exploring Scotland's heritage: Fife, Perthshire and Angus*. 2nd edition. Edinburgh: HMSO, 1996*

Castlehill of Strachan

'Castlehill of Strachan: motte', P A Yeoman, *Discovery and Excavation in Scotland 1980* (1981), 11

'Castlehill of Strachan: motte', P A Yeoman, *Discovery and Excavation in Scotland 1981* (1982), 14–15

'Medieval Britain in 1980', S M Youngs and J Clark, *Medieval Archaeology* 25 (1981), 202

'Medieval Britain in 1981', S M Youngs and J Clark, *ibid* 26 (1982), 219

'Excavations at Castlehill of Strachan, 1980–81', P A Yeoman, *Proceedings of the Society of Antiquaries of Scotland* 114 (1984), 315–64 + microfiche*

Crathes

Crathes Castle & garden. O Thomson. Edinburgh: National Trust for Scotland, 1995*

'Crathes Castle', S M Fraser, *Discovery and Excavation in Scotland* new ser 2 (2001), 8

Dunnottar

Excavations at Urquhart and Dunnottar castles 1983 & 1984: interim reports. S M Foster, S T Driscoll and L Alcock. Glasgow: University of Glasgow, 1985*

Dunnottar Castle: historical and descriptive. W D Simpson. 8th edition. Aberdeen: Wyllies, 1962*; 17th edition, Dunecht: Pearson, 1993*

'Dunnottar Castle', L Alcock, *Discovery and Excavation in Scotland 1985* (1986), 18

'Dunnottar Castle', J Wood, *Discovery and Excavation in Scotland* new ser 6 (2005), 14–15

'Medieval Britain and Ireland in 1984', S M Youngs, J Clark and T Barry, *Medieval Archaeology* 29 (1985), 223–24

'Post-medieval Britain in 1985', G Egan, *Post-Medieval Archaeology* 20 (1986), 337

Glenbervie

'Glenbervie and its castle', W D Simpson, *Proceedings of the Society of Antiquaries of Scotland* 105 (1972–4), 255–61*

Haulkerton

'Mains of Haulkerton Wood', J R MacKenzie, *Discovery and Excavation in Scotland 1993* (1993), 39

'Medieval Britain and Ireland in 1993', B S Nenk, S Margeson and M Hurley, *Medieval Archaeology* 38 (1994), 283

'Post-medieval Britain and Ireland in 1993', M Ponsford, *Post-Medieval Archaeology* 28 (1994), 129

KINROSS-SHIRE

Salter, M. *The castles of the heartland of Scotland.* Wolverhampton: Folly Publications, 1994*

Lochleven

Loch Leven Castle. Anon. Edinburgh: HMSO, 1965*

Lochleven Castle. N Q Bogdan. Edinburgh: HMSO, 1984*

Lochleven Castle. C Tabraham. Edinburgh: Historic Scotland, 1994*

'Loch Leven', J H Lewis, *Discovery and Excavation in Scotland 1982* (1983), 33

'Medieval Britain and Ireland in 1982', S M Youngs, J Clark and T B Barry, *Medieval Archaeology* 27 (1983), 225

'Excavation at Lochleven Castle, 1982', J H Lewis, *Proceedings of the Society of Antiquaries of Scotland* 116 (1986), 577–81*

KIRKCUDBRIGHTSHIRE / STEWARTRY OF KIRKCUDBRIGHT

Bogdan, N and Bryce, I B D. 'Castles, manors, and "town houses" survey', *Discovery and Excavation in Scotland 1991* (1991), 23–24, 25–27, 28–31, 35–37 [arranged by districts]

Feachem, R W. 'Iron Age and early medieval monuments in Galloway and Dumfriesshire. 4. Mottes and homestead moats', *Transactions of the Dumfriesshire and Galloway Natural History and Antiquarian Society* 3 ser 33 (1954–5), 64–65

Gifford, J. *Dumfries and Galloway (The buildings of Scotland)*. London: Penguin Books, 1996*

Maxwell-Irving, A M T. *The border towers of Scotland: their history and architecture. The west march (Dumfriesshire & eastern Galloway)*. Blairlogie: the author, 2000*

RCAHMS. *Eastern Dumfriesshire: an archaeological landscape*. Edinburgh: TSO, 1997* [espec pp 186–220, 'The archaeology of lordship']

Roberts, G. *Towers of stone: the fortified buildings of Dumfries and Galloway*. Dumfries: Dumfries and Galloway Libraries, 1993*; 2nd impression, with corrections, 1993*

Salter, M. *The castles of Grampian and Angus*. Wolverhampton: Folly Publications, 1995*

Stell, G. *Exploring Scotland's heritage: Dumfries and Galloway*. Edinburgh: HMSO, 1986*; 2nd edition, TSO, 1996*

Stell, G. 'Medieval buildings and secular lordship', in R D Oram and G P Stell (eds), *Galloway: land and lordship*, 145–59. Edinburgh: Scottish Society for Northern Studies, 1991*

Tabraham, C J. 'Norman settlement in Galloway: recent fieldwork in the Stewartry', in D J Breeze (ed), *Studies in Scottish antiquity: essays presented to Stewart Cruden*, 87–124. Edinburgh: John Donald, 1984*

Barholm

'Barholm Castle', A Dunn, *Discovery and Excavation in Scotland* new ser 1 (2000), 21*

'Barholm Castle', S Coulter and P Fox, *ibid* new ser 5 (2004), 36

'Post-medieval Britain and Ireland in 2003', M Ponsford, *Post-Medieval Archaeology* 38 (2004), 348

'Post-medieval fieldwork in Britain and Northern Ireland in 2004', M Ponsford, *ibid* 39 (2005), 403–4

Bombie

'Bombie Castle, Kirkcudbright', A E Truckell, *Discovery and Excavation: Scotland 1956* (1957), 17

Buittle

'Buittle motte & bailey castle: excavation summary', Stewartry Archaeological Trust, *Castle Studies Group Newsletter* 16 (2002–3), 64–67*

'Botel bailey', [A Selkirk; source, A Penman], *Current Archaeology* 13.12 (1998), 473–75*

'Buittle Castle, near Dalbeattie', A E Truckell and J Wykes, *Discovery and Excavation in Scotland 1972* (1973), 24

'Buittle Castle bailey', A Penman, *Discovery and Excavation in Scotland 1993* (1994), 22*

'Buittle Castle bailey', A Penman, *Discovery and Excavation in Scotland 1994* (1994), 14*

'Botel Castle bailey (Buittle Castle)', A Penman, *Discovery and Excavation in Scotland 1996* (1997), 28–29*

'Botel Castle bailey', A Penman and E Cochrane, *Discovery and Excavation in Scotland 1998* (1999), 25*

'Botel Castle bailey', A Penman and E Cochrane, *Discovery and Excavation in Scotland 1999* (2000), 21–23

'Botel bailey', A Penman and E Cochrane, *Discovery and Excavation in Scotland* new ser 1 (2000), 19–20

'Botel bailey and fosse', A Penman and E J Penman, *ibid* new ser 2 (2001), 26

'Bailey of Buittle Castle', E J Penman and A Penman, *ibid* new ser 3 (2002), 27–28

'Two medieval jettons from Buittle Castle, Dalbeattie, Kirkcudbrightshire', R B K Stevenson, *Transactions of the Dumfriesshire and Galloway Natural History and Antiquarian Society* 3 ser 49 (1972), 118

'The castle of Buittle', A M T Maxwell-Irving, *ibid* 3 ser 66 (1991), 59–66*

'Dervorgilla, the Balliols and Buittle', R D Oram, *ibid* 73 (1999), 165–81

'Medieval Britain and Ireland in 1993', B S Nenk, S Margeson and M Hurley, *Medieval Archaeology* 38 (1994), 279

'Medieval Britain and Ireland in 1994', B S Nenk, S Margeson and M Hurley, *ibid* 39 (1995), 272

'Medieval Britain and Ireland in 1995', B S Nenk, S Margeson and M Hurley, *ibid* 40 (1996), 305–6

'Medieval Britain and Ireland in 1996', B S Nenk, C Haith and J Bradley, *ibid* 41 (1997), 173

'Medieval Britain and Ireland in 1997', M Gaimster, C Haith and J Bradley, *ibid* 42 (1998), 173

'Medieval Britain and Ireland in 1999', J Bradley and M Gaimster, *ibid* 44 (2000), 328–29

'Medieval Britain and Ireland in 2000', J Bradley and M Gaimster, *ibid* 45 (2001), 353–54

'Medieval Britain and Ireland in 2001', J Bradley and M Gaimster, *ibid* 46 (2002), 229–30

'Post-medieval Britain and Ireland in 1994', M Ponsford and R Jackson, *Post-Medieval Archaeology* 29 (1995), 132

Cardoness
Cardoness Castle. Anon. Edinburgh: HMSO, 1973*

Cardoness Castle and Carsluith Castle. D Grove. Edinburgh: Historic Scotland, 1996*

Cardoness Castle. C J Tabraham. Edinburgh: HMSO, 1983*

Carsluith
Cardoness Castle and Carsluith Castle. D Grove. Edinburgh: Historic Scotland, 1996*

Corra
'Corra Castle, nr Kirkgunzeon', A E Truckell, *Discovery and Excavation: Scotland 1955* (1956), 18

Drumcoltran
Drumcoltran Tower. Anon. Edinburgh: HMSO, n d

Ingleston
'Ingleston motte, New Abbey', J Williams, *Discovery and Excavation: Scotland 1966* (1967), 31

'Ingleston motte', A Penman and E Cochrane, *Discovery and Excavation in Scotland 1997* (1998), 24

'Ingleston motte', A Penman and L Averill, *Discovery and Excavation in Scotland 1998* (1999), 27–28

'Ingleston motte', A Penman and L Averill, *Discovery and Excavation in Scotland* new ser 1 (2000), 20

'Ingleston motte', A Penman and E J Penman, *ibid* new ser 3 (2002), 29

'Ingleston motte', E Penman and A Penman, *ibid* new ser 4 (2003), 45–46

'Ingleston motte', A Penman and R McCubbin, *ibid* new ser 6 (2005), 44

'The Inglistoun motte', R C Reid, *Transactions of the Dumfriesshire and Galloway Natural History and Antiquarian Society* 3 ser 25 (1945–7), 166–72

'Medieval Britain and Ireland in 1997', M Gaimster, C Haith and J Bradley, *Medieval Archaeology* 42 (1998), 173

'Medieval Britain and Ireland in 1999', J Bradley and M Gaimster, *ibid* 44 (2000), 329–30

'Medieval Britain and Ireland in 2000', J Bradley and M Gaimster, *ibid* 45 (2001), 355

'Medieval Britain and Ireland in 2001', J Bradley and M Gaimster, *ibid* 46 (2002), 230–31

'Medieval Britain and Ireland in 2003', J Bradley and M Gaimster, *ibid* 48 (2004), 319–20

'Medieval Britain and Ireland in 2005', M Gaimster and K O'Conor, *ibid* 50 (2006), 367–68

Kenmure

'Kenmure Castle', anon, *Discovery and Excavation in Scotland 1967* (1968), 32

'Kenmure Castle', A M T Maxwell-Irving, *Transactions of the Dumfriesshire and Galloway Natural History and Antiquarian Society* 72 (1997), 41–54*

Kirkcudbright

'Kirkcudbright', R Cachart, *Discovery and Excavation in Scotland 1991* (1991), 17

'Tanpits Lane, Kirkcudbright', R Cachart, *Discovery and Excavation in Scotland 1993* (1993), 23

'62 High Street, Kirkcudbright', D Devereux, *Discovery and Excavation in Scotland* new ser 6 (2005), 44–45

'Kirkcudbright: some vanished landmarks', A Graham, *Transactions of the Dumfriesshire and Galloway Natural History and Antiquarian Society* 3 ser 52 (1976–7), 173–77*

'Medieval Britain and Ireland in 1993', B S Nenk, S Margeson and M Hurley, *Medieval Archaeology* 38 (1994), 279–80

'Medieval Britain and Ireland in 2005', M Gaimster and K O'Conor, *ibid* 50 (2006), 368

'Post-medieval Britain and Ireland in 1993', M Ponsford, *Post-Medieval Archaeology* 28 (1994), 128–29

'Kirkcudbright Castle, its pottery and ironwork', G C Dunning, H W M Hodges and E M Jope, *Proceedings of the Society of Antiquaries of Scotland* 91 (1957–8), 117–38*

McCulloch's

'McCulloch's Castle, Arbigland', A E Truckell, *Discovery and Excavation: Scotland 1962* (1963), 32–33

'McCulloch's Castle, Arbigland', J Scott-Elliot, *Transactions of the Dumfriesshire and Galloway Natural History and Antiquarian Society* 3 ser 41 (1962–3), 118–24*

'Medieval Britain in 1962 and 1963', D M Wilson and D G Hurst, *Medieval Archaeology* 8 (1964), 260

MacLellan's

MacLellan's Castle. D Grove. Edinburgh: Historic Scotland, 1997*

MacLellan's Castle. C J Tabraham. Edinburgh: HMSO, n d*

'The building date of M'Clellan's Castle', R C Reid, *Transactions of the Dumfriesshire and Galloway Natural History and Antiquarian Society* 3 ser 30 (1951–2), 196–97

Orchardton

Orchardton Tower. Anon. Edinburgh: HMSO, 1966

Polchree

'Polchree Farm, Anwoth: possible motte', I F Macleod and E Talbot, *Discovery and Excavation in Scotland 1969* (1970), 29

Rusco

'Rusco Castle', R C Reid, *Transactions of the Dumfriesshire and Galloway Natural History and Antiquarian Society* 3 ser 24 (1945–6), 27–35

'Medieval Britain in 1973', L E Webster and J Cherry, *Medieval Archaeology* 18 (1974), 198

Threave

Threave Castle, Kirkcudbright. W D Simpson. Edinburgh: HMSO, 1967*

Threave Castle. C J Tabraham. Edinburgh: HMSO, 1983*

Threave Castle. C Tabraham. Revised edition. Edinburgh: Historic Scotland, 1993*; 2005*

'The artillery fortifications at Threave Castle, Galloway', C J Tabraham and G L Good, in D A Caldwell (ed), *Scottish weapons and fortifications 1100–1800*, 55–72. Edinburgh: John Donald, 1981*

'Threave Castle', C J Tabraham and G L Good, *Archaeological Excavations 1975*,

131–32. London: HMSO, 1976

'Threave Castle', G L Good and C J Tabraham, *Archaeological Excavations 1976*, 156–57. London: HMSO, 1977

'Threave Castle', G L Good and C J Tabraham, *CBA Calendar of Excavations* summaries 1976 (1977), 5

'Threave Castle, stronghold of the Black Douglas', S G Forman, *Country Life* 106 (1949), 407–8, 411*

'Threave Castle', C J Tabraham, *Discovery and Excavation in Scotland 1974* (1975), 76–77

'Threave Castle', C J Tabraham and G L Good, *Discovery and Excavation in Scotland 1975* (1976), 28

'Threave Castle', G L Good and C J Tabraham, *Discovery and Excavation in Scotland 1976* (1977), 38–39

'Threave Castle', G L Good and C J Tabraham, *Discovery and Excavation in Scotland 1977* (1978), 20

'Threave Castle', G L Good and C J Tabraham, *Discovery and Excavation in Scotland 1978* (1979), 5

'The masons' marks at Threave Castle, Stewartry: a riddle', C Tabraham, *Transactions of the Dumfriesshire and Galloway Natural History and Antiquarian Society* 3 ser 57 (1982), 87–88*

'Threave Castle (Stewartry, Kirkcudbrightshire)', C J Tabraham, *International Journal of Nautical Archaeology and Underwater Exploration* 7 (1978), 237

'Medieval Britain in 1974', L E Webster and J Cherry, *Medieval Archaeology* 19 (1975), 242

'Medieval Britain in 1975', L E Webster and J Cherry, *ibid* 20 (1976), 185

'Medieval Britain in 1976', L E Webster and J Cherry, *ibid* 21 (1977), 238–39*

'Medieval Britain in 1977', L E Webster and J Cherry, *ibid* 22 (1978), 171

'Medieval Britain in 1978', L E Webster and J Cherry, *ibid* 23 (1979), 263

'Excavations at Threave Castle, Galloway, 1974–78', G L Good and C J Tabraham, *ibid* 25 (1981), 90–140*

Urr

'Motte of Urr', anon, *Discovery and Excavation: Scotland 1966* (1967), 32

'Motte of Urr', A Truckell, *Discovery and Excavation in Scotland 1979* (1980), 5

'Excavations at the Motte of Urr. Interim report: 1951 season', B Hope-Taylor, *Transactions of the Dumfriesshire and Galloway Natural History and Antiquarian Society* 3 ser 29 (1950–1), 167–72*

LANARKSHIRE

Mason, G W. *The castles of Glasgow and the Clyde*. Musselburgh: Goblinshead, 2000*

Salter, M. *The castles of south-west Scotland*. Wolverhampton: Folly Publications, 1993*

Stevenson, J B. *Exploring Scotland's heritage: the Clyde estuary and Central Region*. Edinburgh: HMSO, 1985*

Stevenson, J B. *Exploring Scotland's heritage: Glasgow, Clydeside and Stirling*. 2nd edition. Edinburgh: HMSO, 1995*

Tabraham, C. 'Norman settlement in Upper Clydesdale: recent archaeological fieldwork', *Transactions of the Dumfriesshire and Galloway Natural History and Antiquarian Society* 3 ser 53 (1977–8), 114–28*

Ward, T. 'Bastle houses of the Anglo-Scottish borders', *Fortress* 5 (1990), 35–43*

Boghall
'Excavation at Boghall Castle', E Archer, *Discovery and Excavation in Scotland 1975* (1976), 32

'Boghall Castle', E Archer, *Discovery and Excavation in Scotland 1976* (1977), 41

'Boghall Castle', E Archer, *Discovery and Excavation in Scotland 1979* (1980), 39–40

'Boghall Castle', E Archer, *Discovery and Excavation in Scotland 1980* (1981), 34

'Boghall Castle: 17th century house', E Archer, *Discovery and Excavation in Scotland 1981* (1982), 37

'Boghall Castle', E Archer and T Ward, *Discovery and Excavation in Scotland 1984* (1985), 27

'Medieval Britain in 1975', L E Webster and J Cherry, *Medieval Archaeology* 20 (1976), 186

'Post-medieval Britain in 1983', G Egan, *Post-Medieval Archaeology* 18 (1984), 310

Bothwell
Bothwell Castle, Lanarkshire. W D Simpson. Edinburgh: HMSO, 1958; 2nd edition, 1978*

Bothwell Castle. W D Simpson. 3rd edition, revised by D J Breeze and J R Hume. Edinburgh: HMSO, 1985*; 2nd impression (with amendments), 1990*

Bothwell Castle. C Tabraham. Edinburgh: Historic Scotland, 1994*

Bothwell Castle: information and ideas for teachers. F Warnick, edited by M Fry. Edinburgh: Historic Scotland, n d* + poster

'The donjons of Conisborough and Bothwell', W D Simpson, *Archaeologia Aeliana* 4 ser 32 (1954), 100–15*

'Bothwell Castle', G Stell, *Archaeological Journal* 143 (1986), 50–52*

'Bothwell Castle: gatehouse, internal structures', J Lewis, *Discovery and Excavation in Scotland 1981* (1982), 40

'Bothwell Castle', J Lewis, *Discovery and Excavation in Scotland 1993* (1993), 84

'Bothwell Castle', D Murray, *Discovery and Excavation in Scotland 1998* (1999), 89

'Excavations at Bothwell Castle, Lanarkshire, 1981', J H Lewis, *Glasgow Archaeological Journal* 11 (1984), 119–28*

'Bothwell Castle reconsidered', W D Simpson, *Transactions of the Glasgow Archaeological Society* new ser 11 (1947), 97–116*

'Medieval Britain in 1981', S M Youngs and J Clark, *Medieval Archaeology* 26 (1982), 221

'Medieval Britain and Ireland in 1991', B S Nenk, S Margeson and M Hurley, *ibid* 36 (1992), 296

'Scottish medieval pottery: the Bothwell Castle collection', S Cruden, *Proceedings of the Society of Antiquaries of Scotland* 86 (1951–2), 140–70*

'Excavations at Bothwell Castle, North Lanarkshire', J Lewis, *ibid* 127 (1997), 687–95*

Cadzow

'"Cadzow Castle" and "The Castle of Hamilton": an archaeological and historical conundrum', D Pringle, *Château Gaillard* 15 (1992), 277–94*

'Cadzow Castle', D Murray, *Discovery and Excavation in Scotland* new ser 1 (2000), 87*

'Cadzow Castle', R Toolis, *ibid* new ser 2 (2001), 92

'Cadzow Castle', G Ewart, D Murray and D Stewart, *ibid* new ser 2 (2001), 92–93

'Cadzow Castle', G Ewart, *ibid* new ser 3 (2002), 113

'Cadzow Castle', G Ewart, *ibid* new ser 4 (2003), 125–26

'Cadzow Castle', M Márkus, *ibid* new ser 6 (2005), 135–35*

'Medieval Britain and Ireland in 2004', M Gaimster and K O'Conor, *Medieval Archaeology* 49 (2005), 461

'Post-medieval Britain and Ireland in 2000', M Ponsford, *Post-Medieval Archaeology* 35 (2001), 259–60

'Post-medieval Britain and Ireland in 2001', M Ponsford, *ibid* 36 (2002), 272–73

'Post-medieval Britain and Ireland in 2002', M Ponsford, *ibid* 37 (2003), 364–65

'Post-medieval Britain and Ireland in 2003', M Ponsford, *ibid* 38 (2004), 390

Calderwood

'Calderwood Castle', Strathclyde Regional Council, *Discovery and Excavation in Scotland 1991* (1991), 59

SCOTLAND

Camphill, Glasgow

'The earthwork on Camphill in Glasgow', H Fairhurst and J G Scott, *Proceedings of the Society of Antiquaries of Scotland* 85 (1950–1), 146–57*

Castle Hill

'Castle Hill motte, East Kilbride', anon, *Discovery and Excavation in Scotland 1994* (1994), 66

Castlemilk House

'Castlemilk House', R Will, *Discovery and Excavation in Scotland 1991* (1991), 59–60

Cathcart

'Cathcart Castle: towerhouse', J B Kerr, *Discovery and Excavation in Scotland 1981* (1982), 35

'Medieval Britain and Ireland in 1985', S M Youngs, J Clark and T Barry, *Medieval Archaeology* 30 (1986), 193

Covington

'Covington: tower', T Ward, *Discovery and Excavation in Scotland 1983* (1984), 26

'Medieval Britain and Ireland in 1982', S M Youngs, J Clark and T B Barry, *Medieval Archaeology* 27 (1983), 224–25

'Medieval Britain and Ireland in 1983', S M Youngs, J Clark and T B Barry, *ibid* 28 (1984), 262

Craignethan

Craignethan Castle: information and ideas for teachers. M Fry. Edinburgh: Historic Scotland, 1994* + poster

Craignethan Castle. I MacIvor. Edinburgh: HMSO, 1978*

Craignethan Castle. I MacIvor. Revised edition. Edinburgh: Historic Scotland, 1993*

'Craignethan Castle, Lanarkshire: an experiment in artillery fortification', I MacIvor, in M R Apted, R Gilyard-Beer and A D Saunders (eds), *Ancient monuments and their interpretation: essays presented to A J Taylor*, 239–61. Chichester: Phillimore, 1977*

'Craignethan Castle, Lanarkshire', S H Cruden, *Discovery and Excavation: Scotland 1961* (1962), 54

'Craignethan Castle, Lanarkshire', anon, *Discovery and Excavation: Scotland 1963* (1964), 59

'Craignethan Castle: modern stonework', C J Tabraham, *Discovery and Excavation in Scotland 1981* (1982), 36

'Craignethan Castle', J Lewis, *Discovery and Excavation in Scotland 1992* (1992), 70

'Craignethan Castle', J Lewis, *Discovery and Excavation in Scotland 1993* (1993), 91

'Craignethan Castle', H Smith, *Discovery and Excavation in Scotland 1995* (1995), 88

'Craignethan Castle', D Stewart, *Discovery and Excavation in Scotland 1998* (1999), 91

'Craignethan Castle', D Stewart, *Discovery and Excavation in Scotland* new ser 1 (2000), 88

'Craignethan Castle', D Stewart, *ibid* new ser 6 (2005), 136–37

'Craignethan Castle', W D Simpson, *Transactions of the Glasgow Archaeological Society* new ser 15 (1960–7), 33–46*

'Medieval Britain in 1961', D M Wilson and D G Hurst, *Medieval Archaeology* 6–7 (1962–3), 325

'Medieval Britain in 1962 and 1963', D M Wilson and D G Hurst, *ibid* 8 (1964), 260

'Medieval Britain in 1981', S M Youngs and J Clark, *ibid* 26 (1982), 221

'Medieval Britain and Ireland in 1992', B S Nenk, S Margeson and M Hurley, *ibid* 37 (1993), 305

'Post-medieval Britain and Ireland in 1993', M Ponsford, *Post-Medieval Archaeology* 28 (1994), 131

'Post-medieval Britain and Ireland in 1995', M Ponsford and R Jackson, *ibid* 30 (1996), 253–54

'Post-medieval Britain and Ireland in 1998 and 1999', M Ponsford, *Post-Medieval Archaeology* 34 (2000), 368

'Post-medieval Britain and Ireland in 2002', M Ponsford, *ibid* 37 (2003), 365

'Castle in Clydesdale', A M D Henderson-Howat, *Scotland's Magazine* 62 (September1966), 48–49*

'Craignethan: the castle of the Bastard of Arran', C McKean, *Proceedings of the Society of Antiquaries of Scotland* 125 (1995), 1069–90*

'Excavations at Craignethan Castle, 1984 and 1995', J Lewis, E McB Cox and H Smith, *ibid* 128 (1998), 923–36*

Glasgow

Glasgow (The buildings of Scotland). E Williamson, A Riches and M Higgs. London: Penguin Books, 1990*

'Glasgow', J R Kellett, in M D Lobel (ed), *Historic towns*, **1**. Oxford: Lovell Johns-Cook, Hammond and Kell Organization, 1969*

'Glasgow, St James' Road', J McBrien, *Discovery and Excavation in Scotland 1985* (1986), 46

'Cathedral Square, Bishop's Castle', M Clarke and M Thomson, *Discovery and Excavation in Scotland 1987* (1988), 50–51

'Bishop's Castle, Cathedral Square', J H McBrien, *Discovery and Excavation in Scotland 1990* (1990), 35

'Medieval Britain and Ireland in 1988', D R M Gaimster, S Margeson and T Barry, *Medieval Archaeology* 33 (1989), 236

'Medieval Britain and Ireland in 1990', B S Nenk, S Margeson and M Hurley, *ibid* 35 (1991), 226–27

'Post-medieval Britain in 1985', G Egan, *Post-Medieval Archaeology* 20 (1986), 345

'Post-medieval fieldwork in Britain and Northern Ireland in 2004', M Ponsford, *ibid* 39 (2005), 413

'The castles of Glasgow', P McDonald, *Scots Magazine* (June, 1979), 236–46*

'Preserving the Bishop's Palace, Glasgow, 1688–1741', A L Murray, *Proceedings of the Society of Antiquaries of Scotland* 125 (1995), 1143–61*

'The Bishop's Castle, Glasgow, 1598–1744', A L Murray, *ibid* 133 (2003), 343–58*

Hallbar

'Hallbar Tower', E Archer, *Discovery and Excavation in Scotland 1982* (1983), 26

'Hallbar Tower', E Archer, *Discovery and Excavation in Scotland 1983* (1984), 27

'Hallbar Tower', E Archer, *Discovery and Excavation in Scotland 1984* (1985), 26

'Hallbar Tower', E Archer, *Discovery and Excavation in Scotland 1985* (1986), 40

'Hallbar Tower', E Archer, *Discovery and Excavation in Scotland 1986* (1987), 30–31

'Hallbar Tower', E Archer, *Discovery and Excavation in Scotland 1987* (1988), 43–44

'Tower of Hallbar', K Speller, *Discovery and Excavation in Scotland 1999* (2000), 82

'Medieval Britain and Ireland in 1982', S M Youngs, J Clark and T B Barry, *Medieval Archaeology* 27 (1983), 225

'Medieval Britain and Ireland in 1983', S M Youngs, J Clark and T B Barry, *ibid* 28 (1984), 261–62

'Medieval Britain and Ireland in 1984', S M Youngs, J Clark and T Barry, *ibid* 29 (1985), 227

'Medieval Britain and Ireland in 1986', S M Youngs, J Clark and T Barry, *ibid* 31 (1987), 189

'Medieval Britain and Ireland in 1987', S M Youngs [*et al*], *ibid* 32 (1988), 306

'Hallbar Tower', E P Archer, *Scottish Archaeological Gazette* 7 (1985), 4–7*

Hamilton

' "Cadzow Castle" and "the castle of Hamilton": an archaeological and historical conundrum', D Pringle, *Château Gaillard* 15 (1992), 277–94*

Lanark

'Excavations at Lanark Castle', J H Lewis, *Transactions of the Dumfriesshire and Galloway Natural History and Antiquarian Society* 3 ser 53 (1977–8), 129–32*

Mains

'Mains, East Kilbride', T C Welsh, *Discovery and Excavation in Scotland 1970* (1971), 32

'Medieval Britain and Ireland in 1993', B S Nenk, S Margeson and M Hurley, *Medieval Archaeology* 38 (1994), 283

Roberton

'Roberton: motte', G Haggarty, *Discovery and Excavation in Scotland 1979* (1980), 39

'Excavation of a motte near Roberton, Clydesdale, 1979', G Haggarty and C Tabraham, *Transactions of the Dumfriesshire and Galloway Natural History and Antiquarian Society* 3 ser 57 (1982), 51–64*

'Medieval Britain in 1976', L E Webster and J Cherry, *Medieval Archaeology* 21 (1977), 240

'Medieval Britain in 1979', L E Webster and J Cherry, *ibid* 24 (1980), 249

Rough Hill

'Rough Hill: motte', T Welsh, *Discovery and Excavation in Scotland 1980* (1981), 36

'Rough Hill motte', J H McBrien, *Discovery and Excavation in Scotland 1990* (1990), 34–35

'Medieval Britain and Ireland in 1990', B S Nenk, S Margeson and M Hurley, *Medieval Archaeology* 35 (1991), 226

Shiels

'The ditched enclosure at Shiels, Govan, Glasgow', J G Scott, in D Alexander (ed), *Prehistoric Renfrewshire: papers in honour of Frank Newall*, 65–70. Edinburgh: Renfrewshire Local History Forum, 1996*

Strathaven

'Strathaven Castle', anon, *Discovery and Excavation in Scotland 1994* (1994), 65

Torrance

'Torrance: motte', T Welsh, *Discovery and Excavation in Scotland 1983* (1984), 31

Windgate

'Windgate House: tower house', T Ward, *Discovery and Excavation in Scotland 1981* (1982), 37

MIDLOTHIAN

Baldwin, J R. *Exploring Scotland's heritage: Lothian and the Borders*. Edinburgh: HMSO, 1985*

Baldwin, J R. *Exploring Scotland's heritage: Edinburgh, Lothian and the Borders*. 2nd edition. Edinburgh: TSO, 1997*

Clark, N H. 'Twentieth century coastal defences of the Firth of Forth', *Fort* 14 (1986), 49–54*

Coe, G S. *Edinburgh and the Lothians*. Tavistock: COECAST, 2006* (Castle touring guides; 4)

McWilliam, C. *Lothian except Edinburgh (The buildings of Scotland)*. Harmondsworth: Penguin, 1978*

Salter, M. *The castles of Lothian and the Borders*. Wolverhampton: Folly Publications, 1994*

Saunders, A. 'The defences of the Firth of Forth', in D J Breeze (ed), *Studies in Scottish antiquity presented to Stewart Cruden*, 469–80. Edinburgh: John Donald, 1984*

Smith, V. 'Defending the Forth: 1880–1910', *Fort* 13 (1985), 89–102*

Borthwick

'Two Scottish border strongholds. Borthwick Castle, Midlothian: Hermitage Castle, Roxburghshire', O Hill, *Country Life* 104 (1948), 126–29*

Colinton

'Medieval Britain and Ireland in 2005', M Gaimster and K O'Conor, *Medieval Archaeology* 50 (2006), 373

Craigmillar

Look at Craigmillar Castle. Anon. Doncaster: Bessacarr Prints, 1997*

Craigmillar Castle. D Pringle. Edinburgh: HMSO, 1990*

Craigmillar Castle. D Pringle. Revised edition. Edinburgh: Historic Scotland, 1996*

Craigmillar Castle. W D Simpson. Edinburgh: HMSO, 1954*; 2nd edition, 1980*

'Craigmillar Castle', W D Simpson, *Archaeological Journal* 121 (1964), 205

'Craigmillar Castle', G Ewart and A Dunn, *Discovery and Excavation in Scotland 1996* (1997), 38

'Craigmillar Castle', D Stewart, *Discovery and Excavation in Scotland 1998* (1999), 34–35

'Post-medieval Britain and Ireland in 1998 and 1999', M Ponsford, *Post-Medieval Archaeology* 34 (2000), 342

Crichton

Crichton Castle, Midlothian. W D Simpson. Edinburgh: HMSO, 1957*

Crichton Castle. C J Tabraham. 2nd edition, from an original script by W D Simpson. Edinburgh: HMSO, 1987*

'Crichton Castle, Midlothian', A Rowan, *Country Life* 149 (1971), 16–19*

'Crichton Castle', J Cannell, *Discovery and Excavation in Scotland 1985* (1986), 30

'Crichton Castle', S Hogg, *Discovery and Excavation in Scotland* new ser 6 (2005), 91

'Medieval Britain and Ireland in 1985', S M Youngs, J Clark and T Barry, *Medieval Archaeology* 30 (1986), 192

'Post-medieval Britain in 1985', G Egan, *Post-Medieval Archaeology* 20 (1986), 337

'Woodwork from Crichton Castle, Midlothian', W N Robertson, *Proceedings of the Society of Antiquaries of Scotland* 89 (1955–6), 450–51*

'Excavations at Crichton Castle, Midlothian', J Lewis, *ibid* 127 (1997), 697–705*

Dalhousie

'Post-medieval Britain and Ireland in 1997', M Ponsford and R Jackson, *Post-Medieval Archaeology* 32 (1998), 151

Edinburgh

Edinburgh Castle. Anon. Carrbridge: Landmark Press, [1980?]*

Excavations within Edinburgh Castle in 1988–91. S T Driscoll and P A Yeoman. Edinburgh: Society of Antiquaries of Scotland, 1997* (Monograph series; 12)

Edinburgh Castle. R Fawcett, I MacIvor and B Petersen. Edinburgh: HMSO, 1980*; revised edition, 1986*

Edinburgh (The buildings of Scotland). J Gifford, C McWilliam and D Walker. Harmondsworth: Penguin Books, 1984*

Conservation and change on Edinburgh's defences: archaeological investigation and building recording of the Flodden Wall, Grassmarket 1998–2001. J A Lawson and D Reed. Edinburgh: Society of Antiquaries of Scotland, 2003* (Scottish archaeological internet report; 10)

Edinburgh Castle: information and ideas for teachers. L McCready and N Murray, edited by M Fry. Edinburgh: Historic Scotland, 1997*

Edinburgh Castle. I MacIvor. London: Batsford for Historic Scotland, 1993*

Edinburgh under siege 1571–1573. H Potter. Stroud: Tempus, 2003*

Edinburgh Castle. J S Richardson and M Wood. 2nd edition. Edinburgh: HMSO, 1948*; 4th edition. 1953* [3rd and 5th editions have not been traced]

Historic Edinburgh, Canongate and Leith: the archaeological implications of development. S Stevenson, A Turner and N Holmes. Glasgow: University of Glasgow, 1981*

Edinburgh Castle. C Tabraham. Edinburgh: Historic Scotland, 1994*

Edinburgh Castle. C Tabraham. Edinburgh: Historic Scotland, 2003*

Edinburgh Castle: prisons of war. C Tabraham. Edinburgh: Historic Scotland, 2004*

'Edinburgh Castle', in RCAHMS, *An inventory of the ancient and historical monuments of the City of Edinburgh*, 1–25. Edinburgh: HMSO, 1951*

'Excavations at Edinburgh Castle', P Yeoman, *Castle Studies Group Newsletter* 3 (1989), 7–10*

'Edinburgh Castle', [A Selkirk; source P Yeoman and S Driscoll], *Current Archaeology* 11.11 (1992), 460–65*

'Edinburgh Castle', D Grove, *Discovery and Excavation in Scotland 1986* (1987), 19–20

'Edinburgh Castle', P Yeoman, *Discovery and Excavation in Scotland 1988* (1989), 18–19

'Edinburgh Castle', P Yeoman, *Discovery and Excavation in Scotland 1989* (1989), 50–51*

'Edinburgh Castle', S Driscoll, *Discovery and Excavation in Scotland 1992* (1992), 50

'Edinburgh Castle, Johnstone Terrace', D Murray, *Discovery and Excavation in Scotland 1998* (1999), 35

'Edinburgh Castle, Museum Square', D Murray, *ibid* (1999), 35

'Edinburgh Castle, Queen Anne Building', G Ewart and D Murray, *ibid* (1999), 35

'Edinburgh Castle, water tower', D Stewart, *ibid* (1999), 35–36

'Edinburgh Castle, Great Hall S wall', A Dunn, *Discovery and Excavation in Scotland 1999* (2000), 37

'Edinburgh Castle, Hospital Square', D Murray, *ibid* (2000), 37–38

'Edinburgh Castle, Queen Anne Building', D Murray, *ibid* (2000), 38

'Edinburgh Castle sallyport', D Murray, *ibid* (2000), 38

'Edinburgh Castle', A Dunn, *Discovery and Excavation in Scotland* new ser 1 (2000), 34–35

'Edinburgh Castle, Queen Anne's Building', D Murray and G Ewart, *ibid* new ser 2 (2001), 40

'Edinburgh Castle, No 2 Water Tower', D Stewart and G Ewart, *ibid* new ser 2 (2001), 40

'Edinburgh Castle, upper vaults', D Stewart and G Ewart, *ibid* new ser 2 (2001), 40–41

'Edinburgh Castle', G Ewart, J Franklin and D Stewart, *ibid* new ser 3 (2002), 48

'Edinburgh Castle', G Ewart, *ibid* new ser 4 (2003), 69

'Edinburgh Castle, 52 Infantry Brigade Museum', D Sproat, *ibid* new ser 5 (2004), 53

'Edinburgh Castle, Mills Mount Battery', D Stewart, *ibid* new ser 6 (2005), 64

'Edinburgh Castle, Portcullis Gate', A Radley and D Stewart, *ibid*, new ser 6 (2005), 64

'Geological notes on (a) the Nor' Loch and (b) the Fore Well in Edinburgh Castle', D Tait, *Transactions of the Edinburgh Geological Society* 14 (1952), 28–33*

'Geological and geomorphological factors influencing the form and development of Edinburgh Castle', N Ruckley, *Edinburgh Geologist* 26 (1991), 18–25*

'Edinburgh Castle: Iron Age fort to garrison fortress, P A Yeoman, *Fortress* 4 (1990), 22–26*

'"ye toun salbe wallit & stankeit about, with ane substantious wall": mural ideology in 16th century Edinburgh and southern Scotland?', C Wallace, J A Lawson and D Reed, *History Scotland* 4.6 (2004), 35–42*

'The siege of Edinburgh Castle, 1573', H Potter, *ibid* 6.3 (2006), 26–34*

'Medieval Britain and Ireland in 1988', D R M Gaimster, S Margeson and T Barry, *Medieval Archaeology* 33 (1989), 233–34

'Medieval Britain and Ireland in 1989', D R M Gaimster, S Margeson and T Barry, *ibid* 34 (1990), 244–45

'Medieval Britain and Ireland in 1991', B S Nenk, S Margeson and M Hurley, *ibid* 36 (1992), 295

'Medieval Britain and Ireland in 2000', J Bradley and M Gaimster, *ibid* 45 (2001), 357

'Medieval Britain and Ireland in 2003', J Bradley and M Gaimster, *ibid* 48 (2004), 322–23

'Medieval Britain and Ireland in 2004', M Gaimster and K O'Conor, *ibid* 49 (2005), 443

'Medieval Britain and Ireland in 2005', M Gaimster and K O'Conor, *ibid* 50 (2006), 374–75

'Excavations at St Mary's Street, Edinburgh, 1974', N M McQ Holmes, *Post-Medieval Archaeology* 14 (1980), 157–84*

'Post-medieval Britain in 1986', G Egan, *ibid* 21 (1987), 271

'Post-medieval Britain and Ireland in 1988', G Egan, *ibid* 23 (1989), 37–38

'Post-medieval Britain and Ireland in 1989', G Egan, *ibid* 24 (1990), 170–71

'Post-medieval Britain and Ireland in 1992', M Ponsford, *ibid* 27 (1993), 222

'Post-medieval Britain and Ireland in 1998 and 1999', M Ponsford, *ibid* 34 (2000), 342

'Post-medieval Britain and Ireland in 2000', M Ponsford, *ibid* 35 (2001), 207–10

'Post-medieval Britain and Ireland in 2001', M Ponsford, *ibid* 36 (2002), 258

'Post-medieval Britain and Ireland in 2002', M Ponsford, *ibid* 37 (2003), 324–25

'Post-medieval fieldwork in Britain and Northern Ireland in 2004', M Ponsford, *ibid* 39 (2005), 408

'The surrender of Edinburgh Castle, December, 1650', K C Corsar, *Scottish Historical Review* 28 (1949), 43–54

'Excavations south of Edinburgh High Street, 1973–4', J Schofield, *Proceedings of the Society of Antiquaries of Scotland* 107 (1975–6), 155–241*

Hallyards
'Hallyards Castle', C Aliaga-Kelly, *Discovery and Excavation in Scotland 1985* (1986), 28

Hatton House
'Hatton House, Midlothian', W D Simpson, , *Proceedings of the Society of Antiquaries of Scotland* 79 (1944–5), 15–26*

Hawthornden
'Hawthornden Castle, Mid Lothian', C Aslet, *Country Life* 181.21 (1987), 128–31*

Inveresk
'Post-medieval Britain and Ireland in 1993', M Ponsford, *Post-Medieval Archaeology* 28 (1994), 129

Lauriston
'Lauriston Castle', N M McQ Holmes, *Discovery and Excavation in Scotland 1985* (1986), 28

Leith
Historic Edinburgh, Canongate and Leith: the archaeological implications of development. S Stevenson, A Turner and N Holmes. Glasgow: University of Glasgow, 1981*

'Timber Bush/Tower Street, Leith', H Moore and G Wilson, *Discovery and Excavation in Scotland* new ser 2 (2001), 44

'Tower Street, Leith', M Cook, *ibid* new ser 2 (2002), 44

'A map illustrating the siege of Leith: a study of the map of the siege in 1560', S Harris, *Proceedings of the Society of Antiquaries of Scotland* 121 (1991), 359–68*

'Post-medieval Britain and Ireland in 1994', M Ponsford and R Jackson, *Post-Medieval Archaeology* 29 (1995), 133

'Post-medieval Britain and Ireland in 2000', M Ponsford, *ibid* 35 (2001), 216

'Post-medieval Britain and Ireland in 2001', M Ponsford, *ibid* 36 (2002), 261–62

'Post-medieval Britain and Ireland in 2002', M Ponsford, *ibid* 37 (2003), 330–31

'Post-medieval fieldwork in Britain and Northern Ireland in 2004', M Ponsford, *ibid* 39 (2005), 410

Liberton

'Liberton Tower', T Addyman, *Discovery and Excavation in Scotland 1998* (199), 36

'Post-medieval Britain and Ireland in 1998 and 1999', M Ponsford, *Post-Medieval Archaeology* 34 (2000), 344

Rosslyn

'Rosslyn Castle, Lothian: the property of the earl of Rosslyn', R Haslam, *Country Life* 183.15 (1989), 112–15*

MORAY

Bogdan, N and Bryce, I B D. 'Castles, manors, and "town houses" survey', *Discovery and Excavation in Scotland 1991* (1991), 23–24, 25–27, 28–31, 35–37 [arranged by districts]

Oram, R D. 'Castles and colonists in twelfth- and thirteenth-century Scotland: the case of Moray', *Château Gaillard* 22 (2006), 289–98*

Salter, M. *The castles of Grampian and Angus*. Wolverhampton: Folly Publications, 1995*

Shepherd, I A G. *Exploring Scotland's heritage: Grampian*. Edinburgh: HMSO, 1986*

Shepherd, I A G. *Exploring Scotland's heritage: Aberdeen and north-east Scotland*. 2nd edition. Edinburgh: HMSO, 1996*

Brodie

'Post-medieval Britain and Ireland in 1998 and 1999', M Ponsford, *Post-Medieval Archaeology* 34 (2000), 360

'Post-medieval Britain and Ireland in 2000', M Ponsford, *ibid* 35 (2001), 240–41

Darnaway

'The great hall and roof of Darnaway Castle, Moray', G Stell and M Baillie, in W D H Sellar (ed), *Moray: province and people*, 162–86. Edinburgh: Scottish Society for Northern Studies, 1993*

SCOTLAND

Duffus

Duffus Castle and church, Moray. W D Simpson. 2nd edition. Edinburgh: HMSO, 1951*

'Duffus Castle', J Cannell, *Discovery and Excavation in Scotland 1985* (1986), 19

'Duffus Castle', G Ewart and D Stewart, *Discovery and Excavation in Scotland* new ser 3 (2002), 82

'Duffus Castle', G Ewart, *ibid* new ser 3 (2002), 82

'Medieval Britain and Ireland in 1985', S M Youngs, J Clark and T Barry, *Medieval Archaeology* 30 (1986), 191

'Post-medieval Britain and Ireland in 2002', M Ponsford, *Post-Medieval Archaeology* 37 (2003), 350

'The castles of Duffus, Rait, and Morton reconsidered', W D Simpson, *Proceedings of the Society of Antiquaries of Scotland* 92 (1958–9), 10–14

'Excavations at Duffus Castle, Moray', J Cannell and C Tabraham, *ibid* 124 (1994), 379–90*

Elgin

'Medieval Britain in 1973', L E Webster and J Cherry, *Medieval Archaeology* 18 (1974), 198

'The archaeology of Elgin: excavations on Ladyhill and in the High Street, with an overview of the archaeology of the burgh', D W Hall [*et al*], *Proceedings of the Society of Antiquaries of Scotland* 128 (1998), 753–829*

Innes House

'The architectural evolution of Innes House, Moray', C McKean, *ibid* 133 (2003), 315–42*

Spynie

Spynie Palace and the bishops of Moray: history, architecture and archaeology. J Lewis and D Pringle. Edinburgh: Society of Antiquaries of Scotland, 2002* (Monograph series; 21)

Spynie Palace. D Pringle. Edinburgh: Historic Scotland, 1996*

'Spynie Palace', R Fawcett, *Archaeological Excavations 1975*, 132–33. London: HMSO, 1976

'Spynie Palace', J H Lewis, *Discovery and Excavations in Scotland 1987* (1988), 24

'Spynie Palace', J H Lewis, *Discovery and Excavations in Scotland 1988* (1989), 15

'Spynie Palace', J Lewis, *Discovery and Excavations in Scotland 1989* (1989), 25–26*

'Spynie Palace', J Lewis, *Discovery and Excavations in Scotland 1992* (1992), 38–39

'Spynie Palace', J Lewis, *Discovery and Excavations in Scotland 1993* (1993), 41–42

'Spynie Palace', D Reed, *Discovery and Excavations in Scotland 1994* (1994), 32

'Medieval Britain and Ireland in 1986', S M Youngs, J Clark and T Barry, *Medieval Archaeology* 31 (1987), 186–87

'Medieval Britain and Ireland in 1987', S M Youngs [*et al*], *ibid* 32 (1988), 303–4

'Medieval Britain and Ireland in 1988', D R M Gaimster, S Margeson and T Barry, *ibid* 33 (1989), 231

'Medieval Britain and Ireland in 1989', D R M Gaimster, S Margeson and T Barry, *ibid* 34 (1990), 243–44*

'Medieval Britain and Ireland in 1990', B S Nenk, S Margeson and M Hurley, *ibid* 35 (1991), 223

'Medieval Britain and Ireland in 1993', B S Nenk, S Margeson and M Hurley, *ibid* 38 (1994), 283

'Medieval Britain and Ireland in 1994', B S Nenk, S Margeson and M Hurley, *ibid* 39 (1995), 275

NAIRNSHIRE

Close-Brooks, J. *Exploring Scotland's heritage: the Highlands*. Edinburgh: HMSO, 1986*; 2nd edition, 1995*

Salter, M. *The castles of western and northern Scotland*. Wolverhampton: Folly Publications, 1995*

Cawdor
'Cawdor Castle, Nairn', O Hill, *Country Life* 97 (1945), 816–19, 860–63*

Dooket Hill
'Dooket Hill motte', B Glendinning, *Discovery and Excavation in Scotland 1999* (2000), 52

'Medieval Britain and Ireland in 2001', J Bradley and M Gaimster, *Medieval Archaeology* 46 (2002), 241

Rait
'The castles of Duffus, Rait, and Morton reconsidered', W D Simpson, *Proceedings of the Society of Antiquaries of Scotland* 92 (1958–9), 10–14

ORKNEY

Dorman, J. *Orkney coast batteries 1914–1956*. London: the author, 1996*

Gifford, J. *Highland and islands (The buildings of Scotland)*. London: Penguin, 1992*

Hamilton-Baillie, J R E. 'The coast defences of Orkney in two world wars', *Fort* 9 (1981), 21–30*

Ritchie, A. *Exploring Scotland's heritage: Orkney and Shetland*. Edinburgh: HMSO, 1985*

Ritchie, A. *Exploring Scotland's heritage: Orkney*. 2nd edition. Edinburgh: TSO, 1996*

Ritchie, A and Ritchie, G. *The ancient monuments of Orkney*. 2nd edition. Edinburgh: HMSO, 1986*; 3rd edition, 1988*

Ritchie, A and Ritchie, G. *The ancient monuments of Orkney*. Edinburgh: HMSO, 1995*

Salter, M. *The castles of western and northern Scotland*. Wolverhampton: Folly Publications, 1995*

Bu of Cairston

'The 'Castle', Bu of Cairston', in RCAMS, *Twelfth report with an inventory of the ancient monuments of Orkney and Shetland. 2. Inventory of Orkney*, 322–23. Edinburgh: HMSO, 1946*

Cubbie Roo's

'Castle of Cobbie Row', in *ibid* 235–39*

Hackness

'Hackness gun battery, Hoy', D Murray and G Ewart, *Discovery and Excavation in Scotland* new ser 2 (2001), 72

'Hackness gun battery, Hoy', J Millar, *ibid* new ser 2 (2001), 72

'A reassessment of Hackness Gun Battery: the results of excavations 1997–2001', S Halliday and C Moloney, *Scottish Archaeological Journal* 24 (2002), 121–45*

Kirkwall

The castle of Bergen and the Bishop's Palace at Kirkwall. W D Simpson. Edinburgh: Oliver and Boyd, 1961*

The Bishop's Palace and the Earl's Palace, Kirkwall, Orkney. W D Simpson. Edinburgh: HMSO, 1965*

Bishop's Palace and Earl's Palace, Kirkwall, Orkney. W D Simpson. 3rd edition. Edinburgh: HMSO, 1986*

The Bishop's Palace and Earl's Palace, Kirkwall, Orkney. W D Simpson. Revised edition. Edinburgh: Historic Scotland, 2001*

'The Bishop's Palace at Kirkwall', W D Simpson, in K Eldjarn (ed), *Pridii Vikingafundur: third Viking congress, Reykjavik 1956*, 101–6. Reykjavik: Isafoldarprentsmidja, 1958*

'The Bishop's Palace, Kirkwall', in RCAMS, *Twelfth report with an inventory of the ancient monuments of Orkney and Shetland. 2. Inventory of Orkney*, 145–48. Edinburgh: HMSO, 1946*

Longhope

The Longhope battery and towers. R P Fereday. [S l: s n], 1971*

'Longhope gun battery, Hackness, South Walls', S Halliday, *Discovery and Excavation in Scotland 1999* (2000), 68–69

'Post-medieval Britain and Ireland in 1998 and 1999', M Ponsford, *Post-Medieval Archaeology* 34 (2000), 361–62

'Longhope Sound: a taste of the Palmerstonian defences in the Orkneys', I Stevenson, *Redan* 32 (1994), 31–36*

Noltland

Noltland Castle, Westray, Orkney. W D Simpson. 2nd edition. Edinburgh: HMSO, 1951*

Noltland Castle. W D Simpson. Edinburgh: HMSO, 1983*

'Noltland Castle, Westray. A critical study. With notes on some kindred buildings mostly in the North Isles', W D Simpson, in *Charters and other records of the royal burgh of Kirkwall./Noltland Castle*, 121–57. Aberdeen: Third Spalding Club, 1962*

'Noltland Castle', in RCAMS, *Twelfth report with an inventory of the ancient monuments of Orkney and Shetland. 2. Inventory of Orkney*, 345–50. Edinburgh: HMSO, 1946*

Skaill

'Medieval Britain and Ireland in 1984', S M Youngs, J Clark and T Barry, *Medieval Archaeology* 29 (1985), 226

Tuquoy

'Medieval Britain and Ireland in 1982', S M Youngs, J Clark and T B Barry, *ibid* 27 (1983), 224

'Medieval Britain and Ireland in 1983', S M Youngs, J Clark and T B Barry, *ibid* 28 (1984), 261

PEEBLESSHIRE

Baldwin, J R. *Exploring Scotland's heritage: Lothian and the Borders*. Edinburgh: HMSO, 1985*

Baldwin, J R. *Exploring Scotland's heritage: Edinburgh, Lothian and the Borders*. 2nd edition. Edinburgh: TSO, 1997*

Cruft, K, Dunbar, J and Fawcett, R. *Borders (The buildings of Scotland)*. London: Yale University Press, 2006*

Dent, J and McDonald, R. *Warfare and fortifications in the Borders*. Melrose: Scottish Borders Council, 2000*

Salter, M. *The castles of Lothian and the Borders*. Wolverhampton: Folly Publications, 1994*

Barns
'Barns Tower', in RCAHMS, *Peebleshire: an inventory of the ancient monuments*, **2**, 218–20. Edinburgh: HMSO, 1967*

Cardrona
'Cardrona Tower', in *ibid*, **1**, 220–21*

Castlehill
'Castlehill Tower', in *ibid*, **1**, 221–22

Chapelhill
'Chapelhill', in *ibid*, **2**, 222–23*

Drochil
'Drochil Castle', in *ibid*, **2**, 223–29*

'Drochil Castle and the plan *toute une masse*', W D Simpson, *Proceedings of the Society of Antiquaries of Scotland* 86 (1951–2), 70–80*

Drumelzier
'Drumelzier Castle', in RCAHMS, *Peebleshire: an inventory of the ancient monuments*, **2**, 229–32. Edinburgh: HMSO, 1967*

Glentress
'Glentress Tower', in *ibid*, **2**, 233–35*

Langhaugh
'Tower and associated buildings, Langhaugh', in *ibid*, **2**, 237–39*

Lee
'Lee Tower', in *ibid*, **2**, 239*

Neidpath
'Neidpath Castle', in *ibid*, **2**, 243–61*

'Medieval Britain in 1958', D M Wilson and J G Hurst, *Medieval Archaeology* 3 (1959), 309

'Medieval Britain and Ireland in 1993', B S Nenk, S Margeson and M Hurley, *ibid* 38 (1994), 279

Nether Horsburgh
'Nether Horsburgh Castle', in RCAHMS, *Peebleshire: an inventory of the ancient monuments*, **2**, 261–62. Edinburgh: HMSO, 1967*

Peebles

'Peebles castle (site)', in *ibid*, **2**, 263

'Two early medieval timber buildings from castle Hill, Peebles', H Murray and G Ewart, *Proceedings of the Society of Antiquaries of Scotland* 110 (1978–80), 519–27*

Skirling

'Skirling Castle (site)', in RCAHMS, *Peebleshire: an inventory of the ancient monuments*, **2**, 271–72. Edinburgh: HMSO, 1967*

'Border strongholds', E Macdonnell, *Country Life* 171 (1982), 486–87*

'Skirling Castle, Peebleshire', K A Steer, *Discovery and Excavation: Scotland 1962* (1963), 52

'Skirling Castle, Peebleshire', K A Steer, *Discovery and Excavation: Scotland 1963* (1964), 53

'Medieval Britain in 1962 and 1963', D M Wilson and D G Hurst, *Medieval Archaeology* 8 (1964), 260–61

'Excavations at Skirling Castle, Peebleshire, 1962–3', J G Dunbar, *Proceedings of the Society of Antiquaries of Scotland* 96 (1962–3), 237–46*

Tinnis

'Tinnis Castle', in RCAHMS, *Peebleshire: an inventory of the ancient monuments*, **2**, 272–73. Edinburgh: HMSO, 1967*

Winkston

'Winkston', in *ibid*, **2**, 275–76*

PERTHSHIRE

Dalglish, C. 'An age of transition? Castles and the Scottish Highland estate in the 16th and 17th centuries', *Post-Medieval Archaeology* 29 (2005), 243–66*

Gifford, J and Walker, F A. *Stirlingshire and central Scotland (The buildings of Scotland)*. London: Yale University Press, 2002*

Ponsford, M and Jackson, R. 'Post-medieval Britain and Ireland in 1995', *Post-Medieval Archaeology* 30 (1996), 254

RCAHMS. *North-east Perth: an archaeological landscape*. [Edinburgh]: HMSO, 1990* [espec pp 88–93]

RCAHMS. *South-east Perth: an archaeological landscape*. [Edinburgh]: HMSO, 1994* [espec pp 104–7, 138–43]

Salter, M. *The castles of the heartland of Scotland*. Wolverhampton: Folly Publications, 1994*

Stell, G. 'Castles and towers', in N J G Pounds (ed), *The St Andrews area: pro-*

ceedings of the 137th summer meeting of the Royal Archaeological Institute, 1991, 13–15. London: RAI, 1991

Walker, B and Ritchie, G. *Exploring Scotland's heritage: Fife and Tayside*. Edinburgh: HMSO, 1987*

Walker, B and Ritchie, G. *Exploring Scotland's heritage: Fife, Perthshire and Angus*. 2nd edition. Edinburgh: HMSO, 1996*

Balvaird

'Balvaird Castle', J H Lewis, *Discovery and Excavation in Scotland 1988* (1989), 28

'Balvaird Castle', J Lewis, *Discovery and Excavation in Scotland 1990* (1990), 43–44*

'Medieval Britain and Ireland in 1988', D R M Gaimster, S Margeson and T Barry, *Medieval Archaeology* 33 (1989), 237

'Medieval Britain and Ireland in 1990', B S Nenk, S Margeson and M Hurley, *ibid* 35 (1991), 227

'Post-medieval Britain and Ireland in 1990', M Ponsford, *Post-Medieval Archaeology* 25 (1991), 127–29

'Excavations at Balvaird Castle, Perthshire', J Lewis, *Proceedings of the Society of Antiquaries of Scotland* 122 (1992), 365–82*

Barton Hill

'Barton Hill, Kinnaird', M Stewart, *Discovery and Excavation in Scotland 1972* (1973), 56–57

Carnbane

'Carnbane Castle', H B Millar and J Kirkhope, *Discovery and Excavation: Scotland 1965* (1966), 29–30

Castle Cluggy

Castle Cluggy, Ochtertyre', M Roy, *Discovery and Excavation in Scotland* new ser 2 (2001), 80

Castle Huntly

Castle Huntly: its development and history. E A Urquhart. Dundee: Abertay Historical Society, 1956*

Castle Menzies

'Castle Menzies', anon, *Discovery and Excavation in Scotland 1971* (1972), 34

Doune

Doune Castle: ideas and information for teachers. Anon. Edinburgh: Historic Scotland, n d* + poster

Doune Castle. D Grove. Edinburgh: Historic Scotland, 2003*

Doune Castle. R D Pringle. Edinburgh: HMSO, 1987*

Doune Castle. W D Simpson. Privately published, n d*

Doune Castle. W D Simpson. 3rd edition. Derby: Pilgrims Press, 1982*

'Doune Castle', G Stell, *Archaeological Journal* 143 (1986), 23–24*

'Doune Castle', J Cannell, *Discovery and Excavation in Scotland 1986* (1987), 5–6

'Doune Castle', G Ewart and D Stewart, *Discovery and Excavation in Scotland 1998* (1999), 94

'Doune Castle', D Stewart, *Discovery and Excavation in Scotland 1999* (2000), 87

'Doune Castle', D Stewart, *Discovery and Excavation in Scotland* new ser 1 (2000), 90

'Doune Castle', G Ewart, *ibid* new ser 4 (2003), 127

'Medieval Britain and Ireland in 1986', S M Youngs, J Clark and T Barry, *Medieval Archaeology* 31 (1987), 183

Drumlochy

'Drumlochy Castle', T Addyman and K Macfadyen, *Discovery and Excavation in Scotland* new ser 5 (2004), 100*

'Post-medieval fieldwork in Britain and Northern Ireland in 2004', M Ponsford, *Post-Medieval Archaeology* 39 (2005), 418

Edramucky

'Edramucky', I Armit, *Discovery and Excavation in Scotland 1996* (1997), 85

Elcho

Elcho Castle. Anon. Edinburgh: HMSO, 1967

Elcho Castle. I MacIvor. Edinburgh: HMSO, 1984*

Elcho Castle. A MacSween. Edinburgh: Historic Scotland, 2003*

'Elcho Castle', J Cannell, *Discovery and Excavation in Scotland 1987* (1988), 56

Glen Devon

'A motte in Glen Devon, Perthshire', J M Davidson, *Proceedings of the Society of Antiquaries of Scotland* 84 (1949–50), 220–23*

Huntingtower

Huntingtower. R D Pringle, based on an original text by the late J S Richardson. 4th edition. Edinburgh: HMSO, 1987*

Huntingtower. D Pringle. Revised edition. Edinburgh: Historic Scotland, 1996*

Huntingtower, Perthshire. 2nd edition. J S Richardson. Edinburgh: HMSO, 1950*

Huntingtower Castle. J S Richardson. 3rd edition. Edinburgh: HMSO, 1987*

'Huntingtower Castle', D Stewart, *Discovery and Excavation in Scotland* new ser 6 (2005), 119

Methven

'Methven Castle', K L S Murdoch, *Journal of the Perthshire Society of Natural Science* 16 (1991), 6–13*

Perth

'The medieval townscape of Perth', R M Spearman, in M Lynch, M Spearman and G Stell (eds), *The Scottish medieval town*, 42–59. Edinburgh: John Donald, 1988*

'Perth, High Street and Mill Street', N Q Bogdan, *Archaeological excavations 1976*, 168. London: HMSO, 1977

'City of Perth', L Blanchard, R Spearman and N McGavin, *Discovery and Excavation in Scotland 1980* (1981), 39–40

'Perth: Scott Street', J Burrows, *Discovery and Excavation in Scotland 1989* (1989), 63

'Skinnergate, Perth', C F Falconer, *Discovery and Excavation in Scotland 1991* (1991), 72

'Princes Street/Marshall Place, Perth', R Cachart, *ibid*, 72

'Site of Cromwellian citadel, Lesser South Inch, Perth', R Cachart, *Discovery and Excavation in Scotland 1994* (1994), 89

'Horse Cross, Perth', A Cox, *Discovery and Excavation in Scotland* new ser 4 (2003), 111

'Medieval Britain in 1976', L E Webster and J Cherry, *Medieval Archaeology* 21 (1977), 150–51

'Medieval Britain in 1980', S M Youngs and J Clark, *ibid* 25 (1981), 214–15

'Medieval Britain and Ireland in 1985', S M Youngs, J Clark and T Barry, *ibid* 30 (1986), 194

'Medieval Britain and Ireland in 1991', B S Nenk, S Margeson and M Hurley, *ibid* 36 (1992), 297–98

'Medieval Britain and Ireland in 2000', J Bradley and M Gaimster, *ibid* 45 (2001), 363–64

'Medieval Britain and Ireland in 2003', J Bradley and M Gaimster, *ibid* 48 (2004), 331

'Post-medieval Britain and Ireland in 1991', M Ponsford, *Post-Medieval Archaeology* 26 (1992), 113

'Post-medieval Britain and Ireland in 1992', M Ponsford, *ibid* 27 (1993), 223

'Post-medieval Britain and Ireland in 1994', M Ponsford and R Jackson, *ibid* 29 (1995), 134

'Post-medieval Britain and Ireland in 1997', M Ponsford and R Jackson, *ibid* 32 (1998), 152

'Post-medieval Britain and Ireland in 1998 and 1999', M Ponsford, *ibid* 34 (2000), 363

'Post-medieval Britain and Ireland in 2000', M Ponsford, *ibid* 35 (2001), 248–49

'Four excavations in Perth, 1979–84', D Bowler, A Cox and C Smith, *Proceedings of the Society of Antiquaries of Scotland* 125 (1995), 917–99*

'Excavation of the south-western bastion of Cromwell's citadel on the South Inch, Perth', M Roy, *Tayside and Fife Archaeological Journal* 8 (2002), 145–67*

Taymouth

'Medieval Britain and Ireland in 2005', M Gaimster and K O'Conor, *Medieval Archaeology* 50 (2006), 385

RENFREWSHIRE

Mason, G W. *The castles of Glasgow and the Clyde*. Musselburgh: Goblinshead, 2000*

Salter, M. *The castles of south-west Scotland*. Wolverhampton: Folly Publications, 1993*

Stevenson, J B. *Exploring Scotland's heritage: the Clyde estuary and Central Region*. Edinburgh: HMSO, 1985*

Stevenson, J B. *Exploring Scotland's heritage: Glasgow, Clydeside and Stirling*. 2nd edition. Edinburgh: HMSO, 1995*

Welsh, T C. 'Antiquities in eastern Renfrewshire', *Renfrewshire Local History Forum Journal* 12 (2003–4), 12–25*

Barrance

'Barrance: possible motte', T C Welsh, *Discovery and Excavation in Scotland 1982* (1983), 27

'Medieval Britain and Ireland in 1982', S M Youngs, J Clark and T B Barry, *Medieval Archaeology* 27 (1983), 224

Crookston

Crookston Castle. C J Tabraham. Edinburgh: HMSO, 1984*

'Crookston Castle', E J Talbot, *Archaeological Excavations 1975*, 134. London: HMSO, 1976

'Crookston', E Talbot, *Discovery and Excavation in Scotland 1973* (1974), 34

'Crookston Castle', E J Talbot, *Discovery and Excavation in Scotland 1974* (1975), 77–79

'Crookston Castle', E J Talbot, *Discovery and Excavation in Scotland 1975* (1976), 31

'Crookston Castle', D M Maguire, *Discovery and Excavation in Scotland* new ser 1 (2000), 43

'Crookston Castle', S Hogg and D Stewart, *ibid* new ser 6 (2005), 76

'Crookston Castle', W D Simpson, *Transactions of the Glasgow Archaeological Society* new ser 12 (1953), 1–14*

'Medieval Britain in 1973', L E Webster and J Cherry, *Medieval Archaeology* 18 (1974), 198

'Medieval Britain in 1974', L E Webster and J Cherry, *ibid* 19 (1975), 242

'Medieval Britain in 1975', L E Webster and J Cherry, *ibid* 20 (1976), 186

'Medieval Britain and Ireland in 2001', J Bradley and M Gaimster, *ibid* 46 (2002), 241

'Medieval Britain and Ireland in 2005', M Gaimster and K O'Conor, *ibid* 50 (2006), 377

'Excavations at Crookston Castle, Glasgow 1973–75', J Lewis, *Scottish Archaeological Journal* 25.1 (2003), 27–56*

Duchal

'Duchal Castle', D Alexander, *Discovery and Excavation in Scotland 1993* (1993), 84*

'Post-medieval Britain and Ireland in 1993', M Ponsford, *Post-Medieval Archaeology* 28 (1994), 131

'Duchal Castle: an initial survey', D Alexander, *Renfrewshire Local History Forum Newsletter* 5 (1993), 12–21*

Durnflat

'Durnflat: possible motte', T Welsh, *Discovery and Excavation in Scotland 1983* (1984), 30

Eastwood

'Castlehill: motte, possible', T Welsh, *Discovery and Excavation in Scotland 1978* (1979), 29

Elderslie

'Elderslie', A Hallifax Crawford, *Discovery and Excavation: Scotland 1965* (1966), 34

Giffnock

'Wood Farm: castle', T Welsh, *Discovery and Excavation in Scotland 1980* (1981), 35

Glanderston

'Glanderston Woods: possible motte', T Welsh, *Discovery and Excavation in Scotland 1983* (1984), 31

'Glanderston Woods: castle', T Welsh, *ibid* 31–32

'Medieval Britain and Ireland in 1983', S M Youngs, J Clark and T B Barry, *Medieval Archaeology* 28 (1984), 262

Housecraig

'Housecraig: possible castle', T Welsh, *Discovery and Excavation in Scotland 1981* (1982), 39

Johnstone

Johnstone Castle: demonstration excavations – September 1997. B Henry. Paisley: Renfrewshire Local History Forum, [1998]* (Occasional paper; 4)

'Johnstone Castle', B Henry, *Renfrewshire Local History Forum Journal* 9 (1998), 21–25*

King's Inch

'Medieval Britain and Ireland in 2005', M Gaimster and K O'Conor, *Medieval Archaeology* 50 (2006), 385

Langrig

'Langrig: possible castle site', T C Welsh, *Discovery and Excavation in Scotland 1982* (1983), 28

Levan

'Levan Castle', E Talbot and P C Denholm, *Discovery and Excavation in Scotland 1970* (1971), 42

'Excavations at Levan Castle, Gourock, 1960 & 1970–72', P C Denholm, *Glasgow Archaeological Journal* 16 (1989–90), 55–80*

'Medieval Britain in 1970', D M Wilson and S Moorhouse, *Medieval Archaeology* 15 (1971), 151

Newark

Newark Castle. Anon. Edinburgh: HMSO, 1967

Newark Castle. C J Tabraham. Edinburgh: HMSO, 1983*

Newark Castle. C Tabraham. Edinburgh: Historic Scotland, 1996*

'Newark Castle', J Cannell, *Discovery and Excavation in Scotland 1985* (1986), 47

'Medieval Britain and Ireland in 1985', S M Youngs, J Clark and T Barry, *Medieval Archaeology* 30 (1986), 194

'Post-medieval Britain in 1985', G Egan, *Post-Medieval Archaeology* 20 (1986), 337

'The hidden castle on the Clyde', I Rose, *Scotland's Magazine* 70 (March, 1970), 13–15*

'Excavations at Newark Castle, Port Glasgow, 1984 and 1997', J Lewis, *Proceedings of the Society of Antiquaries of Scotland* 128 (1998), 905–21*

Newton Mearns

'Newton Mearns', E Talbot, *Discovery and Excavation in Scotland 1970* (1971), 42

'Paidmyre Gardens', T C Welsh, *Discovery and Excavation in Scotland 1987* (1988), 48–49

'Medieval Britain in 1970', D M Wilson and S Moorhouse, *Medieval Archaeology* 15 (1971), 151

Paisley

'Medieval Britain in 1972', L E Webster and J Cherry, *Medieval Archaeology* 17 (1973), 165

Park

'Park Castle', A Hallifax Crawford, *Discovery and Excavation: Scotland 1961* (1962), 44–45

Pollok

'Pollok Castle', B Ballin-Smith and G MacGregor, *Discovery and Excavation in Scotland* new ser 1 (2000), 32

Polnoon

'Polnoon: castle', T Welsh, *Discovery and Excavation in Scotland 1983* (1984), 30

'Polnoon Castle: the Montgomeries and Eaglesham', G Mason, *Postern* 16 (2004–5), 5–9*

Renfrew

'Renfrew Castle', D Alexander, *Discovery and Excavation in Scotland 1996* (1997), 38

'Renfrew Castle', D Alexander, *Discovery and Excavation in Scotland 1997* (1998), 32

'Medieval Britain and Ireland in 1997', M Gaimster, C Haith and J Bradley, *Medieval Archaeology* 42 (1998), 174

Stanely

The castle and lands of Stanely, Paisley, Renfrewshire. D Topen. Paisley: Renfrewshire Local History Forum, 2003* (Occasional paper; 7)

ROSS AND CROMARTY

Close-Brooks, J. *Exploring Scotland's heritage: the Highlands*. Edinburgh: HMSO, 1986*; 2nd edition, 1996*

Dorman, J. *A visit to Cromarty and Loch Ewe*. [S l]: Kent Defence Research Group, 1996* (Ravelin special; 7)

Gifford, J. *Highland and islands (The buildings of Scotland)*. London: Penguin, 1992*

Miket, R and Roberts, D L. *The medieval castles of Skye & Lochalsh*. Portree: MacLean Press, 1990*

Salter, M. *The castles of western and northern Scotland*. Wolverhampton: Folly Publications, 1995*

Stell, G. 'Architecture and society in Easter Ross before 1707', in J R Baldwin (ed), *Firthlands of Ross and Sutherland*, 99–132. Edinburgh: Scottish Society for Northern Studies, 1986*

Cromarty

'Old Cromarty Castle', W W MacKenzie, *Proceedings of the Society of Antiquaries of Scotland* 82 (1947–8), 60–68*

Dun Lagaidh

'Dun Lagaidh', E Mackie, *Current Archaeology* 2.1 (1969), 8–13*

'Dun Lagaidh', E W Mackie, *Discovery and Excavation in Scotland 1968* (1969), 41–42

Kinkell

Kinkell: the reconstruction of a Scottish castle. G Laing. London: Latimer New Dimensions, 1974*; 2nd edition, Dingwall: Ardullie House, 1984*

Strome

'Strome Castle', S Driscoll, R Will and I Cullen, *Discovery and Excavation in Scotland 1994* (1994), 40

'Medieval Britain and Ireland in 1994', B S Nenk, S Margeson and M Hurley, *Medieval Archaeology* 39 (1995), 276

ROXBURGHSHIRE

Baldwin, J R. *Exploring Scotland's heritage: Lothian and the Borders*. Edinburgh: HMSO, 1985*

Baldwin, J R. *Exploring Scotland's heritage: Edinburgh, Lothian and the Borders*. 2nd edition. Edinburgh: TSO, 1997*

Cruft, K, Dunbar, J and Fawcett, R. *Borders (The buildings of Scotland)*. London: Yale University Press, 2006*

Dent, J and McDonald, R. *Warfare and fortifications in the Borders*. Melrose: Scottish Borders Council, 2000*

Salter, M. *The castles of Lothian and the Borders*. Wolverhampton: Folly Publications, 1994*

Allanmouth

'The Allanmouth Tower and the Scotts of Allanhaugh', M Robson, *Hawick Archaeological Society Transactions* (1977), 12–22

Barnhills

'Barnhills Castle', in RCAMS, *An inventory of the ancient and historical monuments of Roxburghshire*, **1**, 55. Edinburgh: HMSO, 1956*

Branxholme

'Branxholme Castle', in RCAMS, *ibid*, **1**, 138–39*

Burnhead

'Burnhead Tower', in *ibid*, **1**, 136–37*

Cessford

'Cessford Castle', in *ibid*, **1**, 128–31*

'Cessford Castle', G Ewart, *Discovery and Excavation in Scotland* new ser 6 (2005), 123

'Note on Cessford Castle', C S T Calder, *History of the Berwickshire Naturalists' Club* 33 (1953–5), 36–41

'Note on Cessford Castle', A F P Christison, *ibid* 33 (1953–5), 42–43

'Medieval Britain and Ireland in 2004', M Gaimster and K O'Conor, *Medieval Archaeology* 49 (2005), 458

'Medieval Britain and Ireland in 2005', M Gaimster and K O'Conor, *ibid* 50 (2006), 386

'Post-medieval fieldwork in Britain and Northern Ireland in 2004', M Ponsford, *Post-Medieval Archaeology* 39 (2005), 420–21

Cocklaw

'The siege of Cocklaw', D Scott, *Hawick Archaeological Society Transactions* (2003), 51–52

Corbet

'Corbet Tower', in RCAMS, *An inventory of the ancient and historical monuments of Roxburghshire*, **2**, 326. Edinburgh: HMSO, 1956*

Darnick

'Darnick Tower', in RCAMS, *ibid*, **2**, 297–98*

Drumlanrig

'Drumlanrig Tower', J Dent, *Discovery and Excavation in Scotland 1993* (1993), 8

'Drumlanrig Tower', J Dent, *Discovery and Excavation in Scotland 1994* (1994), 6

Ferniehirst

'Ferniehirst Castle', in RCAMS, *An inventory of the ancient and historical monuments of Roxburghshire*, **1**, 218–21. Edinburgh: HMSO, 1956*

'Firniehirst Castle and the Kers', J Renilson, *History of the Berwickshire Naturalists' Club* 31 (1947–9), 208–20

Goldielands

'Goldielands Tower', in RCAMS, *An inventory of the ancient and historical monuments of Roxburghshire*, **1**, 137–38. Edinburgh: HMSO, 1956*

Hawick

'The Mote Hill, Hawick', R E Scott, *History of the Berwickshire Naturalists' Club* 38 (1968–70), 24–17

Hermitage

Hermitage Castle. N Bridgland. Edinburgh: Historic Scotland, 1996*

Hermitage Castle, Roxburghshire. W D Simpson. Edinburgh: HMSO, 1957*

Hermitage Castle. W D Simpson. Revised edition. Edinburgh: HMSO, 1982*; 3rd edition, 1987*

'Hermitage Castle', in RCAMS, *An inventory of the ancient and historical monuments of Roxburghshire*, **1**, 75–85. Edinburgh: HMSO, 1956*

'Hermitage Castle', R Donaldson-Hudson, *History of the Berwickshire Naturalists' Club* 35 (1959–61), 272–73

'Two Scottish border strongholds. Borthwick Castle, Midlothian: Hermitage Castle, Roxburghshire', O Hill, *Country Life* 104 (1948), 126–29*

'Hermitage Castle', P Sharman, *Discovery and Excavation in Scotland 1999* (2000), 75

Hillslap

'Hillslap Tower', in RCAMS, *An inventory of the ancient and historical monuments of Roxburghshire*, **2**, 292. Edinburgh: HMSO, 1956*

'Hillslap Tower: masons and regional traditions', P Dixon, *History of the Berwickshire Naturalists' Club* 40.2 (1975), 128–41*

'Hillslap Tower', J Cannel, *Discovery and Excavation in Scotland 1985* (1986), 1–2

'Post-medieval Britain and Ireland in 1985', G Egan, *Post-Medieval Archaeology* 20 (1986), 336–37

'Excavations at Hillslap Tower, 1983–4', J Cannel and J Lewis, *Proceedings of the Society of Antiquaries of Scotland* 125 (1995), 1119–29*

Langshaw

'Langshaw Tower', in RCAMS, *An inventory of the ancient and historical monuments of Roxburghshire*, **2**, 292–93. Edinburgh: HMSO, 1956*

Lanton

'Post-medieval Britain and Ireland in 2002', M Ponsford, *Post-Medieval Archaeology* 37 (2003), 361

Liddel

'Liddel Castle', in RCAMS, *An inventory of the ancient and historical monuments of Roxburghshire*, **1**, 85. Edinburgh: HMSO, 1956*

'Liddell Castle', R Donaldson-Hudson, *History of the Berwickshire Naturalists' Club* 35 (1959–61), 273–75

Linton

'Linton Tower', L Lawson, *Discovery and Excavation: Scotland 1957* (1958), 32–33

Littledean

'Littledean Tower', in RCAMS, *An inventory of the ancient and historical monuments of Roxburghshire*, **1**, 261–62. Edinburgh: HMSO, 1956*

Roxburgh

'Roxburgh Castle', in *ibid*, **2**, 407–11*

'The wardens of Roxburgh Castle', C H Hunter Blair, *History of the Berwickshire Naturalists' Club* 32 (1950–2), 21–45

'Roxburgh Castle', G W Bennett, *ibid* 37 (1965–7), 24–27

'Two dogs and a bone: the story of Roxburgh Castle', C Tabraham, *Château Gaillard* 17 (1996), 165–67*

'Vanished capital of Scotland: Old Roxburgh', C Martin, *Country Life* 145 (1969), 54–56*

'Roxburgh: uncovering Scotland's lost royal burgh', C Martin and R Oram, *History Scotland* 4.6 (2004), 14–24*

Smailholm

Smailholm Tower. Anon. Edinburgh: HMSO, 1969*

Smailholm Tower. C Henderson and E Falconer, edited by K Traynor. Edinburgh: Historic Scotland, 1991* + set of transparencies [school pack]

Smailholm Tower. C Tabraham. Edinburgh: HMSO, n d*

Smailholm Tower. C Tabraham. Edinburgh: HMSO, 1985*; 2nd impression (with amendments), 1989*

Smailholm Tower. C Tabraham. Revised edition. Edinburgh: Historic Scotland, 1993*

'Smailholm Tower', in RCAMS, *An inventory of the ancient and historical monuments of Roxburghshire*, **2**, 416–17. Edinburgh: HMSO, 1956*

'Smailholm Tower: a Scottish laird's fortified residence on the English border', C Tabraham, *Château Gaillard* 13 (1987), 227–38*

'Smailholm Tower: kitchen range', G L Good, *Discovery and Excavation in Scotland 1979* (1980), 1

'Smailholm Tower: barmkin', G L Good and C J Tabraham, *Discovery and Excavation in Scotland 1980* (1981), 2

'Smailholm Tower: tower-house and barmkin', G L Good and C J Tabraham, *Discovery and Excavation in Scotland 1981* (1982), 3–4

'Post-medieval Britain in 1979', J Cherry, *Post-Medieval Archaeology* 14 (1980), 209

'Post-medieval Britain in 1980', J Cherry, *ibid* 15 (1981), 229–30

'Excavations at Smailholm Tower, Roxburghshire', G L Good and C J Tabraham, *Proceedings of the Society of Antiquaries of London* 118 (1988), 231–66 + microfiche*

Timpendean

'Timpendean Tower', in RCAMS, *An inventory of the ancient and historical monuments of Roxburghshire*, **1**, 216–18. Edinburgh: HMSO, 1956*

SELKIRKSHIRE

Cruft, K, Dunbar, J and Fawcett, R. *Borders (The buildings of Scotland)*. London: Yale University Press, 2006*

Dent, J and McDonald, R. *Warfare and fortifications in the Borders*. Melrose: Scottish Borders Council, 2000*

Salter, M. *The castles of Lothian and the Borders*. Wolverhampton: Folly Publications, 1994*

Blackhouse

'Blackhouse Tower', in RCAMS, *An inventory of the ancient and historical monuments of Selkirkshire*, 60–61. Edinburgh: HMSO, 1957*

Cramalt

'Cramalt Tower: historical survey and excavations 1977–9', A M T Maxwell-Irving, *Proceedings of the Society of Antiquaries of Scotland* 111 (1981), 401–29*

Dryhope

'Dryhope Tower', in RCAMS, *An inventory of the ancient and historical monuments of Selkirkshire*, 60. Edinburgh: HMSO, 1957*

'Dryhope Castle', D Connolly, *Discovery and Excavation in Scotland* new ser 3 (2002), 104*

'Post-medieval Britain and Ireland in 2002', M Ponsford, *Post-Medieval Archaeology* 37 (2003), 361

'Post-medieval Britain and Ireland in 2003', M Ponsford, *ibid* 38 (2004), 385

Elibank

'Elibank Castle', in RCAMS, *An inventory of the ancient and historical monuments of Selkirkshire*, 35–36. Edinburgh: HMSO, 1957*

'Note on Elibank Castle', J Allan, *History of the Berwickshire Naturalists' Club* 33 (1953–5), 44–46

Howden

'Motte, Howden', in RCAMS, *An inventory of the ancient and historical monuments of Selkirkshire*, 50–51. Edinburgh: HMSO, 1957*

'Howden motte', P Fenton, *Discovery and Excavation: Scotland 1957* (1958), 33–34

'Medieval Britain in 1957', D M Wilson and J G Hurst, *Medieval Archaeology* 2 (1958), 196

Kirkhope

'Kirkhope Tower', in RCAMS, *An inventory of the ancient and historical monuments of Selkirkshire*, 54–56. Edinburgh: HMSO, 1957*

Newark

'Newark Castle', in *ibid*, 61–65*

'Notes on Newark Castle', C S T Calder, *History of the Berwickshire Naturalists' Club* 32 (1950–2), 93–98

Oakwood

'Oakwood Tower', in RCAMS, *An inventory of the ancient and historical monuments of Selkirkshire*, 52–54. Edinburgh: HMSO, 1957*

Phenzhopehaugh

'Motte, Phenzhopehaugh', in *ibid*, 57*

Selkirk

'Selkirk Castle and motte', in *ibid*, 47–49*

Tushielaw

'Tushielaw Tower and associated buildings', in *ibid*, 56–57*

SHETLAND

Ball, R G. 'The Shetland garrison, 1665–1668', *Journal of the Society for Army Historical Research* 43 (1965), 5–26*

Fojut, N and Pringle, D. *The ancient monuments of Shetland*. Edinburgh: HMSO, 1993*

Gifford, J. *Highland and islands (The buildings of Scotland)*. London: Penguin, 1992*

Ritchie, A. *Exploring Scotland's heritage: Orkney and Shetland*. Edinburgh: HMSO, 1985*

Ritchie, A. *Exploring Scotland's heritage: Orkney*. 2nd edition. Edinburgh: TSO, 1996*

Salter, M. *The castles of western and northern Scotland*. Wolverhampton: Folly Publications, 1995*

Simpson, W D. 'The castles of Shetland', in W D Simpson (ed), *The Viking congress, Lerwick, July 1950*, 175–83. Edinburgh: Oliver and Boyd, 1954*

Lerwick

'Fort Charlotte', G Ewart, *Discovery and Excavation in Scotland 1993* (1993), 106–7

'Fort Charlotte', G Ewart, *Discovery and Excavation in Scotland 1994* (1994), 93–94

'Fort Charlotte', G Ewart and P Sharman, *Discovery and Excavation in Scotland 1996* (1997), 95

'Post-medieval Britain and Ireland in 1993', M Ponsford, *Post-Medieval Archaeology* 28 (1994), 130

'Post-medieval Britain and Ireland in 1994', M Ponsford and R Jackson, *ibid* 29 (1995), 133

'Post-medieval Britain and Ireland in 1996', M Ponsford and R Jackson, *ibid* 31 (1997), 266

Muness

Muness Castle. Anon. Edinburgh: HMSO, 1965*; 1985*

'Muness Castle, in RCAMS, *Twelfth report with an inventory of the ancient monuments of Orkney and Shetland. 3. Inventory of Shetland*, 129–31. Edinburgh: HMSO, 1946*

'Muness castle', H S Ames, *Archaeological Excavations 1975*, 133–34. London: HMSO, 1976

'The northernmost castle of Britain: Muness Castle, Unst, Shetland', W D Simpson, *Scottish Historical Review* 38 (1959), 1–9*

Scalloway

Scalloway Castle, Shetland. B H St J O'Neil. Edinburgh: HMSO, 1950*

'Scalloway Castle', in RCAMS, *Twelfth report with an inventory of the ancient monuments of Orkney and Shetland. 3. Inventory of Shetland*, 118–20. Edinburgh: HMSO, 1946*

'Scalloway Castle', W Lindsay, *Discovery and Excavation in Scotland 1979* (1980), 27

'Scalloway Castle', D Hall, *Discovery and Excavation in Scotland 1980* (1981), 28

'Excavations at Scalloway Castle, 1979 and 1980', D Hall and W J Lindsay, *Proceedings of the Society of Antiquaries of Scotland* 113 (1983), 554–93*

STIRLINGSHIRE

Gifford, J and Walker, F A. *Stirlingshire and central Scotland (The buildings of Scotland)*. London: Yale University Press, 2002*

Mason, G W. *The castles of Glasgow and the Clyde*. Musselburgh: Goblinshead, 2000*

Salter, M. *The castles of the heartland of Scotland*. Wolverhampton: Folly Publications, 1994*

Stevenson, J B. *Exploring Scotland's heritage: the Clyde estuary and Central Region*. Edinburgh: HMSO, 1985*

Stevenson, J B. *Exploring Scotland's heritage: Glasgow, Clydeside and Stirling*. 2nd edition. Edinburgh: HMSO, 1995*

Airth
'Airth Castle', in RCAHMS, *Stirlingshire: an inventory of the ancient monuments*, **1**, 230–37. Edinburgh: HMSO, 1963*

Almond
'Almond Castle', in *ibid*, **1**, 241–43*

Balcastle
'Motte, Balcastle', in *ibid*, **1**, 173–74*

Bardowie
'Bardowie castle', in *ibid*, **1**, 254–56*

Blairlogie
'The Blair, Blairbogie', in *ibid*, **1**, 223–24*

Bonnybridge
'The motte, Bonnybridge', in *ibid*, **1**, 172–73*

Bruce's
'Bruce's castle', in *ibid*, **1**, 227–28*

Castle Cary
'Castle Cary', in *ibid*, **1**, 243–46*

'Castle Cary', G B Bailey, *Discovery and Excavation in Scotland 1996* (1997), 42

'Post-medieval Britain and Ireland in 1996', M Ponsford and R Jackson, *Post-Medieval Archaeology* 31 (1997), 302

Castle Rankine
'Castle Rankine (site)', in RCAHMS, *Stirlingshire: an inventory of the ancient monuments*, **1**, 268–69. Edinburgh: HMSO, 1963*

527

Colzium

Colzium Castle: interim and final reports. H B Millar. Cumbernauld: Cumbernauld and Kilsyth District Council, 1977–8*

'Colzium Castle', H B Millar, *Discovery and Excavation in Scotland 1977* (1978), 35

'Colzium Castle', H B Millar, *Discovery and Excavation in Scotland 1978* (1979), 26

Craigmaddie

'Craigmaddie Castle', in RCAHMS, *Stirlingshire: an inventory of the ancient monuments*, **1**, 248–49. Edinburgh: HMSO, 1963*

Culcreuch

'Culcreuch Castle', in *ibid*, **1**, 262–64*

Duchray

'Duchray Castle', *ibid*, **1**, 261*

Dunmore

'Dunmore Tower', in *ibid*, **1**, 229–30*

Duntreath

'Duntreath Castle', in *ibid*, **1**, 256–60*

Falkirk

'Medieval Britain in 1959', D M Wilson and J G Hurst, *Medieval Archaeology* 4 (1960), 150

Fintry

'Motte, Fintry', in RCAHMS, *Stirlingshire: an inventory of the ancient monuments*, **1**, 175. Edinburgh: HMSO, 1963*

Garmore

'Motte and bailey, "Maiden Castle", Garmore', in *ibid*, **1**, 174*

Keir Knowe

'Motte, Keir Knowe of Drum', in *ibid*, **1**, 176–78*

'Drum, Stirlingshire', R W Feachem, *Discovery and Excavation: Scotland 1957* (1958), 40

'Medieval Britain in 1957', D M Wilson and J G Hurst, *Medieval Archaeology* 2 (1958), 197

Kilsyth

'Kilsyth Castle', H B Millar, *Discovery and Excavation in Scotland 1976* (1977), 64

'Post-medieval Britain and Ireland in 2002', M Ponsford, *Post-Medieval Archaeology* 37 (2003), 351

Mugdock

'Mugdock Castle', in RCAHMS, *Stirlingshire: an inventory of the ancient monuments*, **1**, 249–54. Edinburgh: HMSO, 1963*

'Mugdock Castle, Stirlingshire', K A Steer, *Discovery and Excavation: Scotland 1958* (1959), 40

'Mugdock Castle', L Main, *Discovery and Excavation in Scotland 1986* (1987), 4

'Mugdock Castle', L Main, *Discovery and Excavation in Scotland 1999* (2000), 88–89

'Medieval Britain and Ireland in 1986', S M Youngs, J Clark and T Barry, *Medieval Archaeology* 31 (1987), 183

Old Sauchie

'Old Sauchie', in RCAHMS, *Stirlingshire: an inventory of the ancient monuments*, **1**, 224–27. Edinburgh: HMSO, 1963*

Plean

'Plean Tower', in *ibid*, **1**, 228–29*

'Plean Castle', R Will, *Discovery and Excavation in Scotland 1993* (1993), 13–14*

Sir John de Graham's

'Motte, Sir John de Graham's Castle', in RCAHMS, *Stirlingshire: an inventory of the ancient monuments*, **1**, 175–76. Edinburgh: HMSO, 1963*

Skaithmuir

'Skaithmuir Tower', in *ibid*, **1**, 239–40*

Slamannan

'Medieval Britain in 1958', D M Wilson and J G Hurst, *Medieval Archaeology* 3 (1959), 309

Stirling

Look at Stirling Castle. Anon. Doncaster: Bessacarr Prints, 1995*

Stirling Castle. R Fawcett. Edinburgh: HMSO, 1983*

Stirling Castle. R Fawcett. [New edition]. Edinburgh: Historic Scotland, 1995*

Stirling Castle. R Fawcett. [3rd edition]. Edinburgh: Historic Scotland, 1999*

Stirling Castle. R Fawcett. London: Batsford, in association with Historic Scotland, 1995*

Stirling Castle: the restoration of the Great Hall. R Fawcett (ed). York: CBA, 2001* (Research report; 130)

Stirling Castle: ideas and information for teachers. C Mair. [2nd edition]. Edinburgh: Historic Scotland, n d* + poster

Stirling Castle. J S Richardson and M E Root. 2nd edition, 8th impression. Edinburgh: HMSO, 1972*; 3rd edition, 1978*

'Stirling Castle', in RCAHMS, *Stirlingshire: an inventory of the ancient monuments*, **1**, 179–223. Edinburgh: HMSO, 1963*

'Stirling Castle', R Fawcett, *Archaeological Excavations 1975*, 131. London: HMSO, 1976

'Stirling Castle', L Main, *Archaeological Excavations 1976*, 156. London: HMSO, 1977

'Stirling Castle', J G Dunbar, *Archaeological Journal* 121 (1964), 178–80*

'Stirling Castle', J G Dunbar, *ibid* 143 (1986), 19–20*

'Stirling Castle: the King's Old Building and the late medieval royal planning', R Fawcett, *Château Gaillard* 14 (1990), 175–93*

'Fortress palace of the north', D Walker, *Country Life* 146 (1969), 372–74*

'Stirling Castle', L Main, *Discovery and Excavation in Scotland 1976* (1977), 62

'Stirling Castle', G Ewart, *Discovery and Excavation in Scotland 1977* (1978), 36–37

'Stirling Castle', C Tabraham, *Discovery and Excavation in Scotland 1978* (1979), 2–3*

'Stirling Castle', J Cannell, *Discovery and Excavation in Scotland 1986* (1987), 5

'Stirling Castle', G Ewart, *Discovery and Excavation in Scotland 1992* (1992), 13–17*

'Stirling Castle', G Ewart, *Discovery and Excavation in Scotland 1993* (1993), 13

'Stirling Castle', G Ewart, *Discovery and Excavation in Scotland 1994* (1994), 11

'Stirling Castle (phases I-IV)', G Ewart [*et al*], *Discovery and Excavation in Scotland 1995* (1995), 15–16

'Stirling Castle', G Ewart [*et al*], *Discovery and Excavation in Scotland 1997* (1998), 81–82

'Stirling Castle', C Aliaga-Kelly, *Discovery and Excavation in Scotland 1998* (1999), 95

'Stirling Castle', G Ewart and D Stewart, *ibid* (1999), 95–96

'Stirling Castle', C Aliaga-Kelly, *Discovery and Excavation in Scotland* new ser 1 (2000), 91

'Stirling Castle, Nether Bailey', D Stewart, *ibid* new ser 1 (2000), 91

'Stirling Castle, palace', G Ewart, *ibid* new ser 4 (2003), 128

'Stirling Castle, palace', G Ewart and D Murray, *ibid* new ser 6 (2005), 140–41

'Medieval Britain in 1970', D M Wilson and S Moorhouse, *Medieval Archaeology* 15 (1971), 158

'Medieval Britain in 1976', L E Webster and J Cherry, *ibid* 21 (1977), 238

'Medieval Britain and Ireland in 1984', S M Youngs, J Clark and T Barry, *ibid* 29 (1985), 222

'Medieval Britain and Ireland in 1986', S M Youngs, J Clark and T Barry, *ibid* 31 (1987), 183–84

'Dendrochronology, documents and the timber trade: new evidence for the building history of Stirling Castle, Scotland', A Crone and R Fawcett, *ibid* 42 (1998), 68–87*

'Medieval Britain and Ireland in 1997', M Gaimster, C Haith and J Bradley, *ibid* 42 (1998), 184

'Medieval Britain and Ireland in 2004', M Gaimster and K O'Conor, *ibid* 49 (2005), 462

'Medieval Britain and Ireland in 2005', M Gaimster and K O'Conor, *ibid* 50 (2006), 391–92

'Post-medieval Britain in 1977', J Cherry, *Post-Medieval Archaeology* 12 (1978), 110

'Excavations at Stirling Castle', G Ewart, *ibid* 14 (1980), 23–51*

'Post-medieval Britain in 1986', G Egan, *ibid* 21 (1987), 271

'Post-medieval Britain and Ireland in 1992', M Ponsford, *ibid* 27 (1993), 220–21

'Post-medieval Britain and Ireland in 1993', M Ponsford, *ibid* 28 (1994), 128

'Post-medieval Britain and Ireland in 1995', M Ponsford and R Jackson, *ibid* 30 (1996), 251–53

'Post-medieval Britain and Ireland in 1996', M Ponsford and R Jackson, *ibid* 31 (1997), 266–67

'Post-medieval Britain and Ireland in 1997', M Ponsford and R Jackson, *ibid* 32 (1998), 152–53

'Post-medieval Britain and Ireland in 1998 and 1999', M Ponsford, *ibid* 34 (2000), 369–70

'Post-medieval Britain and Ireland in 2000', M Ponsford, *ibid* 35 (2001), 265

'Post-medieval Britain and Ireland in 2003', M Ponsford, *ibid* 38 (2004), 391–92

'Post-medieval fieldwork in Britain and Northern Ireland in 2004', M Ponsford, *ibid* 39 (2005), 423–24*

'James's Fort, Stirling', J G Dunbar and I MacIvor, *Proceedings of the Society of Antiquaries of Scotland* 96 (1962–3), 361–63

Torwood

'Torwood Castle', G Bailey, *Discovery and Excavation in Scotland 1999* (2000), 44

'Medieval Britain in 1958', D M Wilson and J G Hurst, *Medieval Archaeology* 3 (1959), 309

Touchadam
'Touchadam: motte', N B Aitchison, *Discovery and Excavation in Scotland 1982* (1983), 7

Woodend
'Motte, Woodend', in RCAHMS, *Stirlingshire: an inventory of the ancient monuments*, **1**, 174–75. Edinburgh: HMSO, 1963*

Woodhead
'Woodhead', in *ibid*, **1**, 246–48*

SUTHERLAND

Close-Brooks, J. *Exploring Scotland's heritage: the Highlands*. Edinburgh: HMSO, 1986*; 2nd edition, 1996*

Gifford, J. *Highland and islands (The buildings of Scotland)*. London: Penguin, 1992*

Salter, M. *The castles of western and northern Scotland*. Wolverhampton: Folly Publications, 1995*

Ardvreck
'Ardvreck Castle', D J R la N Noble, *Discovery and Excavation in Scotland 1969* (1970), 48

Skelbo
'Skelbo Castle, Sutherland', M Salter, *Postern* 2 (1993), 3–4*

WEST LOTHIAN

Baldwin, J R. *Exploring Scotland's heritage: Edinburgh, Lothian and the Borders*. 2nd edition. Edinburgh: TSO, 1997*

Clark, N H. 'Twentieth century coastal defences of the Firth of Forth', *Fort* 14 (1986), 49–54*

Coe, G S. *Edinburgh and the Lothians*. Tavistock: COECAST, 2006* (Castle touring guides; 4)

Gifford, J and Walker, F A. *Stirlingshire and central Scotland (The buildings of Scotland)*. London: Yale University Press, 2002*

McWilliam, C. *Lothian except Edinburgh (The buildings of Scotland)*. Harmondsworth: Penguin, 1978*

Salter, M. *The castles of Lothian and the Borders*. Wolverhampton: Folly Publications, 1994*

Saunders, A. 'The defences of the Firth of Forth', in D J Breeze (ed), *Studies in Scottish antiquity presented to Stewart Cruden*, 469–80. Edinburgh: John Donald, 1984*

Smith, V. 'Defending the Forth: 1880–1910', *Fort* 13 (1985), 89–102*

Stell, G. 'Medieval architecture in West Lothian', in A Morrison (ed), *Rural settlement studies: some recent work*, 46–56. Glasgow: Department of Archaeology, University of Glasgow, 1980.

Abercorn
'Abercorn Castle', A Rae, *Discovery and Excavation: Scotland 1963* (1964), 51

Blackness
The castle of Blackness. Anon. Edinburgh: HMSO, 1969

Blackness Castle. I MacIvor. Edinburgh: HMSO, 1982*; 2nd edition, 1989*

Blackness Castle. I MacIvor. Revised edition. Edinburgh: Historic Scotland, 1993*

'Blackness Castle', G Ewart, *Discovery and Excavation in Scotland 1996* (1997), 41

'Blackness Castle', G Ewart and P Sharman, *Discovery and Excavation in Scotland 1997* (1998), 33

'Medieval Britain ad Ireland in 1997', M Gaimster, C Haith and J Bradley, *Medieval Archaeology* 42 (1998), 175

'Post-medieval Britain and Ireland in 1996', M Ponsford and R Jackson, *Post-Medieval Archaeology* 31 (1997), 265–66

'Scotland's ship-shape castle', J Lennard, *Scotland's Magazine* 65 (May, 1969), 40–41*

Duntarvie
'Duntarvie Castle', R McCullagh, *Discovery and Excavation in Scotland 1999* (2000), 89–90

'Duntarvie Castle', L Dunbar and M Cook, *Discovery and Excavation in Scotland* new ser 1 (2000), 93

'Post-medieval Britain and Ireland in 2000', M Ponsford, *Post-Medieval Archaeology* 35 (2001), 266

Linlithgow
Linlithgow Palace: a historical guide to the royal palace and peel. D Pringle. Edinburgh: Historic Scotland, 1998* (reprint)

Linlithgow Palace. J S Richardson and J Beveridge. Edinburgh: HMSO, 1948*

'Documents concerning the king's works at Linlithgow, 1301–3', A J Taylor, in D J Breeze (ed), *Studies in Scottish antiquity presented to Stewart Cruden*, 187–95. Edinburgh: John Donald, 1984*

'Linlithgow's 'princely palace' and its influence in Europe', I Campbell, *Architectural Heritage* 5 (1994), 1–20*

'Linlithgow Palace', G Ewart, *Discovery and Excavation in Scotland* new ser 3 (2002), 117

'Linlithgow Palace and peel', S Stronach, *ibid* new ser 3 (2002), 117

'Excavations at Linlithgow Palace, West Lothian, 1966–7', L R Laing, *Proceedings of the Society of Antiquaries of Scotland* 99 (1966–7), 111–47*

'Linlithgow Palace: an excavation in the west range and a note on finds from the palace', D Caldwell and J Lewis, *ibid* 126 (1996), 823–69*

Midhope

'Midhope Castle', J K Reid, *Discovery and Excavation in Scotland 1989* (1989), 53

'Post-medieval Britain and Ireland in 1989', G Egan, *Post-Medieval Archaeology* 24 (1990), 169

Niddry

'Winchburgh, Niddrie Castle', Lt-Colonel Hunter, *Archaeological Bulletin for the British Isles 1947* (1950), 63

'Niddry Castle', V Blissland, *Archaeology Today* 8.8 (1987), 18–19*

'Niddry Castle revisited', J Reid, *ibid* 9.3 (1988), 38–45*

'Niddry Castle', J K Reid, *Discovery and Excavation in Scotland 1987* (1988), 33

'Niddry Castle', J K Reid, *Discovery and Excavation in Scotland 1988* (1989), 20

'Niddry Castle', C Kelly, *Discovery and Excavation in Scotland 1989* (1989), 53–54

'Niddry Castle', C J A Kelly, *Discovery and Excavation in Scotland 1990* (1990), 31

'Medieval Britain and Ireland in 1987', S M Youngs [*et al*], *Medieval Archaeology* 32 (1988), 305

'Medieval Britain and Ireland in 1988', D R M Gaimster, S Margeson and T Barry, *ibid* 33 (1989), 234

'Medieval Britain and Ireland in 1989', D R M Gaimster, S Margeson and T Barry, *ibid* 34 (1990), 246

'Medieval Britain and Ireland in 1990', B S Nenk, S Margeson and T Barry, *ibid* 35 (1991), 223–24

'Floor tiles in medieval and post-medieval Scotland', C Aliaga-Kelly, *Medieval Ceramics* 19 (1995), 67–75*

'Niddry Castle: discovery and restoration', P Wright, *Scottish Archaeological Gazette* 16 (1987), 16–20*

'Niddry Castle', J Reid and C Aliaga-Kelly, *ibid* 17 (1988), 18–21*

'Excavations at Niddry Castle, West Lothian, 1986–90', E Proudfoot and C Aliaga-Kelly, *Proceedings of the Society of Antiquaries of Scotland* 127 (1997), 783–842*

WIGTOWNSHIRE

Feachem, R W. 'Iron Age and early medieval monuments in Galloway and Dumfriesshire. 4. Mottes and homestead moats', *Transactions of the Dumfriesshire and Galloway Natural History and Antiquarian Society* 3 ser 33 (1954–5), 64–65

Gifford, J. *Dumfries and Galloway (The buildings of Scotland)*. London: Penguin Books, 1996*

RCAHMS. *Eastern Dumfriesshire: an archaeological landscape*. Edinburgh: TSO, 1997* [espec pp 186–220, 'The archaeology of lordship']

Roberts, G. *Towers of stone: the fortified buildings of Dumfries and Galloway*. Dumfries: Dumfries and Galloway Libraries, 1993*; 2nd impression, with corrections, 1993*

Salter, M. *The castles of south-west Scotland*. Wolverhampton: Folly Publications, 1993*

Stell, G. *Exploring Scotland's heritage: Dumfries and Galloway*. Edinburgh: HMSO, 1986*; 2nd edition, TSO, 1996*

Stell, G. 'Medieval buildings and secular lordship', in R D Oram and G P Stell (eds), *Galloway: land and lordship*, 145–59. Edinburgh: Scottish Society for Northern Studies, 1991*

Stell, G. 'Castles and towers in south-western Scotland: some recent surveys', *Transactions of the Dumfriesshire and Galloway Natural History and Antiquarian Society* 3 ser 57 (1982), 65–77*

Craigcaffie

'Excavations at Craigcaffie Tower, by Stranraer', J Moran and D Pollock, *ibid* 71 (1996), 119–31*

Cruggleton

Cruggleton castle: report of excavations 1978–1981. G Ewart. Dumfries: Dumfriesshire and Galloway Natural History and Antiquarian Society, 1985*

'Cruggleton Castle: motte', C Tabraham, *Discovery and Excavation in Scotland 1979* (1980), 7

'Cruggleton Castle: the motte, timber building, hut circle', G J Ewart, *Discovery and Excavation in Scotland 1980* (1981), 4

'Cruggleton Castle: motte', G J Ewart, *Discovery and Excavation in Scotland 1981* (1982), 9

'Cruggleton', V Cormack, *Discovery and Excavation in Scotland 1983* (1984), 4

'Medieval Britain in 1978', L E Webster and J Cherry, *Medieval Archaeology* 23 (1979), 263

'Medieval Britain in 1980', S M Youngs and J Clark, *ibid* 25 (1981), 202

'Medieval Britain in 1981', S M Youngs and J Clark, *ibid* 26 (1982), 218

'Post-medieval Britain in 1979', J Cherry, *Post-Medieval Archaeology* 14 (1980), 210

Lochnaw

'Lochnaw Castle, Isle of Lochnaw', D Alexander, *Discovery and Excavation in Scotland 1995* (1995), 23*

'Lochnaw Castle, Isle of Lochnaw', D Alexander, *Discovery and Excavation in Scotland 1998* (1999), 28

'Medieval Britain and Ireland in 1999', J Bradley and M Gaimster, *Medieval Archaeology* 44 (2000), 330

'Post-medieval Britain and Ireland in 1998 and 1999', M Ponsford, *Post-Medieval Archaeology* 34 (2000), 335

Park

'Castle of Park, stair, ash pit', C J Tabraham, *Discovery and Excavation in Scotland 1979* (1980), 6

Sorbie

'Sorbie: motte', E Talbot, *Discovery and Excavation in Scotland 1983* (1984), 4

'Sorbie, Old Tower', P Harrington, *Discovery and Excavation in Scotland 1996* (1997), 32–33

'Sorbie Old Tower', P Harrington, *Discovery and Excavation in Scotland 1997* (1998), 26

'Sorbie Tower: a field survey of the surrounding lands', S Grant and J S Wood, *Transactions of the Dumfriesshire and Galloway Natural History and Antiquarian Society* 3 ser 61 (1986), 110–12*

'Medieval Britain and Ireland in 1983', S M Youngs, J Clark and T B Barry, *Medieval Archaeology* 28 (1984), 259

'Medieval Britain and Ireland in 1997', M Gaimster, C Haith and J Bradley, *ibid* 42 (1998), 173

Stranraer

'Stranraer Castle', C J Tabraham and J Lewis, *Discovery and Excavation in Scotland 1979* (1980), 6

'Stranraer Castle', E Ritchie, *Discovery and Excavation in Scotland 1989* (1989), 15

'Medieval Britain in 1978', L E Webster and J Cherry, *Medieval Archaeology* 23 (1979), 263

CHANNEL ISLANDS

Anon. *Verstarkung der Kanalinseln (Reinforcing the Channel Islands) 1941*. Jersey: Channel Islands Occupation Society, 1981*

Anon. 'Hitler's fortification order of 1941', *Channel Islands Occupation Review* (1973), 26–29

Appleby, J C. 'A memorandum on the defence of the Channel Islands, 1627', *Société Jersiaise, Annual Bulletin* 23.4 (1984), 503–8

Barton, K. 'Material evidence for medieval defence of the Channel Islands', in P Johnston (ed), *The archaeology of the Channel Islands*, 142–47. Chichester: Phillimore, 1986

Barton, K. 'The principal fortifications of the Channel Islands before 1750', *Fortress* 3 (1989), 24–32*

Coysh, V. 'Nineteenth century defences in the Channel Islands', *La Société Guernesiaise, Report and Transactions* 18 (1966–70), 297–302*

Gander, T. 'From Sudetenland to the Atlantic Wall', *Fortress* 4 (1990), 53–57*

Gardiner, M and McDowell, J (eds). *The Channel Islands: report and proceedings of the 150th summer meeting of the Royal Archaeological Institute in 2004*. London: RAI, 2005* (supplement to *Archaeological Journal* 161 (2004))

Ginns, M. 'German artillery in the Channel islands 1941–1945', *Channel Islands Occupation Review* (1975), 25–44*

Grimsley, E J. *The historical development of the martello tower in the Channel Islands*. Castel, Guernsey: Sarnian Publications, 1988*

Harlow, D. 'The Iron Duke's hobby-horse: the Duke of Wellington and the defence of the Channel Islands, 18389–1850', *Société Jersiaise, Annual Bulletin* 27.4 (2000), 613–30*

King, D J C. 'John des Roches: a fourteenth century staff officer', *Fort* 17 (1989), 3–5

Luke, M J. 'Atlantic Wall blueprint: German bunkers in the Great War and their influence on World War 2 coastal defences in the Channel Islands', *Channel Islands Occupation Review* (1985), 5–14*

Partridge, M S. 'The defence of the Channel Islands, 1814–1870', *Journal of the Society for Army Historical Research* 64 (1986), 34–42

Rolf, R. 'German defences in the Channel Islands', *Fort* 32 (2004), 4–35*

Salter, M. *Castles and old churches of the Channel Islands*. Malvern: Folly Publications, 2001*

Stevenson, C. *The Channel Islands 1941–45: Hitler's impregnable fortress*. Oxford: Osprey, 2006* (Fortress; 41)

Tough, K. 'German fortifications – argument for and against preservation', *Channel Islands Occupation Review* (1986), 39–40

ALDERNEY

Binney, M. 'Fort forlorn', *Independent Magazine* 114 (1990), 82–84, 86*

Coysh, V. *Alderney*. Newton Abbot: David and Charles, 1974*

Coysh, V. 'The forts of Alderney', *Quarterly Review of the Guernsey Society* 11 (1955), 75–77

Davenport, T. *Festung Alderney: the German defences of Alderney*. Alderney: T Davenport, in association with the Alderney Society and the Guernsey Branch of the Channel Islands Occupation Society, 2003*

Davenport, T G and Partridge, C W. 'The Victorian fortification of Alderney', *Fort* 8 (1980), 21–46*

Davenport, T G and Partridge, C W. 'The Victorian fortification of Alderney', supplement to *Fort* 8 (1980), 7–34*

Fowler, W. 'The Atlantic Wall in Alderney', *Defence Lines* 3 (1995), [9–11]*

Ginns, M. 'A tour of Alderney's German fortifications', *Channel Islands Occupation Review* (1977), 27–49*

Hynes, C A and Partridge, C W. *A guide to the fortifications of Alderney. 1. Pre-Victorian*. Alderney: Alderney Society, 1980*

Hynes, C A and Partridge, C W. *A guide to the fortifications of Alderney. 2. Victorian*. Alderney: Alderney Society, 1980*

Hynes, C A and Partridge, C W. *A guide to the fortifications of Alderney. 1. German*. Alderney: Alderney Society, 1980*

Jervois, J F D. 'Jervois: short description of works proposed and in progress at Alderney Isle', supplement to *Fort* 8 (1980), 35–44

Ouseley, M H. 'The defence of Alderney', *Review of the Guernsey Society* 32 (1976), 52–54

Ouseley, M H. 'The 1804 military survey of Alderney', *ibid* 33.2 (1977), 50–53

Pantcheff, T X H. *Alderney, fortress island: the Germans in Alderney, 1940–1945*. Chichester: Phillimore, 1981*

Partridge, C and Davenport, T. *The fortifications of Alderney*. Alderney: Alderney Publishers, 1993*

Platts, B. 'The forts of Alderney', *Country Life Annual* (1967), 149–55*

GUERNSEY

Anon. *Guernsey's German fortifications*. St Peter Port: Guernsey Tourist Board, [c 1993]*

Anon. *Guernsey's historic fortifications*. St Peter Port: Guernsey Tourist Board, [c 1992]*

Burr, H C. 'A brief note on ancient castles of Guernsey', *Review of the Guernsey Society* 41.1 (1985), 15–17

Coysh, V. 'Guernsey's former defences', *Quarterly Review of the Guernsey Society* 4.3 (1948), 12–13

Coysh, V. 'The defences of Guernsey in 1680', *La Société Guernesiaise, Report and Transactions* 16 (1955–9), 462–8

Gavey, E. *A guide to the fortifications on Guernsey*. Castel: Guernsey Armouries, 1997*; revised edition, 2001*

Halliwell, P. 'Castles of the bailiwick of Guernsey', *Herefordshire Archaeological News* 66 (1996), 48–52*

Hill, M. 'A catalogue of the cliffside fortifications of Guernsey', in H Sabine (ed), *Guernsey connections: archaeological and historical papers in honour of Bob Burns*, 147–66. St Peter Port: La Société Guernesiaise, 1998*

Angle
'L'Angle Tower', C Partridge, *Channel Islands Occupation Review* (1974), 51–54*

Brehon
'Brehon Tower', V H C[oysh], *Quarterly Review of the Guernsey Society* 6.4 (1950–1), 3–6

Castle Cornet
Castle Cornet, Guernsey. Anon. [St Peter Port: Guernsey Museums & Galleries], n d*

The archaeology of Castle Cornet, St Peter Port, Guernsey. K J Barton, edited by N Jee. St Peter Port: Guernsey Museum, 2003* (Guernsey Museum monograph; 7)

Castle Cornet, Guernsey. R Cole. Norwich: Jarrold, 1988*

The building of Castle Cornet, Guernsey. 1. Documents relating to the Tudor reconstruction. J Le Patourel (ed). Manchester: Manchester University Press, 1958*

Castle Cornet, Guernsey. B H St J O'Neil. [S l]: States Ancient Monuments Committee, 1952*

The history of Castle Cornet, Guernsey. B H St J O'Neil. Revised edition. [S l]: States of Guernsey Ancient Monuments Committee, 1981*

'Castle Cornet', K J Barton and D Allen, *CBA Newsletter and Calendar* 6 (1982–3), 155

'Castle Cornet', J Moore, *Current Archaeology* 16.9 (2003), 412–13*

'The first Castle Cornet', J Le Patourel, *Quarterly Review of the Guernsey Society* 5.2 (1949), 3–7

'Supplementary notes on "The first Castle Cornet"', J Le Patourel, *ibid* 6.3 (1950), 10–12

'Explosion at Castle Cornet – 1672', C Ozanne, *ibid* 7.2 (1951), 3–6

'Castle Cornet', E F Laine, *ibid* 8.3 (1952), 11

'The siege of Castle Cornet. Part I – 1643 to 1646', R J Thorne, *ibid* 14 (1958), 6–9

'The siege of Castle Cornet. Part II – 1645 to 1651', R J Thorne, *ibid* 14 (1958), 29–32

'Castle Cornet: excavations, 1953', J and J H Le Patourel, *La Société Guernesiaise, Report and Transactions* 15 (1950–4), 350–61*

Chateau des Marais

'Chateau des Marais', K J Barton, *CBA Newsletter and Calendar* 1 (1977–8), 106

'Chateau des Marais, Guernsey', K J Barton, *ibid* 3 (1979–80), 132

'Excavations at the Chateau des Marais (Ivy Castle), Guernsey', K J Barton, *La Société Guernesiaise, Report and Transactions* 20.5 (1980), 657–702*

Essex

'Essex Castle and the Chamberlain family', A H Ewen, *ibid* 16 (1955–9), 224–67

Fort George

'Fort George, past and present', V Coysh, *ibid* 21.5 (1985), 667–74*

Grey

Fort Grey Maritime Museum. Anon. St Peter Port: Museum and Art Gallery, n d*

Fort Grey Shipwreck Museum. R Cole. Norwich: Jarrold, 1994*

Guet

'Le Guet du Castel', P Girard, *Review of the Guernsey Society* 41.2 (1985), 45–48*

Jerbourg

'The history of the medieval and later fortifications at Jerbourg', R P Hocart, in B Burns, *Excavations at Jerbourg, Guernsey*, 48–51. St Peter Port: Guernsey Museum and Art Gallery, 1988*

'Medieval accounts relating to Jerbourg', J H Le Patourel, in *ibid*, 52

'Battery Strassburg', J H Wallbridge, in *ibid*, 53–56*

'Jerbourg Battery: a multiperiod site in Guernsey', M Atha, *La Société Guernesiaise, Report and Transactions* 24.3 (1998), 492–504*

Perelle Bay

Mirus: the making of a battery. C Partridge and J Wallbridge. Alderney: Ampersand Press, 1983*

'Guide to Perelle Bay defences', C Partridge and D Kreckeler, *Channel Islands Occupation Review* (1976), 35–38*

'The Mirus Battery and its history', G Hearson, *Quarterly Review of the Guernsey Society* 15 (1959), 54–56*

Pleinmont

'Pleinmont Tower, Guernsey', R Heaume, *Channel Islands Occupation Review* (1980), 40–43*

St Peter Port

'The medieval walls of St Peter Port', J Marr, *Review of the Guernsey Society* 41.1 (1985), 5–7*

St Sampson's

'St Sampson's, Guernsey', K Barton, *CBA Newsletter and Calendar* 4 (1980–1), 124

Vale

'The Vale Castle and Mount Crevelt', V Coysh, *Quarterly Review of the Guernsey Society* 19 (1963), 82–85*

'Excavations at Vale Castle, Guernsey, C I', K J Barton, *La Société Guernesiaise, Report and Transactions* 21.4 (1984), 485–538*

Vazon Bay

'Guide to Vazon Bay defences', C Partridge and D Kreckeler, *Channel Islands Occupation Review* (1974), 39–42*

JERSEY

Anon. 'The German fortifications', *Société Jersiaise, Annual Bulletin* 15 (1949–52), 329–31

Ginns, M. 'German tunnels in Jersey', *Channel Islands Occupation Review* (1973), 2–13

Ginns, M. 'Anti-tank walls in Jersey', *ibid* (1974), 57–66*

Ginns, M and Bryans, P. *German fortifications in Jersey*. Privately published, 1975*

Halliwell, P. 'The castles of the bailiwick of Jersey', *Herefordshire Archaeological News* 68 (1997), 23–27*

Pocock, H R S. 'Jersey's martello towers', *Société Jersiaise, Annual Bulletin* 20 (1969–72), 389–98*

Stevenson, I. 'Jersey', *The Redan* 63 (2005), 19–35*

Carrière, La

Resistance post La Carrière. M Costard and M Ginns. Jersey: Channel Islands Occupation Society, n d*

Corbière, La

The La Corbière 10.5 cm casemate bunker. M Costard. Jersey: Channel Islands Occupation Society, n d*

Crête Fort, La

'"A respectable little work": the story of la Crête Fort, Bonne Nuit Bay, Jersey', M Brice, *Société Jersiaise, Annual Bulletin* 26.1 (1993), 63–70*

Elizabeth

Elizabeth Castle. Anon. [St Helier]: Jersey Heritage Trust, n d*

Elizabeth Castle, Jersey. M Brown. Norwich: Jarrold, 1986*

Granadoe! Mortars in the Civil War, the Jersey campaign and the siege of Castle Elizabeth. S Bull. Leigh-on-Sea: Partizan House, [1986]*

A guide to the islet of St Helier and Elizabeth Castle. P Davies. [S l]: States of Jersey, 1968*

The islet of St Helier and Elizabeth Castle, Jersey. N V L Rybot. 3rd edition. [S l]: States of Jersey, 1953*

'Mortars at Elizabeth Castle, Jersey, in 1651', S Bull, *Fort* 13 (1985), 61–68*

'Elizabeth Castle', I Stevenson, *The Redan* 57 (2003), 23–31*

'Interesting local documents. Copy of an order issued by King Charles II concerning the royal castles of Elizabeth and Montorgeuil and St Aubin's Fort, now in the archives of the County Record Office, Shire Hall, Bedford', R Mollet, *Société Jersiaise, Annual Bulletin* 16 (1953–6), 291–92

Gorey

See Mont Orgeuil

Landes, Les

Batterie Moltke, Les Landes. M Ginns. [S l]: Channel Islands Occupation Society, n d*

Mare Hill, La

Resistance nest La Mare Mill. Anon. [S l]: Channel Islands Occupation Society, n d*

'La Mare Sechsschartenturm', D Letto, *Channel Islands Occupation Review* (1988), 71–79*

Millbrook

Resistance point Millbrook. D Letto and M Ginns. [S l]: Channel Islands Occupation Society, n d*

'Preservation progress (4.7 cm casemate – Millbrook, Jersey)', D Letto, *Channel Islands Occupation Review* (1985), 71–77*

Mont Orgueil

Mont Orgueil Castle. Anon. [St Helier]: Jersey heritage Trust, n d*

Guide to Mont Orgueil Castle. M Brown. [S l: s n, *c* 1986]*

Mont Orgueil Castle: guide and history. J E Harris. [S l]: States of Jersey, 1971*

The Mont Orgueil debate: a review, including a full transcript of the debate held in the medieval hall at Mont Orgueil on 25 April 2002. P Marshall. [S l: s n], 2002

Dating buildings of the inner ward at Mont Orgueil Castle. J McCormack. Mont Orgueil: Friends of Mont Orgueil Castle, 2002 (Mont Orgueil studies; 6) [duplicated typescript]

Revisiting Governor Peyton's 1617–1620 disbursements book. M T Myres. Mont Orgueil: Friends of Mont Orgueil Castle, 2001 (Mont Orgueil studies; 1) [duplicated typescript]

Military manpower at Mont Orgueil Castle in 1617. M T Myres. Mont Orgueil: Friends of Mont Orgueil Castle, 2001 (Mont Orgueil studies; 2) [duplicated typescript]

Dating the fortification building programmes at Mont Orgueil Castle from the evidence of peaks of annual expenditures on them, 1547–1594. M T Myres. Mont Orgueil: Friends of Mont Orgueil Castle, 2002 (Mont Orgueil studies; 10) [duplicated typescript]

Reasons why the present "Somerset Tower" at Mont Orgueil Castle was not built, or completed, by 1549: the documentary evidence. M T Myres and N P Molyneux. Mont Orgueil: Friends of Mont Orgueil Castle, 2001 (Mont Orgueil studies; 3) [duplicated typescript]

Henry Cornish's inventory of the ordnance at Mont Orgueil Castle: the role of the artillery in identifying particular gun platforms and their seawards orientation in 1549. M T Myres and N P Molyneux. 3rd, revised, edition. Mont Orgueil: Friends of Mont Orgueil Castle, 2002 (Mont Orgueil studies; 4) [duplicated typescript]

Transition and change in the armaments at Mont Orgueil Castle, 1531–1681: an introduction to the artillery. M T Myres. Mont Orgueil: Friends of Mont Orgueil Castle, 2001 (Mont Orgueil studies; 5) [duplicated typescript]

Evidence from the shape (footprint) of the "Somerset" Tower for Henry Cornish's original purpose for it. M T Myres and N P Molyneux. Mont Orgueil: Friends of Mont Orgueil Castle, 2002* (Mont Orgueil studies; 7) [duplicated typescript]

Mont Orgueil Castle and the defence of Jersey 1540–1630. C Platt. Bognor Regis: Woodfield Publishing for the Friends of Mont Orgueil, 2001*

Dating the Somerset Tower. C Platt. Mont Orgueil: Friends of Mont Orgueil Castle, 2002 (Mont Orgueil studies; 8) [duplicated typescript]

The Mont Orgueil dossier, or who built the Somerset Tower? C Platt. Bognor Regis: Woodfield Publishing, 2003*

Geological examination of the d-shaped and adjacent areas of the inner ward of Mont Orgueil Castle. J Renouf. Mont Orgueil: Friends of Mont Orgueil Castle, 2002* (Mont Orgueil studies; 11) [duplicated typescript]

Mont Orgueil Castle, Jersey: history and architecture. W Rodwell. St Helier: Jersey Heritage Trust, 2006*

Gorey Castle, (Le Château Mont Orgueil), Jersey. N V L Rybot. [S l]: States of Jersey, 1957*

'Excavations in the Middle Ward, Mont Orgueil, Gorey, Jersey', K J Barton, *Archaeological Journal* 141 (1984), 216–42*

'The debate over Mont Orgueil', P Marshall, *Castle Studies Group Newsletter* 16 (2002–3), 48–51.

'Gorey Castle, Jersey, Channel Islands', K J Barton, *CBA Calendar of Excavations* summaries 1976 (1977), 3

'Mont Orgueil', [A Selkirk], *Current Archaeology* 16.3 (2002), 98–106*

'Medieval Britain in 1974', L E Webster and J Cherry, *Medieval Archaeology* 19 (1975), 241

'Gorey Castle', D Ford, *Medieval History Magazine* 8 (2004), 18–23*

'A report on the excavations made in the north-east outer slopes of Mont Orgueil Castle during the latter half of the year 1940', N V L Rybot, *Société Jersiaise, Annual Bulletin* 15 (1949–52), 239–48*

'Medieval and post-medieval pottery from Gorey Castle', K J Barton, *ibid* 22.2 (1977), 60–82*

'Early proposals for fortifying Town Hill', W Davies, *ibid* 23.4 (1984), 509–16*

'Investigations in the lower room of the south-west keep of Mont Orgueil Castle', M B Finlaison, *ibid* 27.1 (1997), 85–102*

'Investigations in the lower room of the south-west keep tower of Mont Orgueil. Part 2: the wall paintings', M B Finlaison, *ibid* 28.1 (2001), 78–87*

'The historical evidence for the sixteenth-century structural remodelling of Mont Orgueil Castle', N S Rushton, *ibid* 28.3 (2003), 351–74*

See also Elizabeth Castle

Noirmont Point

Noirmont observation tower. Anon. [S l]: Channel Islands Occupation Society, n d*

A guide to Batterie Lotharingen, Noirmont Point. P Bryans. [S l]: Channel Islands Occupation Society, 1978*

Batterie Lotharingen. P Burnal. [S l]: Channel Islands Occupation Society Jersey, 2002*

The Noirmont command bunker. M Ginns. [S l]: Channel Islands Occupation Society, n d*

Regent
Fort Regent. W Davies. St Helier: [s n], 1971*

St Aubin's
'Saint Aubin's Fort', N V L Rybot, *Société Jersiaise, Annual Bulletin* 14 (1940–8), 367–98*

See also Elizabeth Castle

SARK

Murphy, C. 'Cannon and musket: the defences of Sark', *La Société Guernesiaise, Report and Transactions* 22.4 (1989), 633–37

Ouseley, M H. 'Sark: military installations', *The Review of the Guernsey Society* 32 (1976), 23–24

ISLE OF MAN

Curphey, R A. 'The coastal batteries of the Isle of Man. 1. The lord's defences to the revestment', *Journal of the Manx Museum* 7.83 (1967), 50–57

Curphey, R A. 'The coastal batteries. II. From the revestment to the twentieth century', *ibid* 7.84 (1968), 89–91*

Dickinson, J R. 'Eliza endangered? Elizabeth I, the Isle of Man and the security of England', *Proceedings of the Isle of Man Natural History and Antiquarian Society* 10.1 (1989–91), 123–40

Halliwell, P. 'The castles of the Isle of Man', *Herefordshire Archaeological News* 65 (1996), 13–17*

Salter, M. *Castles and old churches of the Isle of Man.* Malvern: Folly Publications, 1997*

Smith, R D. 'Early cast-iron ordnance with particular reference to guns on the Isle of Man', *Journal of the Ordnance Society* 3 (1991), 25–45*

Bishopscourt
'Bishopscourt', R A Curphey, *Journal of the Manx Museum* 7.88 (1976), 221–24*

'The fort at Bishopscourt, Isle of Man', R A Curphey, *Post-Medieval Archaeology* 8 (1974), 104–7*

Castle Rushen

Castle Rushen. Anon. Douglas: Manx National Heritage, [199?]*

Excavations in Castletown, Isle of Man 1989–1992. P J Davey, D J Freke and D A Higgins. Liverpool: Liverpool University Press, 1996*

Castle Rushen, Isle of Man. B H St J O'Neil. [S l: s n], 1951*

'Castle Rushen, Isle of Man', B H St J O'Neil, *Archaeologia* 94 (1951), 1–26*

'The development of Castletown 1601 to 1703', J R Roscow, *Proceedings of the Isle of Man Natural History and Antiquarian Society* 11.1 (1997–9), 5–28*

Cronk Howe Mooar

'Cronk Howe Mooar, Rushen', J R Bruce, *ibid* new ser 5 (1942–56), 398

Peel

Peel Castle, Isle of Man. D Craine. [S l: s n], 1958*

Peel Castle. R A Curphey. Douglas: Manx National Heritage, n d*

Peel Castle excavations: 1st interim report 1982–3. D J Freke. [S l]: St Patrick's Isle (I O M) Archaeological Trust, 1983*

Peel Castle excavations: 2nd interim report 1984. D J Freke. [S l]: St Patrick's Isle (I O M) Archaeological Trust, 1985*

Peel Castle excavations: 3rd interim report 1985. D J Freke. [S l]: St Patrick's Isle (I O M) Archaeological Trust, 1985*

Peel Castle excavations: 4th interim report 1986. D J Freke. [S l]: St Patrick's Isle (I O M) Archaeological Trust, 1987*

The Peel Castle dig. D Freke. Douglas: The Friends of Peel Castle for the Friends of Manx National Heritage, 1995*

Excavations on St Patrick's Isle, Peel, Isle of Man, 1982–88: prehistoric, Viking, medieval and later. D Freke. Liverpool: Liverpool University Press, 2002* (Centre for Manx Studies monographs; 2)

Peel Castle excavations: final report (1). The Half Moon Battery. R H White. [S l]: St Patrick's Isle (I O M) Archaeological Trust, 1986*

'Peel, Peel Castle on St Patrick's Isle', B R S Megaw, *Archaeological Bulletin for the British Isles* (1950), 19

'Peel Castle', [A Selkirk], source D Freke, *Current Archaeology* 9.4 (1986), 102–5*

'Peel Castle', D Freke, *ibid* 10.3 (1988), 92–97*

'Excavations at Peel Castle, 1947', M D Wright, *Proceedings of the Isle of Man Natural History and Antiquarian Society* 9.1 (1980–2), 21–57*

'Peel Castle summer excursion: June 1979', R A Curphey, *ibid* 9.1 (1980–2), 59–94*

'Medieval Britain and Ireland in 1984', S M Youngs, J Clark and T Barry, *Medieval Archaeology* 29 (1985), 210–11

'Medieval Britain and Ireland in 1985', S M Youngs, J Clark and T Barry, *ibid* 30 (1986), 180–81

'Medieval Britain and Ireland in 1986', S M Youngs, J Clark and T Barry, *ibid* 31 (1987), 174

'Medieval Britain and Ireland in 1987', S M Youngs [*et al*], *ibid* 32 (1988), 293–94

'Post-medieval Britain in 1986', G Egan, *Post-Medieval Archaeology* 21 (1987), 270–71

ISLES OF SCILLY

Campbell, A (ed). *Heritage unlocked: guide to free sites in Cornwall and the Isles of Scilly*. London: English Heritage, 2004*

O'Neil, B H St J. *Isles of Scilly*. London: HMSO, 1949*

O'Neil, B H St J. *Ancient monuments of the Isles of Scilly*. 2nd edition. London: HMSO, 1961*

O'Neil, B H St J. *Ancient monuments of the Isles of Scilly, Cornwall*. 3rd edition. London: HMSO, 1983*

Ratcliffe, J. *Fieldwork in Scilly 1991 and 1992*. Truro: Cornwall County Council, 1993*

Ratcliffe, J and Johns, C. *Scilly's archaeological heritage*. Revised edition. Truro: Twelveheads Press, 2003*

Ratcliffe J and Sharpe, A. *Fieldwork in Scilly, autumn 1990*. Truro: Cornwall County Council, 1991*

Rowland, A J. 'Fortifications of the Isles of Scilly', *Postern* 12 (2000), 13–18*

Salter, M. *The castles of Devon and Cornwall and forts of the Scilly Isles*. Malvern: Folly Publications, 1999*

Spreadbury, I D. *Castles in Cornwall and the Isles of Scilly*. Redruth: Dyllansow Truran, 1984*

Stevenson, I V. 'Some West Country defences', *Fort* 17 (1989), 11–26*

ST MARY'S

Parkes, C. *Archaeological fieldwork in the Isles of Scilly. March 1990. Early batteries on the Garrison, St Mary's*. Truro: Cornwall County Council, 1990*

Thomas, C. 'The names of the batteries on the Garrison, St Mary's, Isles of Scilly', in M Bowden, D Mackay and P Topping (eds), *From Cornwall to Caithness: some* *aspects of British field archaeology. Papers presented to Norman V Quinnell*, 251–59. Oxford: BAR, 1989* (British series; 209)

Harry's Walls

'Harry's Walls, St Mary's: a new interpretation', A D Saunders, *Cornish Archaeology* 1 (1962), 85–91*

'Harry's Walls, St Mary's', B H St J O'Neil, *The Scillonian* 22.93 (1948), 36–38*

Star

Star Castle and its garrison. F and P Adams. Liskeard: Belvedere Press, 1984*

TRESCO

King Charles's

'A 16th century outwork to King Charles's Castle, Tresco', N V Quinnell, *Cornish Archaeology* 17 (1978), 142–43*

IRELAND

ANTRIM

Brett, C E B. *Buildings of County Antrim*. Belfast: Ulster Architectural Heritage Society and the Ulster Historical Foundation, 1996* [espec ch 1]

McNeill, T E. 'The stone castles of northern County Antrim', *Ulster Journal of Archaeology* 3 ser 46 (1983), 101–28*

Salter, M. *The castles of Ulster*. Malvern: Folly Publications, 2004*

Antrim

'Castle walls, Antrim', P Logue, in I Bennett (ed), *Excavations 1998: summary accounts of archaeological excavations in Ireland*, 11. Bray: Wordwell, 2000

'Antrim town war memorial, Castle Street, Antrim', C McConway, in I Bennett (ed), *Excavations 2000: summary accounts of archaeological excavations in Ireland*, 1. Bray: Wordwell, 2002

'Medieval Britain and Ireland in 1998', J Bradley, M Gaimster and C Haith, *Medieval Archaeology* 43 (1999), 288

'Post-medieval Britain and Ireland in 1998 and 1999', M Ponsford, *Post-Medieval Archaeology* 34 (2000), 311

Ballyaghagan

'A square earthwork in north Belfast: the site of the Ekenhead early 14th century coin-hoard', E M Jope and W A Seaby, *Ulster Journal of Archaeology* 3 ser 22 (1959), 112–15*

Ballydown

'Ballydown', N Crothers, in I Bennett (ed), *Excavations 1996: summary accounts of archaeological excavations in Ireland*, 1. Bray: Wordwell, 1997

Ballygalley

'Balleygalley', D P Hurl, in *ibid*, 1

'Post-medieval Britain and Ireland in 1996', M Ponsford and R Jackson, *Post-Medieval Archaeology* 31 (1997), 300

Belfast

'Donegal Street, Belfast', N F Brannon, in I Bennett (ed), *Excavations 1990: summary accounts of archaeological excavations in Ireland*, 11. Bray: Wordwell, 1991

'Fortification of Belfast', G Müller and G Williamson, *Irish Sword* 19 (1993–5), 306–12*

'Post-medieval Britain and Ireland in 1990', M Ponsford, *Post-Medieval Archaeology* 25 (1991), 126–27

Carncastle

'Carncastle: a fortified islet on the north-east coast of County Antrim', D N Johnson, in J R Kenyon and K O'Conor (eds), *The medieval castle in Ireland and Wales: essays in honour of Jeremy Knight*, 217–37. Dublin: Four Courts Press, 2003*

Carrickfergus

Carrickfergus Castle, County Antrim. A Hamlin. Belfast: HMSO, 1977*

A guide to Carrickfergus Castle. E M Jope. 2nd edition. Belfast: HMSO, 1962*

Carrickfergus Castle, County Antrim. T E McNeill. Belfast: HMSO, 1981*

Irish historic towns atlas. 2. Carrickfergus. P Robinson. Dublin: Royal Irish Academy, 1986*

'Carrickfergus Castle, Carrickfergus', N F Brannon, in I Bennett (ed), *Excavations 1991: summary accounts of archaeological excavations in Ireland*, 1–2. Bray: Wordwell, 1992

'Carrickfergus', R Ó Baoill, in *ibid*, 2–3

'Carrickfergus', R Ó Baoill, in I Bennett (ed), *Excavations 1992: summary accounts of archaeological excavations in Ireland*, 1–2. Bray: Wordwell, 1993

'Carrickfergus Castle', C Donnelly and P McCooey, in I Bennett (ed), *Excavations 1993: summary accounts of archaeological excavations in Ireland*, 3. Bray: Wordwell, 1994

'Carrickfergus', R Ó Baoill, in I Bennett (ed), *Excavations 1995: summary accounts of archaeological excavations in Ireland*, 1. Bray: Wordwell, 1996

'1–3 Joymount, Carrickfergus', C McConway, in I Bennett (ed), *Excavations 1999: summary accounts of archaeological excavations in Ireland*, 2–3. Bray: Wordwell, 2000

'Joymount Manse, Carrickfergus', A Gahan, *ibid*, 3

'First Presbyterian War Memorial Hall, Carrickfergus', A Gahan, in I Bennett (ed), *Excavations 2000: summary accounts of archaeological excavations in Ireland*, 4. Bray: Wordwell, 2002

'Carrickfergus', R Logue, in I Bennett (ed), *Excavations 2002: summary accounts of archaeological excavations in Ireland*, 5. Bray: Wordwell, 2004

'Carrickfergus Castle, Carrickfergus', J Ó Néill, in *ibid*, 5–6

'Carrickfergus and its castle', J C Rutherford, *Belfast Natural History and Philosophical Society, Proceedings and Reports* 2 ser 5 (1955–9), 46–55

'Archaeological excavations in Carrickfergus', N F Brannon and M L Simpson, *Carrickfergus and District Historical Society* 1 (1988), 8–10*

'Carrickfergus Castle', C Donnelly, P McCooey and T E McNeill, *Current Archaeology* 14.3 (1998), 102–3*

'The siege of Carrickfergus Castle, 1315–16', G O Sayles, *Irish Historical Studies* 10 (1956–7), 94–100

'Medieval Britain in 1962 and 1963', D M Wilson and D G Hurst, *Medieval Archaeology* 8 (1964), 262–63

'Excavations in Carrickfergus, Co Antrim, 1972–79: a summary report on the excavations directed by the late T G Delaney', M L Simpson and A Dickson, *ibid* 25 (1981), 78–89*

'Medieval Britain and Ireland in 1991', B S Nenk, S Margeson and M Hurley, *ibid* 36 (1992), 279

'Medieval Britain and Ireland in 1993', B S Nenk, S Margeson and M Hurley, *ibid* 38 (1994), 267

'Medieval Britain and Ireland in 1995', B S Nenk, S Margeson and M Hurley, *ibid* 40 (1996), 294

'De Courcy's castle: new insights into the first phase of Anglo-Norman building activity at Carrickfergus Castle, County Antrim', C Donnelly [*et al*], *ibid* 49 (2005), 311–17*

'Post-medieval Britain and Ireland in 1991', M Ponsford, *Post-Medieval Archaeology* 26 (1992), 111–12

'Post-medieval Britain and Ireland in 1992', M Ponsford, *ibid* 27 (1993), 219–20

'Post-medieval Britain and Ireland in 1995', M Ponsford and R Jackson, *ibid* 30 (1996), 251

'Post-medieval Britain and Ireland in 1998 and 1999', M Ponsford, *ibid* 34 (2000), 312

'Post-medieval Britain and Ireland in 2002', M Ponsford, *ibid* 37 (2003), 307

'Excavations at Carrickfergus, 1949–50', E M Jope, *Ulster Journal of Archaeology* 3 ser 13 (1950), 61–65*

'Excavations at the entrance to Carrickfergus Castle, 1950', D M Waterman, *ibid* 3 ser 15 (1952), 103–18*

Castle Carra

'Castle Carra, Castle Park, Cushendun', D P Hurl, in I Bennett (ed), *Excavations 1995: summary accounts of archaeological excavations in Ireland*, 1. Bray: Wordwell, 1996

'Castle Carra. Cushendun', D Hurl, in I Bennett (ed), *Excavations 2002: summary accounts of archaeological excavations in Ireland*, 6. Bray: Wordwell, 2004

'Life and death in a County Antrim tower house', D P Hurl and E M Murphy, *Archaeology Ireland* 10.2 (1996), 20–23*

'Investigations at Castle Carra, Cushendun', D P Hurl, *Castle Studies Group Newsletter* 17 (2004), 82–83*

'Medieval Britain and Ireland in 1995', B S Nenk, S Margeson and M Hurley, *Medieval Archaeology* 40 (1996), 294

Castle Lug

'A small excavation at Castle Lug, Greenisland, County Antrim', N F Brannon, *Ulster Journal of Archaeology* 3 ser 44–45 (1981–2), 202–3*

Doonbought

'Excavations at Doonbought fort, County Antrim', T E McNeill, *ibid* 3 ser 40 (1977), 63–84*

Dromore

'Excavations at Dromore ring-work, County Antrim', A E P Collins, *ibid* 3 ser 31 (1968), 59–66*

Drumadoon

'Summary report on excavations at Drumadoon td, Co Antrim', B Williams and C McSparron, *Castle Studies Group Newsletter* 17 (2004), 80–81*

Dunineny

'Dunineny Castle, Ballycastle', T McNeill, in I Bennett (ed), *Excavations 2000: summary accounts of archaeological excavations in Ireland*, 1–2. Bray: Wordwell, 2002

'Castle or office block?', S Gormley and T McNeill, *Archaeology Ireland* 15.1 (2001), 30–32*

'Dunineny Castle and the Gaelic view of castle building', T E McNeill, *Château Gaillard* 20 (2002), 153–61*

'Excavations at Dunineny Castle, Co Antrim', T E McNeill, *Medieval Archaeology* 48 (2004), 167–200*

'Post-medieval Britain and Ireland in 2000', M Ponsford, *Post-Medieval Archaeology* 35 (2001), 186–87

Dunluce

A guide to Dunluce Castle, Co Antrim. Anon. Belfast: HMSO, 1966, reprinted 1978*

Dunluce Castle, County Antrim. H Dixon. Belfast: HMSO, 1977*

Dunluce Castle. M Meek. Belfast: Department of the Environment for Northern Ireland, [1993]*

Dunluce Castle. M Meek. Belfast: Environment and Heritage Service, 1997*

'The castle of Dunluce', G Priest, *Country Life* 108 (1950), 1984–85*

'Post-medieval Britain in 1987', G Egan, *Post-Medieval Archaeology* 22 (1988), 193–94

'A seventeenth century inventory from Dunluce Castle, county Antrim', H Mac-Donnell, *Journal of the Royal Society of Antiquaries of Ireland* 122 (1992), 109–27

Dunsilly

'Dunsilly', T E McNeill, in T G Delaney (ed), *Excavations 1974: summary accounts of archaeological work in Ireland*, 8–9. [S l: s n], n d

'Dunsilly', in T G Delaney (ed), *Excavations 1974: summary accounts of archaeological work in Ireland*, 6–7. [S l: s n], n d

'Excavations at Dunsilly, County Antrim', T E McNeill, *Ulster Journal of Archaeology* 3 ser 54–55 (1991–2), 78–112*

Inisloughan

'Inisloughan Fort', in G A Hayes-McCoy (ed), *Ulster and other Irish maps c 1600*, 11–12. Dublin: Stationery Office for the Irish Manuscripts Commission, 1964*

Kilwaughter

'Lissan Rectory, Kilwaughter Castle, and the buildings in the north of Ireland designed by John Nash', E M Jope, *Ulster Journal of Archaeology* 3 ser 19 (1956), 121–30*

Lisburn

'Lisburn's castle and cathedral', J F Burns, *Lisburn Historical Society Journal* 5 (1984), 1–5

Malone

'Aspects of local history in Malone, Belfast', T Carleton, *Ulster Journal of Archaeology* 3 ser 39 (1976), 62–67*

Rathlin

'The archaeology of Rathlin Island', B Williams, *Archaeology Ireland* 4.2 (1990), 47–51*

Slievenacloy

'Post-medieval Britain in 1984', G Egan, *Post-Medieval Archaeology* 19 (1985), 163

Toome

'Toome Castle, Toome', R Ó Baoill, in I Bennett (ed), *Excavations 1991: summary accounts of archaeological excavations in Ireland*, 4. Bray: Wordwell, 1992

'Medieval Britain and Ireland in 1991', B S Nenk, S Margeson and M Hurley, *Medieval Archaeology* 36 (1992), 279

'Post-medieval Britain in 1991', M Ponsford, *Post-Medieval Archaeology* 26 (1992), 112

'Excavations at the site of Toome Castle, Co Antrim', R Ó Baoill, *Ulster Journal of Archaeology* 3 ser 58 (1999), 90–108*

ARMAGH

Brett, C E B. *Buildings of County Armagh*. Belfast: Ulster Architectural Heritage Society, 1997* [espec ch 1]

Jope, E M. 'Moyry, Charlemont, Castleraw, and Richhill: fortification to architecture in the north of Ireland', *Ulster Journal of Archaeology* 3 ser 23 (1960), 97–123*

Salter, M. *The castles of Ulster*. Malvern: Folly Publications, 2004*

Blackwater
'The Blackwater forts', [G A Hayes-McCoy], *Irish Sword* 2 (1954–6), 212–15*

Castleraw
'Castleraw, near Loughgall, Co Armagh', E M Jope, *Ulster Journal of Archaeology* 3 ser 16 (1953), 63–67*

'Two fortified houses at Castleraw, County Armagh', N F Brannon, *ibid* 3 ser 46 (1983), 165–66*

Charlemont
'Charlemont Fort', in G A Hayes-McCoy (ed), *Ulster and other Irish maps c 1600*, 7. Dublin: Stationery Office for the Irish Manuscripts Commission, 1964*

'Charlemont Fort, Co Armagh', P Tohall, *Irish Sword* 3 (1957–8), 182–86*

Coney Island
'Medieval Britain in 1962 and 1963', D M Wilson and D G Hurst, *Medieval Archaeology* 8 (1964), 263

'Medieval Britain in 1964', D M Wilson and D G Hurst, *ibid* 9 (1965), 193–94

'Coney Island, Lough Neagh: prehistoric settlement, Anglo-Norman castle and Elizabethan native fortress: an interim report on excavations in 1962 to 1964', P V Addyman, *Ulster Journal of Archaeology* 3 ser 28 (1965), 78–101*

Mount Norris
'Mount Norris', in G A Hayes-McCoy (ed), *Ulster and other Irish maps c 1600*, 3–4. Dublin: Stationery Office for the Irish Manuscripts Commission, 1964*

Moyry Pass
'The Moyry Pass', in *ibid*, 2*

CARLOW

Brindley, A and Kilfeather, A. *Archaeological inventory of County Carlow*. Dublin: Stationery Office, 1993*

Clarke, T. 'Castles of County Carlow', *Carloviana* 38 (1990–1), 24–26, 31*

Hadden, V. *Come capture castles in County Carlow*. Carlow: A Hadden, 1994*

Hadden, W V. 'Some castles near Carlow', *Carloviana* new ser 1.5 (1956), 14–15

McNeill, T E. 'Early castles in Leinster', *Journal of Irish Archaeology* 5 (1989–90), 57–64*

O'Keeffe, T. 'Ballyloughan, Ballymoon and Clonmore: three castles of c. 1300 in County Carlow', in J Gillingham (ed), *Anglo-Norman studies 23: proceedings of the Battle Conference 2000*, 167–97. Woodbridge: Boydell Press, 2001*

Salter, M. *The castles of Leinster*. Malvern: Folly Publications, 2004*

Taaffe, F. 'Fassnagh Rheban (wilderness of Rheban)', *Carloviana* 32 (1984–5), 10–12*

Ballyloo

'Rathnageeragh and Ballyloo: a study of stone castles of probable 14th and 15th century date in county Carlow', T O'Keeffe, *Journal of the Royal Society of Antiquaries of Ireland* 117 (1987), 28–49*

Ballyloughan

'Ballyloughan', in A Brindley and A Kilfeather, *Archaeological inventory of County Carlow*, 84. Dublin: Stationery Office, 1993*

'Ballyloughan, Ballymoon and Clonmore: three castles of c. 1300 in County Carlow', T O'Keeffe, in J Gillingham (ed), *Anglo-Norman studies 23: proceedings of the Battle Conference 2000*, 167–97. Woodbridge: Boydell Press, 2001*

'Excavations at Ballyloughan Castle', L de Paor, *Journal of the Royal Society of Antiquaries of Ireland* 92 (1962), 1–14*

Ballymoon

'Ballymoon', in A Brindley and A Kilfeather, *Archaeological inventory of County Carlow*, 84–85. Dublin: Stationery Office, 1993*

'Ballyloughan, Ballymoon and Clonmore: three castles of c. 1300 in County Carlow', T O'Keeffe, in J Gillingham (ed), *Anglo-Norman studies 23: proceedings of the Battle Conference 2000*, 167–97. Woodbridge: Boydell Press, 2001*

'Discovering Versailles in the smallness of my own experience', T O'Keeffe, in J Fenwick (ed), *Lost and found: discovering Ireland's past*, 213–24. Bray: Wordwell, 2003*

Carlow

Carlow: architectural heritage. W Garner. Dublin: An Foras Forbatha, 1980*

'Carlow (Carlow town), in A Brindley and A Kilfeather, *Archaeological inventory of County Carlow*, 84. Dublin: Stationery Office, 1993*

'Carlow Castle, Carlow', K O'Conor, in I Bennett (ed), *Excavations 1996: summary accounts of archaeological excavations in Ireland*, 4–5. Bray: Wordwell, 1997*

'The origins of Carlow Castle', K O'Conor, *Archaeology Ireland* 11.3 (1997), 13–16*

'Carlow's feudal fortress', W V Hadden, *Carloviana* new ser 1.6 (1957), 21–25*

'The town walls of Carlow', V Hadden, *ibid* new ser 1.10 (1961), 30–31

'The town walls of Carlow', V Hadden, *ibid* new ser 2.26 (1977–8), 19–21*

'Castle of Carlow: who built and occupied the first castle here?', K O'Conor, *ibid* 46 (1998), 37–42*

'Carlow and its medieval walls', J Feeley and J Sheehan, *ibid* 53 (2004), 16–18*

'Who built Carlow Castle? Hugh de Lacy or William Marshall?', M Purcell, *Carlow Past and Present* 1.1 (1985–6), 8–10*

'Medieval Britain and Ireland in 1996', B S Nenk, C Haith and J Bradley, *Medieval Archaeology* 41 (1997), 303

Castlemore
'Castlemore motte & bailey', C Delaney, *Carloviana* 52 (2003), 81–83*

Clogrennan
Clogrennan Castle', V Hadden, *Carlow Past and Present* new ser 2.26 (1978), 19*

Clonmore
'Clonmore (Rathvilly by)', in A Brindley and A Kilfeather, *Archaeological inventory of County Carlow*, 84. Dublin: Stationery Office, 1993*

'Ballyloughan, Ballymoon and Clonmore: three castles of c. 1300 in County Carlow', T O'Keeffe, in J Gillingham (ed), *Anglo-Norman studies 23: proceedings of the Battle Conference 2000*, 167–97. Woodbridge: Boydell Press, 2001*

'Clonmore Castle', S Leahy, *Carlow Past and Present* 1 (1947–51), 183–85

'Come capture a castle at Clonmore', V Hadden, *ibid* new ser 2.23 (1974), 15–17*

Coolyhune
'Coolyhune', in A Brindley and A Kilfeather, *Archaeological inventory of County Carlow*, 95. Dublin: Stationery Office, 1993*

'Coolyhune star fort', I Doyle, *Carlow Past and Present* 35 (1987–8), 16–17*

'Historical background to Coolyhune star fort', I Doyle, *ibid* 36 (1988–9), 21*

Leighlinbridge
'Leighlinbridge (Leighlinbridge town)', in A Brindley and A Kilfeather, *Archaeological inventory of County Carlow*, 86–87. Dublin: Stationery Office, 1993*

'The river-crossing at Leighlinbridge and its defences', B Kealy, *Carlow Past and Present* 1.17 (1968), 29–30

'Notes on the castle at Leighlinbridge', V Hadden, *ibid* new ser 2.28 (1980), 17

Rathnageeragh

'Rathnageeragh', in A Brindley and A Kilfeather, *Archaeological inventory of County Carlow*, 84–85. Dublin: Stationery Office, 1993*

'Rathnageeragh and Ballyloo: a study of stone castles of probable 14th and 15th century date in county Carlow', T O'Keeffe, *Journal of the Royal Society of Antiquaries of Ireland* 117 (1987), 28–49*

St Mullin's

St Mullin's: an early ecclesiastical site and medieval settlement in County Carlow. C Manning. Bray: Archaeology Ireland, 1999* (Heritage guide; 5)

Tullow

'The castle of Tullow, Co Carlow', T O'Keeffe, *Journal of the Co Kildare Archaeological Society* 16.5 (1985–6), 528–29*

CAVAN

Davies, O. 'The castles of County Cavan, part I', *Ulster Journal of Archaeology* 3 ser 10 (1947), 73–100*

Davies, O. 'The castles of County Cavan, part II', *ibid* 3 ser 11 (1948), 81–126*

McCarthy, J. 'The importance of the tower house in the late medieval society of Breifne', *Breifne* 8.1 (1989–90), 118–35*

O'Donovan, P F. *Archaeological inventory of County Cavan*. Dublin: Stationery Office, 1995*

Salter, M. *The castles of Ulster*. Malvern: Folly Publications, 2004*

Belturbet

'Turbet Island motte and bailey, Belturbet, County Cavan', P O'Donovan, *Ulster Journal of Archaeology* 3 ser 54–55 (1991–2), 129–33*

Clogh Oughter

Clogh Oughter: a medieval island castle in County Cavan. C Manning. Bray: Archaeology Ireland, 1999* (Heritage guide; 7)

'Inishconnell', in P F O'Donovan, *Archaeological inventory of County Cavan*, 227. Dublin: Stationery Office, 1995*

'Clogh Oughter Castle, Lough Oughter', C Manning, in I Bennett (ed), *Excavations 1987: summary accounts of archaeological excavations in Ireland*, 10–11. Bray: Wordwell, 1988

'Clogh Oughter Castle', C Manning, *Breifne* 8.1 (1989–90), 20–61*

'Medieval Britain and Ireland in 1987', S M Youngs [et al], *Medieval Archaeology* 32 (1988), 295

'Post-medieval Britain in 1987', G Egan, *Post-Medieval Archaeology* 22 (1988), 194–95

Lisnamaine
'Lisnamaine Castle', H O'Reilly, *Breifne* 6.23 (1985), 263–76

Tonymore
'Tonymore', in P F O'Donovan, *Archaeological inventory of County Cavan*, 235. Dublin: Stationery Office, 1995*

CLARE

Breen. M. 'A 1570 list of castles in County Clare', *North Munster Antiquarian Journal* 36 (1995), 130–38

Breen, M and Ua Cróinín, R. 'Some north-west Clare tower-houses', *The Other Clare* 21 (1997), 5–14* [see also Ua Cróinín, below]

Breen, M and Ua Cróinín, R. 'Some recently located towerhouse sites, *ibid* 24 (2000), 5–9*

Breen, M and Ua Cróinín, R. 'Some restored towerhouses in the Burren area of Co Clare', *ibid* 26 (2002), 8–15*

Breen, M and Ua Cróinín, R. 'Some more towerhouses in east Clare', *ibid* 28 (2004), 5–9*

Gosling, P. 'The Burren in medieval times', in J W O'Connell and A Korff (eds), *The book of Burren*, 119–34. Kinvara: Tír Eolas, 1991*

Healy, J. 'Kilkeedy parish tower houses', *The Other Clare* 11 (1987), 51–57*

Jones, C. *The Burren and the Aran Islands: exploring the archaeology*. Cork: The Collins Press, 2004*

Marrinan, S. 'The tower houses of south west Clare', *ibid* 8 (1984), 40–44*

O'Donovan, J and Curry, E. *The antiquities of County Clare*. Ennis: CLASP, 1997*

Ó Dálaigh, B, Breen, M and Ua Cróinín, R. 'The Edenvale Survey of Co Clare 1671–79', *North Munster Antiquarian Journal* 45 (20050, 33–49*

Ryan, G. 'Some fresh evidence of Norman occupation in the Bunratty area', *The Other Clare* 5 (1981), 12–13*

Ryan, G. 'Medieval tower houses in the barony of Bunratty Lower', *ibid* 7 (1983), 17–21*

Salter, M. *The castles of north Munster*. Malvern: Folly Publications, 2004*

Sherlock, R. 'Notes on the architectural features of a number of east Clare tower houses', *Sliabh Aughty* 7 (1997), 19–22*

Ua Cróinín, R and Breen, M. 'Disappearing towers', *The Other Clare* 14 (1990), 5–9*

Ua Cróinín, R and Breen, M. 'The hidden towers', *ibid* 16 (1992), 5–10*

Ua Cróinín, R and Breen, M. 'Some obscure tower sites in the Corofin area', *ibid* 17 (1993), 5–12*

Ua Cróinín, R and Breen, M. 'Tower houses in the Corofin area (continued)', *ibid* 18 (1994), 23–27*

Ua Cróinín, R and Breen, M. 'Some Atlantic tower houses', *ibid* 19 (1995), 22–28*

Ua Cróinín, R and Breen, M. 'Some tower houses with bawns in the Burren', *ibid* 20 (1996), 5–13*

Ua Cróinín, R and Breen, M. 'Some tower houses in the vicinity of Ennis', *ibid* 22 (1998), 5–13*

Ua Cróinín, R and Breen, M. 'Some tower houses in east Clare', *ibid* 23 (1999), 5–10*

Ua Cróinín, R and Breen, M. 'Some towerhouses in the Burren area of Co Clare', *ibid* 25 (2001), 5–10*

Ua Cróinín, R and Breen, M. 'Some towerhouse sites inn East Clare', *ibid* 27 (2003), 9–13*

Ua Cróinín, R and Breen, M. 'Some towerhouses in the parish of Kilkeedy', *ibid* 29 (2005), 5–10*

Ballinalacken
'Ballinalacken Castle: a stronghold in Corcomroe', S Spellissy, *ibid* 8 (1984), 27–31*

Ballyalla
'Ballyalla: a partial history of other days', S Spellissy, *ibid* 9 (1985), 51–58*

Ballyally
'Irish siege engines, 1641', C Ó Danachair, *Irish Sword* 1 (1949–53), 230–31

Ballycullen
'Ballycullen Castle', R Ua Cróinín and M Breen, *The Other Clare* 12 (1988), 31–33*

Ballyportry
'Living the past', N Maxwell, *Archaeology Ireland* 17.2 (2003), 28–29*

Beal Boru
'Beal Boru, Co Clare', M J O'Kelly, *Journal of the Cork Historical and Archaeological Society* 67 (1962), 1–27*

Bunratty
Bunratty Castle: an illustrated guide to the historic seat of the earls of Thomond. Anon. Shannon: Shannon Free Airport Development, n d*

Bunratty Castle and folk park: a window on the past. E Healy. Bunratty Castle: Shannon Heritage, 1991*

Bunratty Castle. C Lynch. Dublin: Eason, 1984*

'Penn's expedition to Bonratty [sic] in 1646', J R Powell, *Mariner's Mirror* 40 (1954), 4–20*

'Medieval Britain and Ireland in 1990', B S Nenk, S Margeson and M Hurley, *Medieval Archaeology* 35 (1991), 200–1

'Bunratty mound', J H[unt], *North Munster Antiquarian Journal* 8 (1958–61), 88–89

'Bunratty Castle', J Hunt, *ibid* 8 (1958–61), 103–8*

'Heritage in stone. 7. Bunratty Castle', J Hunt, *ibid* 20 (1978), 75–78*

'The medieval borough of Bunratty', J Bradley, *ibid* 30 (1988), 19–25*

'Archaeological trial excavations at Bunratty, Co Clare', J Bradley and H A King, *ibid* 33 (1991), 16–21*

'An inventory of the contents of Bunratty Castle and the will of Henry, fifth earl of Thomond, 1639', B Ó Dálaigh, *ibid* 36 (1995), 139–65*

'Post-medieval Britain and Ireland in 1990', M Ponsford, *Post-Medieval Archaeology* 25 (1991), 124

Cabhail Mór
'Kilnaboy's forgotten fort: the Cabhail Mór', S Spellissy, *The Other Clare* 10 (1986), 47*

Cahermore
'Cahermore stone fort, Co Clare: survey and excavation', M Fitzpatrick, *North Munster Antiquarian Journal* 41 (2001), 45–64*

Carrigaholt
'Carrigaholt Castle, Carrigaholt', L Dunne, in I Bennett (ed), *Excavations 2002: summary accounts of archaeological excavations in Ireland*, 36–37. Bray: Wordwell, 2004

'Carrigaholt's proud past', U O'Reilly, *The Other Clare* 3 (1979), 12–15*

Castletown
'Window spandrels from Castletown (Doora) Castle, near Ennis', S Ó Murchadh, *North Munster Antiquarian Journal* 36 (1995), 172*

Clare
'A find from the other Clare Castle [Suffolk]', P Holland, *ibid* 30 (1988), 54–55

'A history of Clare Castle, 1248–1891', B Ó Dálaigh, *The Other Clare* 13 (1989), 40–48*

Clarecastle
'Historical notes on Clarecastle', P Stanley, *ibid* 3 (1979), 9–11*

'A reinterpretation of the castle at Clarecastle', B Hodkinson, *ibid* 28 (2004), 55–58*

Clenagh

'Clenagh Castle', R Ua Cróinín and M Breen, *ibid* 13 (1989), 62–63*

Clonroad

'History of an O'Brien stronghold: Clonroad *c* 1210–1626', B Ó Dálaigh, *North Munster Antiquarian Journal* 29 (1987), 16–31*

Daingean ui Bhigin

'Daingean ui Bhigin Castle, Quin, Co Clare', R Ua Cróinín and M Breen, *The Other Clare* 10 (1986), 52–53*

Doonlicka

'Reconstructing the past: charting the destruction of Doonlicka Castle, Co Clare', R M Chapple, *North Munster Antiquarian Journal* 40 (2000), 53–62*

Drimmeen

' "Móin na gCaoineach" tower-house, Drimmeen, Co Clare', M A Timoney, *ibid* 15 (1972), 13–16*

Dromoland

'Old Dromoland Castle', I O'Brien, *The Other Clare* 8 (1984), 58–59

Dromore

'Dromore Castle – Ruan', R Ua Cróinín and M Breen, *ibid* 8 (1984), 14–15*

Dysert O'Dea

'O'Dea's Castle, Dysert', D B Gibson, in I Bennett (ed), *Excavations 1995: summary accounts of archaeological excavations in Ireland*, 3–4. Bray: Wordwell, 1996

'O'Dea's Castle, Dysert', D B Gibson, in I Bennett (ed), *Excavations 1996: summary accounts of archaeological excavations in Ireland*, 7. Bray: Wordwell, 1997

'Dysert O'Dea Castle, Co Clare', R Ua Cróinín and M Breen, *The Other Clare* 9 (1985), 17–18*

'Archaeological excavation at Dysert O'Dea 1995', J O'Dea, *ibid* 20 (1996), 33*

'1996 excavation at O'Dea's Castle, Dysert O'Dea, County Clare: summary report', D B Gibson, *ibid* 21 (1997), 47–48*

Gragan

'Gragan Castle, Gragan West', D Lavelle, in I Bennett (ed), *Excavations 1994: summary accounts of archaeological excavations in Ireland*, 8–9. Bray: Wordwell, 1995

Inchiquin

'Inchiquin Castle', R Ua Cróinín and M Breen, *The Other Clare* 7 (1983), 42

IRELAND

Knappogue

Knappogue: the story of an Irish castle. C O'Carroll. Cork: Mercier Press. 2002*

Leamaneh

'Leamaneh: an O'Brien castle and manor house', J [W] O'Connell and P Gosling, in J W O'Connell and A Korff (eds), *The book of Burren*, 135–40. Kinvara: Tír Eolas, 1991*

'Leamaneh Castle, Leamaneh North', C Grant, in I Bennett (ed), *Excavations 2002: summary accounts of archaeological excavations in Ireland*, 47. Bray: Wordwell, 2004

Lisdoonvarna

'Inscribed stone plaque from Lisdoonvarna Castle', E Rynne, *North Munster Antiquarian Journal* 10 (1966–7), 74–76*

Newtown

'Newtown Castle, Newtown', D Lavelle, in I Bennett (ed), *Excavations 1993: summary accounts of archaeological excavations in Ireland*, 5. Bray: Wordwell, 1994

'Newtown Castle, Newtown', D Lavelle, in I Bennett (ed), *Excavations 1994: summary accounts of archaeological excavations in Ireland*, 9–10. Bray: Wordwell, 1995

'Newtown Castle', P Harbison, *Archaeological Journal* 153 (1996), 346–48*

Quin

'Was Quin Castle completed?', B Hodkinson, *North Munster Antiquarian Journal* 44 (2004), 53–58*

Rine

'Silent guns: two pieces of early 19th century ordnance on the shores of Galway Bay', P Gosling, *Journal of the Galway Archaeological and Historical Society* 42 (1989–90), 139–43*

Rossroe

'Rossroe Castle', R Ua Cróinín and M Breen, *The Other Clare* 6 (1982), 10

Smithstown

'Smithstown or Ballynagowan Castle, Smithstown', R Crumlish, in I Bennett (ed), *Excavations 1996: summary accounts of archaeological excavations in Ireland*, 9–10. Bray: Wordwell, 1997

Urlanmore

'Recent collapse of Urlanmore tower house', R Ua Cróinín, *The Other Clare* 23 (1999), 53*

CORK

Carroll, M J. *The castles and fortified houses of west Cork*. Bantry: Bantry Studio Publications, 2001*

Hartnett, P J. 'Some Imokilly castles', *Journal of the Cork Historical and Archaeological Society* 50 (1945), 42–53*

Healy, J N. *The castles of Cork*. Dublin: Mercier Press, 1988*

Kerrigan, P M. 'Signal towers on the west Cork coast', *Mizen Journal* 11 (2003), 29–45*

Mould, D D C P. *Discovering Cork*. Dingle: Brandon Books, 1991*

O'Keeffe, T. 'Lordship and colony: Anglo-Norman settlement in north Cork', *Mallow Field Club Journal* 22 (2004), 155–66

Ó Laoghaire, P. 'Tower castles of the O Mahonys', *Mizen Journal* 10 (2002), 120–27 [reprint of item below; not illustrated]

Ó Laoghaire, P. 'Tower castles of the O Mahonys', *The O Mahony Journal* 11 (1981), 17–22*

Potter, I N. 'O Mahony castles of Ivagha', *ibid* 2 (1972), 7–11*

Power, D. *Archaeological inventory of County Cork. 1: west Cork*. Dublin: Stationery Office, 1992*

Power, D. *Archaeological inventory of County Cork. 2: east and south Cork*. Dublin: Stationery Office, 1994*

Power, D. *Archaeological inventory of County Cork. 3: mid Cork*. Dublin: Stationery Office, 1997*

Power, D. *Archaeological inventory of County Cork. 4: north Cork*. Dublin: Stationery Office, 2000*

Salter, M. *The castles of south Munster*. Malvern: Folly Publications, 2004*

Samuel, M. 'A tentative chronology for tower houses in west Cork', *Journal of the Cork Historical and Archaeological Society* 103 (1998), 105–24*

Snodgrass, L. 'O Mahony towers on the Mizen peninsula', *The O Mahony Journal* 11 (1981), 40–41*

Stevenson, I. 'The Cork harbour defences', *The Redan* 42 (1998), 18–40*

Aghamarta
'Aghamarta', in D Power, *Archaeological inventory of County Cork. 2: east and south Cork*, 218. Dublin: Stationery Office, 1994

Aghern
'Aghern West', in *ibid*, 214

Ardintenant
'Ardintenant Castle', J Hawkes, *Mizen Journal* 11 (2003), 1–28*

Ashgrove
'Ashgrove', in D Power, *Archaeological inventory of County Cork. 2: east and south Cork*, 218. Dublin: Stationery Office, 1994

Ballinacarriga
'Ballinacarriga', in D Power, *Archaeological inventory of County Cork. 1: west Cork*, 321–22. Dublin: Stationery Office, 1992*

Ballincollig
'Ballincollig', in D Power, *Archaeological inventory of County Cork. 3: mid Cork*, 356–57. Dublin: Stationery Office, 1997*

Ballinoroher
'Ballinoroher', in *ibid*, 322

Ballintotis
'Ballintotis', in D Power, *Archaeological inventory of County Cork. 2: east and south Cork*, 219. Dublin: Stationery Office, 1994

Ballinvard
'Ballinvard', in *ibid*, 322*

Ballyannan
'Ballyannan', in D Power, *Archaeological inventory of County Cork. 2: east and south Cork*, 233. Dublin: Stationery Office, 1994*

Ballyderown
'Ballyderown', in D Power, *Archaeological inventory of County Cork. 4: north Cork*, 515. Dublin: Stationery Office, 2000*

'An early Anglo-Norman castle at Ballyderown, county Cork', T O'Keeffe, *Journal of the Royal Society of Antiquaries of Ireland* 114 (1984), 48–56*

Ballymacphilip
'Ballymacphilip', in D Power, *Archaeological inventory of County Cork. 4: north Cork*, 515–16. Dublin: Stationery Office, 2000*

Ballymaloe More
'Ballymaloe More', in D Power, *Archaeological inventory of County Cork. 2: east and south Cork*, 219–20. Dublin: Stationery Office, 1994

Ballynamona
'Ballynamona', in D Power, *Archaeological inventory of County Cork. 4: north Cork*, 523. Dublin: Stationery Office, 2000*

Baltimore

'In a harbour long ago', C Kelleher, in J Fenwick (ed), *Lost and found: discovering Ireland's past*, 273–86. Bray: Wordwell, 2003*

'An early 17th century map of Baltimore', E J Priestly, *Journal of the Cork Historical and Archaeological Society* 89 (1994), 55–57*

Bandon

Irish historic towns atlas. 3. Bandon. P O'Flanagan. Dublin: Royal Irish Academy, 1988*

'Town walls (Gully townland), Bandon', M F Hurley, in I Bennett (ed), *Excavations 2000: summary accounts of archaeological excavations in Ireland*, 39–40. Bray: Wordwell, 2002

'Gully, Bandon', S Lane, in I Bennett (ed), *Excavations 2001: summary accounts of archaeological excavations in Ireland*, 31. Bray: Wordwell, 2003

'Gully, Bandon', S Lane, in I Bennett (ed), *Excavations 2002: summary accounts of archaeological excavations in Ireland*, 58. Bray: Wordwell, 2004

'Bennett's *History* and the walls of Bandon', P Connolly, *Bandon Historical Journal* 22 (1985), 55–60*

Bantry Bay

Bantry Bay: a fortified landscape in west Cork. C Breen, W Forsythe and R Quinn. Bray: Archaeology Ireland, 2002* (Heritage guide; 19)

Barnahely

'Barnahely', in D Power, *Archaeological inventory of County Cork. 2: east and south Cork*, 220–21. Dublin: Stationery Office, 1994

Barryscourt

Medieval Ireland: the Barryscourt Lectures I-X. J Ludlow and N Jameson (eds). Kinsale: Gandon Editions, 2004*

Barryscourt Castle: an architectural survey. J Monk and R Tobin. Carrigtwohill: Barryscourt Trust, 1991*

Barryscourt Castle and the Irish tower-house. T O'Keeffe. Carrigtwohill: Barryscourt Trust, 1999* (Barryscourt lectures; 1)

The bawn exposed: recent excavations at Barryscourt. D Pollock. Carrigtwohill: Barryscourt Trust, 1999* (Barryscourt lectures; 5)

'Barryscourt', in D Power, *Archaeological inventory of County Cork. 2: east and south Cork*, 221–22. Dublin: Stationery Office, 1994*

'Barryscourt Castle, Barryscourt', O Finch, in I Bennett (ed), *Excavations 1992: summary accounts of archaeological excavations in Ireland*, 5–6. Bray: Wordwell, 1993

'A resistivity survey at Barryscourt Castle, Co Cork', M Byrne, in I Bennett (ed), *Excavations 1994: summary accounts of archaeological excavations in Ireland*, 88–89. Bray: Wordwell, 1995*

'Barryscourt Castle, Barryscourt', D Pollock, in I Bennett (ed), *Excavations 1996: summary accounts of archaeological excavations in Ireland*, 10–11. Bray: Wordwell, 1997

'Barryscourt Castle, Carrigtwohill', D Pollock, in I Bennett (ed), *Excavations 1997: summary accounts of archaeological excavations in Ireland*, 9. Bray: Wordwell, 1998*

'Barryscourt Castle, Carrigtwohill', D Pollock, in I Bennett (ed), *Excavations 1998: summary accounts of archaeological excavations in Ireland*, 15–16. Bray: Wordwell, 2000

'Barryscourt Castle, Carrigtwohill', D Pollock, in I Bennett (ed), *Excavations 1999: summary accounts of archaeological excavations in Ireland*, 24–25. Bray: Wordwell, 2000

'Barryscourt Castle, Carrigtwohill', D Pollock, in I Bennett (ed), *Excavations 2000: summary accounts of archaeological excavations in Ireland*, 41–42. Bray: Wordwell, 2002

'Medieval Britain and Ireland in 1996', B S Nenk, C Haith and J Bradley, *Medieval Archaeology* 41 (1997), 303

'Post-medieval Britain and Ireland in 1996', M Ponsford and R Jackson, *Post-Medieval Archaeology* 31 (1997), 300

Benduff

'Benduff', in D Power, *Archaeological inventory of County Cork. 1: west Cork*, 322. Dublin: Stationery Office, 1992

Bere Island

'Ardagh (Bere Island): martello tower', J Kiely, in I Bennett (ed), *Excavations 2000: summary accounts of archaeological excavations in Ireland*, 38. Bray: Wordwell, 2002

'The misplaced guns of Berehaven', I Stevenson, *The Redan* 37 (1996), 23–37*

Blackrock

'Mahon', in D Power, *Archaeological inventory of County Cork. 2: east and south Cork*, 229–30. Dublin: Stationery Office, 1994*

Blarney

Blarney Castle in the county of Cork, Ireland: a short history and guide. R Colthurst. 11th edition. Killarney: Killarney Printing Works, 1974*

'Blarney', in D Power, *Archaeological inventory of County Cork. 3: mid Cork*, 357–60. Dublin: Stationery Office, 1997*

Camden Fort

'Crosshaven Hill', in D Power, *Archaeological inventory of County Cork. 2: east and south Cork*, 289–90. Dublin: Stationery Office, 1994*

Carrigabrick

'Carrigabrick', in D Power, *Archaeological inventory of County Cork. 4: north Cork*, 525. Dublin: Stationery Office, 2000*

Carrigadrohid

'Carrigadrohid', in D Power, *Archaeological inventory of County Cork. 3: mid Cork*, 360–61. Dublin: Stationery Office, 1997*

Carrigaline

'Carrigaline East', in D Power, *Archaeological inventory of County Cork. 2: east and south Cork*, 215. Dublin: Stationery Office, 1994*

Carriganass

'Carriganass', in D Power, *Archaeological inventory of County Cork. 1: west Cork*, 322–23. Dublin: Stationery Office, 1992

'Carriganass', E Cotter, in I Bennett (ed), *Excavations 2002: summary accounts of archaeological excavations in Ireland*, 63. Bray: Wordwell, 2004

'Carriganass Castle Carriganass', C Breen, in *ibid*, 63

'Carriganass Castle, Carriganass', J Kiely, in *ibid*, 63

Carrignamuck

'Carrignamuck', in D Power, *Archaeological inventory of County Cork. 3: mid Cork*, 362–63. Dublin: Stationery Office, 1997*

Castle Barrett

'Castlebarrett', in D Power, *Archaeological inventory of County Cork. 3: mid Cork*, 354–55. Dublin: Stationery Office, 1997*

Castledonovan

'Castledonovan', in D Power, *Archaeological inventory of County Cork. 1: west Cork*, 324. Dublin: Stationery Office, 1992

'Castledonovan', A Quinn, in I Bennett (ed), *Excavations 2002: summary accounts of archaeological excavations in Ireland*, 65. Bray: Wordwell, 2004

Castle Inch

'Castle Inch, Co Cork', E M Fahy, *Journal of the Cork Historical and Archaeological Society* 62 (1957), 1–13*

Castlemartyr

'Castlemartyr', in D Power, *Archaeological inventory of County Cork. 2: east and south Cork*, 223–25. Dublin: Stationery Office, 1994*

IRELAND

Castleredmond
'Castleredmond, Midleton', S Lane, in I Bennett (ed), *Excavations 2001: summary accounts of archaeological excavations in Ireland*, 49. Bray: Wordwell, 2003

Clodah
'Clodah', in D Power, *Archaeological inventory of County Cork. 3: mid Cork*, 365–67. Dublin: Stationery Office, 1997*

Cloghleagh
'Moorepark,', in D Power, *Archaeological inventory of County Cork. 4: north Cork*, 537–38. Dublin: Stationery Office, 2000*

Conna
'Conna', in D Power, *Archaeological inventory of County Cork. 2: east and south Cork*, 226. Dublin: Stationery Office, 1994*

'Conna Castle, Co Cork', J G Barry, *Irish Sword* 2 (1954–6), 235–37

Coppinger's Court
'Coppinger's Court: a document in stone', M Samuel, *Journal of the Cork Historical and Archaeological Society* 89 (1984), 58–76*

Cork
Cork: our city. Anon. Cork: Musaem Chorcai, 1980*

Haulbowline, Spike and Rocky islands in Cork Harbour. N Brunicardi. Cork: Cork Historical Guides Committee, 1968*

Haulbowline, Spike and Rocky islands. N Brunicardi. 2nd edition. Fermoy: Eigse Books, 1982*

Cork City excavations 1984–2000. R M Cleary and M F Hurley (eds). Cork: Cork City Council, 2003*

Skiddy's Castle and Christ Church, Cork: excavations 1974–77 by D C Twohig. R M Cleary, M F Hurley and E S Twohig (eds). Cork: Cork Corporation, 1997*

Excavations at the North Gate, Cork, 1994. M F Hurley. Cork: Cork Corporation, 1997*

Discover Cork. K McCarthy. Dublin: O'Brien Press, 2003* (City guides)

Discovering Cork. D D C P Mould. Cork: Brandon, 1991*

The archaeology of Cork city and harbour from the earliest times to industrialisation. C Rynne. Cork: Collins Press, 1993* [espec ch 4]

'The topographical development of Scandinavian and Anglo-Norman Cork', J Bradley and A Halpin, in P O'Flanagan and C G Buttimer (eds), *Cork: history and society. Interdisciplinary essays on the history of an Irish county*, 15–44. Dublin: Geography Publications, 1993*

'Cork and Kinsale harbours', in G A Hayes-McCoy (ed), *Ulster and other Irish maps c 1600*, 3–4. Dublin: Stationery Office for the Irish Manuscripts Commission, 1964*

'Municipal borough of Cork, Grand Parade', M Hurley, in C Cotter (ed), *Excavations 1985: summary account of archaeological excavations in Ireland*, 13. Dublin: Irish Academic Publications, 1986

'81–83 Grand Parade, Cork', J Wren, in I Bennett (ed), *Excavations 1992: summary accounts of archaeological excavations in Ireland*, 9. Bray: Wordwell, 1993

'Kyrls Quay/North Main St, Cork', M F Hurley, in *ibid*, 8–9

'North Gate, Cork', M F Hurley, in I Bennett (ed), *Excavations 1994: summary accounts of archaeological excavations in Ireland*, 10. Bray: Wordwell, 1995*

'17 Grattan Street, Cork', M F Hurley, in I Bennett (ed), *Excavations 1997: summary accounts of archaeological excavations in Ireland*, 10. Bray: Wordwell, 1998

'North Main Street/Castle Street/Adelaide Street/Liberty Street/Daunt Square/Paradise Place, Cork', C Power, in *ibid*, 10

'Philips Lane/Grattan Street, Cork', M O'Donnell, in *ibid*, 10–11

'Grattan Street, Cork', T Cummins, in I Bennett (ed), *Excavations 1998: summary accounts of archaeological excavations in Ireland*, 18. Bray: Wordwell, 2000

'14–21 Hanover Street, Cork', S Lane, in I Bennett (ed), *Excavations 2000: summary accounts of archaeological excavations in Ireland*, 43. Bray: Wordwell, 2002

'Grand Parade and Washington Street, Cork', H Kelleher, in I Bennett (ed), *Excavations 2002: summary accounts of archaeological excavations in Ireland*, 69–70. Bray: Wordwell, 2004*

'The medieval town wall of Cork', M Hurley and D Power, *Journal of the Cork Historical and Archaeological Society* 86 (1981), 1–20*

'An antiquary's notebook 3', C J F MacCarthy, *ibid* 87 (1982), 58–63*

'Excavations of part of the medieval city wall at Grand Parade, Cork', M F Hurley, *ibid* 90 (1985), 65–90*

'The Cork suburb of Dungarvan', A Candon, *ibid* 90 (1985), 91–103*

'Excavations in medieval Cork: St Peter's Market', M F Hurley, *ibid* 91 (1986), 1–25*

'Medieval town wall off Lambley's Lane, Cork city', R M Cleary, *ibid* 93 (1988), 104–9*

'The siege of Cork in 1690', D Ó Murchadha, *ibid* 95 (1990), 1–19*

'An antiquary's note book 12: Cork harbour defences', C J F MacCarthy, *ibid* 95 (1990), 159–60

'Excavations in Cork city: Kyrl's Quay/North Main Street and at Grand Parade (part 1)', M F Hurley, *ibid* 100 (1995), 47–90*

'Excavations in Cork city: Kyrl's Quay/North Main Street and at Grand Parade (part 2)', M F Hurley, *ibid* 101 (1996), 26–63*

'An archaeological survey of Elizabeth Fort, a seventeenth-century artillery fortification in Cork City', C Rynne, *ibid* 109 (2004), 199–216*

'Elizabeth Fort, Cork', M Mulcahy [*et al*], *Irish Sword* 4 (1959–60), 127–34*

'Note on the history of Haulbowline', D N Brunicardi, *ibid* 7 (1965–6), 19–33*

'Marlborough's siege of Cork, 1690', J G Simms, *ibid* 9 (1969–70), 113–23*

'Medieval Britain and Ireland in 1983', S M Youngs, J Clark and T Barry, *Medieval Archaeology* 28 (1984), 254–55

'Medieval Britain and Ireland in 1985', S M Youngs, J Clark and T Barry, *ibid* 30 (1986), 183

'Medieval Britain and Ireland in 1990', B S Nenk. S Margeson and M Hurley, *ibid* 35 (1991), 203

'Medieval Britain and Ireland in 1992', B S Nenk. S Margeson and M Hurley, *ibid* 37 (1993), 291

'Medieval Britain and Ireland in 1994', B S Nenk. S Margeson and M Hurley, *ibid* 39 (1995), 265–66

'Medieval Britain and Ireland in 1996', B S Nenk, C Haith and J Bradley, *ibid* 41 (1997), 303

'Medieval Britain and Ireland in 1997', M Gaimster, C Haith and J Bradley, *ibid* 42 (1998), 157, 158

'Medieval Britain and Ireland in 1999', J Bradley and M Gaimster, *ibid* 44 (2000), 316–17

'Medieval Britain and Ireland in 2000', J Bradley and M Gaimster, *ibid* 45 (2001), 340

'Medieval Britain and Ireland in 2004', M Gaimster and K O'Conor, *ibid* 49 (2005), 424

'Post-medieval Britain and Ireland in 1992', M Ponsford, *Post-Medieval Archaeology* 27 (1993), 218

Cregg
'Cregg North', in D Power, *Archaeological inventory of County Cork. 4: north Cork*, 532–33. Dublin: Stationery Office, 2000*

Curbeigh
'Medieval Britain and Ireland in 1982', S M Youngs, J Clark and T B Barry, *Medieval Archaeology* 27 (1983), 216

Doonanore
'Ballyieragh, Clear Island', in D Power, *Archaeological inventory of County Cork. 1: west Cork*, 322. Dublin: Stationery Office, 1992

Downdaniel
'Skevanish', in *ibid*, 321

Downmacpatrick
'Downmacpatrick or Old Head', in D Power, *Archaeological inventory of County Cork. 2: east and south Cork*, 227–28. Dublin: Stationery Office, 1994

'Downmacpatrick or Old Head', R M Cleary, in I Bennett (ed), *Excavations 1996: summary accounts of archaeological excavations in Ireland*, 12. Bray: Wordwell, 1997

Drishane
'Drishane More', in D Power, *Archaeological inventory of County Cork. 3: mid Cork*, 367–68. Dublin: Stationery Office, 1997*

Dromaneen
'Dromaneen', in D Power, *Archaeological inventory of County Cork. 4: north Cork*, 541–42. Dublin: Stationery Office, 2000*

'Dromaneen Castle: an O'Callaghan stronghold', D Power, *Mallow Field Club Journal* 17 (1999), 5–17*

Dun Mic Oghmainn
'The castle of Dun Mic Oghmainn and the overlordship of Carbery', D Ó Murchadha, *Journal of the Cork Historical and Archaeological Society* 93 (1988), 73–82*

Dunasead
'Dunasead Castle, Baltimore', E Cotter, in I Bennett (ed), *Excavations 1998: summary accounts of archaeological excavations in Ireland*, 13–14. Bray: Wordwell, 2000

'Baltimore', E Cotter, in I Bennett (ed), *Excavations 2002: summary accounts of archaeological excavations in Ireland*, 57–58. Bray: Wordwell, 2004

Dunboy
'Dunboy', E M Fahy, in T G Delaney (ed), *Excavations 1972: summary reports of archaeological excavations in Ireland*, 7. [S l]: Association of Young Irish Archaeologists, n d

'Dunboy', E M Fahy, in T G Delaney (ed), *Excavations 1973: summary reports of archaeological excavations in Ireland*, 7. [S l: s n], n d

'Dunboy Castle, Dunboy', E Klingelhöfer, in I Bennett (ed), *Excavations 1989: summary accounts of archaeological excavations in Ireland*, 15–16. Bray: Wordwell, 1990

'Dunboy Castle, Co Cork', E M Fahy and M Gowen, *Journal of the Cork Historical and Archaeological Society* 83 (1978), 1–49*

'The Renaissance fortifications at Dunboy Castle, 1602: a report of the 1989 excavations', E Klingelhöfer, *ibid* 97 (1992), 85–96*

'Post-medieval Britain and Ireland in 1989', G Egan, *Post-Medieval Archaeology* 24 (1989), 166–67

Dunalong
'Farranacoush, Skerkin Island', in D Power, *Archaeological inventory of County Cork. 1: west Cork*, 327. Dublin: Stationery Office, 1992

Dundeady
'Dundeady', in *ibid*, 325–26

Dunlough
'Dunlough', in *ibid*, 325–26*

Dunmanus
'Dunmanus West', in *ibid*, 326*

'Dunmanus Castle', J Hawkes, *Mizen Journal* 7 (1999), 4–19*

Glanworth
Glanworth: a medieval castle, friary and town in County Cork. C Manning. Bray: Archaeology Ireland, 2000* (Heritage guide; 9)

'Boherash', in D Power, *Archaeological inventory of County Cork. 4: north Cork*, 516. Dublin: Stationery Office, 2000

'Medieval Britain and Ireland in 1982', S M Youngs, J Clark and T B Barry, *Medieval Archaeology* 27 (1983), 216

'Medieval Britain and Ireland in 1983', S M Youngs, J Clark and T B Barry, *ibid* 28 (1984), 254

'Medieval Britain and Ireland in 1984', S M Youngs, J Clark and T Barry, *ibid* 29 (1985), 213

'Rectangular keeps of the thirteenth century at Grenan (Kilkenny) and Glanworth (Cork)', D M Waterman, *Journal of the Royal Society of Antiquaries of Ireland* 98 (1968), 67–73*

Ightermurragh
'Ightermurragh', in D Power, *Archaeological inventory of County Cork. 2: east and south Cork*, 234. Dublin: Stationery Office, 1994*

Kanturk
'Paal East', in D Power, *Archaeological inventory of County Cork. 4: north Cork*, 544. Dublin: Stationery Office, 2000*

'Kanturk Castle', J Bolton, *Heritage Outlook* winter/spring (2006–7), 30–31*

Kilbolane
'Kilbolane', in D Power, *Archaeological inventory of County Cork. 4: north Cork*, 517–18. Dublin: Stationery Office, 2000*

Kilcoe

'Kilcoe', in D Power, *Archaeological inventory of County Cork. 1: west Cork*, 328. Dublin: Stationery Office, 1992*

'Kilcoe Castle, Kilcoe', E Cotter, in I Bennett (ed), *Excavations 1998: summary accounts of archaeological excavations in Ireland*, 20. Bray: Wordwell, 2000

'Kilcoe Castle, Kilcoe', J Kiely, in I Bennett (ed), *Excavations 1999: summary accounts of archaeological excavations in Ireland*, 24–25. Bray: Wordwell, 2000

'Kilcoe', E Cotter, in I Bennett (ed), *Excavations 2001: summary accounts of archaeological excavations in Ireland*, 44. Bray: Wordwell, 2003

'Kilcoe Castle and the clan Dermod MacCarthy', J Hawkes, *Mizen Journal* 8 (2000), 4–27*

Kilcolman

'Kilcolman Castle', D N Johnson, in A C Hamilton (gen ed), *The Spenser encyclopaedia*, 417–22. Toronto: University of Toronto Press; London: Routledge, 1990*

'Kilcolman Castle, Kilcolman Middle', E Klingelhöfer, in I Bennett (ed), *Excavations 1994: summary accounts of archaeological excavations in Ireland*, 13–14. Bray: Wordwell, 1995*

'Kilcolman Castle, Kilcolman Middle', E Klingelhöfer, in I Bennett (ed), *Excavations 1995: summary accounts of archaeological excavations in Ireland*, 7–8. Bray: Wordwell, 1996

'Kilcolman Castle, Kilcolman Middle', E Klingelhöfer, in I Bennett (ed), *Excavations 1996: summary accounts of archaeological excavations in Ireland*, 13–14. Bray: Wordwell, 1997

'Castle of the *Faerie Queene*: probing the ruins of Edmund Spenser's Irish home', E Klingelhöfer, *Archaeology* 52.2 (1999), 48–52*

'Medieval Britain and Ireland in 1996', B S Nenk, C Haith and J Bradley, *Medieval Archaeology* 41 (1997), 303–4

'Edmund Spenser at Kilcolman Castle: the archaeological evidence', E Klingelhöfer, *Post-Medieval Archaeology* 39 (2005), 133–54*

Kilmeedy

'Kilmeedy East', in D Power, *Archaeological inventory of County Cork. 3: mid Cork*, 369–70. Dublin: Stationery Office, 1997*

Kilnatoora

'Kilnatoora', in D Power, *Archaeological inventory of County Cork. 2: east and south Cork*, 228–29. Dublin: Stationery Office, 1994

Kinsale

Charles Fort, Kinsale, Co Cork. Anon. Dublin: National Parks and Monuments Service, 1979*

Charles Fort visitors' guide. Anon. Dublin: Dúchas The Heritage Service, n d*

Desmond Castle visitors' guide. Anon. Dublin: Dúchas The Heritage Service, n d*

The battle of Kinsale. H Morgan (ed). Bray: Wordwell, 2004*

A short history of Kinsale. M Mulcahy. Cork: Cork Historical Guides Committee, 1966*

Kinsale: Spanish intervention in Ireland at the end of the Elizabethan wars. J J Silke. Liverpool: Liverpool University Press, 1970*

'Old-Fort: James's Fort', in D Power, *Archaeological inventory of County Cork. 2: east and south Cork*, 288. Dublin: Stationery Office, 1994*

'Old-Fort: blockhouse', in *ibid*, 291

'The siege of Kinsale', in G A Hayes-McCoy (ed), *Ulster and other Irish maps c 1600*, 22–23. Dublin: Stationery Office for the Irish Manuscripts Commission, 1964*

'Castle Park, Kinsale', in *ibid*, 33*

'Charles Fort, Forthill, Kinsale', M McCarthy, in I Bennett (ed), *Excavations 1998: summary accounts of archaeological excavations in Ireland*, 20–21. Bray: Wordwell, 2000

'James's Fort, Old-Fort, Kinsale', M O'Donnell, in *ibid*, 21–22

'James Fort, old-fort', M G O'Donnell, in I Bennett (ed), *Excavations 2003: summary accounts of archaeological excavations in Ireland*, 71. Bray: Wordwell, 2006

'The fortifications of Kinsale, Co Cork', P M Kerrigan, *An Cosantóir* 32 (1972), 239–45*

'Excavations at James Fort, Kinsale, 1974–98', M G O'Donnell, *Journal of the Cork Historical and Archaeological Society* 107 (2002), 1–70*

'del Aguila's defence of Kinsale (1601–1602)', H Mangan, *Irish Sword* 1 (1949–53), 218–24

'An indictment of Don Juan del Aguila', F M Jones, *ibid* 2 (1954–6), 217–23, with comments by H Mangan on pp 220–23

'A vindication of Don Juan del Aguila', H Mangan, *ibid* 2 (1954–6), 343–51

'Charles Fort, Kinsale', P M Kerrigan, *ibid* 13 (1978–9), 323–38*

'Charles Fort – history', anon, *Oibre: Bulletin of the Commissioners of Public Works* 14 (1980), 23–48

Liscarroll

'Liscarroll', in D Power, *Archaeological inventory of County Cork. 4: north Cork*, 520–21. Dublin: Stationery Office, 2000*

Lisgriffin

'Lisgriffin', in D Power, *Archaeological inventory of County Cork. 4: north Cork*, 543–44. Dublin: Stationery Office, 2000*

Lohort

'Castlelohort demesne', in D Power, *Archaeological inventory of County Cork. 4: north Cork*, 528–29. Dublin: Stationery Office, 2000*

Mallow

'Castlelands', in *ibid*, 540–41.

'Mallow Castle', K Myers, *Mallow Field Club Journal* 13 (1995), 5–19*

Mashanaglass

'Mashanaglass', in D Power, *Archaeological inventory of County Cork. 3: mid Cork*, 370–71. Dublin: Stationery Office, 1997*

Mogeely

'Mogeely Lower', in D Power, *Archaeological inventory of County Cork. 2: east and south Cork*, 216–17. Dublin: Stationery Office, 1994*

'Elizabethan settlements: Mogeely Castle, Curraglass, and Carrigeen, Co Cork (part I)', E Klingelhöfer, *Journal of the Cork Historical and Archaeological Society* 104 (1999), 97–110*

'Medieval Britain and Ireland in 1991', B S Nenk, S Margeson and M Hurley, *Medieval Archaeology* 36 (1992), 280

Monkstown

'Monkstown', in D Power, *Archaeological inventory of County Cork. 2: east and south Cork*, 235–36. Dublin: Stationery Office, 1994*

Newtown

'Newtown: 17th-century fort and village', C Breen, in I Bennett (ed), *Excavations 2000: summary accounts of archaeological excavations in Ireland*, 50–51. Bray: Wordwell, 2002

Raheen

'Raheen', in D Power, *Archaeological inventory of County Cork. 1: west Cork*, 329. Dublin: Stationery Office, 1992

Rathbarry

'Rathbarry Castle, Castlefreke', R Crumlish, in I Bennett (ed), *Excavations 1993: summary accounts of archaeological excavations in Ireland*, 7–8. Bray: Wordwell, 1994

Ringmahon

'Mahon', in D Power, *Archaeological inventory of County Cork. 2: east and south Cork*, 230. Dublin: Stationery Office, 1994*

Rosslague

'Rosslague: martello tower', in D Power, *Archaeological inventory of County Cork. 2: east and south Cork*, 293–94. Dublin: Stationery Office, 1994*

Shanagarry

'Shanagarry Castle, Shanagarry', E Cotter, in I Bennett (ed), *Excavations 1994: summary accounts of archaeological excavations in Ireland*, 15. Bray: Wordwell, 1995

Spike

'Spike: HQ of the Coastal Defence Artillery', D MacCarron, *An Cosantóir* 48.7 (1988), 18–19*

Youghal

'The college grounds, Emmet Place, Youghal', C Power, in I Bennett (ed), *Excavations 1995: summary accounts of archaeological excavations in Ireland*, 9. Bray: Wordwell, 1996

'Hill Cottage, Gaol Steps, Youghal', D Noonan, in I Bennett (ed), *Excavations 2002: summary accounts of archaeological excavations in Ireland*, 95–96. Bray: Wordwell, 2004

'54 Main Street North, Youghal', D Noonan, in I Bennett (ed), *Excavations 2003: summary accounts of archaeological excavations in Ireland*, 78. Bray: Wordwell, 2006

'P Burk(e)'s painting of Youghal: the earliest known signed townscape by an Irish artist', P Harbison, *Journal of the Cork Historical and Archaeological Society* 78 (1973), 66–79*

'Penn's attempt to relieve Youghal, 1645', J R Powell, *Irish Sword* 2 (1954–6), 83–87

'Medieval Britain and Ireland in 1995', B S Nenk, S Margeson and M Hurley, *Medieval Archaeology* 40 (1996), 295

DONEGAL

Anon. 'Why Lough Swilly was defended', *An Cosantóir* 38 (1978), 201*

Clements, W H. 'Captain Sir William Augustus Smith 1751–1831', *Irish Sword* 22.89 (2001), 265–67 [re Lough Swilly]

Lacy, B. 'Castles and fortified buildings to the 17th century', in B Lacy, *Archaeological survey of County Donegal: a description of the field antiquities of the county from the Mesolithic period to the 17th century AD*, 350–84. Lifford: Donegal County Council, 1983*

McKay, R. 'The fortifications of Lough Swilly and Lough Foyle: temporary expedients, 1798–1800', *Donegal Annual* 12.1 (1977), 40–48

Ní Loingsigh, M. 'An assessment of castles and landownership in late medieval north Donegal', *Ulster Journal of Archaeology* 3 ser 57 (1994), 145–58*

Rowan, A. *North west Ulster (The buildings of Ireland)*. Harmondsworth: Penguin Books, 1979*

Salter, M. *The castles of Ulster*. Malvern: Folly Publications, 2004*

Barnesmore
'An eighteenth century redoubt in County Donegal', J C T MacDonagh, *Irish Sword* 1 (1949–53), 338–40

Buncrana
'Tullynarvan: Buncrana Castle', in B Lacy, *Archaeological survey of County Donegal: a description of the field antiquities of the county from the Mesolithic period to the 17th century AD*, 380–81. Lifford: Donegal County Council, 1983*

Burt
'Grange: Burt Castle', in *ibid*, 370–71*

Caol Uisce
'Caol Uisce and Domnach Mór: two medieval mysteries by the Erne', D Ó Seaneachain, *Donegal Annual* 56 (2004), 116–25*

Carrickabraghy
'Carrickabraghy: Carrickabraghy Castle', in B Lacy, *Archaeological survey of County Donegal: a description of the field antiquities of the county from the Mesolithic period to the 17th century AD*, 353–55. Lifford: Donegal County Council, 1983*

Castle Bawne
'Ballyness: Castle Bawne', in *ibid*, 353–54*

Doe
'Castledoe: Doe Castle', in *ibid*, 356–59*

'Doe Castle', H A King, in I Bennett (ed), *Excavations 1998: summary accounts of archaeological excavations in Ireland*, 29. Bray: Wordwell, 2000

'Ghosts of a forgotten castle', G Priest, *Country Life* 107 (1950), 1200–1*

'The story of Doe Castle', J C T MacDonagh, *Donegal Annual* 2.2 (1952), 381–402*

Donegal
Donegal Castle visitors' guide. Anon. Dublin: OPW, n d*

'Donegal: Donegal Castle', in B Lacy, *Archaeological survey of County Donegal: a description of the field antiquities of the county from the Mesolithic period to the 17th century AD*, 361–65. Lifford: Donegal County Council, 1983*

'Donegal Castle, Donegal', F Moore, in I Bennett (ed), *Excavations 2002: summary accounts of archaeological excavations in Ireland*, 111–12. Bray: Wordwell, 2004

'Donegal Castle', T E McNeill and M A Wilkin, *Ulster Journal of Archaeology* 3 ser 58 (1999), 81–89*

Dunree

The guns of Dunree Military Museum – Fort Dunree. D O'Carroll. [S l: s n], n d*

'The Heather Fort', J Fitzgerald, *Donegal Annual* 12.3 (1979), 427–34*

Faugher

'Faugher: Faugher House', in B Lacy, *Archaeological survey of County Donegal: a description of the field antiquities of the county from the Mesolithic period to the 17th century AD*, 367–69. Lifford: Donegal County Council, 1983*

Fortstewart

'Fortstewart: Fortstewart', in *ibid*, 369–70*

Greencastle

'Eleven Ballyboes: Greencastle', in *ibid* 365–67, 380*

'Greencastle', R Ó Baoill and E Halpin, in I Bennett (ed), *Excavations 1996: summary accounts of archaeological excavations in Ireland*, 15. Bray: Wordwell, 1997

'Medieval Britain and Ireland in 1996', B S Nenk, C Haith and J Bradley, *Medieval Archaeology* 41 (1997), 304

'Greencastle, Co Donegal', D M Waterman, *Ulster Journal of Archaeology* 3 ser 21 (1958), 74–88*

Inch

'Castle Quarter: Inch Castle', in B Lacy, *Archaeological survey of County Donegal: a description of the field antiquities of the county from the Mesolithic period to the 17th century AD*, 355–56. Lifford: Donegal County Council, 1983*

Kilbarron

'Cloghbolie: Kilbarron Castle', in *ibid*, 359–61*

Knockalla

'A Napoleonic fort in Donegal', M Donelly, *Country Life* 158 (1975), 748–49*

Lenan

'The coastal defences in Lenan during the Emergency', J Campbell, *Donegal Annual* 43 (1991), 109–17

Lougheask

'Lougheask Demesne: castle', in B Lacy, *Archaeological survey of County Donegal: a description of the field antiquities of the county from the Mesolithic period to the 17th century AD*, 371–72. Lifford: Donegal County Council, 1983* in *ibid*, 371–72*

Lough Eske

'Corveen: Lough Eske Island Castle', in *ibid*, 361* [illustration on p 349]

McSwyne's

'Rahan Near: McSwyne's Castle', in *ibid*, 376–77*

Mongavlin

'Mongavlin: Mongavlin Castle', in *ibid*, 372–74*

'Mongavlin Castle, Co Donegal', E M Jope, *Ulster Journal of Archaeology* 3 ser 17 (1954), 169–72*

Moross

'Moross: Moross Castle', in B Lacy, *Archaeological survey of County Donegal: a description of the field antiquities of the county from the Mesolithic period to the 17th century AD*, 374–76. Lifford: Donegal County Council, 1983*

Northburgh

'Medieval and modern castles in County Donegal', J C T MacDonagh, *Donegal Annual* 3.2 (1956), 123–26

Raphoe

'Raphoe Town Parks: Bishop's Palace', in B Lacy, *Archaeological survey of County Donegal: a description of the field antiquities of the county from the Mesolithic period to the 17th century AD*, 376–79. Lifford: Donegal County Council, 1983*

Termon McGrath

'Aghnahoo Glebe: Termon McGrath Castle', in *ibid*, 351–53*

DOWN

Archaeological Survey. 'Mottes and raised raths', 'Stone castles with keep and bailey', 'Tower-houses' and 'Artillery works', in *An archaeological survey of County Down*, 116–27. Belfast: HMSO, 1966*

Brett, C E B. *Buildings of north County Down*. Belfast: Ulster Architectural Heritage Society, 2002* [espec ch 1]

McErlean, T, McConkey, R and Forsythe, W. *Strangford Lough: an archaeological survey of the maritime cultural landscape*. Belfast: Blackstaff Press: Environment and Heritage Service, 2002* [espec pp 413–17, 587–88]

McNeill, T E. 'County Down in the later Middle Ages', in L Proudfoot (ed), *Down: history and society. Interdisciplinary essays on the history of an Irish county*, 103–22. Dublin: Geography Publications, 1997*

Salter, M. *The castles of Ulster*. Malvern: Folly Publications, 2004*

Ardglass

'Ardglass Castle', in *An archaeological survey of County Down*, 220–22. Belfast: HMSO, 1966*

'Three medieval buildings in the port of Ardglass, Co Down', T E McNeill, *Proceedings of the Royal Irish Academy* 105C (2005), 1–21*

Ardkeen

'Ardkeen', in *An archaeological survey of County Down*, 197–98, 225. Belfast: HMSO, 1966*

'The Castle Hill', P Breen, *Journal of the Upper Ards Historical Society* 7 (1983), 11–14

Ardquin

'Ardquin: the Abbacy', in *An archaeological survey of County Down*, 255–56. Belfast: HMSO, 1966*

Ards

'The baronies of Upper and Lower Ards, Co Down', in G A Hayes-McCoy (ed), *Ulster and other Irish maps c 1600*, 7. Dublin: Stationery Office for the Irish Manuscripts Commission, 1964*

Audley's

Three tower-houses: Audley's Castle, Strangford Castle, Portaferry Castle, County Down. H Dixon. Belfast: HMSO, 1980*

'Audley's Castle', in *An archaeological survey of County Down*, 225–27. Belfast: HMSO, 1966*

'Audley's Castle and the Lecale Audleys', A V Sterritt, *Lecale Miscellany* 4 (1986), 3–6*

Ballydugan

'Ballydugan Td: bawn', in *An archaeological survey of County Down*, 257–59. Belfast: HMSO, 1966*

Ballyfounder

'Excavations at Ballyfounder rath, Co Down', D M Waterman, *Ulster Journal of Archaeology* 3 ser 21 (1958), 39–61*

Ballymaghan

'Medieval Britain in 1966', D M Wilson and D G Hurst, *Medieval Archaeology* 11 (1967), 291

Ballmaghery

'Ballymaghery Td', in *An archaeological survey of County Down*, 190. Belfast: HMSO, 1966*

Ballynarry

'Ballynarry Td', in *ibid*, 191–92*

'Excavations at Ballynarry rath, Co Down', B K Davison, *Ulster Journal of Archaeology* 3 ser 24–5 (1961–2), 39–87*

Ballyroney

'Ballyroney Td', in *An archaeological survey of County Down*, 198. Belfast: HMSO, 1966*

'Excavations at Seafin Castle and Ballyroney motte and bailey: the identification of the castle of Magh Cobha in the light of recent research', D M Waterman, *Ulster Journal of Archaeology* 3 ser 18 (1955), 83–104*

Ballyspurge

'The White House, Ballyspurge', D P Hurl, in I Bennett (ed), *Excavations 1996: summary accounts of archaeological excavations in Ireland*, 15. Bray: Wordwell, 1997

'Post-medieval Britain and Ireland in 1996', M Ponsford and R Jackson, *Post-Medieval Archaeology* 31 (1997), 300

Bonecastle

'Bonecastle Td: Bonecastle', in *An archaeological survey of County Down*, 228. Belfast: HMSO, 1966

Carlingford

'Carlingford Lough: fort', in *ibid*, 228–30*

Castleboy

'Castleboy: Castleboy Td', in *ibid*, 230*

Castle Bright

'Castle Bright: Bright Td', in *ibid*, 230–31*

Castle Island

'Castle Island Td: castle', in *ibid*, 231*

Castlereagh

'The castle of Castlereagh, Co Down', T E McNeill, *Ulster Journal of Archaeology* 3 ser 50 (1987), 123–27*

Castleskreen

'Castleskreen Td: rath 2', in *An archaeological survey of County Down*, 198–200. Belfast: HMSO, 1966*

'Castleskreen', in *ibid*, 231*

'Excavation of a rath with motte at Castleskreen, Co Down', C W Dickinson and D M Waterman, *Ulster Journal of Archaeology* 3 ser 22 (1959), 67–82*

'Excavations at Castleskreen, Co Down', *ibid* C W Dickinson and D M Waterman, 3 ser 23 (1960), 63–77*

Castle Ward

'Castle Ward Td: Castle Ward', in *An archaeological survey of County Down*, 231–

33. Belfast: HMSO, 1966*

Clough

'Clough Td', in *ibid*, 200–3*

'Excavations at Clough Castle, Co Down', D M Waterman, *Ulster Journal of Archaeology* 3 ser 17 (1954), 103–63*

Cowd

'Ardglass: Cowd Castle', in *An archaeological survey of County Down*, 222. Belfast: HMSO, 1966*

Downpatrick

Irish historic towns atlas. 8. Downpatrick. R H Buchanan and A Wilson. Dublin: Royal Irish Academy, 1997*

'Downpatrick', in *An archaeological survey of County Down*, 202–3. Belfast: HMSO, 1966*

Dromore

'Dromore: Ballyricknacally Td', in *ibid*, 203–4*

'Dromore: tower', in *ibid*, 233*

'Excavations at Dromore motte, Co Down', D M Waterman, *Ulster Journal of Archaeology* 3 ser 17 (1954), 164–68*

Dundonald

'Church Quarter', N F Brannon, in 'Excavations bulletin 1977–1979: summary accounts of archaeological excavations in Ireland', *Journal of Irish Archaeology* 4 (1987–8), 71

Dundrum

Dundrum Castle, County Down. A Hamlin. Belfast: HMSO, 1977*

'Dundrum Castle', in *An archaeological survey of County Down*, 207–11. Belfast: HMSO, 1966*

'The Windsor of Ulster', G Priest, *Country Life* 112 (1952), 1555*

'Excavations at Dundrum Castle, 1950', D M Waterman, *Ulster Journal of Archaeology* 3 ser 14 (1951), 15–29*

'A note on Dundrum Castle, Co Down', D M Waterman, *ibid* 3 ser 21 (1958), 63–66*

'The water supply at Dundrum Castle, Co Down', D M Waterman, *ibid* 3 ser 27 (1964), 136–39*

Duneight

'Duneight Td 2', in *An archaeological survey of County Down*, 205–6. Belfast: HMSO, 1966*

'Medieval Britain in 1962 and 1963', D M Wilson and D G Hurst, *Medieval Archaeology* 8 (1964), 263

'Excavations at Duneight, Co Down', D M Waterman, *Ulster Journal of Archaeology* 3 ser 26 (1963), 55–78*

Greencastle

'Greencastle', in *An archaeological survey of County Down*, 211–17, 219. Belfast: HMSO, 1966*

'Grim fortress or picturesque ruin? Greencastle, Co Down', in A Hamlin and C Lynn (eds), *Pieces of the past: archaeological excavations by the Department of the Environment for Northern Ireland 1970–1986*, 66–69. Belfast: HMSO, 1988*

'Greencastle', C J Lynn, in T Delaney (ed), *Excavations 1971: summary reports of archaeological excavations in Ireland*, 10–11. [S l]: Association of Young Irish Archaeologists, n d

'Greencastle', C J Lynn, in T Delaney (ed), *Excavations 1972: summary reports of archaeological excavations in Ireland*, 11. [S l]: Association of Young Irish Archaeologists, n d

'Greencastle', R Ó Baoill, in I Bennett (ed), *Excavations 2001: summary accounts of archaeological excavations in Ireland*, 72–73. Bray: Wordwell, 2003

'Greencastle', C J Lynn, in 'Excavations bulletin 1977–1979: summary accounts of archaeological excavations in Ireland', *Journal of Irish Archaeology* 4 (1987–8), 72

'Medieval Britain in 1966', D M Wilson and D G Hurst, *Medieval Archaeology* 11 (1967), 291

'Medieval Britain in 1967', D M Wilson and D G Hurst, *ibid* 12 (1968), 181

'Medieval Britain and Ireland in 1982', S M Youngs, J Clark and T B Barry, *ibid* 27 (1983), 215–16

'Post-medieval Britain and Ireland in 2001', M Ponsford, *Post-Medieval Archaeology* 36 (2002), 244–45

'Excavations at Greencastle, Co Down, 1951', D M Waterman and A E P Collins, *Ulster Journal of Archaeology* 3 ser 15 (1952), 87–102*

'Metallographic and chemical studies on a group of iron artifacts from the excavations at Greencastle, County Down', B G Scott, *ibid* 3 ser 39 (1976), 42–52*

'Excavations at Greencastle, County Down, 1966–70', C Gaskell Brown, *ibid* 3 ser 42 (1979), 51–65*

Grey Point Fort

Grey Point Fort, County Down. I Gailey and H Dixon. Belfast: HMSO, 1987*

'The guns of Grey Point Fort', P F Nowlam, *Irish Sword* 21.85 (1999), 349*

Hillhall

'Hillhall Td: bawn and house', in *An archaeological survey of County Down*, 259–60. Belfast: HMSO, 1966*

Hillsborough

Historic monuments in Hillsborough, County Down. H Dixon. Belfast: HMSO, 1977*

'The rath in Hillsborough Fort, County Down', C Gaskell Brown, *Ulster Journal of Archaeology* 3 ser 41 (1978), 78–87*

Jordan's

A guide to Jordan's Castle, Ardglass, County Down. Anon. Belfast: HMSO, 1963*

Jordan's Castle, Ardglass, County Down. H Dixon. Belfast: HMSO, 1977*

'Ardglass: Jordan's Castle', in *An archaeological survey of County Down*, 223–25. Belfast: HMSO, 1966*

'Jordan's Castle, Ardglass', M Gardiner, in I Bennett (ed), *Excavations 1998: summary accounts of archaeological excavations in Ireland*, 31. Bray: Wordwell, 2000

Kilclief

'Kilclief Castle', in *An archaeological survey of County Down*, 233–35. Belfast: HMSO, 1966*

Killyleagh

'Killyleagh Castle', in *ibid*, 236–38*

King's

'King's Castle', in *ibid*, 225*

Kirkistown

'Kirkistown Castle', in *ibid*, 238–41*

'Kirkistown Castle', E J C Lyttle, *Journal of the Upper Ards Historical Society* 7 (1983), 18–19*

Lismahon

'Ballykinler Lower Td: Lismahon', in *An archaeological survey of County Down*, 186–87. Belfast: HMSO, 1966*

'Excavations at Lismahon, Co Down', D M Waterman, *Medieval Archaeology* 3 (1959), 139–76*

Mahee

'Mahee Castle, Mahee Island', R Ó Baoill, in I Bennett (ed), *Excavations 2001: summary accounts of archaeological excavations in Ireland*, 74–75. Bray: Wordwell, 2003*

'Mahee Castle, Mahee Island', P Macdonald, in I Bennett (ed), *Excavations 2002:*

summary accounts of archaeological excavations in Ireland, 119–20. Bray: Wordwell, 2004

'Post-medieval Britain and Ireland in 2001', M Ponsford, *Post-Medieval Archaeology* 36 (2002), 245

Margaret's
'Ardglass: Margaret's Castle', in *An archaeological survey of County Down*, 222–23. Belfast: HMSO, 1966*

Narrow Water
A guide to Narrow Water Castle, County Down. D M Waterman. Belfast: HMSO, 1975*

'Narrow Water Castle: Narrow Water Td', in *An archaeological survey of County Down*, 241–43. Belfast: HMSO, 1966*

Nendrum
'Nendrum Castle: Mahee Island', in *ibid*, 244–45*

Newry
'Bagenal's Castle, Newry', J Ó Néill, in I Bennett (ed), *Excavations 2000: summary accounts of archaeological excavations in Ireland*, 65. Bray: Wordwell, 2002

'Bagenal's Castle, Newry', C MacManus, in I Bennett (ed), *Excavations 2003: summary accounts of archaeological excavations in Ireland*, 102–4. Bray: Wordwell, 2006

'The rediscovery of Bagnal's Castle, Newry', C Foley, *Archaeology Ireland* 11.2 (1997), 5

'Bagenal's Castle, Newry: an Elizabethan tower-house and cemetery', G Dawkes and L Buckley, *ibid* 20.4 (2006), 31–33*

'Post-medieval Britain and Ireland in 2000', M Ponsford, *Post-Medieval Archaeology* 35 (2001), 187–88*

'Nicholas Bagnall's castle at Newry, County Down', J J Ó Néill, *Ulster Journal of Archaeology* 3 ser 61 (2002), 117–24*

Newtownards
'Newtownards: Castle Garden', in *An archaeological survey of County Down*, 260. Belfast: HMSO, 1966*

'Post-medieval Britain and Ireland in 1998 and 1999', M Ponsford, *Post-Medieval Archaeology* 34 (2000), 313

Piper's Fort
'Farranfad Td: Piper's Fort', in *An archaeological survey of County Down*, 195–96. Belfast: HMSO, 1966*

'Piper's Fort, Farranfad, Co Down', D M Waterman, *Ulster Journal of Archaeology* 3 ser 22 (1959), 83–87*

Portaferry

Three tower-houses: Audley's Castle, Strangford Castle, Portaferry Castle, County Down. H Dixon. Belfast: HMSO, 1980*

'Portaferry Castle', in *An archaeological survey of County Down*, 245–46. Belfast: HMSO, 1966*

Quoile

'Quoile Castle', in *ibid*, 247–48*

Rathfriland

'Rathfriland Castle', in *ibid*, 248*

Rathmullan

'Rathmullan: castle, site of', in *ibid*, 248

'Slices through time: Rathmullan, Co Down', in A Hamlin and C Lynn (eds), *Pieces of the past: archaeological excavations by the Department of the Environment for Northern Ireland 1970–1986*, 48–50. Belfast: HMSO, 1988*

'Excavations of Rathmullan mound', C J Lynn, *Lecale Miscellany* 2 (1984), 19–23*

'The excavation of Rathmullan, a raised rath and motte in County Down', C J Lynn, *Ulster Journal of Archaeology* 3 ser 44–5 (1981–2), 65–171*

'The excavation of Rathmullan, County Down: addenda', C J Lynn, *ibid* 3 ser 48 (1985), 130–32

'Four medieval iron objects from Rathmullan, County Down', I Goodall, *ibid* 3 ser 48 (1985), 132–33*

'The dating of late 12th and early 13th century pottery in Ireland', J G Hurst, *ibid* 3 ser 48 (1985), 138–41

'Observations on the radiocarbon dates from Rathmullan', R B Warren, *ibid* 3 ser 48 (1985), 142–43

Ringhaddy

'Ringhaddy Castle', in *An archaeological survey of County Down*, 248–50. Belfast: HMSO, 1966*

Seafin

'Seafin Castle', in *ibid*, 218–20*

'Excavations at Seafin Castle and Ballyroney motte and bailey: the identification of the castle of Magh Cobha in the light of recent research', D M Waterman, *Ulster Journal of Archaeology* 3 ser 18 (1955), 83–104*

Sketrick

'Sketrick Castle', in *An archaeological survey of County Down*, 250–52. Belfast: HMSO, 1966*

'Sketrick Castle', N Crothers, in I Bennett (ed), *Excavations 2001: summary accounts of archaeological excavations in Ireland*, 77–78. Bray: Wordwell, 2003

'Post-medieval Britain and Ireland in 2001', M Ponsford, *Post-Medieval Archaeology* 36 (2002), 246

Strangford

Three tower-houses: Audley's Castle, Strangford Castle, Portaferry Castle, County Down. H Dixon. Belfast: HMSO, 1980*

'Strangford Castle', in *An archaeological survey of County Down*, 252–53. Belfast: HMSO, 1966*

'A note on Strangford Castle, Co Down', D M Waterman, *Ulster Journal of Archaeology* 3 ser 30 (1967), 83–86*

Walshestown

'Walshestown Castle', in *An archaeological survey of County Down*, 253–55. Belfast: HMSO, 1966*

White House

'The White House: Ballyspurge Td', in *ibid*, 256–57*

Woodgrange

'Woodgrange Td: remains of tower in rath', in *ibid*, 255

DUBLIN

Cairns, H. 'Martello towers', *Bray Journal* (1985), 33–34*

Corlett, C. *Antiquities of old Rathdown*. Bray: Wordwell, 1999*

Johnson, D N. *Dublin castles*. Dublin: University College, 1988* (The Resource Source: exploring Dublin 13)

Kerrigan, P M. 'Minorca and Ireland – an architectural connection: the martello towers of Dublin Bay', *Irish Sword* 15 (1982–3), 192–96*

McKenna, R. 'Martello towers', in *Balbriggan: a history for the millennium*, 84–86. Balbriggan: Balbriggan & District Historical Society, 1999*

McKenna, R. 'Martello towers and other coastal defenders of the 19th century', *Time & Tide* 3 (2001), 105–12*

O'Keeffe, T. 'Medieval frontiers and fortifications: the pale and its evolution', in F H A Aalen and K Whelan (eds), *Dublin, city and country: from prehistory to present. Studies in honour of J H Andrews*, 57–78. Dublin: Geography Publications, 1992*

Salter, M. *The castles of Leinster*. Malvern: Folly Publications, 2004*

Baldongan

'From Kildare to Baldongan: Fr Conor Donnagh and the siege of Baldongan, 1642', M Ní Mhurchadha, *Journal of the County Kildare Archaeological Society* 19.2 (2002–3), 269–88*

Ballymount Great

'The archaeology of Ballymount Great, Co Dublin', G Stout, in C Manning (ed), *Dublin and beyond the Pale: studies in honour of Patrick Healy*, 145–54. Bray: Wordwell, 1998*

Ballyowen

'Ballyowen Castle, Ballyowen Lane, Lucan', L Simpson, in I Bennett (ed), *Excavations 1995: summary accounts of archaeological excavations in Ireland*, 28. Bray: Wordwell, 1996

'Medieval Britain and Ireland in 1995', B S Nenk, S Margeson and M Hurley, *Medieval Archaeology* 40 (1996), 296

Bremore

'Bremore Castle', T Coughlan, in *Balbriggan: a history for the millennium*, 39–48. Balbriggan: Balbriggan & District Historical Society, 1999*

'Bremore Castle, Bremore', in I Bennett (ed), *Excavations 1995: summary accounts of archaeological excavations in Ireland*, 11. Bray: Wordwell, 1996

'Bremore, Balbriggan', F O'Carroll, in I Bennett (ed), *Excavations 2001: summary accounts of archaeological excavations in Ireland*, 78–79. Bray: Wordwell, 2003

'Bremore, Balbriggan', F O'Carroll, in *ibid*, 79–80

Carrickmines

'A much disputed land: Carrickmines and the Dublin marches', E O'Byrne, in S Duffy (ed), *Medieval Dublin IV: proceedings of the Friends of Medieval Dublin symposium 2002*, 229–52. Dublin: Four Courts Press, 2003*

'Heritage, rhetoric, identity: critical reflections on the Carrickmines Castle controversy', T O'Keeffe, in M McCarthy (ed), *Ireland's heritages: critical perspectives on memory and identity*, 139–51. Aldershot: Ashgate, 2005*

'Carrickmines Castle, Carrickmines Great', N Brady, in I Bennett (ed), *Excavations 2000: summary accounts of archaeological excavations in Ireland*, 71–72. Bray: Wordwell, 2002

'Carrickmines Castle, Carrickmines Great', M Clinton, *ibid*, 72

'Carrickmines Great', M Clinton, in I Bennett (ed), *Excavations 2001: summary accounts of archaeological excavations in Ireland*, 85–87. Bray: Wordwell, 2003

'Carrickmines Castle, Carrickmines Great', M Clinton, in I Bennett (ed), *Excavations 2002: summary accounts of archaeological excavations in Ireland*, 131. Bray: Wordwell, 2004

'On the frontier: Carrickmines Castle and Gaelic Leinster', E O'Byrne, *Archaeology Ireland* 16.3 (2002), 13–15*

'The Walshes and the massacre at Carrickmines', E O'Byrne, *ibid* 17.3 (2003), 8–11*

Cherrywood
'Post-medieval Britain and Ireland in 1995', M Ponsford and R Jackson, *Post-Medieval Archaeology* 30 (1996), 251

Clontarf
'Clontarf Castle, Clontarf', E O'Donovan, in I Bennett (ed), *Excavations 1996: summary accounts of archaeological excavations in Ireland*, 17–18. Bray: Wordwell, 1997

'Post-medieval Britain and Ireland in 1996', M Ponsford and R Jackson, *Post-Medieval Archaeology* 31 (1997), 263

Colmanstown
'Colmanstown Castle and church sites', M McCabe, *Dublin Historical Record* 53 (2000), 38–45*

Corr
'Corr Castle, Howth Road, Howth', R Swan, in I Bennett (ed), *Excavations 1998: summary accounts of archaeological excavations in Ireland*, 60–61. Bray: Wordwell, 2000

'A towerhouse in north County Dublin', A Daly, *Trowel* 1 (1988), 27–28

Dalkey
Medieval Dalkey in the 1760s. C Corlett. Bray: Archaeology Ireland, 2006* (Heritage guide; 33)

'59 Castle Street, Dalkey', C McConway, in I Bennett (ed), *Excavations 1997: summary accounts of archaeological excavations in Ireland*, 29. Bray: Wordwell, 1998

'62 Castle Street, Dalkey', J Kavanagh, in I Bennett (ed), *Excavations 2003: summary accounts of archaeological excavations in Ireland*, 115–16. Bray: Wordwell, 2006

Dalkey Island
Dalkey Island – an island on the tides of time. Landscape Archaeology Research Group. Bray: Archaeology Ireland, 2001* (Heritage guide; 16)

Drimnagh
'Drimnagh Castle, Ballyfermot', C Mullins, in I Bennett (ed), *Excavations 1992: summary accounts of archaeological excavations in Ireland*, 14. Bray: Wordwell, 1993

'Excavations at Drimnagh Castle, Drimnagh', C Mullins, in I Bennett (ed), *Excavations 1993: summary accounts of archaeological excavations in Ireland*, 13–14. Bray: Wordwell, 1994

'Drimnagh Castle, Drimnagh', R Swan, in *ibid*, 14

Dublin

Caislean Bhaile Atha Cliath/Dublin Castle. Anon. Dublin: Commissioners of Public Works, n d*

Viking Dublin exposed: the Wood Quay saga. J Bradley (ed). Dublin: O'Brien Press, 1984*

Dublin: the city within the Grand and Union canals and the circular road with the Phoenix Park (The buildings of Ireland). C Casey. London: Yale University Press, 2005*

Dublin c 840–1540: the medieval town in the modern city. H B Clarke. Dublin: Ordnance Survey and Friends of Medieval Dublin, 1978*

Irish historic towns atlas. 11. Dublin part 1, to 1610. H B Clarke. Dublin: Royal Irish Academy, 2002*

Dublinia: the story of medieval Dublin. H Clarke, S Dent and R Johnson. Dublin: O'Brien Press, 2002*

Dublin Castle in the life of the Irish nation. P Costello. Dublin: Wolfhound Press, 1999*

Dublin Castle: at the heart of Irish history. D McCarthy. Dublin: Stationery Office, 2004*

Dublin Castle: historical background and guide. J B Maguire. Dublin: Stationery Office, n d*

The Powder Tower, Dublin Castle. C Manning. Bray: Archaeology Ireland, 2001* (Heritage guide; 14)

Excavations at Isolde's Tower, Dublin. L Simpson. Dublin: Temple Bar Properties, 1994*

Archaeological excavations at Patrick, Nicholas and Winetavern streets, Dublin. C Walsh. Dingle: Brandon, 1997*

'Dublin Castle', in G A Hayes-McCoy (ed), *Ulster and other Irish maps c 1600*, 11–12. Dublin: Stationery Office for the Irish Manuscripts Commission, 1964*

'The mapping of medieval Dublin: a case-study in thematic cartography', H Clarke, in H B Clarke and A Simms (eds), *The comparative history of urban origins in non-Roman Europe: Ireland, Wales, Denmark, Germany, Poland and Russia from the ninth to the thirteenth century*, 617–43. Oxford: BAR, 1985* (International series; 285)

'Edward II and the murage of Dublin: English administrative practice versus Irish custom', J S Hamilton, in J S Hamilton and P J Bradley (eds), *Documenting the past: essays in medieval history presented to George Peddy Cuttino*, 85–97. Woodbridge: Boydell Press, 1989

'Dublin's north-eastern city wall: early reclamation and development at the Poddle-Liffey confluence', N Burke, in H Clarke (ed), *Medieval Dublin: the making of a metropolis*, 142–61, 282–85. Blackrock: Irish Academic Press, 1990*

'The town walls of Dublin', P Healy, in *ibid*, 183–92, 288–89*

'Seventeenth-century plans of Dublin Castle', J B Maguire, in *ibid*, 193–201, 289*

'Dublin's southern town defences, tenth to fourteenth centuries: the evidence from Ross Road', C Walsh, in S Duffy (ed), *Medieval Dublin II: proceedings of the Friends of Medieval Dublin symposium 2000*, 88–127. Dublin: Four Courts Press, 2001*

'Excavations at Dublin Castle, 1985–7', A Lynch and C Manning, in *ibid*, 169–204*

'The earthen banks and walled defences of Dublin's north-east corner', G Scally, in S Duffy (ed), *Medieval Dublin III: proceedings of the Friends of Medieval Dublin symposium 2001*, 11–33. Dublin: Four Courts Press, 2002*

'Dublin Castle in the Middle Ages', J Lydon, in *ibid*, 115–27

'The Record Tower, Dublin Castle', C Manning, in J R Kenyon and K O'Conor (eds), *The medieval castle in Ireland and Wales: essays in honour of Jeremy Knight*, 72–95. Dublin: Four Courts Press, 2003*

'Dublin Castle', A Lynch, in C Cotter (ed), *Excavations 1985: summary accounts of archaeological excavations in Ireland*, 22. Dublin: Irish Academic Publications, 1986

'Dublin Castle, Royal Exchange Ward', C Manning, in C Cotter (ed), *Excavations 1986: summary accounts of archaeological excavations in Ireland*, 17–18. Dublin: Irish Academic Publications, 1987

'Winetavern Street, South City Ward', M McMahon, in I Bennett (ed), *Excavations 1989: summary accounts of archaeological excavations in Ireland*, 21. Bray: Wordwell, 1990

'Christchurch Place, Wood Quay Ward', M Gowen, in *ibid*, 22

'Patrick St/Nicholas St/Winetavern St, South City Ward, Dublin', C Walsh, in I Bennett (ed), *Excavations 1990: summary accounts of archaeological excavations in Ireland*, 28–29. Bray: Wordwell, 1991

'Exchange Street Lower/Parliament Street/Essex Quay, Dublin', M Gowen, in *ibid*, 30

'Nicholas St, Dublin', C Walsh, in I Bennett (ed), *Excavations 1991: summary accounts of archaeological excavations in Ireland*, 13. Bray: Wordwell, 1992 [2 entries]

'Francis St/Cornmarket/Back Lane, Dublin', A Halpin, in *ibid*, 12–13*

'Bridge St Upr, Dublin', A Hayden, in I Bennett (ed), *Excavations 1992: summary accounts of archaeological excavations in Ireland*, 18. Bray: Wordwell, 1993

'Jury's Hotel site, Christchurch Place, Dublin', A Hayden, in *ibid*, 20

'Cornmarket/Francis St/Lamb Alley, Dublin', A Hayden, in *ibid*, 20–21

'Christchurch Place, Dublin', C Walsh and A Hayden, in I Bennett (ed), *Excavations 1993: summary accounts of archaeological excavations in Ireland*, 16–17. Bray: Wordwell, 1994

'Isolde's Tower, Exchange St, Dublin', L Simpson, in *ibid*, 21–22

'The 'West End' of Temple Bar, Dublin', M Gowen, in *ibid*, 26–28

'Augustine St, Dublin', A Hayden, in I Bennett (ed), *Excavations 1994: summary accounts of archaeological excavations in Ireland*, 20. Bray: Wordwell, 1995

'Back Lane/Lamb Alley, Dublin', M Gowen, in *ibid*, 14–15*

'Davis Place, Dublin', M Conway, in I Bennett (ed), *Excavations 1996: summary accounts of archaeological excavations in Ireland*, 22–23. Bray: Wordwell, 1997

'1 Essex Gate/10 Exchange Street Upper, Dublin', G Scally, in *ibid*, 23–24

'Augustine Street/Oliver Bond Street, Dublin', C Walsh, in I Bennett (ed), *Excavations 1997: summary accounts of archaeological excavations in Ireland*, 31–32. Bray: Wordwell, 1998

'City Hall, Cork Hill, Dublin', H Kehoe, in I Bennett (ed), *Excavations 1999: summary accounts of archaeological excavations in Ireland*, 65. Bray: Wordwell, 2000

'14–15 Werburgh Street, Dublin', L Simpson, in I Bennett (ed), *Excavations 2000: summary accounts of archaeological excavations in Ireland*, 99. Bray: Wordwell, 2002

'2–6 Longford Street Little/Dawson Court, Dublin', J Ó Néill, in I Bennett (ed), *Excavations 2001: summary accounts of archaeological excavations in Ireland*, 105–6. Bray: Wordwell, 2003

'Mother Redcap's Market, Lamb Alley, Dublin', H Kehoe, in I Bennett (ed), *Excavations 2002: summary accounts of archaeological excavations in Ireland*, 149. Bray: Wordwell, 2004

'Dublin Castle - the archaeological project', A Lynch and C Manning, *Archaeology Ireland* 4.2 (1990), 65–68*

'Dublin Castle: the building of a royal castle in Ireland', C Manning, *Château Gaillard* 18 (1998), 119–22*

'The Pigeon House Fort, Ringsend (a forgotten outpost of empire)', J Cooke, *An Cosantóir* 48.9 (1988), 33–36*

'Dublin Castle – 1', J Cornforth, *Country Life* 148 (1970), 284–87*

'The walls of Dublin', D Goodbody, *Dublin Historical Record* 17 (1961–2), 126–32, 141–42

'The site of Isolde's Tower', K Murray, *ibid* 41 (1987–8), 98–100

'Dublin Castle: preservation and presentation of the excavated remains', C Manning, *Europa Nostra Bulletin* 58 (2004), 75–82*

'The defence of Dublin, 1794–95', K Murray, *Irish Sword* 2 (1954–6), 332–38*

'Medieval Britain and Ireland in 1986', S M Youngs, J Clark and T Barry, *Medieval Archaeology* 31 (1987), 177–78

'Medieval Britain and Ireland in 1989', D R M Gaimster, S Margeson and M Hurley, *ibid* 34 (1990), 228–29, 230

'Medieval Britain and Ireland in 1990', B S Nenk, S Margeson and M Hurley, *ibid* 35 (1991), 205, 206–7

'Medieval Britain and Ireland in 1991', B S Nenk, S Margeson and M Hurley, *ibid* 36 (1992), 280–82

'Medieval Britain and Ireland in 1992', B S Nenk, S Margeson and M Hurley, *ibid* 37 (1993), 294

'Medieval Britain and Ireland in 1993', B S Nenk, S Margeson and M Hurley, *ibid* 38 (1994), 271–72

'Medieval Britain and Ireland in 1994', B S Nenk, S Margeson and M Hurley, *ibid* 39 (1995), 267

'Medieval Britain and Ireland in 1995', B S Nenk, S Margeson and M Hurley, *ibid* 40 (1996), 296–97

'Medieval Britain and Ireland in 1996', B S Nenk, C Haith and J Bradley, *ibid* 41 (1997), 305

'Medieval Britain and Ireland in 2000', J Bradley and M Gaimster, *ibid* 45 (2001), 341

'Medieval Britain and Ireland in 2005', M Gaimster and K O'Conor, *ibid* 50 (2006), 355

'Post-medieval Britain and Ireland in 1994', M Ponsford and R Jackson, *Post-Medieval Archaeology* 29 (1995), 131

'The Exchequer documents from the reign of Henry the Third', J F Lydon, *Proceedings of the Royal Irish Academy* 65C (1966–7), 1–27

'Dublin's north-eastern city wall: early reclamation and development at the Poddle-Liffey confluence', N Burke, *ibid* 74C (1974), 13–32*

'Seventeenth century plans of Dublin Castle', J B Maguire, *Journal of the Royal Society of Antiquaries of Ireland* 104 (1974), 5–14*

'Dublin Castle: three centuries of development', J B Maguire, *ibid* 115 (1985), 13–39*

'The rebuilding of Dublin Castle: thirty critical years, 1661–1690', R Loeber, *Studies* 69 (1980), 45–69*

'A new document in the Public Record Office: defensive houses in medieval towns', E M Jope and W A Seaby, *Ulster Journal of Archaeology* 3 ser 22 (1959), 115–18*

'A note on the medieval walls and gates of Dublin', anon, *ibid* 3 ser 23 (1960), 138

Dundrum

'Dundrum Castle, Dundrum', E O'Brien, in I Bennett (ed), *Excavations 1987: summary accounts of archaeological excavations in Ireland*, 13–14. Bray: Wordwell, 1988

'Dundrum Castle, Dundrum', E O'Brien, in I Bennett (ed), *Excavations 1989: summary accounts of archaeological excavations in Ireland*, 19. Bray: Wordwell, 1990

'Dundrum Castle, Dundrum', E O'Brien, in I Bennett (ed), *Excavations 1990: summary accounts of archaeological excavations in Ireland*, 25–26. Bray: Wordwell, 1991

'Dundrum Castle, Dublin', E O'Brien, in I Bennett (ed), *Excavations 1991: summary accounts of archaeological excavations in Ireland*, 15–16. Bray: Wordwell, 1992

'Excavations at Dundrum Castle, Dundrum, Co Dublin', E O'Brien, *Archaeology Ireland* 3.4 (1989), 136–37

'Medieval Britain and Ireland in 1987', S M Youngs [*et al*], *Medieval Archaeology* 32 (1988), 296

'Medieval Britain and Ireland in 1988', D R M Gaimster, S Margeson and T Barry, *ibid* 33 (1989), 223

'Medieval Britain and Ireland in 1989', D R M Gaimster, S Margeson and M Hurley, *ibid* 34 (1990), 231

'Medieval Britain and Ireland in 1990', B S Nenk, S Margeson and M Hurley, *ibid* 35 (1991), 208

'Medieval Britain and Ireland in 1991', B S Nenk, S Margeson and M Hurley, *ibid* 36 (1992), 282–83

'Post-medieval Britain and Ireland in 1991', M Ponsford, *Post-Medieval Archaeology* 26 (1992), 110

Dún Laoghaire

'John Murray and the building of the Dún Laoghaire Martello towers', A Horner, *Irish Sword* 24.98 (2005), 426–34*

Dunsoghly

'Dunsoghly Castle, Dunsoghly', D Murphy, in I Bennett (ed), *Excavations 1994:*

summary accounts of archaeological excavations in Ireland, 32. Bray: Wordwell, 1995

'Dunsoghly Castle and St Margaret's well', M J Tutty, *Dublin Historical Record* 32.4 (1979), 155–57

Finglas

'King William's Rampart, Finglas West', C Cotter, in I Bennett (ed), *Excavations 1991: summary accounts of archaeological excavations in Ireland*, 16. Bray: Wordwell, 1992

'Patrickswell Place, Finglas', E Halpin, in I Bennett (ed), *Excavations 1995: summary accounts of archaeological excavations in Ireland*, 25. Bray: Wordwell, 1996

'Patrickswell Lane, Finglas', N Dunne, in I Bennett (ed), *Excavations 1998: summary accounts of archaeological excavations in Ireland*, 224. Bray: Wordwell, 2000

Killiney Bay

'The French are one the sea ... A military history of Killiney Bay from 1793–1815', P Ó Duibhir, *Irish Sword* 12 (1975–6), 55–61*

Lehaunstown Park

'Lehaunstown Park, Co Dublin: a forgotten tower house', L Swan, in C Manning (ed), *Dublin and beyond the Pale: studies in honour of Patrick Healy*, 163–68. Bray: Wordwell, 1998*

Little Bray

'Little Bray Castle', C Martin, *Bray Historical Record* 1.1 (1986), 28

Malahide

War and peace: the survival of the Talbots of Malahide 1641–1671. J Byrne. Dublin: Irish Academic Press, 1997* (Maynooth studies in local history; 13)

Malahide Castle. [M Wynne]. Dublin: Eason, 1978*

'Malahide Castle', M J Tutty, *Dublin Historical Record* 31.3 (1978), 93–96

Newtown

'Newtown', F Rooney, in I Bennett (ed), *Excavations 2001: summary accounts of archaeological excavations in Ireland*, 136. Bray: Wordwell, 2003

Oldcourt

'Killininy, Oldcourt', D L Swan, in I Bennett (ed), *Excavations 1990: summary accounts of archaeological excavations in Ireland*, 27. Bray: Wordwell, 1991

Rathfarnham

'Rathfarnham Castle', C Scantlebury, *Dublin Historical Record* 12 (1951), 20–30

'Rathfarnham Castle', anon, *ibid* 41 (1987–8), 21–23

'Post-medieval Britain and Ireland in 1994', M Ponsford and R Jackson, *Post-Medieval Archaeology* 29 (1995), 131–32

Seapoint

'Seapoint', C Corlett, in I Bennett (ed), *Excavations 2003: summary accounts of archaeological excavations in Ireland*, 180–81. Bray: Wordwell, 2006

'Some features uncovered at Seapoint Martello Tower, Co Dublin', C Corlett, *Journal of the Royal Society of Antiquaries of Ireland* 131 (2001), 140–43*

Swords

'The archbishop's residence at Swords: castle or country retreat?', R Stalley, in S Duffy (ed), *Medieval Dublin VII: proceedings of the Friends of Medieval Dublin symposium*, 152–76. Dublin: Four Courts Press, 2006*

'Swords Castle', T Fanning, in T Delaney (ed), *Excavations 1971: summary reports of archaeological excavations in Ireland*, 12. [S l]: Association of Young Irish Archaeologists, n d

'The Pound licensed premises, Bridge St, Swords', D L Swan, in I Bennett (ed), *Excavations 1993: summary accounts of archaeological excavations in Ireland*, 33. Bray: Wordwell, 1994

'Swords Castle, Bridge Street, Swords', E E Sullivan, in I Bennett (ed), *Excavations 2001: summary accounts of archaeological excavations in Ireland*, 141–42. Bray: Wordwell, 2003

'An Irish medieval tile pavement: recent excavations at Swords Castle, county Dublin', T Fanning, *Journal of the Royal Society of Antiquaries of Ireland* 105 (1975), 47–82*

Tallaght

'Medieval Britain and Ireland in 1990', B S Nenk, S Margeson and M Hurley, *Medieval Archaeology* 35 (1991), 207

Turvey

'Turvey House, Turvey', D Murtagh, in I Bennett (ed), *Excavations 1993: summary accounts of archaeological excavations in Ireland*, 33–34. Bray: Wordwell, 1994

Tymon

'Tymon: a lost Pale castle recorded', D N Johnson, in G Mac Niocaill and P F Wallace (eds), *Keimelia: studies in medieval archaeology and history in memory of Tom Delaney*, 557–72. Galway: Galway University Press, 1988*

FERMANAGH

Johnston, J D. 'Settlement and architecture in County Fermanagh, 1610–41', *Ulster Journal of Archaeology* 3 ser 43 (1980), 79–89*

Rowan, A. *North west Ulster (The buildings of Ireland)*. Harmondsworth: Penguin Books, 1979*

Salter, M. *The castles of Ulster*. Malvern: Folly Publications, 2004*

Agheeghter
'Agheeghter Castle, Co Fermanagh', D M Waterman, *Ulster Journal of Archaeology* 3 ser 30 (1967), 87–88*

Castle Archdale
'Castle Archdale, Co Fermanagh', D M Waterman, *ibid* 3 ser 22 (1959), 119–23*

Castle Balfour
'Castle Balfour, Lisnaskea, Co Fermanagh', D M Waterman, *ibid* 3 ser 31 (1968), 71–76*

Enniskillen
Enniskillen Castle, County Fermanagh. H Dixon and J Johnston. Belfast: HMSO, 1980*

'Castle Barracks, Enniskillen', E Halpin, in I Bennett (ed), *Excavations 1990: summary accounts of archaeological excavations in Ireland*, 32. Bray: Wordwell, 1991

'Medieval Britain and Ireland in 1990', B S Nenk, S Margeson and M Hurley, *Medieval Archaeology* 35 (1991), 200

'Post-medieval Britain in 1987', G Egan, *Post-Medieval Archaeology* 22 (1988), 194

'Post-medieval Britain and Ireland in 1990', M Ponsford, *ibid* 25 (1991), 127

'Enniskillen water-gate: a further note', E M Jope, *Ulster Journal of Archaeology* 3 ser 16 (1953), 68

'Excavations at Enniskillen Castle, Co Fermanagh', E Halpin, *ibid* 3 ser 57 (1994), 119–44*

Monea
Monea Castle and Derrygonnelly Church, County Fermanagh. H Dixon. Belfast: HMSO, 1977*

Portora
'Portora Castle, Enniskillen', N Brannon, in I Bennett (ed), *Excavations 1997: summary accounts of archaeological excavations in Ireland*, 63. Bray: Wordwell, 1998

'Portora Castle, near Enniskillen', E M Jope, *Ulster Journal of Archaeology* 3 ser 21 (1958), 107–8*

Trannish Island
'An artillery fort on Trannish Island, County Fermanagh', B B Williams, *Clogher Record* 9 (1976–7), 295–96*

Tully

Tully Castle, County Fermanagh. M Meek. Belfast: Department of the Environment for Northern Ireland, 1984*

'Tully Castle', B Williams, in I Bennett (ed), *Excavations 2002: summary accounts of archaeological excavations in Ireland*, 194. Bray: Wordwell, 2004

'Tully Castle, Co Fermanagh', D M Waterman, *Ulster Journal of Archaeology* 3 ser 22 (1959), 123–26*

Tullykelter

'Tullykelter Castle, Co Fermanagh', D M Waterman, *ibid* 3 ser 22 (1959), 127–29*

GALWAY

Alcock, O, de hÓra, K and Gosling, P. *Archaeological inventory of County Galway. 2. North Galway*. Dublin: Stationery Office, 1999*

Gosling, P. *Archaeological inventory of County Galway. 1. West Galway (including Connemara and the Arran Islands)*. Dublin: Stationery Office, 1993*

Holland, P. 'Anglo-Normans and their castles in County Galway', in G Moran (ed), *Galway: history and society. Interdisciplinary essays on the history of an Irish county*, 1–26. Dublin: Geography Publications, 1996*

Holland, P. 'The Anglo-Normans in Co Galway: the process of colonization', *Journal of the Galway Archaeological and Historical Society* 41 (1987–8), 73–89

Holland, P. 'Anglo-Norman Galway: rectangular earthworks and moated sites', *ibid* 46 (1994), 203–11*

Holland, P. 'The Anglo-Norman landscape in County Galway: land-holding, castles and settlements', *ibid* 49 (1997), 159–93*

Jones, C. *The Burren and the Aran Islands: exploring the archaeology*. Cork: The Collins Press, 2004*

Lynn, C J. 'Some 13th-century castle sites in the west of Ireland: note on a preliminary reconnaissance', *Journal of the Galway Archaeological and Historical Society* 40 (1985–6), 90–113*

O'Connell, J W. 'Invasion anticipated: Colonel W Robertson's "Plans for the defence of the Irish coasts & foreign invasion & to prepare for security, taken occasionally in 1796, 97 & 98"', *ibid* 50 (1998), 10–36*

Salter, M. *The castles of Connacht*. Malvern: Folly Publications, 2004*

Spellissy, S. *The history of Galway*. Limerick: Celtic Bookshop, 1999*

Stanley, C. *Castles and demesnes: gleanings from Kilconieran and Clostoken*. Athenry: the author, 2000*

Anbally

'Anbally/Anbhaile', in O Alcock, K de hÓra, and P Gosling, *Archaeological inventory of County Galway. 2. North Galway*, 393, 398, 400. Dublin: Stationery Office, 1999*

Annaghadown

'Annaghadown Castle', D Delany, in I Bennett (ed), *Excavations 2000: summary accounts of archaeological excavations in Ireland*, 125–26. Bray: Wordwell, 2002

Ardamullivan

'Ardamullivan', F Rooney, in I Bennett (ed), *Excavations 2001: summary accounts of archaeological excavations in Ireland*, 143. Bray: Wordwell, 2003

'Ardmullivan', F Rooney, in I Bennett (ed), *Excavations 2002: summary accounts of archaeological excavations in Ireland*, 195. Bray: Wordwell, 2004

'Ardmullivan', M Fitzpatrick, in *ibid*, 195

'A spectacular revelation: medieval wall paintings at Ardamullivan', K Morton, *Irish Arts Review Yearbook* 18 (2002), 104–13*

Arkin

'Arkin Fort: the military history of a garrison outpost on Inis Mór', P Walsh, in J Waddell, J W O'Connell and A Korff (eds), *The book of Aran: the Aran Islands*, 148–58. Kinvara: Tír Eolas, 1994*

'Arkin: an outpost in Aran', J R W Goulden, *Irish Sword* 1 (1949–53), 262–67

Athenry

'Athenry', C Foley, in T G Delaney (ed), *Excavations 1972: summary reports of archaeological excavations in Ireland*, 12. [S l]: Association of Young Irish Archaeologists, n d

'Athenry', E Rynne, in C Cotter (ed), *Excavations 1985: summary accounts of archaeological excavations in Ireland*, 24. Dublin: Irish Academic Publications, 1986

'Athenry Castle, Athenry', C Papazian, in I Bennett (ed), *Excavations 1990: summary accounts of archaeological excavations in Ireland*, 32–33. Bray: Wordwell, 1991 [1989 excavation]

'Excavations at Athenry Castle, Co Galway', C Papazian, *Journal of the Galway Archaeological and Historical Society* 43 (1991), 1–45*

'Medieval Britain and Ireland in 1989', D R M Gaimster, S Margeson and M Hurley, *Medieval Archaeology* 34 (1990), 231–32*

Aughnanure

Aughnanure Castle, Oughterard, Co Galway. Anon. Dublin: National Parks and Monuments Service, n d*

'Aughnanure/Achadh na Niúr', in P Gosling, *Archaeological inventory of County Galway. 1. West Galway (including Connemara and the Arran Islands)*, 156–57. Dublin: Stationery Office, 1993*

Ballindooley
'Post-medieval Britain and Ireland in 1989', G Egan, *Post-Medieval Archaeology* 24 (1990), 167

Ballinsnave
'Foster and Ballinsnave Castle: a query', P Harbison, *Journal of the Galway Archaeological and Historical Society* 48 (1996), 161*

Ballybrit
'Ballybrit/Baile an Bhriotaigh', in P Gosling, *Archaeological inventory of County Galway. 1. West Galway (including Connemara and the Arran Islands)*, 157–58. Dublin: Stationery Office, 1993*

Castlegar
'Castlegar Castle, Castlegar', J Higgins, in I Bennett (ed), *Excavations 1997: summary accounts of archaeological excavations in Ireland*, 64. Bray: Wordwell, 1998

Claregalway
'Claregalway', A Carey, in I Bennett (ed), *Excavations 2002: summary accounts of archaeological excavations in Ireland*, 199. Bray: Wordwell, 2004

Claretuam
'Claretuam Castle, Claretuam', in I Bennett (ed), *Excavations 1995: summary accounts of archaeological excavations in Ireland*, 31. Bray: Wordwell, 1996

Cloghaun
'Cloghaun Castle, Kilkreest', A Connolly, in I Bennett (ed), *Excavations 1996: summary accounts of archaeological excavations in Ireland*, 40–41. Bray: Wordwell, 1997

Clonbrock
'Clonbrock Demesne/Diméin Chluain Broc', in O Alcock, K de hÓra, and P Gosling, *Archaeological inventory of County Galway. 2. North Galway*, 404. Dublin: Stationery Office, 1999*

Dunguaire
'Model house in an ancient tower: Dunguaire Castle, Co Galway', M Girouard, *Country Life* 133 (1963), 664–65*

Dunmore
'Castlefarm/Páirc an Chaisleáin', in O Alcock, K de hÓra, and P Gosling, *Archaeological inventory of County Galway. 2. North Galway*, 401. Dublin: Stationery Office, 1999*

Galway

Archaeological investigations in Galway City, 1987–1998. E FitzPatrick, M O'Brien and P Walsh. Bray: Wordwell, 2004*

Galway: architectural heritage. W Garner. Dublin: An Foras Forbartha, 1985*

Discover Galway. P Walsh. Dublin: O'Brien Press, 2001* (City guides)

'Lynch's Castle, Galway city: a reassessment', D N Johnson, in C Manning (ed), *Dublin and beyond the Pale: studies in honour of Patrick Healy*, 221–51. Bray: Wordwell, 1998*

'The topography of the town of Galway in the medieval and early modern periods', P Walsh, in G Moran (ed), *Galway: history and society. Interdisciplinary essays on the history of an Irish county*, 27–96. Dublin: Geography Publications, 1996*

'Merchant's Road, Townparks', G Walsh, in I Bennett (ed), *Excavations 1987: summary accounts of archaeological excavations in Ireland*, 15–16. Dublin: Wordwell, 1988

'Barrack lane, Townparks', M Clyne, in I Bennett (ed), *Excavations 1989: summary accounts of archaeological excavations in Ireland*, 28. Dublin: Wordwell, 1990

'Merchants Road II, Townparks', D Delany, in *ibid*, 28–29

'Eglinton Street, Townparks, Galway', M Clyne, in I Bennett (ed), *Excavations 1990: summary accounts of archaeological excavations in Ireland*, 34–35. Bray: Wordwell, 1991

'Merchants Road III, Townparks, Galway', D Delany, in *ibid*, 35 [1989 excavation]

'Merchants Road IV, Townparks, Galway', D Delany, in *ibid*, 35–36

'Quay Street, Townparks, Galway', M Casey, in *ibid*, 36

'St Augustine Street, Townparks, Galway', C O'Regan, in *ibid*, 36

'St Augustine Street/Merchants Road, Townparks, Galway', M Clyne, in *ibid*, 36–37

'Bollingbrook Fort, Galway', H Kieley, in I Bennett (ed), *Excavations 1991: summary accounts of archaeological excavations in Ireland*, 20. Bray: Wordwell, 1992

'Merchants Rd/Abbeygate St Lower, Galway', D Delany, in I Bennett (ed), *Excavations 1992: summary accounts of archaeological excavations in Ireland*, 29–30. Bray: Wordwell, 1993*

'17–21 Eyre St, Galway', L Simpson, in I Bennett (ed), *Excavations 1995: summary accounts of archaeological excavations in Ireland*, 34. Bray: Wordwell, 1996

'17–21 Eyre St, Galway', L Simpson, in I Bennett (ed), *Excavations 1996: summary accounts of archaeological excavations in Ireland*, 42. Bray: Wordwell, 1997

'Custom House, Court House Lane, Galway', G Walsh, in I Bennett (ed), *Excavations 1997: summary accounts of archaeological excavations in Ireland*, 65–66. Bray: Wordwell, 1998

'Custom House, Court House Lane/Flood Street, Galway', D Delany, in *ibid*, 66–69*

'Flood Street/New Dock Street, Galway', F Rooney, in I Bennett (ed), *Excavations 1998: summary accounts of archaeological excavations in Ireland*, 79–80. Bray: Wordwell, 2000

'Custom House, Flood Street/Courthouse Lane, Galway', D Delany, in I Bennett (ed), *Excavations 1999: summary accounts of archaeological excavations in Ireland*, 99–100. Bray: Wordwell, 2000

'Bollingbrook Fort, Seán Mulvoy Road, Galway', D Delany, in I Bennett (ed), *Excavations 2000: summary accounts of archaeological excavations in Ireland*, 132–34. Bray: Wordwell, 2002*

'Recent trial excavations in Galway city', M Casey, *Archaeology Ireland* 3.1 (1989), 17–20*

'Galway in the Jacobite war', S Mulloy, *Journal of the Galway Archaeological and Historical Society* 40 (1985–6), 1–19*

'Trial excavations in Galway city, 1987', M Casey, *ibid* 41 (1987–8), 114–19*

'Galway and the 'new' system of fortifications 1643–50', P Lenihan, *ibid* 48 (1996), 69–91*

'Galway and the Jacobite war', H Murtagh, *Irish Sword* 12 (1975–6), 1–14*

'Medieval Britain and Ireland in 1989', D R M Gaimster, S Margeson and M Hurley, *Medieval Archaeology* 34 (1990), 233

'Medieval Britain and Ireland in 1990', B S Nenk, S Margeson and M Hurley, *ibid* 35 (1991), 208

'Medieval Britain and Ireland in 1992', B S Nenk, S Margeson and M Hurley, *ibid* 37 (1993), 294–95

'Post-medieval Britain in 1987', G Egan, *Post-Medieval Archaeology* 22 (1988), 195–96

'Post-medieval Britain and Ireland in 1989', G Egan, *ibid* 24 (1990), 167–68

'Post-medieval Britain and Ireland in 1990', M Ponsford, *ibid* 25 (1991), 124

'Post-medieval Britain and Ireland in 1992', M Ponsford, *ibid* 27 (1993), 218–19

Gort

'Gort inse Guaire, a royal residence in south Galway', A Ryan, *Journal of the Galway Archaeological and Historical Society* 42 (1989–90), 143–50*

Inishbofin

'Port Island/Oileán an Phoirt', in P Gosling, *Archaeological inventory of County Galway. 1. West Galway (including Connemara and the Arran Islands)*, 164, 166. Dublin: Stationery Office, 1993*

'Cromwell's Barrack: a Commonwealth garrison fort on Inishbofin, Co Galway', P Walsh, *Journal of the Galway Archaeological and Historical Society* 42 (1989–90), 30–71*

'Inishbofin – the ultimate stronghold', S Mulloy, *Irish Sword* 17 (1987–8), 105–15

Inisheer

'Inisheer/Inis Oírr', in P Gosling, *Archaeological inventory of County Galway. 1. West Galway (including Connemara and the Arran Islands)*, 160–61. Dublin: Stationery Office, 1993*

Jenning's

'Castlegrove East/Garrán an Chaisleáin Thoir', in O Alcock, K de hÓra, and P Gosling, *Archaeological inventory of County Galway. 2. North Galway*, 395, 401, 414, 416. Dublin: Stationery Office, 1999*

Loughrea

'Fairgreen, Loughrea', A Hayden, in I Bennett (ed), *Excavations 1987: summary accounts of archaeological excavations in Ireland*, 15. Dublin: Wordwell, 1988

' 'The Sycamores', Main Street, Loughrea', M Jones, in I Bennett (ed), *Excavations 2003: summary accounts of archaeological excavations in Ireland*, 202. Bray: Wordwell, 2006*

'Excavations on the line of the medieval town defences of Loughrea, Co Galway', A Hayden, *Journal of the Galway Archaeological and Historical Society* 41 (1987–8), 1–4–13*

'Medieval Britain and Ireland in 1987', S M Youngs [*et al*], *Medieval Archaeology* 32 (1988), 296

Merlin

'Merlin Park, Galway', M Fitzpatrick, in I Bennett (ed), *Excavations 2002: summary accounts of archaeological excavations in Ireland*, 203–4. Bray: Wordwell, 2004

Moylough

'Moylough/Maigh Locha', in O Alcock, K de hÓra, and P Gosling, *Archaeological inventory of County Galway. 2. North Galway*, 415. Dublin: Stationery Office, 1999*

'Moylough Castle, Co Galway', D M Waterman, *Journal of the Royal Society of Antiquaries of Ireland* 86 (1956), 73–76*

IRELAND

Mutton Island

' "The old castle" on Mutton Island', J Mitchell, *Journal of the Galway Archaeological and Historical Society* 48 (1996), 98–103*

Pallas

'Pallas', M Fitzpatrick, in I Bennett (ed), *Excavations 2001: summary accounts of archaeological excavations in Ireland*, 155–56. Bray: Wordwell, 2003

Portumna

Portumna Castle visitors' guide. Anon. Dublin: Dúchas The Heritage Service, n d*

Portumna Castle. M Craig, Dublin: Gifford and Geaves, 1976*

Portumna Castle and its lords. M MacMahon. [S l]: the author, 1983*

Portumna Castle and priory, Co Galway. H A Wheeler. Dublin: National Parks and Monuments Service, [1985]*

'Portumna Castle: a little-known early survey and some observations', D N Johnson, in J Bradley (ed), *Settlement and society in medieval Ireland: studies presented to F X Martin o s a*, 477–503. Kilkenny: Boethius Press, 1988*

'Portumna Castle, Portumna', D Murphy, in I Bennett (ed), *Excavations 1995: summary accounts of archaeological excavations in Ireland*, 37–38. Bray: Wordwell, 1996*

'Portumna Castle, Portumna', D Murphy, in I Bennett (ed), *Excavations 1996: summary accounts of archaeological excavations in Ireland*, 46. Bray: Wordwell, 1997

'Portumna Castle, Portumna', D Murphy, in I Bennett (ed), *Excavations 1997: summary accounts of archaeological excavations in Ireland*, 77–78. Bray: Wordwell, 1998

'Portumna Castle, Portumna', D Murphy, in I Bennett (ed), *Excavations 1998: summary accounts of archaeological excavations in Ireland*, 87–88. Bray: Wordwell, 2000

'Portumna restored', J Fenlon, *Irish Arts Review* 20.3 (2003), 110–17*

'Post-medieval Britain and Ireland in 1996', M Ponsford and R Jackson, *Post-Medieval Archaeology* 31 (1997), 263–64

'Post-medieval Britain and Ireland in 1997', M Ponsford and R Jackson, *ibid* 32 (1998), 150

Rinmore

'Rinmore Fort: a seventeenth century fortification at Renmore [*sic*], Galway', P Walsh, *Journal of the Galway Archaeological and Historical Society* 41 (1987–8), 120–25*

Rossaveal

'Silent guns: the two pieces of early 19th century ordnance on the shores of Galway Bay', P Gosling, *ibid* 42 (1989–90), 139–43*

KERRY

Barrington, T J. *Discovering Kerry: its history, heritage and topography*. Monkstown: Blackwater Press, 1976*

Bradley, J. 'The medieval towns of Kerry', *North Munster Antiquarian Journal* 28 (1986), 28–39*

Cuppage, J. *Archaeological survey of the Dingle Peninsula/Suirbhé se-andálaíochta Chorca Dhuibhne: a description of the field antiquities of the Barony of Corca Dhuibhne from the Mesolithic period to the 17th century*. Bally-ferriter: Oidreacht Chorca Dhuibhne, 1986*

Mac Curtain, M. 'A lost landscape: the Geraldine castles and tower houses of the Shannon estuary', in J Bradley (ed), *Settlement and society in medieval Ireland: studies presented to F X Martin o s a*, 429–44. Kilkenny: Boethius Press, 1988*

Mould, D P. 'The barracks of Ballinskelligs Bay', *Archaeology Ireland* 8.2 (1994), 22–24*

O'Sullivan, A and Sheehan, J. *The Iveragh Peninsula: an archaeological survey of south Kerry*. Cork: Cork University Press, 1996*

Salter, M. *The castles of south Munster*. Malvern: Folly Publications, 2004*

Toal, C. *North Kerry archaeological survey*. Dingle: Brandon, 1995*

Ballinskelligs

'Ballinskelligs Castle, Ballinskelligs', J Sheehan, in I Bennett (ed), *Excavations 1991: summary accounts of archaeological excavations in Ireland*, 23. Bray: Wordwell, 1992

'Post-medieval Britain and Ireland in 1988', G Egan, *Post-Medieval Archaeology* 23 (1989), 35–36

Ballycarbery

'Ballycarbery Castle', M S, *Journal of the Kerry Archaeological and Historical Society* 30 (1997), 49–56

Barrow

'Ye castel at Barrow', C Donaghy, *Trowel* 2 (1989), 8–9*

Carrigafoyle

'Carrigafoyle Castle (Co Kerry)', R Stalley, *Archaeological Journal* 153 (1996), 328–29

Dingle

' "The Canon's Garden", Green Street, Dingle', I Bennett, in I Bennett (ed), *Excavations 1998: summary accounts of archaeological excavations in Ireland*, 90–91. Bray: Wordwell, 2000

'Main Street, Dingle', L Dunne, in *ibid*, 91

'Medieval Britain and Ireland in 1999', J Bradley and M Gaimster, *Medieval Archaeology* 44 (2000), 319

Gallarus

'Gallarus: Gallarus Castle', in J Cuppage, *Archaeological survey of the Dingle Peninsula …*, 372–75. Ballyferiter: Oidreacht Chorca Dhuibhne, 1986*

Kilcoleman

'An unrecorded tower house in Kilcoleman parish, Co Kerry with some notes on the Godrey family', V M McK Bary, *Journal of the Kerry Archaeological and Historical Society* 18 (1985), 224–35*

Listowel

'Listowel Castle, Listowel', F M Hurley, in I Bennett (ed), *Excavations 1998: summary accounts of archaeological excavations in Ireland*, 94. Bray: Wordwell, 2000

Minard

'Kilmurry: Minard Castle', in J Cuppage, *Archaeological survey of the Dingle Peninsula …*, 375–78. Ballyferiter: Oidreacht Chorca Dhuibhne, 1986*

Ross

Ross Castle visitors' guide. Anon. Dublin: Dúchas The Heritage Service, n d*

'A few impressions of Ross Castle', S Wells, *Journal of the Kerry Archaeological and Historical Society* 29 (1996), 31–39*

Smerwick

'Smerwick: Dún an Óir', in J Cuppage, *Archaeological survey of the Dingle Peninsula …*, 424–26. Ballyferiter: Oidreacht Chorca Dhuibhne, 1986*

'The plan of the Golden Fort at Smerwick, 1580', F M Jones, *Irish Sword* 2 (1954–56), 41–42*

'Dún an Óir', O Snoddy, *Journal of the Royal Society of Antiquaries of Ireland* 102 (1972), 247–48

Tarbert

'The fort at Tarbert, Co Kerry', A Dillon, *Irish Sword* 3 (1957–8), 286

Tralee

'Abbey Court, Tralee', L Dunne, in I Bennett (ed), *Excavations 2003: summary accounts of archaeological excavations in Ireland*, 224. Bray: Wordwell, 2006

'The siege of Tralee, 1642', J Caball, *Irish Sword* 2 (1954–6), 315–17

KILDARE

McNeill, T.E. 'Early castles in Leinster', *Journal of Irish Archaeology* 5 (1989–90), 57–64*

O'Keeffe, T. 'Tower-houses of the Pale in east County Kildare', *Oughterany: Journal of the Donadea Local History Group* 1.2 (1995), 4–11*

Salter, M. *The castles of Leinster*. Malvern: Folly Publications, 2004*

Taaffe, S. 'The role of the castle in Kildare 1169–1550', *Journal of the County Kildare Archaeological Society and Surrounding Districts* 18.4 (1998–9), 516–32

Athy
'The evidence for town walling at Athy, Co Kildare', S Taaffe, *Trowel* 4 (1993), 26–31*

Ballyshannon
'Ballyshannon Fort, Co Kildare, 1642–1650', D Bryan, *Irish Sword* 4 (1959–60), 93–98

Barberstown
'Barbarstown [*sic*] Castle, Straffan', F O'Carroll, in I Bennett (ed), *Excavations 1995: summary accounts of archaeological excavations in Ireland*, 48. Bray: Wordwell, 1996

'The owners and tenants of Barberstown Castle', M J Kelly, *Journal of the Co Kildare Archaeological Society* 16.1 (1977–8), 61–67*

Castledermot
'Castledermot', H G Leask, *Archaeological Journal* 117 (1960), 164

Castlefarm
'Castlefarm', C Mullins, in I Bennett (ed), *Excavations 1995: summary accounts of archaeological excavations in Ireland*, 44–45. Bray: Wordwell, 1996

Confey
'The church and castle of Confey, Co Kildare', T O'Keeffe, *Journal of the Co Kildare Archaeological Society* 16.5 (1985–6), 408–17*

'An illustration of Confey Castle, Co Kildare', C Manning, *Journal of the Royal Society of Antiquaries of Ireland* 131 (2001), 143–45*

Dunganstown
'Dunganstown Castle', P J Murray, *Journal of the Co Kildare Archaeological Society* 13 (1946–63), 342–44*

Grange
'Grange Castle, Grange', D Pollock, in I Bennett (ed), *Excavations 1998: summary accounts of archaeological excavations in Ireland*, 105–6. Bray: Wordwell, 2000

'Grange Castle', W Cumming, *Journal of the Co Kildare Archaeological Society* 17 (1987–91), 222–25*

Kildare

Irish historic towns atlas. 1. Kildare. J H Andrews. Dublin: Royal Irish Academy, 1986*

'Kildare Castle, Kildare', F O'Carroll, in I Bennett (ed), *Excavations 1989: summary accounts of archaeological excavations in Ireland*, 32–33. Dublin: Wordwell, 1990

'The Norman castle of Kildare', A J Mullowney, *Journal of the Co Kildare Archaeological Society* 18.3 (1996–7), 301–15*

Kilkea

'Kilkea Castle', anon, *Carloviana* new ser 1.14 (1965), 28–30*

Kilteel

'The Pale Boundary at Cupidstown, Co Kildare', M G O'Donnell, in R M Cleary, M F Hurley and E A Twohig (eds), *Archaeological excavations on the Cork-Dublin gas pipeline (1981–82)*, 106–10. Cork: University College Cork, 1987* (Cork archaeological studies; 1)

'Medieval Britain and Ireland in 1982', S M Youngs, J Clark and T B Barry, *Medieval Archaeology* 27 (1983), 218

Ladycastle Lower

'Ladycastle Lower', A Wallace, in I Bennett (ed), *Excavations 2002: summary accounts of archaeological excavations in Ireland*, 257–58. Bray: Wordwell, 2004

Leixlip

'Leixlip Castle, Co Kildare', J Musson, *Country Life* 195.29 (2001), 98–103*

Maynooth

Maynooth Castle visitors' guide. Anon. Dublin: Dúchas The Heritage Service, n d*

Irish historic towns atlas. 7. Maynooth. A Horner. Dublin: Royal Irish Academy, 1995*

'Maynooth Castle, Maynooth', A Hayden, in I Bennett (ed), *Excavations 1996: summary accounts of archaeological excavations in Ireland*, 52. Bray: Wordwell, 1997

'Maynooth Castle, Maynooth', A Hayden, in I Bennett (ed), *Excavations 1999: summary accounts of archaeological excavations in Ireland*, 132–33. Bray: Wordwell, 2000

'Medieval Britain and Ireland in 1996', B S Nenk, C Haith and J Bradley, *Medieval Archaeology* 41 (1997), 306

'Medieval Britain and Ireland in 2000', J Bradley and M Gaimster, *ibid* 45 (2001), 343–44

Naas

'Moatville, Abbey Road, Naas', E O'Brien, in I Bennett (ed), *Excavations 1990: summary accounts of archaeological excavations in Ireland*, 38. Bray: Wordwell, 1991

'Corban's Lane/South Main Street, Naas', F O'Carroll, in I Bennett (ed), *Excavations 1996: summary accounts of archaeological excavations in Ireland*, 54. Bray: Wordwell, 1997

'Dublin Road, Naas', M E Byrne, in I Bennett (ed), *Excavations 1999: summary accounts of archaeological excavations in Ireland*, 134. Bray: Wordwell, 2000

'The castles of Naas', B Murtagh, *Journal of the Co Kildare Archaeological Society* 16.4 (1983–4), 355–61*

'St David's Castle: a fortified town house, Naas, Co Kildare', B Murtagh, *ibid* 16.5 (1985–6), 468–78*

'The north and south moats of Naas', W H Gibson, *ibid* 17 (1987–91), 49–58*

Oughterard

'Medieval agriculture and settlement in Oughterard and Castlewarden, Co Kildare', D N Hall, M Hennessy and T O'Keeffe, *Irish Geography* 18 (1985), 16–25*

Pitchfordstown

'A turreted enclosure at Pitchfordstown, County Kildare', S Cullen and T O'Keeffe, *Journal of the Royal Society of Antiquaries of Ireland* 124 (1994), 215–17*

Pollardstown

'Pollardstown', T Fanning, in T Delaney (ed), *Excavations 1971: summary reports of archaeological excavations in Ireland*, 16. [S l]: Association of Young Irish Archaeologists, n d

'Excavation of a ringfort at Pollardstown, Co Kildare', T Fanning, *Journal of the Co Kildare Archaeological Society* 15 (1971–6), 251–61*

Skerries

'Earthwork at Skerries, Athy, Co Kildare', M P Flynn, *ibid* 18.3 (1996–7), 397–98

Timolin

'Timolin', M E Byrne, in I Bennett (ed), *Excavations 2001: summary accounts of archaeological excavations in Ireland*, 201. Bray: Wordwell, 2003

KILKENNY

Birthistle, D. 'Some tower houses in the barony of Gowran, County Kilkenny', in J Kirwan (ed), *Kilkenny studies in honour of Margaret M Phelan*, 28–44. [Kilkenny]: Kilkenny Archaeological Society, [1997]*

De Loughry, R. 'Castles of north Kilkenny', *Old Kilkenny Review* new ser 1 (1974–8), 33–37

Empey, C A. 'County Kilkenny in the Anglo-Norman period', in W Nolan and K Whelan (eds), *Kilkenny: history and society. Interdisciplinary essays on the history of an Irish county*, 74–95. Dublin: Geography Publications, 1990*

Harbison, P. 'Beranger's copies of eighteenth-century views of Kilkenny', in J Kirwan (ed), *Kilkenny studies in honour of Margaret M Phelan*, 98–103. [Kilkenny]: Kilkenny Archaeological Society, [1997]*

Manning, C. 'Delusions of grandeur: the pictorial forgeries of Sheffield Grace', in *ibid*, 112–28*

Murtagh, B. 'Kilmurry Castle and other related sites in Slieverue parish', *Old Kilkenny Review* 52 (2000), 26–108*

Salter, M. *The castles of Leinster*. Malvern: Folly Publications, 2004*

Shine, L. 'The manor of Earlstown, county Kilkenny: an interdisciplinary approach', in J Lyttleton and T O'Keeffe (eds), *The manor in medieval and early modern Ireland*, 40–69. Dublin: Four Courts Press, 2005*

Callan
'Fair Green Lane, Callan', B Murtagh and R Elliott, in I Bennett (ed), *Excavations 2002: summary accounts of archaeological excavations in Ireland*, 547–48. Bray: Wordwell, 2004

'The finding of the Civil Survey of Inistioge and Callan', C Manning, *Archaeology Ireland* 14.3 (2000), 18–23*

'The Civil Survey of Inistioge and Callan', C Manning, *Journal of the Royal Society of Antiquaries of Ireland* 128 (1998), 48–73*

'Cromwell in Callan', J Kennedy, *Old Kilkenny Review* 2 ser 3.1 (1984), 47–51*

Castletobin
'Castletobin', D Sutton, in T Delaney (ed), *Excavations 1974: summary accounts of archaeological work in Ireland*, 18. [S l: s n], n d

Clara
'Clara Castle', M Hegarty, *Old Kilkenny Review* 17 (1965), 9–14

Clonmantagh
'Clonmantagh Castle, Clonmantagh', D Delany, in I Bennett (ed), *Excavations 1999: summary accounts of archaeological excavations in Ireland*, 140–41. Bray: Wordwell, 2000*

Coolhill
'Coolhill Castle', E W Hughes, *Old Kilkenny Review* 9 (1956–7), 42–47

Dysart
'Dysart, Dysart', B Murtagh, in I Bennett (ed), *Excavations 1991: summary accounts of archaeological excavations in Ireland*, 27–28. Bray: Wordwell, 1992*

'Medieval Britain and Ireland in 1991', B S Nenk, S Margeson and M Hurley, *Medieval Archaeology* 36 (1992), 286

'Archaeological excavations at Dysart, Co Kilkenny 1989–1994: an interim report', B Murtagh, *Old Kilkenny Review* 4.6 (1994), 78–94*

Earlstown

'The manor of Earlstown, county Kilkenny: an interdisciplinary approach', L Shine, in J Lyttleton and T O'Keeffe (eds), *The manor in medieval and early modern Ireland*, 40–69. Dublin: Four Courts Press, 2005*

Foulksrath

Foulksrath Castle. J Brennan. Kilkenny: Kilkenny Archaeological Society, 1979*

Galmoy

'Castletown, Galmoy', P Stevens, in I Bennett (ed), *Excavations 1999: summary accounts of archaeological excavations in Ireland*, 141–42. Bray: Wordwell, 2000

Gorteens

'Gorteens', H A King, in I Bennett (ed), *Excavations 1993: summary accounts of archaeological excavations in Ireland*, 48–49. Bray: Wordwell, 1994

'Gorteens Castle, Gorteens', F Walsh, in I Bennett (ed), *Excavations 2003: summary accounts of archaeological excavations in Ireland*, 260. Bray: Wordwell, 2006

'Post-medieval Britain and Ireland in 1993', M Ponsford, *Post-Medieval Archaeology* 28 (1994), 128

Grenan

'Rectangular keeps of the thirteenth century at Grenan (Kilkenny) and Glanworth (Cork)', D M Waterman, *Journal of the Royal Society of Antiquaries of Ireland* 98 (1968), 67–73*

Instioge

'A seventeenth-century map of Instioge, Co Kilkenny', D Edwards and C Manning, *ibid* 131 (2001), 38–55*

Kells

The Augustinian priory of Kells, Co Kilkenny: an exploration. D Tietzsch-Tyler. [S l]: Kells Region Economic & Tourism Enterprise, 1993*

'The sacred and the secular: the Augustinian priory of Kells in Ossory, 1193–1541', C A Empey, *Irish Historical Studies* 24 (1984–5), 131–51

'A case study of the primary phase of Anglo-Norman settlement: the lordship of Kells', C A Empey, *Old Kilkenny Review* 2 ser 3.1 (1984), 32–40

'Kells motte, County Kilkenny', T B Barry, E Culleton and C A Empey, *Proceedings of the Royal Irish Academy* 84C (1984), 157–70*

Kilbline

'Kilbline tower-house', D Malone, *In the Shadow of the Steeple* 3 (1992), 89–101*

Kilkenny

Kilkenny Castle. Anon. Dublin: Stationery Office, 1978*

Discover Kilkenny. J Bradley. Dublin: O'Brien Press, 2000* (City guides)

Irish historic towns atlas. 10. Kilkenny. J Bradley. Dublin: Royal Irish Academy, 2000*

The medieval walls of Kilkenny City. I Doyle. Bray: Archaeology Ireland, 2005* (Heritage guide; 32)

Kilkenny Castle. P Friel. Dublin: Stationery Office, [1991]*

Kilkenny Castle. K M Lanigan. Kilkenny: Kilkenny Archaeological Society, 1966*

Kilkenny city walls: conservation plan. J Munby and R Tyler. Dublin: Heritage Council, 2005*

'The early development of the medieval town of Kilkenny', J Bradley, in W Nolan and K Whelan (eds), *Kilkenny: history and society. Interdisciplinary essays on the history of an Irish county*, 62–71. Dublin: Geography Publications, 1990*

'Kilkenny', P D Sweetman, in T Delaney (ed), *Excavations 1975–76: summary accounts of archaeological work in Ireland*, 13. [S l : s n], n d

'Pennyfeather Lane/Pudding Lane, St Mary's/St Patrick's Ward, Kilkenny', H A King, in I Bennett (ed), *Excavations 1990: summary accounts of archaeological excavations in Ireland*, 40–41. Bray: Wordwell, 1991

'Talbot Bastion, Townparks, Kilkenny', E C Bourke, in *ibid*, 41

'Kilkenny Castle, Kilkenny', B Murtagh, in I Bennett (ed), *Excavations 1991: summary accounts of archaeological excavations in Ireland*, 29–30. Bray: Wordwell, 1992

'Kilkenny Castle, Kilkenny', B Murtagh, in I Bennett (ed), *Excavations 1992: summary accounts of archaeological excavations in Ireland*, 39–40. Bray: Wordwell, 1993*

'68/69 John Street, Kilkenny', E O'Donovan, in I Bennett (ed), *Excavations 1996: summary accounts of archaeological excavations in Ireland*, 58–59. Bray: Wordwell, 1997

'Abbey Street, Kilkenny', P King, in I Bennett (ed), *Excavations 1997: summary accounts of archaeological excavations in Ireland*, 99. Bray: Wordwell, 1998

'Kilkenny Castle, The Parade, Kilkenny', B Murtagh, in *ibid*, 102–4

'Bridge House, 87–89 John Street Lower, Kilkenny', P Stevens, in I Bennett (ed), *Excavations 1999: summary accounts of archaeological excavations in Ireland*, 144–45. Bray: Wordwell, 2000

'Kilkenny Castle, The Parade, Kilkenny', B Murtagh, in I Bennett (ed), *Excavations 1999: summary accounts of archaeological excavations in Ireland*, 146–47. Bray: Wordwell, 2000

'Plan of Kilkenny Castle 1767', M Kenealy, *Journal of the Butler Society* 3.1 (1986–7), 63–64*

'Medieval Britain and Ireland in 1990', B S Nenk. S Margeson and M Hurley, *Medieval Archaeology* 35 (1991), 210

'Medieval Britain and Ireland in 1991', B S Nenk, S Margeson and M Hurley, *ibid* 36 (1992), 286–87*

'Medieval Britain and Ireland in 1997', M Gaimster, C Haith and J Bradley, *ibid* 42 (1998), 164

'Medieval Britain and Ireland in 1998', J Bradley, M Gaimster and C Haith, *ibid* 43 (1999), 290

'Medieval Britain and Ireland in 1999', J Bradley and M Gaimster, *ibid* 44 (2000), 319

'Cromwell's siege of Kilkenny', T J Clohosey, *Old Kilkenny Review* 8 (1955), 34–46

'The Cromwellian siege of Kilkenny', J F K Keane, *ibid* 16 (1964), 75–82

'The town wall of Kilkenny, part I', J Bradley, *ibid* new ser 1 (1974–8), 85–103*

'The town wall of Kilkenny, part II', J Bradley, *ibid* new ser 1 (1974–8), 209–18*

'The discovery of a portion of 13th century wall at Kilkenny Castle', C Foley, *ibid* new ser 1 (1974–8), 103

'The castle is open again', K Lanigan, *ibid* new ser 1 (1974–78), 248–53

'Plan of Kilkenny Castle 1767', M Kenealy, *ibid* new ser 2 (1982), 343–46*

'The Kilkenny Castle archaeological project 1990–1993: interim report', B Murtagh, *ibid* 4.5 (1993), 1101–17*

'Work begins on Talbot Tower, Kilkenny', B Murtagh, *ibid* 55 (2003), 26–29*

'Excavation of a riverside circular tower in College Park, Kilkenny City', I W Doyle, *ibid* 57 (2005), 32–42*

'Post-medieval Britain and Ireland in 1990', M Ponsford, *Post-Medieval Archaeology* 25 (1991), 125

'Post-medieval Britain and Ireland in 1991', M Ponsford, *ibid* 26 (1992), 111

'Some late seventeenth-to-eighteenth-century finds from Kilkenny Castle', P D Sweetman, *Proceedings of the Royal Irish Academy* 81C (1981), 249–66*

Kilmurry

'Kilmurry Castle and other related sites in Slieverue parish', B Murtagh, *Old Kilkenny Review* 52 (2000), 26–108*

Knocktopher

'Medieval Britain in 1973', L E Webster and J Cherry, *Medieval Archaeology* 18 (1974), 197

Neigham

'Neigham Castle', K M Lanigan, *Old Kilkenny Review* new ser 22.3 (1981), 250–52*

Newtown

'The manor of Earlstown, county Kilkenny: an interdisciplinary approach', L Shine, in J Lyttleton and T O'Keeffe (eds), *The manor in medieval and early modern Ireland*, 40–69. Dublin: Four Courts Press, 2005*

Purcell's Inch

'A newly discovered Anglo-Norman ringwork castle from Purcell's Inch townland, Kilkenny', P J H Neary, *Old Kilkenny Review* 57 (2005), 106–8*

Thomastown

'The Bridge Castle, Thomastown, Co Kilkenny', B Murtagh, in G Mac Niocaill and P F Wallace (eds), *Keimelia: studies in medieval archaeology and history in memory of Tom Delaney*, 536–56. Galway: Galway University Press, 1988*

'Brady's Castle, Thomastown: a 14th-century fortified town house', J Bradley and B Murtagh, in J R Kenyon and K O'Conor (eds), *The medieval castle in Ireland and Wales: essays in honour of Jeremy Knight*, 194–216. Dublin: Four Courts Press, 2003*

Threecastles

'Threecastles', T P Lyng, *Old Kilkenny Review* 16 (1964), 64–72*

LAOIS

Bradley, J. 'Early urban development in County Laois', in P G Lane and W Nolan (eds), *Laois: history and society. Interdisciplinary essays on the history of an Irish county*, 257–82. Dublin: Geography Publications, 1999*

Cunningham, G. *Illustrated guide: Roscrea and district. Monuments and antiquities*. Roscrea: Parkmore Press, 1976*

Feehan, J. *Laois: an environmental history*. Ballykilcavan: Ballykilcavan Press, 1983* [espec ch 8]

Loeber, R. 'Warfare and architecture in County Laois through seventeenth century eyes', in P G Lane and W Nolan (eds), *Laois: history and society. Interdisciplinary essays on the history of an Irish county*, 377–414. Dublin: Geography Publications, 1999*

O'Conor, K. 'Anglo-Norman castles in Co Laois', in *ibid*, 183–211*

Salter, M. *The castles of Leinster*. Malvern: Folly Publications, 2004*

Sweetman, P D, Alcock, O and Moran, B. *Archaeological inventory of County Laois*. Dublin: Stationery Office, 1995*

Aghaboe
'Aghaboe', in P D Sweetman, O Alcock and B Moran, *Archaeological inventory of County Laois*, 101. Dublin: Stationery Office, 1995*

Ballagh
'Ballagharahin', in *ibid*, 110, 112–13*

Ballaghmore
'Ballaghmore Lower', in *ibid*, 110*

Ballinaclogh Lower
'Archaeological investigations in the environs of a motte and bailey at Ballinaclogh Lower, near Timahoe, Co Laois', H A King, E Grogan and J Bradley, *Journal of the Co Kildare Archaeological Society* 18.1 (1992–3), 8–19*

Dunamase
Anglo-Norman Dunamase: the Rock of Dunamase. D Delany and E O'Leary. Vicarstown: Courtyard Book, 1996* [the O'Leary section, on the Rock, was first published in 1909]

'A summary of recent work at the Rock of Dunamase, Co Laois', B Hodkinson, in J R Kenyon and K O'Conor (eds), *The medieval castle in Ireland and Wales: essays in honour of Jeremy Knight*, 32–49. Dublin: Four Courts Press, 2003*

'Park or Dunamase', in P D Sweetman, O Alcock and B Moran, *Archaeological inventory of County Laois*, 108–9. Dublin: Stationery Office, 1995*

'Rock of Dunamase', B J Hodkinson, in I Bennett (ed), *Excavations 1993: summary accounts of archaeological excavations in Ireland*, 50–51. Bray: Wordwell, 1994

'Rock of Dunamase', B Hodkinson, in I Bennett (ed), *Excavations 1994: summary accounts of archaeological excavations in Ireland*, 51–52. Bray: Wordwell, 1995

'Rock of Dunamase', B J Hodkinson, in I Bennett (ed), *Excavations 1995: summary accounts of archaeological excavations in Ireland*, 53. Bray: Wordwell, 1996

'Rock of Dunamase', B Hodkinson, in I Bennett (ed), *Excavations 1996: summary accounts of archaeological excavations in Ireland*, 62. Bray: Wordwell, 1997

'Dunamase', B Hodkinson, in I Bennett (ed), *Excavations 1997: summary accounts of archaeological excavations in Ireland*, 108. Bray: Wordwell, 1998

'Rock of Dunamase', B Hodkinson, *Archaeology Ireland* 9.2 (1995), 18–21*

'Dunamase Castle', K O'Conor, *Journal of Irish Archaeology* 7 (1996), 97–115*

'The sources for the history of Dunamase Castle in the medieval period', B J Hodkinson, *Laois Heritage Society Journal* 1 (2003), 6–20*

'The outer gate house at Dunamase Castle, Co Laois', T E McNeill, *Medieval Archaeology* 37 (1993), 236–39*

'Medieval Britain and Ireland in 1995', B S Nenk, S Margeson and M Hurley, *ibid* 40 (1996), 300

'Medieval Britain and Ireland in 1996', B S Nenk, C Haith and J Bradley, *ibid* 41 (1997), 307

'Medieval Britain and Ireland in 1997', M Gaimster, C Haith and J Bradley, *ibid* 42 (1998), 164–65

Maryborough
'Maryborough', in P D Sweetman, O Alcock and B Moran, *Archaeological inventory of County Laois*, 117. Dublin: Stationery Office, 1995

Portlaoise
'Portlaoise', D Delany, in I Bennett (ed), *Excavations 2003: summary accounts of archaeological excavations in Ireland*, 297. Bray: Wordwell, 2006

Watercastle
'Watercastle rediscovered', D Delany, *Laois Heritage Society Journal* 2 (2004), 49–57*

LEITRIM

Condit, T and Gibbons, M. 'An introduction to County Leitrim', *Archaeology Ireland* 3.1 (1989), 6–9*

McCarthy, J. 'The importance of the tower house in the late medieval society of Breifne', *Breifne* 8.1 (1989–90), 118–35*

Moore, M J. *Archaeological inventory of County Leitrim*. Dublin: Stationery Office, 2003*

Salter, M. *The castles of Connacht*. Malvern: Folly Publications, 2004*

Jamestown
'Jamestown', F Ryan, in I Bennett (ed), *Excavations 2001: summary accounts of archaeological excavations in Ireland*, 226. Bray: Wordwell, 2003

'A gate to Connacht: the building of the fortified town of Jamestown, County Leitrim, in the era of plantation', R Loeber, *Irish Sword* 15 (1982–3), 149–52*

Parke's
Parke's Castle visitors' guide. Anon. Dublin: OPW, 1990*

'Kilmore', C Foley, in T G Delaney (ed), *Excavations 1972: summary reports of archaeological excavations in Ireland*, 19–20. [S l]: Association of Young Irish Archaeologists, n d

'Kilmore', C Foley, in T G Delaney (ed), *Excavations 1974: summary accounts of archaeological work in Ireland*, 20. [S l: s n], n d

LIMERICK

Carroll, M J. *The castles of County Limerick*. Bantry: Bantry Studio Publications, 2005*

Donnelly, C J. 'Decline and adaptation: the medieval Irish tower house in early modern County Limerick', in G Malm (ed), *Archaeology and buildings: papers from a session held at the European Association of Archaeologists fifth annual meeting in Bournemouth 1999*, 7–17. Oxford: Archaeopress, 2001* (BAR international series; 930)

Donnelly, C J. 'Tower houses and late medieval secular settlement in County Limerick', in P J Duffy, D Edwards and E FitzPatrick (eds), *Gaelic Ireland c. 1250-c. 1650: land, lordship and settlement*, 315–28. Dublin: Four Courts Press, 2001*

Donnelly, C [J]. 'Disappearing towerhouses: the evidence from County Limerick', *Archaeology Ireland* 7.4 (1993), 13–14*

Donnelly, C J. 'Passage or barrier? Communication between bawn and tower house in late medieval Ireland – the evidence from County Limerick', *Château Gaillard* 21 (2004), 57–64*

Donnelly, C J. 'Sectionally constructed tower-houses: a review of the evidence from County Limerick', *Journal of the Royal Society of Antiquaries of Ireland* 128 (1998), 26–34*

Donnelly, C J. 'A typological study of the tower houses of County Limerick', *ibid* 129 (1999), 19–39*

Hill, J. *The building of Limerick*. Cork: Mercier Press, 1991*

Keegan, M. 'The archaeology of manorial settlement in west county Limerick in the thirteenth century', in J Lyttleton and T O'Keeffe (eds), *The manor in medieval and early modern Ireland*, 17–39. Dublin: Four Courts Press, 2005*

Kirwan, S. 'County Limerick', *Archaeology Ireland* 5.1 (1991), 8–11*

Mac Curtain, M. 'A lost landscape: the Geraldine castles and tower houses of the Shannon estuary', in J Bradley (ed), *Settlement and society in medieval Ireland: studies presented to F X Martin, o s a*, 429–44. Kilkenny: Boethius Press, 1988*

Marrinan, S. 'Castles and schools in the Roxborough area', *North Munster Antiquarian Journal* 30 (1988), 26–28

O'Connor, P J. *Exploring Limerick's past: an historical geography of urban development in county and city*. Newcastle West: Oireacht na Mumhan Books, 1987*

Salter, M. *The castles of north Munster*. Malvern: Folly Publications, 2004*

Adare

'Adare', P D Sweetman, in T G Delaney (ed), *Excavations 1975–76: summary accounts of archaeological work in Ireland*, 14. [S l: s n], n d

'Adare Castle, Adare', L Dunne, in I Bennett (ed), *Excavations 2001: summary accounts of archaeological excavations in Ireland*, 228–29. Bray: Wordwell, 2003

'Adare Castle, Adare', L Dunne, in I Bennett (ed), *Excavations 2002: summary accounts of archaeological excavations in Ireland*, 293–95. Bray: Wordwell, 2004

'Adare Castle, Adare', J Kiely, in I Bennett (ed), *Excavations 2003: summary accounts of archaeological excavations in Ireland*, 304–5. Bray: Wordwell, 2006

'Archaeological excavations at Adare Castle, Co Limerick', P D Sweetman, *Journal of the Cork Historical and Archaeological Society* 85 (1980), 1–6*

'Was Desmond Castle, Adare, erected on a ringfort?', E Rynne, *North Munster Antiquarian Journal* 8 (1958–61), 193–202*

Ardmore Point
'Fort Shannon: a case history in Anglo-Irish co-operation during the Second World War', D de Cogan and S Swords, *Irish Sword* 22.90 (2001), 432–55*

Aughinish Island
'Aughinish Island: site 7', A Lynch, in T G Delaney (ed), *Excavations 1974: summary accounts of archaeological work in Ireland*, 22. [S l: s n], n d

Ballysimon
Excavation of a medieval ringwork at Ballysimon, County Limerick. T Collins and T Cummins. Limerick: Aegis Archaeology, 2001* (Aegis Archaeology reports: 1)

'Limerick ringwork excavations', T Cummins, *Archaeology Ireland* 14.1 (2000), 23*

Bulgaden Eady
'Bulgaden Eady', K Wiggins, in I Bennett (ed), *Excavations 2003: summary accounts of archaeological excavations in Ireland*, 307. Bray: Wordwell, 2006

Fantstown
'Newly recorded figurative carvings on tower houses in County Limerick', R Sherlock, *North Munster Antiquarian Journal* 44 (2004), 15–23*

Glin
Glin Castle: a guide. The Knight of Glin. Privately published, n d*
'Glin Castle, Co Limerick – I', M Girouard, *Country Life* 135 (1964), 446–50*

Kilmallock
'Abbeyfarm, Kilmallock', J O'Connor, in I Bennett (ed), *Excavations 2000: summary accounts of archaeological excavations in Ireland*, 192. Bray: Wordwell, 2002

'An Elizabethan map of Kilmallock', J H Andrews, *North Munster Antiquarian Journal* 11 (1968), 27–35*

Limerick

King John's Castle, Limerick visitors' guide. Anon. Dublin: OPW, n d*

Souvenir book of the tercentenary commemoration of the siege of Limerick, 1651. F Finegan. Limerick: Limerick Commemoration Committee, 1951*

The sieges and Treaty of Limerick. F Noonan. Dublin: Eason, 1991* (Irish heritage series; 70)

Historic Limerick: and city and its treasures. L Walsh. Dublin: Eason, 1984*

Anatomy of a siege: King John's Castle, Limerick, 1642. K Wiggins. Woodbridge: Boydell Press; Bray: Wordwell, 2001*

King John's Castle, Limerick, Ireland: bridging the centuries. K Wiggins. Limerick: Tom Sheedy & Associates, 2004*

'The siege of Limerick, 1690', J G Simms, in E Rynne (ed), *North Munster studies: essays in commemoration of Monsignor Michael Moloney*, 308–14. Limerick: Thomond Archaeological Society, 1967

'Ambrose and archaeology', K Wiggins, in J Fenwick (ed), *Lost and found: discovering Ireland's past*, 255–64. Bray: Wordwell, 2003*

'The constables of Limerick Castle', K Wiggins, in M Meek (ed), *The modern traveller to our past: Festschrift in honour of Ann Hamlin*, 264–73. [Southport]: DPK, 2006*

'Limerick city', P D Sweetman, in T G Delaney (ed), *Excavations 1975–76: summary accounts of archaeological work in Ireland*, 33. [S l: s n], n d

'Charlotte's Quay, Abbey C Ward', C Tarbett and K Wiggins, in I Bennett (ed), *Excavations 1989: summary accounts of archaeological excavations in Ireland*, 35–37. Dublin: Wordwell, 1990

'King's Island, John's Ward B', B Hodkinson, in *ibid*, 37

'King John's Castle, St Mary's parish', K Wiggins, in I Bennett (ed), *Excavations 1990: summary accounts of archaeological excavations in Ireland*, 35–37. Bray: Wordwell, 1991

'King John's Castle, Limerick', K Wiggins, in I Bennett (ed), *Excavations 1993: summary accounts of archaeological excavations in Ireland*, 52. Bray: Wordwell, 1994

'Milk Market, Limerick', C O Rahilly, in *ibid*, 52–53

'King John's Castle, Limerick', K Wiggins, in I Bennett (ed), *Excavations 1994: summary accounts of archaeological excavations in Ireland*, 56–58. Bray: Wordwell, 1995*

'Island Row, Limerick', B J Hodkinson, in I Bennett (ed), *Excavations 1995: summary accounts of archaeological excavations in Ireland*, 54. Bray: Wordwell, 1996

'King John's Castle, Limerick', K Wiggins, in I Bennett (ed), *Excavations 1996: summary accounts of archaeological excavations in Ireland*, 69. Bray: Wordwell, 1997

'King John's Castle, Limerick', K Wiggins, in *ibid*, 54–55

'Athlunkard Street to Sir Harry's Mall (northern relief road, phase 2), Limerick', C O Rahilly, in I Bennett (ed), *Excavations 1997: summary accounts of archaeological excavations in Ireland*, 116–17. Bray: Wordwell, 1998

'King John's Castle, Limerick', K Wiggins, in I Bennett (ed), *Excavations 1998: summary accounts of archaeological excavations in Ireland*, 135–36. Bray: Wordwell, 2000

'Verdant Place/Island Gate, Limerick', C O Rahilly, in *ibid* 136–37

'King John's Castle, Limerick', K Wiggins, in *ibid*, 120

'Sir Harry's Mall/Long Lane/Fish Lane (site K.I.16), Limerick', C O Rahilly, in I Bennett (ed), *Excavations 1999: summary accounts of archaeological excavations in Ireland*, 175–77. Bray: Wordwell, 2000

'Abbey River/George's Quay, Limerick', E O'Donovan, in I Bennett (ed), *Excavations 2000: summary accounts of archaeological excavations in Ireland*, 193–94. Bray: Wordwell, 2002

'Cathedral Place/New Road/Lelia Street, Limerick', C O Rahilly, in *ibid*, 194–95

'Nicholas Street/Mary Street, Limerick', C O Rahilly, in *ibid*, 196–97

'Sheep Street, Limerick', C O Rahilly, in *ibid*, 197–98

'Sheep Street, Limerick', T Collins, in I Bennett (ed), *Excavations 2003: summary accounts of archaeological excavations in Ireland*, 314. Bray: Wordwell, 2006

'King John's Castle', L Irwin, *Archaeological Journal* 153 (1996), 354

'Recent research in Limerick city', C O Rahilly, *Archaeology Ireland* 2.4 (1988), 140–44*

'Strange changes at King John's Castle', K Wiggins, *ibid* 5.3 (1991), 13–15*

'King John's Castle (1976) … Revisited', K Wiggins, *ibid*, 7.3 (1993), 26–28*

'Wiggins rebuked', D Sweetman, *ibid*, 7.4 (1993), 19–20*

'Church property dumped in Limerick Castle', E Whyte, *ibid* 10.1 (1996), 14–16*

'Something to crow about', K Wiggins and E Whyte, *ibid* 14.3 (2000), 30–33* [but see letter in same journal, 18.2 (2004), 40–41]

'The surrender of Limerick, 1691', J G Simms, *Irish Sword* 2 (1954–6), 23–28

'Hugh Dubh O'Neill's defence of Limerick, 1650–1651', J G Simms, *ibid* 3 (1957–8), 115–23

'The castle of Limerick', S Harbison, *ibid* 18.72 (1991), 199–204*

'Medieval Britain and Ireland in 1987', S M Youngs [*et al*], *Medieval Archaeology* 32 (1988), 297

'Medieval Britain and Ireland in 1989', D R M Gaimster, S Margeson and M Hurley, *ibid* 34 (1990), 235

'Medieval Britain and Ireland in 1990', B S Nenk, S Margeson and M Hurley, *ibid* 35 (1991), 211–12

'Medieval Britain and Ireland in 1998', J Bradley, M Gaimster and C Haith, *ibid* 43 (1999), 291

'Medieval Britain and Ireland in 2001', J Bradley and M Gaimster, *ibid* 46 (2002), 219–20

'Archaeological investigation of the site of a star-shaped fort at Singland, Garry-owen, Limerick city', R M Cleary, *North Munster Antiquarian Journal* 37 (1996), 131–34*

'A possible gunport in Irishtown, Limerick', B Hodkinson, *ibid* 45 (2005), 141–42*

'King John's Castle', W W Gleeson, *Old Limerick Journal* 12 (1982), 13*

'The topography of the siege', K Hannan, *ibid* 28 (1990), 37–39*

'The siege of Limerick, 1690', J G Simms, *ibid* 28 (1990), 52–56*

'Report on the fortifications of Limerick, 1685', T Phillips, 28 (1990), 72–73

'The walls of Limerick', K Hannan, *ibid* 28 (1990), 210–11*

'Post-medieval Britain and Ireland in 1990', M Ponsford, *Post-Medieval Archaeology* 25 (1991), 121

'Archaeological excavations at King John's Castle, Limerick', P D Sweetman, *Proceedings of the Royal Irish Academy* 80C (1980), 207–29*

'Excavations of the medieval town defences at Charlotte's Quay, Limerick', A Lynch, *ibid* 84C (1984), 281–331*

Lough Gur

'The siege of Lough Gur Castle, 1641', M Quinlan, *Lough Gur and District Historical Society Journal* (1985), 3–6*

Newcastle West

'Desmond Castle, Newcastle West', K Hanley, in I Bennett (ed), *Excavations 1996: summary accounts of archaeological excavations in Ireland*, 71–72. Bray: Wordwell, 1997 [report on work in 1995]

'Desmond Castle, Newcastle West', L Dunne, in I Bennett (ed), *Excavations 2001: summary accounts of archaeological excavations in Ireland*, 239–40. Bray: Wordwell, 2003

'Desmond Castle, Newcastle West', T Cummins, in I Bennett (ed), *Excavations 2003: summary accounts of archaeological excavations in Ireland*, 315–16. Bray: Wordwell, 2006

'Medieval Britain and Ireland in 1995', B S Nenk, S Margeson and M Hurley, *Medieval Archaeology* 40 (1996), 300–1*

Raheen
'Earthworks at Raheen Castle, Co Limerick', T Fanning and K O'Brien, *North Munster Antiquarian Journal* 16 (1973–4), 29–32*

Shanid
'Shanid Castle', P Fullam, *The Annual Observer* (1980), 20–22*

Singland
'Cromwell's Fort, Singland', R M Cleary, in I Bennett (ed), *Excavations 1996: summary accounts of archaeological excavations in Ireland*, 72. Bray: Wordwell, 1997

Springfield
'Newly recorded figurative carvings on tower houses in County Limerick', R Sherlock, *North Munster Antiquarian Journal* 44 (2004), 15–23*

LONDONDERRY/DERRY

Curl, J S. *The Londonderry plantation 1609–1914: the history, architecture and planning of the estates of the City of London and its livery companies in Ulster*. Chichester: Phillimore, 1986*

McNeill, T E. 'The archaeology of Gaelic lordship east and west of the Foyle', in P J Duffy, D Edwards and E FitzPatrick (eds), *Gaelic Ireland c. 1250-c. 1650: land, lordship and settlement*, 346–56. Dublin: Four Courts Press, 2001*

Rowan, A. *North west Ulster (The buildings of Ireland)*. Harmondsworth: Penguin Books, 1979*

Salter, M. *The castles of Ulster*. Malvern: Folly Publications, 2004*

Bellaghy
'Bellaghy bawn, Bellaghy', N F Brannon, in I Bennett (ed), *Excavations 1990: summary accounts of archaeological excavations in Ireland*, 21. Bray: Wordwell, 1991

'Post-medieval Britain and Ireland in 1989', G Egan, *Post-Medieval Archaeology* 24 (1990), 168–69

'Post-medieval Britain and Ireland in 1990', M Ponsford, *ibid* 25 (1991), 127

Brackfield
'Excavation at Brackfield bawn, County Londonderry', N F Brannon, *Ulster Journal of Archaeology* 3 ser 53 (1990), 8–14*

Coleraine
'Where history and archaeology unite: Coleraine, Co Londonderry', in A Hamlin and C Lynn (eds), *Pieces of the past: archaeological excavations by the Depart-*

ment of the Environment for Northern Ireland, 1970–1986, 78–79. Belfast: HMSO, 1988*

'Londonderry and Coleraine: walled towns, epitome or exception', A Thomas, in G O'Brien (ed), *Derry and Londonderry: history and society. Interdisciplinary essays on the history of an Irish county*, 259–78. Dublin: Geography Publications, 1999*

'Coleraine', N F Brannon, in 'Excavations bulletin 1977–1979: summary accounts of archaeological excavations in Ireland', *Journal of Irish Archaeology* 4 (1987–8), 70

'Post-medieval Britain and Ireland in 1998 and 1999', M Ponsford, *Post-Medieval Archaeology* 34 (2000), 313

'Post-medieval Britain and Ireland in 2002', M Ponsford, *ibid* 37 (2003), 307

Dungiven

'Archaeological excavations at Dungiven Priory and bawn', N Brannon, *Benbradagh* 15 (1985), 15–18*

'Dungiven Castle – the site over three centuries', F Smith, *ibid* 18 (1988), 10–13*

'Dungiven bawn re-edified?', N F Brannon and B S Blades, *Ulster Journal of Archaeology* 3 ser 43 (1980), 91–96*

Londonderry/Derry

Londonderry: guide to the city walls. Anon. Belfast: HMSO, 1970*

Maps and views of Derry 1600–1914: a catalogue. W S Ferguson. Dublin: Royal Irish Academy, in association with Derry City Council, 2005*

The siege of Derry. C Gébler. London: Little, Brown, 2005*

Derry's walls. P Hippsley. Derry: Guildhall Press, 1989*

The sieges of Derry. W Kelly (ed). Dublin: Four Courts Press, 2001

The siege of Derry. B Lacy. Dublin: Eason, 1989*

Discover Derry. B Lacey. Dublin: O'Brien Press, 1999* (City guides)

The walls of Derry. C D Milligan. 2 parts. Londonderry: Sentinel, 1948–50*

The walls of Derry: their building, defending, and preserving. Parts 1 & 2. C D Milligan. Lurgan: Ulster Society (Publications), 1996* [new edition of the above]

Derry – Londonderry. A Thomas. Dublin: Royal Irish Academy, 2005* (Irish historic towns atlas; 15)

'The siege: its history and legacy, 1688–1889', T G Fraser, in G O'Brien (ed), *Derry and Londonderry: history and society. Interdisciplinary essays on the history of an Irish county*, 379–404. Dublin: Geography Publications, 1999*

'Londonderry and Coleraine: walled towns, epitome or exception', A Thomas, in *ibid*, 259–78*

'Millennium Theatre, Derry', P Logue, in I Bennett (ed), *Excavations 1999: summary accounts of archaeological excavations in Ireland*, 38. Bray: Wordwell, 2000

'St Columb's Hall, Orchard Street, Derry', C McConway, in I Bennett (ed), *Excavations 2002: summary accounts of archaeological excavations in Ireland*, 106. Bray: Wordwell, 2004

'Rescue archaeology in Londonderry, Ireland', B Lacy, *Archaeology* 33 (1980), 52–54*

'The siege of Derry', J G Simms, *Irish Sword* 6 (1963–4), 221–33

'Londonderry', B Lacy, in 'Excavations bulletin 1977–1979: summary accounts of archaeological excavations in Ireland', *Journal of Irish Archaeology* 4 (1987–8), 70–71

'Post-medieval Britain and Ireland in 1983', G Egan, *Post-Medieval Archaeology* 18 (1984), 168–308

'Post-medieval Britain and Ireland in 1998 and 1999', M Ponsford, *ibid* 34 (2000), 314

'Five excavations in Ulster 1978–1984', N F Brannon, *Ulster Journal of Archaeology* 3 ser 49 (1986), 89–98*

Mountsandel
'Mountsandel', A E P Collins, in T G Delaney (ed), *Excavations 1975–76: summary accounts of archaeological work in Ireland*, 10–11. [S l: s n], n d

Movanagher
'Post-medieval Britain and Ireland in 1998 and 1999', M Ponsford, *Post-Medieval Archaeology* 34 (2000), 315

LONGFORD

Casey, C and Rowan, A. *North Leinster: the counties of Longford, Louth, Meath and Westmeath (The buildings of Ireland)*. London: Penguin Books, 1993*

Doran, L. 'Aspects of Anglo-Norman secular settlement in Longford and Roscommon *c* 1300', *Irish Sword* 24.98 (2005), 361–96*

Salter, M. *The castles of Leinster*. Malvern: Folly Publications, 2004*

LOUTH

Buckley, V M. *Archaeological inventory of County Louth*. Dublin: Stationery Office, 1986*

Buckley, V M and Sweetman, P D. *Archaeological survey of County Louth*. Dublin: Stationery Office, 1991*

Casey, C and Rowan, A. *North Leinster: the counties of Longford, Louth, Meath and Westmeath (The buildings of Ireland)*. London: Penguin Books, 1993*

Salter, M. *The castles of Leinster*. Malvern: Folly Publications, 2004*

Stout, G and O'Reilly, M. 'Pillboxes on the Boyne (1939–45)', *Journal of the Old Drogheda Society* 12 (2000), 244–55*

Sweetman, P D. 'Aspects of early thirteenth century castles in Leinster', *Château Gaillard* 15 (1992), 325–33*

Ardee

Ardee Castle. D MacIvor. Dundalk: Co Louth Archaeological and Historical Society, n d

'Townparks (Ardee)', in V M Buckley and P D Sweetman, *Archaeological survey of County Louth*, 345–50. Dublin: Stationery Office, 1991*

'Ardee Castle, Ardee', K Campbell, in I Bennett (ed), *Excavations 1997: summary accounts of archaeological excavations in Ireland*, 123. Bray: Wordwell, 1998

'Ardee: an archaeological study', J Bradley, *Journal of the County Louth Archaeological and Historical Society* 20.4 (1984), 267–96*

'Hatch's Castle, Ardee, County Louth: a fortified town house of the Pale', B Murtagh, *ibid* 22.1 (1989), 36–48*

'Medieval Britain and Ireland in 2000', J Bradley and M Gaimster, *Medieval Archaeology* 45 (2001), 341

Athclare

'Athclare', in V M Buckley and P D Sweetman, *Archaeological survey of County Louth*, 302–3. Dublin: Stationery Office, 1991*

'Athclare Castle, Dunleer', D Murphy, in I Bennett (ed), *Excavations 1999: summary accounts of archaeological excavations in Ireland*, 217–18. Bray: Wordwell, 2000

Ballug

'Ballug', in V M Buckley and P D Sweetman, *Archaeological survey of County Louth*, 302–3. Dublin: Stationery Office, 1991*

Balregan

'Balregan', in *ibid*, 304–7*

Carlingford

Carlingford town: an antiquarian's guide. P Gosling. [Carlingford]: County Louth Heritage Trust, 1992*

King John's Castle, Carlingford. H G Leask. Dublin: Stationery Office, n d*

'Liberties of Carlingford', in V M Buckley and P D Sweetman, *Archaeological sur-*

vey of County Louth, 320–29, 352–53. Dublin: Stationery Office, 1991*

'Taaffe's Castle, Carlingford', D G Moore, in I Bennett (ed), *Excavations 1995: summary accounts of archaeological excavations in Ireland*, 57–58. Bray: Wordwell, 1996*

'Medieval Britain and Ireland in 1994', B S Nenk, S Margeson and M Hurley, *Medieval Archaeology* 39 (1995), 269

'Medieval Britain and Ireland in 1995', B S Nenk, S Margeson and M Hurley, *ibid* 40 (1996), 300–1

Carntown

'Carntown', in V M Buckley and P D Sweetman, *Archaeological survey of County Louth*, 307–8. Dublin: Stationery Office, 1991*

Castle Guard

'Castle Guard motte, Dawson's Demesne, Ardee', F O'Carroll, in I Bennett (ed), *Excavations 2000: summary accounts of archaeological excavations in Ireland*, 208. Bray: Wordwell, 2002

'Castle Guard motte, Dawson's Demesne, Ardee', F O'Carroll, in I Bennett (ed), *Excavations 2000: summary accounts of archaeological excavations in Ireland*, 208–9. Bray: Wordwell, 2002*

Castletown

'Castletown', in V M Buckley and P D Sweetman, *Archaeological survey of County Louth*, 308–10. Dublin: Stationery Office, 1991*

Drogheda

The medieval town walls of Drogheda. C Brady. Bray: Archaeology Ireland, 2003* (Heritage guide; 23)

'[Drogheda town]', in V M Buckley and P D Sweetman, *Archaeological survey of County Louth*, 352–59. Dublin: Stationery Office, 1991*

'Drogheda', K Campbell, in C Cotter (ed), *Excavations 1985: summary accounts of archaeological excavations in Ireland*, 29. Dublin: Irish Academic Publications, 1986

'Drogheda town', K Campbell, in I Bennett (ed), *Excavations 1994: summary accounts of archaeological excavations in Ireland*, 63. Bray: Wordwell, 1995

'Duleek gate, Duleek St/Priest's Lane, Drogheda', D L Swan, in I Bennett (ed), *Excavations 1995: summary accounts of archaeological excavations in Ireland*, 59. Bray: Wordwell, 1996

'Millmount, Drogheda', B Ó Riordáin, in *ibid*, 60

'Moneymore, Drogheda', D Murphy, in I Bennett (ed), *Excavations 1996: summary accounts of archaeological excavations in Ireland*, 76–77. Bray: Wordwell, 1997

'Millmount, Drogheda', D Murphy, in I Bennett (ed), *Excavations 1998: summary accounts of archaeological excavations in Ireland*, 144. Bray: Wordwell, 2000

'Millmount, Drogheda', D Murphy, in I Bennett (ed), *Excavations 1999: summary accounts of archaeological excavations in Ireland*, 202. Bray: Wordwell, 2000*

'Drogheda, 1574', A Thomas, *Journal of the County Louth Archaeological and Historical Society* 18 (1973–6), 179–86*

'The topography and layout of medieval Drogheda', J Bradley, *ibid* 19.2 (1978), 98–127*

'When the walls came tumbling down', M Corcoran, *Journal of the Old Drogheda Society* 8 (1992), 18–25*

'Recent archaeological discoveries in Drogheda', D Murphy, *ibid* 11 (1998), 6–17*

'Medieval Britain and Ireland in 1982', S M Youngs, J Clark and T B Barry, *Medieval Archaeology* 27 (1983), 218–19

'Medieval Britain and Ireland in 1988', D R M Gaimster, S Margeson and T Barry, *ibid* 33 (1989), 223

'Medieval Britain and Ireland in 1995', B S Nenk, S Margeson and M Hurley, *ibid* 40 (1996), 301–2

'Medieval Britain and Ireland in 1996', B S Nenk, C Haith and M Hurley, *ibid* 41 (1997), 308

'Medieval Britain and Ireland in 1998', J Bradley, M Gaimster and C Haith, *ibid* 43 (1999), 291

'Medieval Britain and Ireland in 2003', J Bradley and M Gaimster, *ibid* 48 (2004), 310–11

Dundalk

A survey and report on the archaeology of the town and district. P Gosling. Dundalk: Dundalk Urban District Council, 1983, 3 vols*

'Clanbrassil Street, Dundalk', C McConway, in I Bennett (ed), *Excavations 1995: summary accounts of archaeological excavations in Ireland*, 62–63. Bray: Wordwell, 1996

'Rothe's Castle, Dundalk and Hugh O'Neill: a sixteenth century map', H O'Sullivan, *Journal of the County Louth Archaeological Society* 15 (1961–4), 281–91*

'From Dún Delca to Dundalk: the topography and archaeology of a medieval frontier town AD *c* 1187–1700', P Gosling, *Journal of the County Louth Archaeological and Historical Society* 22.3 (1991), 221–353* [espec ch 7, 253–62]

'The site of Warren's Gate, Dundalk', N Ross, *ibid* 23.2 (1994), 214–17*

'Medieval Britain and Ireland in 1983', S M Youngs, J Clark and T B Barry, *medieval Archaeology* 28 (1994), 256

'Medieval Britain and Ireland in 1997', M Gaimster, C Haith and J Bradley, *ibid* 42 (1998), 204

Dunmahon

'Dunmahon', in V M Buckley and P D Sweetman, *Archaeological survey of County Louth*, 311–13. Dublin: Stationery Office, 1991*

'The sack of Dunmahon Castle', G F Paterson, *Co Louth Archaeological Journal* 11 (1945–8), 164–68

Glaspistol

'Glaspistol', in V M Buckley and P D Sweetman, *Archaeological survey of County Louth*, 313–15. Dublin: Stationery Office, 1991*

Haynestown

'Haynestown', in *ibid*, 315–18*

Killincoole

'Killincoole', in *ibid*, 318–20*

Knockabbey

'Knockabbey, Thomastown', D O'Donovan, in I Bennett (ed), *Excavations 1999: summary accounts of archaeological excavations in Ireland*, 222–24. Bray: Wordwell, 2000*

Louth

'The medieval borough of Louth: an archaeological study', J Bradley, *Journal of the County Louth Archaeological and Historical Society* 21.1 (1985), 8–22*

Mayne

'Mayne', C Ó Drisceoil, in I Bennett (ed), *Excavations 2001: summary accounts of archaeological excavations in Ireland*, 265–66. Bray: Wordwell, 2003

Mellifont

'Mellifont', in V M Buckley and P D Sweetman, *Archaeological survey of County Louth*, 359–60. Dublin: Stationery Office, 1991*

Milltown

'Milltown', in ibid, 329–33*

Roche

'Roche', in *ibid*, 333–37*

Roodstown

'Roodstown', in *ibid*, 337–38*

Termonfeckin

'Termonfeckin', in *ibid*, 340–42*

MAYO

Corlett, C. *Antiquities of West Mayo*. Bray: Wordwell, 2001*

Lavelle, D. *An archaeological survey of Ballinrobe and district, including Lough Mask and Lough Carra*. [S l]: Lough Mask and Lough Carra Tourist Development Association, 1994*

Lynn, C J. 'Some 13th-century castle sites in the west of Ireland: note on a preliminary reconnaissance', *Journal of the Galway Archaeological and Historical Society* 40 (1985–6), 90–113*

Salter, M. *The castles of Connacht*. Malvern: Folly Publications, 2004*

Burrishoole

'A magnetic survey of Burrishoole Castle, Co Mayo', P Morris and C English, *Kosmos* 6 (1968), 20–21*

Turin

'Turin', R Crumlish, in I Bennett (ed), *Excavations 1999: summary accounts of archaeological excavations in Ireland*, 231. Bray: Wordwell, 2000

'Turin', M Fitzpatrick, in I Bennett (ed), *Excavations 2000: summary accounts of archaeological excavations in Ireland*, 252. Bray: Wordwell, 2002

MEATH

Casey, C and Rowan, A. *North Leinster: the counties of Longford, Louth, Meath and Westmeath (The buildings of Ireland)*. London: Penguin Books, 1993*

Galway, F. 'Meath tower houses', *Ríocht na Midhe* 7.4 (1985–6), 28–59*

Moore, M J. *Archaeological inventory of County Meath*. Dublin: Stationery Office, 1987* [a selection of the entries from this volume has not been made due to their brevity]

Prior, S. *A few well-positioned castles: the Norman art of war*. Stroud: Tempus, 2006*

Salter, M. *The castles of Leinster*. Malvern: Folly Publications, 2004*

Seaver, M. 'Practice, spaces and places: an archaeology of boroughs as manorial centres in the barony of Slane', in J Lyttleton and T O'Keeffe (eds), *The manor in medieval and early modern Ireland*, 70–104. Dublin: Four Courts Press, 2005*

Sweetman, P D. 'Some ringwork castles in County Meath', in T Condit and C Corlett (eds), *Above and beyond: essays in memory of Leo Swan*, 393–98. Bray: Wordwell, 2005*

Sweetman, P D. 'Aspects of early thirteenth century castles in Leinster', *Château Gaillard* 15 (1992), 325–33*

IRELAND

Ashbourne

'Ashbourne town centre', E O'Donovan and W O Frazer, in I Bennett (ed), *Excavations 2002: summary accounts of archaeological excavations in Ireland*, 399–400. Bray: Wordwell, 2004

Castle Jordan

'Castle Jordan Castle', R R Callary, *Ríocht na Midhe* 1.2 (1956), 21–35*

Clonard

'Excavation of medieval 'field boundaries' at Clonard, county Meath', P D Sweetman, *Journal of the Royal Society of Antiquaries of Ireland* 108 (1978), 10–22*

Galtrim

'The internal structure of Galtrim motte, County Meath, as revealed by ground-penetrating radar and electrical resistivity geophysical techniques', P J Gibson and R Breen, *Ríocht na Midhe* 16 (2005), 23–28*

Kells

Irish historic towns atlas. 4. Kells. S Simms and K Simms. Dublin: Royal Irish Academy, 1990*

Kilbeg Upper

'Medieval Britain and Ireland in 1991', B S Nenk, S Margeson and M Hurley, *Medieval Archaeology* 36 (1992), 289

Killeen

'Killeen', R Meenan, in I Bennett (ed), *Excavations 1996: summary accounts of archaeological excavations in Ireland*, 87. Bray: Wordwell, 1997

Navan

'Abbey Road, Navan', I Russell, in I Bennett (ed), *Excavations 2002: summary accounts of archaeological excavations in Ireland*, 426. Bray: Wordwell, 2004

'Recent excavations at Navan', E P Kelly, *Ríocht na Midhe* 7.2 (1982–3), 76–85*

Ratoath

'Main Street, Ratoath', R Meenan, in I Bennett (ed), *Excavations 2002: summary accounts of archaeological excavations in Ireland*, 434. Bray: Wordwell, 2004

Trim

Trim Castle visitors' guide. Anon. Dublin: Dúchas The Heritage Service, n d*

Trim. M Hennessy. Dublin: Royal Irish Academy, 2004* (Irish historic towns atlas; 14)

Trim Castle. J P Kelly. Privately published, 1965*

Trim Castle, Co Meath. K O'Brien and J Fenlon. Dublin: Dúchas The Heritage Service, 2002*

Medieval Trim: history and archaeology. M Potterton. Dublin: Four Courts Press, 2005* [espec ch 6]

'Trim', H A Wheeler, *135th annual meeting, 1985: programme*, CAA, 1985, 45–47

'Trim', P D Sweetman, *Excavations 1971*, 22–23. [S l]: Association of Young Irish Archaeologists, n d

'Trim', P D Sweetman, *Excavations 1972*, 25–26. [S l]: Association of Young Irish Archaeologists, n d

'Trim', P D Sweetman, in T G Delaney (ed), *Excavations 1973*, 23. [S l: s n], 1974

'Trim', P D Sweetman, in T G Delaney (ed), *Excavations 1974: summary accounts of archaeological work in Ireland*, 26. [S l: s n], n d

'Trim Castle, Trim', A Hayden, in I Bennett (ed), *Excavations 1995: summary accounts of archaeological excavations in Ireland*, 73–75. Bray: Wordwell, 1996*

'Trim', R Meenan, in I Bennett (ed), *Excavations 1996: summary accounts of archaeological excavations in Ireland*, 89. Bray: Wordwell, 1997

'Trim Castle, Trim', A Hayden, in *ibid*, 89–90

'Trim Castle, Trim', A Hayden, in I Bennett (ed), *Excavations 1998: summary accounts of archaeological excavations in Ireland*, 169. Bray: Wordwell, 2000

'Emmet Street, Trim', A Hayden, in I Bennett (ed), *Excavations 2001: summary accounts of archaeological excavations in Ireland*, 338–39. Bray: Wordwell, 2003

'Emmet Street, Trim', A Hayden, in *ibid*, 339

'Trim Castle', H G Leask, *Archaeological Journal* 117 (1960), 179–82*

'Trim Castle, Co Meath: the first three generations', T E McNeill, *ibid* 147 (1990), 308–36*

'The Anglo-Norman keep at Trim: its architectural implications', R Stalley, *Archaeology Ireland* 6.4 (1992), 16–19*

'Rings of truth at Trim Castle, Co Meath', T Condit, *ibid* 10.3 (1996), 30–33*

'The development of Trim Castle in the light of recent research', P D Sweetman, *Château Gaillard* 18 (1998), 223–30*

'The castle of Trim, Co Meath', H G Leask, *Irish Sword* 5 (1961–2), 94–97*

'Trim', P D Sweetman, in 'Excavations bulletin 1977–1979: summary accounts of archaeological excavations in Ireland', *Journal of Irish Archaeology* 4 (1987–8), 77

'Medieval Britain and Ireland in 1996', B S Nenk, C Haith and J Bradley, *Medieval Archaeology* 41 (1997), 309

'Trim Castle archaeological excavation (preliminary report)', P D Sweetman, *Ríocht na Midhe* 5.4 (1974), 68–77*

'Archaeological excavations at Trim Castle, Co Meath, 1971–1974', P D Sweetman, *Proceedings of the Royal Irish Academy* 78C (1978), 127–98*

MONAGHAN

Brindley, A L. *Archaeological inventory of County Monaghan*. Dublin: Stationery Office, 1986* [a selection of the entries from this volume has not been made due to their brevity]

Salter, M. *The castles of Ulster*. Malvern: Folly Publications, 2004*

Maghernacloy

'Maghernacloy Castle: a 16th century fortified house', L McDermott, *Clogher Record* 17.3 (2002), 781–84*

Mannan

'Mannan Castle, Donaghmoyne', E Moore, in I Bennett (ed), *Excavations 1999: summary accounts of archaeological excavations in Ireland*, 252–54. Bray: Wordwell, 2000

'Mannan Castle, Donaghmoyne', E Moore, in I Bennett (ed), *Excavations 2000: summary accounts of archaeological excavations in Ireland*, 269. Bray: Wordwell, 2002

'Mannan Castle, Donaghmoyne', E Moore, in I Bennett (ed), *Excavations 2001: summary accounts of archaeological excavations in Ireland*, 341. Bray: Wordwell, 2003

Monaghan

'Monaghan', in G A Hayes-McCoy (ed), *Ulster and other Irish maps c 1600*, 16–17. Dublin: Stationary Office for the Irish Manuscripts Commission, 1964*

'Westenra Arms Hotel, The Diamond, Monaghan', D J O'Connor, in I Bennett (ed), *Excavations 2003: summary accounts of archaeological excavations in Ireland*, 401–2. Bray: Wordwell, 2006

'Westenra Arms Hotel, The Diamond, Monaghan', D J O'Connor, in *ibid*, 402

OFFALY

Cunningham, G. *The Anglo-Norman advance into the south-west midlands of Ireland 1185–1221*. Roscrea: Parkmore Press, 1987*

Cunningham, G. *Illustrated guide: Roscrea and district. Monuments and antiquities*. Roscrea: Parkmore Press, 1976*

Kerrigan, P M. 'Castles and fortifications of County Offaly, *c* 1500–1815', in W Nolan and T P O'Neill (eds), *Offaly: history and society. Interdisciplinary essays on the history of an Irish county*, 393–438. Dublin: Geography Publications, 1998*

O'Brien, C. 'The earthwork castles of Anglo-Norman Offaly', in *ibid*, 153–80*

O'Brien, C and Sweetman, P D. *Archaeological inventory of County Offaly*. Dublin: Stationery Office, 1997*

Salter, M. *The castles of Leinster*. Malvern: Folly Publications, 2004*

Sheehy, M. 'Architecture in Offaly', *Journal of the Co Kildare Archaeological Society* 14 (1964–70), 1–28*

Ballinlough

'Ballinlough (Clonlisk By.)', in C O'Brien and P D Sweetman, *Archaeological inventory of County Offaly*, 140. Dublin: Stationery Office, 1997*

Ballymooney

'Oakleypark', in *ibid*, 159–60*

Banagher

'Banagher Fort, Kylebeg or Banagher', B Cassidy, in I Bennett (ed), *Excavations 1990: summary accounts of archaeological excavations in Ireland*, 50. Bray: Wordwell, 1991

'Kylebeg, Banagher', J Higgins, in I Bennett (ed), *Excavations 1998: summary accounts of archaeological excavations in Ireland*, 173. Bray: Wordwell, 2000

'Post-medieval Britain and Ireland in 1990', M Ponsford, *Post-Medieval Archaeology* 25 (1991), 125–26

Birr

'Birr Castle, Co Offaly – I', M Girouard, *Country Life* 137 (1965), 410–14*

Castletown

'The rare survival of a defensive mud enclosure at Castletown-Clonyn-Rahyn (Co Offaly)', R Loeber, M Stouthamer-Loeber and M Stout, *Offaly Heritage* 1 (2003), 12–21*

Clonmacnoise

Clonmacnoise. C Manning. Dublin: Stationery Office, 1994*

'Clonmacnoise', in C O'Brien and P D Sweetman, *Archaeological inventory of County Offaly*, 136–37. Dublin: Stationery Office, 1997*

'Clonmacnoise Castle', K O'Conor and C Manning, in H A King (ed), *Clonmacnoise studies. 2. Seminar papers 1998*, 137–65. Dublin: Stationery Office, 2003*

Clonony

'Clonony Castle, Clonony More', D Noonan, in I Bennett (ed), *Excavations 2003: summary accounts of archaeological excavations in Ireland*, 416. Bray: Wordwell, 2006

Coole

'Revealing a private inscription', C Manning, *Archaeology Ireland* 8.3 (1994), 24–26*

Dungar

'Dungar', in C O'Brien and P D Sweetman, *Archaeological inventory of County Offaly*, 145–47. Dublin: Stationery Office, 1997*

Knockbarron

'Medieval objects from Knockbarron motte, Co Offaly', J Dooley, *Ríocht na Midhe* 5.3 (1973), 85–90*

Leap

'Leap', in C O'Brien and P D Sweetman, *Archaeological inventory of County Offaly*, 150–51. Dublin: Stationery Office, 1997*

Monasteroris

'From Anglo-Norman manor to plantation estate: an archaeological survey of Monasteroris, county Offaly', S Armstrong-Anthony, in J Lyttleton and T O'Keeffe (eds), *The manor in medieval and early modern Ireland*, 105–31. Dublin: Four Courts Press, 2005*

Shannonbridge

'The Shannonbridge fortifications', P M Kerrigan, *Irish Sword* 11 (1973–4), 234–45*

Srah

'Ballydrohid', in C O'Brien and P D Sweetman, *Archaeological inventory of County Offaly*, 139, 141. Dublin: Stationery Office, 1997*

ROSCOMMON

Dockery, L. 'Towerhouses in Co Roscommon', *Co Roscommon Historical and Archaeological Society Journal* 6 (1996), 17–18*

Doran, L. 'Aspects of Anglo-Norman secular settlement in Longford and Roscommon *c* 1300', *Irish Sword* 24.98 (2005), 361–96*

Graham, B J. 'Medieval settlement in County Roscommon', *Proceedings of the Royal Irish Academy* 88C (1988), 19–38*

Lynn, C J. 'Some 13th-century castle sites in the west of Ireland: note on a preliminary reconnaissance', *Journal of the Galway Archaeological and Historical Society* 40 (1985–6), 90–113*

O'Conor, K. 'The morphology of Gaelic lordly sites in north Connacht', in P J Duffy, D Edwards and E FitzPatrick (eds), *Gaelic Ireland c 1250-c 1650: land, lordship and settlement*, 329–45. Dublin: Four Courts Press, 2001*

Salter, M. *The castles of Connacht*. Malvern: Folly Publications, 2004*

Ballinsnave

'Foster and Ballinsnave Castle: a query', P Harbison, *Journal of the Galway Archaeological and Historical Society* 48 (1996), 161

Ballintubber

'Ballintubber Castle, Co Roscommon', J A Claffey, *Journal of the Old Athlone Society* 1 (1969–75), 218–21

Cartron

'Cartron', L Morahan, in C Cotter (ed), *Excavations 1985: summary accounts of archaeological excavations in Ireland*, 33. Dublin: Irish Academic Publications, 1986

Cloonfree

'The moated site at Cloonfree, Co Roscommon', T Finan and K O'Conor, *Journal of the Galway Archaeological and Historical Society* 54 (2002), 72–87*

Donamon

'Donamon Castle: some aspects of its chequered history', M Kenny, *Co Roscommon Historical and Archaeological Society Journal* 5 (1994), 47–48

Gailey

'Gailey Castle', J Kerrigan, *Co Roscommon Historical and Archaeological Society Journal* 6 (1996), 103–4*

Rindown (Rindoon)

'Note on Rindoon Castle', A S, *ibid* 2 (1988), 14*

'Rindown Castle: a royal fortress in Co Roscommon', S Harbison, *Journal of the Galway Archaeological and Historical Society* 47 (1995), 138–48*

Roscommon

'Roscommon Castle, Roscommon', D Murphy, in I Bennett (ed), *Excavations 2002: summary accounts of archaeological excavations in Ireland*, 458–60. Bray: Wordwell, 2004

'Castle Street Lower, Cloonbracknagh, Roscommon', C Read, in I Bennett (ed), *Excavations 2003: summary accounts of archaeological excavations in Ireland*, 426. Bray: Wordwell, 2006

'Roscommon Castle, Roscommon', D Murphy, in *ibid*, 428–29

'Roscommon Castle: underestimated in terms of location?', M Murphy, *Journal of the Galway Archaeological and Historical Society* 55 (2003), 38–49*

Tulsk

'The earthwork at Tulsk, Co Roscommon: topographical and geophysical survey and preliminary excavation', N Brady and P Gibson, in *Discovery Programme reports 7. North Roscommon in the later medieval period: an introduction*, 59–75. Dublin: Royal Irish Academy, 2005*

SLIGO

Lynn, C J. 'Some 13th-century castle sites in the west of Ireland: note on a preliminary reconnaissance', *ibid* 40 (1985–6), 90–113*

Salter, M. *The castles of Connacht*. Malvern: Folly Publications, 2004*

Ballymote

'Archaeological excavations at Ballymote Castle, Co Sligo', P D Sweetman, *Journal of the Galway Archaeological and Historical Society* 40 (1985–6), 114–24*

Grange

'Grange', L Morahan, in I Bennett (ed), *Excavations 2001: summary accounts of archaeological excavations in Ireland*, 369–70. Bray: Wordwell, 2003*

Sligo

'Archaeological excavation at Sligo Town Hall Gate Lodge, June 2002', E Halpin, in M A Timoney (ed), *A celebration of Sligo: first essays for Sligo Field Club*, 193–94. Sligo: Sligo Field Club, 2002*

'Sligo's de Burgo castle of 1310: an addendum', P E O'Brien and M A Timoney, in *ibid*, 195–98*

'Sligo Castle', K D O'Conor, in *ibid*, 183–92.

'The Green Fort, Fort Hill, Sligo', E Halpin, in I Bennett (ed), *Excavations 1993: summary accounts of archaeological excavations in Ireland*, 72. Bray: Wordwell, 1994

'Gate Lodge, Quay Street, Sligo', E Halpin, in I Bennett (ed), *Excavations 2001: summary accounts of archaeological excavations in Ireland*, 374. Bray: Wordwell, 2003

'Quay Street, Sligo', E Halpin, in I Bennett (ed), *Excavations 2002: summary accounts of archaeological excavations in Ireland*, 468–69. Bray: Wordwell, 2004

'Sligo in the Jacobite war, 1689–91', J G Simms, *Irish Sword* 7 (1965–6), 124–35*

TIPPERARY

Bradley, J. 'The medieval towns of Tipperary', in W Nolan (ed), *Tipperary: history and society. Interdisciplinary essays on the history of an Irish county*, 34–59. Dublin: Geography Publications, 1985*

Butler, D J. 'Defence from the dispossessed: the state-sponsored garrisoning of the south Tipperary landscape *c* 1650 – *c* 1730', *Irish Sword* 24.95 (1004), 45–56*

Cairns, C T. *Irish tower houses: a Co Tipperary case study*. [S l]: Group for the Study of Irish Historic Settlement, 1987*

Cairns, C T. 'Guns and castles in Tipperary', *Irish Sword* 16 (1984–6), 110–16*

Cunningham, G. *The Anglo-Norman advance into the south-west midlands of Ireland 1185–1221*. Roscrea: Parkmore Press, 1987*

Cunningham, G. *Illustrated guide: Roscrea and district. Monuments and antiquities*. Roscrea: Parkmore Press, 1976*

Farrelly, J and O'Brien, C. *Archaeological inventory of County Tipperary. 1. North Tipperary*. Dublin: Stationery Office, 2002*

Salter, M. *Castles of north Munster*. Malvern: Folly Publications, 2004*

Stout, G T. *Archaeological survey of the Barony of Ikerrin*. Roscrea: Roscrea Heritage Society, 1984*

Ardcrony
'Ardcrony', in J Farrelly and C O'Brien, *Archaeological inventory of County Tipperary. 1. North Tipperary*, 353–54. Dublin: Stationery Office, 2002*

Ballydoyle
'Earthworks around Ballydoyle Castle, Co Tipperary', E Rynne, *North Munster Antiquarian Journal* 10 (1966–7), 72–74*

Ballynakill
'Balynakill', in J Farrelly and C O'Brien, *Archaeological inventory of County Tipperary. 1. North Tipperary*, 358–59. Dublin: Stationery Office, 2002

'Ballynakill 5 (castle – in ruins)', in G T Stout, *Archaeological survey of the Barony of Ikerrin*, 125–27. Roscrea: Roscrea Heritage Society, 1984*

Ballynamoe
'Ballynamoe 2 (Ballynamoe Castle – in ruins)', in *ibid*, 127–28*

Ballytarsna
'Ballytarsna Castle', B Hodkinson, in I Bennett (ed), *Excavations 1999: summary accounts of archaeological excavations in Ireland*, 283–84. Bray: Wordwell, 2000

''Ballytarsna', B Hodkinson, in I Bennett (ed), *Excavations 2001: summary accounts of archaeological excavations in Ireland*, 377. Bray: Wordwell, 2003

Beakstown House
'Beakstown House, Holycross', P Stevens, in I Bennett (ed), *Excavations 2000: summary accounts of archaeological excavations in Ireland*, 321. Bray: Wordwell, 2002

Boolabaun
'Boolabaun 2 (castle – in ruins)', in G T Stout, *Archaeological survey of the Barony of Ikerrin*, 129–30. Roscrea: Roscrea Heritage Society, 1984*

Borrisnafarney
'Borrisnafarney 1 (battery)', in *ibid*, 114*

Cahir (Caher)
Cahir Castle, Cahir, Co Tipperary. Anon. Dublin: National Parks and Monuments Service, n d*

Cahir Castle, Co Tipperary. Based on an original script by H A Wheeler, with additional text by D Pollock and contributions by J Fenlon, edited by C Manning and A O'Shaughnessy. Dublin: Dúchas The Heritage Service, 1999*

'Cahir', J F Reynolds, *Excavations 1972*, 26. [S l]: Association of Young Irish Archaeologists, n d

'Cahir Castle, County Tipperary', P Harbison, *Ireland of the Welcomes* 32.2 (1983), 26–28*

'A contemporary plan of the siege of Caher Castle, 1599, and some additional remarks', D N Johnson, *Irish Sword* 12 (1975–6), 109–15*

'Cahir Castle', anon, *Journal of the Butler Society* 4 (1972–3), 237–44*

'A carving in Cahir Castle, County Tipperary', P Holland, *North Munster Antiquarian Journal* 30 (1988), 14–18*

'The thirteenth-century remains at Cahir Castle, Co Tipperary', P Holland, *ibid* 35 (1993–4), 62–71*

'Caher Castle', anon, *Oibre: Bulletin of the Commissioners of Public Works* 9 (1972), 9–10*

'A pipeline trench at Cahir Castle', P Holland, *Tipperary Historical Journal* (1991), 215–17*

Carneycastle

'Carneycastle', in J Farrelly and C O'Brien, *Archaeological inventory of County Tipperary. 1. North Tipperary*, 362–63. Dublin: Stationery Office, 2002*

Carrick on Suir

Ormonde Castle, Carrick on Suir, Co Tipperary. Anon. Dublin: Stationery Office, n d*

Ormond Castle. J Fenlon. Dublin: Stationery Office, 1996*

Carrick-on-Suir and its people. P C Power. Dun Laoghaire: The Carrick Society and Anna Livia Books, 1976*

Ormonde Castle, Carrick-on-Suir: an anthology. J Maher (ed). Clonmel: Nationalist Newspaper Co, 1970*

'The decorative plasterwork at Ormond Castle: a unique survival', J Fenlon, *Architectural History* 41 (1998), 67–81*

'Carrick-on-Suir Castle, Co Tipperary', anon, *Oibre: Bulletin of the Commissioners of Public Works* 8 (1970), 15*

'Carrick-on-Suir: its origins and growth', P C Power, *Tipperary Historical Journal* (1992), 86–96*

Cashel

'44–46 Main St, Cashel', S Stevens, in I Bennett (ed), *Excavations 1990: summary accounts of archaeological excavations in Ireland*, 51. Bray: Wordwell, 1991

'Our Lady's Hospital, The Green, Cashel', M G O'Donnell, in I Bennett (ed), *Excavations 2003: summary accounts of archaeological excavations in Ireland*, 460. Bray: Wordwell, 2006

'The walls of Cashel', R W Jackson, *North Munster Antiquarian Journal* 6 (1949–52), 24–25*

'The medieval town defences of Cashel', T E Collins, *Tipperary Historical Journal* (1997), 124–30*

Castleleiny

'Castleleiny 3 (castle – in ruins)', in G T Stout, *Archaeological survey of the Barony of Ikerrin*, 121–22. Roscrea: Roscrea Heritage Society, 1984*

Clonakenny

'Clonakenny 6 (castle – in ruins)', in *ibid*, 130*

Clonamicklon

'Clonamicklon Castle, Gurtnahoe', J Moran, in I Bennett (ed), *Excavations 1996: summary accounts of archaeological excavations in Ireland*, 105. Bray: Wordwell, 1997

Cloncannon

'Cloncannon 6', in G T Stout, *Archaeological survey of the Barony of Ikerrin*, 111–12. Roscrea: Roscrea Heritage Society, 1984*

Clonmel

'Emmet Street, Burgagery Lands-West, Clonmel', S Zajac, in I Bennett (ed), *Excavations 1990: summary accounts of archaeological excavations in Ireland*, 51. Bray: Wordwell, 1991

'Kickham Street, Clonmel', J Channing, in I Bennett (ed), *Excavations 1991: summary accounts of archaeological excavations in Ireland*, 42–43. Bray: Wordwell, 1992

'5–7 New Quay, Clonmel', O M B Scully, in I Bennett (ed), *Excavations 1992: summary accounts of archaeological excavations in Ireland*, 58. Bray: Wordwell, 1993

'5–7 New Quay, Clonmel', O M B Scully, in I Bennett (ed), *Excavations 1993: summary accounts of archaeological excavations in Ireland*, 74. Bray: Wordwell, 1994

'Ruined wall-tower at the NE angle of Clonmel burgh', P Lyons, *Journal of the Royal Society of Antiquaries of Ireland* 75 (1945), 258*

'Medieval Britain and Ireland in 1996', B S Nenk, C Haith and J Bradley, *Medieval Archaeology* 41 (1997), 311

'Medieval town wall at Emmet Street, Clonmel', R M Cleary, *Tipperary Historical Journal* (1993), 194–98*

'Clonmel excavations – 1. Medieval town wall: Dowd's Lane site', H Opie, *ibid* (1995), 152–68*

'Clonmel excavations – 2. Medieval town wall: Dowd's Lane site', M Henry, *ibid* (1995), 169–74*

'Clonmel excavations – 3. South-east corner of medieval walled town: test investigations', O Scully, *ibid* (1996), 175–78*

Cranagh

'Cranagh 2 (Cranagh Castle)', in G T Stout, *Archaeological survey of the Barony of Ikerrin*, 131–33. Roscrea: Roscrea Heritage Society, 1984*

Derryleigh

'Castle Amery', B Hodkinson, *North Munster Antiquarian Journal* 45 (2005), 149–50 67uy

Drumlummin

'Drumlummin, Co Tipperary', R M Cleary, in R M Cleary, M F Hurley and E A Twohig (eds), *Archaeological excavations on the Cork-Dublin gas pipeline (1981–82)*, 116–45. Cork: University College, 1987*

Farrenroy

'Farrenroy tower-house, County Tipperary: a gentleman's home', R Clutterbuck, *Trowel* 9 (1998–9), 7–9*

Fethard

Fethard, Co Tipperary: a guide to the medieval town. T O'Keeffe. Fethard: Fethard Historical Society, 1997*

Fethard. T O'Keeffe. Dublin: Royal Irish Academy, 2003* (Irish historic towns atlas; 13)

'Medieval Britain and Ireland in 1991', B S Nenk, S Margeson and M Hurley, *Medieval Archaeology* 36 (1992), 290

Kilcash

Kilcash: a history, 1190–1801. J Flood and P Flood. Dublin: Geography Publications, 1999*

Kilfeakle

'Kilfeakle and Knockgraffon mottes, Co Tipperary', P Lyons, *Journal of the Royal Society of Antiquaries of Ireland* 80 (1950), 263–68*

Killoskehan

'Killoskehan 27 (Killoskehan Castle)', in G T Stout, *Archaeological survey of the Barony of Ikerrin*, 133–34. Roscrea: Roscrea Heritage Society, 1984*

Kiltinan

'Kiltinan Castle, Fethard', D Pollock, in I Bennett (ed), *Excavations 1997: summary accounts of archaeological excavations in Ireland*, 162. Bray: Wordwell, 1998

'Kiltinan Castle, Kiltinan', D Pollock, in I Bennett (ed), *Excavations 1998: summary accounts of archaeological excavations in Ireland*, 195. Bray: Wordwell, 2000

'Kiltinan Castle, County Tipperary: a Butler stronghold, 1452–1650', Lord Dunboyne, *Journal of the Butler Society* 1 (1968), 52–55

Knockane

'Knockane (Templedowney Par)', in J Farrelly and C O'Brien, *Archaeological inventory of County Tipperary. 1. North Tipperary*, 373–74. Dublin: Stationery Office, 2002*

Knockgraffon

'Kilfeakle and Knockgraffon mottes, Co Tipperary', P Lyons, *Journal of the Royal Society of Antiquaries of Ireland* 80 (1950), 263–68*

Lackeen

Lackeen (Abbeville td): a late medieval and later settlement in Tipperary, North Riding. D Sweetman and C O'Brien. Bray: Wordwell, 1999* (Heritage guide; 6)

'Abbeville', in J Farrelly and C O'Brien, *Archaeological inventory of County Tipperary. 1. North Tipperary*, 351–52. Dublin: Stationery Office, 2002

Lorrha

'Lorrha motte, County Tipperary', E J Talbot, *North Munster Antiquarian Journal* 15 (1972), 8–16*

Moatquarter

'Moatquarter 1', in G T Stout, *Archaeological survey of the Barony of Ikerrin*, 112–13. Roscrea: Roscrea Heritage Society, 1984*

Moorstown

'Moorstown Castle: a neglected tower-house near Clonmel', L Wallace, *Tipperary Historical Journal* (1989), 17–19*

Moycarky

'Moycarky', in J Farrelly and C O'Brien, *Archaeological inventory of County Tipperary. 1. North Tipperary*, 375–78. Dublin: Stationery Office, 2002*

Nenagh

The castle and manor of Nenagh. D F Gleeson and H G Leask. Revised edition. [Nenagh]: Wordsnare Publications, 1976*

Nenagh Castle: chronology and architecture. N Murphy. Nenagh: Relay Publications, 1993*

'Nenagh North', in J Farrelly and C O'Brien, *Archaeological inventory of County Tipperary. 1. North Tipperary*, 312–13. Dublin: Stationery Office, 2002

'Nenagh Castle, Nenagh', B Hodkinson, in I Bennett (ed), *Excavations 1996: summary accounts of archaeological excavations in Ireland*, 107. Bray: Wordwell, 1997

'Nenagh Castle', B Hodkinson, in I Bennett (ed), *Excavations 1997: summary accounts of archaeological excavations in Ireland*, 178–79. Bray: Wordwell, 1998

'Nenagh Castle', G Butler, *Journal of the Butler Society* 3 (1970–1), 208*

'Nenagh Castle: some interesting documents relating to it', N Murphy, *ibid* 2.4 (1985), 436–41*

'Medieval Britain and Ireland in 1996', B S Nenk, C Haith and J Bradley, *Medieval Archaeology* 41 (1997), 311

'Medieval Britain and Ireland in 1997', M Gaimster, C Haith and J Bradley, *ibid* 42 (1998), 170

'Excavations in the gatehouse of Nenagh Castle, 1996 and 1997', B Hodkinson, *Tipperary Historical Journal* (1999), 162–82*

'The two Sir George Hamiltons and their connections with the castles of Roscrea and Nenagh', C Manning, *ibid* (2001), 149–54*

Oldcastle
'Oldcastle', in G T Stout, *Archaeological survey of the Barony of Ikerrin*, 114–15. Roscrea: Roscrea Heritage Society, 1984*

Pallas Upper
'A tower house and ringfort at Pallas Upper, Borrisoleigh', D O'Regan, *Tipperary Historical Journal* (1992), 206–9*

Rathnaveoge
'Rathnaveoge Lower 6 (castle – in ruins)', in G T Stout, *Archaeological survey of the Barony of Ikerrin*, 134–36. Roscrea: Roscrea Heritage Society, 1984*

Roscrea
Roscrea visitors' guide. Anon. Dublin: Dúchas The Heritage Service, n d*

Excavations at Roscrea Castle. C Manning (ed). Dublin: Stationery Office, 2003* (Department of the Environment, Heritage and Local Government archaeological monograph; 1)

'Townparks (Roscrea par)', in J Farrelly and C O'Brien, *Archaeological inventory of County Tipperary. 1. North Tipperary*, 314–15. Dublin: Stationery Office, 2002

'Roscrea Castle', in G T Stout, *Archaeological survey of the Barony of Ikerrin*, 116–21. Roscrea: Roscrea Heritage Society, 1984*

'Roscrea Castle, Townparks', C Manning, in I Bennett (ed), *Excavations 1989: summary accounts of archaeological excavations in Ireland*, 46. Dublin: Wordwell, 1990

'Roscrea Castle, Townparks', C Manning, in I Bennett (ed), *Excavations 1990: summary accounts of archaeological excavations in Ireland*, 52–53. Bray: Wordwell, 1991

'Roscrea Castle, Roscrea', J Wren, in I Bennett (ed), *Excavations 1992: summary accounts of archaeological excavations in Ireland*, 59. Bray: Wordwell, 1993

'King John's Tower, Roscrea Castle, Roscrea', A Hayden, in I Bennett (ed), *Excavations 1998: summary accounts of archaeological excavations in Ireland*, 202. Bray: Wordwell, 2000*

'The king's castle of Roscrea', C Manning, *Archaeology Ireland* 18.1 (2004), 20–23 [issue was mis-numbered 17.4]

'Trial excavations at Roscrea Castle, Co Tipperary', G Stout, *Eile* 2 (1983–4), 29–42*

'Excavations at Roscrea Castle, Co Tipperary', C Manning, *Europa Nostra Bulletin* 55 (2001), 115–20*

'Medieval Britain and Ireland in 1982', S M Youngs, J Clark and T B Barry, *Medieval Archaeology* 27 (1983), 220–21

'Medieval Britain and Ireland in 1989', D R M Gaimster, S Margeson and M Hurley, *ibid* 34 (1990), 230

'Medieval Britain and Ireland in 1990', B S Nenk, S Margeson and M Hurley, *ibid* 35 (1991), 213

'Medieval Britain and Ireland in 1991', B S Nenk, S Margeson and M Hurley, *ibid* 36 (1992), 290

'Post-medieval Britain and Ireland in 1990', M Ponsford, *Post-Medieval Archaeology* 25 (1991), 126

'The two Sir George Hamiltons and their connections with the castles of Roscrea and Nenagh', C Manning, *Tipperary Historical Journal* (2001), 149–54*

Summerhill

'Summerhill 5', in G T Stout, *Archaeological survey of the Barony of Ikerrin*, 115–16. Roscrea: Roscrea Heritage Society, 1984*

Terryglass

'Terryglass', in J Farrelly and C O'Brien, *Archaeological inventory of County Tipperary. 1. North Tipperary*, 313–14. Dublin: Stationery Office, 2002*

Thurles

'Black Castle Theatre, Thurles', M Gowen, in I Bennett (ed), *Excavations 1995: summary accounts of archaeological excavations in Ireland*, 83. Bray: Wordwell, 1996

Tullow

'Tullowmacjames', in J Farrelly and C O'Brien, *Archaeological inventory of County Tipperary. 1. North Tipperary*, 315–16. Dublin: Stationery Office, 2002

'Tullowmacjames 4 (Tullow Castle – tower in ruins)', in G T Stout, *Archaeological survey of the Barony of Ikerrin*, 136–37. Roscrea: Roscrea Heritage Society, 1984*

TYRONE

Roulston, W. 'Seventeenth-century manors in the barony of Strabane', in J Lyttleton and T O'Keeffe (eds), *The manor in medieval and early modern Ireland*, 160–87. Dublin: Four Courts Press, 2005*

Rowan, A. *North west Ulster (The buildings of Ireland)*. Harmondsworth: Penguin Books, 1979*

Salter, M. *The castles of Ulster*. Malvern: Folly Publications, 2004*

Augher

'Augher Fort', in G A Hayes-McCoy (ed), *Ulster and other Irish maps c 1600*, 18–19. Dublin: Stationery Office for the Irish manuscripts Commission, 1964*

Blackwater

'Armagh and the third Blackwater fort', in *ibid*, 5–6*

The Bonn

'Excavation at a farmyard in the Bonn townland, County Tyrone', N F Brannon, *Ulster Journal of Archaeology* 3 ser 47 (1984), 177–81*

Castlecaulfield

'Castlecaulfield, Co Tyrone', E M Jope, *ibid* 3 ser 21 (1958), 101–7*

Castle Curlews

'Sir John Davies and his Ulster buildings: Castlederg and Castle Curlews, Co Tyrone', D M Waterman, *ibid* 3 ser 23 (1960), 89–96*

Castlederg

'Castlederg Castle, Castlessaigh', C Newman, in I Bennett (ed), *Excavations 1991: summary accounts of archaeological excavations in Ireland*, 43–44. Bray: Wordwell, 1992

'Castlederg Castle, Castlederg', E Halpin, in I Bennett (ed), *Excavations 1992: summary accounts of archaeological excavations in Ireland*, 59. Bray: Wordwell, 1993

'Sir John Davies and his Ulster buildings: Castlederg and Castle Curlews, Co Tyrone', D M Waterman, *Ulster Journal of Archaeology* 3 ser 23 (1960), 89–96*

Dungannon

'Dungannon, Tullahoge and a crannog', in G A Hayes-McCoy (ed), *Ulster and* *other Irish maps c 1600*, 8–10. Dublin: Stationery Office for the Irish manuscripts Commission, 1964*

'Castle Hill, Dungannon', R M Chapple, in I Bennett (ed), *Excavations 2003: summary accounts of archaeological excavations in Ireland*, 486–87. Bray: Wordwell, 2006*

'Excavations at Castle Hill, Dungannon, Co Tyrone', R M Chapple, *Archaeology Ireland* 17.3 (2003), 24–29*

Harry Avery's
'Medieval Britain in 1962 and 1963', D M Wilson and D G Hurst, *Medieval Archaeology* 8 (1964), 263

'Harry Avery's Castle, Newtownstewart, Co Tyrone: excavations in 1950', E M Jope, H M Jope and E A Johnson, *Ulster Journal of Archaeology* 3 ser 13 (1950), 81–92*

'Recent work at Harry Avery's Castle, Co Tyrone', S G Rees-Jones and D M Waterman, *ibid* 3 ser 30 (1967), 76–82*

Mountjoy
'Mountjoy Fort', in G A Hayes-McCoy (ed), *Ulster and other Irish maps c 1600*, 13. Dublin: Stationery Office for the Irish manuscripts Commission, 1964*

Newtownstewart
'Newtownstewart Castle, Newtownstewart', R Ó Baoill, in I Bennett (ed), *Excavations 1999: summary accounts of archaeological excavations in Ireland*, 291–92. Bray: Wordwell, 2000

'Post-medieval Britain and Ireland in 1998 and 1999', M Ponsford, *Post-Medieval Archaeology* 34 (2000), 315–16

'Post-medieval Britain and Ireland in 2000', M Ponsford, *ibid* 35 (2001), 189

'The castle at Newtownstewart, Co Tyrone', H Meek and E M Jope, *Ulster Journal of Archaeology* 3 ser 21 (1958), 109–14*

Sessiamagaroll
'Sessia and Sessiamagaroll fort', P Ó Conlain, *Dúiche Néill: Journal of the O Neill County Historical Society* 1.1 (1986), 12–21*

WATERFORD

Moore, M. *Archaeological inventory of County Waterford*. Dublin: Stationery Office, 1999*

Power, P C. *History of Waterford, city and county*. Dublin: Mercier Press, 1990*

Salter, M. *The castles of south Munster*. Malvern: Folly Publications, 2004*

Walton, J C. 'A check-list of the castles of Co Waterford', *Decies* 6 (1977), 3–6

Walton, J C. 'Checklist of Waterford castles', *ibid* 8 (1978), 14–15

IRELAND

Ballyclohy

'Ballyclohy', in M Moore, *Archaeological inventory of County Waterford*, 220. Dublin: Stationery Office, 1999*

Clonea

'The castle at Clonea-Power', T Nolan, *Decies* 35 (1987), 18–23*

Dungarvan

'Ballyknock Upper/Dungarvan', in M Moore, *Archaeological inventory of County Waterford*, 213–14. Dublin: Stationery Office, 1999*

'St Augustine Street (Friary Street), Dungarvan Urban District', C Power, in I Bennett (ed), *Excavations 1989: summary accounts of archaeological excavations in Ireland*, 48. Dublin: Wordwell, 1990

'Dungarvan Castle, Dungarvan', D Pollock, in I Bennett (ed), *Excavations 1995: summary accounts of archaeological excavations in Ireland*, 84–85. Bray: Wordwell, 1996*

'Dungarvan Castle, Dungarvan', D Pollock, in I Bennett (ed), *Excavations 1996: summary accounts of archaeological excavations in Ireland*, 110–11. Bray: Wordwell, 1997

'Dungarvan Castle, Dungarvan', D Pollock, in *ibid*, 111

'Tannery, Dungarvan', D Pollock, in *ibid*, 111

'Dungarvan Castle, Dungarvan, D Pollock, in I Bennett (ed), *Excavations 1997: summary accounts of archaeological excavations in Ireland*, 184–85. Bray: Wordwell, 1998*

'Dungarvan Castle, Dungarvan', D Pollock, in I Bennett (ed), *Excavations 1998: summary accounts of archaeological excavations in Ireland*, 206–7. Bray: Wordwell, 2000*

'Carberry's Lane, Dungarvan', D Pollock, in I Bennett (ed), *Excavations 1999: summary accounts of archaeological excavations in Ireland*, 292–93. Bray: Wordwell, 2000*

'Dungarvan Castle, Dungarvan', D Pollock, in *ibid*, 293–94*

'Dungarvan Castle, Dungarvan', D Pollock, in I Bennett (ed), *Excavations 2000: summary accounts of archaeological excavations in Ireland*, 333. Bray: Wordwell, 2002*

'Castle Street, Dungarvan', D Pollock, in I Bennett (ed), *Excavations 2002: summary accounts of archaeological excavations in Ireland*, 488. Bray: Wordwell, 2004

'MacGrath's Castle, Abbeyside, Dungarvan', W Fraher, *Decies* 49 (1994), 38–44*

'Medieval Britain and Ireland in 1995', B S Nenk, S Margeson and M Hurley, *Medieval Archaeology* 40 (1996), 304–5*

'Medieval Britain and Ireland in 1996', B S Nenk, C Haith and J Bradley, *ibid* 41 (1997), 311

'Post-medieval Britain and Ireland in 1996', M Ponsford and R Jackson, *Post-Medieval Archaeology* 31 (1997), 264

'Excavations in Dungarvan: a medieval town wall', C Power, *Tipperary Historical Journal* (1995), 183–201*

Kilbarry

'Cromwell's Camp at Kilbarry?', J S Carroll, *Decies* 1 (1976), 3

Lisfinny

'Lisfinny', in M Moore, *Archaeological inventory of County Waterford*, 225–26. Dublin: Stationery Office, 1999*

Mayfield

'Mayfield or Rocketscastle', in *ibid*, 227–28*

Passage

'Aspects of Passage East: part I', J C Walton, *Decies* 10 (1979), 21–28*

'Aspects of Passage East: part II', J C Walton, *ibid* 11 (1979), 17–25*

'The fortifications of Waterford, Passage and Duncannon 1495 to 1690', P M Kerrigan, *ibid* 29 (1985), 12–23*

Rathgormack

'Notes on Rathgormack Castle', [D Cowman], *ibid* 16 (1981), 52–60*

Sheanmore

'Shean More', in M Moore, *Archaeological inventory of County Waterford*, 228–29. Dublin: Stationery Office, 1999*

Waterford

Reginald's Tower visitors' guide. Anon. Dublin: Dúchas The Heritage Service, n d*

Late Viking age and medieval Waterford: excavations 1986–1992. M F Hurley and O M B Scully. Waterford: Waterford Corporation, [1997]* [espec pp 20–33]

Discover Waterford. E McEneaney. Dublin: O'Brien Press, 2001* (City guides)

Reginald's Tower and the story of Waterford. P Mackey. [S l]: South Eastern Regional Tourism Organisation, 1980*

'Waterford Fort', in G A Hayes-McCoy (ed), *Ulster and other Irish maps c 1600*, 8–10. Dublin: Stationery Office for the Irish manuscripts Commission, 1964*

'Waterford City', in M Moore, *Archaeological inventory of County Waterford*, 207–212. Dublin: Stationery Office, 1999*

'The topographical development of Scandinavian and Anglo-Norman Waterford', J Bradley and A Halpin, in W Nolan and T P Power (eds), *Waterford: history and* *society. Interdisciplinary essays on the history of an Irish county*, 105–30. Dublin: Geography Publications, 1992*

'Grady's Yard, John Street', B Murtagh, in C Cotter (ed), *Excavations 1985: summary accounts of archaeological excavations in Ireland*, 39–40. Dublin: Irish Academic Publications, 1986

'Grady's Yard, John Street, Ward of Mount Sion', B Murtagh, in C Cotter (ed), *Excavations 1986: summary accounts of archaeological excavations in Ireland*, 36. Dublin: Irish Academic Publications, 1987

'Custom House B Ward', B Murtagh, in I Bennett (ed), *Excavations 1989: summary accounts of archaeological excavations in Ireland*, 47. Dublin: Wordwell, 1990

'Bakehouse Lane 11, Custom House Ward, Waterford', O M B Scully, in I Bennett (ed), *Excavations 1990: summary accounts of archaeological excavations in Ireland*, 53. Bray: Wordwell, 1991

'Double Tower, Castle Street, Ward of Mount Sion, Waterford', B Murtagh, in *ibid*, 53–54*

'The Watch Tower, Railway Square/Manor Street, Ward of Mount Sion, Waterford', B Murtagh, in *ibid*, 54–55*

'Beach Tower, Jenkins Lane, Waterford', O M B Scully, in I Bennett (ed), *Excavations 1996: summary accounts of archaeological excavations in Ireland*, 111–12. Dublin: Wordwell, 1997

'Reginald's Tower, The Quay, Waterford', B Murtagh, in I Bennett (ed), *Excavations 1997: summary accounts of archaeological excavations in Ireland*, 186–87. Bray: Wordwell, 1998

'Waterside Motors Ltd, Waterside, Waterford', A Gittins, in I Bennett (ed), *Excavations 1998: summary accounts of archaeological excavations in Ireland*, 208. Bray: Wordwell, 2000

'Waterford', O Scully, in I Bennett (ed), *Excavations 2000: summary accounts of archaeological excavations in Ireland*, 340. Bray: Wordwell, 2002

'Lady Lane, Waterford', J Wren, in *ibid*, 341–42

'Grady's Yard, John Street, Waterford', D Pollock, in I Bennett (ed), *Excavations 2001: summary accounts of archaeological excavations in Ireland*, 390–91. Bray: Wordwell, 2003*

'Lifetime Day Care Centre, Lady Lane, Waterford', R Tobin, in *ibid*, 391 [1995 excavation]

'Lady Lane, Waterford', J Wren, in *ibid*, 391–92

'Lady Lane, Waterford', J Wren, in I Bennett (ed), *Excavations 2002: summary accounts of archaeological excavations in Ireland*, 496. Bray: Wordwell, 2004

'Waterford's Watergate', B Murtagh, *Archaeology Ireland* 15.2 (2001), 28–33*

'The walls and defences of Waterford', J S Carroll, *Decies* 4 (1977), 16–18

'The walls and defences of Waterford, part II', J S Carroll, *ibid* 5 (1977), 6–10*

'The archaeology of Waterford. 2. City walls and gateway at site of St Martin's Castle', M Moore, *ibid* 23 (1983), 49–61*

'Reginald's Tower', J S Carroll, *ibid* 26 (1984), 22–27*

'The fortifications of Waterford, Passage and Duncannon 1495 to 1690', P M Kerrigan, *ibid* 29 (1985), 12–23*

'The city wall at 118–119 Parade Quay, Waterford', C Sheehan, *ibid* 50 (1994), 8–16*

'The Watergate and excavations at Grady's Yard, Waterford', B Murtagh, *ibid* 57 (2001), 9–41*

'New evidence for the form and nature of Colbeck gate: an archaeological excavation at Colbeck Street, Waterford', B Mac Domhnaill, *ibid* 61 (2005), 151–66*

'Cromwell's siege of Waterford, 1649', J G Simms, *Irish Sword* 4 (1959–60), 171–79

'Medieval Britain and Ireland in 1983', S M Youngs, J Clark and T B Barry, *Medieval Archaeology* 28 (1984), 257–58

'Medieval Britain and Ireland in 1984', S M Youngs, J Clark and T Barry, *ibid* 29 (1985), 216–18*

'Medieval Britain and Ireland in 1985', S M Youngs, J Clark and T Barry, *ibid* 30 (1986), 188

'Medieval Britain and Ireland in 1986', S M Youngs, J Clark and T Barry, *ibid* 31 (1987), 180–81

'Medieval Britain and Ireland in 1987', S M Youngs [*et al*], *ibid* 32 (1988), 299

'Medieval Britain and Ireland in 1988', D R M Gaimster, S Margeson and T Barry, *ibid* 33 (1989), 226

'Medieval Britain and Ireland in 1989', D R M Gaimster, S Margeson and M Hurley, *ibid* 34 (1990), 239

'Medieval Britain and Ireland in 1990', B S Nenk, S Margeson and M Hurley, *ibid* 35 (1991), 216

'Medieval Britain and Ireland in 1993', B S Nenk, S Margeson and M Hurley, *ibid* 38 (1994), 277–78

'Medieval Britain and Ireland in 1994', B S Nenk, S Margeson and M Hurley, *ibid* 39 (1995), 271

'Medieval Britain and Ireland in 1996', B S Nenk, C Haith and J Bradley, *ibid* 41 (1997), 312

'Medieval Britain and Ireland in 1997', M Gaimster, C Haith and J Bradley, *ibid* 42 (1998), 170–71

'Medieval Britain and Ireland in 1998', J Bradley, M Gaimster and C Haith, *ibid* 43 (1999), 293–94

'Medieval Britain and Ireland in 2000', J Bradley and M Gaimster, *ibid* 45 (2001), 349

'Post-medieval Britain and Ireland in 1990', M Ponsford, *Post-Medieval Archaeology* 25 (1991), 126

WESTMEATH

Casey, C and Rowan, A. *North Leinster: the counties of Longford, Louth, Meath and Westmeath (The buildings of Ireland)*. London: Penguin Books, 1993*

Salter, M. *The castles of Leinster*. Malvern: Folly Publications, 2004*

Athlone

Irish historic towns atlas. 6. Athlone. H Murtagh. Dublin: Royal Irish Academy, 1994*

'The North Gate, Athlone', A M Ireland, in T Condit and C Corlett (eds), *Above and beyond: essays in memory of Leo Swan*, 461–72. Bray: Wordwell, 2005*

'The town wall fortifications of Athlone', H Murtagh, in H Murtagh (ed), *Irish midland studies: essays in commemoration of N W English*, 89–106. Athlone: Old Athlone Society, 1980*

'Athlone Castle, Athlone', A Halpin, in I Bennett (ed), *Excavations 1991: summary accounts of archaeological excavations in Ireland*, 45. Bray: Wordwell, 1992

'Bastion Street, Athlone', P Stevens, in I Bennett (ed), *Excavations 1998: summary accounts of archaeological excavations in Ireland*, 208. Bray: Wordwell, 2000

'Northgate Street, Athlone', M E Byrne, in *ibid*, 208–9*

'Athlone Westside Main Drainage Scheme', M E Byrne, in I Bennett (ed), *Excavations 1999: summary accounts of archaeological excavations in Ireland*, 296. Bray: Wordwell, 2000

'Northgate Street, Athlone', M E Byrne, in *ibid*, 296

'The work at the Double Tower, Waterford', B Murtagh, *Decies* 60 (2004), 1–18*

'Athlone, Aughrin and Arklow', anon, *Irish Sword* 1 (1949–53), 268*

'A diary of the siege of Athlone, 1691', anon, *ibid* 4 (1959–60), 88–92

'A report on the castle of Athlone, 1793', anon, 4 (1959–60), 180–81*

'The medieval castle of Athlone', J A Claffey, *Journal of the Old Athlone Society* 1 (1969–75), 55–60

'The siege of Athlone 1690', H Murtagh, *ibid* 1 (1969–75), 84–87

'The siege of Athlone 1691', H Murtagh, *ibid* 1 (1969–75), 172–83

'A report of the castle of Athlone 1793', anon, *ibid* 1 (1969–75), 250–53*

'The batteries, Athlone', P M Kerrigan, *ibid* 1 (1969–75), 264–70*

'The batteries – some additional notes', P M Kerrigan, *ibid* 2.5 (1978), 24–25

'Thomas Phillip's plan of Athlone', H Murtagh, *ibid* 2.6 (1985), 133–35*

'The siege of Athlone', D Murtagh, *Journal of the Royal Society of Antiquaries of Ireland* 83 (1953), 58–81*

'Post-medieval Britain and Ireland in 1991', M Ponsford, *Post-Medieval Archaeology* 26 (1992), 123

Ballymore

'Map of Ballymore Fort, County Westmeath: a seventeenth-century error rectified', H L Wood, *Irish Sword* 19 (1993–95), 344–46*

'Ballymore and the Jacobite war', H Murtagh, *Journal of the Old Athlone Society* 1 (1969–75), 242–46*

Castletown

'Anglo-Norman change and continuity: the castle of Telach Cail in Delbna', M T Flanagan, *Irish Historical Studies* 28 (1992–5), 385–89

Fore

Fore, Co Westmeath. H G Leask. Dublin: Stationery Office, n d*

Kilkenny

'Kilkenny Castle, Kilkenny West', K Campbell, in I Bennett (ed), *Excavations 1996: summary accounts of archaeological excavations in Ireland*, 112. Bray: Wordwell, 1997

Mullingar

Irish historic towns atlas. 5. Mullingar. J H Andrews and K M Davies. Dublin: Royal Irish Academy, 1992*

WEXFORD

Colfer, B. *Arrogant trespass: Anglo-Norman Wexford 1169–1400*. Enniscorthy: Duffry Press, 2002*

Colfer, B. *The Hook Peninsula, County Wexford*. Cork: Cork University Press, 2004*

Colfer, B. 'Anglo-Norman settlement in County Wexford', in K Whelan (ed), *Wexford: history and society. Interdisciplinary essays on the history of an Irish county*, 65–101. Dublin: Geography Publications, 1987*

Hadden, G. 'Some earthworks in Co Wexford', *Journal of the Cork Historical and Archaeological Society* 69 (1964), 118–22

Harbison, P. 'Barralet and Beranger's antiquarian sketching tour through Wicklow and Wexford in the autumn of 1780', *Proceedings of the Royal Irish Academy* 104C (2004), 131–90*

Jeffrey, W H. *The castles of Co Wexford (notes compiled from various sources)*. [Wexford]: Old Wexford Society, 1979

Jordan, A J. 'Date, chronology and evolution of the County Wexford tower house', *Journal of the Wexford Historical Society* 13 (1990–1), 30–81*

Loeber, R and Stouthamer-Loeber, M. 'The lost architecture of the Wexford plantation', in K Whelan (ed), *Wexford: history and society. Interdisciplinary essays on the history of an Irish county*, 173–200. Dublin: Geography Publications, 1987*

McNeill, T E. 'Early castles in Leinster', *Journal of Irish Archaeology* 5 (1989–90), 57–64*

Moore, M J. *Archaeological inventory of County Wexford*. Dublin: Stationery Office, 1996*

O'Callaghan, J. 'The fortified houses of the 16th century in south Wexford', *Journal of the Old Wexford Society* 8 (1980–1), 1–51*

Salter, M. *The castles of Leinster*. Malvern: Folly Publications, 2004*

Sweetman, P D. 'Aspects of early thirteenth century castles in Leinster', *Château Gaillard* 15 (1992), 325–33*

Baginbun

'A reinterpretation of the earthworks at Baginbun, Co Wexford', K O'Conor, in J R Kenyon and K O'Conor (eds), *The medieval castle in Ireland and Wales: essays in honour of Jeremy Knight*, 17–31. Dublin: Four Courts Press, 2003*

Ballyhack

'A mid seventeenth-century pottery group and other objects from Ballyhack Castle, Co Wexford', J G Hurst, *Proceedings of the Royal Irish Academy* 75C (1970), 103–18*

Ballyhire

'Ballyhire Castle, St Helens', E O'Donovan, in I Bennett (ed), *Excavations 1997: summary accounts of archaeological excavations in Ireland*, 194. Bray: Wordwell, 1998

Butlerstown

'Butlerstown Castle', anon, *Journal of the Butler Society* 3.4 (1994), 561*

Coolhull

'Coolhull', in M J Moore, *Archaeological inventory of County Wexford*, 180–81. Dublin: Stationery Office, 1996*

Danescastle

'Danescastle', in *ibid*, 172*

Deeps

'Castle of the Deeps', J O'Callaghan, *Journal of the Old Wexford Society* 2 (1969), 26–38*

Duncannon

Dún Conáin: Duncannon Fort. P Kerrigan. [S l]: Irish Tourist Board, n d*

'Duncannon', in M J Moore, *Archaeological inventory of County Wexford*, 191. Dublin: Stationery Office, 1996*

'Duncannon Fort, Duncannon', M Reid, in I Bennett (ed), *Excavations 1993: summary accounts of archaeological excavations in Ireland*, 79. Bray: Wordwell, 1994

'Duncannon Fort, Duncannon', S McCutcheon, in I Bennett (ed), *Excavations 1997: summary accounts of archaeological excavations in Ireland*, 192. Bray: Wordwell, 1998

'Duncannon Fort', D O'Shea, *An Cosantóir* 46.9 (1986), 29*

'The fortifications of Waterford, Passage and Duncannon 1495 to 1690', P M Kerrigan, *Decies* 29 (1985), 12–23*

'The *Great Lewis* and the siege of Duncannon, 1645', K Downes, *ibid* 60 (2004), 115–16.

'Operations of the Parliamentary squadron at the siege of Duncannon in 1645', J R Powell, *Irish Sword* 2 (1954–6), 17–21*

'Duncannon', P J Sinnot, *Journal of the Old Wexford Society* 3 (1970–1), 62–80*

'Fort Duncannon, County Wexford', R Morgan, *Postern* 16 (2004–5), 13–17*

'Post-medieval Britain and Ireland in 1993', M Ponsford, *Post-Medieval Archaeology* 28 (1994), 128

Ferns

'The chronology and formal affinities of the Ferns *donjon*, Co Wexford', T O'Keeffe and M Coughlan, in J R Kenyon and K O'Conor (eds), *The medieval castle in Ireland and Wales: essays in honour of Jeremy Knight*, 133–48. Dublin: Four Courts Press, 2003*

'Castleland', in M J Moore, *Archaeological inventory of County Wexford*, 155–56. Dublin: Stationery Office, 1996*

'Ferns', P D Sweetman, *Excavations 1972*, 28–29. [S l]: Association of Young Irish Archaeologists, n d

'Ferns', P D Sweetman, in T G Delaney (ed), *Excavations 1973*, 27–28. [S l]: Association of Young Irish Archaeologists, 1974

'Ferns', P D Sweetman, in T G Delaney (ed), *Excavations 1974: summary accounts of archaeological work in Ireland*, 28. [S l]: Association of Young Irish Archaeologists, n d

'Archaeological excavations at Ferns Castle, Co Wexford', P D Sweetman, *Proceedings of the Royal Irish Academy* 79C (1979), 217–45*

Ferrycarrig

'Ferrycarrig, Newtown', C Cotter, in C Cotter (ed), *Excavations 1986: summary accounts of archaeological excavations in Ireland*, 37. Dublin: Irish Academic Publications, 1987

'Ferrycarrig, Newtown', C Cotter, in I Bennett (ed), *Excavations 1987: summary accounts of archaeological excavations in Ireland*, 30. Dublin: Wordwell, 1988

'Preliminary archaeological excavations at Ferrycarrig ringwork, Newtown td, Co Wexford', I Bennett, *Journal of the Old Wexford Society* 10 (1984–5), 24–43*

'Medieval Britain and Ireland in 1984', S M Youngs, J Clark and T Barry, *Medieval Archaeology* 29 (1985), 219

'Medieval Britain and Ireland in 1986', S M Youngs, J Clark and T Barry, *ibid* 31 (1987), 181

Fethard-on-Sea

Fethard Castle – a manorial centre cum episcopal residence in County Wexford. B Murtagh. Bray: Archaeology Ireland, 2004* (Heritage guide; 25)

'Survey of Fethard-on-Sea Castle, Co Wexford', B Murtagh, in I Bennett (ed), *Excavations 1993: summary accounts of archaeological excavations in Ireland*, 83. Bray: Wordwell, 1994

Hook

'The Tower of Hook', W Colfer, *Journal of the Wexford Society* 10 (1984–5), 69–78*

Kilcloggan

'Kilcloggan', in M J Moore, *Archaeological inventory of County Wexford*, 173–74. Dublin: Stationery Office, 1996*

New Ross

'The walling of New Ross: a thirteenth-century poem in French', H Shields, *Long Room* 12–13 (1975–6), 24–28

Old Ross

'The Quay, New Ross', M E Byrne, in I Bennett (ed), *Excavations 2000: summary accounts of archaeological excavations in Ireland*, 356–57. Bray: Wordwell, 2002

'The Norman motte at Old Ross: method of construction', E Culleton and W Colfer, *Journal of the Old Wexford Society* 5 (1974–5), 22–25*

Rathmacknee

'Rathmacknee Great', in M J Moore. *Archaeological inventory of County Wexford*, 177. Dublin: Stationery Office, 1996*

'Rathmacknee Castle, Co Wexford', H G Leask, *Journal of the Royal Society of Antiquaries of Ireland* 83 (1953), 37–45*

Rathshillane

'Rathshillane', in M J Moore, *Archaeological inventory of County Wexford*, 181. Dublin: Stationery Office, 1996*

'Rathshillane', C Ó Drisceoil, in I Bennett (ed), *Excavations 2003: summary accounts of archaeological excavations in Ireland*, 536–37. Bray: Wordwell, 2006

Rosslare

'Rosslare Fort and its people', G Kehoe, *Journal of the Old Wexford Society* 4 (1972–3), 43–52

'Rosslare: its fort and lifeboat', J Turner, *The Past* 9 (1972), 52–56

Sigginstown

'Sigginstown', in M J Moore, *Archaeological inventory of County Wexford*, 178. Dublin: Stationery Office, 1996*

Slade

'Slade Castle, Co Wexford', H G Leask, *Journal of the Royal Society of Antiquaries of Ireland* 81 (1951), 198–201*

Wexford

'Wexford', M Cahill and M Ryan, in T G Delaney (ed), *Excavations 1975–76: summary accounts of archaeological work in Ireland*, 37. [S l]: Association of Young Irish Archaeologists, n d

'Westgate/Slaney Street/Temperance Road/Redmond Place, Townparks, Wexford', E C Rourke, in I Bennett (ed), *Excavations 1990: summary accounts of archaeological excavations in Ireland*, 57. Bray: Wordwell, 1991

'Wexford town', J Wren, in I Bennett (ed), *Excavations 1993: summary accounts of archaeological excavations in Ireland*, 83. Bray: Wordwell, 1994 *

'George [*sic*] St area, Wexford', D G Moore, in I Bennett (ed), *Excavations 1995: summary accounts of archaeological excavations in Ireland*, 89. Bray: Wordwell, 1996

'Georges St, Wexford', J Moran, in *ibid*, 89

'Gasworks, Trinity St, Wexford', C McConway, in *ibid*, 90

'An investigation of the town wall at Abbey Street, Wexford', M Cahill and M Ryan, *Journal of the Old Wexford Society* 8 (1980–1), 56–64*

'Medieval Wexford', B Colfer, *Journal of the Wexford Society* 13 (1990–1), 4–29*

Threecastles
'Threecastles', in M J Moore. *Archaeological inventory of County Wexford*, 191. Dublin: Stationery Office, 1996*

WICKLOW

Corlett, C. *Antiquities of old Rathdown*. Bray: Wordwell, 1999*

Grogan, E and Kilfeather, A. *Archaeological inventory of County Wicklow*. Dublin: Stationery Office, 1997*

Harbison, P. 'Barralet and Beranger's antiquarian sketching tour through Wicklow and Wexford in the autumn of 1780', *Proceedings of the Royal Irish Academy* 104C (2004), 131–90*

Salter, M. *The castles of Leinster*. Malvern: Folly Publications, 2004*

Shanahan, B. 'The manor in east county Wicklow', in J Lyttleton and T O'Keeffe (eds), *The manor in medieval and early modern Ireland*, 132–59. Dublin: Four Courts Press, 2005*

Simpson, L. 'Anglo-Norman settlement in Ui Briúin Cualann, 1169–1350', in K Hannigan and W Nolan (eds), *Wicklow: history and society. Interdisciplinary essays in the history of an Irish county*, 191–235. Dublin: Geography Publications, 1994*

Bray
Irish historic towns atlas. 9. Bray. K M Davies. Dublin: Royal Irish Academy, 1998*

'The castle of Bray', K M Davies, *Journal of the Cualann Historical Society* (1986), 22–25*

Burgage More
'Burgage More', in E Grogan and A Kilfeather, *Archaeological inventory of County Wicklow*, 187–88. Dublin: Stationery Office, 1997*

Carnew
'Carnew castle', T Foley, in T Condit and C Corlett (eds), *Above and beyond: essays in memory of Leo Swan*, 423–34. Bray: Wordwell, 2005*

Fassaroe
'Fassaroe', in E Grogan and A Kilfeather, *Archaeological inventory of County Wicklow*, 189. Dublin: Stationery Office, 1997*

Kindlestown
'Dublin's southern frontier under siege: Kindlestown Castle, Delgany, County

Wicklow', L Simpson, in S Duffy (ed), *Medieval Dublin IV: proceedings of the Friends of Medieval Dublin symposium 2002*, 279–368. Dublin: Four Courts Press, 2003*

'Kindlestown Castle, Delgany', L Simpson, in I Bennett (ed), *Excavations 2001: summary accounts of archaeological excavations in Ireland*, 418–21. Bray: Wordwell, 2003*

'Medieval Britain and Ireland in 2001', J Bradley and M Gaimster, *Medieval Archaeology* 46 (2002), 221

Oldcourt
'Oldcourt', in E Grogan and A Kilfeather, *Archaeological inventory of County Wicklow*, 190. Dublin: Stationery Office, 1997*

'Solid as a rock? Oldcourt Castle, Co Wicklow', S Pavin and J Bolton, *Archaeology Ireland* 13.2 (1999), 15–18*

Powerscourt
'Powerscourt Demesne', D Delany, in I Bennett (ed), *Excavations 2001: summary accounts of archaeological excavations in Ireland*, 427. Bray: Wordwell, 2003

Rathdown
'Rathdown Castle, Rathdown Upper', M Gowen, in I Bennett (ed), *Excavations 1993: summary accounts of archaeological excavations in Ireland*, 86–87. Bray: Wordwell, 1994

Threecastles
'Three Castles: a sentinel in stone watching the north-west frontier of Gaelic Leinster', K Ferguson, *Irish Sword* 22.88 (2000), 121–24*

APPENDIX

This appendix lists material that has come to my attention since the submission of the main text in January 2007, up to the beginning of September 2007. It includes some items that were actually published in 2007, but many date to the end of 2006 or even earlier. It was particularly unfortunate, given my place of work, to come across some Welsh material in March that I had not picked up, though in one case this was due to the publishing society not sending the National Museum of Wales the last few issues of its annual journal.

PART 1 (A) GENERAL – BOOKS AND PAMPHLETS

Castleden, R
Castles of the Celtic lands: the historic castles of Ireland, Scotland and Wales. London: Quercus, 2006*

English castles: a photographic history. London: Quercus, 2006*

Emery, A
Discovering medieval houses in England and Wales. Princes Risborough: Shire, 2007* (Discovering; 297)

Gravett, C and Hook, A
The castles of Edward I in Wales 1277–1307. Oxford: Osprey, 2007* (Fortress; 64)

Hislop, M
John Lewyn of Durham: a medieval mason in practice. Oxford: John and Erica Hedges, 2007* (BAR British series; 438)

Humphrys, J
Enemies at the gate: English castles under siege from the 12th century to the Civil War. Swindon: English Heritage, 2007*

Kenyon, J R
Castle studies: recent publications – 20. [S1]: Castle Studies Group, 2007

Nossov, K
Ancient and medieval siege weapons: a fully illustrated guide to siege weapons and tactics. Staplehurst: Spellmount, 2006*

Osborne, M
20th century defences in the London area: London within the M25, Berkshire,

Buckinghamshire, Hertfordshire and Oxfordshire. Market Deeping: Concrete Publications, 2006*

Ronnes, H
Architecture and élite culture in the United Provinces, England and Ireland, 1500–1700. Amsterdam: University of Amsterdam Press, 2006*

Stierlin, H
Unfolding history: castles, fortresses and citadels. London: Thames & Hudson, 2006*

PART 1(B) GENERAL – PERIODICAL ARTICLES

Davis, P
'Bastles of northern England', *Castle Studies Group Journal* 20 (2006–7), 224–25*

'Licences to crenellate: information on sources and some analysis', *ibid* 20 (2006), 226–33*

'Licences to crenellate 1199–1264', *ibid* 20 (2006), 234–45

Donnelly, C [et al]
'Timber castles and towers in sixteenth-century Ireland: some evidence from Ulster', *Archaeology Ireland* 21.2 (2007), 22–25*

Kenyon, J R
'Richard Avent and castle studies', *Castle Studies Group Journal* 20 (2006–7), 282–83

Murtagh, H
'Thomas Phillips' prospects of Ireland 1684–5', *Irish Arts Review* 24.1 (2007), 104–9*

O'Reilly, W
'Charles Vallancey and the *Military Itinerary* of Ireland', *Proceedings of the Royal Irish Academy* 106C (2006), 125–217*

O'Sullivan, M and Downey, L
'Know your monuments: mottes', *Archaeology Ireland* 21.1 (2007), 19–21*

Tierney, A
'The Gothic and the Gaelic: exploring the place of castles in Ireland's Celtic revival', *International Journal of Historical Archaeology* 8 (2004), 185–98*

PART 1(C) GENERAL – ESSAYS IN BOOKS

Halsall, T J
'Geological constraints on the siting of fortifications: examples from medieval Britain, in E P F Rose and C P Nathanail (eds), *Geology and warfare: examples of*

the influence of terrain and geologists on military operations, 3–31. Bath: Geological Society, 2000*

McKean, C
'Castles, palaces and fortified houses', in G Stell, J Shaw and S Storrier (eds), *Scotland's buildings*, 27–47. East Linton: Tuckwell Press, 2003* (Scottish life and society: a compendium of Scottish ethnology; 3)

Murphy, K
'Military defences', in A Davidson (ed), *The coastal archaeology of Wales*, 76–80. York: CBA, 2002* (Research report; 131)

Ruckley, N A
'Public defences' in G Stell, J Shaw and S Storrier (eds), *Scotland's buildings*, 381–420. East Linton: Tuckwell Press, 2003* (Scottish life and society: a compendium of Scottish ethnology; 3)

PART 2 – TOPOGRAPHICAL

ENGLAND

BERKSHIRE

Osborne, M. *20th century defences in the London area: London within the M25, Berkshire, Buckinghamshire, Hertfordshire and Oxfordshire*. Market Deeping: Concrete Publications, 2006*

Windsor
Edward III's Round Table at Windsor: the House of the Round Table and the Windsor festival of 1344. J Munby, R Barber and R Brown. Woodbridge: Boydell Press, 2007*

'The Catherine Room, Windsor Castle', A Ballantyne, in R Gowing and R Pender (eds), *All manners of murals: the history, techniques and conservation of secular wall paintings*, 115–20. London: Archetype Publications, in association with English Heritage and the Institute of Conservation, 2007*

BUCKINGHAMSHIRE

Osborne, M. *20th century defences in the London area: London within the M25, Berkshire, Buckinghamshire, Hertfordshire and Oxfordshire*. Market Deeping: Concrete Publications, 2006*

CAMBRIDGESHIRE

Cambridge
'Cambridge: historic city centre revealed', sources: A Dickens and C Cessford, *Current Archaeology* 18.4 (2007), 22–27, 30–31*

FORTIFICATIONS BIBLIOGRAPHY

DERBYSHIRE

Bolsover

'Bolsover Castle', R Sheppard, in 'Fieldwork in Derbyshire by Trent & Peak Archaeological Unit in 2004–2006', *Derbyshire Archaeological Journal* 127 (2007), 115–20*

DEVON

Fox, H. 'Two Devon estuaries in the Middle Ages: fisheries, ports, fortifications and places of worship', *Landscapes* 8 (2007), 39–68*

Exeter

'Post-medieval fieldwork in Britain and Northern Ireland in 2005', M Ponsford, *Post-Medieval Archaeology* 40 (2006), 337

Salcombe

'Post-medieval fieldwork in Britain and Northern Ireland in 2005', M Ponsford, *ibid* 40 (2006), 337–38*

DORSET

Bridport

'Bridport's 13th-century defences: archaeological observations to the rear of 41 and 43 East Street, Bridport', P S Bellamy, *Proceedings of the Dorset Natural History and Archaeological Society* 127 (2005), 59–66*

DURHAM

Barnard

Acts of perception: a study of Barnard Castle in Teesdale. D Austin. Durham: Architectural and Archaeological Society of Durham and Northumberland, in association with English Heritage, 2 vols, 2007* (AASDN research report; 6)

ESSEX

Bettley, J and Pevsner, N. *Essex (The buildings of England)*. London: London: Yale University Press, 2007*

Nash, F. 'World War Two defences in Essex project', *Essex Archaeology and History* 34 (2003), 262–63*

Nash, F. 'World War Two defences in Essex project', *ibid*, 35 (2004), 159–60*

Nether Hall

'Nether Hall: a fortified manor of the Wars of the Roses', D D Andrews, *Essex Archaeology and History* 35 (2004), 78–97*

APPENDIX

Waltham Abbey

'World War One anti-aircraft gun sites of Waltham Abbey', F Nash, *Essex Archaeology and History* 34 (2003), 263–65*

HAMPSHIRE

Carisbrooke

'Carisbrooke Castle', C Young, in M Gardiner and D Tomalin (eds), *The Isle of Wight: report and proceedings of the 152nd summer meeting of the Royal Archaeological Institute in 2006*, 24–36. London: RAI, 2007* (supplement to *Archaeological Journal* 163 for 2006)

Hurst

'Hurst Castle', J Coad, in *ibid*, 56–61*

Needles

'The Needles Batteries', J Coad, in *ibid*, 51–54*

Portsmouth

'Post-medieval fieldwork in Britain and Northern Ireland in 2005', M Ponsford, *Post-Medieval Archaeology* 40 (2006), 371

Victoria

'Fort Victoria', J Coad, in M Gardiner and D Tomalin (eds), *The Isle of Wight: report and proceedings of the 152nd summer meeting of the Royal Archaeological Institute in 2006*, 61. London: RAI, 2007 (supplement to *Archaeological Journal* 163 for 2006)

Yarmouth

'Yarmouth Castle', J Coad, in *ibid*, 62–65*

HEREFORDSHIRE

Yates, S (ed). *Heritage unlocked: guide to free sites in the Midlands*. London: English Heritage, 2006*

Ewyas Harold

Ewyas Harold Castle. A Boucher. Hereford: Archaeological Investigations, 2007*

Hereford

The Castle Green at Hereford: a landscape of ritual, royalty and recreation. D Whitehead. Almeley: Logaston Press, 2007*

'Hereford, Castle Pool', A Boucher, *West Midlands Archaeology* 48 (2005), 29–30*

HERTFORDSHIRE

Osborne, M. *20th century defences in the London area: London within the M25, Berkshire, Buckinghamshire, Hertfordshire and Oxfordshire*. Market Deeping: Concrete Publications, 2006*

FORTIFICATIONS BIBLIOGRAPHY

Hertford

The chronicles of Hertford Castle. H C Andrews. Hertford: Austin, 1947*

KENT

Dover

Dover Castle. J Coad. London: English Heritage, 2007*

LEICESTERSHIRE

Ashby de la Zouch

'Investigating a Tudor garden', S Newsome, *The Archaeologist* 63 (2007), 18–19*

'Ashby de la Zouch Castle. News of the landscape investigations: a summary', T Way, *Castle Studies Group Journal* 20 (2006–7), 144–46*

'A late medieval/Renaissance garden at Ashby de la Zouch', P Pattison [*et al*], *Research News: Newsletter of the English Heritage Research Department* 5 (2006–7), 40–43*

LINCOLNSHIRE

Yates, S (ed). *Heritage unlocked: guide to free sites in the Midlands*. London: English Heritage, 2006*

LONDON AND MIDDLESEX

Osborne, M. *20th century defences in the London area: London within the M25, Berkshire, Buckinghamshire, Hertfordshire and Oxfordshire*. Market Deeping: Concrete Publications, 2006*

City Defences

The London Wall walk. H Chapman, J Hall and G Marsh. London: Museum of London, 1985*

Civil War Defences

'London's Fort Royal', D Flintham, *Casemate* 80 (2007), 16–18*

Tower of London

Unfolding history: castles, fortresses and citadels. H. Stierlin. London: Thames & Hudson, 2006*

'Officials and moneyers at the Tower of London in 1433', J Freeman, *British Numismatic Journal* 76 (2006), 303–11

NORTHUMBERLAND

Dunstanburgh

Dunstanburgh Castle. A Oswald and J Ashbee. London: English Heritage, 2007*

APPENDIX

OXFORDSHIRE

Osborne, M. *20th century defences in the London area: London within the M25, Berkshire, Buckinghamshire, Hertfordshire and Oxfordshire*. Market Deeping: Concrete Publications, 2006*

Oxford

'The Augustinian canons and the University of Oxford: the lost college of St George', J Barron, in C M Barron and J Stratford (eds), *The church and learning in later medieval society: essays in honour of R B Dobson. Proceedings of the 1999 Harlaxton Symposium*, 228–54. Donington: Shaun Tyas, 2002 (Harlaxton medieval studies; 11)

'Post-medieval fieldwork in Britain and Northern Ireland in 2005', M Ponsford, *Post-Medieval Archaeology* 40 (2006), 369

SHROPSHIRE

Yates, S (ed). *Heritage unlocked: guide to free sites in the Midlands*. London: English Heritage, 2006*

Fordhall

'Monastic enterprise in town and countryside: two case studiers from north-east Shropshire', M Fradley, *Landscape History* 28 (2006), 5–33*

Oswestry

'Oswestry, land off Chapel Street', P Frost, *West Midlands Archaeology* 48 (2005), 41–43*

Stokesay

'Medieval masterpiece', L Lambton, *Heritage Today* 77 (2007), 21–23*

'Post-medieval fieldwork in Britain and Northern Ireland in 2005', M Ponsford, *Post-Medieval Archaeology* 40 (2006), 376–77

'Stokesay Castle, the gatehouse chimney', D Rouse, *West Midlands Archaeology* 48 (2005), 47–48

'Stokesay, Stokesay Castle chimney stage 2', D Rouse and S Mayes, *ibid* 48 (2005), 48–49*

Tyrley (Market Drayton)

'Monastic enterprise in town and countryside: two case studiers from north-east Shropshire', M Fradley, *Landscape History* 28 (2006), 5–33*

SOMERSET

Nether Stowey

The historic landscape of the Quantock Hills. H Riley. Swindon: English Heritage, 2006* [espec pp 91–92]

FORTIFICATIONS BIBLIOGRAPHY

STAFFORDSHIRE

Tutbury

'The Tutbury project: an interim report', M Hislop and G Williams, *Castle Studies Group Journal* 20 (2006–7), 170–213*

'Tutbury, Tutbury Castle and park pale', M Hislop, *West Midlands Archaeology* 48 (2005), 67–68

SUFFOLK

Hegarty, C and Newsome, S. *Suffolk's defended shore: coastal fortifications from the air*. Swindon: English Heritage, 2007*

SURREY

Reigate

'Reigate Fort', P W Sloan, *Surrey Archaeological Society Bulletin* 400 (2007), 11–12

SUSSEX

Lewes

'Brack Mount keep: searching for new evidence', A Gammon, *Sussex Past & Present* 111 (2007), 6–7*

WARWICKSHIRE

Coventry

'Coventry, Bond Street', P Mason and D McAree, *West Midlands Archaeology* 48 (2005), 122–24*

Kenilworth

'Kenilworth, Kenilworth Castle gatehouse', B Gethin, *ibid* 48 (2005), 92–93

'Kenilworth, Kenilworth Castle, Gallery Tower', C Jones, *ibid* 48 (2005), 93–94*

'Kenilworth, Kenilworth Castle, keep', C Coutts, *ibid* 48 (2005), 93

WORCESTERSHIRE

Brooks, A and Pevsner, N. *Worcestershire (The buildings of England)*. London: Yale University Press, 2007*

YORKSHIRE

Scarborough

'Post-medieval fieldwork in Britain and Northern Ireland in 2005', M Ponsford, *Post-Medieval Archaeology* 40 (2006), 368

APPENDIX

WALES

ANGLESEY

Aberlleiniog
'Castell Aberlleiniog, Anglesey and Cronk Howe Mooar, Isle of Man: related monuments?', S Smith, *Anglesey Antiquarian Society and Field Club Transactions* (2004), 31–45*

CAERNARVONSHIRE

Conwy
Conwy Castle and town walls. J A Ashbee. Cardiff: Cadw, 2007*

CARMARTHENSHIRE

Carmarthen
Castell Caerfyrddin/Carmarthen Castle. N Ludlow. Carmarthen: Carmarthenshire County Council, 2007*

Dinefwr
Dinefwr Castle, Dryslwyn Castle. S E Rees and C Caple. Revised edition. Cardiff: Cadw, 2007*

Dryslwyn
Dinefwr Castle, Dryslwyn Castle. S E Rees and C Caple. Revised edition. Cardiff: Cadw, 2007*

DENBIGHSHIRE

Denbigh
Denbigh Castle, Denbigh town walls, Lord Leicester's Church, St Hilary's Chapel, Denbigh Friary. L Butler. Revised edition. Cardiff: Cadw, 2007*

GLAMORGAN

Hull, L. *The castles of Glamorgan*. Almeley: Logaston Press, 2007* (Monuments in the landscape; 12)

Ridge, M, Ridge, R and Morris, B. *Castles of Gower*. Revised edition. Swansea: The Gower Society, 2005*

Caerphilly
Unfolding history: castles, fortresses and citadels. H Stierlin. London: Thames & Hudson, 2006*

Llanilid
'*Apud castellum de Sancta Julitta*: a castle of the Reigny family in Glamorgan', B Coplestone-Crow, *Morgannwg* 50 (2006), 43–60

MONMOUTHSHIRE

Newport

'Did Newport have a town wall?', R Trett, *S.O.S.: the Newsletter of the Friends of the Newport Ship* 11 (2007), 6–8*

PEMBROKESHIRE

Driver, T. *Pembrokeshire: historic landscapes from the air*. Aberystwyth: RC-AHMW, 2007*

SCOTLAND

ABERDEENSHIRE

Castle Fraser

'Post-medieval fieldwork in Britain and Northern Ireland in 2005', M Ponsford, *Post-Medieval Archaeology* 40 (2006), 388

Fetternear

'Excavation report: medieval bishop's palace and tower-house, Fetternear 2005–2006', P Z Dransart and W J Lindsay, *Castle Studies Group Journal* 20 (2006–7), 214–15*

Huntly

Huntly Castle. A Rutherford. Edinburgh: Historic Scotland, 2006*

ANGUS

Edzell

Edzell Castle. W D Simpson, revised by C Tabraham. Revised edition. Edinburgh: Historic Scotland, 2007*

AYRSHIRE

Davis, M C. *The castles and mansions of Ayrshire*. Ardrishais: privately published, 1991*

Culzean

'Post-medieval fieldwork in Britain and Northern Ireland in 2005', M Ponsford, *Post-Medieval Archaeology* 40 (2006), 405

Dundonald

'Dundonald Castle excavations: further information on the finds', D H Caldwell, N Holmes and F Hunter, *Scottish Archaeological Journal* 28.1 (2006), 75–80

APPENDIX

BANFFSHIRE

Auchindoun
'Auchindoun Castle', H Sands, *History Scotland* 7.5 (2007), 51–52*

CAITHNESS

Castle Sinclair
'Post-medieval fieldwork in Britain and Northern Ireland in 2005', M Ponsford, *Post-Medieval Archaeology* 40 (2006), 401

DUMFRIESSHIRE

Caerlaverock
Caerlaverock Castle. D Grove and P Yeoman. Revised edition. Edinburgh: Historic Scotland, 2006*

DUNBARTONSHIRE

Dumbarton
Dumbarton Castle. C Tabraham. Revised edition. Edinburgh: Historic Scotland, 2007*

'Post-medieval fieldwork in Britain and Northern Ireland in 2005', M Ponsford, *Post-Medieval Archaeology* 40 (2006), 406

EAST LOTHIAN

Dirleton
Dirleton Castle and gardens. C Tabraham. Revised edition. Edinburgh: Historic Scotland, 2007*

Tantallon
Tantallon Castle. C Tabraham. Revised edition. Edinburgh: Historic Scotland, 2007*

INVERNESS-SHIRE

Miket, R and Roberts, D L. *The medieval castles of Skye and Lochalsh*. New edition. Edinburgh: Birlinn, 2007*

Castle Tioram
'The Castle Tioram debate: the background', N Guy, *Castle Studies Group Journal* 20 (2006–7), 266

'Historic Scotland Board meeting 21st August 2006 HSB 19/06 Castle Tioram', M Cooper, *ibid* 20 (2006–7), 267–74*

'Castle Tioram: Geoffrey Stell's "final statement"', G Stell, *ibid* 20 (2006–7), 275–81*

FORTIFICATIONS BIBLIOGRAPHY

Fort George

Fort George, Ardersier. I MacIvor, revised by D Grove. Revised edition. Edinburgh: Historic Scotland, 2006*

KINCARDINESHIRE

Dunnottar

'Post-medieval fieldwork in Britain and Northern Ireland in 2005', M Ponsford, *Post-Medieval Archaeology* 40 (2006), 388

KINROSS-SHIRE

Gifford, J. *Perth and Kinross (The buildings of Scotland)*. London: Yale University Press, 2007*

KIRKCUDBRIGHTSHIRE

Threave

Threave Castle. C Tabraham. Revised edition. Edinburgh: Historic Scotland, 2007*

MIDLOTHIAN

Colinton

'Post-medieval fieldwork in Britain and Northern Ireland in 2005', M Ponsford, *Post-Medieval Archaeology* 40 (2006), 395

Craigmillar

Craigmillar Castle. C Tabraham. Revised edition. Edinburgh: Historic Scotland, 2007*

Edinburgh

'Post-medieval fieldwork in Britain and Northern Ireland in 2005', M Ponsford, *Post-Medieval Archaeology* 40 (2006), 395

Leith

'Post-medieval fieldwork in Britain and Northern Ireland in 2005', M Ponsford, *ibid* 40 (2006), 396

PERTHSHIRE

Gifford, J. *Perth and Kinross (The buildings of Scotland)*. London: Yale University Press, 2007*

Huntingtower

Huntingtower Castle. D Pringle, revised by C Tabraham. Revised edition. Edinburgh: Historic Scotland, 2007*

Taymouth

'Post-medieval fieldwork in Britain and Northern Ireland in 2005', M Ponsford, *Post-Medieval Archaeology* 40 (2006), 401

APPENDIX

ROSS AND CROMARTY

Miket, R and Roberts, D L. *The medieval castles of Skye and Lochalsh*. New edition. Edinburgh: Birlinn, 2007*

ROXBURGHSHIRE

Cessford

'Post-medieval fieldwork in Britain and Northern Ireland in 2005', M Ponsford, *Post-Medieval Archaeology* 40 (2006), 404

Smailholm

Smailholm Tower. C Tabraham. Revised edition. Edinburgh: Historic Scotland, 2007*

STIRLINGSHIRE

Stirling

'Post-medieval fieldwork in Britain and Northern Ireland in 2005', M Ponsford, *Post-Medieval Archaeology* 40 (2006), 406*

CHANNEL ISLANDS

JERSEY

Carter, J. 'Forts and towers', *The Heritage Magazine* (2006), 62–68*

Davies, W. *The coastal towers of Jersey*. St Helier: Société Jersiaise, 1991*

Ginns, M. *Jersey's German defences*. St Ouen: Channel Islands Occupation Society (Jersey), 1999, reprinted 2004* (Archive book; 9)

Mont Orgueil

Mont Orgueil Castle: a souvenir guide. D Ford. St Helier: jersey Heritage Trust, 2007*

'Mont Orgueil Castle and General Conway: the lost chapter', C Platt and R Mesch, *Société Jersiaise, Annual Bulletin* 29.1 (2005), 99–115*

'The high-vaulted room at Mont Orgueil; hall, chamber or chapel?', J McCormack, *ibid* 29.2 (2006), 184–94*

'A note on the chapels of St Mary and St George at Mont Orgueil Castle', C Platt, *ibid* 29.2 (2006), 195–201*

Noirmont Point

A guide to Batterie Lothringen. M Costard. [S l]: Channel Islands Occupation Society (Jersey), 2007*

ISLE OF MAN

Cronk Howe Mooar

'Castell Aberlleiniog, Anglesey and Cronk Howe Mooar, Isle of Man: related monuments?', S Smith, *Anglesey Antiquarian Society and Field Club Transactions* (2004), 31–45*

THE SCILLY ISLES

St Mary's

'The St Mary's Garrison project', M Fletcher [et al], *Research News: Newsletter of the English Heritage Research Department* 6 (2007), 20–23*

IRELAND

ANTRIM

Carrickfergus

Carrickfergus, Co Antrim: a walled town in the seventeenth century. R Ó Baoill. Dublin: Archaeology Ireland, 2007* (Heritage guide; 36)

'Recent excavations in medieval Carrickfergus', R Ó Baoill, *Carrickfergus and District Historical Journal* 7 (1993), 54–63*

'Further excavations in medieval Carrickfergus: a summary account', R Ó Baoill, *ibid* 9 (1998), 25–32*

Castle Lug(g)

'A note on Castle Lugg, west division, Carrickfergus', S Speers, *ibid* 2 (1986), 55–57*

CORK

MacCotter, P. 'Anglo-Normans in the Mallow area', *Mallow Field Club Journal* 22 (2004), 49–60*

Sherlock, R. 'Mural domestic bread ovens: evidence for the medieval-post-medieval architectural transition', *Journal of the Cork Historical and Archaeological Society* 111 (2006), 107–24*

LIMERICK

Limerick

'Thom Cor Castle: a 14th century tower house in Limerick City?', B Hodkinson, *Journal of the Royal Society of Antiquaries of Ireland* 135 (2005), 119–29*

'St John's Gate and the Citadel in Irishtown, Limerick', B Hodkinson, *North Munster Antiquarian Journal* 46 (2006), 129–31*

Londonderry/Derry

'Excavations at Bishop's Street Without: 17th century conflict archaeology in Derry City', P Logue and J O'Neill, *Journal of Conflict Archaeology* 2 (2006), 49–75*

LOUTH

Faughart

Faughart, Co Louth: the hill of heroes, saints, battles and boundaries. T Condit and V Buckley. Dublin: Archaeology Ireland, 2007* (Heritage guide; 37)

OFFALY

Leap

'The Gothic and the Gaelic: exploring the place of castles in Ireland's Celtic revival', A Tierney, *International Journal of Historical Archaeology* 8 (2004), 185–98*

TIPPERARY

Harbison, P. 'J. J. Barralet's antiquarian sketching tour of Tipperary in 1780', *Irish Architectural and Decorative Studies* 9 (2006), 246–65*

INDEX OF AUTHORS

The compilation of this index has been fraught with problems, primarily in trying to verify whether authors with the same surname and initials are one and the same or two different people. I have not been able to resolve all such issues, **so anyone consulting this index needs to be aware that the references under a single author's name may be to more than one person**. 'G H Williams' is a case in point, as is John Hawkes, the latter name appearing under both Somerset and County Cork. There are also cases where the same author may appear under two entries where again it has not been possible to discover to verify the full name. For example, H Hannaford and H R Hannaford, writing on sites in adjacent counties, are likely to be one and the same person, but my rule has been that if there is any doubt, create two records. Another example is E Shepherd and L Shepherd writing on Norwich Castle (Elizabeth and Liz), where gut instinct would assume that they are one and the same, and probably also the same as E Shepherd Popescu. *Country Life* was not able to confirm whether articles in the magazine by A Oswald (Arthur) and A S Oswald were by one and the same person.

Some authors have changed their names due to marriage or other reasons, but the index lists the surname as given in the publication. Examples of these are R McNeil and R McNeil-Sale, B Lacey and B Lacy.

Occasionally I have included the forename in brackets where it has been possible to differentiate authors with the same surname and initial. There are several instances where an author varies the use of his or her forenames. For example, papers and guidebooks by the Edwardian castle scholar Arnold Taylor might appear as A Taylor or A J Taylor. In such circumstances, and where it is known that the two forms equate with the one and the same individual, the full name appears in the index (Taylor, A J). Authors such as Bill Wilson and Tony Wilmott have been entered as Wilson, B and Wilmott, T, rather than Wilson, W and Wilmott, A, as for all I know the B and the T may be their actual initials.

Where a work has more than three authors cited, only the first name appears in the bibliography, and hence in this index.

It is important to note that the names of editors of books from which articles have been taken are included, but excluded are the names of the compilers/editors of the national annual excavation and fieldwork round-ups that appear in the journals *Medieval Archaeology* and *Post-Medieval Archaeology*, as well as the volumes summarising work in Ireland.

The arrangement of the index is letter by letter, but surnames beginning with Mac and Mc have been treated in one sequence, under Mac.

Aalen, F H A, 5, 80
ab Alun, A, 359
Abels, R P, 82, 84
Aberg, A, 338
Adams, B, 5
Adams, F, 549
Adams, P (Pam), 549
Adams, P (Paul), 209
Addyman, P V, 88, 89, 97, 123, 276, 280, 324, 346, 555
Addyman, T, 440, 454, 460, 461, 468, 469, 506, 514
Adkin, M, 5
Aikman, C W H, 483
Ainslie, A D, 5
Ainsworth, S, 86, 236, 245
Aitchinson, N B, 532
Akerman, J B, 383
Albarella, U, 105
Alcock, E A, 452
Alcock, L, 53, 69, 271, 357, 358, 381, 383, 385, 388, 391, 392, 406, 407, 452, 486, 487, 488
Alcock, N W, 213, 316
Alcock, O, 599, 600, 601, 604, 616, 617
Aldred, D, 5
Aldsworth, F G, 167, 168, 306, 308, 310
Alebon, P H, 101
Alexander, C, 5
Alexander, D, 463, 466, 477, 500, 517, 519, 536
Alexander, J A, 97, 240, 241, 243
Alexander, J S, 259
Alexander, M, 300
Algar, D J, 327
Aliaga-Kelly, C, 505, 530, 534, 535
Allan, J, 525
Allan, J P, 124, 128, 132
Alldridge, N J, 101
Allen, C, 260
Allen, D, 157, 162, 541
Allen, J, 296
Allen, J R L, 399, 403
Allibone, J, 6, 245
Allison, K, 333, 336
Ambrus, V, 6
Ames, H S, 305, 526
Amos, S, 107, 109

Amt, E, 88
Anderson, D, 442
Anderson, I, 191, 192
Anderson, M, 103
Anderson, S, 157
Anderson, W, 6
Anderson, W A, 455
Andersson, H, 70
Anderton, M J, 37, 282
Anderton, S, 246
Andrew, J, 107
Andrews, D (D), 141, 143, 662
Andrews, E A, 131, 133
Andrews, H C, 664
Andrews, J H, 609, 619, 652
Andrews, P, 323
Annis, R G, 111
Anniss, G, 98
Anthony, M, 411
ap Hywel, E, 69
Appleby, J C, 538
Appleton-Fox, N, 184
Apted, M R, 111, 115, 199, 207, 226, 314, 354, 364, 413, 441, 444, 445, 478, 479, 497
Archaeological Survey of Co Down, 580 (*passim* Co Down section)
Archer, E P, 495, 499
Ardagh, P, 6
Aris, M, 6
Armit, I, 514
Armitage, E S, 6
Armitage, P L, 118
Armstrong, P, 336
Armstrong-Anthony, S, 635
Arnold, C J, 285, 365, 368, 414, 415, 420, 421, 423, 424
Arrol, A, 272
Arscott, D, 303
Ascot-Symms, J, 269
Ash, M, 437
Ash, P, 115
Ashbee, J, 37, 129, 176, 201, 203, 227, 249, 250, 355, 356, 405, 664, 667
Ashmore, F M, 401
Ashmore, P J, 401
Ashwin, T, 233
Aslet, P C, 201, 505

Brown, R, 661
Brown, R A, 7, 8, 39, 70, 71, 73, 195, 197, 202, 215, 224, 225, 226, 231, 256, 295, 296, 314, 315, 433
Brown, R L, 383
Brown, R R, 304
Brown, S (Sarah), 92
Brown, S (Stewart), 118, 127
Brown, T (Tony), 96
Brown, T M, 278
Browne, D M, 352, 360, 429, 433
Brownsword, R, 234, 319
Browse, R G, 109
Bruce, D, 39
Bruce, J R, 547
Bruce-Mitford, R L S, 297
Brunicardi, D N, 569, 571
Bryan, D, 608
Bryans, P, 542, 545
Bryant, J, 8
Bryce, I B D, 39, 436, 438, 461, 462, 489, 506
Buchanan, R H, 583
Buckingham, C, 190
Buckland, P C, 334
Buckley, D G, 140
Buckley, L, 586
Buckley, R J, 212, 213
Buckley, V M, 625, 626, 627, 629, 673
Buckmaster, R A, 205
Bühler, C F, 158
Buisseret, D, 69
Bull, S, 136, 543
Bulmer, C G, 113
Bulmer, W, 253
Bu'lock, J D, 208
Bur, M, 8, 39, 71, 79,
Burchill, R, 148
Burgess, L A, 168, 170
Burke, J, 8, 39, 71
Burke, N, 592, 594
Burke, T, 209
Burl, A, 82
Burnal, P, 545
Burne, R V H, 39
Burnett, R J A, 345
Burnham, H, 349, 361, 370, 372, 414, 432
Burns, J, 6

Burns, J F, 554
Burns, R (Bob), 541
Burr, H C, 540
Burridge, D, 39, 188, 194, 195, 197, 198, 199, 201, 205
Burrington, P A, 340
Burrow, I, 121, 287
Burrows, J, 515
Burton, N, 8
Burton, P A, 340
Bury, J, 39
Bush, R, 286
Butchart, C B R, 155, 159
Buteux, S, 278
Butler, D J, 637
Butler, G, 643
Butler, J, 222
Butler, L A S, 40, 72, 331, 339, 341, 342, 345, 356, 370, 371, 372, 397, 415, 416, 421, 667
Butler, R F, 147
Butler, R M, 262, 344, 345, 346
Buttery, D, 317
Buttimer, C G, 40, 569
Buttimer, J, 40
Buttimer, N, 227
Byatt-Price, E M, 219
Byrne, J, 596
Byrne, M E, 567, 610, 651, 655
Bythell, D, 135

Caball, J, 607
Cachart, R, 445, 446, 472, 476, 492, 515
Cadman, G, 237, 238
Cadw: Welsh Historic Monuments, 8
Caen Colloquy, 40
Cahill, M, 656, 657
Caiger, J E L, 202
Cain, R, 434
Cairns, C T, 8, 40, 637
Cairns, H, 588
Calder, C S T, 521, 525
Caldwell, D H, 8, 40, 79, 84, 85, 247, 458, 463, 464, 475, 476, 478, 493, 534, 668
Caldwell, H, 458
Callaghan, R, 306
Callary, R R, 631
Calvert, D, 307

Fraher, W, 647
Frame, R, 258
France, J, 75
Francis, E, 116
Francis, M, 365, 386
Francis-Wemyss, P, 375
Franklin, G, 258
Franklin, J, 475, 504
Fraser, C M, 253
Fraser, H, 458
Fraser, R, 253
Fraser, S, 14
Fraser, S M, 440, 488
Fraser, T G, 624
Frazer, W O, 631
Freeman, A Z, 45
Freeman, J, 664
Freeman, M D, 427, 432
Freeman, P W M, 73, 75
Freethy, R, 208
Freke, D J, 214, 307, 547
Frere, S S, 190, 433
Friar, S, 14
Friel, P, 613
Frodsham, P, 244, 245, 249, 251, 256, 470
Frost, P, 433, 665
Fry, M, 440, 445, 470, 476, 477, 486, 495, 497
Fry, M F, 45
Fry, P S, 14, 224
Fulford, M, 168, 309
Fullam, P, 623
Fullbrook-Leggatt, L E W O, 152
Funari, P P A, 78
Furtado, P, 14

Gabra-Sanders, T, 465
Gahan, A, 551
Gailey, I, 584
Gaimster, D, 72, 289
Gaines, B, 75
Gale, F, 370, 371, 373
Gale, J, 290
Galer, D, 306
Galinié, H, 69, 417 f
Gallagher, D, 470
Galway, F, 630
Gamble, G S, 278

Gammon, A, 666
Gander, T, 14, 538
Gardiner, M, 585, 663
Gardiner, M (Margaret), 45
Gardiner, M (Mark), 307, 310, 538
Gardner, K S, 123, 149
Gardner, W, 399
Garlick, T, 331
Garner, K, 227
Garner, M F, 169
Garner, W, 556, 602
Garner-Lahire, J, 467
Garnett, E D, 306
Garnett, O, 119, 176
Garratt, B, 163
Garrod, A P, 151, 152, 153
Garton, S J, 343
Gascoigne, B, 14
Gascoigne, C, 14
Gaskell Brown, C, 126, 584, 585
Gater, J A, 340
Gathercole, P W, 269
Gaunt, P, 14, 421
Gavey, E, 540
Gébler, C, 624
Geddes, J, 256
Gee, E, 45, 345
George, M S F, 87
Gerrard, C, 15
Gerrard, S, 426
Gethin, B, 666
Gething, P, 246
Giannazza, G, 15
Gibb, J H P, 284
Gibbons, M, 617
Gibbs, K, 198
Gibson, A, 447
Gibson, A (Alex), 422, 424, 432
Gibson, D B, 562
Gibson, L I, 208
Gibson, P, 636
Gibson, P J, 631
Gibson, W H, 610
Gies, F, 15
Gies, J, 15
Gifford, J, 467, 468, 469, 474, 478, 483, 489, 502, 508, 512, 519, 525, 527, 532, 535, 670
Gifford, P R, 136

Papazian, C, 600

Papworth, M, 129, 130

Parfitt, K, 196, 197, 198, 199

Park, D, 93, 100, 101, 102

Parker, R, 127

Parker, W E J, 131

Parkes, C, 548

Parkes, L N, 409

Parkhouse, J, 95, 384, 385, 395

Parkin E W, 204

Parkinson, A J, 349

Parks, P, 299

Parnell, G, 221, 225, 226, 227, 228

Parrish, E J, 298

Parry, C, 370

Parry, G, 355

Parsons, A, 391

Parsons, D, 81, 216

Partridge, C W, 539, 540, 542

Partridge, J, 139

Partridge, M S, 26, 210, 538

Passmore, A, 127

Paterson, C, 247

Paterson, G F, 629

Patterson, A T, 156

Patterson, B H, 165

Patterson, E M, 461

Patterson, S W, 372

Pattison, P, 75, 86, 91, 102, 103, 141, 142, 145, 146, 194, 198, 200, 202, 205, 236, 245, 296, 664

Patullo, N, 27

Pavin, S, 658

Pavry, F H, 96

Pawsey, J T, 137, 229, 293

Payne, A, 115

Peachey, S, 148

Pearce, D J, 384

Pearce, S M, 83

Pearson, A W, 433

Pearson, N, 346

Pearson, T, 343, 344

Pearson, V, 212, 237

Peberdy, P, 168

Peers, C, 159, 184, 212, 285, 309, 335, 339, 341

Pegden, B K, 60

Pelham, R A, 170

Pender, R, 93, 661

Pendleton, C, 294

Penman, A, 490, 491, 492

Penman, E J, 490, 492

Penn, S A C, 149

Percival, D, 429

Perks, J C, 81, 82, 130, 367, 392, 403, 404, 407, 426, 428, 429

Perriam, D R, 110, 111, 112, 320,

Perry, D R, 445, 476, 479, 480, 486

Perryman, J, 408

Petchey, M R, 144, 185

Peters, E, 27

Petersen, B, 502

Petre, J, 113

Petrie, G, 60

Pettifer, A, 27

Peverley, J R, 196, 197

Pevsner, N, 87, 90, 95, 97, 99, 104, 110, 114, 116, 128, 133, 137, 156, 174, 184, 186, 208, 211, 214, 220, 229, 238, 244, 257, 263, 269, 270, 281, 287, 293, 297, 302, 311, 320, 322, 331, 662, 666

Phillips, A, 103, 187

Phillips, A (Alan), 348, 353, 355, 398

Phillips, A (Andrew), 352

Phillips, B, 323

Phillips, B (Barty), 60

Phillips, C T, 390

Phillips, C W, 97

Phillips, G (Georgeana), 27

Phillips, G (Gervase), 27

Phillips, K, 431

Phillips, N, 174, 400, 401, 407, 412

Phillips, R, 323

Phillips, T, 622

Phillips-Birt, D, 156

Philp, B, 197

Pike, A, 95

Pike, H H M, 157

Pilkington-Rowland, H, 162

Pinder, A, 89

Pinsent, M (L), 60, 131, 133

Piper, J, 60

Pitt, E, 319

Pitte, D, 237

Place, C, 303

Planel, P, 27, 124, 284, 325

249, 251, 303, 320, 334, 335, 436, 437, 438, 439, 440, 441, 442, 443, 445, 451, 452, 454, 456, 457, 459, 466, 471, 473, 476, 478, 483, 486, 488, 493, 495, 496, 498, 501, 502, 505, 507, 508, 509, 510, 511, 514, 517, 522, 526, 668

Simpson, W G, 219

Sinclair Williams, C L, 139, 271

Singer, V A, 312

Sinnot, P J, 654

Sitch, B, 336

Sitwell, S, 64

Sivier, D, 148

Skelton, R A, 64

Skurdenis, J, 64

Slade, C F, 91

Slade, H G, see Gordon Slade, H

Slade, R M, 209

Slater, T R, 83

Slater, W D, 118

Sloan, P W, 666

Small, A, 335

Smallwood, J P, 237

Smith, C (Catherine), 516

Smith, C (Chris), 371

Smith, C E, 409

Smith, E, 138

Smith, F, 624

Smith, G, 326

Smith, H, 480, 485, 498

Smith, J B, 350, 367, 391, 397

Smith, J S, 31, 73, 74, 83, 84, 86, 437

Smith, J T, 75, 278, 319, 352

Smith, Ll B, 397

Smith, M, 169

Smith, N, 95

Smith, P (Penny), 284

Smith, P (Peter), 376

Smith, R, 235

Smith, R D, 94, 304, 546

Smith, S G, 372, 667, 672

Smith, T P, 64, 216, 222, 232, 233

Smith, V (Mrs), 200

Smith, V T C, 31, 64, 137, 138, 189, 193, 194, 199, 200, 201, 202, 205, 223, 224, 282, 297, 478, 501, 533

Smith, W J, 421

Smithers, D W, 189

Smyth, J, 270

Snape, J W, 277

Snell, A, 272

Sneyd, S, 64, 332, 336

Snoddy, O, 607

Snodgrass, L, 564

Snow, D, 198

Sockett, E W, 341

Soden, I, 240, 288, 314

Solomon, A, 365

Somerville, R, 292

Sorrell, A, 31

Soulsby, I, 31, 412

Southern, M K, 146

Southworth, E, 69, 221

South Yorkshire County Archaeology Service, 345

Sparkes, I G, 138, 145

Speak, S, 136

Spearman, R M, 84, 446, 515

Speers, S, 672

Speight, M, 18

Speight, S, 64, 258, 262

Speller, K, 499

Spellissy, S, 560, 561, 599

Spence, K E, 321

Spence, R T, 344

Spicer, S, 115

Spiteri, S C, 64

Sprack, P, 155, 161, 162, 167, 168

Sprackling, G, 174

Spratt, A, 476, 478

Spreadbury, I D, 104, 548

Sproat, D, 504

Spry, N P, 151

Spurgeon, C J, 84, 270, 271, 275, 279, 280, 350, 351, 358, 360, 361, 362, 371, 373, 378, 379, 380, 381, 384, 385, 386, 387, 389, 390, 391, 392, 393, 394, 395, 396, 398, 399, 400, 415, 420, 421, 423, 424, 429, 433

Spurrell, M, 92

Stacey, M, 283

Stalley, R A, 31, 64, 84, 597, 606, 632

Stammers, M, 353

Stamper, P A, 72, 157, 158,

Stanford, C, 64, 183, 345

Stanford, C H, 433

Williams, J H, 240, 241, 321
Williams, N J, 325
Williams, R, 102, 393
Williams, S, 384
Williams, S E, 155
Williams, T C, 387
Williams, V A, 380
Williams, W, 35
Williams-Jones, K, 353, 356
Williamson, E, 269, 498
Williamson, G, 550
Williamson, P, 76
Williamson, P R, 332
Williamson, T, 35
Willoughby, R, 162
Wills, H, 35, 68
Wills, J, 155, 330
Wilmott, T, 220, 340
Wilshere, J, 212
Wilson, A, 328
Wilson, A (Anthony), 583
Wilson, A E, 305
Wilson, B (Barbara), 346
Wilson, B (Bill), 229
Wilson, C, 93
Wilson, D, 225
Wilson, D H, 425
Wilson, E M, 444
Wilson, G, 505
Wilson, J, 191, 201, 203, 444, 447, 472
Wilson, J D, 137, 190
Wilson, M, 314
Wilson, P, 407
Wilson, P A, 321
Wilson, P R, 336
Wilson, R, 234
Wilson, S, 406
Wilson, T, 138, 140
Wilson-North, W R, 75, 117, 122, 282, 284, 304
Wilton, J W, 229
Wilton, P, 128
Winchester, A J L, 35
Winer, M, 81
Winstock, L S, 74
Winter, M J, 211
Wise, M, 330
Wise, T, 35

Witten, F H, 310
Wolfe, M, 10, 73
Wood, D, 68, 194
Wood, D A, 36, 296
Wood, H L, 652
Wood, J, 208, 485, 488
Wood, J (Jason), 68, 210
Wood, J S, 536
Wood, M (Margaret), 36, 90, 159
Wood, M (Marguerite), 502
Wood, M (Maureen), 118
Wood, M A, 110
Wood, P N, 246
Wood, R G E, 137
Wood, S, 36
Wood, T, 36
Woodburn, C W (Bill), 302
Woodfield, C, 313
Woodhouse, E, 315
Woodhouse, R, 134, 332
Woodward, A, 131
Woodward, D, 139
Woodward, F (W), 104, 117, 125, 126
Woodward, P, 89
Woolgar, C M, 36
Woolner, A, 122
Woolner, D, 122
Worcester Archaeological Service, 328
Worcestershire County Museum, 327
Wordsworth, J, 462, 481
Worrall, D H, 386
Worsley, G, 113, 227, 246, 484
Worsley, L, 114
Worssam, B C, 190, 203
Worthington, M J, 405
Wrathmell, S (Stuart), 396, 409, 410
Wrathmell, S (Susan), 396
Wren, J, 570, 644, 649, 656
Wright, A C, 138
Wright, M D, 547
Wright, N, 36
Wright, P, 535
Wright, S, 163
Wykes, J, 490
Wynne, M, 596

Yarrow, A, 129, 303, 307
Yates, S, 99, 134, 208, 320, 663, 664, 665

INDEX OF PLACES